Britain: standard regions and sub-divisions

Regional Development
in
Britain

Regional Development
in
Britain

GERALD MANNERS
Reader in Geography, University College London

DAVID KEEBLE
Lecturer in Geography, University of Cambridge

BRIAN RODGERS
Professor of Geography, University of Manchester

KENNETH WARREN
Lecturer in Geography, University of Oxford

JOHN WILEY & SONS

London · New York · Sydney · Toronto

Library of Congress Catalog Card No. 74-37115

ISBN 0 471 56765 5

Composed in Monophoto Times New Roman by
Thomson Press (India) Limited, Faridabad, Haryana

Printed in Great Britain by
Unwin Brothers Limited, Woking and London

Contents

Contents

Preface

Regional contrasts in the nature and the pace of economic development have increasingly captured the public imagination in recent years. The resurgence of Celtic nationalism during the nineteen sixties, the creation of the regional economic planning councils and the subsequent burst of official surveys, studies and strategies have all been influential in this development. But above all it has been the persistence of a group of economic and social problems which have a primarily regional rather than national expression that have ensured a quickening interest in and a wider familiarity with the changing geography of opportunity in Britain. Partly in response to this interest, this book describes and interprets the trends, the problems and the uncertainties that are associated with the evolving pattern of regional economic change; it evaluates the political response to them and it affords a benchmark for contemplating something of the prospective geography of Britain in the nineteen seventies. The first and last chapters provide an important national perspective without which the intermediate regional chapters, making up the greater part of the book, would be less intelligible. Chapter 1 seeks to summarize and clarify in a highly generalized fashion the principal forces that have shaped the economic geography of Britain over the last three or so decades. It examines *inter alia* the economic characteristics of, and the regional planning reaction to the problems in, the more prosperous parts of southern England, the less prosperous 'older' industrial economies of the north and the west, and the intermediate or grey areas juxtaposed between the two. Chapter 11 briefly focusses upon some of the dilemmas which continue to challenge the government in the field of regional development and planning.

The regional division that has been adopted in this book mainly follows the lead set by the government in its delimitation of new 'standard economic regions', a map of which appears on the back end-paper. These are regions which received a good deal of official study and interpretation in recent years, and for which a widening range of socio–economic statistics is readily available (especially in the annual *Abstract of Regional Statistics* prepared by the Central Statistical Office). It was judged, however, that many of the problems associated with regional development can be better understood through a slightly modified regionalization. For example, without denying the historical identity and the political integrity of the Principality of Wales, it is widely accepted that many of the development problems—and certainly the prospective economic opportunities—of the southern counties can best be understood in the context of a Severnside region spanning

vii

both sides of the Bristol Channel; similarly, the close economic and social associations between the counties of North Wales and the Merseyside conurbation, and the growing recreational and overspill links between Central Wales and the West Midlands, confirm the advantage of considering the three main spatial components of the Principality alongside their neighbouring English regions for the purposes of this volume. Likewise, it is evident that the future development of Cumberland and Westmoreland lies in the strengthening of their relationships with Lancashire rather than with North East England, a region with which they have been officially associated through the Northern Economic Planning Council and Regional Planning Board since 1965. Within each of the regions discussed, once again it has been found preferable generally to make use of the official sub-divisions (shown on the back end-paper) rather than any alternative spatial disaggregation. Not only has this allowed the use of readily available official data, but it has minimized the amount of space devoted to a discussion of regional and sub-regional boundaries. Only where spatial disaggregation poses particularly delicate issues for the interpretation of data and developments—as, for example, in the East Midlands—is any extended attention given to them.

The geographical balance of the book, and especially the heavy emphasis placed upon the South East, demands a word of explanation. In the broad allocation of space to the discussion of different parts of the country, it was decided that population and economic importance rather than area should provide an initial yardstick, and that the complexity of spatial problems would afford a secondary criterion. On this basis, the 17 million people living in the South East more than justify the two chapters devoted to their geography and problems; on these criteria, also, the difficulties facing the sparcely populated Highlands and Islands of Scotland could also be given critical examination. The decision to omit Northern Ireland from the book was taken with some regret; however, it was judged that the many unique economic and political characteristics of the Province demand its exclusion from many generalizations appropriate to the rest of the United Kingdom, and that its development problems justify rather more sensitive and extended treatment than would have been possible in this volume.

A study of contemporary affairs inevitably runs the risk of being quickly overtaken by events. In the case of regional development the problem is compounded by the time-lag in the collection and processing of statistics which means that, in the case of occupational data for example, an eight year gap can widen between events and the last census material; it will be 1973 before the shifting geography of office employment can be updated for the period 1966–1971. Inevitably, therefore, much of the present book must be seen as a reflection of evidence and understanding *circa* 1970. Nevertheless it has been possible to include in the text some of the preliminary results of the 1971 Census, and to update the record of major developments and government decisions to the middle of 1972, including the principal proposals contained in the White Paper on *Industrial and Regional Development* (Cmnd. 4942), presented to Parliament by the Secretary of State for Trade and Industry in March 1972.

Although I have acted as general editor of this volume, *Regional Development in Britain* is the product of four authors, each of whom naturally prefers the maximum freedom from editorial constraints. In consequence, no stamp of uniformity has been imposed upon the regional chapters, and the interpretation of development characteristics and problems in different parts of the country has been approached from a variety of personal standpoints. Such contrasts as may be found in the focus and accent of those chapters reflect their author's intellectual stance as well as the distinctiveness of the regions themselves. Nevertheless, the reader will find that in all cases the emphasis is upon the problems of industrial and urban development, to the relative neglect of rural and agricultural affairs. This is a bias that springs logically from the first of the two yardsticks noted earlier. The reader might also find the book at times unfairly sceptical towards the objectives and achievements of regional planning in Britain. This is in no way meant to understate the considerable successes which the government might reasonably claim, or to overlook the admiration for British policies that is to be found overseas. Rather it stems from a belief that only by approaching the record and problems of regional development in a critical frame of mind can the student—and this book is primarily intended for those in the early stages of higher education—come to a fuller understanding of the issues involved and perhaps in time make some contribution to their solution.

University College London   GERALD MANNERS

List of Tables

List of Figures

xiv

Back end-paper   Britain : standard regions and sub-divisions

All the figures were drawn by Trevor Allen in the Cartographic Unit of the Department of Geography, University College London.

CHAPTER 1

National Perspectives

GERALD MANNERS

1.1 Introduction

At the root of changes in the economic geography of an advanced industrial society lies the evolution of its consumer demands. Motor cars and washing machines, carpets and television sets, lawn mowers and refrigerators have all been purchased in ever increasing quantities as the people of Britain have increased and redistributed their wealth over the past twenty-five years. Simultaneously, families have come to spend an increasing proportion of their income on travel and entertainment, on sport and recreation and upon a widening range of personal services. As a consequence, the number of jobs available in these growing manufacturing and service activities has steadily increased; and firms engaged therein have frequently been faced with an embarrassing shortage of labour. In other sections of the economy, however, the story has been quite different for the steady growth of national affluence has by no means affected all industries in the same way. The demand for some manufactures and services is relatively inelastic; thus, a decreasing proportion of the nation's income has been spent on clothing and household goods, on food and tobacco, and upon such services as public transport and cinemas. The market for others—for example, steam locomotives, slate tiles and domestic servants—has contracted severely. Jobs in these industries, as a result, have shrunk both relatively and absolutely.

Of course, the changing structure of employment opportunities in an advanced and 'open' economy is also influenced by the shifting nature of the world political economy, by developments in international markets and the domestic entrepreneurial response to them, and by those technological developments which influence the extent to which capital is substituted for labour. Whilst trade between Britain and the rest of Western Europe has increased in both relative and absolute importance over the last quarter-century, transactions between Britain and the countries of the Commonwealth have become relatively less significant. In parallel, overseas sales of cars and lorries, of aircraft engines and electronic equipment, and of a variety of professional and scientific services have increased persistently and profitably. At the same time many of the more 'traditional' exporting activities of the country, such as cotton textile manufacture, coal mining and much entrepôt trade, progressively have come to be less profitable and thus have come to play a much

1

smaller role in Britain's international trade. Jobs in these industries as a consequence
have shown a persistent tendency to decline. In addition, technological developments in
which capital has been rapidly substituted for labour have simultaneously accelerated
the reduction of employment opportunities in many of these contracting export-oriented
activities—as well as in other trades such as iron and steel manufacture and shipbuilding
that have experienced a more buoyant demand, plus a third group of industries including
the railways that serve an essentially domestic market. Without such a contraction,
however, it is difficult to see how the growth industries could in fact have been manned.

1.1.1 *Changing Locational Preferences*

Each industry has its distinctive set of locational characteristics. Changes in the structure
of an economy, therefore, inevitably feed through into the geographical pattern of employment opportunities. Sometimes the decline of an industry in a particular town or region
is quickly and spontaneously counterbalanced by the expansion of another. It has been
a characteristic of British economic growth, however, that most of the newer industries
which have expanded particularly vigorously since 1945—and, indeed, even since the
turn of the present century—have exhibited different locational preferences from many
of the older industries which were the foundation of the country's economy in the nineteenth century. During that period of rapid and precocious industrialization one of the
important influences upon the geography of enterprise and employment was the ready
availability of coal, and its particular attraction for firms when it was found in association
with other industrial raw materials. As a consequence, major manufacturing and urban
concentrations emerged in Central Scotland, South Wales, South Lancashire, the East
and West Midlands, West Yorkshire and on the North East coast. Their specialisms,
besides coal mining, were iron and steel production, shipbuilding, cotton and wool textile
manufacture, and heavy engineering. The development of these regional economies
afforded a geographical counterbalance to London, which was not only the seat of the
Imperial Government and the Court but also a major industrial centre in its own right,
the country's largest port and the focus of its commercial activities. They generated as a
consequence a major redistribution of population within the country. The nineteenth
century pattern of urban settlement was filled out with a traditional scatter of market
towns related principally to the agricultural economy, and a rash of new coastal resorts
which stretched from Brighton to the Clyde coast and satisfied the growing holiday
demands of the burgeoning industrial areas.

Since Edwardian times, the attractions of the coal-fields for the establishment and
expansion of industrial enterprise have steadily weakened, and other factors have become
progressively more important in the location of economic activity. Proximity to large or
specialized consumer markets, or to the suppliers of component parts or sub-assemblies,
has emerged as one of the most decisive factors for manufacturing industry. That proximity is strongly conditioned by the geography of the country's most modern transport

facilities—major roads, railways and ports. These facilities were found most readily in southern England generally, and especially in Greater London and the West Midlands. As a consequence it was there that the new industries making vacuum cleaners and electric heaters, cookers and refrigerators, radios and television sets, typewriters and adding machines, cosmetics and pharmaceuticals, computers and data processing equipment, motor cycles and motor cars, and all the paraphernalia of modern life first came to be located. It was there also that they subsequently preferred to expand.

This is not to deny the importance of a variety of other factors in the location of twentieth century industrial enterprise. The availability of appropriately skilled labour, the importance of a variety of natural endowments and the role of innovation and enterprise, for example, are not to be discounted. Nor is it to overlook the importance of changes in transport technology, and the persistent reduction in the real costs of movement. These have eroded the importance of distance, and have simultaneously permitted the utilization of a new and wider range of sites for economic development in the present century. Nevertheless, whereas at one time it was the railway which attracted to its vicinity the greater part of manufacturing and even office activities, the new arterial road and motorway system, together with the country's major international airports, have progressively assumed a comparable if not greater importance (Figure 1a). The geography of these new transport facilities is crucial. In common with the first phase of liner train developments by British Rail (Figure 1b), with the 400 kV grid of the Central Electricity Generating Board, with the bulk transmission pipelines of both the Gas Council and the petroleum industry, and with the first major deep sea container facilities, their concentration within southern England is outstanding. As a result, the nodality and the relative attractiveness of the London-Midlands zone for economic activity has steadily increased.

The distribution of population within Britain is intimately linked to the geography of economic opportunity and employment. Apart from minor differences in local demographic characteristics and activity rates, interregional shifts in the two have been virtually identical. Intraregional changes in the distribution of population and employment, on the other hand, have exhibited important contrasts even though they have been moulded by somewhat similar forces for change. Especially since 1945 the rising level of national wealth has in part been invested in improved housing at lower residential densities. Such an investment could only be made following the simultaneous acceptance of the necessity for and the costs of constructing homes further away from centres of employment, and a lengthening of the daily journey to work. Rising levels of personal wealth have also created demands for a widening range of facilities and services, the more specialized of which can only be provided economically in larger urban centres. Combined, therefore, these characteristics have led to a growing concentration of people in a handful of larger and yet ever more sprawling conurbations and cities, the evolution of which has rested heavily upon innovation in and the improvement of both public and private transport. The tram and the bus, the tube and the trolley-bus, the electric railway and the urban motorway have each in their time and distinctive fashion permitted a growing separation

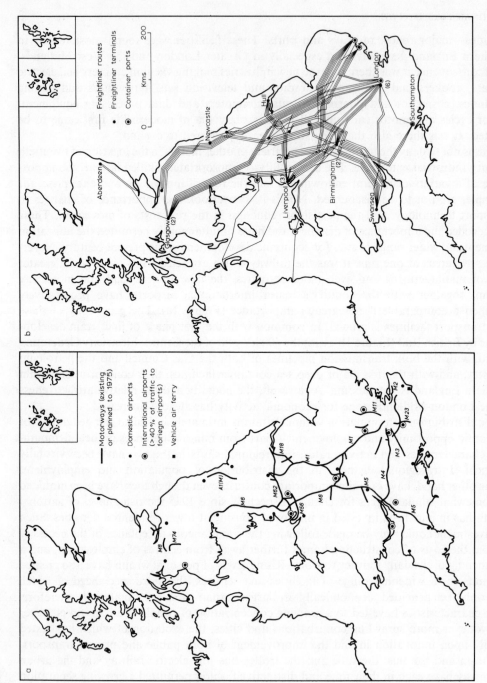

Figure 1   Britain: principal transport facilities, 1971. (a) motorways and airports, (b) railway freightliner routes and terminals.
Sources: Department of the Environment; British Rail.

of work and home, and have powerfully moulded the urban geography of twentieth century Britain.

These spatial tendencies—for both employment opportunities and people to move away from the coal-field industrial areas into the London-Midlands centre of national economic gravity, and for a relatively low density form of urban and suburban development with a lengthening journey to work to become increasingly prevalent—represent the two principal features of the changing economic geography of Britain today. They reflect both the individual and the collective decisions of many people concerning the best locations for their businesses, their work and their homes. However, these decisions, taken in the perceived self-interest of individuals or groups of individuals, have presented the community as a whole with a number of major problems. Two of these stand out above the rest, and are closely interrelated. First, by creating some regions of relatively rapid and often highly localized economic development, the new locational preferences have presented certain parts of the country with a complex set of difficulties which stem from the progressive concentration of both people and traffic, from an intense and increasing competition for the use of land, and from the necessity for the government to resolve the most appropriate size, location and timing of new and frequently costly infrastructural investments. Whilst these problems have had to be faced in many parts of the country, in one way or another, they have been posed in their most acute and urgent form throughout the South East and in the West Midlands. Second, the same spatial economic forces have simultaneously left certain areas and regions of the country with a generally slow rate of economic growth, and occasionally with the characteristics of stagnation and decay. These regions have experienced a persistently higher than average rate of unemployment, low activity rates and a steady loss of population—and they are located particularly in the north and the west of the country (Table 1).

These, then, are the two principal sets of problems posed by the dynamics of Britain's economic geography. Regional planning, initially concerned primarily with ameliorating the worst effects of these developments, increasingly seeks to recognize, interpret and selectively to use the underlying forces for change in order to create a better physical, economic and social environment. In the process it tries to reconcile a wide range of frequently conflicting considerations relating to the growth of population, the propensity for migration, industrial and commercial efficiency, alternative urban and sub-regional patterns of settlement, investment in transport and communications and many matters of social welfare. Intraregionally, for example, it is deeply concerned with shaping and at times containing the spread of large urban areas, seeking to balance considerations of transport efficiency with environmental quality, and of industrial and commercial needs for land with agricultural and recreational requirements. Interregionally, regional planning seeks to influence the distribution of employment and population, attempting selectively to increase the rate of growth, to lower the unemployment rates, to check the out-migration and to raise the activity rates of the less prosperous parts of the country. Changes in their function, their relative importance and their economic geography are of course inevitable;

Table 1. Britain : population 1971; and population change and net migration, by regions, 1951–1971

	Mid-year estimated home population '000s				Total population growth 1951–1971		Net migration 1951–1966	
	1971[1]	1966[2]	1961[2]	1951[2]	'000s	%	'000s	%
BRITAIN	53,821.4	53,176.1	51,380.0	48,917.5	4,903.9	10.02	131	0.3
More prosperous regions	31,057.9	30,321.3	29,170.7	27,190.8	3,867.1	14.22	1,028	4.1
South East	17,133.3	17,006.3	16,345.5	15,216.4	1,916.9	12.60	542	3.6
East Anglia	1,666.0	1,581.7	1,489.2	1,387.6	278.4	20.06	86	6.2
West Midlands	5,104.7	4,998.9	4,760.6	4,426.1	678.6	15.33	82	1.9
East Midlands	3,385.8	3,298.6	3,139.3	2,913.3	472.5	16.22	94	3.2
South West	3,768.1	3,634.8	3,436.0	3,247.4	520.7	16.03	223	6.9
Less prosperous regions	22,763.5	22,653.8	22,209.3	21,706.7	1,056.8	4.87	−897	−4.1
North West	6,726.3	6,712.8	6,545.3	6,416.8	309.5	4.82	−152	−2.4
Yorkshire and Humberside	4,793.6	4,731.2	4,595.9	4,488.3	305.3	6.80	−112	−2.5
Northern	3,292.3	3,316.9	3,249.0	3,130.3	162.0	5.18	−116	−3.7
Wales	2,723.6	2,704.1	2,635.2	2,588.8	134.8	5.21	−39	−1.5
Scotland	5,227.7	5,190.8	5,183.8	5,102.5	125.2	2.45	−478	−9.4

Sources : 1. Office of Population Censuses and Surveys, *Census* 1971, *Preliminary Report* (1971); 1971 boundaries.
2. Central Statistical Office, *Abstract of Regional Statistics, No.* 6, 1970 (1970); 1966 boundaries.

but evidence is not lacking to support the belief that some public intervention to accelerate the adjustment of these regions to a new national and international role is both economically and socially advantageous for the country as a whole.

1.1.2 *The Political Response*

Over a number of years now, in fact, there has been a significant political element in the forces moulding the country's economic geography. The Royal Commission on the Distribution of Industrial Population (1940) studied these matters, and in its famous report stressed the social, economic and strategic disadvantages of the further growth of London and the continued decline of the older industrial areas. It therefore endorsed the objectives of the earlier 1934 Special Areas legislation (McCrone, 1969, pp. 91 ff), and accelerated the creation of a Ministry of Town and Country Planning in 1943 which was charged with 'securing consistency and continuity in the framing and the execution of a national policy with respect to the use and development of land'. A few years later in the spate of legislation which followed World War II—the Distribution of Industry Acts of 1945 and 1949, the New Towns Act of 1946, and the Town and Country Planning Act of 1947 in particular (Self, 1957)—there was secured for Britain one of the most comprehensive bodies of regional and environmental planning legislation in the whole world. The basic notions behind this legislation initially were twofold. First, it was assumed that locally and regionally the uncontrolled use of land could be wasteful and socially undesirable—the worst aspects of nineteenth century industrial development, urban growth and land dereliction were sufficient to make this point—and that some measure of public supervision over its use was both possible and desirable in the best interests of the community. Indeed, considering the relatively high density of population in Britain, and the limited land resources of the country, many argued that tighter controls over the use of land had become an urgent necessity. The second primarily humanitarian notion was that there existed a social responsibility, through the government, to provide all members of the community with the opportunity of employment; attempts should be made therefore to create jobs in those parts of the country that were suffering from (or appeared likely to suffer from) economic collapse and high levels of unemployment. Subsequently the associated policies were endorsed by economic, environmental and political arguments, all of which merit attention.

In several exercises conducted by public bodies during the early nineteen sixties as part of successive attempts to accelerate the national rate of economic growth (National Economic Development Council, 1963), it was reasoned that regional policies could help to make fuller use of the country's productive resources. For example, it was argued that regional planning—by lowering the rates of localized unemployment, by raising the characteristically low female activity rates and by helping to shift labour out of less productive and into more productive work—could both increase the quantity and improve the quality of the labour inputs into the national economy. The National Economic Development Council on one occasion estimated that a 50 per cent reduction in the difference between regional unemployment and activity rates and the national average could add 1.3 per cent to the national labour force. To make use of such a labour reserve would cost money. But calculations demonstrated how central government expenditure on such a policy would quickly generate a more than ample return. It was also urged that the less prosperous parts of the country, in addition to their underutilized manpower, had considerable resources of social capital in the form of houses, roads, schools, churches and the like, resources which could be more fully utilized through regional policies. Such arguments were weakened by a realization that the built environment of the coal-field industrial areas urgently needed a major overhaul, and that despite their characteristic of net outmigration the total population within them was continuing to increase. Moreover, theoretically attractive though the labour reserve argument may have remained, remedial policies for the less prosperous regions failed to bring about a significant reduction in their unemployment levels; indeed, the late nineteen sixties in fact experienced an increase rather than a decrease in the national and especially the regional rates. Partly this was a consequence of international uncertainties and of balance of payment difficulties, plus the imperfections of national economic management; partly it was a function of accelerating structural change in the British economy.

One of the persistent macroeconomic dilemmas of the British economy in the years since 1945 has been the way in which, at each upswing of the business cycle, inflationary pressures allegedly generated in the more prosperous parts of the country have increased the national propensity to import and have demanded measures to dampen down aggregate home demand—thereby curtailing a rate of national economic growth which was already slow by international standards. Whilst temporarily ameliorating a balance of payments problem in this way, successive governments have thus been denied the opportunity of exploiting the underutilized resources of labour and capital in the less prosperous regions. A further economic argument for regional planning, therefore, came to rest upon the assumption that inflation could be better controlled and national economic growth accelerated by deflecting some resource demands away from southern England and into the less prosperous regions (First Secretary of State, 1965, p. 11; Department of Economic Affairs, 1969, pp. 91–94). In some measure, regional policy came legitimately to be regarded in part as a new attempt to manage, with rather more sensitive tools than conventional fiscal and monetary policies, the level of aggregate demand in the national economy. To the extent that these policies were able also to reduce interregional migration, it was suggested by some observers (Needleman and Scott, 1964) that inflationary pressures in southern England would be further checked, since the investment required by migrants is likely in the short run to increase the income of the more prosperous regions rather faster than their output. The inflationary effects of population movement remain unproven. The argument rests primarily upon the assumption that a reduction in interregional migration is likely to reduce the amount of social overhead and productive investment required by the economy. The poor state of much social capital in the less prosperous regions, and the need to restructure their economies, hints that this might not be the case. Indeed, to the extent that the income generated in the coal-field industrial economies by major infrastructural investments (which are a feature of some regional programmes) is not in the short run matched by a commensurate increase in output, it can be suggested that regional planning has contributed to, rather than checked, inflationary tendencies in the national economy.

On another level, the economic case for public intervention in the space economy was endorsed by the realization that market forces are frequently imperfect for determining the best location of at least some economic activities. For example, by comparison with the cost variations of their other inputs and outputs, many industries exhibit such small differences in their locational costs that a low priority is rightly accorded to questions of location in investment decisions. Many managements therefore treat these questions superficially, as a result of which 'adequate' or 'convenient' rather than 'the best' places are often selected for their operations. Even when firms—and it is usually the larger ones—take the trouble to calculate the costs and benefits of alternative locations, they are naturally concerned solely with their own efficiency, and pay no attention to any costs which might be transferred to the community as a whole. By its decision to operate in a particular place, a firm may impose upon a local authority the need to construct a wider road, a larger hospital, or a new school. These are expenses which might be only partly covered by the contribution the firm makes to local public income. It has been suggested that there are considerable social costs generated by the excessive concentration of economic activities in large metropolitan areas that are not borne by the industries primarily responsible for them. As a result the expansion of those urban areas continues, in spite of the (alleged) diseconomies involved.

Closely related to such an economic argument for regional planning is a series of equally important environmental justifications. Increasingly it has come to be realized that the wealth of a society can not be measured solely in conventional money terms. Indeed, if the pursuit of maximum financial gain is carried to the extreme, the quality of the urban-industrial environment can deteriorate very rapidly indeed. The relatively untamed search for 'wealth' in the northern industrial centres of Britain during the nineteenth century created many a bleak urban environment and hectares of industrial spoil and dereliction. Unrestrained, a similar set of values today would almost certainly underprovide parkland and other amenities in towns; it would pollute rivers and the atmosphere beyond their already sadly high levels; it would allow land and air traffic noise to exceed tolerable proportions; and it would probably litter the countryside with advertisements. Whilst it has for many decades been acknowledged that town planning can materially contribute to the well being and true wealth of the community, it is only more recently that sub-regional and regional planning have begun to be similarly recognized. The debate surrounding the location of the Third London Airport is a particularly good example. While regional planning from this standpoint imposes upon both individuals and the community at large certain recognizable costs—especially through the delays incurred in development and the restraints surrounding enterprise—its reputation frequently suffers from the less tangible nature of its benefits and achievements.

Any interpretation of contemporary attitudes towards regional planning would be incomplete without some mention of their purely political content. It is natural for Members of Parliament elected from constituencies in the less prosperous regions of the country to press for and expect some public assistance for their communities. The middle nineteen sixties, however, experienced a new political development, resulting from a growing disenchantment with central government. This was the emergence of a more articulate regional spirit in Provincial England, and an increasingly vocal nationalistic spirit in Scotland and Wales. The development was given expression, and possibly was even encouraged, by the creation (in 1964–1965) of the Regional Planning Boards and Regional Economic Councils. The Boards comprise civil servants from central government departments who are responsible for the activities of the latter in particular regions. The Economic

Councils are nominated by the government from various sections of the community—in particular from business, the trades unions, local government and the universities—to advise on the implications and directions of government policies as they affect their regions. The existence of these bodies has created a situation in which central government policies are now more than ever carefully scrutinized for their spatial implications, and regional dissatisfaction can thus be given a more formal expression. Whatever reforms eventually emerge from the Crowther Commission on the Constitution, there can be no doubt that a public awareness of the several regions and nations that comprise Britain is greater today than for many decades past. The growing recognition of the importance of regional planning throughout the nineteen sixties was undoubtedly related in part to this new political phenomenon.

1.2 The More Prosperous Regions

Between 1951 and 1971, the British population increased by about 10 per cent, or some 4.9 million. Of this increase, 3.9 million were to be found in the five more prosperous regions in the south and midlands of England (see Table 1). The South East alone increased by 1.9 million people, of which more than 0.5 million was the result of net interregional and international migration; at an even faster rate the population of the West and East Midlands increased by 1.1 million. The concentration of the British people in the southern parts of the country, and more particularly in the London and Birmingham city regions, undoubtedly reflects the private advantages of locating economic developments there. The economic structure of the two regions is by no means identical. Yet both are characterized by a wide diversity of industrial and commercial activities, amongst which rank a large percentage of growth industries satisfying the rapidly expanding sectors of both the national and international markets. Their economic evolution has been conditioned by the existence of a set of recognizable advantages which are to be found in many localities of continuing urban growth but which are particularly abundant in the South East and West Midlands regions. One of these is an ease of access to markets.

A large percentage of firms—particularly in their early innovatory years, if not subsequently—elect to serve the whole of the national market from a single place of production. Because most manufacturers absorb the costs of distributing their final products to the consumer through selling at a (nationally) uniform delivered price, it is clearly advantageous for them to be located where these transport costs are at a minimum. The long-standing concentration of the British population in southern England, therefore, affords manufacturing industries there a considerable advantage. Distribution costs are at their lowest and convenient access to consumers is most likely to be assured. More especially in the case of a wide range of service activities, there can be very little doubt as to the primacy of London in the national market. As a yardstick of this advantageous market accessibility of southern England, Clark (1966) has produced an index of 'economic potential'. This index measures the relative proximity of a place to total purchasing power as it is distributed geographically throughout the country. Purchasing power is broadly defined as the net earned income of the resident population, although account is taken of the advantage of accessibility to export outlets by allotting a notional overseas income to the country's main ports. Proximity is measured not in terms of geographical distance, but of tapered freight transport rates. Clark's calculations (Figure 2a) reveal that the place with greatest 'economic potential' in Britain, measured in this way, is in fact London. From the metropolis, economic potential values, and hence relative accessibility to the markets for goods and services, fall in all directions. Birmingham has a value 7 per cent below that of London, Leeds 15 per cent below and Glasgow 30 per cent below. An advantage of this sort, translated into increased sales through lower transport costs and closer contact with customers, helps considerably to explain the remarkable growth of London and the West Midlands in the present century. Prospectively, it suggests the relative advantage of southeast England within an enlarged European Economic Community (Clark, Wilson and Bradley, 1969) (Figure 2b).

Although it is rooted in the distribution of the British population, this pattern of market *Access* accessibility is also a function of the country's transport facilities and costs. As has been seen, the geography of road and rail transport in Britain affords a unique and advantageous nodality to both London and Birmingham. In the case of London, however, the outstanding importance of its ports must also be recognized. Historically the most important single geographical advantage promoting the development of the capital was its position at the head of ocean navigation on the most important estuary in the country. Today, the focus of Western European trade is increasingly coming to be concentrated upon both the great and the smaller ports of the 'Narrows'—London, Southampton, Le Havre, Antwerp and Rotterdam, Felixstowe, Harwich, Seaford, Dunkirk and Ostend. Their industrial hinterlands, which extend from Birmingham in the north to Paris in the south, and from the Ruhr in the east to South Wales in the west, form the economic heart of Western Europe today. The economies of Greater London and the West Midlands, therefore, especially through the use they make of the *ports* of London (which include Felixstowe, Harwich, the Medway, Dover, Folkestone and in certain respects even Southampton), need to be considered as part of a greater North West European economic complex and not solely in domestic terms. In addition to its seaports, London also has the advantage of the major international airport at Heathrow. Not only is this the third most important port in the country in terms of the value of goods handled, but it has also been a major stimulus to economic development in southeast England. Directly employing about 45,000 people, it has been calculated that the airport, through the attraction of employments into its sub-region and through the various employment and population multipliers, has come to 'generate' an associated population of between 200,000 and 250,000.

The relative advantage of the London and Birmingham city regions in attracting growth *Labour* industries also stems from the characteristics of their labour markets. As a consequence of their economic history, the long standing diversity of manufacturing employments in London, and the concentration of pioneering engineering activities in the West Midlands,

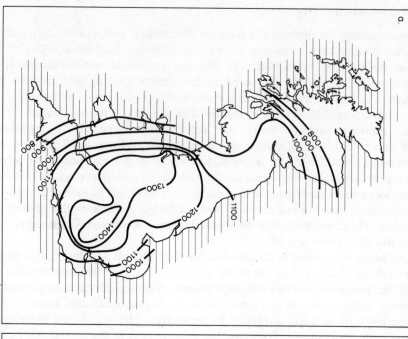

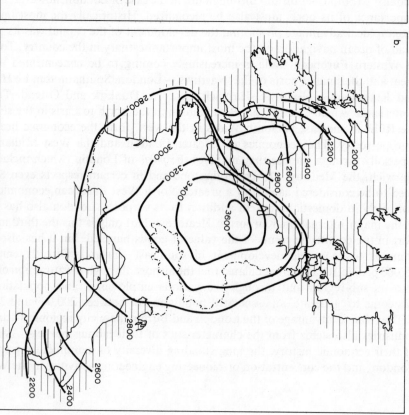

Figure 2 Britain and Western Europe: indices of economic potential, *circa* 1965.

Note: Economic potential is an abstract index of the relative proximity of a place to total purchasing power as it is distributed spatially throughout a country or region: see pp. 10 and 11.

Sources: Clark, 1966; Clark, Wilson and Bradley, 1969.

these regions afford unique advantages for the development of modern industries. The range of skills which are available to an entrepreneur, and the supplementary training and educational facilities which are available to him and his work force, are of outstanding importance. In addition, the very size of the labour markets in London and West Midlands means that the possibility of attracting the right sort of skills when and where they are wanted is much greater than anywhere else in the country. Although major interregional differentials in the cost of labour are severely constrained by the growing tendency for wages to be bargained and agreed at a national level, these metropolitan labour markets are undoubtedly relatively expensive. It is reasonable to assume, however, that for many firms the greater diversity and larger size of these labour markets permit an efficiency of operation and the possibility of growth, which more than justifies the marginally higher costs that have to be paid for employees there. In the service sector, of course, the position is even more extreme. Central London by the middle nineteen sixties had some 16.6 million square metres (179 million square feet) of office space, and the rest of the South East region a further 22.0 million square metres (237 million square feet); together these represented about half of the total office space in England and Wales. As a consequence the South East Economic Planning region provides employment for about half of the 4.6 million office workers in England and Wales, and some 0.8 million are employed in Central London alone. It is naturally very difficult for any other part of the country to compete with such a remarkable concentration of skills.

A further set of advantages for economic development in southern England are what might be loosely grouped under the heading of 'external economies'. A large number of firms regularly purchase from other firms such supplementary services as transport and sub-contracting, advertising and market consultancy, specialized broking, computer facilities and the like. The fact that London especially, but also the West Midlands, offer these services in greater variety than other parts of the country is an important asset in their economic development. New firms can take advantage of them. And the arrival of these new firms both enlarges the market for such activities and also signals the possibility of yet further external economies by permitting the emergence of even more specialized facilities and services. The type of firm said to benefit most from such externalities is the relatively small business producing goods or services for a fluctuating market; in a large metropolitan economy it is in a position to share with other firms in the industry, or with the metropolitan economy in general, activities and costs which it might elsewhere be required to internalize. However, there are no theoretical reasons why comparable benefits should not be available to firms of different sizes, organization and technology. Normally, the hire of additional lorries to meet a temporary upsurge of demand can more readily be arranged by a London firm than by its counterpart in Grimsby, and the stocks or inventories carried by a Birmingham motor component manufacturer need to be very much smaller than those of a similar enterprise in the Central Valley of Scotland.

The traditions of vigorous entrepreneurship and innovation that have characterized the two main conurbations of southern England for many generations further assist in their economic growth. Moreover, the relative ease with which capital can be raised there, and the impressively wide range of social, cultural, and educational amenities, which are associated with London in particular, play a significant role in regional economic development. There can also be little doubt that the location of the central government in London, plus the fact that the greater number of its research establishments are within easy reach of the capital, gives the South East a further economic advantage. These and other considerations are discussed further in Chapters 2 to 4. It is necessary, of course, to acknowledge explicitly that these many advantages of southern England in general, and of the London and Birmingham city regions in particular, are purely relative. Nevertheless, they have been decisive in creating there a distinctive set of development characteristics which are shared in smaller measure with the other more prosperous regions, but which are more elusive in the rest of the country. Since nothing breeds success like success, they would undoubtedly have been even more influential but for the intervention of public policy.

These advantages are partly offset by a number of outstanding problems that are posed by rapid economic and physical growth in the South East and the West Midlands. Their precise expression, and the 'received' interpretation of them, however, has changed through time. The Royal Commission on the Distribution of Industrial Population in 1940 was of an opinion that the continuing growth of London in particular presented the country with strategic as well as economic and social problems; yet it is rare to hear a military strategist arguing against the further growth of urban areas in southern England today. Again, at one time there was some evidence to suggest that large conurbations generally had a rather poorer record of physical health than other parts of the country; this is certainly no longer the case, although it has been suggested that the social and psychological stresses of living in large urban communities are not without their costs. Packman (1968, p. 170), for example, has demonstrated the greater prevalence of deprived children in southeast England compared with the northwest. The Barlow Commission also asserted that the London area faced a major problem of 'congestion', a perjorative indictment which has subsequently appeared regularly both in government reports and private writings, yet one which invariably has lacked a precise meaning. In so far as the concentration of people and their work in urban areas is likely to afford considerable benefits of agglomeration, it is obviously confusing to regard all centres of concentrated activity as 'congested'. The word is better reserved either for those situations in which certain minimum standards of housing, employment conditions, or noise level are exceeded, or for those instances in which the costs resulting from agglomeration demonstrably exceed the simultaneously generated benefits. In this context, therefore, such sweeping Barlow phrases as 'congested and insanitary urban areas', and a 'sprawling agglomeration of humanity', read less impressively and relevantly today than they did thirty years ago. Nevertheless, two complex sets of problems stemming from rapid and extensive urban growth remain as continuing intellectual and practical challenges to the urban and regional planner.

The first is the task of ensuring certain minimum environmental standards for the whole of the urban population. The need to clear slums, to reduce housing densities, to improve residential environments, to eliminate factories with poor working conditions, to improve such social investments as schools and health centres, and to increase recreational space is as much a task of the nineteen seventies as it was of the nineteen forties. Within the city region, the zones of decay change. For the community in general, acceptable standards of environment persistently rise. Yet within both the public and private purse, the amount of money available for environmental improvements is perennially limited. The attempt to achieve minimum environmental standards for all, therefore, not only persists but also continues to be limited by rigorous financial constraints. The second continuing urban dilemma relates to the improvement of mobility and circulation. In an age of increasing private car ownership and use, the internal transport problems of any town, city or metropolitan area raise complex questions concerning the most appropriate forms of traffic management, and the most desirable level and type of public transport investment. Yet there can be little doubt that the difficulties are at their most acute in the larger urban areas. The techniques for their examination, such as those used in the metropolitan transport surveys (Greater London Council, 1966; 1969a), are both highly sophisticated and very costly. Yet such controversial matters as the degree and style of public transport subsidies, and the trade-off between road and rail improvements, still remain unresolved. The size of the investments required are outstandingly high—the Greater London Council has suggested the need for an expenditure of £725 million at 1967 prices on road system improvements in its area alone. Yet at the end of the day—*vide* the controversy over the London Motorway box (pp. 126ff)—there is no unanimity concerning the wisdom of the decisions taken.

1.2.1 *Public Policy Responses : Restraining Economic Growth*

Partly in response to these problems of environment and mobility in the London and Birmingham city regions (particularly in their conurbation cores), and partly as a result of perceived but not necessarily proven disadvantages of continued economic expansion there, public policy since 1945 has sought to steer the physical development and restrain the economic growth of the country's most dynamic city and economic regions. In the process the policy has not only sought to prevent the merging of the two into a single English megalopolis, but it has also helped to alleviate the problems of the less prosperous parts of the country.

Although the Barlow Commission had advocated a ban upon further industrial developments in London, after 1945 the government embraced a policy which sought merely to restrain the pace of economic development there and in the West Midlands. Under the 1947 Town and Country Planning Act, local planning authorities (the counties and county boroughs) were given the power to prohibit changes in the use of land from one activity to another. Rural or residential land, therefore, could not be converted to industrial

Table 2. United Kingdom : employment resulting from principal movements of manufacturing industry, by regions, end-1966
(thousands)

origin	destination				
	South East and East Anglia	West Midlands	Rest of England	Peripheral Areas	United Kingdom
(A) Moves taking place in 1945–1951 (lower limit for inclusion : emp. of 8,000)					
Greater London	53	—	—	65	124
Rest of South East Region	—	—	8	19	34
East Anglia	—	—	—	—	8
West Midlands Conurbation	—	13	—	17	36
Rest of West Midlands	—	—	—	18	22
East Midlands	—	—	9	14	23
North West ex Merseyside	—	—	—	18	22
Yorkshire and Humberside	—	—	11	24	36
Abroad	—	—	—	41	45
All Origins (inc. others not detailed above)	67	16	53	237	373
(B) Moves taking place in 1952–1959 (lower limit for inclusion : emp. of 6,000)					
Greater London	92	—	7	15	115
Rest of South East Region	11	—	9	6	27
West Midlands Conurbation	—	8	—	7	17
Rest of West Midlands	—	—	—	—	11
East Midlands	—	—	6	—	10
North West ex Merseyside	—	—	—	6	13
South West ex Devon and Cornwall	—	—	—	9	12
Yorkshire and Humberside	—	—	7	—	11
Abroad	12	—	10	18	41
All Origins (inc. others not detailed above)	123	16	56	79	274

Table 2. (*Continued*)

origin	destination				
	South East and East Anglia	West Midlands	Rest of England	Peripheral Areas	United Kingdom
(C) Moves taking place in 1960–1965 (lower limit for inclusion: emp. of 4,000)					
Greater London	49	—	5	35	89
Rest of South East Region	7	—	4	26	37
West Midlands Conurbation	—	4	—	15	24
Rest of West Midlands	—	—	—	8	13
East Midlands	—	—	—	—	6
North West ex Merseyside	—	—	—	5	8
Yorkshire and Humberside	—	—	—	5	8
Abroad	4	—	—	17	23
All Origins (inc. others not detailed above)	65	6	30	122	223

Source : Howard (1968), p. 19.

purposes without their permission. By far the most important means of control over industrial development, however, was the industrial development certificate (i.d.c.) which was a natural successor to various wartime and immediate post-war government controls. From 1947 this had to be issued by the Board of Trade for any industrial building over 465 square metres (5,000 square feet) or representing a 10 per cent addition to existing industrial premises. By withholding certificates in South East England and the West Midlands, the Board thus came to exert a powerful influence over industrial movement in, and the economic geography of, the country. In addition, various financial and other incentives were made available to manufacturers moving to or located in the less prosperous regions (pp. 49ff). There was no blanket refusal of i.d.c. applications in southern England. Each application was 'viewed on its merits'. It was also viewed in the light of shifting planning doctrines and development priorities. The Board (subsequently absorbed into the Department of Trade and Industry) was much more reluctant to grant certificates in the period to 1949, and from about 1960 to 1969, than it was during the intervening or subsequent period when successive governments tended to discount the value of regional planning, or were desperate for new industrial investment wherever it might be encouraged. In the early nineteen seventies nearly 90 per cent of all i.d.c. applications in the South East region received approval. Howard (1968) has fully demonstrated the much slower pace of industrial movement away from the South East and West Midlands during the nineteen fifties (see Table 2).

Not only changing political attitudes limited the effectiveness of policies designed to steer manufacturing industry away from the more prosperous regions through i.d.c. refusals. The certificates relate to factory floor space. But a large proportion of manufacturing enterprises take up less than 465 square metres (5,000 square feet), and hence lay outside of the Board of Trade's control. New, pioneering and rapidly growing firms especially are found in this category. And many other firms, which might well have taken up more space, deliberately kept their size below 465 square metres simply in order to avoid the inconvenience of moving away from southern England. It is quite possible that the efficiency of some firms suffered as a result. In 1966 the government responded to this situation by temporarily reducing the size of plant needing an i.d.c. to first 280 square metres (3,000 square feet) and then to 93 square metres (1,000 square feet); by 1971, however, the limit was raised to 465 square metres again, and a year later to 930 square metres in the South East and 1395 metres in the Midlands. More fundamentally, however, it is clear that an administrative tool regulating industrial floor space is bound to be a somewhat insensitive device for the control of employment opportunities, which is what the policy fundamentally sought to achieve. Further, when a firm elected to move out of London or Birmingham its premises were invariably taken over by another manufacturing enterprise. The policy thus had little chance of stabilizing, let alone reducing, the number of jobs available in manufacturing industry either regionally or sub-regionally in southern England. Only if public authorities had bought up vacated industrial sites at market prices could this have been achieved—but the cost was too high.

Some expansion of manufacturing job opportunities in the London and Birmingham city regions was in any case both necessary and unavoidable. Quite apart from the employment needs of the new and expanding communities in the Outer Metropolitan Area (O.M.A.) of the South East and on the periphery of the West Midlands conurbation, the population of both regions was growing—as a result of natural increase as well as immigration—and it needed an expanding economic base. Moreover, there are some firms which primarily serve markets in Greater London or the West Midlands; others are highly dependent upon a site near to an international airport or seaport for their efficiency; a third group are closely tied to other firms in southern England. All of these firms could produce powerful and acceptable economic arguments for their location or expansion in the south. There was also a need to renew and redevelop industrial premises and zones within the conurbations if working conditions there were not to remain or fall below acceptable standards. Judged by its original intentions, therefore, the policy of seeking to check the economic expansion of the more prosperous regions of Britain through land use and i.d.c. controls over manufacturing industry, although it had a marked impact upon the economic structure of the less prosperous regions (pp. 61–62) and accelerated the rate of industrial decentralization into the O.M.A., met with only qualified success. By 1970, the South East and the West Midlands remained without question the power houses of British manufacturing industry, in terms of their size, their growth and their ability to generate new firms and activities.

As time went on, however, misgivings were increasingly expressed concerning the wisdom of these policies. In particular it was felt that they were having a debilitating effect upon the long-term prospects of the manufacturing sector in southern England, and especially within the conurbations there. To the protesting voices of many West Midlands' industrialists and the reservations expressed by the Confederation of British Industries (which nevertheless applauded the broad objectives of government regional policies), there was added in 1969 the disquiet of the Greater London Council (G.L.C.). In common with many other large metropolitan areas in the world, it had come to be alarmed by the steady decentralization of its manufacturing activities (Chapters 2 and 3). Sooner or later, it was feared, this was bound to present the central city and its inner suburbs with a long-term threat to their economic base. The plea in the G.L.C.'s *Development Plan* (1969b, p. 78 ff), therefore, was for a new approach by central government towards i.d.c. applications, and preferably for the control to be handed over to the strategic planning authority (the G.L.C. in the London case) which would accept only those industries with a record of relatively high productivity in conurbation locations. It was a plea which represented a major challenge to a fundamental element in the regional planning procedures of post-war Britain.

Throughout the nineteen forties and nineteen fifties, the attempts to curb the rate of economic growth in southern England were related entirely to the manufacturing sector of the economy. Yet the fastest growing employments were services. In the late nineteen fifties, jobs in Greater London were estimated to be growing at 45,000 per year, and those in central London at 20,000; of the latter, 15,000 were in offices. In response, a policy was initiated in 1963 designed to persuade offices to move out of London, and in that year the Location of Offices Bureau (L.O.B.) was established 'to encourage the decentralization of office employment from congested *(sic)* central London to suitable centres elsewhere'. In particular, it sought to publicise the relatively high cost of office floor space in London (Table 3), and the Bureau offered free advice to management on the advantages of alternative locations. Simultaneously, the government began to disperse some of its own activities from the capital. Parts of Customs and Excise were moved to Southend; much of the routine tax work for the London area was transferred to provincial centres; and the Post Office Savings Bank was moved to Glasgow. The *Economist* (1962, December 8, p. 989) even advocated the creation of an entirely new national capital—Elizabetha—somewhere in the Vale of York.

Controls were soon added to persuasion in the private sector. Following the 1965 Control of Offices and Industrial Development Act, an office development permit (o.d.p.)

Table 3. Britain : variations in office rentals, by towns and regions, mid-1970

	Rent per square metre (£)	Rent per square foot (£)
Central London	64.50–107.00	6.00–10.00
The South East		
Aldershot	10.75	1.00
Andover	9.40	0.90
Basildon	11.30	1.05
Brentwood	13.45	1.25
Brighton	7.50–10.75	0.70–1.00
Maidenhead	13.45	1.25
Maidstone	13.45–14.80	1.25–1.40
Margate	9.10	0.85
Reading	8.05	0.75
Slough	22.05	2.05
Southampton	8.05–14.80	0.75–1.40
The Midlands		
Birmingham	12.10	1.15
Leamington Spa	10.75	1.00
Leicester	10.20	0.95
Nottingham	5.40–9.65	0.50–0.90
Stratford upon Avon	10.75	1.00
South West England and South Wales		
Bristol	8.90–11.55	0.80–1.10
Cardiff	16.10–26.85	1.50–2.50
Cheltenham	10.75	1.00
Exeter	6.45	0.60
Swindon	12.10	1.15
The North		
Bootle	10.75	1.00
Bradford	4.30	0.40
Gateshead	8.65	0.80
Leeds	8.05–11.85	0.75–1.10
Liverpool	12.10	1.15
Newcastle upon Tyne	10.75–19.40	1.00–1.80
Oldham	7.25	0.70
Runcorn	10.75	1.00
Scotland		
East Kilbride	15.05	1.40
Glasgow	12.10	1.15

Source : Location of Offices Bureau.

had to be granted by the Board of Trade, and more recently the Ministry of Local Government and Development within the new Department of the Environment, before any new office building or conversion exceeding 353 square metres (3,000 square feet) could be undertaken. The control initially applied only to the London Metropolitan Region and to the West Midlands conurbation, but it was soon extended (in 1966) to the whole of the South East and to both the East and West Midlands; however, the exemption limits were raised outside the London Metropolitan Region to 929 square metres (10,000 square feet) in 1967. The decentralization of central government offices—as well as the devolution of some administrative responsibilities to the Regional Planning Boards and the newly-created Welsh Office—in the meantime was pursued more vigorously (Daniels, 1969).

The transitional costs of moving an office from central London are perhaps higher than generally realized—£560 per employee was quoted in a 1967 survey. On the other hand, the operating expenses of a decentralized office can be as much as 20 per cent below its central London counterpart as a result of lower rents, lower salaries and a lower rate of staff turnover. However, there is no continuous cost gradient with increasing distance from London, and the savings in expenses do not generally increase beyond the O.M.A.; indeed the cost of office space in some provincial centres is relatively high by O.M.A. standards (Table 3). It was not unnatural therefore for office developers and decentralizing employers to show a particular interest in such places as Basingstoke, Brighton, Bletchley, Chichester, Croydon, Guildford, Horley, Reading, Reigate, Southend, Worthing and the London new towns—rather than places further from London. The number of jobs moved out of central London under the auspices of L.O.B. (and these probably represent about one half of the total private and government moves, since not all decentralizers contact the Bureau) rose to a peak of 14,000 in 1967–1968. But despite the office controls the greater number of the office employers—representing 82 per cent of the jobs associated with L.O.B. between 1963 and 1969—were reluctant to move their activities more than about 130 kilometres (80 miles) from London; only 1 per cent were willing to move into a Development Area where a 25 per cent building grant was available (Figure 3).

After 1967–1968, however, the rate of private office decentralization from central London began to fall (Table 4). The amount of vacant office space both in London and the country as a whole contracted severely, and the cost of office accommodation in the centre of the capital rose quite dramatically. The dilemma facing the government became clear. Whilst its policies were restricting the short distance movement of offices out of central London through the imposition of floor space controls in the South East and the Midlands, there remained insufficient encouragement for office employers to move longer distances into the provinces and Development Areas. Meanwhile, of course, the population of Greater London continued to disperse outwards in search of homes and amenity. Without a parallel movement of jobs in the longer run, such a trend implied an overall lengthening of the journey to work, a prospect which received planning doctrine certainly abhorred. L.O.B. (1970, p. 28–9) called for 'the relaxation of the control on

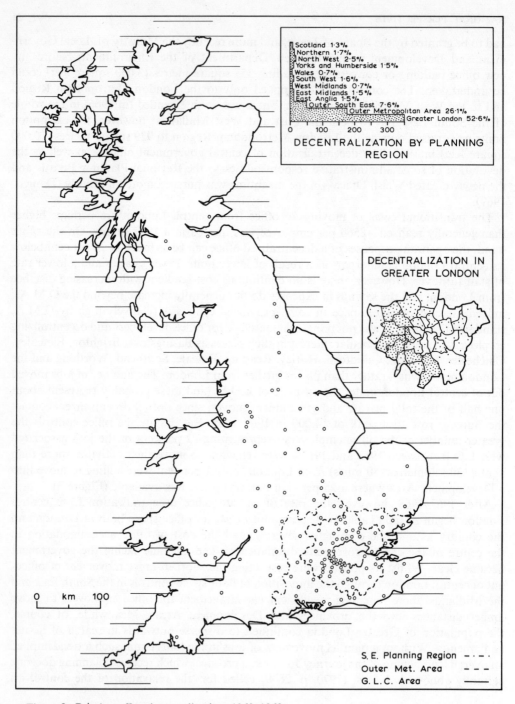

Legend within map:

Scotland 1·3%
Northern 1·7%
North West 2·5%
Yorks and Humberside 1·5%
Wales 0·7%
South West 1·6%
West Midlands 0·7%
East Midlands 1·5%
East Anglia 1·5%
Outer South East 7·6%
Outer Metropolitan Area 26·1%
Greater London 52·6%

0   100   200   300

DECENTRALIZATION BY PLANNING
REGION

DECENTRALIZATION IN
GREATER LONDON

0   km   100

S. E. Planning Region — · — ·
Outer Met. Area   — — —
G. L. C. Area   ————

Figure 3 Britain: office decentralization, 1963–1969.
Note : dots indicate the location of decentralized offices recorded by the Location of Offices
Bureau, plus the location of decentralized government offices.
Source : Daniels, 1969.

Table 4. Britain : office decentralization from central London, 1963–1970

Years	Enquiries	Jobs to be moved as represented by enquiries	Firms moved	Jobs moved
(A) Moves assisted by the Location of Offices Bureau				
1963/64	354	36,000	7	291
1964/65	522	56,221	97	6,342
1965/66	408	43,412	146	10,768
1966/67	308	29,543	162	11,564
1967/68	253	21,772	191	14,002
1968/69	203	14,182	146	10,996
1969/70	172	15,920	129	9,367
TOTAL	2,220	217,050	878	63,330
(B) Estimated independent moves				
1963–70	—	—	approx. 600	approx. 100,000
(C) Government departments and British Rail				
1963–70	—	—	74	20,059
GRAND TOTAL	—	—	approx. 2,200	approx. 180,000

Source : Location of Offices Bureau.

office development in Greater London so as to permit substantial additions to the western boroughs such as Kingston, Ealing and Brent; the "new town" of Thamesmead and lesser amounts in other strategic town centres of the Greater London Development Plan ... Outside Greater London, the Bureau would like to see the present control lifted and matters left to normal planning procedures.' It became increasingly evident, therefore, that only by offering considerably greater financial inducements could the government hope to secure from the private office sector a contribution to the solution of the inter-regional development problem comparable to that being made by the civil service (Rhodes and Kan, 1971). Intraregionally, office policy clearly needed to be more closely geared to the strategic planning goals of the South East; and with o.d.p. controls lifted outside the region in 1970 (and applying only to projects of more than 929 square metres in the South East) this manifestly become the intention of the Government.

1.2.2 *Public Policy Responses : Constraining Physical Expansion*

Paralleling the attempt to control economic growth in southern England was the decision, made possible by the immediate post-war land use planning legislation, to control the physical extension of the Greater London and the West Midlands conurbations. The idea of constraining the growth of London by physical controls was by no means new (Thomas, 1970). The Elizabethan 'Cordon Sanitaire' and the ideas of Pepler were the natural forerunners of the green belt proposed in Abercrombie's plan for Greater London in 1944. The intention was that within this 'sterilized' zone—which could offer recreational opportunities for Londoners—only developments which conformed to the existing pattern of primarily rural land uses were to be allowed. As a result the continuing outwards sprawl of the conurbation, which had been a persistent feature of the inter-war years, could be checked. To a large extent the policy succeeded. A variety of associated problems nevertheless gradually emerged. Since land uses within the green belt were from the outset mixed in character—villages and towns, quarries and sand pits, airfields and public buildings, as well as parks and farmland—the definition of 'conforming uses' proved far from easy in the day-to-day administration of the policy. The initial pressures for urban and suburban developments there were considerable. They increased as the population of Greater London grew, as the land initially designated for housing was gradually used up, and as regional planning decisions were avoided during the fifties. Local planning authorities and the Ministry of Housing and Local Government nevertheless defended the policy well into the next decade. By that time, however, the doctrine of the green belt was the subject of increasing scepticism and criticism. First, it came to be recognized that with population growth, with the 'fission' of households and with the redevelopment of central residential areas at lower densities, there had been a considerable underestimation in the immediate post-war years of the need for housing land within the conurbation. Abercrombie, for example, had mistakenly assumed a static London population in his plan. It was argued by some, therefore, that more land should be released for housing, and that at least some of this should come from the green belt, especially those parts which demonstrably had little recreational value. At the same time questions arose as to whether the green belt was in fact being used for those recreational purposes that were in part its justification. Above all, there developed a sense that urban areas are dynamic and need to 'grow', and that without conclusive evidence on the optimum size of cities at various levels of the urban hierarchy this requirement should not be frustrated.

A new school of planning thought thus began to emerge. It argued the advantages of allowing the physical expansion of urban areas along their major radial lines of communication, saw green wedges between those growth sectors as an alternative to the green belt, and advocated the deliberate creation of parks within the green wedges to serve metropolitan recreational needs. The wisdom of the green belt policy was first questioned in an official publication in the South East Study of 1964; its long-term value was further challenged in the 1966 Strategy for the South East in which 'country zones', wedged between radial sectors of urban expansion, were given the role of shaping metropolitan growth and affording recreational opportunities. Neither publication, however, had an operational status, and it was only with the approval of the 1970 *Strategic Plan for the South East* that a retained green belt was officially wedded to bolder notions of countryside preservation over much larger tracts of the region (see Chapter 3).

The physical containment of urban growth in the West Midlands has had a somewhat different history. There, it was rivalries and disagreements between the several local authorities responsible for the physical planning of the Birmingham city region which more than anything else prevented the transfer of land to urban uses and restrained the outward spread of the conurbation. By 1965, however, a ministerially approved green belt had been agreed and drawn upon the map. It was shaped not only to restrain the outward growth of the main built up areas within this polynuclear urban complex, but also to keep them apart. Thus, besides helping to maintain the identity of such places as Nuneaton and Bedworth, it also serves to separate towns like Redditch, Bromsgrove, Kidderminster and Stafford from the mass of the West Midlands conurbation. Curiously, therefore, whilst the usefulness of a green belt for the London Metropolitan region was being challenged, the idea was being more firmly embraced in the West Midlands. It was nevertheless made clear in the 1965 West Midlands *Regional Study* by the Department of Economic Affairs that the precise boundaries of the green belt might have to be adjusted in the light of further transport and land use studies; it is also noteworthy that the concept of sectoral growth is not absent from the strategic thinking of some planners concerned with urban growth in the West Midlands (see Chapter 5).

1.2.3 *Public Policy Responses: the Overspill Arrangements*

Intimately related to the policies designed to restrain the economic and physical growth of the London and Birmingham city regions were the arrangements made to provide the opportunity, and indeed deliberately to foster, the growth of population at specific places beyond their green belts. This was the policy of overspill. Even on Abercrombie's assumption of a static London population, it was recognized that the redevelopment of the inner areas of the conurbation would necessitate the designation of an area of land for housing which was simply not available within the London contained by the green belt. Naturally some new, and quite major, housing estates or 'satellites' could be built within what is now Greater London—Roehampton and St. Mary Cray are two examples—but additional accommodation was also clearly required. This need was wedded to the ideas of Ebenezer Howard and the new towns movement, which deplored many aspects of Victorian and Edwardian urbanization, and sought to create new self-contained and balanced communities for working and living. By 1949, with prototypes already built and financed by private capital at Letchworth (1903) and Welwyn Garden City (1920), the government had designated eight new towns in southeast England under the 1946 New Towns Act (Figure 4). For each, a Development Corporation was appointed and charged with the responsibility of acquiring land, preparing plans, and administering the overspill of industry and population from the inner parts of London.

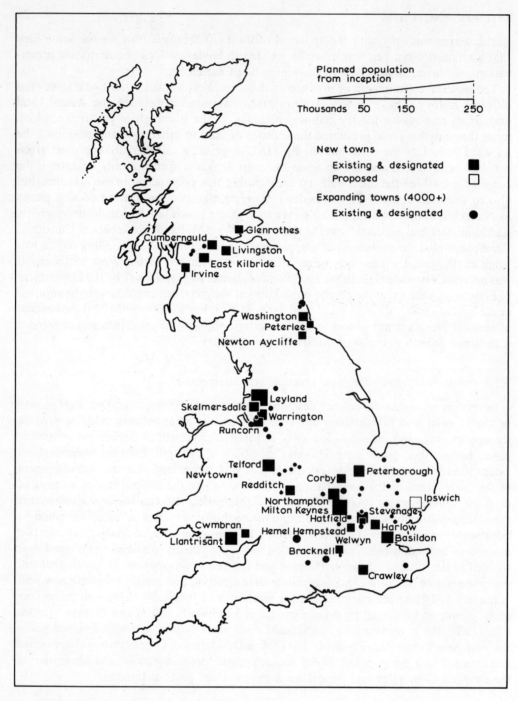

Figure 4 Britain: new and expanded towns, 1971.
Source : *Town and Country Planning,* January 1971.

NB A seems to have miscalc? all along the line.

Only three of the ten sites preferred by Abercrombie were in fact selected, and alternative locations were chosen that were either more accessible to London, or better able to serve various physical planning objectives as well as overspill. After a somewhat slow start, which was inevitable for such a pioneering programme within a mixed economy, by the early nineteen sixties the new towns were becoming significant centres of economic and population growth (Thomas, 1969). They developed an expanding and frequently high wage industrial base; in time they came to be attractive to decentralizing offices; the quality of their social amenities was outstanding in relation to their size; and they proved to be a financial success. By early 1971 they had a total population of 471,000, of which some 372,000 represented the overspill component (Table 5), and their revised target population was over 628,000.

NT. 9c early '60s

Although the new towns idea was taken up and adapted in several of the Development Areas during the nineteen forties and fifties (p. 59), none were built for the West Midlands conurbation. Throughout the period local pressure groups such as the Midlands New Towns Society urged the necessity for providing adequate overspill facilities beyond the (as yet undesignated) green belt. However, the same lack of cooperation between the local planning authorities which had plagued the region's green belt policy prevented any agreement until 1963. In that year Dawley was selected as the first new town for the city region. Subsequently Redditch was also designated and the scale of the Dawley proposals enlarged to make the new planned city of Telford (pp. 212ff).

No N.T's in W. Mids

Dawley ↓ Tlford.

Throughout the nineteen fifties, successive Ministers of Housing and Local Government were reluctant to approve further new town schemes on the grounds of their initially high capital cost, plus a belief that existing towns could also make a substantial and less expensive contribution to the process of metropolitan overspill. Financial assistance was first made available for expanded towns under the 1952 Town Development Act, and the London County Council made a large number of arrangements with such places as Thetford and Haverhill, Ashford and Andover, Aylesbury and Banbury (see Figure 4). Similarly, the Birmingham authorities agreed to encourage the movement of industry and population to several Staffordshire towns, to Shrewsbury and to a number of Welsh communities. Although these arrangements facilitated the decentralization of some conurbation activities and people, the Town Development Act in retrospect has left only a relatively small imprint upon the urban geography of Britain (see Table 5). Only in the case of Swindon, where the urgent need to restructure the local economy (following the contraction of jobs in the town's principal source of employment, the railway workshops) was fortuitously combined with rare local authority initiative, and at a later stage in the case of Basingstoke, did the Act serve as a mechanism for large scale overspill.

prtcl initial high cap cost, & NB new notion. Finance a) Govt b) City.

Modest effect.

By the early nineteen sixties, therefore, a crisis in the land use and regional planning of the London and Birmingham city regions was becoming all too apparent. The earlier miscalculations concerning the population growth and the housing needs of the conurbations, the continuing net immigration which could not be checked, and the powerful

Crisis :
1)
2)

Table 5. Britain : progress in the new and expanded towns, 1971

A. New Towns

	Date of designation	Population			Total employment (est.)[1]			
		Original	Proposed	31 Dec. 1970 (est.)	Males	Females	Total	Date
LONDON RING								
Basildon	4 Jan. 1949	25,000	134,000	83,000	24,000	14,400	38,400	Dec. 1970
Bracknell	17 June 1949	5,140	60,000	37,300	10,850	6,350	17,200	June 1970
Crawley	9 Jan. 1947	9,100	120,000	67,800	28,745	14,683	43,428	June 1968
Harlow	25 Mar. 1947	4,500	90,000+	76,500	21,200	13,600	34,800	Sept. 1970
Hatfield	20 May 1948	8,500	29,500	26,300	16,370	8,061	24,431	June 1969
Hemel Hempstead	4 Feb. 1947	21,000	80,000	70,000	18,400	12,100	30,500	June 1969
Stevenage	11 Nov. 1946	6,700	105,000	66,300	21,700	11,250	32,950	Dec. 1970
Welwyn Garden City	20 May 1948	18,500	50,000	43,630	17,646	11,085	28,731	June 1969
TOTAL, LONDON RING	—	98,440	668,500+	470,830	158,911	91,529	250,440	—
OTHERS IN ENGLAND & WALES								
Aycliffe	19 Apr. 1947	60	45,000	24,000	342	684	1,026[2]	Nov. 1970
Corby	1 Apr. 1950	15,700	83,000	50,500	18,794	6,355	25,149[3]	—
Cwmbran	4 Nov. 1949	12,000	55,000	46,400	10,013	5,776	15,789	June 1969
Milton Keynes	12 Jan. 1967	44,000	250,000	50,000	13,450	6,850	20,300	Dec. 1970
Newtown	18 Dec. 1967	5,700	13,000	5,500	2,000	1,000	3,000	June 1969
Northampton	14 Feb. 1968	131,120	260,000	130,612	39,271	25,964	65,235	June 1968
Peterborough	1 Aug. 1967	82,910	187,890	88,400	34,095	15,905	50,000	Dec. 1970
Peterlee	10 Mar. 1948	200	30,000	24,000	2,731	3,872	6,603	Sept. 1970
Redditch	10 Apr. 1964	32,000	90,000	39,800	—	—	22,000	Oct. 1970
Runcorn	10 Apr. 1964	30,000	90,000	36,440	11,260	4,990	16,250	Dec. 1970
Skelmersdale	9 Oct. 1961	10,000	80,000	27,300	5,777	2,379	8,156	June 1969
Telford	12 Dec. 1968	70,000	250,000	78,000	—	—	33,000	Dec. 1970
Warrington	26 Apr. 1968	122,300	209,000	133,000	40,536	22,468	63,004	Dec. 1970
Washington	26 July 1964	20,000	80,000	26,006	7,138	2,502	9,640	Dec. 1970
TOTAL, OTHERS IN ENGLAND & WALES	—	575,990	1,722,890	759,958	185,407	98,745	339,152	—

1. Figures for male and female employment total less than total employment because male and female breakdown not available in all cases.
2. The Aycliffe industrial estate adjacent to but not within the designated area, employs 6,702 males.
3. The British Steel Corporation adjacent to but outside the designated area, employs 13,292 persons.

Table 5. (*Continued*)

	Date of designation	Population			Total employment (est.)[2]			
		Original	Proposed	31 Dec. 1970 (est.)	Males	Females	Total	Date
SCOTLAND								
Cumbernauld	9 Dec. 1955	3,000	100,000	32,400	6,413	3,776	10,189	Sept. 1970
East Kilbride	6 May 1947	2,400	100,000	66,300	14,415	10,326	24,741	Sept. 1970
Glenrothes	30 June 1948	1,100	75,000	30,000	5,700	4,800	10,500	Dec. 1970
Irvine	9 Nov.1966	34,600	120,000	42,000	9,200	5,600	14,800	Sept. 1970
Livingston	17 Apr. 1962	2,000	100,000	14,000	2,700	1,200	3,900	Dec. 1970
TOTAL, SCOTLAND	—	43,100	495,000	184,700	38,429	25,702	64,130	—
BRITAIN, GRAND TOTAL		717,530	2,886,390	+1,415,488	382,746	215,976	653,722	—

B. Expanded Towns (summary table)

Dispersing area	Number of schemes agreed	Dwellings		
		To be built	Completed	Under construction
ENGLAND & WALES				
Greater London	31	89,453	41,445	5,916
Birmingham	15	21,222	7,485+	1,763
Bristol	4	2,278	2,278	—
Liverpool	4	18,526	4,970	1,063
Manchester	4	8,514	1,361	15
Newcastle upon Tyne	2	10,517	1,513	657
Salford	1	4,518	4,518	—
Walsall	2	444	444	—
Wolverhampton	4	4,527	4,327+	60
TOTAL, ENGLAND & WALES	67	159,999	68,341	9,474
GLASGOW	42	18,205	9,780	—
BRITAIN, GRAND TOTAL	109	178,204	78,121+	9,474

Table 5. (*Continued*)

C. Expanded Towns (details)

Dispersing area	Expanding towns	Dwellings		
		To be built	Completed[4]	Under construction
Greater London	Andover B	6,000	1,526	617
	Ashford UD	4,250	1,953	—
	Aylesbury B	3,000	1,969	41
	Banbury B	2,236	1,070	147
	Basingstoke B	11,500	5,122	1,624
	Bletchley UD	5,000	3,551	288
	Bodmin B	500	67	50
	Braintree and Bocking UD	1,200	113	71
	Burnley CB	700	64	§
	Bury St Edmunds B	3,000	1,167	62
	Canvey Island UD	414	414	—
	Frimley and Camberley UD	1,177	1,177	—
	Gainsborough UD	1,000	78	72
	Grantham B	500	21	—
	Haverhill UD	4,500	2,110	301
	Huntingdon and Godmanchester B	2,450	1,755	84
	King's Lynn B	3,500	1,238	86
	Letchworth UD	1,500	1,174	146
	Luton CB	1,000	1,000	—
	Luton RD	3,896	1,396	271
	Melford RD	750	739	—
	Mildenhall RD	2,000	475	70
	Peterborough B	300	132	—
	Plymouth CB	300	6	—
	St Neots UD	2,000	683	90
	Sandy UD	700	—	—
	Sudbury B	1,500	—	386
	Swindon B	8,580	7,480	110
	Thetford B	3,000	2,178	405
	Wellingborough UD	10,000	1,572	630
	Witham UD	3,000	1,215	365
	TOTAL FOR GREATER LONDON	89,453	41,445	5,916
Birmingham	Aldridge-Brownhills UD	2,500	913	—
	Banbury B	235	235	—
	Cannock UD	500	461	39
	Daventry B	5,275	1,370	33
	Droitwich B	2,000	960	316
	Leek UD	100	—	—
	Lichfield B	1,200	838	48
	Lichfield RD	500	66	—
	Rugeley UD	300	123	23
	Stafford B	750	320	—
	Stafford RD	300	—	—
	Tamworth B	6,500	1,309	1,138

Table 5. (*Continued*)

C. Expanded Towns (details)

Dispersing area	Expanding towns	Dwellings		
		To be built	Completed[4]	Under construction
	Tutbury RD	60	49	—
	Uttoxeter UD	200	200	—
	Weston super Mare B	802	636	166
	TOTAL FOR BIRMINGHAM	21,222	7,485	1,763
Bristol	Keynsham UD	642	642	—
	Sodbury RD	136	136	—
	Thornbury RD	500	500	—
	Warmley RD	1,000	1,000	—
	TOTAL FOR BRISTOL	2,278	2,278	—
Liverpool	Burnley CB	2,200	62	—
	Ellesmere Port B	5,500	2,134	360
	Widnes B	4,160	493	361
	Winsford UD	6,666	2,281	342
	TOTAL FOR LIVERPOOL	18,526	4,970	1,063
Manchester	Burnley CB	2,700	12	—
	Crewe B	4,000	35	15
	Macclesfield B	1,250	750	—
	Winsford UD	564	564	—
	TOTAL FOR MANCHESTER	8,514	1,361	15
Newcastle upon Tyne	Seaton Valley UD (Cramlington)	6,500	803	7
	Longbenton UD (Killingworth)	4,017	710	650
	TOTAL FOR NEWCASTLE UPON TYNE	10,517	1,513	657
Salford	Worsley UD	4,518	4,518	—
Walsall	Aldridge UDC	215	215	—
	Brownhills UDC	229	229	—
	TOTAL FOR WALSALL	444	444	—
Wolverhampton	Cannock RD	400	200	60
	Seisdon RD	1,546	1,546	—
	Tettenhall UD	131	131	—
	Wednesfield UD	2,450	2,450	—
	TOTAL FOR WOLVERHAMPTON	4,527	4,327	60

Table 5. (*Continued*)

C. Expanded Towns (details)

Dispersing area	Expanding towns	Dwellings		
		To be built	Completed[4]	Under construction
Glasgow	Alloa	75	67	—
	Alva	50	2	—
	Arbroath	398	193	—
	Barrhead	210	210	—
	Bathgate	277	193	—
	Bonnyrigg and Lasswade	100	70	—
	Denny and Dunipace	500	306	—
	Dumbarton	272	72	—
	Dumfries	100	12	—
	Dunbar	196	124	—
	Dunbarton County	349	124	—
	Forfar	150	—	—
	Fort William	200	100	—
	Galashiels	100	100	—
	Galston	100	3	—
	Girvan	700	50	—
	Grangemouth	697	681	—
	Haddington	250	250	—
	Hamilton	388	254	—
	Hawick	118	132	—
	Invergordon	50	1	—
	Inverkeithing	400	254	—
	Inverness County	100	108	—
	Irvine	1,239	744	—
	Jedburgh	250	—	—
	Johnstone (3 agreements)	1,920	1,671	—
	Kelso	75	25	—
	Kilsyth	102	62	—
	Kirkintilloch (2 agreements)	1,016	891	—
	Maybole	360	—	—
	Midlothian	750	157	—
	Newmilns and Greenholm	100	12	—
	Peebles	132	52	—
	Peebles County	20	20	—
	Renfrew County (3 agreements)	4,725	1,719	—
	Selkirk	65	22	—
	Stevenston	50	47	—
	Stewarton	400	181	—
	Sutherland County	50	—	—
	West Lothian (Blackburn)	300	300	—
	Whitburn	571	571	—
	Wick	300	—	—
	TOTAL FOR GLASGOW	18,205	9,780	—

Source : *Town and Country Planning*, January 1971.   4. By 30 June 1970.

natural forces encouraging the decentralization of employment and population together
rendered the existing overspill arrangements grossly inadequate. The scale of the problem
was such that it was decided to experiment with the creation of not only new cities with
a planned population of about ¼ million but also—and once again using the Development
Corporation mechanism—to expand some existing large towns by 100 per cent or more.
Although the designated area of Milton Keynes includes several small communities,
one of which (Bletchley) already had an overspill agreement with the G.L.C. under the
1952 Act, this scale of urban development represented a major innovation in British
planning. Similarly, the decision rapidly to double the size of Peterborough and Northampton made an entirely new use of the 1946 New Towns Act.

Ideas about planned overspill have changed in several respects since 1945. Quite apart
from the need to revise notions concerning the layout of new communities, and especially
the need for architects and urban planners to come to better terms with the motor car,
three changes are particularly outstanding. The first is the revision of the size of community
considered both desirable and feasible for an overspill population. Whereas the pre-war,
private enterprise new towns were designed as communities of about 30,000 people,
the first generation of new towns under the 1946 Act (although including two of only
25,000—Harlow and Bracknell) were planned to be significantly larger and in the 55,000
to 80,000 range. The largest, Basildon, was initially intended for a population of rather
more than 100,000. Subsequently the population targets of several of these towns were
revised upwards. Stevenage, for example, where the original design was for 60,000 people,
revised its plans to cater for 135,000; Crawley's plan was altered to house 120,000 rather
than 56,000. The new cities designated in the middle nineteen sixties marked yet a further
increase in the scale of the planned components in metropolitan overspill. In addition,
feasibility studies have been commissioned to examine the implications of the expansion
of South Hampshire into an enlarged urban complex of 1 million people. The growing
size of individual overspill plans is partly a matter of economics, for it has been shown
that the unit (public and private) costs of developing a community of 150,000 are lower
than those of a smaller community of 100,000. It is also related to the fact that the increasingly specialized demands of a progressively more affluent society require larger
communities to provide a satisfactory range of services and amenities. In addition, the
more recently designated overspill communities are further away from major metropolitan
centres than their earlier counterparts. Hence they are in locations which central place
theory would suggest are spatially suited to larger urban centres.

A second change which can be noted in overspill arrangements is the development of
ideas concerning the economic base of the planned communities. Immediately after
1945, the new towns were considered primarily a place for manufacturing industry,
plus those services which were required by the local community. With time, however,
research establishments connected either with local industry or with the associated metropolitan economy came to be established, and they were quickly followed by service industries and offices which had both a regional and even a national market. With the movement

of the Meteorological Office to Bracknell, British Petroleum to Harlow and Kodak to Hemel Hempstead, for example, not only has the economic base, but also the social structure, of the new towns gradually been changed. Later, when the prospective employment and social structure of Milton Keynes was analysed, it was accepted from the outset that offices and service jobs would in all probability provide a driving force of expansion there.

The third major change in ideas on metropolitan overspill concerns the spatial role of the new communities. The thinking of Abercrombie, like that of Howard before him, envisaged the creation of towns which in large measure would be self-contained in employment and services. The new towns have gone some considerable way to achieve this objective. Most of the people living in these communities also work there. However, the continuing erosion of the costs, and hence the importance, of distance has led (and will doubtless increasingly lead) to a greater movement of people in and out of the towns for work and for the provision of services. Whilst new town houses are generally made available to the workers of an incoming factory or office, should they be requested, there is nothing to stop a tenant subsequently looking for and taking work in a nearby town or even in London. The rest of his household are in the same position. Hence, the vastly improved commuter services between the new towns and central London, and the accessibility of many of the new communities to the radial motorways, have not only enormously enhanced the attractiveness of these places for industrial and commercial development, but also more firmly embraced them in the metropolitan labour market. There is no inherent virtue in increasing the distance travelled to work. Yet it is often the price that has to be paid for choice, opportunity and specialization in matters of employment and leisure. It is a development which is likely to increase rather than diminish. This feature, and also the recognition of the strong industrial and commercial linkages which exist between the new towns and other communities (particularly in their parent conurbation), stress the need to reinterpret metropolitan green belt and overspill policies primarily as a means of moulding and shaping urban growth—rather than as a devise for stopping it in order to create separate and smaller urban communities.

These changing ideas on the most appropriate scale, the potential economic base and the ultimate spatial role of overspill communities have been paralleled by a growing conviction of the advantages of the Development Corporation as a mechanism for their creation and growth. These statutory bodies, now appointed by the Secretary of State for the Environment, gain from their relatively easy access to government funds and hence to the large sums of capital which are required for initiating and completing large scale urban development of this sort. They are geographically flexible, and thus are able to handle developments which cut across established local authority boundaries. They can also advantageously combine within the same organization research, decision making and executive functions. The Regional Development Agencies, proposed (but never accepted) in the Steering Group's Report in *Traffic in Towns* (Ministry of Transport, 1963) as a means of adjusting existing urban areas to widespread motor car ownership and use, were consciously based upon the new town Development Corporations and their success. By comparison—and this was the main weakness of the Town Development Act—existing local authorities and more especially the smaller ones generally neither have, nor can afford, the expertise required to combine research and executive skills, and to initiate major development schemes. Development Corporations naturally have to work alongside existing local authorities, a requirement which proved to be difficult at times even when the latter were small urban districts and boroughs; only time will tell whether this problem is greater when the Corporations for the new cities have to deal with boroughs and county boroughs of much greater size, independence and importance.

1.2.4 *Public Policy Responses : Further Components*

There were three further components in the public policy response to the problems posed by urban growth in southern England. One was a changing set of policies relating to urban transport. Initially transport policy was not considered as part of the metropolitan growth problem, and attitudes towards the improvement of roads and public transport services were discussed and then adopted outside of a regional planning context. But with the growing ownership and use of cars, plus all the problems of road congestion which this development entails, increasingly was it realized that decisions affecting transport facilities and costs have fundamental implications for the geography of urban growth. To put it at its simplest, the further urban circulation shifts away from public and towards private transport, the greater will be the tendency towards a geographical dispersion of metropolitan development. By the middle nineteen sixties, therefore, there had been initiated in Greater London, in the West Midlands and in several smaller communities such as the Leicester sub-region major traffic and land use surveys which sought to relate the two sides of the urban development coin. Although the *South East Study* of 1963, and the *South East Strategy* of 1967, had both to be formulated without any clear assurances from the Ministry of Transport and other authorities concerning prospective road and public transport improvement schemes, the Greater London Development Plan of 1969 did have the benefit of the London Traffic Survey behind it. Similarly the 1970 *Strategic Plan* was evaluated against a set of specified transport objectives. By this date the Greater London Council was in the process of assuming overall responsibility for London (passenger) Transport, and arrangements for much closer cooperation with British Rail in regard to the planning of commuter services were being put in hand. The crucial importance of welding traffic and land use proposals together, and in particular the advantages of blending public transport policy with regional and sub-regional plans, caused the government to create under the 1969 Transport Act several passenger transport authorities in the provinces, amongst which was one for the West Midlands. These bodies are responsible to the local authorities in their respective areas, and they are charged with the task of framing policy and supervising finance. By settling the broad lines of metropolitan transport strategy—including such matters as fare structures, subsidies and the quality of service—the transport authorities are thus in a powerful position to assist in the realization of the broad land use objectives set by local and regional planning bodies. Earlier, in 1968, the two Whitehall ministries primarily concerned with regional and transport planning were brought together for the first time under a single Department (Local Government and Regional Planning), subsequently re-styled the Department of the Environment.

A critical element in metropolitan land use and transport planning in general is the specific set of dilemmas facing the central city in which the authorities face the huge task of appropriately renewing its fabric. Quite apart from the extensive tracts of central London which needed to be rebuilt after the bombing of World War II, economic and social blight afflicts considerable areas of older properties adjacent to the central business districts in all major cities. Both public and private initiatives are required for their reconstruction. Simultaneously the transport needs of those same areas change with time, and it is frequently possible to combine urban renewal with a redesigned circulation system within the city. All this—the speed at which, and the way in which, blighted areas at the centre of cities are renewed—has a considerable bearing upon the rate of population overspill and the pattern of metropolitan geography as a whole. Since 1945, public policy has sought to give urban renewal a reasonably high priority in central city affairs. Aided by a substantial subsidy on high rise accommodation, the inner London boroughs and Birmingham authorities have been able to retain a much larger population than might otherwise have been the case. Legislation has also allowed the compulsory purchase by local authorities of extensive tracts of central area land for comprehensive redevelopment. Not only has this substantially assisted in the redevelopment process and permitted a higher standard of urban design, but it has also allowed investment in major (if local) improvements in traffic flow. Whilst all the issues and dilemmas of urban renewal are somewhat tangential to the focus of this book, therefore, their relationship to the metropolitan development process can not be overlooked.

The geographical framework and organization of planning is the final component in public policy demanding attention at this point. The Development Corporations of the new towns apart, the spatial structure of land use planning in southern England has been shaped out of the traditional local government areas dating from the late nineteenth century. With the changing nature of economic life, and particularly with the changing technology of transport, however, the arrangement whereby counties and county boroughs were primarily responsible for making land use plans became increasingly obsolete. Until 1964 the traditional structure had to serve. In that year, however, the major reorganization of London's local government, proposed by the Herbert Commission in 1960, was put into effect with the creation of the G.L.C. which was given responsibility for the structure plan of its area. This represented a considerable advance on the previous situation—although there were many who argued that such a responsibility should have been commissioned on an even larger scale in order to embrace the whole of the city region. Meanwhile, County Councils had begun to cooperate in their regional planning research and decisions. In 1959, the County Planning Officers Conference was founded under the general guidance of the Ministry of Housing and Local Government to provide at least an official channel of communication in regional planning matters. Then in 1962 the Standing Conference on London and South East Regional Planning was created; serving twentyone local planning authorities it supports joint research and examines mutual problems. Similar cooperative moves were slower to develop in the Midlands, but by 1970 several liaison bodies bridging the gap between the geography of local government and the scale of economic and social life relevant for decision making in regional planning had come into existence. By 1965, in addition, the Regional Economic Councils and Planning Boards provided an intermediate level of advice and (in the case of the Boards) executive authority between central Government and the local authorities. The outmoded geography of the latter, however, remained. It was left to the Royal Commission on Local Government in England in 1969 to point to the need for, and the possibilities of, a major reorganization in the nineteen seventies. The government, however, elected to pursue a less radical reform in which 1,210 local authorities will be replaced in 1974 by rather less than 400, including 62 (provincial and metropolitan) counties and 66 metropolitan districts with major planning functions (Secretary of State for the Environment, 1971). Under the new arrangements, planning will be a three-tier affair: at the top is the regional strategy, formulated by joint teams representing the regional boards and councils, the Department of the Environment and the local authorities; next, constrained by the strategy, the counties will prepare structure plans for their areas; and at the local level the (county and metropolitan) districts will prepare the detailed land use plans.

In sum, therefore, public policies aimed at restraining and shaping economic and urban development in southern England demand interpretation at two levels. These can be broadly differentiated in terms of the government departments primarily concerned, the stated policy objectives and the reception areas for the 'shifted' growth. Concerned with decentralizing economic and physical growth a short distance away from the two major conurbations, intraregional policies were largely in the hands of the Ministry of Local Government and Development (formerly the Ministry of Housing and Local Government, and now within the Department of the Environment). They sought to reduce 'the congestion' and allow urgent redevelopment at the heart of the conurbations, and generally to improve the quality of urban life through the control of changes in land use. The reception centres were especially the new and expanded towns, although the decentralization of economic and social life exhibited other forms as well. Once the somewhat static approach to the planning of the London and Birmingham city regions (based upon the assumption of relatively little or no population growth) had been abandoned in favour of a more dynamic mode of strategic planning rooted in an acceptance of modest population growth, the tensions between regional planning and economic and demographic reality lessened. Nevertheless, many of the problems of metropolitan planning remained; the contrasting approaches of the various local and regional authorities in southern England are exposed in later chapters.

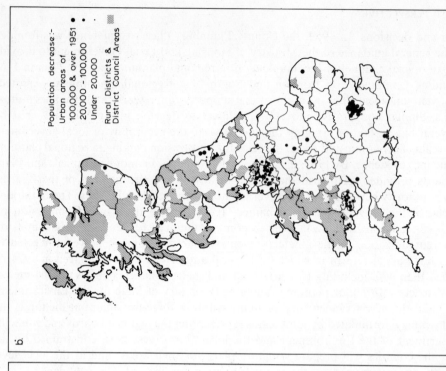

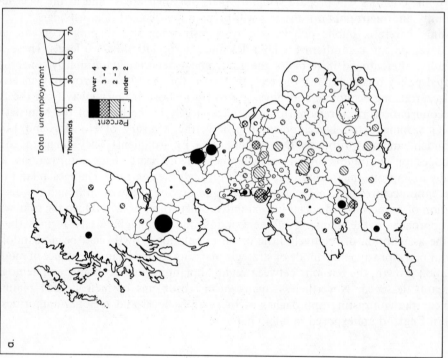

Figure 5 Britain : (a) unemployment 1968, and (b) areas of persistent population decrease 1951–1966.
Source : Secretary of State for Economic Affairs, 1969, Figs. 4 & 9.

On another level, interregional policies were concerned with attempts to shift some of the economic growth—but not the population—of southern England north and west. Their administration was largely in the hands of the Board of Trade and, since 1970, the new Department of Trade and Industry. For a few years this field was also the concern of the erstwhile Department of Economic Affairs. These policies sought to bring about a 'proper' distribution of industry and a better 'balance' between regions—without exactly specifying the meaning of either 'proper' or 'better'. It was to the various development areas and districts that the greater part of this longer distance dispersal was steered. The next section is devoted to a consideration of these policies.

1.3 The Less Prosperous Regions

In contrast to the widening economic opportunities and growth of southern England, for over fifty years now the less prosperous north and west of the country has been unable to throw off a set of complex economic problems. Since the end of the World War I, relatively high levels of unemployment, low activity rates and a steady net out-migration of people have characterized much of industrial North East England, North West England, the central valley of Scotland, and the industrial areas of Wales (Table 6). All these regions have suffered from the same basic inability to provide enough jobs for the people living there. With these coal-field industrial areas must be associated the rural parts of Northern England, Scotland, Wales, and the South West of England, which have also experienced a steady depopulation as a consequence of the changing structure and the contracting labour inputs of agriculture (Figure 5).

The high level of local unemployment in these less prosperous—and in relation to the national market, peripheral—regions has naturally varied through time. Their worst experience of unemployment was during the inter-war years, and more particularly during the years of the depression. It was then that Wales had 36.5 per cent of its labour force unemployed, whilst the other peripheral industrial areas all had unemployment levels above 27 per cent; the national figure in 1932 was, of course, as high as 22.2 per cent. Since 1945, the national rate of unemployment has remained very much lower. It has ranged between 1.5 and 2.5 per cent, although by early 1972 an adjusted monthly figure of 3.8 per cent was recorded. However, the differential between the national percentage and those of the less prosperous regions—albeit narrowing slightly—has remained. In Scotland, for example, unemployment has varied between 2.4 and 4.8 per cent—levels which would have been greater but for the steady movement of people out of the region (see Table 1). During the period 1923–1931, the average annual migration of people from Scotland was between 35,000 and 40,000; during the period 1964–1967 the annual net loss rose briefly again to about 40,000, but more recently the figure has fallen to just over 20,000, of which about one third went overseas. In addition, the proportion of the potential labour force in the less prosperous regions which is actually employed has remained persistently lower than in South East England and the West Midlands. The

Table 6. Britain : selected economic indicators, by regions, 1961–1970

	Employment				Male employment				Proportion of women at work 1966		
	1970 '000s	Change 1966–1970 %	1966 '000s	Change 1961–1966 %	1970 '000s	Change 1966–1970 %	1966 '000s	Change 1961–1966 %	%	%	%
BRITAIN	22,919	−3	23,550	+4	14,275	−5	14,900	+2	40	41	38
More prosperous regions :											
South East	7,812	−3	8,070	+5	4,775	−1	5,390	+4	43	44	42
East Anglia	649	+5	620	+13	414	+4	400	+11	36	33	32
West Midlands	2,299	−4	2,390	+6	1,458	−5	1,540	+5	42	44	43
East Midlands	1,422	−1	1,440	+6	898	−3	930	+4	40	40	38
South West	1,342	−1	1,360	+6	847	−3	870	+4	33	33	31
Less prosperous regions :											
North West	2,914	−4	3,030	+1	1,788	−4	1,870	Nil	42	43	43
Yorkshire and Humberside	2,028	−4	2,110	+3	1,285	−6	1,360	+2	39	40	39
Northern	1,326	−1	1,340	+2	850	−3	880	−1	36	35	33
Wales	968	−4	1,010	+3	635	−7	680	−1	31	30	27
Scotland	2,159	−1	2,190	+1	1,325	−3	1,370	−2	41	40	38

Table 6. (*Continued*)

	Total net personal income 1968–1969		Average income per week 1968–1969		Male earnings relative to Britain 1964–1965	Average weekly expenditure per person 1968–1969	Unemployment range		Additional employment from i.d.c. approvals 1956–1967
	£ mill.	%	£ per person	£ per household	%	£	1966–1970 %	1961–1966 %	'000s
BRITAIN	26,005	100.0	10.55[1]	31.22[1]	100.0[1]	8.67	2–3	1–2	1,245.2
More prosperous regions :									
South East	10,208	39.4	12.32	35.26	109.9	10.07	1–2	1–2	278.0
East Anglia	709	2.7	10.35	29.46	91.7	8.57	1–2	1–2	48.3
West Midlands	2,543	9.8	10.73	32.28	102.7	8.60	2–3	1–2	86.3
East Midlands	1,516	5.8	10.41	30.77	95.8	8.27	1–2	1–2	53.1
South West	1,636	6.3	9.81	30.07	93.9	8.48	2–3	1–2	76.0
Less prosperous regions :									
North West	2,975	11.4	10.30	30.22	96.2	8.36	2–3	1–2	204.6
Yorkshire and Humberside	2,147	8.3	9.54	28.07	93.9	7.59	2–3	1–2	82.6
Northern	1,285	4.9	9.57	28.23	92.1	8.25	4–5	3–4	147.6
Wales	1,000	3.9	9.10	27.20	94.9	7.77	3–4	2–3	104.8
Scotland	1,986	7.6	9.56	29.11	89.6	8.03	3–4	3–4	166.0

1. U.K. average.

(see over for notes)

NOTES

Table 6. (*Continued*)

Data	Notes	Source
Employment and Male Employment :	Employees are classified by place of work, and include the unemployed classified by residence, but exclude the self employed and forces. The numbers of employees have been rounded to the nearest ten thousand, and the percentage change to the nearest integer.	Department of Employment
Proportion of Women at Work :	Female employees are related to adult females (15+) classified by residence : the rates are therefore affected by travel to work across sub-regional boundaries.	
Unemployment :	Numbers of wholly unemployed, including school leavers. Unemployed classified by residence; the numbers of employees, on which the percentages are based, are classified by workplace. Unemployment rates, particularly in or near city areas, are affected by travel to work across sub-regional boundaries. Unemployment rates are not strictly annual averages, but the averages of the rates for January and June of each year.	
Earnings :		
Net personal income :		Inland Revenue
Household Income and Expenditure :		Family Expenditure Survey
Industrial Development Certificates :	When an application is made, the applicant estimates the additional employment which will be provided by the new project at that site when complete and fully manned. There is evidence from other sources —the follow-up of firms moving from one region to another—of some bias in the employment estimates which are thought likely to be pitched high in development areas, but low in other regions. The estimates are to some extent dependent upon the general economic circumstances prevailing at the time the estimate is made. These may alter before the building is complete and affect the additional numbers actually employed.	Department of Trade and Industry

latter had rates of 58.9 and 60.9 per cent respectively (in 1963); the figures for Wales, the Northern region and Scotland in contrast were 48.0, 52.6 and 56.1 per cent. The resultant inability of these areas to hold on to all of the natural increase in their population and their continuing experience of net out-migration is illustrated in Table 1. These then are the principal symptoms of the malaise in the north and the west of the country that demand explanation.

Throughout the present century—as has already been noted—the British economy has been subject to persistent and fundamental structural and geographical changes. Resources of capital and labour have been pulled out of those industries which changing technology and comparative economic advantage have left as misfits in the contemporary scene. These industries, characterized especially by their production of specialized, high-quality, almost craft products in limited quantities, have been replaced by modern industries which have been subject to contrasting locational forces. Based upon rapidly advancing technologies and concerned especially with the mass production of standardized goods, these new industries appeared, succeeded and subsequently expanded in southern England. In consequence the coal-field economies of the North and the West were left with the larger part of the country's old, stagnant and contracting employments. The considerable resources of capital and labour of these peripheral economies—capital assets which had for the most part been invested in the heyday of Victorian expansion—came thereby to be underemployed. Even when some of the older and traditional industries of the less prosperous regions were able to retain a substantial market for their products, changing economics often demanded the substitution of capital for labour. As a result, there was frequently a divergence between their record of production and trends in the employment opportunities which they could afford. In the late nineteen sixties, for example, the iron and steel industry was in a position whereby only through planning for a severe reduction in its labour force—a reduction of about one-third, or some 100,000 men—could it realistically envisage competitive success and an expansion of its markets and output (Manners 1968b).

Historical, economic and social forces were at work to produce these regions of relative, and in some cases absolute, depression. One of the historical reasons why a new economic base failed to emerge in the less prosperous economies was the fact that many of the new industries grew out of the existing lighter engineering trades which had never been well represented on the coal-fields. It was especially important that the quality of the labour force of these trades—their diverse skills, their distinctive traditions, and their apprenticeship and training schemes, for instance—provided a natural springboard from which new enterprises could readily develop in southern England. The carriage trade of London, for example, was not only a forerunner of the modern motor industry in a technological sense; it had also nurtured over the years a skilled labour force which could easily be adapted to the new industry's requirements. However, these were skills which coalminers, shipbuilders, the operatives in heavy engineering industries, tinplate workers and the like could not immediately offer prospective employers. The less prosperous regions did have, of course, the compensating advantage of a large amount of unemployed labour readily available for new industries. These men and women could have been cheaply trained and utilized by new manufacturers. But in the formative inter-war years, when aggregated demand in the British economy was low, adequate supplies of labour were always available in southern England either indigenously or through migration; there was consequently no incentive for the growth industries to move north in search of it.

A second historical factor explaining the plight of the peripheral regions is the lack of indigenous enterprise there. Few observers would doubt that, with a little local initiative, new factories could have been established in these areas and a large number would have succeeded. The profitability of the many enterprises induced by the government into the peripheral economies since 1936 is evidence enough. But enterprise was not forthcoming. One of the reasons for this lay in the industrial history of the less prosperous regions, and the nature of the economy and society that had been powerfully shaped by events in the nineteenth century. With the industrial revolution, these regions attracted and prospered with a group of industries, which by and large were oligopolistic in structure, and in which entrepreneurial decisions were concentrated in relatively few hands. Their societies, as a consequence, were denied a widespread tradition of enterprise, and contrasted vividly with the type of highly entrepreneurial society which was to be found in London and Birmingham. Also stemming from their traditional economic structures was the relative scarcity of entrepreneurial capital. Despite the small size of Britain, there is some evidence to suggest that these older industrial regions did not develop institutions and traditions which made capital readily available to the small man anxious to pioneer a new enterprise. Unlike London and Birmingham, therefore, where a long tradition of highly competitive, small scale industries spawned both formal and informal means of making relatively small amounts of risk capital available to the entrepreneur, the peripheral economies inherited yet another factor deficiency which hindered their industrial adjustment and revival.

These historical forces shaping Britain's changing industrial geography were endorsed by a second group of primarily economic factors. The most important of these was the geography and influence of the home market. The relative advantages of southern England, that were noted earlier, were of course the relative disadvantages of the less prosperous north and west of the country. Whereas in the nineteenth century Britain in her industrial precocity had been able to open up huge export markets with little difficulty, after 1918 industry had to face increasingly severe overseas competition. To this was added during the inter-war years economic nationalism, currency chaos and a world economic depression. In consequence, the growth industries of this period were established primarily to serve the home market. Characterised by their low inputs of raw materials and by their assembly of components and high value sub-assemblies, they experienced little attraction to locate on or near to the country's coal-fields which were generally eccentric to the centre of the national market. Since the cost of transporting most manufactured goods from factory to the domestic wholesaler, retailer or consumer normally represents only about

2 to 4 per cent of the total production and marketing costs—even in the case of Scottish manufacturers (Report of a Committee, 1961, p. 73)—this matter needs to be kept in perspective. Nevertheless, the fact that industry in the less prosperous regions (particularly before the construction of the motorway network and the introduction of freightliner and other improved services by British Rail) was relatively ill-served with transport and communication facilities to the rest of the British market did impose an additional inconvenience and higher costs upon its operations. Moreover, as exports increasingly became important after 1945, the relative inaccessibility of the coal-field industrial areas (south Lancashire apart) to the country's major ports stood further to their disadvantage. This transport situation was just one aspect of the relative absence of external economies which faced manufacturers in the peripheral regions of Britain.

Reinforcing these historical and economic forces were also a number of social factors. In the matter of amenities, for example, the less prosperous regions were in no position to offer the employer or the employee an urban environment and social capital equal to that of southern England. With relatively little new investment after 1914, even by the late nineteen fifties these areas were characterized by an essentially Victorian urban

Table 7. England and Wales : housing conditions, by regions, 1967–1968
(Estimated percentage of an area's housing stock)

Regions	Date of Estimate	Dwellings statutorily unfit %	% Dwellings lacking exclusive use of	
			an internal w.c.	a fixed bath
TOTAL ENGLAND AND WALES	Feb. 1967	12	19	13
South East	Feb. 1967	6	11	9
Northern, Yorkshire and Humberside and North West	Feb. 1967	15	25	17
Rest of England and Wales	Feb. 1967	14	20	14
Conurbations				
English conurbations	Feb. 1967	11	18	14
West Midlands	Dec. 1967	10	23	12
South East Lancashire	Dec. 1967	15	28	18
Merseyside	June 1968	9	20	14
(Liverpool)	June 1968	(12)	(28)	(22)
Tyneside	June 1968	8	24	16

Source : Secretary of State for Economic Affairs (1969), p. 29.

inheritance. All the relevant indices of social progress—the age and condition of housing (Table 7), the quality of the schools, the area of derelict land (Table 8), the availability of recreational facilities, and the like—recorded and perpetuated the disadvantage of the coal-field economies. In terms of cultural facilities too, such as concert halls and theatres, art collections and museums, the assets of the less prosperous regions were scattered and relatively poor. Undoubtedly, these deficiencies were reflected in their failure to attract sufficient alternative employments. The ease of access which the regions afforded to natural environments of high quality—the Brecon Beacons in South Wales and Cheviots in North East England for example—was too small a compensating factor, at least until the middle nineteen sixties. This is not to deny the importance of these natural amenities as assets likely to prove attractive to many entrepreneurs in the long run.

Manufacturing, of course, provides less than one half of the total number of the jobs in Britain, and as the economy matures so do service activities become relatively more important. Some services are clearly related to local needs, and their distribution has tended to parallel interregional shifts in manufacturing employment. There are in addition, however, a large number of service activities which serve both regional and national markets. Once again for historical, economic and social reasons, these have been little attracted to the less prosperous regions. All service jobs have a tendency to gravitate towards a central place in the market which they serve. With improvements in communi-

Table 8. Britain : estimates of derelict land, by regions, *circa* 1965

	Hectares	Acres
BRITAIN	34,041	84,113
More prosperous regions	9,960	24,726
South East	1,527	3,772
East Anglia	694	1,714
West Midlands	4,032	9,964
East Midlands	2,172	5,367
South West	1,582	3,909
Less prosperous regions	24,034	59,387
North West	3,961	9,788
Yorkshire and Humberside	2,926	7,253
Northern	6,100	15,074
Wales	5,371	13,272
Scotland	5,666	14,000

Source : Secretary of State for Economic Affairs (1969), p. 29.

cations, service activities tend to increase the spatial extent of their market areas and thus cause a centralization of related employments. During the last fifty years, as a result, with Greater London standing as the focal point in the domestic and international transport network, the relative role of the less prosperous regions in matters of trade, commerce, banking, finance, government and law has tended to decline. The Bank of England no longer operates a branch in Swansea. The provincial commodity markets have virtually disappeared. With this relative decline of employment opportunities in the service trades has developed a scarcity of readily available skilled, white collar labour in the less prosperous regions upon which any reversal of past trends could be based.

1.3.1 *Public Policy Responses: National Economic Management*

The nature and the magnitude of the difficulties experienced by the less prosperous regions varied through space and altered with time. Their problems were, and remain, relative and not absolute. It must never be forgotten that these are all regions of increasing population, despite their characteristic of net out-migration. In a very real sense, therefore, they are also areas of growth. Nevertheless, the difficulties of the less prosperous regions are equally real and they persisted into the nineteen seventies, despite some thirty-five years of government policies which have sought to ameliorate the problems of the coalfield industrial areas in particular.

Several major components can be recognized in the programmes of public assistance to the less prosperous regions. The first has been the maintenance of a relatively high level of aggregate demand in the economy as a whole. The amelioration of the problems of the peripheral economies undoubtedly still owes a considerable debt to Keynesian economics. This may, of course, be only a temporary palliative for, even with a Keynesian stability superimposed upon advanced economy, it could well be that in future the problem of structural unemployment will grow as a direct consequence of rapid technological change. This is certainly American experience. Macrodemand management, therefore, could well become relatively less important in ameliorating the problems of less prosperous regional economies in the future than it has been in the past.

1.3.2 *Public Policy Responses: Assistance to Staple Industries*

A second component of public policy has been the various measures which have sought to assist the major staple industries of the less prosperous regions—in order either to slow down their rate of decline, or to restructure these traditional activities into a more appropriate contemporary form. Since it reached its peak production in 1955, the coal industry has been a major beneficiary of such policies. Various *ad hoc* measures have been used to protect the markets for coal. These include the tax on fuel oil and the government's restraining influence over the Central Electricity Generating Board when the latter sought to switch coal-fired stations to burning oil. Following the publication of the 1967 White Paper on a national *Fuel Policy* (Minister of Power, 1967), considerable sums of public money have been made available to permit the National Coal Board (N.C.B.) to plan a dignified retreat from many of the country's energy markets. By writing off the coal industry's debts, by decelerating the rate of mine closures, by offering money to assist the movement of miners to the lower cost coal-fields and by providing special assistance to attract new industries to locate on the coal-fields in the Special Development Areas, the government has spent vast sums of money to assist this waning industry. Simultaneously, public capital has helped to reorganize the N.C.B. and to permit the concentration of its remaining production upon the most efficient units, especially the mines of the East Midlands and South Yorkshire. In 1970, the British coal industry, for the first time in twenty-five years open to overseas competition (following the Minister of Power's decision to lift the ban upon coal imports), was of a size and offered a scale of employment opportunity that owed a great deal to public policies.

In the case of the steel industry, until 1967 largely in private ownership, the government again intervened to influence its geography, its investments and the magnitude of its employments (Manners, 1971, pp. 95–98; Warren, 1970). After World War II, the government retained the right to supervise all major investment decisions in the industry. This allowed public intervention in the siting of some works—for instance, the decision to locate two major tinplate plants in Swansea and Llanelli rather than adjacent to the new integrated strip mill at Port Talbot—and in the regional allocation of major investments. In 1959, for example, the cabinet insisted that new strip mill capacity should be shared between Llanwern in Wales and Ravenscraig in Scotland. Following the nationalization of the greater part of the industry in 1967, investments under the initial corporate planning programme of the British Steel Corporation were clearly formulated in the light of the best economic and commercial evidence available. However, it remained clear that any attempt to establish integrated steelmaking capacity on a large scale in southern England (locations on Thamesside and Southampton Water have been proposed) would have to overcome substantial political objections. The cotton industry also received substantial public assistance. Under a 1960 Act of Parliament government money was made available to assist in the reorganization of the industry into fewer but individually larger units, in the expectation that it would then be better able to face the increasing severity of international competition (see Chapter 7). In the case of the shipbuilding industry, successive government measures—initially to help the industry in general to survive, but subsequently to assist only where the industry was prepared to rationalize its structure—were also fundamental to the industry's geography in 1970 (see pp. 379–380, 393–395).

No aggregate figure is readily available which quantifies the scale of public assistance over the years to the older staple industries that at one time flourished on the coal-fields, and that still remain major sources of especially male employment there. It is impossible to be at all certain of the size and the geography of these trades had there not been substantial public intervention in their affairs. These uncertainties, however, must not blind

us to the enormous cost and significance of the assistance provided by the government
to these industries in the overall strategy of regional development.

1.3.3 *Public Policy Responses : Development Area Policies*

In addition to assisting the older trades there, public money has also been used to
diversify and restructure the peripheral economies. It was as early as 1934, following
the Special Areas (Development and Improvement) Act, that the government embarked
upon an enduring, though not always consistent, attempt to lessen the dependance of the
less prosperous regions upon the old, declining industries which had been the success
stories of Victorian times. The policies of the nineteen thirties created a number of non-
profit making industrial estates, and also financed the construction of standard factories
(by government agencies) in advance of demand. These policies amounted to a set of
inducements designed to 'steer' industrialists away from southern England. This was
probably the most that could be achieved in the political climate of the time. With the
outbreak of World War II, however, the government was able quickly to acquire rather
greater powers. In particular, it was able to direct industry away from southern England
for strategic and defence purposes, and thus came to possess a much more powerful
weapon for the manipulation of the country's industrial geography. The 'war' industries
which arrived in South Wales, North East England, North West England and Scotland
between 1939 and 1945—aluminium and aircraft production, ordnance and vital engineering activities, for example—were an important foundation for the subsequent diversification of those regional economies.

After 1945, the government sought a middle course. It rejected the geographical direction
of industry as a solution to the problem. Instead, it armed itself with a stronger and more
varied set of weapons to influence industrial location than those available during the
inter-war years. Under the Distribution of Industry Act of 1945 and the Town and Country
Planning Act of 1947, the government was given wide powers to attract industry to the
peripheral economies. It extended the system of industrial estates, built factories ahead
of demand, and subsidized their rents. In addition, the government was able to offer
grants and loans to industrialists locating or expanding in the less prosperous economies,
and (later) to offer certain tax concessions to new enterprises there. The magnitude and
nature of these inducements varied through time, although by 1964 they represented
grants of 10 per cent on the cost of buildings and 25 per cent on the cost of machinery;
in addition, the government allowed free depreciation, which meant that the whole of
an industrial investment could be written off immediately against tax.

Between 1965 and 1967, the inducements to industrial development in the less prosperous
regions were substantially increased, and they were strongly biased towards offsetting the
capital costs of manufacturing industry. The keystone of assistance was a 40 per cent
investment grant, which was 20 per cent higher than that available in southern England.
In addition the government was prepared occasionally to give a 35 per cent building

grant for the purchase of land by a manufacturer. Construction grants of 25 per cent were also available from the Board of Trade, but they could be increased to 35 per cent if the firm proposed to employ a high proportion of male labour. Advance factories, which could be bought or rented from the Board of Trade at prices below those charged on the open market, were also made available in greater numbers; in the Special Development Areas these were made available rent free for five years. Money was also made available to firms following a move into a Development Area in order to provide an adequate cash-flow during the sometimes difficult settling-in period. The investment grants, which applied to plant and machinery, were made available under the Industrial Development Act of 1966; the other forms of assistance stemmed from the several Local Employment Acts between 1960 and 1966. Criticism that this 'package' of government assistance was too heavily biased towards subsidizing capital expenditure, whereas the regions concerned had a problem of labour surplus, were met under a clause in the 1967 Finance Act. This gave manufacturers in the peripheral economies a Regional Employment Premium (R.E.P.)—a device whereby their labour costs were subsidized to the weekly value of £1.79 per man employed, and a rather smaller sum for other employees. In addition, special financial assistance was made available through the Department of Employment to train employees in skills required by new industries. This scheme was designed to supplement the labour retraining facilities provided in the government centres which were established under the 1964 Industrial Training Act. Yet two further items of public assistance to the less prosperous regions were the provision of housing for those 'key' workers who were required to transfer to the regions with their firms, and the preference given by both government departments and the nationalized industries to firms located in development areas when contracts were being placed.

As a consequence of all these measures, government expenditure to assist in the attraction of new employments to the less prosperous regions rose from £80 million in 1966–1967 to £259 million in 1968–1969 (Table 9; Figure 6). It was estimated that in the nineteen forties and fifties the government spent approximately £1,000 per job *directly* created by its distribution of industry policies in the less prosperous regions, a figure which almost certainly was less than the alternative costs of unemployment benefits and public assistance. This figure, of course, does not take into account any large infrastructural investments in those regions which have undoubtedly aided in their recovery. Simultaneously, however, it neglects the additional employment gains in those areas generated by the local and regional multiplier effects of the new industries. It could well be that £1,000 per job considerably overestimates the costs of the policies at that time. As the level of public expenditure in the less prosperous regions rose in the middle nineteen sixties, however, the costs per job clearly rose in parallel. Estimates vary but at one extreme is an observation that in the Northern Development Area public assistance at a large capital intensive plant represented over £20,000 per additional job. Although this was clearly well above the average cost of creating employment in the peripheral regions, it naturally raised questions about the cost-effectiveness of the government's programme. Nevertheless,

the 1972 initiative on regional problems (Secretary of State for Trade and Industry, 1972)
proposed *inter alia* free depreciation plus a 20 per cent grant on plant, machinery and
buildings in the Development Areas, the grants alone representing an annual exchequer
cost of £250–£300 million.

These inducements to industrialists to locate in the peripheral economies were, of
course, powerfully reinforced by the policy of refusing i.d.c.s, in southern England.
There was, in other words, both a 'push' as well as a 'pull' element to the regional development programmes. The main emphasis of policy however was upon moving manufacturing
industry. The R.E.P. was paid only for manufacturing employees, for example. It
only gradually that the service industries came to be seen as having a role to play in the

Table 9. Britain : level of differential government expenditure on the Development Areas, 1966–1969

	1966–67 £m.	1967–68 £m.	1968–69 (Estimated) £m.
Free depreciation	35.0	Negligible	Negligible
Regional differential element of investment grants		70([1])	80
Regional Employment Premium		34.1([2])	99
Selective Employment Tax Premium for Development Areas	—	—	25.0
Local Employment Acts assistance	43.3	43.8	50.0
Development Area Training Grants	0.8	0.9	2.0
Additional craft/technician training and off-the-job training places for semi-skilled workers	—	Nil	0.8
Highlands and Islands Development Board	0.75	1.45	1.8
Development Commission loans to small hotels			0.4
SET refunds to hotels in certain rural areas			0.3([3])
TOTAL	80	150	259
Clearance of derelict land([4])	0.5	1.2	1.6
Provision of basic services([4])	Negligible	0.05	0.1

1. Free Depreciation in Development Districts was replaced in 1966 by the regionally differentiated investment grant. Estimated figure only.
2. Part financial year only. Payments began with effect from September 1967.
3. In a full year the cost of the SET refund to hotels is estimated to be £1m.
4. The figures on clearance of derelict land and provision of basic services are for total expenditure on these items in Development Areas. Similar facilities are also available, although on a different basis, outside the Development Areas, and it is not feasible to put a figure on the expenditure arising from arrangements which apply to the Development Areas only.

Source : Secretary of State for Economic Affairs (1969), p. 236.

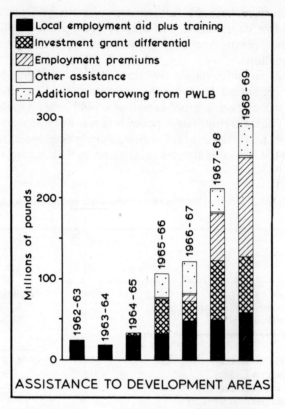

Figure 6   Britain: assistance to the Development Areas, 1962/1963–1968/1969.
Source: Board of Trade.

solution of the problems of the less prosperous regions. The government's initiative in transferring an increasing number of its own administrative activities into the development areas has already been noted; the unsuccessful attempt to persuade private offices to move there without financial incentives has also been noted earlier. However, the hotel trade was able to take advantage of some assistance which it was given in the less prosperous regions, and the universities there were excluded from the general restraints on public expenditure which followed the balance of payments crises in 1967 and 1968.

The rationale of all these policies aimed at the diversification of the economic structure and the employment opportunities in northern England, Wales and Scotland had three principal elements. First, it was believed that the private costs of the industries steered into the less prosperous regions would, after a short initial settling-in period, be no higher than in southern England. Location theory suggested, and various empirical studies such as those conducted by Luttrell (1962), Tothill (Report of a Committee, 1961) and Cameron (1966) demonstrated, that a wide range of manufacturing enterprise was in this category and could generically be termed 'footloose'. Second, in so far as locational questions ranked relatively low in the investment decision-making considerations of many firms (if they ranked at all), the possibility existed that some entrepreneurs might be forced by these policies to discover a location which had in fact a private cost advantage. Third, there was a significant social gain to be obtained from the policy for reasons already discussed (pp. 7ff). With the Board of Trade (and later the Department of Trade and Industry) handling each i.d.c. application 'on its merits', the probability was strong that those firms whose costs were relatively insensitive to location could be more easily persuaded to take up a location in a development area (granted the package of incentives); others, which had strong economic reasons for remaining in southern England, were often allowed to do so. Even by 1971, however, research was not available to demonstrate just how much of manufacturing and service industry is relatively insensitive to locational costs, and what proportion could advantageously be steered by public policies away from metropolitan centres to the less prosperous regions and the new towns. The location of employment policy, as a result, had to proceed on the somewhat unsatisfactory assumption that there would be 'enough' mobile enterprise to achieve its objectives.

Paralleling these general policies of regional employment diversification, some industries were clearly subject to rather more direct political pressures than others in making their investment and locational decisions. One such industry was motor car manufacture, which in the period 1958–1960 was about to embark upon a major expansion programme. After lengthy negotiations with the Board of Trade, often at very high levels of government, each of the major assembly firms were persuaded to put a significant part of their new capacity in the development areas—in return for which they were granted i.d.c.s for some expansion of plant at or near their major West Midlands or London factories. Again, in 1966–1967, the aluminium smelting industry for the first time expressed an interest in British locations and, after a great deal of political manoeuvring, agreement was reached to construct three relatively small plants in North Wales, North East England and Scotland; the public and private costs of this new industry, some commentators believe, will consequently be particularly high in the long as well as the short term (Manners, 1968a).

All these policies of 'regional protection' were subject to important historical and geographical variations. It is possible to specify three phases during which the government's distribution of industry policies have been relatively effective. The pre-1939 years were comparatively unimportant. Inducements (in the north) without controls (in the south) brought only limited results. In any case the economy as a whole was not growing at a particularly fast rate, and there were only a few entrepreneurs who were looking for sites and whose locational decisions could in fact be influenced. The war years, however, were quite different. The dispersal of strategic industries away from southern England was achieved speedily and on a considerable scale. This movement was to be of fundamental importance later, for with it the less prosperous regions acquired not only a substantial amount of capital plant and a labour force with new skills; but they also gained the invaluable evidence that many manufacturing activities other than those of their Victorian legacy could be successfully pursued there.

Immediately after 1945 there was a marked burst of Board of Trade activity to steer industry into the peripheral economies. A high level of aggregate demand in the national economy, and a large number of firms wishing to reestablish themselves after the war, meant that factory space, industrial sites and permission to build new plants were all at a premium. The result was that the government was able easily to steer industrialists away from southern England and the economies of the less prosperous regions were injected with much new life. After 1947, however, it was necessary to reduce the rate of capital investment in the economy, and the amount of new factory construction fell abruptly. Moreover, with a fairly high level of employment persisting throughout the country, the government showed progressively less interest in the location of industry policies and devoted its energy to other things. This situation continued into the late the nineteen fifties, by which time the use of the i.d.c. to influence the location of manufacturing industry had been all but abandoned. It was in fact possible to build a factory almost anywhere in the country provided local planning permission could be obtained.

By 1960, therefore, any success which the government might have claimed for having helped to rehabilitate the peripheral economies owed much to three factors in particular. First, the country had a substantial amount of experience in matters concerning the relocation of industry dating back to the inter-war years, but more especially from the war years. Second, the Barlow and other government war-time reports ensured that a body of effective legislation was on the statute book to influence industrial location very shortly after 1945. Third, immediately after the war there was elected into office a government which firmly believed in exerting an influence over the distribution of employment.

After a lapse of a decade, however, industrial location policies were revived once again. With the 1958–1959 recession, the level of unemployment in the peripheral economies rose sharply. As a result the government instructed the Board of Trade both to issue i.d.c. approvals in southern England with discretion once again, and to start building more factories in the less prosperous regions (either for lease to specific firms planning expansion there or ahead of actual demand). This policy was endorsed in 1963 with the White Papers on *North East England* and *Central Scotland*. It was yet further strengthened in the middle and late sixties as unemployment levels rose nationally, and as a further set of major structural adjustments began to affect the British economy. The effectiveness of the policy was constrained, of course, by the slow rate of national economic growth and the limited amount of new investment throughout the whole country.

The work of Howard (1968) has demonstrated something of these historical variations in location policies (see Table 2). His evidence shows how the total volume of industrial movement involved about 53,000 jobs per year in the period 1945–1951, 35,000 per year in the period 1952–1959 and 46,000 per year in the period 1960–1965. It demonstrates how the less prosperous regions received some two-thirds of all manufacturing movement (in terms of employment) in the first period, but how during the following eight years the main flow of jobs was from Greater London to the rest of southeast England. Between 1960 and 1965, however, the peripheral areas were once again the principal destination of firms on the move. Howard's research also underlines the regional importance of the development area policies by showing that nearly 30 per cent of all employment in manufacturing industry in Wales in 1965 was attributable to moves into the Principality during the previous twenty-one years; the corresponding proportion of the Northern region's jobs was about one-fifth, and of Scotland's one eighth.

1.3.4 *Public Policy Responses: The Geography of Assistance*

Programmes to assist the less prosperous parts of the country have to be applied to clearly defined geographical areas. These too have changed with time. With the 1934 legislation, four 'Special Areas' were designated (see Figure 7). These were South Wales, North East England, Cumberland and Central Scotland. Their extent was determined by local levels of unemployment. Because the major towns there—Cardiff and Swansea in South Wales, Newcastle in North East England, etc.—recorded lower rates of unemployment than their hinterlands, however, these regional capitals were excluded from the benefits of the special areas legislation. After 1945, this geography of protection was changed. The Special Areas became 'Development Areas' (see Figure 7). More regions were included, such as Merseyside and the North Wales coal-field. The delimitation of these areas was again determined by their (inter-war and immediate post-war) record of unemployment, but by this date the problem was interpreted as regional rather than local in nature; hence the regional capitals were included in the areas made eligible for government help. By 1958, however, it was realized that other parts of the country were suffering persistently from unemployment but, because they were outside the Development Areas, they were not eligible for public assistance. In response, the Distribution of Industry (Industrial Finance) Act was passed to make help available to any such areas through the Development Areas Treasury Advisory Committee (D.A.T.A.C.). Nearly all these additional areas were geographically peripheral once again; their unemployment problems tended to be either seasonal, or a response to changes in agriculture and rural depopulation. The greater geographical and functional flexibility of this programme was seen to be so advantageous that in 1960 all the previous distribution of industry legislation was replaced by a new Local Employment Act. Under its provisions, any locality (that is any Department of Employment exchange area) in which unemployment existed, or appeared lightly to exist, became eligible for help as a Development District (see Figure 7); however, once the level of unemployment fell below about 4 per cent, the locality was immediately removed from the list of districts and assistance was withdrawn. The flexibility offered

a. THE 'SPECIAL' AREAS 1934-39

Linlithgow
Haltwhistle
Newcastle
South Shields
Hartlepool
Glasgow
Kilmarnock
Workington
Pembroke
Swansea

b. THE DEVELOPMENT AREAS 1945-60

Inverness
Dundee
Glasgow
Newcastle
Middlesbrough
Carlisle
North-east Lancashire
Wigan-St.Helens
Merseyside
Wrexham
Pembroke
Swansea
Newport

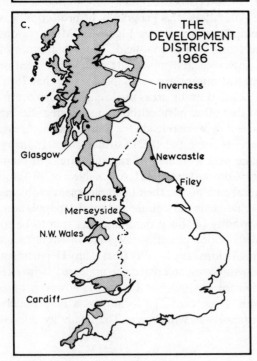

c. THE DEVELOPMENT DISTRICTS 1966

Inverness
Glasgow
Newcastle
Filey
Furness
Merseyside
N.W. Wales
Cardiff

Figure 7 Britain: the changing geography of assistance to the less prosperous regions, 1934–1966.

Figure 8 Britain: the Development and Intermediate Areas, January 1971.
Source : Department of Trade and Industry.

by this legislation had certain administrative advantages. Soon, however, it created grave problems for the less prosperous regions. Government assistance became even less consistent than before with the problems of structural economic change coming to be viewed in a local, rather than in the more appropriate regional, context once again.

In handling the location of industry policy in the years immediately after 1945, the Board of Trade attempted to strike a geographical balance between two possible extremes within the coal-field industrial economies. On the one hand, it could have sought to steer new jobs as near as possible to the sources of surplus labour there—that is to the colliery villages and the cotton mill towns—and to what were often amongst the least attractive localities from the viewpoint of a modern manufacturer. On the other hand, the Board could have insisted that the labour should move, either daily or permanently, towards new sources of employment sited at the best locations within the less prosperous regions. There are always some localities where the relative disadvantages of these regions are at a minimum—sites in or near the regional capitals tend to be particularly attractive. Yet invariably these were not the worst areas affected by unemployment and out-migration. The middle course steered by the Board of Trade was inherently quite flexible in its spatial emphasis. Where possible the Board encouraged the construction of factories, and the location of new industry, in places which for a modern manufacturing concern were certainly not the best within the peripheral economies; but they were by no means the worst locations, and they often committed the indigenous labour force to a certain amount of daily commuting. Thus, in South Wales, an emphasis was placed upon steering industry to the mouths of the coalmining valleys, rather than allowing all new industry to collect in and around the relatively attractive Cardiff-Newport area, or forcing the newcomers to site themselves in the narrow, constricted and isolated valleys themselves (see p. 00). However, the 1960 Local Employment Act required the Board to insist that government assistance was only available to firms who were prepared to locate in (what were in effect) the least attractive parts of the less prosperous regions. These were localities which persistently had the highest rates of unemployment and were classified as Development Districts. Meanwhile, good industrial sites only a few kilometres away were ineligible for the government help which might have attracted firms and jobs there. The inherent weaknesses of this approach were soon exposed. Its validity was quickly challenged in the press and in Parliament, and within three years it was virtually abandoned. From 1963, government attitudes towards the planning and development of the peripheral economies, as a consequence, took on another new look.

About this time, not only did interregional planning suddenly become respectable—it was given the blessing of the National Economic Development Council and the Federation of British Industries, and the President of the Board of Trade assumed the additional title of Minister for Regional Development—but with the publication of the White Papers on *North East England* and *Central Scotland* a new emphasis was given to the rehabilitation of the problem economies in the north and the west. The 1960 Act remained on the Statute Book. Funds continued to be available to assist the less attractive parts of the less prosperous regions. But the decision was taken to channel the greater part of the public effort and expenditure into the most attractive—and what are potentially the most rewarding— places in the peripheral economies from the viewpoint of contemporary development. These are invariably adjacent to the larger and more accessible communities within the regions. They are the towns and cities which have access to the largest labour force and the widest range of labour skills. They are places which afford the greatest opportunity to exploit the limited external economies and social amenities of these problem regions. In some instances, new towns, such as Livingston near Edinburgh or Washington near Newcastle, were designated where it was judged a new urban environment would help to attract contemporary enterprise. In this process, 'growth points' came to be defined in Central Scotland, and a 'growth zone' was delimited in North East England. In these areas funds were made available to improve the infrastructure, to provide additional trading estates, to invest in new transport facilities, and to modernize the environment. By taking advantage of the best endowed localities within the peripheral economies, government policies thus took on what many regarded as a more realistic and more forward-looking character. And it was clearly the intention of the government to extend this philosophy of planning to South Wales, North West England and other problem regions.

In 1964, however, there was a change of government. As a result both the strategy and style of regional planning in Britain was subject to yet a further major reappraisal. The planning machine was re-organized once again. Whilst the Board of Trade still retained its role as the administrator of the distribution of industry policy, and the Ministry of Housing and Local Government remained responsible for the preparation of land use plans, the coordination of government action with reference to regional development passed into the hands of the newly created Department of Economic Affairs. For the first time Britain was divided into ten planning regions, with the intention that each would prepare studies and (subsequently) plans that would be integrated within a National Plan. It was hoped that the new structure would permit a reconciliation of competing regional ambitions, and allow much more co-operation in the regions between different government departments and local authorities than had been common in the past. Simultaneously, the government extended the areas eligible for assistance under the Local Employment Acts, especially in Wales and in North West England. It was significant, however, that only the relatively less attractive parts of these regions were included. It became increasingly clear that, at least overtly, the growth point philosophy of 1963 was meeting strong political opposition.

Under the subsequent 1966 Industrial Development Act, the Development Districts were in fact abandoned in favour of a new set of Development Areas (Figure 8). These were defined to include the whole of Scotland (except a small area around Edinburgh), the whole of the Northern region, the whole of Wales (except the northeastern and south-eastern parts of the Principality), and a large area in the remoter part of South West England. A year later, and following the publication of the White Paper on *Fuel Policy,* additional assistance was made available to a number of Special Development Areas in the coal-fields, where the problems of mine closures and unemployment were particularly acute. Later still, Millom was added, and then in the spring of 1971 much of West Central Scotland (including Glasgow), Tyneside and Wearside, Peterlee, Harlepool and additional parts of South Wales were made Special Development Areas. For these localities, there were normal Development Area aids plus a subsidy of 30 per cent on wage and salary costs during the first three years of a plant's operation and a rent-free period of five years in government factories. Nevertheless, the essential characteristic of Development Area policy from the middle sixties was the extensive availability of assistance throughout the less prosperous regions. This approach was based upon the argument that, above all else, geographical flexibility was required in the administration of regional development policies. In particular, it permitted the various regional authorities to elect their own spatial priorities if they so desired. For example, in the Northern Region opinion continued to favour the concentration of development in the growth zone of 1963, and more especially in its Tyneside and Teesside components. Indeed, the North East Development Council adopted a policy of welcoming new firms to the region regardless of their sub-regional preferences. In Wales, on the other hand, the opportunities for development on Severnside were foregone in favour of a policy which continued to steer industrial development and employment opportunities to the west of Cardiff, and hence nearer to those communities experiencing high levels of local unemployment. These and other contrasts in the geography of regional development in recent years emerge more clearly in Chapters 6–10.

1.3.5 *Public Policy Responses : Further Components*

To complete this review of the public policy response to the dilemmas of the less prosperous regions, three other components in the government's strategy must also be noted. First, for many years, very little public money was spent on the retraining of labour, except perhaps through the N.C.B. whose training schemes tended to benefit other industries in the Development Areas as much as the coal industry itself; many of the Board's electricians, fitters and the like moved out of mining once they had acquired a marketable skill. Since the early nineteen sixties, however, a growing volume of resources has been spent on facilities for the retraining of labour. The impact of the 1964 Industrial Training Act was outstanding in this respect, as to a lesser extent was the Coal Industry Act of 1967 which made special provisions for redundant miners. Second, throughout the period large sums of public money were spent upon improvements to the infrastructure of the less prosperous regions, more especially upon their road systems; in this regard the 1963 White Papers were singularly important in the evolution and prospects of at least two of the peripheral regional economies. Third, an effort to improve the amenities and the environment of the less prosperous economies was also made, especially in the nineteen sixties. The designation of new towns, the redevelopment of provincial city centres, the extension of the activities of the regional arts councils, the clearing and planting of derelict land, and the like, all served to enhance the attractions of these regions from a development point of view.

1.3.6 *Public Policy Responses : Some Results*

The sum of all these policies aimed at ameliorating the problems of the less prosperous regions eludes quantification. Demonstrably, their higher than average levels of structural unemployment remains, the net out-migration continues, a considerable reliance upon the country's declining industries persists and signs of self-perpetuating growth are only occasionally to be found. Since it is impossible to judge what would have happened in these areas without government assistance, however, it is equally impossible to spell out with any clarity the full implications of public intervention in their development. Yet the point cannot be evaded that in a number of important respects government policies in the less prosperous regions—policies which were frequently designed primarily to cure the principal symptom of their economic distress, unemployment—left some of the fundamental causes of their long standing problems relatively untouched. This is not to imply that the difficulties could necessarily have been completely overcome with alternative policies. In regard to the problem of labour quality in the Development Areas, for example, whilst government initiatives certainly increased the variety and the size of the skilled labour force available to incoming industry and employers, and considerably improved the quality of the training and educational facilities available there, the reality remains that the range of skills in none of these areas can compare with that available to entrepreneurs in (say) the West Midlands; their relative disadvantage consequently persists. Again, in regard to the problems posed by the relative absence of enterprise and entrepreneurial capital in the Development Areas, the characteristic firm arriving and succeeding there has tended to be large—a branch plant of a London or a Midlands firm— but it has elected to retain its head office and decision making functions in southern England. The capital requirements of such firms have tended to be satisfied either from their own resources or on the London capital market. Manufacturers such as these, therefore, can make only a limited contribution to the solution of a regions' lack of entrepreneurial skills and capital. Similarly, as far as external economies and amenities in the peripheral economies are concerned, the fundamental interregional contrasts remain.

It is also clear that many of the policies of public assistance to the less prosperous regions continue to be pursued in the shadow of a number of unresolved yet fundamental questions. It is still not clear what the socially 'optimum' speed of workforce contraction for a declining industry might be. In the case of the coal industry, Lord Robens argued that the rate of rundown of manpower should not exceed 10 per cent each year; it is a view unsubstantiated, however, by clear evidence. The social as well as economic worth of preserving old communities is another unknown in the matter of regional policy. Obviously some balance has to be struck between the movement of people and the movement of jobs, both interregionally and intraregionally, but evidence on the best mix has still to be demonstrated. In restructuring a regional economy, questions remain concerning the most appropriate degree of specialization or diversification of the new activities being encouraged there; it is argued by some that, since the historical strength of the coal-field economies derived from their highly specialized Victorian industrial structures, it is unwise to diversify them indiscriminately and thereby to deny them the external economies of a more specialized style of regional redevelopment. Increasingly, too, there is the question of cost. As expenditure in the Development Areas has risen, the effectiveness of the alternative means which might be used to induce industrial and other growth there has come to demand much more thorough investigation than has been given it in the past. Then, behind all these dilemmas of regional policy lies the even more burdensome problem of the slow pace of national economic growth—for the rate of new industrial and other investment in the less prosperous regions is tightly constrained by the speed of national economic development.

Nevertheless, the economic disadvantages of the less prosperous regions are today much less than they were a decade or more ago. This change is in part the result of developments in the nature and geography of the country's markets, and the changing characteristics of national transport facilities and costs. Improvements in national living standards have naturally been reflected in all of the country's regions; as a result they have created new markets in the less prosperous parts of Britain to which enterprise can respond. In addition, better and still improving road, rail and air communications have steadily eroded the effective distance between the Development Areas and the rest of the British market, and, with the aid of extensive government and regional advertising, have altered the perceptions of many businessmen concerning the range of locational alternatives. The relative transport advantages of southern England naturally remain, more especially with the growing economic links between Britain and continental Europe. With transport a permissive rather than a dynamic factor in regional development, however, the improved facilities have made it very much easier for the government to steer industry and employments away from southern England. Given the existence of distribution of employment policies, transport improvements must be regarded as a principal catalyst in the revival of the peripheral economies.

Despite the continuing relative disadvantage of the less prosperous regions in seeking to attract a 'reasonable' share of national economic growth, therefore, it is clear that government policies over the years have assisted considerably in removing some of the more fundamental constraints upon their economic growth. The factor endowments of the regions have been much improved. New and vigorous export bases are slowly being forged. The image of the regions—and this is important in convincing management and key workers of the desirability of moving to them—is steadily being enhanced. Indeed, in view of the rather inconsistent application of government policies through time, it is quite remarkable that so much has in fact been achieved. Some details of this success are recorded in later chapters.

1.4 The Intermediate Areas, the Growth Estuaries and the Rural Communities

Whilst the division of Britain into only two major spatial components—the more prosperous and the less prosperous regions—provides many valuable insights into the country's evolving pattern of economic activities and changing population distribution, it is of course a gross over-simplification. The geography of economic life does not simply comprise areas that are either 'black' or 'white'. In reality, the regional and sub-regional economies of Britain reflect every shade of 'grey'. Within the more prosperous regions, for example, there are huge contrasts between the scale and the nature of growth experienced by Greater London and the Outer Metropolitan Area and the more consistent prosperity of the East Midlands; similarly, the prospects and problems of the West Midlands demand a different interpretation from those of the more accessible northern parts of the South West in and around Bristol. Moreover, there are to be found within the more prosperous regions, localities and districts of falling job opportunities and relatively high levels of unemployment; parts of inner London and eastern Kent and the Potteries sub-division of the West Midlands, for example, fall into this category. Within the peripheral economies, likewise, the economic and social problems of some districts are very much worse than those of others. For this reason the delimitation of the several Development Areas (or Districts) has never been identical to the broadly defined less prosperous regions noted in Table 1. Thus, whilst the various programmes of public assistance for the coal industry have been of some benefit to Yorkshire, since World War II that county has generally been ineligible for the larger package of incentives for new industry which the government has provided in, say, Durham and central Scotland. The rest of this chapter discusses three further types of region, a recognition of which can contribute substantially to an understanding of British regional development.

1.4.1 *The Intermediate Areas*

In offering development assistance, problems are inevitably posed regarding the most appropriate criteria to be used for defining the eligible areas upon a map. The dilemmas become considerably magnified when the level of public assistance to a development locality is substantial. It was not surprising therefore that following the introduction of the new range of benefits for the Development Areas in the period 1965 to 1967, the so-called 'grey areas' and their difficulties were for the first time given wide publicity. Some of these areas were quite small in extent. Located adjacent to the existing Development Areas, they included some districts that were clearly losing new investment and potential sources of employment to nearby communities which were offering considerable sums of public money and other incentives to new enterprises. The estuarine strip in the south-east of South Wales was one case in point (see Chapter 6). Critics of the government's policies could point to the difficulties presented to such places as Cardiff, Newport and Cwmbran in their search for new industry when they were outside the Welsh Development Area, and when substantial assistance was available to manufacturers only a few kilometres away. Indeed, not a few firms in this estuarine zone elected to move into the Development Area in order to take advantage of the subsidies available there (p. 259).

More important, however, were the problems posed by those more extensive areas in the north of England which were excluded from the Development Areas, and yet which for some time had experienced serious economic problems. Their difficulties were spelled out most fully by the Hunt Committee which reported in 1969 on *The Intermediate Areas*. Hunt pointed to ten 'causes for concern' (Secretary of State for Economic Affairs, 1969, pp. 5 ff). These were the sluggish or falling levels of employment experienced in many parts of these regions; the slow appearance of new industrial developments; above average levels of unemployment; low or declining proportions of women at work; low average earnings per head by national standards; a heavy reliance upon industries whose demand for labour was growing slowly or even falling; relatively poor communications; a decayed or inadequate environment; and a substantial net outward migration of population. The Intermediate Areas, then, were those regions and localities in which unemployment was below a level which would justify their inclusion in a Development Area, yet whose recent experience of, and prospects for, growth were singularly gloomy. They exhibited many of the fundamental problems of the Development Areas, such as inappropriate labour skills for growth industries, relatively inconvenient access to the national market, and a largely Victorian and Edwardian legacy of a comparatively unattractive urban environment. Although they may have had within their factor endowments and economic structures a potential for recovery—perhaps more than the designated Developments Areas—this was more than offset by the local absence of government assistance, plus its availability elsewhere. Few disagreed with the observation that 'The distinction between black and grey Britain is too sharply drawn at present, and Development Area policy is much too blunt an instrument to ensure a rational and fair distribution of new industrial investment' (Rodgers, 1969, p. 8).

Although its Report was not unanimous, the Hunt Committee advocated some measure of public assistance to the Intermediate Areas. It urged, however, the continuing exclusion of southeast South Wales and the Plymouth area from any benefits on the grounds that, provided appropriate transport and communication improvements were forthcoming, their inherent growth potential would in time overcome any existing difficulties. For the more extensive grey areas in northern England, the Committee proposed the introduction of government aid in the form of industrial building grants, financial assistance for industrial training and education, and a determined effort to reclaim derelict land. The Committee also advocated that the Economic Planning Councils of the North West and of Yorkshire and Humberside should identify potential growth zones within their regions, and that priority should be given to the provision of the necessary infrastructure for their accelerated development. In this, the Committee leaned heavily upon the philosophy of the 1963 White Papers on *North East England* and *Central Scotland*.

On the same day that the Hunt Committee's *Report* was published, the government announced its plans. Contrary to the advice of the Committee, assistance was in fact offered to those problem localities bordering on the Development Areas in southeast South Wales, the South West (Plymouth) and Scotland (Leith). The subsidies that were offered included factory building grants of 25 per cent, government built factories financed on the same basis as in the Development Areas, and the full range of Development Area training grants and other training assistance for new industries. The same package of assistance was offered to certain larger localities outside the Development Areas in northern England (see Figure 8). However, the government refused to endorse the growth zone idea, and allocated its assistance geographically by criteria of 'need'—defined by the character and level of local unemployment and the rate of outward migration—rather than 'opportunity'. Thus, the Yorkshire coal-field, the Erewash valley of Derbyshire, parts of Humberside and the main industrial areas of North East Lancashire (to the east of the proposed new city of Leyland-Chorley) were all made eligible for assistance. The decision was disquieting to those favouring a more forward-looking set of proposals. Three years later, however, the whole of Yorkshire and Humberside and the North West region (outside Merseyside), plus northeast Wales, were given Intermediate Area status, with a 20 per cent development grant on buildings only (see front end-paper).

1.4.2 *The Growth Estuaries*

Curiously enough, whilst the government was rejecting the Hunt Committee's ideas on growth areas in the Intermediate Areas, the Ministry of Housing and Local Government was completing its reports on the growth potential of three of the country's relatively undeveloped estuaries. These studies dated from about 1965 when the projections of the Registrar General indicated that the population of Britain by the end of the century would have increased by some 20 million people. In response to this somewhat alarming prospect, the government set up an interdepartmental special committee, the Central Unit for Environmental Planning, to investigate its land use and regional planning implications. Out of their deliberations came a decision to examine the possibility of stimulating large, new urban complexes in several parts of the country which were relatively lacking in development, but which at first sight appeared capable of sustaining a major expansion of population. The three areas which came under government scrutiny were Humberside, Severnside and Tayside. Economic, land use and traffic studies were initiated in relation to their development potential. The first of the three studies to be completed—that for *Humberside*—was published in 1969. Demonstrating the existing and potential attractions of that section of eastern England, it predictably indicated the possibility of large-scale urban development there provided the appropriate infrastructural investments were made. Although the government was not immediately willing to commit itself to all these investments, it did decide to programme the construction of a new road bridge across the river Humber, one of the keystones in any large scale development of the sub-region (see Chapter 8). In 1970, the Tayside study was also published (see Chapter 10) and a year later the results of the Severnside enquiry were made public (see Chapter 6). However, by then something of the urgency for such new estuarine developments had been dissipated following the downward revision of the Registrar General's population forecasts, and with the emergence of a national economic situation in which the possibility of committing large sums of infrastructural capital for such schemes became more difficult to envisage.

1.4.3 *The Rural Communities*

Within both the more prosperous and the less prosperous regions of Britain there are extensive rural areas. Although the emphasis of this book is upon the problems of industrial and urban change, the relationship of the latter to the rural economy cannot be overlooked. As a consequence both of improving communications and of higher living standards, Britain's increasingly mobile population has placed many rural areas under growing development and especially recreational pressures. Simultaneously, the changing structure and characteristics of agriculture, with its burgeoning inputs of capital and its declining job opportunities, have posed major problems for large areas of the countryside. In the South West, East Anglia, Mid-Wales, the Cheviots, and in large tracts of northern Scotland, the story is the same : the declining manpower requirements of agriculture have generated a steady rural depopulation and, especially in the more remote parts where an offsetting countermovement of middle-class commuters is not to be found, posed problems for those running public and social services. Transport and hospitals, utilities and education, are all increasingly expensive to provide there by comparison with the costs of provision in the more urbanized parts of the country. Although there is a general acceptance of the need to subsidize these and other rural services, the quality of those provided tends to lag behind that in other parts of the country. In consequence, local authorities in rural areas have sought to ameliorate their problems by initiating moves in two directions.

First, they have sought to agree upon the spatial concentration of many services and amenities in fewer villages and towns. Second, they have attempted to create alternative sources of non-agricultural employment. The Mid-Wales Industrial Development Association, for example, has sought to encourage lighter industries to move into the towns of Mid-Wales and so to provide a wider economic base for the population there. Also of particular importance is the work supported by the Development Commissioners appointed under the Development and Road Improvement Fund Acts of 1909 and 1910 who have access to certain funds under the 1960 Local Employment Act, and also the Industrial Estates Corporations of England, Scotland and Wales which have powers to build factories in rural areas. Deliberate attempts have also been made to widen the recreational role of many rural communities and to make further provision for tourism. Both national bodies, such as the Countryside Commission, and local associations have played an important role in these matters.

The shifting patterns of regional development and society's response to their associated dilemmas demand understanding at more than one scale. This chapter has presented a broad, comprehensive framework within which something of the diverse nature, the problems and the plans of the component parts of Britain in the matter of economic development might be better understood. It is a level of economic and political generalization that affords a preliminary grasp of the spatial development process. However, regional change also requires understanding at more intimate scales. Strong contrasts exist both between and within each of the more prosperous regions; the problems and prospects of the several less prosperous economies vary likewise; and each of the Intermediate, 'growth' and rural areas can only be interpreted sensitively within its own unique regional and sub-regional setting. The chapters which follow reveal something of the geographical variety that characterizes the economic features and the development problems of the several regions of Britain.

REFERENCES

Caesar, A. A. L. (1964). Planning and the geography of Great Britain. *Advancement of Science*, **21**, 230–240.

Cameron, G. & Clark, D. B. (1966). *Industrial Movement and the Regional Problem*, Oliver and Boyd, Glasgow.

Chisholm, M. (1962a). The common market and British industry and transport. *Journal of the Town Planning Institute*, **48**, 10–13.

Chisholm, M. (1962b). *Location of Industry*, Political and Economic Planning, London.

Clark, C. (1966). Industrial location and economic potential. *Lloyds Bank Review*, **82**, 1–17.

Clark, C., Wilson, F., & Bradley, J. (1969). Industrial location and economic potential in Western Europe. *Regional Studies*, **3**, 197–212.

Coates, B. E. and Rawstron, E. W. (1966). Regional variations in incomes. *Westminster Bank Review* February, 28–46.

Coates, B. E. and Rawstron, E. W. (1971). *Regional Variations in Britain*, Batsford, London.

Daniels, P. W. (1969). Office decentralisation from London—policy and practice, *Regional Studies* **3**, 171–78.

Department of Economic Affairs (1969). *The Task Ahead, Economic Assessment to 1972*, H.M.S.O., London.

Department of Economic Affairs (1965). *The West Midlands, a Regional Study*, H.M.S.O., London.

Department of the Environment (1971). *Long Term Population Distribution in Great Britain—A Study*, H.M.S.O., London.

First Secretary of State and Secretary of State for Economic Affairs (1965). *The National Plan* (Cmnd. 2764), H.M.S.O., London.

First Secretary of State and Secretary of State for Economic Affairs (1966). *Investment Incentives* (Cmnd.2874), H.M.S.O., London.

First Secretary of State and Secretary of State for Economic Affairs (1967). *The Development Areas— Regional Employment Premium* (Cmnd.3310), H.M.S.O., London.

Greater London Council (1966). *London Traffic Survey*, Vol. 2, G.L.C., London.

Greater London Council (1969a). *London Transportation Study—Movement in London*, G.L.C., London.

Greater London Council (1969b). *Development Plan; Report of Studies*, G.L.C., London.

Hemming, M. F. W. (1963). The regional problem, *National Institute Economic Review*, **25**, 40–57.

Holmans, A. E. (1964). Industrial development certificates and the control of the growth of employment in South East England. *Urban Studies*, **1**, 138–152.

Howard, R. S. (1968). *The Movement of Manufacturing Industry in the United Kingdom*, 1945–65, H.M.S.O., for Board of Trade, London.

Hunter, L. C. (1963). Employment and unemployment in Great Britain : some regional considerations. *The Manchester School*, **31**, 21–38.

Location of Offices Bureau (1964 onwards). *Annual Report*. L.O.B., London.

London County Council (1964). *London Traffic Survey*. Vol. 1, L.C.C., London.

Luttrell, W. F. (1962). *Factory Location and Industrial Movement*, N.I.E.S.R., London.

McCrone, G. (1969). *Regional Policy in Britain*, Allen and Unwin, London.

Manners, G. (1968a). Misplacing the smelters. *New Society*, 16 May, 712–713.

Manners, G. (1968b). Reshaping steel. *New Society*, 19 December, 907–908.

Manners, G. (1971). *The Changing World Market for Iron Ore*, 1950–1980, Johns Hopkins, Baltimore.

Ministry of Housing and Local Government (1964a). *The Green Belts*, H.M.S.O., London.

Ministry of Housing and Local Government (1964b). *The South East Study*, 1961–81, H.M.S.O., London.

Ministry of Power (1967). *Fuel Policy* (Cmnd.3438), H.M.S.O., London.

Ministry of Transport (1963). *Traffic in Towns*, H.M.S.O., London.

National Economic Development Council (1963a). *Growth in the United Kingdom Economy to* 1966, H.M.S.O., London.

National Economic Development Council (1963b). *Conditions Favourable to Faster Growth*, H.M.S.O., London.

Needleman, L. (1965). What are we to do about the regional problem? *Lloyds Bank Review*, January, 45–58.

Needleman, L. and Scott, B. (1964). Regional problems and location of industry policy. *Urban Studies*, **1**, 153–173.

Nevin, E. (1966). The case for regional policy, *The Three Banks Review*, **72**, 30–46.

Packman, J. (1968). *Child Care : Needs and Numbers*. Allen and Unwin, London.

Report of a Committee (1961). *Inquiry into the Scottish Economy*, 1960–61, (Chairman : J. N. Toothill), Scottish Council, Edinburgh.

Rhodes, J. and Kan, A. (1971). *Office Dispersal and Regional Policy*. Cambridge University Press, Cambridge.

Rodgers, H. B. (1969). The Hunt Report : prospects for Pennine England. *Area*, **3**, 1–9.

Royal Commission on the Distribution of Industrial Population (1940). *Report*, (Chairman : Sir M. Barlow), (Cmnd.6153), H.M.S.O., London.

Royal Commission on Local Government in Greater London (1960). *Report*, (Chairman : Sir Edwin Herbert), (Cmnd.1164), H.M.S.O., London.

Royal Commission on Local Government in England (1969). *Report*, (Chairman : Lord Redcliffe-Maud), (Cmnd.4040), H.M.S.O., London.

Secretary of State for Economic Affairs (1969). *The Intermediate Areas*. (Chairman : Sir Joseph Hunt), (Cmnd.3998), H.M.S.O., London.

Secretary of State for the Environment (1971). *Local Government in England; Government Proposals for Reorganisation*. (Cmnd.4584), H.M.S.O., London.

Secretary of State for Scotland (1971). *Reform of Local Government in Scotland*, (Cmnd.4583), H.M.S.O., Edinburgh.

Secretary of State for Trade and Industry (1972). *Industrial and Regional Development* (Cmnd.4942), H.M.S.O., London.

Secretary of State for Wales (1971). *The Reform of Local Government in Wales : the Consultative Document*, H.M.S.O., Cardiff.

Self, P. (1957). *Cities in Flood,* Faber and Faber, London.

South East Economic Planning Council (1967). *A Strategy for the South East.* H.M.S.O., London.

South East Joint Planning Team (1970). *Strategic Plan for the South East.* H.M.S.O., London.

Thomas, D. (1970). *London's Green Belt.* Faber and Faber, London.

Thomas, R. (1969). *London's New Towns.* P.E.P., London.

Tress, R. C. (1969). The next stage in regional policy. *The Three Banks Review,* **81,** 3–30.

Warren, K. (1970). *The British Iron and Steel Industry since* 1840, Bell, London.

CHAPTER 2

The South East and East Anglia

I. The Metropolitan Region

David Keeble

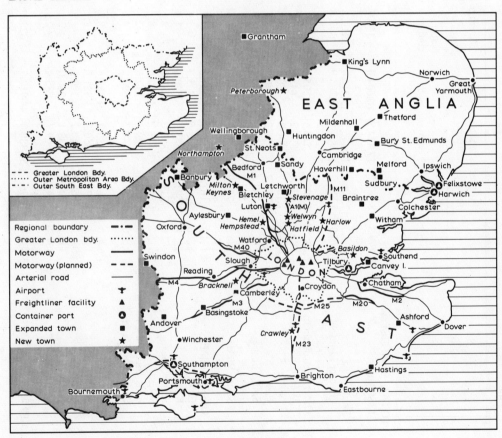

Figure 9 The South East and East Anglia : location map.
Note : Motorways and motorway proposals within Greater London are shown on Figure 14.

Table 10. The South East and East Anglia : selected regional and sub-regional indicators

A. Population :   Thousands

	Mid-year estimates home population				Average annual change 1961–1966			Average annual change 1951–1961		
	1971[1]	1966[2]	1961[2]	1951[2]	Natural change	Armed forces change	Net migration change	Natural change	Armed forces change	Net migration change
TOTAL, South East and East Anglia	**18,799.3**	**18,588.0**	**17,834.7**	**16,604.0**	**+118.9**	**+1.0**	**+37.7**	**+72.9**	**+3.8**	**+46.5**
South East	17,133.3	17,006.3	16,345.5	15,216.4	+110.2	+1.1	+20.8	+66.4	+2.8	+43.8
Greater London	7,379.0	7,836.2	7,980.4	8,208.9	+52.3	+1.3	−82.7	+33.3	+4.8	−61.0
Outer Metropolitan Area	5,290.3	5,009.0	4,517.6	3,505.7	+43.4	+0.2	+54.8	+24.2	−0.5	+77.5
West	983.6	934.4	826.2	648.3	+9.1	−0.5	+13.0	+4.8	+0.2	+12.8
North	1,171.7	1,105.7	1,006.3	729.1	+11.5	+0.1	+8.3	+6.6	+0.6	+20.5
East	945.9	884.2	779.7	540.3	+7.5	—	+13.4	+4.2	+0.1	+19.6
South East	774.3	733.8	659.9	586.1	+5.9	+0.5	+8.4	+3.0	−0.9	+5.3
South	628.3	597.1	561.5	437.0	+3.1	—	+4.1	+1.8	+0.1	+10.6
South West	786.5	753.9	684.0	564.8	+6.3	—	+7.6	+3.7	−0.6	+8.8
Outer South East	4,464.0	4,161.2	3,847.7	3,501.8	+14.5	−0.5	+48.7	+8.9	−1.6	+27.3
Essex	407.6	362.7	328.6	305.3	+1.6	−0.4	+5.7	+0.7	—	+1.6
Kent	621.8	591.6	545.6	520.6	+1.0	—	+8.2	+1.0	−0.6	+2.0
Sussex coast	962.0	913.7	859.0	782.8	−3.1	+0.2	+13.8	−2.6	+0.3	+9.9
Solent	1,641.7	1,554.3	1,443.2	1,290.6	+8.1	+0.4	+13.7	+5.3	−0.4	+10.3
Beds. and Bucks.	305.3	251.6	229.5	212.6	+2.1	—	+2.3	+1.1	−0.6	+1.2
Berks. and Oxon.	525.6	487.2	441.7	390.0	+4.8	−0.6	+4.9	+3.3	−0.3	+2.2
East Anglia	1,666.0	1,581.7	1,489.2	1,387.6	+8.7	−2.1	+11.9	+6.5	+1.0	+2.7
South East	384.3	371.7	350.2	321.8	+2.1	−0.4	+2.6	+1.6	+0.5	+0.8
North East	605.2	565.9	540.2	520.5	+1.9	−0.7	+3.9	+1.6	—	+0.4
North West	309.1	301.9	289.1	260.0	+2.1	−0.6	+1.0	+1.8	+0.6	+0.5
South West	367.4	342.2	309.7	285.4	+2.5	−0.4	+4.4	+1.5	−0.1	+1.0
BRITAIN	53,821.4	53,176.1	51,380.0	48,917.5	+328.2	−0.5	+22.6	+231.4	+12.9	+1.9

1. 1971 Census; 1971 boundaries.   2. 1966 boundaries.

B. Employment :

	Employment		Male employment		Proportion of women at work		Unemployment range		
	1966 '000s	Change 1961–1966 %	1966 '000s	Change 1961–1966 %	1966 %	Change 1961–1966 %	1968 %	1967 %	1961–1966 %
TOTAL South East and East Anglia	**8,690**	**+5**	**5,390**	**+4**	**42**	**+2**	**1–2**	**1–2**	**1–2**
South East	8,070	+5	4,990	+4	44	+2	1–2	1–2	1–2
Greater London	4,700	Nil	2,880	−1	55	+2	1–2	1–2	1–2
Outer Metropolitan Area	1,890	+8	1,180	+17	35	+4	1–2	1–2	0–1
Outer South East									
Essex	120	+11	80	+8	28	+2	2–3	2–3	1–2
Kent	200	+9	120	+8	30	+2	3–4	3–4	2–3
Sussex Coast	300	+3	170	+3	29	Nil	2–3	2–3	2–3
Solent	580	+9	370	+6	33	+3	2–3	2–3	1–2
Beds., Bucks., Berks. and Oxon	290	+7	190	+4	36	+2	1–2	1–2	0–1
East Anglia	620	+13	400	+11	34	+2	2–3	2–3	1–2
South East	140	+13	100	+10	31	+2	2–3	1–2	1–2
North East	240	+13	150	+12	35	+2	2–3	2–3	2–3
North West	120	+15	80	+11	33	+4	2–3	2–3	1–2
South West	120	+14	80	+11	34	+1	1–2	1–2	0–1
BRITAIN	23,550	+4	14,900	+2	40	+2	2–3	2–3	1–2

C. Industrial Development Certificates :

	Total	Annual averages		
	1956–1967 '000s	1964–1967 '000s	1960–1963 '000s	1956–1959 '000s
TOTAL South East and East Anglia	**326.3**	**21.8**	**30.9**	**28.9**
South East	278.0	16.3	26.9	26.3
Greater London	48.3	2.8	4.0	5.3
Outer Metropolitan Area	121.0	6.0	12.1	12.0
Outer South East				
Essex	6.1	0.6	0.6	0.3
Kent	21.8	1.4	2.8	1.3
Sussex Coast	16.9	1.0	1.6	1.6
Solent	53.2	3.7	5.1	4.5
Beds., Berks., Bucks. and Oxon	10.7	0.7	0.7	1.3
East Anglia	48.3	5.5	4.0	2.6
South East	8.3	0.9	0.7	0.5
North East	18.1	1.9	1.6	0.9
North West	10.8	1.4	0.8	0.5
South West	11.1	1.2	0.9	0.6
BRITAIN	1,245.2	121.8	108.1	81.2

Sources : See Table 6.

2.1 Introduction

Whatever definition of its boundaries is adopted, South East England represents the single most populated, economically important and prosperous region of Britain. Within the 3 million hectares (6.77 million acres) of the South East standard region, comprising only 11 per cent of the country's land area, are crowded no less than 17.1 million people, or over 31 per cent of the nation's total population. East Anglia, which is becoming increasingly linked to and part of South East England, by contrast, contains only 3 per cent of the country's population living within more than 5 per cent of the total land area.

The huge concentration of people in the South East is partly a response to, and partly a cause of, the greatest single cluster of economic activity and jobs in the country. Greater London and its surrounding towns comprise Britain's most important manufacturing region, with over 2.5 million workers (or 29 per cent of the national total) engaged in the production of industrial goods. In a whole host of industries, such as food, drink and tobacco, chemicals, electrical and mechanical engineering, vehicles and aircraft, furniture, clothing, and paper and printing, South East factories employ more workers and produce goods of greater total value than those in any other region. Some of these industries are in fact remarkably concentrated in the South East relative to other parts of the country. South East manufacturing industries with over half the country's total workforce in that industry include pharmaceutical and toilet preparations (61 per cent), scientific, surgical and photographic instruments (69 per cent), radio and other electronic apparatus (60 per cent), fur (78 per cent), women's tailored clothing (59 per cent), and printing and publishing (53 per cent). A wide range of others account for more than 40 per cent of British total employment, the main ones being office machinery, furniture, toys and games, and plastics. Not surprisingly, the South East's manufacturing industries are also of particular importance from the viewpoint of national exports, and the country's balance of payments. Whereas nineteenth century Britain relied for exports and prosperity upon the coal, steel, ships and textiles of such coastal regions as the North East and South Wales, the twentieth century has witnessed the growth of the South East as the greatest single export manufacturing region of the country, providing about one-third by value of national visible exports. Many of these are shipped through the Port of London and London (Heathrow) Airport, which now rank amongst the country's three leading export outlets, measured by value of goods handled.

Yet the dominance of the South East's manufacturing industries *vis-a-vis* those of other regions is in many ways surpassed by that of its so-called service trades. Within the standard region these employ 5.3 million people, twice as many as are engaged in manufacturing, and 39 per cent of the British total. Many South East service industries are of course largely if not wholly concerned simply with supplying the needs of the region's resident population. Good examples are the provision of basic medical facilities, primary and secondary education, local government, the building industry, and the distribution of electricity. But a significant number, nearly all of which are clustered in the great office and service centre of London, fulfil national and international roles of the greatest importance for the economic well-being of Britain as a whole.

The most obvious example of a London-based service industry supplying national needs is probably national government administration. National, as opposed to local, government departments and ministries employ nearly 300 thousand workers in the South East, or 48 per cent of the national total. About half of these work in the huge government offices which cluster around the Houses of Parliament in the West End of central London. Even more concentrated in London, however, are the country's insurance, banking and financial services, centred upon the City of London, with its great financial institutions such as the Stock Exchange and Bank of England. No less than 56 per cent of the country's workers in this group of service industries are to be found in the South East : and about half of these (nearly 200 thousand in all) journey each day to work in the City. Again, as with manufacturing, this London-based group of industries is of major importance to the economic prosperity of the nation; the City's financial, insurance and shipping firms are responsible for a large share of the country's net foreign exchange earnings on 'invisible exports', estimated at a record £540 million (out of a national total of £1,370 million) in 1971. Wholesaling is yet another important service activity traditionally concentrated in Greater London, with the South East as a whole accounting for 45 per cent of total national employment in this industry. By contrast, retailing is spread much more evenly throughout the country in relation to the distribution of population, and the South East's three-quarters of a million workers represent only 37 per cent of the total. The fact that this is somewhat higher than the region's share of population (31 per cent) does however bear witness to London's role as a national (and international) retailing centre, and the attractions of such world-famous shopping districts as Oxford and Regent Street, Savile Row and Carnaby Street.

Less easy to categorize, but of major and growing importance in the South East are a whole host of service activities loosely classified as 'professional and scientific' and 'miscellaneous'. The region provides employment for over 900 thousand workers in each of these two very diverse groups of industries, accounting for 36 and 43 per cent respectively of the national total. Many of the firms and activities involved—ranging from theatre, cinema and hotel companies to advertising agencies, consulting engineers, and medical, legal, architectural and other professional bodies of many different kinds—fulfil important national and even international needs. Some of those which are especially concentrated in South East England include legal services, centred upon London's famous Law Courts and legal colleges (45 per cent of national employment), accountancy (46 per cent), scientific research institutions and professional bodies (59 per cent), and the television, broadcasting, theatre and cinema industry. Nearly two-thirds (62 per cent) of the country's jobs in this last industry are found in the South East, the majority of them of course in London.

The growth and concentration of a very remarkable range of manufacturing and service industries in the South East owes a great deal to the region's unrivalled nodality, both nationally and internationally, in terms of communications. In view of the importance

of London's airports and docks, it is perhaps not surprising that the transport and communications industries of the South East employ a high proportion—40 per cent, or 650
thousand workers—of the national workforce in these activities. South East jobs in the
air transport industry alone account for no less than 86 per cent of the British total.

A final index of the contemporary importance of the South East vis-a-vis other regions
is the relative wealth of its inhabitants. One measure of this is the value of retail sales in
the region's shops, expressed as pounds per head of the regional population. In 1961,
together the South East and East Anglian regions recorded retail sales worth £193 per
head of the resident population. Concealed within this average is a remarkably high
Greater London figure of £217 per head of the conurbation's population. These values
were by far the highest for any region or major urban area in the country, and were significantly greater than the British average of £174 per head. Another index of the relative
prosperity of the South East compared to the rest of the country is provided by tax data
on personal incomes. In the financial year 1966–1967, so-called net earned income per
head of the taxable population in the South East was no less than £1,112, higher than
any other region. In the country as a whole, it was only £1,043—and this national figure
was of course boosted by the relatively high incomes earned by residents in the South
East. By contrast, workers in East Anglia received on average only £979, one of the lowest
regional values in the country (see Table 6).

Although complex, the reasons for the apparent relative prosperity of the South East,
and the low incomes of East Anglia, are undoubtedly partly a result of the types of jobs
available in each region. Agricultural workers, for example, who make up 10 per cent
of East Anglia's labour force, are notoriously poorly-paid. Professional posts, large
numbers of which are available in the South East, are in contrast generally well-paid.
Another probable reason is the very low post-war rate of unemployment in the South
East, standing at between 1 and 2 per cent of the total workforce in most years, compared
to a national average of double this figure. East Anglia, although better off in this respect
than regions such as Wales, Scotland or the North East, has however experienced higher
unemployment rates than the South East, with values closer to the national average.
Unemployed workers, of course, generally receive lower incomes in the form of state
payments, than employed workers. Whatever the reasons, however, the geography of
prosperity in Britain is undoubtedly dominated by a concentration of wealth in England's
south eastern corner, a fact of considerable significance for population and industrial
growth.

The contemporary importance of the South East is paralleled by the twentieth century
tendency for British population, employment and wealth to become more concentrated
within the region. Figure 10 indicates that in 1901, what is now the South East standard
region possessed a population of only 10.5 million, and that this had grown to 17.0
million by 1966. What the graph does not show, however, is that the South East's population has also grown at a consistently faster rate throughout the twentieth century
than that of Britain as a whole, so that the region's share of the country's population has

steadily increased, from 27.5 per cent in 1901, to 29.4 per cent in 1931, 30.3 per cent in
1951 and 31.2 per cent in 1966. The provisional 1971 figures, suggesting a slight decline
to 31.0 per cent, are suspect because of problems of under-enumeration in London—
although a levelling-off between 1966 and 1971 in the rate of increase of the true percentage
share is very probable. Although East Anglia's share of national population fell slightly

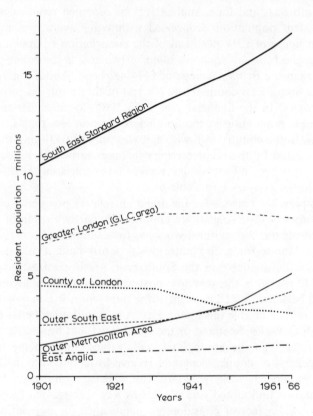

Figure 10 The South East and East Anglia:
population trends, 1901–1966.

between 1901 (3.0 per cent) and 1966 (2.9 per cent), the whole of this relative decline
occurred during the early years of the century; since 1931 (2.7 per cent), its share too has
grown. The provisional 1971 figures suggest further growth to 3.0 per cent.

If anything, the twentieth century rate of growth of manufacturing activity and, to a lesser extent, services in South East England has probably been faster than that of population. Although accurate figures are very difficult to obtain, the general trend of increasing concentration of economic activity in the South East is clearly evident. For instance, in 1923, London and the so-called Home Counties (Bedfordshire, Buckinghamshire, Essex, Hertfordshire, Kent, Middlesex and Surrey) accounted for 18.7 per cent of manufacturing employment in Britain. By 1937, very rapid industrial growth had increased the share of this area, which is not a great deal smaller than the present South East standard region, to 23.4 per cent of the national total. A similar trend has continued since World War II. Figures compiled by Martin (1966, pp. 217–220) show that the 'London Region' (comprising the London and Home Counties area defined above, plus Hampshire and Sussex) accounted for 24.7 per cent of Britain's manufacturing employment in 1951, and 26.9 per cent in 1962. The importance of South East England as a manufacturing region has thus steadily increased throughout the twentieth century. Service activities have also become more concentrated there, albeit at a slower rate than manufacturing.

Dynamic population and economic growth in South East England is intimately related to the increasing localization of prosperity and wealth in the region relative to other parts of the country. Although figures do not exist for the years before World War II, some evidence for this is provided by post-1945 retail trade data. If Britain is divided into two parts, the South East plus East Anglia, and the rest of the country, the value of retail sales per head of their resident population in 1950 was £116 and £100 respectively. By 1961, sales per head in the two areas had risen, to £193 and £164 respectively. The difference between the 1950 values is 16.0 per cent; that between the 1961 values is 17.7 per cent. In other words, the gap between the prosperity of these two areas, as measured by per capita retail sales, appears to have widened over the eleven-year period. A similar conclusion may be drawn from income tax data on regional changes in personal incomes per (taxable) head during the nineteen fifties.

2.2 The Planning Problems

2.2.1 Housing and Land Shortages

The twentieth century growth of population, industry and wealth in the South East is the product of very powerful forces whose character and operation are discussed elsewhere (pp. 10–15). One major result of this growth, however, has been the development of serious planning problems, involving both the provision of what is often called 'social overhead capital' (housing, roads and railways, schools, hospitals, etc.), and the efficiency of economic activity. These problems are largely confined to the vast built-up mass of Greater London, whose population of approximately 7.4 million people (1971) is crowded into an area of only about 1,800 square kilometres (700 square miles). This bald fact immediately draws attention to the single greatest obstacle to the proper provision of modern housing, roads and other forms of social overhead capital in London today—the enormous pressure on, and competition for, land.

Pressure on urban land resources through fierce competition for sites from building developers is common to great cities throughout the world. It reflects the many economic and social advantages which sites within a large urban area offer both for residence and a variety of economic activity—industry, offices and shops. Up to a point, such competition may have beneficial effects, in that it provides a mechanism for the allocation of particular plots of land to those functions which can make the best use of them, as measured by profits. Thus, for example, department stores are able to pay a higher price than most other users for very accessible and hence desirable sites at the centres of cities, because of the higher income they are able to generate there. Manufacturing firms, on the other hand, tend to locate further out where land prices are lower, since their income does not depend nearly as much on accessibility to urban customers or suppliers. Thus, competition for urban land between different economic activities such as these tends to result in a reasonably appropriate arrangement of land use within the city. Unfortunately, however, this is not nearly so true when housing, the provision and arrangement of which needs to be assessed in social as well as economic terms, is considered. For example, poorer families generally cannot afford to live very far from the workplace of the head of the family, because of commuting costs. Yet many jobs in a great city like London are in or near to the centre, where land values are highest. It is thus very difficult to provide adequate, reasonably priced housing for such families without some sort of public subsidy.

In London, pressure on land for housing is acute. Indeed, a shortage of housing, the product of a serious imbalance between the demand for and supply of dwellings in the metropolis, probably represents London's greatest single planning problem. The magnitude of the housing shortage is a matter of some debate. The *South East Study*, 1961–1981 (Ministry of Housing and Local Government, 1964, p. 32) estimated that in 1961, London's 2¾ million 'families' had to make do with only 2½ million separate dwellings. Allowing for 'families' made up of single individuals, whose need is for lodgings rather than separate homes, this calculation suggested a 1961 housing shortage of around 150 thousand dwellings. The Greater London Council's *Development Plan*. (1969b, p. 19), on the other hand, was able to use information from a special 1967 housing survey, and concludes that the real shortfall in 1967 may well have been of the order of 270 thousand homes. This represents an infinitely greater housing shortage, both absolutely and in proportion to population, than that experienced by any other conurbation in England or Wales. Moreover, if measured by numbers of London families actually homeless, or living in shared accommodation (1.4 million people in 1966), the situation seems to have worsened during the 1960s. The number of homeless London families living in temporary hostels increased by no less than 77 per cent, 1964–70, to involve a total of 13,000 people (Greve, Page and Greve, 1971).

The existence for many years of a serious housing shortage in London has rightly been a major consideration shaping post-1945 planning policies for the South East. However, some authorities have argued that the shortage could be eliminated in the near future. The Greater London Development Plan (1969b, p. 29) estimates that sufficient vacant land still exists in London to provide space for over 200 thousand new dwellings. If gains from redevelopment of older low-density residential areas, and from the sub-division of large houses into flats, are included, between 230 and 330 thousand new homes might be provided. In other words, the present housing shortages apparently could be eliminated within a decade. However, this assumes that there will be no further increase in the number of London households requiring homes, an assumption which is tentatively accepted by the Greater London Development Plan, and which is not unreasonable given the continuing decline in London's total population (p. 96). Moreover, the finding ignores the special problem of the lack of geographical correspondence within London between areas of present housing demand, and those of future dwelling construction. It further assumes that finance will be available, and that London's building industry, both public and private, can actually construct this number of dwellings by 1981; in view of the massive additional need for the replacement of at least 200 thousand obsolete homes during the next decade, and of the sharp decline in local authority house building and slum clearance which occurred in the late 1960s (Greve, Page and Greve, 1971), this is a very bold if not unrealistic assumption. In short, though apparently feasible, the successful elimination within the not-too-distant future of London's longstanding and serious housing problem must remain in doubt.

This shortage of houses, and more particularly of land on which to build them, has had four outstanding effects. The most important, up to 1939, was the outward extension of bricks and mortar in a remarkable process of urban sprawl around the edge of the built-up area. During the nineteen thirties, for example, no less than 85 thousand houses were built each year in the London and Home Counties region: and the bulk of these were constructed, often in vast estates, on the conurbation's periphery. Popular revulsion to this wholesale and haphazard sterilization of farmland resulted in post-1945 planning legislation which effectively stemmed further outward growth. Thus, in many places the present boundaries of built-up London represent, in almost fossilized form, the limits reached by the tidal wave of metropolitan expansion during the nineteen thirties. The second effect—one most pronounced during the last two decades—has been the construction of tall blocks of flats and office skyscrapers, especially in or near to central London. The redevelopment of the East End, for example, has seen the construction of numerous 'high-rise' blocks of flats, such as the now notorious 23-storey block at Ronan Point, in place of narrow terraced housing. The height of office blocks is even more striking. The recently opened Euston Tower, soaring to 125 metres (410 feet), may soon be surpassed as London's highest office skyscraper by an 183-metre (600-foot) block proposed for a site in the City of London as the headquarters of the National Westminster Bank.

Building upwards instead of outwards has been accelerated by a third effect of the imbalance between the supply and demand of land—its increasing cost. Exceptionally as expensive as in the Euston Tower development (up to £1.2 million per hectare—£0.5 million per acre), land values have risen rapidly in London in recent years, especially when compared with other parts of the country. In 1969, one hectare of private sector housing land in London cost on average £77,200; this figure was nearly five times the average for England and Wales as a whole (£16,100). Partly as a result, houses in Greater London are much more expensive than those elsewhere. A recent building society survey showed that in the second quarter of 1971, the average price of older houses in London (£6,090) was nearly double that in regions such as North East England (£3,132) and Northern Ireland (£3,248). London prices had increased by 172 per cent since 1952, compared to increases of between 61 and 150 per cent in all other regions of the country. Undoubtedly, the high cost of housing in London partly offsets the higher monetary incomes enjoyed by many of the city region's inhabitants. A further corollary of high and rising land costs, and a last effect of imbalanced land supply and demand, is the relatively small size of many of the 'town houses' and flats built in London since 1945. Where land is scarce and expensive, both private and public developers are forced to plan in terms of minimum rather than desirable space requirements for rooms, gardens, and the like.

The shortage and high cost of land also gravely hinders the provision of other kinds of social overhead capital, such as roads, schools and hospitals. Thus, the construction of the innermost 40 kilometre urban motorway (Ringway 1) proposed by the Greater London Council (1969b, pp. 198–201) is likely to cost over £12.0 millions per kilometre (£19 million per mile); and exactly 30 per cent (£144 million) of the total cost is expenditure on land and buildings lying in the motorway's path. A related problem with this type of infrastructure investment is the highly concentrated character of land uses in London, and the resultant need for the compulsory purchase and destruction of existing buildings. The Greater London Council admitted, for example, that the 1967 urban motorway plan for London, if approved, will involve the destruction of approximately 20,000 dwellings, and the rehousing of a similar number of families.

In addition to these huge yet tangible problems, pressure on land and high density development may create other intangible but no less real difficulties for urban dwellers. The shortage of open spaces and parkland, and distance from attractive countryside, undoubtedly rank high as drawbacks to residence in London for many of its inhabitants. Despite slum area redevelopment and the existence of such famous amenities as Regent's and Hyde Parks, parts of inner London such as Islington, Shoreditch and Southwark still have little or no public open space. Traffic congestion aggravates the problem of sheer distance from the countryside, enforcing laborious journeys of an hour or more's driving upon inner London residents spending a day in the country. More controversial than these amenity matters is the question of urban living and mental health. Various studies (Faris and Dunham, 1965) have revealed that residence in the inner built-up areas of large cities is commonly associated with unusually high rates of certain types of mental illness. In the case of London, a recent survey revealed that East End districts such as Stepney possess an incidence of schizophrenia two-and-a-half times the national average, and one of depressive illness nearly twice as great. While the reasons for this pattern are undoubtedly complex, it does seem at least possible that the physical character of the centres of large cities, with their cramped and often dilapidated buildings, plays some part.

Although competition for land provides part of the explanation for the relatively high housing densities of inner London, equally important is the historical timing of housing construction in this area. Despite redevelopment, probably half to two-thirds of all dwellings in inner London were built before 1900. Many of these are found to the east and north of the City, in the form of narrow terraces or congested tenement blocks, built to provide the bare minimum of space for nineteenth century working class families. Others, though built for middle class families on a more spacious scale as for example in the Notting Hill-North Kensington area, are now sub-divided into numerous small dwellings. In very many cases, nineteenth century housing in inner London is cramped, overcrowded, lacking in such basic facilities as baths and lavatories, and in urgent need of replacement or renovation. In terms of the proper provision of social overhead capital, herein lies a planning problem second only to that of pressure on land—although the exact extent of inner London's so-called 'twilight' housing areas, and the number of houses in need of replacement, are matters of considerable debate. A 1955 Ministry of Housing and Local Government survey yielded a ridiculously narrow estimate of 21,000 slum dwellings in the old County of London (i.e. inner London). More recently, Westergaard (Glass and Westergaard, 1965, p. 83) has used 1961 Census data to suggest a more realistic total of nearly 300 thousand 'obsolete' dwellings in this same area, while Hall (1969, p. 107), on a still wider definition, arrives at a 1961 figure of 465 thousand inner London homes in need of replacement or renovation. The last estimate represents almost exactly half of the total number of dwellings in the old County of London. The most recent view is provided by the Greater London Development Plan (1969b, p. 8), which calculates that no less than 220 thousand dwellings will need to be pulled down and replaced between 1967 and 1981. The problems of overcrowding and housing obsolescence, and the need for urban redevelopment in London—although proportionately less serious than in some northern and Scottish cities—are nevertheless of massive scale and importance.

2.2.2 *Transport*

A further group of planning problems relating to London's social overhead capital concerns the provision of transport facilities, both public and private. London's public transport system, comprising London Transport's underground and bus services, and British Rail's suburban lines, has been faced with major problems in recent years. The most important is a steady decline in passenger use, largely due to increasing car ownership, but also to falling population. Use of London's buses, for example, measured in passenger-kilometres, fell by 20 per cent between 1962 and 1967. To cover costs, fares have therefore had to be increased steeply (by 33 per cent, 1962–67), which in turn has encouraged increased use of private cars in a vicious spiral (Greater London Council, 1969b, pp. 156, 180).

The financial difficulties facing London's public transport services have been aggravated for many years by the markedly peaked nature of demand for transport in connection with journeys to work. Massive rush-hour demands for transport are related to the huge size of the conurbation and its surrounding labour catchment area, coupled with the concentration of jobs—especially office jobs—at its centre. A crude indication of the extent of the resultant geographical imbalance between jobs and homes is given by the fact that, in 1961, the old County of London housed 20 per cent of the population of the South East standard region, but provided 35 per cent of total regional jobs. Thus, although the great majority of journeys to work in London are over only short distances, significant medium and long distance rush-hour flows of workers to and from the centre do occur. Indeed, the commuting hinterland of London's central area has widened since 1945, and now extends up to 100 kilometres (60 miles) in most directions from Charing Cross (see Figure 12).

Despite a massive growth in motor car ownership, most of these flows have to be handled by the South East's tube, rail and bus system, including the notoriously overburdened Southern Region network of British Rail. Since these flows are naturally concentrated into two relatively short periods of the day (between 07.00 and 10.00 hours in the morning, and between 16.30 and 19.00 hours in the evening), the public transport system has to meet the considerable expense of vehicles, rolling stock, equipment and staff which are fully used only during the rush-hour periods. Passed on to the users, the increased costs per kilometre have tended to encourage a further loss of off-peak traffic to private transport, and have widened the existing cost/revenue gap.

Admittedly, various attempts to solve the financial problems of London's public transport system, in addition to raising fares, have been made in recent years. One of these is direct government subsidy. Following the Transport Act of 1968, British Rail was given a government grant of £15 million a year towards the cost of otherwise uneconomic London suburban services. This represented about one quarter of all government subsidies for uneconomic lines throughout Britain but was withdrawn in 1971–1972 following a decision to terminate all such subsidies. Another approach has been through increased investment in modern equipment, in an attempt to win back passengers by providing better services. The main problem here is the scale of investment needed. In January 1970, the new London Transport Executive estimated that it would need £600 million over the next five to ten years for modernization and improvement of its tube (£400 million) and bus (£200 million) services. A third approach has been administrative. Under the Transport (London) Act of 1969, which came into force on January 1st, 1970, responsibility for the policy and financial solvency of London Transport, now renamed the London Transport Executive, has been vested in the G.L.C., London's own elected government. Whether, however, the G.L.C. will prove any more capable of solving the basic economic problems of London's public transport system than previous bodies seems doubtful, at least without some form of direct or indirect subsidy.

The planning problems associated with private (road) transport in London centre around the exceptionally high cost of road improvements, which has already been discussed, and the growth of traffic congestion. Despite new traffic management schemes, average off-peak traffic speeds in the central area of London, for example, fell from 20 kilometres (12.4 miles) per hour in 1962 to 17 kilometres (10.7 miles) per hour in 1966. G.L.C. estimates suggest that by the latter year, traffic congestion throughout the conurbation may have been costing Londoners and London firms as much as £150 million per annum (Greater London Council, 1969b, p. 172). The obvious cause of increased congestion is steady growth in the volume of traffic crowding onto London's inadequate road network. Between 1952 and 1964, traffic volumes in congested central London increased by over 50 per cent: in outer London, the percentage and absolute growth was almost certainly even greater. The actual number of vehicles owned by Londoners, as measured by vehicle licences issued in the G.L.C. area, has been increasing by as much as 10 per cent per annum in recent years. Statistics such as these suggest the need for rapid implementation of some sort of radical road improvement plan for London, if acute levels of traffic congestion are not to cripple vehicle movement within the capital in the next couple of decades.

The solution of London's transport problems is made the more difficult by the divergence of what may be called private as opposed to community costs and benefits arising from transport improvements. In many cases, economic decisions by private individuals or firms involve significant but indirect transport costs which do not have to be borne by the firm or individual concerned, but by the community as a whole. Thus, for example, growth of service employment in central London in recent decades has inevitably increased peak hour demands for public transport, aggravated the financial problems of London Transport and British Rail to a point where direct government subsidies have been necessary, and increased social costs generally in the form of time wasted in commuting. Yet, as the subsidies show, only part of these additional costs has had to be met, in the form of increased wage payments, by the service firms whose locational decisions lie at the root of the problem. This is particularly true of the cost of time spent, and apparently wasted, in commuting to the centre. Although recent figures are not available, a 1954 survey revealed that the average door-to-door journey time between home and work for people living within Greater London and working in the centre was no less than 47 minutes.

In terms of the whole working population of central London, this represents a colossal daily expenditure of time and energy, borne more by the community as a whole than by the firms basically responsible. The same problem arises over the provision of modern roads, and their use by private cars. It is generally agreed that in inner London at least, private car users are not at present charged anything like the whole cost of road provision and vehicle movement in the area. Most of the high cost of special traffic management systems, of new or widened roads, and of environmental deterioration through traffic noise and fumes, has to be borne by the community as a whole or by individuals other than the car driver himself. It may well be that London's transport problems will not really be solved until this divergence between private and community costs and benefits is reduced, perhaps by wholly new transport pricing methods.

2.2.3 *Manufacturing and Services*

The growth and prosperity of Greater London in recent decades has also created serious economic problems for the conurbation's manufacturing and service industries. Chief amongst them, as with housing, is the shortage and the resultant high cost of land and buildings. In the case of both manufacturing and service industries, shortages are as much a product of post-1945 government planning policy—which has deliberately restricted the building of new factories and offices in London—as of sheer physical congestion and unabated demand. Soaring prices and rents for commercial and industrial buildings have greatly increased production and operation costs for many London firms. In some cases, small manufacturing concerns have even been forced out of business by such increases, notably in a few areas where planned redevelopment has replaced dilapidated but cheap premises with expensive modern factories. Restrictions on the construction of new buildings has also meant that many manufacturing and office firms still operate in relatively old premises, which are cramped and poorly designed for modern needs.

A further set of problems and costs arise from acute shortages of labour. Despite the enormous size of London's workforce, and the range of skills available, many firms— especially manufacturing firms—have experienced severe shortages of workers in the last two decades. These shortages are a reflection of the very low regional unemployment rate. They are also a product of the steadily increasing demand for labour from the conurbation's 'growth industries', set against a background of population decline within Greater London. This phenomenon, illustrated by Figure 10, is of major significance not just in terms of past and present labour shortages, but also in planning for London's future. Labour shortages have led to additional problems. In many firms, labour turnover has risen, and the quality of workers filling particular posts has declined. Most important of all, wages and labour payments of all kinds have risen steeply, to reach and be maintained at levels significantly higher than in other regions. A recent government survey revealed that in 1967–1968 average weekly earnings by male manual workers in the South East were 8 per cent higher than the British average, and nearly 17 per cent higher than in the Northern region and Scotland. This situation imposes additional costs upon London firms. Whether, as some economists argue, it also generates an inflationary wage and price spiral which is transmitted to other regions is, however, debatable (p. 8).

Although primarily the result of competition for labour, the high and rising level of wage payments to London workers probably also owes something to the unusually high cost of daily commuting. Government statistics reveal that the average weekly cost to Greater London families of journeys to work and transport in general over the years 1965–1967 was no less than £3.45, or 13.3 per cent of total weekly family expenditure. This was the highest absolute amount and proportion spent on transport in any region of the country, the British average being only £2.70, or 12.2 per cent. Unusually high commuting expenses thus probably represent an extra hidden cost, included in higher overall wage payments, to London firms.

These extra costs vary in their intensity and importance with different types of firms. Some activities, notably headquarters and specialized offices, seem able to bear rising building and labour costs more readily than others, particularly manufacturing industries. Within the manufacturing sector, larger firms, those requiring unusual amounts of space, and those employing above-average proportions of female workers (with the exception of the clothing industry) seem to have suffered most from rising costs, and have therefore taken part to an unusual degree in recent industrial migration from the metropolis. Although lack of detailed research prevents definitive conclusions, it is clear that the impact of these costs is selective, a fact with important implications for the future economic structure and perhaps prosperity of London.

2.2.4 *Rural and coastal periphery*

Undoubtedly, the greatest planning problems facing South East England are those which stem from the region's exceptional population concentration and economic growth. This is true even in many rural areas where increasing immigration, often of London commuters, generates new housing demands, and where farmers face both labour shortages and rising land prices associated with local urban and industrial growth. However, some rural and coastal districts in the peripheral parts of the South East, and more particularly East Anglia, are suffering from the very different problems of economic stagnation and decline. One major reason for this is over-reliance upon industries, notably agriculture, in which employment is contracting through technological change. Agricultural jobs in the South East standard region outside Greater London have been falling by 4,500 workers, or 3.7 per cent, per annum, in recent years. In East Anglia, where agriculture is locally even more important, the decline has been even faster, averaging 2,500 workers or 4.8 per cent, per annum.

At the same time, many of the rural areas concerned contain too small a population, dispersed over too wide an area, to justify the provision locally of what are called 'higher-order' services. On the market-town level, this means the absence of cinemas, theatres, hospitals, secondary schools, and branches of national chain or department stores. On the village or farmhouse level, it means a lack of main drainage, piped gas, a local primary school, and many other services. Since these are just the type of services increasingly regarded as basic essentials for modern living, their absence accelerates still further the drift of younger people away from these areas to London and other large towns, leaving behind smaller and ageing populations which are even less capable of supporting both these and sometimes lower order services.

The third reason for economic stagnation or decline in these fringe areas is undoubtedly their very peripherality. Isolation from Greater London, the dominant focus of employment and economic growth in the South East, greatly inhibits any influx of new economic activity or population. The only major exception to this is the South Coast, especially in Sussex, which has become the country's greatest single retirement area since the war. Even here, however, the age and low purchasing power of the average retirement migrant militate against significant local economic growth as a result of local population expansion. A further problem here, and in the other coastal areas of the South East and East Anglia, is the markedly seasonal nature of employment in the holiday resort industry. High winter unemployment results. Unlike the problems discussed earlier, however, which affect the millions who live or work in London, these rural planning problems concern only a relatively small number of people, even though they have a surprisingly wide geographical occurrence.

2.3 The Policy Response

2.3.1 *Decentralization*

The planning problems which have been discussed in relation to London have been evident for at least forty years. In a society which has come to accept the need for some government intervention in economic and urban development in what is, after all, a relatively small and crowded island, these problems provide one major explanation for the adoption by successive post-1945 governments of what can broadly be termed a decentralization planning policy for London. The economic, social and political bases of this policy, which has been aimed at promoting the outward movement of both population and economic activity from London, are considered in Chapter 1 (pp. 6ff). Its implicit assumption has been that the economic vitality of Greater London, the country's greatest single concentration of economic activity, will not be significantly damaged by continued government-sponsored industrial and office decentralization. Indeed, at no time has any government publication ever specified what total amount of economic movement from London is desirable in the long run, even though the policy has now been in force for over thirty years.

Decentralization planning policy has operated at two distinct levels, differentiated in terms of the reception areas, the official statements and the government departments involved. At the interregional level, it has long been public policy to promote the long-distance decentralization of economic activity, but not population, from London to the less prosperous regions of the country. Expressing government concern over the high levels of unemployment and slow economic growth there, this policy has been largely the responsibility of the Board of Trade (and more recently the Department of Trade and Industry), and has been viewed almost entirely in terms of manufacturing industry. Only since 1963 has the decentralization of service activities, in particular offices, been accepted as a major goal of policy at this inter-regional level.

Although the policy has also been applied to the West Midlands, South East England in general and Greater London in particular have constituted by far the largest single source of migrant manufacturing firms which have been persuaded to begin production in the less prosperous regions. This is clear from Board of Trade data, which reveal that South East England and Greater London provided no less than 39 per cent (445) and 28 per cent (320), respectively, of all manufacturing establishments set up for the first time between 1945 and 1965 in one of the less prosperous regions (Howard, 1968). In terms of the resultant new industrial employment in these regions, the respective proportions were 38 and 26 per cent. No other single region of the country provided more than 12 per cent of total moves to the national economic periphery, or 16 per cent of total new industrial employment there. Many of the London firms involved have been major expanding concerns, with household names such as Hoover, Glaxo, Ford and Heinz. Their impact upon the economies of particular less prosperous regions such as Wales, where half of all the immigrant firms have come from the South East, has been profound. In contrast, very few London office concerns have so far transferred their activities to the peripheral regions. The chief exceptions are government departments, notably the Post Office, which has moved the Savings Certificate Division and Savings Headquarters to Durham (2,500 jobs) and the Savings Bank to Glasgow (7,500 jobs).

The second level at which the government's policy of decentralization has operated is the intraregional level. As far as South East England is concerned, post-1945 planning at this level stems almost entirely from the thinking and proposals of Sir Patrick Abercrombie's *Greater London Plan* (1945). Abercrombie himself was a member of the Barlow Commission, and was obviously much influenced by the evidence presented to, and recommendations of, that body. However, his plan, commissioned by the then coalition government, was concerned entirely with the optimum geographical arrangement of population and economic activity within South East England, and government intraregional location policy.

Abercrombie's thinking was dominated by essentially metropolitan planning problems. His central recommendation was the massive decentralization of both people and industry from Greater London to other parts of the South East. The transfer of no less than 1¼ million Londoners was to be effected chiefly through government action, in the form of the planned expansion of existing towns (525 thousand migrants) and the creation of wholly new towns (380 thousand migrants) along lines successfully pioneered by Ebenezer Howard and his 'garden cities' of Welwyn and Letchworth (see Howard, 1965). Migration on this scale, Abercrombie claimed, would reduce the conurbation's population to little more than 7 million, and permit the redevelopment of inner congested housing areas at lower net residential densities.

At least three considerations were fundamental to Abercrombie's proposals. The first was that the government would take powers to prevent any further outward extension of the built-up area of London. To this end, the conurbation would be encircled by a green belt, about eight kilometres (five miles) wide, within which new urban development would be very strictly controlled. The second was the assumption that further growth

of the South East's total population would not take place. In 1944, government demo-
graphers forecast a balancing-out of births and deaths, with a falling birth rate as in the
1930s; and Abercrombie assumed that net immigration to the South East would cease
as a result of the government's regional development policies. The third consideration
was the considerable emphasis placed on the movement of employment, interpreted
almost wholly as manufacturing industry, to outlying parts of the South East. This was
regarded as an essential corollary of population migration. As Abercrombie rightly
stressed, the decanting of people but not employment from London would simply result
in increased long-distance commuting to the metropolis, and would intensify rather than
ameliorate the existing journey to work problems.

Abercrombie's recommendations were in principle accepted by the government: and,
since 1945, a remarkable centrifugal shift in the geographical distribution of the South
East's population and industry has indeed occurred. In many ways this shift represents
the most striking single change in the human geography, not just of the region, but of the
country as a whole. Between 1951 and 1966, the population of Greater London (the area
of the Greater London Council) fell by approximately 370 thousand, or 4.5 per cent,
to *circa* 7.8 million. Given a natural increase in Greater London's population by excess
of births over deaths of perhaps 40 thousand per annum, this decline represents a net
average annual out-migration from London of no less than 60 thousand people. In the
last few years, the rate has quickened considerably, to about 90 thousand net migrants
per annum. However, while London's population has been falling, that of the rest of
the South East standard region has been growing at an explosive rate. Again, between
1951 and 1966, the resident population of this outer area increased by no less than 2.2
million, or 31 per cent. This represented approximately half of the absolute increase
in the country's total population over the period. The provisional 1971 census figures
suggest that the rate of population decline in London has increased dramatically since
1966, the five year period witnessing a fall of *circa* 400 thousand, or 6.0 per cent, in the
resident population of the G.L.C. area. Population in the rest of the South East rose by
over 600 thousand (or 7 per cent) to 9.75 million.

Although part of this phenomenal growth around London represents the natural
increase of the population already living in the area, a very significant share has been
contributed by people moving out from London to buy new homes beyond the boundaries
of the conurbation. In the middle nineteen sixties, no less than 160 thousand Londoners
moved out annually to settle in the rest of the South East. Since only about 70 thousand
people each year moved in the opposite direction (from the rest of the South East back
into London), the net balance of migration was very clearly in favour of the outer part
of the South East, at a net immigration rate of 90 thousand Londoners a year. This rate
seems to have quickened considerably since then.

Massive decentralization has not been confined to population alone. Since 1945,
economic activity, and in particular manufacturing industry, has also been growing at a
phenomenal rate in the outer part of the South East. Between 1951 and 1966, for example,

employment in manufacturing firms in this area increased by about 400 thousand workers. The rate of growth—55 per cent—was even faster than that of population. Simultaneously, manufacturing employment in London itself fell by about 70 thousand workers (5 per cent) between these two dates. Once again, the chief single reason for this remarkable shift in the geographical distribution of manufacturing activity within the South East was the migration of manufacturing firms from London to new factories in South East towns outside the conurbation. Although the figures are not strictly comparable with those from the Censuses of Population given above, Board of Trade records (Howard, 1968) suggest that the London firms which have moved out in this way since 1945 were providing jobs for at least 180 thousand people by 1966. A further 9 thousand manufacturing jobs went to East Anglia.

These facts and figures suggest that Abercrombie's planning policy has been implemented with great success. This view is also supported by other evidence. For example, London's further outward growth has undoubtedly been prevented by the designation of an official green belt around the conurbation (Figure 11), and by strict planning controls over new development within this zone. Redevelopment of some of the worst slum areas in inner London has been carried out, most notably in such East End districts as Stepney and Poplar. Most strikingly of all, Abercrombie's new town proposals have borne fruit in the shape of eight such towns, located in a ring about 50 kilometres (30 miles) from the metropolis. By 1969, these communities housed some 350 thousand immigrants, the bulk of whom had moved directly from London. Their industrial growth had also been considerable, with the establishment of over 400 manufacturing firms, three-quarters of them migrants from London.

Despite these achievements of the decentralization policy, at least two important qualifications concerning the implementation of Abercrombie's proposals must be made. One stems from the inaccuracy of his basic assumption of a static regional population. As subsequent commentators have been delighted to point out (Hall, 1969, pp. 92–93), this expectation has been totally falsified by events. Although falling until 1955, the birth rate in the country as a whole and the South East in particular then rose rapidly and unexpectedly until 1964. As a result, the region's population grew through natural increase by nearly 1.2 million people between 1951 and 1966. This was augmented, despite the Board of Trade's efforts to stem the drift of population from regions of higher unemployment, by net immigration of over half-a-million new residents. The effects of this unexpected surge of population growth in terms of the implementation of Abercrombie's proposals have been to slow down, at least until *circa* 1964, the rate of population decline in London, at the same time as speeding up population growth in the rest of the South East. Until the late nineteen sixties, the planners thus found it more difficult than expected to redevelop inner London at lower population densities, while an insatiable demand for new houses in such counties as Hertfordshire, Essex and Berkshire forced them to permit building development there on a larger scale than Abercrombie envisaged.

The other qualification to the apparent success of Abercrombie's policy is that decen-

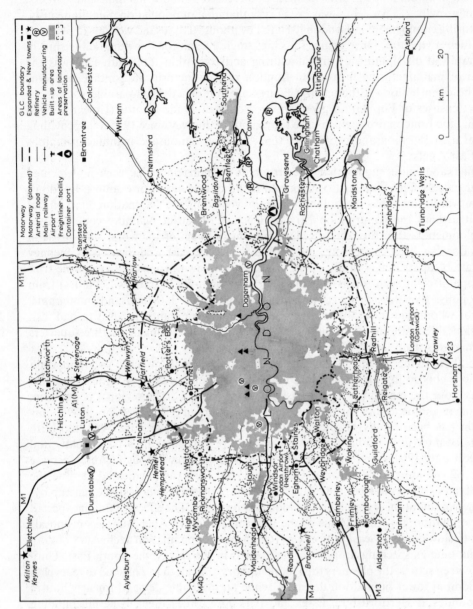

Figure 11 Inner South East England: principal economic and land use features, 1971.
Notes : 'Areas of landscape preservation' are mainly the Metropolitan green belt, but also include certain
areas of outstanding natural beauty. Motorways and motorway proposals within the G.L.C.
area are shown on Figure 14.

tralization has been in many ways as much a product of very powerful natural forces as
of deliberate government action. This view is supported by various kinds of evidence.
For example, only about 400 thousand people, or 18 per cent of the total 1951–1966
growth in population outside London, have actually been housed in government-sponsored
new or expanded towns. The great mass of new residents in the outer parts of the South
East live outside these planned reception areas, which Abercrombie proposed should
take four-fifths of future population growth. Indeed, in recent years only one in eight
actual migrants from London to the outer parts of the South East has settled in these
official overspill centres, the remainder moving entirely of their own volition to other
towns and villages. Even industrial decentralization seems to be less influenced by South
East planning policy than by natural forces. Although accurate figures are very hard to
obtain, official records suggest that only about 40 per cent of all the South East factories
set up by migrant London firms post-1945 are located in the new towns; and various
surveys reveal that apart from the occasional displacement by housing redevelopment
schemes, the basic reasons for industrial movement from London have more to do with
building congestion and labour shortages than with local planning policies.

In sum, the tidal wave of post-1945 decentralization from London seems to reflect not
only the operation of regional planning policy, but also, and to a greater extent, the
continuing impact of the same natural centrifugal forces which extended London's
built-up area before 1939. The difference lies in the much wider geographical area affected
by recent decentralization, and its concentration by planning controls into existing or
new towns separated by open land from the bricks and mortar of London itself.

The two aspects of decentralization policy in the South East—interregional and intraregional—thus possess rather different origins and aims, and contrasting means of imple-
mention. It is not perhaps surprising, therefore, that in certain ways and at certain times
they have been in conflict. This is most clearly the case with industrial movement from
London. As was noted in Chapter 1, during at any one time period only a limited number
of London firms have been willing actively to consider relocating outside the metropolis.
Yet both the Board of Trade, on behalf of the less prosperous regions, and the South East
planning authorities—such as the erstwhile London County Council, the Greater London
Council and the new town Development Corporations—have been anxious to attract
as many industrial firms as possible to their respective reception areas. Although the
Board, which has over-riding powers in this respect through its control of i.d.c.s. has treated
sympathetically many applications for movement to new and expanded towns in the South
East, a conflict of interest has at times been apparent.

Office decentralization policy also reveals conflicting aims. Recent years have seen a
virtual government ban on new office building throughout the South East, as a new aspect
of interregional decentralization policy. At the same time, however, the government-
sponsored Location of Offices Bureau has been striving to encourage intraregional office
decentralization from congested central London to the outer suburbs and new towns,
where service employment is welcome and journey to work problems are lessened.

The Bureau's earlier successes along these lines owed much to the construction of new, often speculative, office blocks in areas such as outer West London and Croydon. After 1964, however, the supply of intraregional 'decentralized' accommodation began to dry up, with strict enforcement of o.d.p. controls over the whole region. As a result, intraregional office decentralization became much more difficult. Since very few central London office firms appeared willing to consider interregional movement, by 1971 the net effect of this conflict between the two decentralization policies had been significantly to reduce outward movement within the region, with little or no compensating increase in long-distance transfers. Government policy was therefore modified (Manners, 1972).

2.3.2 *Reassessment*

Government decentralization planning policies and natural economic and social forces have therefore combined to bring about a considerable dispersal of people and economic activity from the built-up area of London to other parts of South East England since 1945. This dispersal has been large enough to offset natural growth, producing a significant decline in Greater London's population and manufacturing employment. The former has now been falling for some 30 years (see Figure 10), the latter since about 1960. Moreover, the rate of decline of both seems to have quickened considerably in recent years. These trends are of course exactly those which planners operating the traditional decentralization policy have aimed at for nearly thirty years. Yet as so often happens, the very success of this policy has begun to alter the climate of opinion in which it has hitherto operated.

One of the most interesting, and in many ways surprising, aspects of traditional policy has been the readiness with which London's own planning authorities have cooperated in measures to disperse population and economic activity from their own areas—for the immediate benefit of towns far beyond London itself. The achievement at last of a rate of decline which promises a very significant drop in the level of London's population and perhaps even economic activity over the next ten or twenty years, has however brought with it the first major reassessment of the assumptions and validity of traditional decentralization policy. Not surprisingly, this reassessment has been carried out by the planning authority most intimately concerned with Greater London—the Greater London Council. Set up in 1965 under the provisions of the 1963 London Government Act, the Council is the first official body ever to be made statutorily responsible for the planning strategy of Greater London as a whole. The wide ranging review and evaluation of current trends and planning policies in London which was therefore begun by its Planning Department in 1965 found expression in the 1969 publication (Greater London Council 1969a; 1969b) of the draft *Greater London Development Plan* (G.L.D.P.).

The challenge contained in the G.L.D.P. is based, not so much on Abercrombie-type physical planning considerations, as upon economic arguments which Abercrombie and subsequent South East planning proposals have largely ignored. The Plan's starting point is an assessment of the vital economic importance of Greater London to the national economy. The Council points out that in terms of exports, both visible and invisible, and the whole question of the country's balance of payments and rate of economic growth, the contribution of London-based firms is significantly greater than that which might be expected simply from the capital's share of national population. As the country's greatest centre of economic innovation, as the principal channel through which new ideas and technology from abroad are disseminated to other cities and regions, as the industrial complex in which labour productivity in manufacturing appears to be higher than in any other part of the country, London represents in many ways Britain's greatest single economic asset. The Council therefore argues that its primary responsibility must be to safeguard and encourage the economic vitality of the metropolis. At the very outset, it accepts as fundamental to its policy the need 'to foster the commercial and industrial prosperity of London', a viewpoint on which it 'offers no compromise' (Greater London Council, 1969a, p. 10).

This approach, wholly different in character from that of Abercrombie, with his preoccupation over lack of amenity, urban sprawl, and housing congestion, immediately raises two major questions. Can this viewpoint be reconciled with traditional industrial and commercial decentralization policy, and what are its implications for policy concerning the future rate of population dispersal? The Plan's fundamentally pro-London approach inevitably leads it to question many aspects of received opinion. While accepting the value of decentralizing those industries, offices and other economic activities to which a London location is not essential, it points out that a number of important manufacturing industries seem to function more efficiently in London, as measured by a significantly higher average labour productivity, than anywhere else in Britain. Census of Production records reveal, for example, that in 1958 at least ten London manufacturing industries, including vehicles, clothing, printing, timber and furniture, and other metal goods, achieved a significantly higher labour productivity than their counterparts in the nearest comparable area, the rest of the South East (plus East Anglia). London's overall value of net output per employee in manufacturing was therefore greater than in any other region except Wales (Greater London Council, 1969b, pp. 73–75). The same pattern is probably even more true of central London's office activity, although here the absence of data prevents quantitative comparison.

Admittedly, as the G.L.D.P. itself is at pains to point out, this very interesting labour productivity argument can be challenged on various grounds. Thus the exclusion of capital, for which regional data are not available, renders the G.L.D.P.'s analysis partial rather than complete as an authoritative study of regional variations in returns to all the factors of production. Again, demonstrable differences in labour productivity measure more than the locational advantages for a given industry of a particular region; variations in labour costs and hence degree of capital substitution, age of plant, and quality of management also influence the calculation. A third criticism is that the analysis perforce deals only with average productivities, whereas locational policy ought to be based on a knowledge of marginal productivities and returns to marginal production increments in different regions.

These criticisms indicate the great need for data and detailed research on interregional variations in productivity as a basis for location policy-making in Britain. In the absence of such data and research, however, the G.L.D.P.'s carefully-qualified productivity analysis, the conclusions of which seem to be corroborated by independent academic research (Brown, 1969, p. 767), does appear to be of value in this respect. On this and other general grounds, the Plan therefore uncompromisingly rejects any policy of wholesale dispersal, even though this is implied by some of the 'blanket' controls which have been used to promote economic decentralization since 1945. In its view, 'any attempt to interfere drastically with the main functions of London as developed over the centuries would bring incalculable and possibly disastrous consequences for the country'. In particular, the Council clearly feels that government controls over new office floorspace should be operated much more selectively, lest 'shortage of space for legitimate expansion' impair the efficiency of London's unique office complex (Greater London Council, 1969a, p. 10). Its thinking here, though obviously influenced by the needs of indigenous 'City' offices engaged in the earning of invisible exports, probably also owes much to a recognition of the capital's increasing role as a European market base for North American and other international office organizations. If London is to compete successfully with Brussels, Paris and other centres for future European-oriented service firms, a flexible office distribution policy would seem essential. The Plan therefore announced the Council's intention to discuss with government the possibility of removal or modification of o.d.p. or i.d.c. controls as they at present apply to the capital.

The G.L.D.P. also views population decentralization policy from a new, economic, standpoint. It fully accepts that post-1945 'reduction of population has had many good results' (Greater London Council, 1969a, p. 10), and that existing commitments to outlying expanded towns must be met. But it points out that 'continuing and perhaps accelerating decline could be harmful' to the economy of London and therefore to the nation, through its effect upon the level of London's resident labour force (Greater London Council, 1969a, p. 15). With a significant and steady fall in the birthrate since 1964—in England and Wales as a whole from 876 thousand live births in 1964 to 805 thousand in 1969—and with increased out-migration, the population of the G.L.C. area is now falling by 90 thousand people each year. If this rate of decline continues unchecked, the capital's population could well fall to a level significantly less than 7 million by 1981. For demographic reasons, this dramatic decline would involve an even steeper reduction in the resident workforce, to a total of perhaps little more than 3.1 million. The acute labour shortage which could well result might seriously threaten the economic vitality and efficiency of those many industries which need to be located in London, most notably its 'vitally important central functions'. Such shortages might also have a serious inflationary effect, and stimulate greatly increased commuting pressure on the South East's already strained communications system.

Taking all these factors into account, therefore, the Plan argues strongly that a limit must be set to population decline. This limit may well be reached during the nineteen seventies. The Plan as a result concludes that the Council's policy 'must aim at a population for Greater London which is not so great that it militates against the creation of good living conditions nor so small that it gives rise to difficulties in the maintenance of the labour force. For that purpose, and on present evidence, the Council considers that the population of Greater London in 1981 should be around 7.3 millions (Greater London Council, 1969a, p. 10). In effect, the Plan is suggesting that from an economic viewpoint Abercrombie's original 'target' population for London (translated in terms of the Greater London Council area) was too small by over half-a-million people. The controversy which these views and proposals have inevitably stimulated will doubtless rage for years rather than months.

2.4 The London City Region

2.4.1 Character and Extent

Despite major differences in their approach and date, the plans produced by Abercrombie and the Greater London Council share one common feature. Both accept that neither Greater London nor the remainder of the South East can be planned in isolation from each other. Both quite explicitly view the whole of South East England as one functional region, whose various formally dissimilar parts—the built-up areas of Greater London, the surrounding commuter towns, the rural areas of Kent, Hampshire, Berkshire, Essex, the south coast ports—are intimately linked by regular if not daily flows of people, goods and information. Any plan for part of the South East will therefore inevitably have considerable effects on the rest of the region as well.

The links and flows which bind the South East into a single functional region centre of course, both geographically and in terms of their intensity, upon London. It is the presence of one of the world's greatest cities at the heart of the region, coupled with a basically radial pattern of communications connecting all parts of the South East to the centre, which really ties the area together. The dominance of London in this respect finds expression in the phrase 'the London city region', an aphorism which increasingly is used to describe the areas lying up to 80 or 95 kilometres (50 or 60 miles) from the capital —in other words, virtually the whole of South East England. The phrase embodies a view of modern cities in general, and London in particular, which sees them as much wider entities than the zone of continuous bricks-and-mortar traditionally labelled 'London', 'Birmingham' or 'Manchester'. It acknowledges that in a functional sense, most great cities today extend over much wider areas than that covered by their central built-up core. Fundamentally, London's citizens are the people who look to the metropolis for employment, for specialized shopping, for entertainment and culture. Its industries are those which regard easy access to metropolitan customers, material and component suppliers, banking and financial firms, even workers, as essential to their activities. As such, the capital's citizens and industries are almost as likely to reside or operate today in Brighton or Basingstoke as in Holborn or Hounslow. Such has been the effect of the twentieth century spread of London's influence, population and industry to formerly more isolated towns and villages in South East England.

Acceptance of the functional unity of the London city region immediately raises two important questions. How far does this region extend outwards from London, and what types of flows and functional links are involved? Unfortunately, no clear-cut answer can be given to the first of these questions. The problem here is that, as with many other spatial patterns in human geography, the influence of London exhibits what is known as a 'field' phenomenon. The impact of the metropolis on the lives and activities of people in South East England, like the power of the magnet, is greatest at the centre, and declines in all directions away from it. Unlike a magnetic field, however, London's influence decreases at different rates in different directions, depending upon the existence or other-wise of competing larger towns, the ease of movement along particular radial communication links, and such random factors as the local planned colonization by London overspill population and industry. Thus, for example, the expanded Norfolk town of Thetford, 127 kilometres (79 miles) from Charing Cross, is as much a part of the London city region as, say, the commuting centre of Haslemere, located only 69 kilometres (43 miles) from the metropolis : whereas Portsmouth, though not much more than 100 kilometres (60 miles) away, is perhaps best considered as outside it.

The limits of London's city region vary both according to the type of influence, and the type of population, considered. Commuting to the centre of London for employment decreases fairly rapidly with distance from the capital, whereas London's influence as a market and source of materials and components for industry is still felt strongly 80 or 95 kilometres (50 or 60 miles) away. Again, higher incomes enable many more managerial and professional workers to travel to London for work or entertainment from distant high-income residential areas—southern Sussex, Margate, Clacton-on-Sea—than semi-skilled or unskilled workers living in nearby lower-income districts.

In short, as a field phenomenon involving different and sometimes even intangible types of influence, London's city region cannot easily be defined in terms of clear-cut, formal boundaries. What can be said, however, is that taking into account the various functional relationships which do exist between London and the surrounding area, the capital's influence today is felt sufficiently strongly by towns and villages up to about 95 kilometres (60 miles) from the centre to warrant their inclusion in any working definition of its city region. This qualitative conclusion is supported by what quantitative evidence exists on the spatial extent of different types of influence, such as flows of commuters to London (see Figure 12), and frequency of telephone calls to and from the metropolis. Maps of the latter (Standing Conference, 1968) reveal the remarkable dominance of London as the source or destination of virtually all major flows of telephone calls in the South East. They also indicate that with the exception of calls to Birmingham and South Hampshire, very few major flows take place between London and towns located further than 100 kilometres (60 miles) from Charing Cross.

2.4.2 *Communications* (Lon City Reg²)

Logic suggests that the wide spatial extent of London's city region reflects more than anything else the ease with which it is possible to travel between London and other South East towns. If this is so, there are strong grounds for believing that, even though it is difficult to specify precise boundaries, the distance over which the influence of contemporary London is felt is significantly greater than it was only thirty years ago. In other words, the London city region has grown in size in response to the rapid improvements in the number and quality of radial communications between London and the rest of the South East over the last twenty years. These improvements have been far more substantial than those made to the rather limited circumferential, or 'orbital', routes around London, and reflect the fact that nearly all major flows by rail or road in the South East take place along the radial routes.

As far as roads are concerned, the most striking recent and projected improvements involve the new South East motorways. Britain's first full-scale motorway, the M1, the M4 from Brentford towards South Wales, the new M40 stretch on the London-Oxford road, the A1(M) north of Stevenage, the M2 between Rochester and Faversham, and the newly-opened section of the M3 between Ascot and Basingstoke, have already greatly increased speed and ease of road access from London to outlying South East towns and villages; in all, over 240 kilometres (150 miles) of radial motorway have so far been built in South East England. With the exception of the 45-kilometre (28-mile) stretch of the South Coast motorway (M27) between Portsmouth and Southampton, and the low-priority M25 (see Figure 9), all the projected motorway developments in the South East outside London are also of a radial nature. In addition to the remaining stretches of the M3 from London to Winchester, three motorways are envisaged. The M23 will run from inner south London to Crawley, bringing central Sussex even closer in touch with the capital. The M11 will replace the congested A11 as the route from north-east London to Bishop's Stortford and the Cambridge sub-region; and the short M12, running eastwards from Ilford through Greater London, will speed flows to central Essex. Construction of these new motorway stretches will add about 160 kilometres (100 miles) of first class radial highway to the South East's road network.

The same trend characterizes recent improvements in rail communications. Most striking of these has been the expensive electrification of the Waterloo-Bournemouth and Euston-Lancashire main lines. The total cost of the latter, over one-quarter of which traverses the South East, was £160 million. The former, with all its 160 kilometres (100 miles) of track in the South East, cost £15 million. The justification for electrification was, of course, the heavy traffic already carried by these lines. In turn, the much-shortened journey times made possible by electrification and track realignment are attracting even greater flows of passengers and freight. Southampton and Bournemouth are now only 70 and 100 minutes respectively from London, while the fastest non-stop services to Bletchley take only 37 minutes to cover the 73 or so kilometres (45 miles) from Euston. Areas on the very periphery of the South East have thus been brought considerably closer to London in terms of journey time. Once again it has been the radial routes linking London with its city region, rather than orbital lines between outlying towns, which have been improved, while the same is true of planned rail improvements, such as the electrification of Kings Cross suburban services to Welwyn, Stevenage and Hitchin, on the model of the successful Liverpool Street to Bishop's Stortford electrification scheme further east. The Kings Cross scheme, to be completed by 1977, will cost £35 million, and is financed by a 75 per cent government grant. Thus, the extent of London's influence in South East England and the neighbouring parts of East Anglia has increased, is increasing, and is unlikely to be diminished.

2.4.3 *Commuting*

Discussion of the changing city region boundaries has already touched on the second question raised earlier concerning the types of flows, functional links and interrelationships which bind the outer parts of London's city region to its central core. The most obvious and easily measured is the daily journey to work. The influence of London in this respect upon many of the inhabitants of its city region has long been recognized, and often deplored. Although concerned primarily with the daily surge of suburban commuters into and out of central London, Sir Halford Mackinder's classic 1902 description captures most vividly the vitality of a phenomenon now involving many who live outside the conurbation. 'The life of the great metropolis ... exhibits a daily throb as of a huge pulsating heart. Every evening half-a-million men are sent in quick streams, like corpuscles of blood in the arteries, along the railways and the trunk roads outward to the suburbs. Every morning they return, crowding into the square mile or two wherein the exchanges of the world are finally adjusted' (pp. 257–8).

In discussing commuting to the highly distinctive office concentration of central London, Mackinder was describing the more important of the two main types of daily movement which take place between London and its region. In recent years, the journey to work in London's central area has involved as many as 230 thousand long-distance commuters from South East towns and villages outside the conurbation. This number represents a very significant increase, of over 70 per cent, compared with that obtaining in the nineteen forties. Not surprisingly, such an increase has gone hand-in-hand with a widening of the catchment area from which the long-distance commuters are drawn. Before 1939 really long-distance flows to central London originated from only a few especially attractive residential areas, notably Brighton and Hove. By 1961, however, the latter were sending no less than $4\frac{1}{2}$ thousand commuters daily into the offices of inner London, while over 200 commuters were travelling from centres as far away from London as Southampton and Portsmouth in Hampshire, Saffron Walden and Dunmow in Essex, and Broadstairs and Margate in Kent.

The other main type of commuting which links together London and its city region is relatively short distance radial movement of workers to jobs in London's suburban industrial, office and shopping zones. The industrial areas of west London—Hayes, Willesden, Brentford—draw on workers from Buckinghamshire and Berkshire; the office and industrial centre of Croydon employs labour from Surrey, Kent and even Sussex.

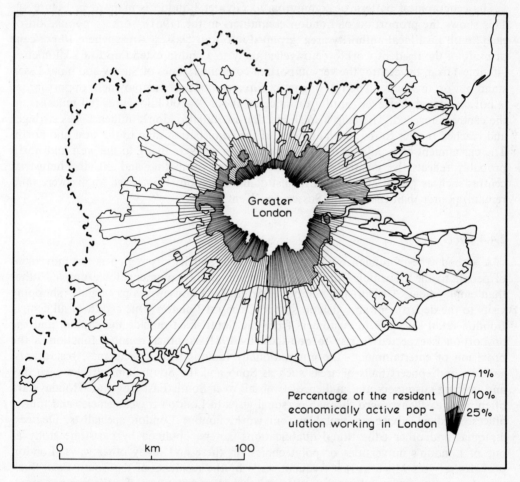

Figure 12   The South East : commuting hinterland of Greater London, 1961.
  Source :   Report of Standing Conference on London and South East Regional Planning, Technical Panel, LRP 1180, 17 July 1968.

Short distance journeys to work of this kind, virtually all of which originate in the Outer Metropolitan Area (see Figure 9), have involved a further 240 thousand commuters in recent years. Altogether, therefore, London's city region outside the conurbation each day despatches almost half-a-million (470 thousand) people to jobs in Greater London, and thus provides just over 10 per cent of the capital's total workforce. Looked at in another way, one in every ten workers living in South East England outside Greater London travels every day to a job in the metropolis. No wonder the overloaded rail and road system of the South East is so often in the news because of traffic jams and rail delays.

The geographical pattern of commuting to Greater London is mapped in Figure 12. This shows the proportion of London commuters in the (1961) working population of each South East local authority area, grouped into four classes. Areas where 10 per cent or more of the resident workforce travelled daily to London extend up to 65 kilometres (40 miles) from the centre; the very important commuter zones of Surrey and inner Essex stand out on this score. The full impact of Greater London's employment opportunities is not dissipated, however, until a distance of about 95–100 kilometres (60 miles) from the centre is reached. The map also shows that in 1961 London's influence was stronger and reached further to the south and east of the conurbation than to the west and north. The curtailment of London's relative impact upon workers living to the west and north probably reflects the greater development there of competing and thriving industrial centres such as Luton and Slough, whilst communications from East Anglia were (and remain) poorer than those from Sussex and Kent.

2.4.4 *Other Links*

A second type of influence which links London and its city region is the movement of people to the metropolis for purposes—retailing, entertainment, for example—other than employment. A surprising number of South East housewives pay regular shopping visits to the department and fashion stores of central London. One-eighth of all central London retail sales are to customers from the South East outside the capital, and the proportion is expected to rise to one-sixth by 1981. Another regional function is the provision of entertainment—the internationally famous theatres, cinemas, restaurants, galleries and concert halls of areas such as Soho and the South Bank attract each day and evening customers and audiences from all over South East England. Holidays are often more easily arranged through personal visits to London travel agencies and tourist offices. Medical advice is available from world famous London specialists. Degrees, diplomas and other educational qualifications can be obtained by part-time study at one of London's universities or polytechnics. In these and many other ways, London provides services which attract frequent visits by the residents of the South East. Such trips have almost certainly increased in volume in recent years, if only because many former Londoners, accustomed to patronizing London services, have migrated to the remainder of the region.

London's influence upon economic activity, especially manufacturing, in its city region is also profound. Within the boundary of the Greater London Council is located the largest concentration of material and component suppliers, the greatest market, and the most important advertising, financial and communications centre in Britain, let alone the South East. As a result, most South East industrial towns—such as Brighton, Rochester, Slough and Stevenage—possess stronger links with London, in the form of flows of industrial materials, components and finished goods, than with any other urban centre. Moreover, as in the case of population movement, links of this kind have tended to increase in recent years as a result of the considerable dispersal of London firms to the rest of the South East. Board of Trade records (Howard, 1968) show that at least 750 new factories were set up in the outer parts of the South East by London firms in the twenty years to 1965. A further 80 such factories were established in East Anglia. Although forced to leave the capital, for reasons discussed later (p. 120), the vast majority of these factories have retained very strong links with London, receiving the bulk of their materials and components from there, relying on London firms for specialized processing, and dispatching much of their production to metropolitan customers. A significant number— established often as far away as Margate, Salisbury or Thetford—are subsidiary branches of London firms and send daily lorry-loads of semifinished goods or components to their parent factory. The colonization of the rest of the South East and East Anglia by London manufacturing industry has thus strengthened and widened the geographical extent of the capital's influence over its surrounding city region.

As far as non-manufacturing economic activity is concerned, London's dominance over its city region is probably most strongly felt in the areas of agriculture, wholesale functions, office activity and regional news media. Proximity to the huge urban market of Greater London is undoubtedly the dominant influence shaping the present-day character of farming in South East England. This is most evident in the recurrent emphasis on horticulture and market-gardening. Even in an era of declining transport costs, these farm activities still benefit to some extent from a location close to an urban market of such huge dimensions. The Lee Valley, especially around Cheshunt, still contains Britain's greatest single concentration of commercial glasshouses, producing flowers, tomatoes and other greenhouse crops. Equally dependent upon metropolitan demand are the small-fruit area of Botley in Hampshire, the intensive market-gardening district around Sandy in Bedfordshire, and the fruit-growing region of Dartford and Swanley in Kent. Proximity to London also encourages many South East farmers outside these areas to grow cash crops of vegetables, fruit or flowers as valuable side-lines. This sort of urban-oriented farming is by no means new to South East England. Vegetable production for the London market was being carried on in the Sandy district, for example, as early as the seventeenth century. But its importance has grown during the twentieth century with the expansion of London, and with new demands from its increasingly wealthy inhabitants for farm products previously regarded as luxuries. The development of an intensive poultry-fattening industry in Sussex over the last fifteen years is another typical response.

Closely related is the development of part-time farming in South East England. Wealthy migrants, whose main employment is in London, have gradually begun to displace the traditional farming population in many of the attractive rural yet residential areas of Surrey and Sussex. Engaging in farming only part-time, and tending to regard it partly as a hobby, they have invested large sums of capital in rather specialized activities such as the keeping of pedigree cattle. As a consequence, and especially in some farming localities close to London, rural land prices have risen and forced yet further changes upon both the type of rural population and the type of farming practiced.

Parallel to these spatial relationships in the agricultural sector of the economy are links between South East shops and London wholesalers. London's role as the country's greatest wholesaling centre is symbolized by the world famous markets of Covent Garden and Spitalfields (fruit, flowers and vegetables), Smithfield (meat) and Billingsgate (fish). Employing as many as 3½ thousand workers and handling as much as one million tons of goods a year (Covent Garden), these markets supply retailers in the many towns surrounding London, as well as in the metropolis itself and in the country as a whole. A similar relationship operates within certain large London-based retailing companies, such as Sainsbury's, which until recently supplied its numerous South East branches from a central wholesale depot at Blackfriars. In addition, local shops throughout the region use the services of London wholesalers specializing in the storage and distribution of carpets, furniture, clothing and almost every type of retail good.

London's influence over office activity in its city region is most commonly felt through the control exercised by headquarters in the capital over branch offices in such towns as Southampton, Oxford and Ipswich. Good illustrations are provided by the insurance, banking and other commercial services. In several cases, London's influence in this respect seems to be growing, as a result of technological and organizational developments which lead to more centralized information handling procedures. An excellent example was the introduction of a London-based computer accounts system for all its South East branches by Lloyds Bank in 1969, replacing former local accounting procedures.

A rather different but also recent trend strengthening London's influence over commercial activity in the region has been office decentralization. Since 1945, at least 240 separate office establishments have moved out of the conurbation to such South East towns as Reading, Watford, Maidenhead and Southend (Daniels, 1969). Though forced to move by a combination of government action, high office rents and labour shortages (see pp. 19ff), most of these offices retain very close links with central London, in the form of frequent telephone, telex and personal contacts. These links are particularly strong in cases where the head office functions remain in the capital and the more routine departments—responsible for records, accounts, data processing and the like—are moved out.

A final component in the London city region's web of interactions is the various news media, the most influential of which is probably regional broadcasting. Although East Anglia and South Hampshire have their own services, the regional news programmes of both the B.B.C. and I.T.V. undoubtedly foster a sense of regional identity throughout the rest of the South East. The natural predominance of news items about London, the source of the broadcasts, obviously strengthens the capital's influence over its surrounding region. So too does the distribution of London-produced and London-focused evening papers, which are sold as far away as Cambridge, Southend and Portsmouth.

2.5 Summary

This chapter has had three main aims. One has been to demonstrate the enormous importance of South East England to the economic life, growth and prosperity of Britain as a whole. Another has been to outline the planning problems which have arisen, especially in London, as a result of growth, and to discuss the effects and recent criticisms of the government's 'traditional' policy of encouraging decentralization of population and economic activity from the metropolis. The third has been to emphasise the intricate, powerful and possibly growing links which bind together London and its surrounding settlements into one functional unit—the London city region. Given this initial treatment of the South East as a whole, it is now time to turn to detailed discussion of the human geography, economic character and planning problems of different parts of the one region.

REFERENCES :

Abercrombie, P. (1945). *Greater London Plan* 1944, H.M.S.O., London.
Brown, A. J. (1969). Surveys of Applied Economics : Regional Economics, with Special Reference to the United Kingdom, *Economic Journal*, **79,** 759–796.
Daniels, P. W. (1969). Office Decentralization from London—Policy and Practice. *Regional Studies,* **3,** 171–178.
Faris, R. E. L. and Dunham, H. W. (1965). *Mental Disorders in Urban Areas,* University of Chicago Press, Chicago.
Glass, R. and Westergaard, J. (1965). *London's Housing Needs,* Centre for Urban Studies, University College, London.
Greater London Council (1969a). *Greater London Development Plan : Statement,* G.L.C., London.
Greater London Council (1969b). *Greater London Development Plan : Report of Studies,* G.L.C., London.
Greve, J., Page, D. and Greve, S. (1971). *Homelessness in London,* Scottish Academic Press, Edinburgh.
Hall, P. (1969). *London* 2000, 2nd edition, Faber and Faber, London.
Hillman, J. (ed.) (1971). *Planning for London,* Penguin, Harmondsworth.
Howard, E. (1965). *Garden Cities of To-morrow.* Faber and Faber, London. (First published in 1902).
Howard, R. S. (1968). *The Movement of Manufacturing Industry in the United Kingdom* 1945–1965, H.M.S.O., for the Board of Trade, London.
Manners, G. (1972). On the Mezzanine Floor : Some Reflections on Contemporary Office Location Policy. *Town and Country Planning,* April, 210–215.
Martin, J. E. (1966). *Greater London : an Industrial Geography,* Bell, London.
Ministry of Housing and Local Government (1964). *The South East Study,* 1961–1981, H.M.S.O., London.
Standing Conference on London and South East Regional Planning (1968). *Economic and Social Linkages within the Conference Area—Analysis of Telephone Calls* 1958. (Technical Panel Report LRP 1192), S.C.L.S.E.R.P., London.

CHAPTER 3

The South East and East Anglia

II. The Zonal Structure

David Keeble

3.1 The Zonal Structure of the South East

Given that London's influence, and the impact of recent changes in population and employment distribution, decline outwards from the metropolis, the most appropriate sub-division of the region is into three roughly circular zones. The first of these is the built-up mass of Greater London itself, virtually all of which is contained within the area administered by the Greater London Council. Although a zone of population decline (see Figure 10), London nonetheless contains approximately 7.4 million people, or 43 per cent of the South East standard region's population, together with the country's greatest concentration of industrial and commercial activity. The second zone comprises the Outer Metropolitan Area (O.M.A.), which contains a population of approximately 5.3 million. This zone (see Figure 9) completely encircles Greater London, extending from the boundary of the Greater London Council area at some 24 kilometres (15 miles) from central London, out to between 65 and 75 kilometres (40 to 50 miles) from the centre. The O.M.A. thus comprises the bulk of London's city region outside the metropolis. Indeed, planners use the phrase 'the Metropolitan Region' to describe Greater London and the O.M.A. combined. The O.M.A. contains most of the green belt, and all London's new towns. During the last twenty years, its population and industry have been growing faster and in greater absolute numbers than those in any other area of comparable size in Britain (see Figure 15). In many ways, this is the London of the future.

The third and last zone comprises the remainder of the South East region, known by planners as 'the Outer South East', together with East Anglia. Though still in many ways part of London's city region, towns in the more isolated, peripheral, O.S.E. do possess

107

more independence from the metropolis than their counterparts in the O.M.A. Perhaps one measure of this is the significantly greater size of such O.S.E. centres as Southampton, Portsmouth, Bournemouth and Brighton. Population and industry in the O.S.E. have been growing quite rapidly in recent years (see Figure 10), while at least one major new city, Milton Keynes, is planned for this area. The present population of the O.S.E. is about 4.5 million. Although it will be discussed for convenience largely as one unit within this third zone, East Anglia could more realistically be divided into two parts. The southern area of South Cambridgeshire and Suffolk, with its expanded towns and good communications with London, is already strongly influenced by the metropolis. Cambridge, after all, is only the same distance from London as Brighton. Urban population and industry have been growing fairly rapidly in this area in recent years (see Figure 15). In contrast, the northern half of East Anglia, comprising the Fens and Norfolk, is much more isolated, with greater problems of rural depopulation, and limited employment opportunities outside agriculture. East Anglia's total population is now about 1.7 million.

3.2 Greater London : the National Metropolis

3.2.1 *The Scale and Growth of Manufacturing Industry*

Despite the unique importance of London's office and service industries, it would seem probable that the larger part of the income which Greater London earns from other regions and countries arises from the sales of goods manufactured in the metropolis. That its economic base depends rather more on manufacturing than on services is suggested by the greater geographical extent of the former's markets. The Greater London Council's 1967 Employment Survey (G.L.C., 1969, p. 38) discovered that 59 per cent of manufacturing firms despatched at least one-fifth of production to customers outside London, compared to only 27 per cent of service firms. For this reason, therefore, the present discussion of London's economy begins with consideration of its manufacturing sector.

At least three characteristics of metropolitan manufacturing render London unique among British industrial centres. One is its size, another its diversity, and the third its twentieth century vitality and growth, at least until the nineteen sixties. London is the leading industrial centre in the United Kingdom, and one of the greatest in the world. In 1963, its 21 thousand manufacturing firms employed no less than 1.3 million workers, or 16.3 per cent of the country's total manufacturing work force. Its share of industrial production, measured by net output, was even greater, at 17.6 per cent. No other British conurbation or city approached these proportions. Connected with its scale is the fact that London's manufacturing industry is also more varied than that of any other large British industrial centre. The capital's remarkable range of industries includes almost every conceivable aspect of food and drink manufacturing, the production of chemicals, toilet preparations and pharmaceuticals, electrical and mechanical engineering, vehicle making, printing and publishing, clothing and furniture manufacture, the rubber and musical instrument industries, and so on.

This diversity can of course be measured. For example, every single specialist category of manufacturing recognized by the official Standard Industrial Classification (111 in all) is represented in London, only six of these categories employing less than 500 workers. Another way of measuring the capital's industrial diversity is by a Lorenz curve, as in Figure 13. The three Lorenz curves in the diagram (for England and Wales, Greater London and Tyneside) record the proportionate contribution of each manufacturing category to total industrial employment in each area, plotted as a cumulated percentage against the number of industrial categories (17 in this case). In constructing each curve, categories are ranked by employment size from smallest (bottom left-hand corner) to

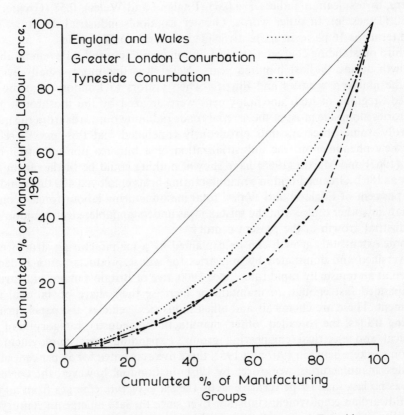

Figure 13   England and Wales, Greater London and Tyneside:
Lorenz curves of industrial diversification, 1961.

largest (top right-hand corner). Thus the more diversified and balanced an area's industrial structure is, the closer the curve should lie to the diagonal (which indicates exactly equal employment shares for each category).

The graph shows that England and Wales as a whole has a more diversified manufacturing structure than Greater London, while London is more diversified than Tyneside, a conurbation selected to represent the other major industrial concentrations of the country. Tyneside's specialization on shipbuilding and mechanical engineering (41 per cent of manufacturing employment) explains the greater 'sag' in its curve away from the diagonal. Actual measurement from the graph of an index of diversification for each region involves comparing the area enclosed by each curve and the righthand and bottom axes of the graph with the total area of the triangle represented by these axes and the diagonal line. Complete diversification, in the sense of equal proportions of all industry groups, would thus yield an index of 1.00. For the 17-category industrial classification used here, diversification indices are 0.65 (England and Wales), 0.58 (Greater London) and 0.50 (Tyneside). In other words, Greater London's industrial structure, measured in these terms, is 16 per cent more diversified than that of Tyneside.

The third outstanding characteristic of London manufacturing is its remarkable vitality and growth during the last hundred years. Never was this more visually evident than during the nineteen twenties and thirties, when visitors to London from the so-called depressed regions of high unemployment were amazed by the mushroom growth of new factories alongside most of the arterial roads radiating outwards from the metropolis. Admittedly, some observers thus erroneously concluded that this growth reflected an entirely new phenomenon, the industrialization of a hitherto non-industrial city: but, as Hall (1962) and Martin (1966) have shown, nothing could be further from the truth. As early as 1861, Greater London's manufacturing firms employed 470 thousand workers, or 14.9 per cent of England and Wales' total manufacturing labour force—considerably more than any other centre. But the mistake was understandable, given London's remarkable industrial growth in the present century.

To some extent, this growth can be explained by a manufacturing structure which is both diversified and dominated by industries for whose products national demand has expanded at an unusually rapid rate. Since 1900, five of Britain's major industrial groups have expanded fast enough to maintain or increase their share of national industrial employment. These are chemicals and allied industries, vehicles, the paper, printing and publishing trades, the so-called 'other' manufacturing industry category, and the huge mechanical and electrical engineering group. Expanding their employment by over 3½million workers between 1907 and 1957, these five accounted for 58 per cent of England and Wales' manufacturing workforce by 1961. In London, however, the corresponding figure was no less than 69 per cent. Exactly the same picture emerges from an examination of Edwardian employment statistics. Ever since the late nineteenth century, Greater London has enjoyed an unusually favourable industrial structure in terms of the most modern growth industries of the period. As new industries have developed in Britain—

road vehicles, aircraft, radio, television, computer electronics—Greater London has nearly always been in the forefront of the areas in which these industries have first appeared and subsequently grown fastest. As a result, its total manufacturing capacity, measured for want of a better index by employment, has increased faster than that of England and Wales as a whole, the relative figures over the 1861 to 1961 period being +214 per cent (1.00 million workers) and +142 per cent (4.55 million workers), respectively (Hall, 1962, p. 185).

The explanation of London's industrial growth in terms of a favourable industrial structure, however, in many ways begs the real question. Why, after all, has London had a favourable structure? What explains the initial attraction of growth industries to the capital? One major factor is London's status as the country's leading *innovation centre*. Recent geographical research on the spatial spread of new ideas, techniques and activities within countries suggests that many innovations affecting new types of manufacturing production and demand are first adopted and tested in the largest urban centre of a particular country (Hagerstrand, 1968). They then spread to other cities and towns according to the principle of 'hierarchical diffusion'. This means that they then appear at the next level of urban centre in the hierarchy—Birmingham, Manchester, Liverpool in the British case—then at the next level, and so on.

The explanation for this pattern lies in the related problems of risk and cost. By definition, innovations are new, perhaps completely untried, ideas or products. To adopt them involves the entrepreneur in much greater financial risks than does the implementation of more traditional ideas or technology. These risks are, however, reduced if the innovation is first introduced and tested in the country's 'safest' market—its largest urban centre. In such a centre, the size and average wealth of the population which can be reached by the innovation are greater than anywhere else, while its more cosmopolitan and progressive character increases the likelihood of innovation acceptance. Dominant urban centres like London thus tend to pioneer the adoption of innovations, and only later does diffusion to smaller centres become financially feasible.

This simple theory of innovation origin and diffusion may account for much of London's twentieth century industrial growth. In a modern competitive world, the firm or area which first succeeds in launching a new product, or utilizing a new technology, tends to cream the profits; subsequent immitators are generally forced to accept much lower rates of return for the same product. As Berry has pointed out, 'biggest means first, earliest means most'. Thus the high profits and growth rates characteristic of the industrial pioneer may in part explain London's remarkable industrial vitality. In this context, the dramatic twentieth century rise in national importance of the new lighter industries (electrical and instrument engineering, vehicles and aircraft, pharmaceuticals and plastics) so typical of London is noteworthy. These now account for more than double the share of national output contributed by the classic nineteenth century industries (iron and steel, ship-building, textiles) of the less prosperous regions. Innovations in the former have clearly played a much greater part in national industrial growth than those in the latter.

Specific evidence for this *innovation centre* hypothesis concerns both indigenous innovations, and those imported from abroad. That London has led the way in the creation or adoption of 'British-made' innovations affecting manufacturing production is confirmed by two considerations. The first is the remarkable twentieth century concentration of industrial and scientific research in and around the capital. One government report (D.S.I.R., 1958, p. 19) revealed that, in 1955, no less than 45.4 per cent of the United Kingdom's total number of research workers in private industrial and scientific research establishments were employed in the South East (plus East Anglia). In contrast, the region's share of the country's overall industrial labour force was only 28.8 per cent. More recently, Buswell and Lewis (1970) have estimated that the South East alone contains 49 per cent of all research establishments in the United Kingdom. The reasons for this striking geographical concentration of research activity include the attractiveness of residence in South East England for highly qualified research personnel, the existing concentration of modern technologically oriented industry there, the unrivalled role of London as the country's leading university city and centre for scientific conferences, and its unparalleled international communications nodality. Its effect is to encourage a greater volume of industrial and technological innovations in the region, and particularly in London, than in other regions or centres.

The second consideration stems from London's leadership over other British centres in the adoption of non-manufacturing innovations. Many examples of this can be cited. One of the most obvious is broadcasting. Radio broadcasting began in London in 1922, programmes only being available in other regions after 1925 and the opening of the Daventry transmitter. Television broadcasts from Alexandra Palace in north London began in 1936; a second, Birmingham, transmitter was not inaugurated until 13 years later. In other words, the London area led the way in radio and television transmission and reception. The same pattern of initial innovation acceptance by London is evident in such contrasting spheres as civil aviation and the opening of clothing 'boutiques'. The first-ever scheduled civil aviation service in Britain began operation in 1919 between London and Paris, symbolizing the dominance which London exerted over commercial and private flying in Britain from the earliest days of powered flight. More recently, the 'boutique' phenomenon of the nineteen sixties began entirely in, and is still dominated by, London, with the world famous boutique centres of Carnaby Street and King's Road, Chelsea, dictating fashion changes in teenage clothing throughout the country.

London's innovating role in each case reflects its position as the country's largest, most affluent, and hence lowest-risk market. The key point here, however, is the fact that leadership in non-manufacturing innovation has resulted in leadership also in associated manufacturing. Thus, London's dominance over early broadcasting, at a period when equipment was bulky, fragile and undergoing rapid technological change, resulted in a remarkable concentration of radio manufacturing in London. By 1939, 80 per cent of British employment in the radio and television industry was provided by factories in the capital. Again, the concentration, from the very beginning, of civil aviation services in London inevitably encouraged the growth of aircraft manufacturing in and around the metropolis. Such famous firms as De Havilland, Handley Page, Napier, Sopwith and Hawker all began life in London, which was the country's leading aircraft manufacturing centre up to the early nineteen twenties. Lastly, London's innovating role in the sale of boutique clothing has more recently benefited the capital's garment industry, both by the reflected prestige of a 'Made in London' label, and by its ability to respond rapidly to fashion changes which is made possible by daily contact with Carnaby Street and the other London boutique districts.

Further evidence for the *innovation centre* hypothesis concerns the many important manufacturing innovations which have been imported from abroad during the twentieth century; for London's unrivalled international nodality, coupled with its geographical proximity to Europe, has meant that most of these imported innovations have reached Britain through the capital. In other words, London firms have been unusually well-placed to adopt and profit by foreign innovations before their competitors elsewhere in the country. An excellent example of London's leadership in importing innovations from abroad concerns the development of road vehicle manufacturing. Early car making in Britain was greatly influenced by technological developments in France and Germany. These developments, together with imported components such as the famous French De Dion engine, reached Britain through London. Not surprisingly, London's vehicle firms were thus able to lead the way in adopting and adapting foreign innovations, while several French firms such as Darraq, Citroen and Aster established or licensed London factories to manufacture their products for the first time in Britain. Another illustration is afforded by the early motion-picture manufacturing industry. In this instance it was American technological innovations which reached Britain through London, and the resultant leadership in their adoption, particularly by the London scientific instrument maker Robert Paul, helped the capital to become the unrivalled centre for motion-picture and camera manufacturing in the country.

London's role as Britain's outstanding innovation centre thus goes far to explain the resilience and vitality of its industry. However, other locational advantages afforded by the capital have also stimulated metropolitan industrial growth. One of the most important of these is *market accessibility*. Not only does this help explain London's leading role as an innovation centre, but it has directly encouraged the location and growth in London of the many lighter industries now untrammelled by transport cost ties to fuel, raw material or break-of-bulk locations.

London's unrivalled market accessibility partly results from its location at the centre of Britain's most affluent and concentrated regional market. The South East contains no less than 31 per cent of the country's population, and commands 39 per cent of national purchasing power measured by personal incomes. Location at the centre of this market area permits some consumer goods firms to achieve production scale economies greater than those possible in smaller regions, thereby increasing their profits and market strength. London's capital goods firms benefit both from easy access to the South East's 32 thousand manufacturing firms, and from proximity to the unique concentration of headquarter offices in central London's West End, where numerous purchasing decisions are taken concerning government and private spending on equipment of all kinds.

London's exceptional nodality in terms of the national pattern of road, rail and air communications also increases its market accessibility. Access to the national market, 80 per cent of which is in any case found within 200 miles of London, is easier from London via the motorways, trunk roads and express rail services which lead directly to Bristol, Birmingham, Liverpool, Sheffield, Newcastle and Edinburgh, than from almost any other British city, with the possible exception of Birmingham. Lastly, export markets for manufactured goods are also more accessible from London than from any other centre. The geographical range and frequency of sailings and flights from the Port of London and London (Heathrow) Airport, respectively, far surpass those from other British sea and air ports. Sales contact with, and deliveries to, foreign customers are therefore undoubtedly easier and quicker from London than from other industrial areas. It is not surprising that South East firms now contribute one-third of all national exports by value.

In sum, the London area provides manufacturing firms with easier access to South East, national and international markets than any other part of the country. The extent of this advantage has been measured quantitatively by Clark's 'economic potential' index (Clark, 1966; see p. 10 and Figure 2) which reveals that the place with the greatest economic potential in Britain (measured in this fashion) is London; from London economic potential values fall in all directions. Exceptional market accessibility, translated into increased sales through closer contact with customers, helps considerably to explain London's remarkable industrial growth. There are other explanations too.

Greater London's *manufacturing labour force* is larger and more concentrated geographically than that of any other industrial centre in Britain. Despite some decline since 1961, the Greater London area provided employment in 1966 for over 1.3 million manufacturing workers, at an average density of 800 workers per square kilometre (2,100 per square mile). This remarkable concentration of workers has almost certainly assisted the twentieth century expansion of manufacturing industry in the capital, in various ways. The sheer size and compactness of this labour pool ensure the availability of sufficient workers within easy commuting distance of any expanding London firm, provided of course that the firm is willing to pay the wages necessary to attract employees from other firms. The remarkable range of skills represented in London's workforce means that expanding firms requiring almost any type of skill or training can find it, providing again that they are willing to pay high enough wages; and the general quality of the workforce is probably exceptionally high, given the unusually large proportions of younger people and those whose full-time education has continued beyond the age of 20 amongst migrants to London from the rest of the country (Brown, 1968, pp. 49–50). That migration to the capital has been markedly selective, as suggested by Myrdal (1957, p. 27) for industrial growth centres generally, was certainly shown by the 1961 population census, which revealed that 66 per cent of London migrants in 1960–1961 were in the 15 to 44 age group, compared with only 39 per cent in England and Wales as a whole.

More specific advantages afforded by London's labour pool stem from the unusual concentration of engineering workers, scientific and industrial research personnel, and highly trained management staff. Concentration of each type of worker can be shown by their Location Quotients (L.Q.). For any area the L.Q. of a group of workers is obtained by calculating the percentage of the national total of such workers which are found in the area, and the percentage of the national total of all workers which are found there. The former is then divided by the latter. An L.Q. greater than 1.00 means that the area's labour force is unusually biassed towards that group. The 1961 Greater London L.Q.s (England and Wales base) for skilled precision instrument and chronometer makers, and for electrical and electronic engineering workers, were 1.70 and 1.12 respectively. For the special subcategory of electrical and electronic assemblers, the L.Q. rose to 1.65. Those for professional and research engineering workers, and for industrial managers (including sales managers) were 1.24 and 1.31 respectively. In all cases, the inclusion of the many such workers who live immediately around, and travel in daily to, the capital would raise these values still further. The significance of these high L.Q.s lies in the fact that the workers involved are precisely those most in demand by manufacturers in the country's leading growth industries—engineering and electrical goods, and other 'science-based' industries. The greater relative availability of such skills in London has thus almost certainly encouraged the contemporary concentration of these industries in and around the capital.

That London contains an unusual concentration of potential *entrepreneurs*—individuals who bear the financial risks and responsibility of establishing and directing new firms— is also highly probable, though it is difficult to prove conclusively. Certainly it is suggested by the bias in the capital's work force towards skilled workers and managers, by the high proportion of younger, and hence perhaps more progressive, people amongst the immigrants to London and by the attraction London has afforded to refugees and migrants from Europe. That such migrants—German and Polish Jews, Czechs, Hungarians and many others—are far more concentrated in London that any other centre is shown by a 1966 Greater London (G.L.C. area) L.Q. of no less than 2.21 for residents reporting a European birthplace. Unusually biassed towards professional and managerial workers, this migrant group has produced a surprising number of entrepreneurs, to the benefit of metropolitan manufacturing growth.

In all discussions of the growth of huge urban-industrial centres, the importance of what are called *agglomeration economies* is rightly stressed. Such economies are cost savings accrueing to firms because of the sheer scale of economic activity of all kinds within a relatively small area, and the ability of a firm in effect to share some of its external expenses with others. One type of agglomeration economy enjoyed by London's manufacturing firms results from the remarkable concentration of over 24 thousand separate factory buildings within the capital. As a result, manufacturing entrepreneurs anxious to set up in business for the first time, or firms wishing to expand, can usually find suitable premises within easy reach of their homes or former factories; and establishment or movement costs may be reduced quite substantially. Another type of agglomeration economy occurs through the development of metropolitan industrial linkages. Manufacturing plants are said to be industrially linked when flows of semifinished goods and components take place between them. In other words, one firm acts as a market for the semifinished products of another. Many small London firms, especially in the clothing, furniture and engineering industries, are vitally dependent for their prosperity and growth upon linkages of this kind with other metropolitan firms. At the same time, they, through specialization, may be able to achieve production economies which are then passed on through lower charges to their customers. The latter may also be able to respond quickly to rapid increases in demand, despite an immediate shortage of production space, by putting out work to nearby small sub-contractors. Although difficult to quantify, such local industrial linkages, stimulated by the vast scale and geographical compactness of London's manufacturing industry, may yield considerable agglomeration economies to metropolitan firms.

Other more general agglomeration economies stem from the concentration of non-manufacturing economic activity in London. Certain ancillary trades have grown up in London directly to serve manufacturing industry. These include raw material stockholders, firms engaged in packaging and despatching manufactured exports, road haulage specialists, industrial development and market research consultants, and machinery service firms. Such services are undoubtedly more readily available to London manufacturers than to those in smaller industrial centres. This external economy confers a useful advantage on the former in competition with the latter. Other advantages which are also more readily available in London arise from the massive development of services less specifically geared to manufacturing, such as the insurance, banking and financial trades, advertising and publishing, and the provision of gas, electricity, effluent disposal and other services. The enormous range of minor agglomeration economies enjoyed by London firms undoubtedly helps to explain the remarkable growth of industry, especially new kinds of industry, in the capital.

3.2.2 *The Spatial Pattern of Manufacturing Industry*

The capital's greatest single cluster of industry is found in *inner London*, in the form of a crescentic belt of factories encircling the commercial centre north of the Thames (see Figure 14). This cluster, which dates from the nineteenth century, has been named by Hall (1962, p. 32) 'the Victorian Manufacturing Belt'. Other small inner London industrial zones are found just south of the Thames, to the east alongside the river, and towards the northeastern and northwestern suburbs. The industrial importance of inner London is evident both in terms of employment and factory floorspace. The old County of London plus the Borough of Newham—the boundary of which roughly represents the limit of London's built-up area at the turn of the century and of contemporary inner London—provided employment for 640 thousand manufacturing workers, or 48 per cent of London's industrial work force, in 1966. Its industrial premises accounted for the same proportion of the capital's 1966 factory floorspace. Although it is still London's most important industrial zone, however, inner London in general—and the Victorian Belt in particular—now appears to face decline. Inner London's manufacturing employment fell by no less than 20 thousand jobs each year between 1961 and 1966, while its stock of factory space declined by 15 million square feet between 1957 and 1966. The rate of employment decline has quickened still further in the last few years. The reasons for this decline will be considered later (pp. 120ff).

As Martin (1964) and Hall (1962) have shown, manufacturing in inner London is typically different from that of outer London. Firms are smaller. They occupy older, multistoreyed, premises. Most important, inner London's most characteristic industries—clothing, furniture and printing—are only poorly developed outside the centre. A legacy of the nineteenth century, these industries have remained in inner London because of locational ties to central sites. These ties are most evident in the remarkable industrial 'quarters' of inner north London, small districts with an intense concentration of particular industries. Most of the quarters possess precise boundaries, although wider districts or 'sectors' of secondary concentration do fan out from some—such as the East End clothing quarter—on their northern sides. The clustering together of small firms in this way is sometimes referred to as 'industrial swarming', a phenomenon typified by the East and West End clothing quarters, the Fleet Street and Shoreditch printing quarters, the Clerkenwell precision engineering and printing quarter, and the Shoreditch/Bethnal Green furniture quarter.

The most important locational factor producing swarming is local industrial linkage. In turn, this results from the small size of the firms involved. In 1955, for example, four-fifths of the factories in the East End clothing quarter employed less than 24 operatives. Their small size reflects a relative ease of entry into these industries in terms of capital requirements, as well as the greater flexibility of small firms when catering, as in clothing, for rapid changes of fashion. Being small, however, firms in the quarters often cannot afford to employ skilled workers for specialist processes. They therefore put out such work to local specialists, who in turn owe their existence to the local concentrated demand. Both types of firm as a result benefit. Excellent examples of this sort of local industrial linkage occur in the East End, where specialist button-holing, pleating and belt-making firms serve the many women's clothing manufacturers of the quarter. Similarly, furniture quarter specialists carry out milling, glass work, upholstering and polishing.

Another major tie of industry to the inner London quarters is the local availability of cheap, rentable and often multistoreyed premises. Such premises, often tucked away down back streets or jumbled up with terraced houses, may not easily be recognized as factories at first glance, but their availability and cheapness have encouraged a high local birth rate of new small firms, and contributed much to the persistence of the quarters over time. So too has market proximity. Despite an average factory size much greater than that of the other classic trades of inner London, the persistence of Fleet Street's newspaper printing quarter reflects a need for the closest possible access to foreign and domestic news, and for the fastest possible despatch to customers via its nearby national rail termini. Similarly, the proximity of the West End fashion market and central London clothing wholesalers is a major bond tying clothing firms to inner London, especially in view of the rapid changes of fashion so characteristic of that industry.

The last factor explaining the development and persistence of inner London's industrial quarters is the availability of trained manufacturing workers. The East End depends upon skilled Jewish clothing workers from Whitechapel, Bethnal Green and Shoreditch. Local concentrations of skilled printers and engineering workers are vital to the operation of the Fleet Street and Shoreditch printing quarters. The precision trades—optical and measuring instruments, jewellery and the like—of the historically-important Clerkenwell quarter, and the Kings Cross and Camden Town districts would collapse without their adjacent and uniquely skilled supplies of labour.

Industry in *outer London* is the product of the capital's twentieth century industrial growth. Indeed, many suburban firms originated in inner London, and migrated outwards as a result of growth and increased needs for factory space. Since this migration has been highly selective in character, outer London industry differs from that in the inner areas in certain important respects. The relationship between migration and growth has resulted in an industrial structure dominated not by clothing or printing, but by the growth industries of twentieth century Britain—electrical engineering, vehicles, pharmaceuticals. The firms are larger. They occupy single-storeyed buildings more suited to modern 'flow-line' production. And most interesting of all, the spatial pattern of manufacturing is different.

In outer London, the roughly concentric Victorian manufacturing belt gives way to a pattern of radial industrial areas (see Figure 14). Fairly discrete clusters of manufacturing firms radiate outwards from inner London like beads on a string, following the major road and rail communications. The Park Royal, Perivale, Greenford, Northolt sequence provides a good example. Moreover, whereas in inner London the bulk of manufacturing is found to the east and northeast of the centre, in outer London the weight is towards the west and northwest. Thus the outer northwest sector of the Greater London Council area (Hounslow, Hillingdon, Ealing, Brent, Harrow, Barnet, Haringey and Enfield) accounted for 29 and 27 per cent respectively of London's 1966 industrial employment and floorspace; this compares with only 11 per cent in both cases in the second most important sector, the outer northeast. The two southern sectors combined accounted for only 12 per cent of employment and 14 per cent of floorspace. Although inclusion of the important Lee Valley manufacturing zone, which in certain respects more properly belongs to the outer northeast, inflates the outer northwest total, the bias towards northwest London is clear.

Suburban industrial clustering differs from that in inner London in at least one important respect—the much reduced significance of local industrial linkage. Unlike their counterparts in inner London's quarters, suburban firms do not usually exhibit a marked dependence upon other local firms. True, linkages are important to many engineering firms in northwest London and the Lee Valley. But the areal scale over which these linkages operate is regional or even national, rather than local. In other words, considerations other than linkage explain industrial clustering in outer London.

Chief amongst these is the role of industrial estate companies. During the nineteen twenties and thirties, factory building in outer London was largely controlled by a few specialist construction companies. Present day suburban industrial clustering as a result simply reflects the fact that these companies found it advantageous to buy up blocks of land, and develop them as discrete industrial estates. The fact that many of these were sited close to radial communication links reflects both the lower land prices there and the demand by industrial firms for easy access to suppliers, customers and workers. The prestige advertising opportunities afforded by sites fronting arterial roads, such as Brentford's 'Golden Mile' along the Great West Road, is a further explanation of the radial, communications-oriented, pattern of suburban industrial development.

Estate company development, however, does not explain the marked sectoral bias in this development towards the northwest. At least three different factors are involved here. One was the sheer availability of open space. The development of the huge west London Park Royal estate after 1919, for example, largely reflected its position at that time as the nearest large area of unused land to central London. In south London, prior housing development ruled out large-scale factory estate construction at a comparable distance from the centre. Another factor was the radial orientation of industrial migration. Because inner London firms tended to move outwards in the same radial sector as that in which they had originated, outer north London received far more migrant industry than outer south London. Differences in the industrial structure are also partly explained by this tendency; the Lee Valley, for example, received more clothing and furniture firms, whilst the northwest benefited from the migration of Clerkenwell and West End engineering, vehicle and 'luxury' goods firms.

The third factor is market accessibility, which varies not only between London and other centres, but also between different sectors of outer London. Firms supplying both the London market and customers in other regions of the country have undoubtedly been attracted to outer north and west London by the greater geographical proximity of these sectors (via major trunk routes such as the A4 (M4), A5 (M1) and A1) to Britain's other urban centres. In contrast, outer southeast London is both further and more physically isolated from these centres by the built-up mass of London itself. The importance of this differential in market accessibility is clearly illustrated by the remarkable development of market-oriented branch factories of foreign firms in outer northwest London between 1920 and 1940; over half of all American plants set up in Britain in the nineteen thirties, for example, were located here or in Slough.

A third and distinctive component in the spatial pattern of London's manufacturing industry is *Thameside*. Within the capital, the Thames is fronted by several industrial zones whose firms make use of waterborne materials, or have historical connections with the river. Grain milling, sugar refining, saw milling and boat repairing are carried on in Millwall and Limehouse; chemical plants occupy formerly isolated marshland sites in Stratford and Silvertown; the Ford Motor Company imports iron ore and coking coal by water for use in its Dagenham blast furnace. Though generally dependent, like other London industry, upon the huge London market, these water-oriented industrial districts warrant special mention.

3.2.3 *The Movement of Manufacturing Industry*

Much of the preceding discussion centres around the role of London as the country's leading twentieth century industrial growth centre. Between 1861 and 1961, successive censuses recorded steady expansion in the capital's manufacturing labour force; the whole century witnessed a growth of a million extra workers. However, it now is clear that the nineteen sixties represent something of a water-shed in the history of metropolitan industry. For, between 1961 and 1966, for the first time in census history, the level of manufacturing employment in Greater London actually fell—by no less than 125 thousand workers, from 1,451 to 1,326 thousand. Moreover, since 1966 this rate of decline has almost certainly speeded up, to over 30 thousand manufacturing jobs per year.

This apparent decline in London's manufacturing industry has undoubtedly influenced the thinking behind the proposed strategy of the 1969 *Greater London Development Plan* (pp. 94–97). For, to the extent that the decline has resulted from the siphoning-off of the capital's most virile, expanding firms to other areas, genuine doubts are raised concerning its long-term industrial employment prospects. It must be stressed, however, that decline could be more apparent than real. Other indices of manufacturing capacity— perhaps nowadays more meaningful—in fact contradict this notion of decline as suggested by employment data. After all, a continued growth of manufacturing employment is only possible so long as extra people are available to be employed. When the supply of extra workers dries up, as it seems to have done in a London whose population is falling, firms may well decide to maintain and increase production by substituting capital, in the form of more automated machinery and new buildings, for labour. Although very difficult to measure, this may be what is happening in London today. London's stock of factory floorspace, a very crude index of capital investment in manufacturing, has been growing, not falling, by about 90 thousand square metres (1 million square feet) per annum in recent years (Greater London Council, 1969, p. 68). Industrial output may well be growing at a faster rate than this.

In aggregate, therefore, London's manufacturing capacity and output may still be growing. However, in inner London a significant decline is occurring both in industrial capacity (measured by floorspace) and in employment. This reflects various factors. One is planned redevelopment; the rebuilding of old mixed residential-industrial districts in areas such as Stepney and Poplar has eliminated many small firms. Simultaneously, firms remaining in inner London's quarters are facing increased competition from larger, more automated, plants elsewhere. Lastly—though perhaps of first importance—inner London is losing by emigration many of its most progressive, expanding firms.

Movements of manufacturing firms from both inner and outer London have occurred on a remarkable scale in recent years. Since 1945, no less than 1,300 new factories and 330 thousand jobs have been provided outside London by migrant metropolitan firms (Howard, 1968, p. 15). Some of these jobs are in branch plants of firms whose main factories have remained in London. But a significant proportion, about 30 per cent, have involved complete moves from the metropolis. Diversion of growth on this massive scale, involving employment equivalent to one-quarter of London's present manufacturing work force, accounts in large part for manufacturing decline in inner London.

Migration is basically a response to restrictions on growth imposed by a London location (Keeble, 1968). As a result, most of the firms involved are expanding firms, drawn from growth industries such as engineering and electrical goods, chemicals and pharmaceuticals. The restrictions on expansion, which have increasingly offset the advantages of a location within London's built-up area since 1945, fall into three groups. One is the shortage (up to *circa* 1965), the age and high cost of factory premises. A century of industrial growth has bequeathed a legacy of severely cramped factory sites, and of many old, badly designed and dilapidated buildings. And competition for available premises or land has raised factory prices to exorbitant levels, such as £60 or more per square metre (£5 or more per square foot).

Labour problems also severely handicap expansion. Acute labour shortages, evident in a London unemployment rate usually half that of the country as a whole, together with high wage costs resulting from fierce competition for manufacturing workers, have encouraged many expanding firms to set up factories outside London. The third restriction upon expansion is, of course, public policy. The Board of Trade's i.d.c. control over factory building has both indirectly aggravated the shortage of industrial premises, and directly prevented the expansion of many metropolitan firms as part of the government's decentralization objectives. Despite a few parallels, the situation has been different in the case of service industries, however.

3.2.4 *The Growth and Movement of Service Industry*

In Greater London, service industries employ no less than 2.79 million workers, over twice the number in manufacturing. Moreover, unlike manufacturing, service employment continued to grow between 1961 and 1966, increasing by 140 thousand workers or 5 per cent—although this rise may have been reversed since then. Many of London's service establishments—local shops, schools, cinemas, medical centres—exist as in other cities solely to supply the needs of local residents. But as the highest-order central place in the country, London also possesses specialist services catering for people outside the capital on a scale unrivalled by any other British city. Thus in London are to be found the nation's leading orchestras, ballet and opera companies, art galleries, theatres and sports grounds. At the heart of London are sited the country's main teaching hospitals, its biggest university, and its leading department and fashion stores. To London's unique concentration of hotels come more tourists than to any other British tourist centre. Within the metropolis are the country's main international communication facilities, in the shape of London airport (Heathrow) and London docks. Most important of all, London is the seat of national government, and the headquarters of many of the country's major industrial and commercial undertakings, as well as of national radio and T.V. broadcasting.

London's unrivalled dominance of many nationally important service activities quite naturally arouses frequent regional resentment. Regional critics argue, for example, that its share of the nation's cultural cake is out of all proportion to the needs of other areas. Why should London possess four national orchestras, when some large British cities have none? Similarly, national government is frequently regarded as being too London-oriented, a viewpoint which has led to growing demands in recent years for greater regional administrative autonomy. Anti-London criticism has been further stimulated by a continuing concentration since 1945 of new, nationally important, service facilities in the London area—such as the huge South Bank cultural complex and the new National Theatre, the headquarters of such new public bodies as the National Coal Board, the Gas Council and the British Steel Corporation, and (prospectively near London) a new main international airport.

Increased regional hostility to London's preeminence, whether justified or not, has strengthened separatist movements in other regions of Britain. For proper political reasons, therefore, recent governments have attempted to encourage the growth of specialized service facilities in other British cities. Unfortunately, however, the hard facts of economics and economic geography which lie behind London's preeminence in service activity are very difficult to gainsay. The focus of the most affluent and densely populated region of Britain, the unrivalled hub of national and international communications, and one of the greatest historic, cultural and economic centres of Europe and the world, London's natural attractions for new specialized services requiring very large threshold populations are far more powerful than those of any other British city.

Perhaps the most important aspect of London's preeminence in service industry is in terms of its unique central office complex. This complex, divided into the two sub-centres of the City of London and the West End (including Westminster), is remarkable for its size, its recent growth, and its national importance in terms of invisible exports. As far as the latter is concerned, estimates suggest that the City of London alone has earned as much as £540 million in one recent year (1971) for Britain through its international financial and trading transactions. Office firms in the central area employ three-quarters of a million workers and occupy 16.6 million square metres (179 million square feet) of office space. The remarkable scale of this concentration is revealed by the fact that, in 1963, the rateable value of offices in the old County of London accounted for no less than three-quarters of the total value of all offices in England and Wales (Hammond, 1964, p. 132).

The characteristic of this concentration which has attracted most attention recently, however, is its post-1945 growth. Visually evident in the construction of towering office blocks such as those in the Barbican scheme around St. Paul's, this growth, according to many official and academic commentators during the early nineteen sixties, involved annual employment increments of *circa* 15 thousand new workers each year (e.g. Ministry of Housing and Local Government, 1964, p. 41). As a result, so some commentators argued, peak-hour commuter pressure on rail, tube and road transport services to and from central London was likely to become intolerable (Hall, 1969, pp. 68–69). The effect of these comments was to encourage the government to establish in 1963 the Location of Offices Bureau with the task of stimulating office decentralization from central London; this was followed by the imposition in 1964 of wholly new government controls on office building in the London Metropolitan Region, with o.d.p.s now being required for all new buildings of over 350 square metres (3,000 square feet). Administered earlier by the Board of Trade and now by the Department of the Environment, this new type of decentralization policy was initiated largely with a view to encouraging interregional office decentralization (pp. 19–23).

In fact, however, the statistical basis of the arguments which led to the institution of this policy has been since proved inaccurate. Census figures not available until recent years reveal that office jobs in central London expanded during the nineteen fifties only by about 7 thousand workers per year, not 15 thousand (Evans, 1967). More striking still, growth has now been replaced by stability or even decline. Office jobs there seem to have reached a peak about 1963, and has been tending to fall slightly ever since. Office employment in the whole of the capital fell by 20 thousand, 1966–1969, to about 1.51 million workers. Moreover, the growth which did take place during the nineteen fifties resulted from the expansion of just those central London office activities which have the greatest claim to such a location, in terms of their national and international economic importance. While West End office employment in public administration fell by 10 thousand workers between 1951 and 1961, central London's insurance, banking and finance trades and professional, scientific and miscellaneous services expanded their work force by about 80 thousand employees, chiefly in the City of London. Thus, although the growth was significant, it was nowhere as great as the government had believed, and it involved nationally important economic functions.

Government office decentralization policy, and the natural economic tendencies towards increased office rents and labour shortages in central London, have had two effects. The first is a decentralization of office activity. Although accurate figures are very difficult to obtain, a recent L.O.B. estimate suggests that between mid-1963 and late-1969, no less than 2,800 office organizations were involved in moves from central London affecting 180 thousand jobs there (Table 4). However, it is also clear that many—perhaps half—of these moved no further than London's suburbs, while only a small proportion moved to regions outside the South East. In fact, most interregional long distance office moves, as noted earlier (p. 21), have involved government departments employing fairly large numbers of people. Perhaps 20 thousand government office jobs have thus been moved to other regions. But, by and large, office decentralization—unlike industrial migration— has involved short distance moves within the South East. Most have been by fairly small office firms or departments, which retain important links with offices remaining in central London and therefore cannot afford to move far away.

The most striking result of office decentralization has been the post-1960 rise to importance as suburban office centres of Croydon and parts of outer west London. Croydon's recently constructed central office district now employs over 25 thousand workers; sixty of its firms have moved from central London. In west London, office blocks in Hounslow, Ealing and Richmond house about a hundred migrant establishments from the centre. The selection of these particular boroughs as new office centres is partly due to planning action, and partly to speculative office developers choosing locations thought to be attractive to prospective clients. Their locational attractions include excellent rail links with central London; a large local pool of office labour; nearness to London airport (Heathrow); and a relative proximity to desirable residential areas for managers and executives. And, until *circa* 1968, office rents in these suburban office centres were only a third or less of those in central London. Outside Greater London, smaller office complexes housing decentralized firms have also developed at Reading, Southend, Maidenhead and Basingstoke.

The other main effect of the government's office decentralization policy is more recent than the first. This is the drastic restriction of new office building by means of the post-1964 o.d.p. controls, not only in central London but also in the suburbs. Admittedly, central London office space continued to expand after this date whilst previously unused permissions were taken up. The City and Westminster added 260 thousand square metres (2.8 million square feet), or 2 per cent, to their stock of office space between 1965 and 1967; but by 1969 the supply of new space anywhere in London had shrunk drastically. As a result central rents for new offices soared from £26 to the staggering figure of £150 per square metre (£2.25 to £14 per square foot) between 1963 and 1970. Office growth generally, therefore, has been severely curbed, and suburban decentralization, one of the main aims of the Location of Offices Bureau, has considerably declined.

The drastic effects of the government's blanket controls on central London office growth have alarmed the Greater London Council with its concern for London's future prosperity. The Council has thus argued for a much more selective, and hence less restrictive, approach to central office controls. Its case is based upon the national economic importance of much central office activity, and its strong economic ties to existing central sites. However, an important distinction must be drawn here between the West End and the City office sub-centres within the central office complex. The West End has developed largely during the twentieth century as a diversified 'prestige' office district, catering for a wide variety of office functions. Most important are national and local government offices, clustering around the Houses of Parliament, together with a remarkable concentration of the headquarter offices of national industrial concerns. The West End also houses many of the headquarters of learned societies, publishing firms, and such relatively new activities as television and cinema organizations, air transport and advertising companies. In other words, the West End contains a heterogeneous mixture of office activities, which possess limited functional ties to each other, play little direct part in the earning of invisible exports, and have probably chosen to locate there for such reasons as an advantageous accessibility to customers and workers, plus an element of prestige.

The City sub-centre, on the other hand, presents a different picture. Although it boasts only about half of the West End's office space, and three-quarters of the latter's office workers, the financial activities of the 'Square Mile' are of enormous importance to Britain's economy and balance of payments (Greater London Council, 1969, pp. 70–73). Moreover, its characteristic office functions, which are wholly different from those found in the West End, are bound to each other by very strong functional ties (Dunning, 1969, pp. 208–212). For centuries, the City has performed a dual role as a centre for commodity trading and shipping activity on the one hand, and for finance, insurance and banking on the other. Its shipping and trading interests cluster around the commodity markets of Mincing Lane whilst its function as one of the world's greatest financial centres is symbolized by the presence at its heart of such institutions as the Bank of England, the Stock Exchange and Lloyds. The distinctive localization of these activities in the City partly reflects historical connections with the Port of London, and an ease of access to office workers throughout London and its city region. But the main justification for its present-day existence is the vital need on the part of its constituent firms for frequent, rapid and 'face-to-face' contact with other firms and institutions within the Square Mile. A very high intensity of local contacts, necessitated by rapid, almost hour-by-hour, changes in international financial affairs, represents a vital functional bond tying many financial firms to a City location.

This fact, perhaps more than any other, explains the limited impact of the government's office decentralization policy in this area. At the same time, as critics of that policy point out, a more vigorous approach could damage the long-term economic vitality of activities which are perforce tied to the City, by inhibiting their growth, forcing them to occupy outdated premises, and increasing their costs through soaring rents. The Greater London Council is not alone in urging a revision of o.d.p. policy and a more selective approach to the control of office growth in London (Hall, 1969, pp. 78–82; Dunning, 1969, p. 230).

3.2.5 *Communications* (City London)

In recent years, more controversy has raged over planning proposals for new communications in or near London—the Greater London Council's ringway scheme and the third London airport, for example—than over any other aspect of South East planning. At the heart of such controversy is the problem of the high cost of communication development, especially in London, together with the adverse local environmental effect of motorway and airport construction.

London's very dense rail network is basically radial in nature, catering particularly for passenger flows in and out of major central London termini such as Victoria, Waterloo, Liverpool Street and Euston stations. The very high cost of providing for the peak-hour tidal surge of commuters has already been noted (p. 84). On British Rail's Southern Region, investment of approximately £10 million a year during the nineteen sixties proved insufficient to maintain existing standards and services. Largely because of the uneconomic nature of peak-hour flows, at least £14 million a year was needed by 1971; and improved services would cost £22 million each year during the nineteen seventies. While successful, the electrification of such routes as Waterloo-Bournemouth and Euston-Bletchley has also been very expensive. Most prospective electrification schemes are, therefore, less ambitious, involving short commuter lines in inner Essex, Hertfordshire and Sussex. The chief exception is the Kings Cross-Royston electrification scheme, government approval for which was announced in 1971. The total cost of this scheme, due for completion in 1977, is no less than £35 million. London Transport's separate underground rail system, though heavily used, also fails to make a profit. The recently-constructed £70 million Victoria line between Brixton and Walthamstow will not yield sufficient revenue to repay in full interest charges on borrowed capital, although fares are expected to cover operating costs. The recently-approved section of the Fleet Line, to connect Baker Street and the Strand by 1977, will cost a further £35 millions. In short, the high cost of providing adequate rail services for the existing pattern of passenger flows in London still represents a major justification for traditional decentralization policy.

London's intricate road network covers no less than 11 per cent of the total area of the metropolis. Nearly all major routes carrying heavy flows of vehicles—the A4, A40, A11 and A13—are radial in character, the only important exception being the orbital North Circular Road. In general, London's road system has grown up haphazardly over the centuries, and is now very poorly designed for modern levels and speeds of vehicle movement. Despite this, the capital possesses the second highest level of car ownership amongst British conurbations, with over 1.3 million private cars, and over 2 million road vehicles of all kinds. The rapid annual growth in these numbers, coupled with the high cost of road building in such a densely built-up area, lies at the root of London's road traffic problems. Steadily increasing flows of private vehicles not only necessitate expensive road improvements—such as the elevated M4 motorway at Brentford, or the multilevel Brent Cross flyover crossing the North Circular Road—but partly account for the declining use and hence economic viability of London Transport's bus services. In terms of passenger-kilometres, usage of these services fell by 20 per cent between 1962 and 1967.

The capital's road traffic problems permit of no easy solution. Interim measures such as the designation of extensive one-way traffic systems, and the use of computers to control traffic lights and flows, have helped to maintain speeds in the face of the rising tide of vehicle movements. Not until 1967, however, was an official comprehensive road development scheme proposed, in the shape of the Greater London Council's ringway plan. This plan has aroused fierce opposition. Estimated by the Council to cost no less than £1,700 million by the late nineteen nineties, it involves a new 'primary' urban motorway network dominated by three orbital routes, Ringways 1, 2 and 3 (Figure 14). Incoming radial motorways, such as the M1, M4 and M23, will terminate at the inner and most

expensive orbital route, Ringway 1. This primary network will be designed to handle a
quarter of all vehicle journeys and half the total vehicle-kilometres forecast for Greater
London in the nineteen eighties. Improved secondary roads will feed into the primary
network.

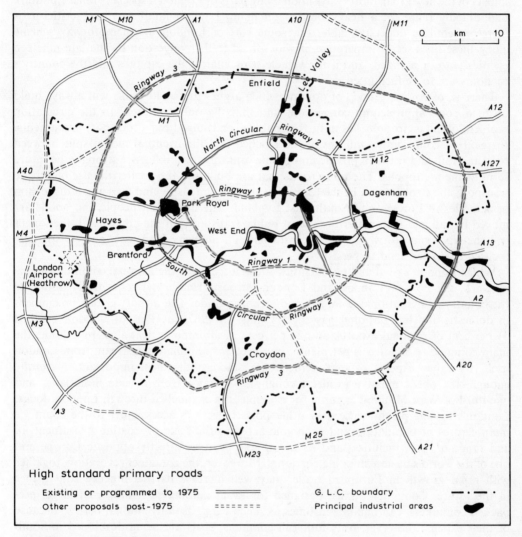

Figure 14   Greater London: motorway proposals and industrial areas, 1971.
Sources :   G.L.C. and Martin (1964, p. 122).

The economic and social costs of this ringway scheme will be considerable. Although by national standards the relative cost envisaged—£30 per year for each London car owner—is entirely reasonable, the huge capital sums involved will be difficult to raise. An entirely new London retail sales tax has been suggested as a possible (though improbable) source. Socially, the loss of 20 thousand dwellings, and the disrupting environmental impact of the new urban motorways upon many parts of London (especially inner London), undoubtedly represent a heavy burden on many London families. Fierce criticism is therefore entirely understandable, but some sort of London urban motorway scheme along these lines seems imperative, if widespread traffic congestion by the late nineteen eighties is to be avoided, and if the vehicle trips vital to the capital's and the country's economy are to be facilitated.

There is, of course, a body of opinion which argues that road traffic will always build up to a point approaching congestion, and that the only 'solution' to the circulation problem of the metropolis lies in further public—and subsidized—transport investments. In reality a compromise will always be reached and the eventual modal split between road and rail, and between private and public, transport will influence strongly the future form of the metropolis. The more roads that are built and the greater the use of private transport, the stronger will be the forces towards low intensity land uses and a dispersion of activities in London and South East England. The more that people and goods are moved by rail and the greater the use of public transport, on the other hand, the longer will the traditional form of the city, with its high intensity land uses, and its spatially focused character, tend to persist.

Whilst London's road and rail facilities afford a focus for the national communications network, the Port of London and London Airport (Heathrow) respectively dominate the country's international seaborne and airborne trade. The airport is also preeminent in domestic and international passenger flights. In 1967, the Port of London handled 31 per cent of national exports, and 28 per cent of all imports, by value. In volume, the main commodity handled is petroleum, imported for refining downstream from London itself. By value, exports of road vehicles are amongst the most important. Naturally enough, the port's massive export throughput is drawn from a wide hinterland, and one-third of West Midland exports, for example, are channelled through London docks. London's trading preeminence over other ports reflects its accessibility to the country's main centres of population and economic activity; the scale of existing investment in, and range of, port facilities; and its favourable position directly opposite Europe and one of the world's busiest shipping corridors. Moreover, the container revolution, together with rapid growth in European trade, may well increase its preeminence still further in the future. Container berths, designed for rapid automated handling of large, prepacked containers, can handle ten times as much cargo as conventional berths. Because of their expense, however, only four full container ports are being developed in South East England, at Felixstowe, Harwich, Southampton and London (Tilbury). Despite labour problems, the Tilbury container port is already by far the most important of these, £27 million having so far been invested there.

London Airport (Heathrow) is even more important for international air communications than the Port of London is for shipping services. In 1968, Heathrow handled no less than 65 per cent of all air passenger traffic to and from Britain, as well as no less than 11 per cent of the country's exports and reexports and 9 per cent of its imports— far more than any other airport. Moreover, passenger and freight movements to and from Heathrow are growing at the phenomenal rate of 20 and 30 per cent per annum respectively. As with the Port, Heathrow's dominance reflects its central and accessible position relative to the country's main concentrations of population, together with the huge amounts of capital invested in runways, buildings, navigation equipment, and facilities of all kinds. Its new 65 hectares (160-acre) cargo terminal alone cost £23 million. As with Tilbury, this sort of investment only serves to increase Heathrow's advantages vis-a-vis other airports, attracting more freight and passengers and thereby justifying yet further investment, in a cumulative spiral of growth. Developments in the Port of London and at Heathrow thus illustrate a natural trend towards the concentration and centralization of communication facilities within South East England, a development which is at some odds with the government's traditional decentralization policy. So too is the massive stimulus to local population growth afforded by employment expansion at Heathrow, where no less than 45 thousand workers now travel daily to jobs at the airport, and create demands for goods and services which are satisfied by at least an equal number of local workers.

3.3 The Outer Metropolitan Area: the New Outer London

3.3.1 *Growth and Vitality*

Since 1945 the Outer Metropolitan Area (see Figure 9), which extends for about 50 kilometres (30 miles) from the edge of Greater London, has been the scene of the most remarkable surge of population and employment growth in the country. Between 1951 and 1966, the area's population soared from 3.51 million to 5.01 million, an annual rate of increase of 3 per cent. Provisional census estimates suggest a further increase, to 5.3 million, by 1971. Although comparable (Census) employment figures are not yet available, Department of Employment estimates suggest that jobs in the O.M.A. grew at a similar rate (*circa* 2.9 per cent per annum) throughout the nineteen sixties, with a slightly faster rate of growth of service industry (3.2 per cent) then manufacturing (3.0 per cent). This very high rate of employment growth has been achieved despite a rapid decline (−4.0 per cent per annum) in employment in primary industry, notably agriculture. In many ways, therefore, the O.M.A.—now with three-quarters of a million workers in manufacturing industry and a total employment approaching the 2 million mark—represents Britain's newest major industrial and economic region.

This acknowledged, it is impossible to explain growth in the O.M.A. as though it were a relatively self-sufficient economic region like, say, Scotland (which contains an almost identical volume of population and industry). For this growth fundamentally represents a spilling-over of people and economic activity from London into outer parts of the capital's functionally dependent city region. The same centrifugal forces which produced London's suburban sprawl between 1920 and 1940 lie behind post-1945 O.M.A. expansion. The only difference lies in the wider geographical area involved, and the effect of planning controls in shaping the spatial pattern of development. In many ways, the O.M.A., one-sixth of whose employed residents actually work in the capital, may be regarded as the new, though more diffuse, outer London of the nineteen seventies and eighties.

The massive population migration from London to the O.M.A. reflects both push and pull factors. As a residential area, London appears to be becoming steadily less attractive to many younger couples and families. High house prices, old housing, cramped living conditions and traffic congestion, all encourage movement out of the capital. Conversely, the availability of new housing, more space, the quiet and psychological attractions of small towns and semirural areas, plus lower house prices, pull people to the O.M.A. House price differentials between Greater London and the O.M.A. are particularly noteworthy. Housing land values in the early nineteen sixties for example fell from £13,000 per hectare within 16 kilometres of central London, to £7,000 between 16 and 32 kilometres, and £3,500 between 32 and 48 kilometres (£32,000, £17,000 and £8,500 per acre, respectively). Given easy access to London jobs via improved communications, many former London families have as a result opted for residence in the O.M.A., and government intraregional decentralization policy expressed in new and expanded towns has accentuated this trend. Largely because an unusually high proportion of migrants are young couples, natural population increase in the O.M.A. is also high, and accounted for 30 per cent of the area's total population growth between 1951 and 1966.

Although service industry growth in the O.M.A. reflects principally the need to provide local services for the area's expanding population, the decentralization of manufacturing industry from London once again provides the chief explanation for the area's manufacturing boom. Although exact figures are not available, at least 100 thousand manufacturing jobs have been created since 1945 in the O.M.A. by migrant London firms. The restrictions forcing expanding firms out of London have already been outlined (pp. 120–121). The O.M.A.'s main attractions to these firms are relative proximity to London compared with the other regions of the country, and available modern factories or industrially-zoned land. Proximity is essential to the many of the smaller migrant firms which need to retain close links with customers, suppliers, sales offices, port and airport facilities, and even parent factories, in the capital. Until at least the middle nineteen sixties, new factories or land on which to build them have been available in many parts of the O.M.A. for purchase by determined London firms, despite government interregional decentralization policy. Low factory costs have not played much part in migration, since new premises in the O.M.A., at about £43 per square metre (£4 per square foot) in the early nineteen sixties, were not much cheaper than in London.

The established connection between industrial expansion and migration means that O.M.A. manufacturing is dominated, as is that in outer London, by the country's 'growth' industries. In 1960, the heterogeneous engineering and electrical goods group, which in the O.M.A. includes many electronics firms, accounted for 37 per cent of O.M.A. manufacturing employment; vehicles and aircraft provided another 17 per cent; chemicals, and the paper, printing and publishing group—two other post-war growth industries—accounted for 6 per cent and 12 per cent respectively. The industrial structure of the O.M.A. is thus heavily biassed towards expanding industries, and a considerable future growth of manufacturing in the area seems inevitable.

3.3.2 *Town and Country Planning*

The capital's explosive growth between 1920 and 1940 produced an unplanned, chaotic and inefficient jumble of housing, industry and roads in outer London. Since 1945, South East planners have sought to prevent a recurrence of this pattern in the much larger O.M.A., using new powers over changes in the use of land, and following the broad strategy laid down by Abercrombie. Their response to the challenge of growth in the O.M.A. has included both negative and positive elements.

The chief negative element has been the designation and maintenance of the *green belt* around London (see Figure 11). Abercrombie's proposals for such a belt, designed to supplement earlier action by the London County Council, were accepted by the government in 1946 and they were given statutory definition in county and county borough development plans approved after 1954. The basic purpose of this belt was (and is) to check the further outward sprawl of London, although more recent government statements have also stressed its amenity value for recreation. Local planning authorities have power to refuse permission for building in the belt; the Secretary of State for the environment can, however, over-rule them as in the celebrated case of Span's New Ash Green village development in the middle nineteen sixties. In fact, as Thomas (1970, p. 135) has shown, as much as 30 per cent of green belt land is used for purposes other than agriculture, while the belt is punctured by large 'holes' occupied by towns such as Watford and St. Albans. Nevertheless, in general it has so far preserved land close to London from large scale building development or urban sprawl, unlike the situation in most other European and North American metropolitan regions.

Positive O.M.A. planning has shaped the spatial pattern of the area's residential and industrial growth in two ways. The more important has been the release of building land in conformity with the local *development plans*. These plans, drawn up in terms of the basic strategy recommended by Abercrombie (1945), have largely determined the location of new houses erected by private builders. Such dwellings make up two-thirds of all new South East homes outside London in recent years. The plans have also controlled the location of new industry. Many new industrial estates have been designated by local authorities to provide nearby jobs for an expanding population. In general this has resulted in considerable expansion of most existing O.M.A. towns, especially those on major commuter routes to London, whilst intervening villages and rural areas have been preserved from large scale development.

The most striking aspect of positive O.M.A. planning, however, has been the creation of eight *new towns* (see Figure 9), in accordance with Abercrombie's principles, in or just beyond the green belt. Housing no less than 350 thousand people, these new towns are exciting symbols of the government's intraregional decentralization policy. Nearly all have succeeded in attracting a stable yet virile economic base, in the form of manufacturing industry. Indeed, with over 400 manufacturing firms all told, the O.M.A. new towns are more dependent upon manufacturing than most ordinary towns of their size. Where new town manufacturing is particularly specialized, of course, this dependence can be dangerous. For example, manufacturing employment in Hatfield, over 70 per cent of which was in aircraft manufacturing in 1960, actually declined by 9 per cent between 1960 and 1966, because of difficulties in this industry. On the other hand, manufacturing in Basildon and Harlow, which is more diversified yet orientated to growth industries, expanded by no less than 13 thousand (130 per cent) and 6 thousand (50 per cent) workers respectively over the same period (see Table 5).

The successful development of an employment base in the new towns, largely through industrial migration from London, has eliminated the need for large-scale commuting into the capital—even though this is a common feature of many other towns located up to 50 kilometres (30 miles) away. True, the 1961 census recorded out-commuter percentages as high as 40 per cent and 34 per cent of the employed residents for Basildon and Hemel Hempstead respectively, but only a few of these (for example, 9 per cent from Basildon) travelled to central London. Most journeyed to nearby towns, as is normal in urbanized regions today. In Stevenage, the out-commuting and central London percentages were as low as 14 and 2 per cent respectively. Further successful aspects of the new towns include a good provision of open spaces and sportsfields, and the construction of road systems and car parks which, despite original government underestimation of future levels of car ownership, nevertheless do cater for modern traffic more efficiently and safely than those in traditional towns.

One criticism which has been levied at the O.M.A.'s new towns is that, despite the initial planners' desire for 'social balance' there, they have remained essentially artisan and failed to attract as residents the highest paid managers, directors and professional workers whose activities are an integral part of their economies. Thus, for example, a 1964 survey in Stevenage revealed that only one in ten executives of the big Hawker Siddeley plant there actually resided in the town (Brown, 1966). However, other more recent studies (Heraud, 1968; Thomas, 1969) have now demonstrated that this criticism is in fact invalid as a general assessment of the O.M.A. new towns. As early as 1960, for example, 26 per cent of Hemel Hempstead residents were in Social Classes I and II (professional and intermediate professional), whilst the comparable (1961) figures for Greater London and England and Wales were 20.6 and 19.2 per cent respectively (Heraud, 1968). Moreover, the new town figures relate only to the occupants of Corporation-built housing; the addition of data on private housing within and immediately beyond the designated area might well increase the proportion of residents in these Social Classes. Since 1960, too, the new towns have received a significant influx of service employment, while Development Corporations have been empowered to sell homes to existing tenants and to set aside more land for private building. With the notable exception of Basildon (Thomas, 1969, p. 417), such developments may well be shifting the class balance of these new communities yet further away from the national norm, but in a direction contrary to that suggested by earlier critics.

A more substantial criticism of the new towns is that their original target populations, ranging from 25 thousand (Bracknell and Hatfield) to 97 thousand (Basildon), were in general too small to justify the local provision of many expensive services and facilities such as a large general hospital, a theatre, a department store or a branch of Marks and Spencer. Only with an increase in their target populations (to as high as 134, 120 and 105 thousand at Basildon, Crawley and Stevenage), which was partly necessitated by the unexpected surge in the South East's birth rate after 1955, have the largest of the towns been able to attract some of these facilities.

Pressure to increase their size has revealed a further defect in this first generation of new towns. For reasons of design and siting, the population of these communities can not be expanded very much above their original targets. The architect-planners' adoption of a roughly circular shape with roads radiating out from a central, residentially-enclosed, shopping zone, renders large scale expansion of central facilities, car parks and road capacities difficult and expensive, largely because of lack of space. Moreover, the original selection of sites fairly close to other urban centres, as at Stevenage and Hemel Hempstead, has inhibited expansion for fear of urban coalescence. While successful, and increasingly diversifying their employment structures, the O.M.A. new towns will thus be unable to make as substantial a contribution to the housing of natural population growth in the region as many planners had hoped.

3.3.3 *Spatial Patterns*

Three superimposed patterns may be detected in the map of recent O.M.A. population and employment growth. The first, and perhaps most obvious, pattern is *zonal*. Since 1945, there has been a broad tendency for growth to be greatest in the ring of areas close to or bordering London, and to decline with distance outwards from the metropolis. This is certainly the most striking feature of the small-scale aggregate map of population change between 1951 and 1961 (Figure 15a). Immediately around London, the concentric zone of inner Kent, Surrey, Berkshire, Buckinghamshire, Hertfordshire and Essex experienced local authority population growth rates which were amongst the highest in the country (over 20 per cent). Outwards from this, however, rates declined to between 5 and 15 per cent in the remainder of the O.M.A. Although more nucleated, industrial and employment growth during the nineteen fifties revealed the same zonal tendency.

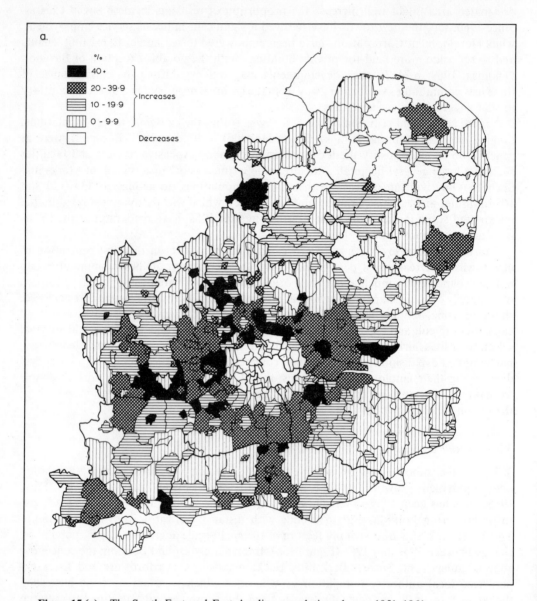

Figure 15 (a)   The South East and East Anglia: population change 1951–1961.

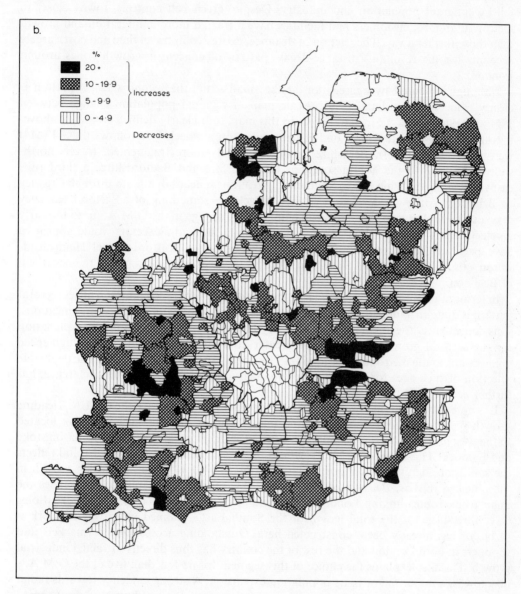

Figure 15 (b)   The South East and East Anglia: population change 1961–1966.

This pattern of course results directly from the need for continued contact with London felt by emigrant population and industry. Despite green belt controls, towns closer to metropolitan jobs, customers and facilities have attracted more immigration and growth than those further away. The friction of distance, expressed in travel time and cost, largely accounts for the resultant 'distance-decay' pattern of concentric growth zones around London.

Although obscured by aggregation at the small scale, the second *sectoral* pattern is clearly evident in the detailed large-scale map of regional population change between 1951 and 1961 (Jones & Sinclair, 1968). In this map, four clearly-defined sectors of above-average growth radiate from London like spokes on a wheel. One follows the A4 (M4) westwards into southern Berkshire; another, slightly more fragmented, travels north-westwards close to the M1 in southern Hertfordshire and Bedfordshire; a third runs eastwards along the main line to Southend; and a fourth heads due south through Crawley to Brighton. Although accurate evidence is lacking, something of a sectoral tendency may also have characterized industrial employment change in the O.M.A. up to the early nineteen sixties (Martin, 1966, pp. 226–227). Again, the leading sectors would appear to have been to the northwest of London, along a broad Watford-Hemel Hempstead-Luton axis, to the west from Slough to Reading, and eastwards embracing the new town of Basildon.

In terms of population growth at least, the clarity of this detailed nineteen fifties sectoral pattern is quite striking. So also is its close coincidence with major radial communications. This coincidence, together with actual survey findings, suggests that a major explanation for the sectoral growth pattern is the greater attractiveness of centres with high-speed connections to the metropolis for migrant Londoners and ex-London firms. The deliberate selection of such sites for new town development, in anticipation of this preference, has further accentuated this relationship.

It is noteworthy that in absolute and to some extent relative terms, the O.M.A.'s leading growth sectors for both population and manufacturing activity since 1945 are located to the west and northwest of London, in a broad segment enclosed by lines to Basingstoke and Baldock. This above-average growth to the west and northwest of the capital reflects the same considerations as those which encouraged west London's suburban growth in the nineteen thirties. Because of its position, this segment is nearer to, and carries the main trunk routes linking London with, Britain's other major cities and conurbations. Over three-fifths of the total length of the South East's planned motorway network is to be, or has already been, constructed here. Outstanding accessibility to markets and suppliers in both London and the rest of the country has thus directly attracted industrial growth. This also explains the choice of this segment for no less than five of the O.M.A.'s new towns, a major factor in its population expansion. A strong tendency towards radial industrial migration from the capital has also benefited the northwest of the O.M.A. much more than, say, Kent and Surrey, since south London's industrial areas are much smaller than those of London's west and northwest suburbs. The desirability of living in such attractive residential zones as the Chilterns or Thames valley may also have encouraged population and industrial expansion in the segment.

Below-average growth to the south east of London may conversely be explained by Kent's relatively isolated position. However, this segment also embraces the south bank of the Thames estuary, which with the opposite shore possesses unique locational advantages for industrial development orientated to water transport. As a result, considerable growth has at least occurred since 1945 in the oil refining industry. Lower Thameside, with sites capable of handling 70,000 dwt tankers fully laden (and even larger vessels for which it is the second port of discharge) is now the leading oil refining centre in the country with major refineries at Shell Haven (with a 1970 capacity of 10.00 million tons), Coryton (6.25 mt), and the Isle of Grain (11.95 mt); in prospect are an expansion at Shell Haven and a further refinery on Canvey Island (with a proposed capacity of 10.00 mt). New oil burning power stations have been built or are planned on the lower Thames, and as the upstream docks of the Port of London Authority close Tilbury is rapidly developing as a major container and specialized cargo (grain, wood etc.) port. But even allowing for these changes, development on anything like the scale evident just across the Channel at Rotterdam-Europoort is conspicuously absent. The difference in part reflects contrasts in the hinterlands of the two ports; but it also mirrors contrasts in public policies. The Dutch have deliberately encouraged the development of trade and industry—and perhaps even subsidized the infrastructure costs—of the port of Rotterdam. Thameside, on the other hand, has undoubtedly suffered from the British government's preoccupation with the needs of the less prosperous regions, the resultant restrictive planning and i.d.c. policies, and the politically and socially motivated inertia in the choice of new plant locations by the country's older raw material importing and processing industries such as iron and steel. Whether the recent establishment of a small (180 thousand ton) privately-owned steel plant at Sheerness, based on an electric-arc furnace and South East scrap, is any kind of omen for a future large-scale Thameside development in this industry remains to be seen. Certainly Lower Thameside in general was considered as a possible location for a large 'greenfield' steel complex by the British Steel Corporation until the Government ruled it out on regional planning grounds in 1972.

The third, and perhaps most significant, superimposed pattern of recent O.M.A. growth is *nucleated*. Since 1945, natural forces and planning policies have channelled much of the population and industrial migration from London into existing O.M.A. towns. Probably the main single influence here has been the designation of the metropolitan green belt, which has diverted growth from the O.M.A.'s many attractive rural areas to relatively few existing urban centres. But other major factors have been new town policy, the natural tendency for the region's largest, higher-order, service centres to generate above-average local employment and therefore population growth, and the predilection of industrialists for urban areas possessing good road and rail communications and a relatively large supply of labour. Up to a dozen O.M.A. towns—including Guildford, Slough, Watford, Reading, Luton, Chelmsford and Maidstone—have thus expanded considerably over the last twenty years and become increasingly important as sub-regional employment and service centres.

Nucleated growth has been particularly characteristic of O.M.A. manufacturing. Most of the area's individual manufacturing industries cluster in a relatively few locations. Even the giant engineering and electrical goods group, the biggest and most widespread, is particularly concentrated in a dozen or so centres, the chief of which are Chelmsford, Luton, Slough, Letchworth, Crawley, Dartford and the Medway towns. Extremely localiz-ed is furniture manufacture, which is dominated by High Wycombe firms, whose ten thousand furniture employees account for one-third of the O.M.A. total. Road vehicle manufacturing is equally strongly concentrated in Luton and Dunstable, the headquarters of the Vauxhall company; while Weybridge, Hatfield and Stevenage contain the bulk of the O.M.A.'s important aircraft industry. Bracknell has developed in recent years as a major electronics centre. Slough stands out on the map of both food and light chemicals manufacturing as one of the O.M.A.'s two main centres of each industry, as does Reading (food) and Welwyn Garden City (chemicals). As already pointed out, O.M.A. employment in heavy chemicals is dominated by Thameside oil-refining, while the adjoining Dartford-Gravesend-Maidstone area contains the biggest concentration of paper and cement plants in the country. Industrial clustering thus characterizes most O.M.A. industries, reflecting varied locational forces which include the impact of individual giant firms (such as Vaux-hall), local concentrations of skilled workers (High Wycombe), and the special transport advantages of break-of-bulk sites (Thameside).

The recent growth in sub-regional importance of the O.M.A.'s largest towns, both as manufacturing and service centres, raises a most important and intriguing question. To what extent may it be true that the nineteen sixties represented something of a watershed in the history of London's domination of its surrounding city region, and that in future, regional economic and population growth will focus decreasingly upon London, and increasingly upon outlying centres both in the O.M.A. and Outer South East? In other words, is the spatial structure of population and economic activity in South East England now tending towards a polynuclear pattern, focused on a series of dispersed major urban nodes, as compared with the traditional pattern of domination by a single central nucleus, in the form of London?

This hypothesis, recently suggested in general terms by Hall (1969, pp. 82–83), is in many ways at variance with the evidence presented in Chapter 2 (pp. 97–105). Radial communication improvements, the growth of commuting to London, and colonization of outer areas by London manufacturing firms, all point to increased rather than reduced functional dominance by the capital of surrounding areas, both in the recent past and immediate future. However, other rather conflicting evidence does offer some support for this intriguing polynuclear hypothesis, especially as a longer-term forecast relating to the next twenty or thirty years. Not least, of course, is the rapid current decline in London's population, coupled with the equally rapid growth of outlying urban centres already described. As Hall (1969, pp. 120–122) has pointed out, the nineteen sixties seem to have witnessed the dissolution of the earlier zonal pattern of population change around London, into a much more fragmented distribution of population growth, focused not upon the capital, but upon these major outlying centres (Figure 15b). A similar shift characterizes employment growth in general, and manufacturing change in particular (Keeble and Hauser, 1971, p. 241; Keeble, 1969, p. 852). At the same time, the influence of the outlying towns upon commuting and shopping trips from areas up to 24 kilometres (15 miles) away is undoubtedly growing, probably at a faster rate than that of London. Lastly, future planning policies, which incorporate such major nucleated developments as the Milton Keynes new city of 250 thousand people, and expansion in the Southampton-Portsmouth zone to a population of well over one million, are bound to encourage this trend. Though the evidence is conflicting, growth in the relative importance of the South East's outlying centres as major employment nodes, and as foci for regional population and economic growth, may now be challenging the traditional dominance of London in these terms.

3.4 The Outer South East and East Anglia : the Stage for Future Growth?

3.4.1 *General Development*

Although the exact boundary line between them is arbitrary, the Outer South East and East Anglia (see Figure 9) differ from the O.M.A. in several important respects. Towns, though somewhat larger, are separated by much more extensive rural areas in which agriculture and its associated industries are more important than in the O.M.A. A proximity to the coast has encouraged greater development of water-oriented activities (such as small shipbuilding and tourism) and of retirement immigration. Links with London for employment, shopping or manufacturing needs are less strong, and, most important of all, the outward tide of metropolitan decentralization has only recently begun to affect this outer zone on a large scale. Between 1951 and 1966, total O.S.E. population grew from 3.50 million to 4.16 million, or by 19 per cent (see Figure 10). Up to 1961, however, the annual growth rate was only 0.9 per cent, whereas between 1961 and 1966 it rose to 1.5 per cent. (In contrast, the O.M.A. rate, though significantly higher in both periods, actually declined from 2.6 per cent in the former to 2.1 per cent in the latter.) Provisional census figures suggest an O.S.E. growth rate, 1966–1971, of 1.4 per cent per annum, thus making a 1971 population of 4.46 million. East Anglia's population also grew rapidly between 1951 and 1966, from 1.39 to 1.58 million (an increase of 14 per cent); as with the O.S.E., the annual rate of growth between 1961 and 1966 (+1.2 per cent) was considerably faster than that during the nineteen fifties (+0.7 per cent). By 1971, East Anglia's population had reached 1.67 millions. Quickening growth rates also characterize manufacturing and service industry in these areas; manufacturing employment in both expanded by 3 per cent per annum during the nineteen sixties.

As with the O.M.A., the recent growth in these areas owes much more to net immigration of people and industry than to natural expansion. Again, the largest single source of immigrants is Greater London, although the O.M.A. itself is now exporting some firms and population to outlying centres. As with movement to the O.M.A., migration other than to the South Coast tends to be dominated by younger couples and families. Similarly, incoming industry is made up largely of firms in growth industries such as engineering and electrical goods. In 1960, the latter already accounted for 36 per cent of O.S.E. manufacturing employment, with a further 20 per cent in vehicles, and 8 per cent in paper, printing and publishing. Declining or static industries such as clothing and footwear, and furniture and timber, accounted for only 4 and 5 per cent respectively of O.S.E. manufacturing employment. East Anglia was less well off in this respect, with 13 per cent of its manufacturing jobs in the declining footwear and clothing trades, and only 32 and 9 per cent respectively in engineering and electrical goods, and vehicles. Both areas, of course, have suffered from a significant decline in agricultural employment since 1945, although heavy investment in machinery and fertilizers has enabled East Anglia to maintain its leadership as the nation's most important arable farming region.

3.4.2 The Rural Periphery

The most meaningful socio–economic division of the O.S.E. and East Anglia, however, is into two zones, here termed the rural and coastal peripheries. The rural periphery comprises the western, north western and north eastern parts of the O.S.E., together with most of East Anglia. Its most significant spatial characteristic is its organization into eight or so reasonably distinct and independent local city regions. These are centred upon the towns of Norwich, Ipswich, Colchester, Cambridge, Peterborough, Bedford, Oxford and Swindon. Limited areas of functional dependence also surround certain smaller, more isolated, centres such as King's Lynn, Newbury and Bury St. Edmunds. The larger towns provide both higher-order services for rural populations up to 48 kilometres (30 miles) away, and industrial and other non-agricultural job opportunities for commuters living within about 24 kilometres (15 miles). Thus, most are important retail centres with department, multiple and specialist stores; most contain regional hospitals, technical colleges, and fire and police services; and most are foci of a radial local communications and bus service network. Nearly all these towns also possess a significant manufacturing base, supplemented as far as Oxford, Cambridge, Norwich and Colchester are concerned by employment in major universities. As with O.M.A. towns, their industries are often highly specialized. Oxford is famous for motor vehicle manufacturing (British Leyland) which employs 27 thousand workers and Cambridge for radio, television and scientific instrument production. Ipswich is the country's leading agricultural engineering centre, Norwich possesses an important (though declining) footwear industry and Swindon, located only just outside the South East's boundary and diversified in the course of its expansion under the Town Development Act, is still noted for its railway engineering.

The Bedford/Bletchley and Peterborough districts are the country's leading brick producers, using the local Oxford Clay.

The chief planning problems of the rural periphery occur in its more isolated parts, lying 24 kilometres (15 miles) or more from one of the major towns. These problems include low agriculturally-dependent wage levels, declining agricultural employment, rural depopulation, ageing population structures, and the high cost of providing adequate social facilities. At least until the nineteen sixties, rural depopulation, the most easily measurable of these, was extremely widespread. No less than three-fifths of East Anglia's 1,250 rural parishes recorded a decline in population between 1951 and 1961 (see Figure 15a). The parishes recording substantial population growth were nearly all located within 8 to 16 kilometres (5 to 10 miles) of a major town, reflecting the lure of cheaper housing, more space, and the attraction of rural living conditions to those urban workers who are willing to commute daily to their jobs, generally by private car. Although growth has replaced decline in quite a number of East Anglian parishes more recently, two-fifths of the total still recorded a population loss between 1961 and 1966 (see Figure 15b).

3.4.3 *The Coastal Periphery*

Although such towns as Southampton, Portsmouth, Bournemouth and Brighton also dominate extensive local city regions (in terms of shopping and commuting ties), the character, functions and problems of the coastal periphery of the South East and East Anglia are generally different from those of its rural counterpart. Moreover, differences within the coastal periphery demand the separate discussion of its three main sub-regions.

South Hampshire—comprising the cities of Portsmouth, Southampton, and Bournemouth, with their surrounding urban and rural districts—contains the South East's largest local concentration of population after Greater London itself. By 1966, no less than 1.2 million people were living there; and this total was growing as a result of natural increase and net immigration by over 10 thousand new residents each year. The area's economic base is in process of transformation from a heavy dependence upon declining or highly seasonal activities (such as shipbuilding, ship repairing and tourism) to a manufacturing economy biassed towards both labour and capital intensive growth industries. The expansion of manufacturing job opportunities at a rate of 2.9 per cent per annum between 1960 and 1966 was dominated by a very rapid development of engineering and electrical goods firms; in addition there was some growth of employment in chemicals, paper, printing and publishing, and so-called 'other' manufacturing activities. The movement from London of labour-intensive industries, such as those manufacturing electronic components, television sets, and cosmetics, hoping to benefit from a local surplus of female workers, has been a most important component in this growth. It is not surprising, therefore, that some planners (Ministry of Housing and Local Government, 1964, pp. 72–73) have looked to the population and industrial expansion of this area as a possible future 'counter-magnet' to London.

Others (Davies and Robinson, 1968) have stressed the emergence of close functional ties—for shopping, commuting, higher order services and the like—within South Hampshire, and have viewed the sub-region as an incipient polynuclear metropolis in its own right. Certainly the considerable local population and industrial movement outwards, from Portsmouth and Southampton to surrounding centres such as Havant, Fareham and Chandlers Ford, is producing a wider and more complex pattern of interdependent settlements in the Southampton-Portsmouth zone. The improvement of local communications, such as the South Coast motorway (M27) to be built between Portsmouth, Southampton and Bournemouth, and the electrified Bournemouth-Southampton rail link, will encourage this trend still further.

The interdependence of the sub-region's several parts is also connected with local economic specialization. Waterfront Southampton is almost entirely given over to the harbour installations, warehouses and passenger terminals indicative of its longstanding role as Britain's leading passenger port. Its recent selection as one of Britain's four deep sea container ports reflects its unique natural advantage in terms of a double high-water for berthing big ships, its proximity to Europe and ocean trading routes, problems of labour relations in the Port of London, and its accessibility from London and the Midlands. Since 1945 the west bank of Southampton Water has been transformed into one of the country's main oil refining and power generating centres. Esso's £125-million, 16.25 million ton Fawley refinery, sited with regard to the local sheltered deep-water harbourage, is the largest in Britain. Dependent on it are nearby petrochemical works (synthetic rubber) and two oil burning power stations. Portsmouth has traditionally been dependent upon its male-employing naval dockyards, and Bournemouth upon its retirement role and summer tourism. Eastleigh is still an important railway engineering centre, while many modern labour-intensive engineering firms have sprung up since 1945 in Poole and Havant, as well as at Southampton.

One of the chief planning problems facing South Hampshire is the need to preserve the area's exceptional natural recreational amenities—the New Forest, the Channel coasts, the yachting areas of Southampton Water, Beaulieu and Hamble—in the face of rapidly-increasing pressure from expanding population and industry. Fawley's steel chimneys and refining plant where once there were only fields and trees, Southampton's new 200-hectare (500-acre) peripheral housing development athwart the Romsey road, and the Central Electricity Generating Board's search for a water-oriented 2,000 MW nuclear power station site close to Southampton or Portsmouth, all indicate the attractiveness of the area to industry and population and the continuing need to preserve the area's superb natural and recreational heritage by skillful planning.

An identical preservation problem faces coastal Sussex and Kent. Here, however, the growth of population is as much the result of retirement migration as of manufacturing expansion. Indeed, although immigrant growth firms producing electrical goods, pharmaceuticals and the like have expanded rapidly in various South Coast towns in the last fifteen years, manufacturing employment in Brighton, the zone's largest industrial centre, actually declined between 1960 and 1966. The considerable movement of retired people to the South Coast since 1945 reflects the attractions of its relatively warm and sunny climate, the scenic beauty of Weald, the Downs and the coast, and its general accessibility to London. The resultant population expansion has been greatest in Sussex's Littlehampton-Hastings belt, which housed 650 thousand people by 1966. The fairly rapid growth here (1 per cent per annum between 1951 and 1966) is due solely to immigration, since the unusually aged population (44 per cent of Bexhill's population is over 60) produces a local death rate which is higher than the birth rate (see Table 10).

The pressure on the South Coast's superb natural amenities—the North and South Downs, and the coast itself—is further aggravated by the demands of the tourist industry, and to a much lesser extent cross-Channel communications. A huge summer influx of holiday-makers benefits hotels throughout the area, from the Isle of Wight in the west to Herne Bay in the east. However, although lucrative in season, tourism affords a poor local economic base because of its associated high winter unemployment. A heavy dependence locally upon tourism, therefore, represents a further planning problem. The rapid growth in the cross-Channel carriage of cars and passengers in recent years has also placed increasing strain on local communications and interchange centres such as Dover and Lydd. The projected cross-Channel rail tunnel might relieve some of this pressure.

The responses of planners to these problems include special land use controls and industrial promotion. Although Dungeness now has a nuclear power station, pressures for the development of unspoilt coastal sites have often been checked by the designation of Areas of Outstanding Natural Beauty, or Coastal Protection Areas. These now include the Downs, and much of the Isle of Wight and east Kent coast. Planning permission for development in these areas is very hard to obtain. A heavy reliance locally on tourism has in places been reduced by planned industrial immigration, generally from London. Although partly due to local initiative, as exemplified by the expanded town status of Ashford and Hastings, this migration also owes much to the former Board of Trade, notably in the case of movement to East Kent and the Isle of Wight. Concerned primarily with interregional decentralization, the Board has nevertheless at times acknowledged the need of certain peripheral South East and East Anglian resorts for more stable, industrial, employment; and its greater willingness to grant i.d.c.s in these areas has led to a marked migration of industrial firms from London. Thus, manufacturing employment in east Kent (east of a Dover-Canterbury-Sheerness line) expanded by nearly 9 thousand workers (55 per cent) between 1960 and 1966; although on a much smaller scale, the same type of movement has also taken place to the Isle of Wight.

Unlike the South Coast, East Anglia's coastal areas have not experienced a massive influx of migrants to retirement. Although one or two southerly towns, such as Clacton-on-Sea and Frinton, have grown quite rapidly, the colder east-facing North Sea coast, with its low clay and gravel cliffs, is much less attractive to retired couples. The main problems here, therefore, are the imbalanced, tourist-dominated and highly seasonal employment opportunities, coupled with pressures for the development of large scale tourist facilities—such as caravan parks, holiday camps and yachting marinas—both close to the coast and in the Norfolk Broads. Except in the case of Lowestoft, East Anglia's leading fishing centre, the problems of seasonal unemployment have been aggravated by the decline in the area's traditional fishing industry. Although some industrial migration from London has helped, the main economic development assisting coastal East Anglia recently has been the rapid expansion of several of its smaller ports, notably Harwich and Felixstowe. Their excellent position in relation to London, the Midlands and European ports, plus good labour relations, have attracted many container and 'unitized' shipments— and their imports and exports now represent about 5 per cent of the country's foreign trade by value.

3.4.4 *The Shape of Things to Come*

Although the planning response to some of the specific problems facing the O.S.E. and East Anglia has already been outlined, certain planning strategies with wider implications for both the coastal and rural peripheries demand attention. At the *local scale,* for example, one suggested solution to the twin problems of rural depopulation and the high cost of social facilities is what might be called the 'growth village' strategy proposed in the Cambridgeshire County Council's 1965 Development Plan review. Although eventually rejected by the Minister, this review proposed a strategy based on the selection of eight outlying and well-dispersed Cambridgeshire villages. All are fairly large, with some local industry, secondary schools and shops. All but one are surrounded by areas of rural depopulation. The strategy envisaged the channelling of what local population growth did occur, as well as expanding industry from Cambridge itself, into these growth villages. Increasing size, it was hoped, would in turn attract or justify shops, services or firms which require a larger local market or labour supply, and had not existed in these areas before. In this way, a wider range of services and job opportunities would have been made available to rural dwellers within about 16 kilometres (10 miles) of these selected villages than would otherwise have been possible. Though officially rejected, such a strategy seems both realistic and plausible in the context of a rural area such as East Anglia. Certainly some sort of growth village pattern does seem to be emerging in outer Cambridgeshire, where for example the population of Melbourne, one of the villages originally proposed as an expansion centre, doubled between 1956 and 1970 to 2,900 inhabitants, with associated growth of local shops, schools and light industry.

At the *sub-regional scale,* a rather similar planning strategy has recently been proposed for East Anglia by the region's Economic Planning Council (1968, pp. 20–25). This strategy is based upon the existing spatial organization of the area into four main city regions, focused upon Cambridge, Ipswich, Norwich and Peterborough. The Council points out that East Anglia's sub-regional planning problems include the cost of higher-order services for a widely scattered population; the small scale of industrial employment; the inadequate capacity of intraregional communications; and, above all, provision for very rapid future population growth. Official South East decentralization schemes envisaged in 1968, for example, would have resulted in a 27 per cent increase in East Anglia's population between 1961 and 1981, compared with a rate of only 11 per cent in England and Wales. These problems can best be tackled, the Council argues, in terms of a spatial planning framework based on the four 24-kilometre (15-mile) wide city regions noted above, together with three smaller 'town regions' around King's Lynn, Great Yarmouth-Lowestoft and Bury St. Edmunds. Although inadequately spelt out in terms of its practical implications, the Council's proposal seems to imply that the provision of the necessary facilities for new population, the attraction of industry and improvements in communications will be easier if growth is channelled to or around the cities and towns specified. By virtue of their organizing role, growth in these centres will benefit in turn the whole city or town region around them. Such a strategy, based squarely on an acceptance of powerful economic trends and established spatial patterns, seems logical and applicable to much of the rural periphery.

However, by far the most important type of planning strategy affecting the O.S.E. and East Anglia concerns the *regional scale* of analysis. For this zone represents the reception area most favoured until recently by regional decentralization strategists for housing future regional population growth. It is thus of crucial significance in current discussions of the optimum urban form for South East England as a whole, and of present and future regional planning policy.

The earliest decentralization proposals affecting this zone were of course embodied in Abercrombie's new and expanded town strategy. Although all eight new towns designated before 1950 were located in the O.M.A., the great majority of the 32 expanded towns which have signed or are negotiating agreements with the Greater London Council under the Town Development Act of 1952 lie further out (see Figure 9), especially in East Anglia (9) and the O.S.E. (8). Most are small market centres, seeking and only capable of limited expansion. Most overspill agreements have been in force for less than 10 years, and involved protracted negotiations. The contribution of expanded towns to planned decentralization has thus so far been small, involving only about 120 thousand Londoners. Admittedly, the local impact of planned immigration has often been considerable, especially in East Anglia where job opportunities outside agriculture are scarce. Thus Thetford's 20-thousand population, swollen by Londoners, is now four times what it was only 12 years ago, while over 50 immigrant firms provide local manufacturing employment. However, the general effect of the Abercrombie-type strategy upon the zone's urban structure has so far been limited, and has created only a dispersed pattern of small-scale settlement growth (see Table 5).

A realization by decentralization planners of the limitations of this traditional town expansion approach—and of the implications for future housing demand in South East England of the post-1955 surge in the birth rate—led to the counter-magnet strategy of the 1964 *South East Study*. This document, prepared by the Ministry of Housing and

Local Government, represented the first major official review of overall regional planning problems in the South East and East Anglia since Abercrombie. One of its main conclusions was that, despite massive postwar decentralization to the O.M.A., the rapid natural increase in population would necessitate the transfer from the capital of a further one million Londoners between 1961 and 1981. Homes would also be needed outside London for a further 2½million people, comprising immigrants from other regions and the natural increase of the rest of the South East. The problem was 'where?'.

The Study's answer was in some respects vague, in other respects bold and clear (see Figure 16a). It was vague—even confused—in that it claimed that the local planning authorities in the O.M.A. could cater for most of this growth, yet failed to suggest any guiding strategy for its spatial arrangement within this zone. It was clear, on the other hand, in that it called urgently for a second generation of much bigger London overspill towns, to be located entirely in or beyond the O.S.E. or East Anglia as potential counter-magnets to the capital. Compared with the first generation new towns, these large centres would be cheaper to build (in terms of cost per household); they would provide a much wider range of facilities, services and jobs; and in the case of the expansion of existing large towns, they would be able to attract London population and industry from the outset by providing good shops, schools and services. By locating them outside the O.M.A., undue pressure on this already rapidly-expanding zone could be avoided. The Study thus suggested the creation of three new cities, one in the Bletchley area (for 150 thousand overspill immigrants), one at Newbury (150 thousand) and one (250 thousand) between Southampton and Portsmouth; two large new towns (100 thousand each) were proposed for Ashford and Stansted; and major expansions, involving from 50 to 100 thousand migrants each were suggested for Peterborough, Ipswich, Northampton and Swindon. The latter two are strictly just outside the South East (see Figure 9). These schemes, greater than almost anything previously envisaged or attempted anywhere in the world, implied a rate of planned industrial movement over twice as fast as that achieved with the earlier new towns.

In effect, therefore, the Study's proposals aimed at the creation of a polynuclear city region in the South East, with the continued expansion of towns in the O.M.A., and with the creation of major new outlying cities, one or two of which would be big enough to act as counter-magnets to London. Its failure to spell out in detail any strategy for natural growth within the O.M.A. has since been remedied by the contrasting proposals of the Standing Conference on London and South East Regional Planning, and the South East Economic Planning Council. The former, representing local planning authorities, suggested in 1967 what might be called a 'growth-concentration' planning strategy for the South East, based upon the proposition that population and employment growth should be concentrated in a few areas of limited agricultural and landscape value. The possible consequences for the spatial pattern of future population growth were illustrated by three, alternative, maps. Although all include growth areas around Bletchley and Southampton-Portsmouth, two anticipate the heaviest expansion to occur around a number of existing O.M.A. settlements sited on relatively poor land to the southwest and northwest of London. In other words, the primary consideration behind this strategy seems to be a desire to concentrate growth, for economic and physical planning reasons, into areas of relatively low quality land, many of which are within the O.M.A.

The South East Economic Planning Council's 'growth-sector' strategy, on the other hand, as outlined in its 1967 report *A Strategy for the South-East*, was based on an entirely different principle. The Council argued that the spatial pattern of future South East growth should be closely related to that of the region's main road and rail communications. In other words, development should be channelled into sectors, radiating outwards along major lines of communication from London (see Figure 16b). Such a strategy clearly conforms closely to recent trends in O.M.A. growth. It is also adaptable to major infrastructural investments with implications for urban expansion, a case in point being the proposed Third London Airport (T.L.A.). In the late nineteen sixties, the British Airports Authority forecast the need for a major international airport in the London area to supplement the facilities at Heathrow and Gatwick. Following the success of local opposition to the government's initial selection of Stansted (Essex), four main sites were short-listed by the special Roskill Commission for detailed consideration as sites for a T.L.A. Three of them—Foulness (Essex), Thurleigh (Bedfordshire) and Cublington (Buckinghamshire)—each lay within one of the growth sectors suggested by the Council; and each of the surrounding localities could have absorbed the considerable urbanization which will be associated with such a major investment. Some studies have suggested that the employment generated at the airport itself might range between 45 and 65 thousand workers by the year 2,000, which in turn might be associated through multipliers with an urbanization in the airport sub-region of no less than 400 thousand people. Adoption of a growth sector strategy would thus have facilitated planning for population growth associated with a T.L.A. at three of the short-listed sites; the fourth at Nuthampstead (Hertfordshire) was in a rural sector where little urbanization has occurred, and was never a realistic possibility. In the event, of course, the Roskill Commission's recommendation of Cublington was rejected by the government, and the airport is now to be built at Foulness—but called Maplin.

However, at least two theoretical justifications also exist for a growth-sector strategy. On the one hand, the very high cost of public investment in modern communications is warranted only if they are heavily used. Location of new housing and industrial areas close to new motorways and electrified rail routes would help to ensure that these expensive communications were used intensively. On the other hand, the South East's increasingly affluent population is becoming increasingly mobile, and demanding rapid access to jobs, shops and leisure facilities—many of which are in London. Industry, too, needs good communications with the capital, and a wide labour catchment area. Thus, by locating housing and industry close to major radial communications both people and firms are able to benefit.

The other arguments in favour of a sector strategy include the possibility of more easily preserving wide tracts of unspoilt countryside, and the ease with which this strategy may be grafted onto the older counter-magnet proposals. Thus three of the Council's four major growth sectors led to counter-magnet cities proposed in the *South-East Study*. One ran southwest to Southampton-Portsmouth; another followed the M1 northwest to Milton Keynes (the new city in the Bletchley area); a third led northeast to Ipswich; and the fourth ran southeast to Canterbury. Minor growth sectors—to Swindon, Peterborough, Southend and Ashford—paralleled each major sector and a fifth, isolated, minor sector led to Brighton.

What concrete results have so far emerged from this succession of alternative South East planning strategies? One of the most important has been the government's acceptance of a modified form of counter-magnet strategy, based on the thinking of the South East Study. The most dramatic decision here was the designation (in 1967) of a site at Milton Keynes in Buckinghamshire (see Figure 9) for a wholly new city of 250 thousand people. The design team's 1970 masterplan anticipates that three-fifths of these will come from London, as will the city's manufacturing industry. The site already houses 40 thousand people, in settlements such as Bletchley and Wolverton, and contains the headquarters of the Open University. In addition, designation orders have been made (and plans drawn up) for major overspill expansions at Swindon, Northampton and Peterborough, each of which will eventually have populations of over 200 thousand. The last two have been designated official new towns under the New Towns Act 1965.

On the other hand, the idea of major planned overspill expansion at Newbury, Ashford and Stansted, and most recently in the Ipswich and Southampton-Portsmouth areas, has been abandoned. Strong local opposition partly accounts for these decisions. But a major factor is also the need to cut back public investment generally, for national economic reasons, coupled with a realization of the massive strain which an acceptance of all the South East Study's proposals would have placed upon the existing machinery for South East overspill. A downward revision of estimates concerning the magnitude of overspill facilities required—such as those produced by the Greater London Council—has also played its part in the government's decisions. In the case of South Hampshire, however, a feasibility study by Professor Buchanan (1966) of new city development has led to the establishment of a special local planning unit to cope with the area's considerable anticipated natural growth.

The other major result of the controversy over the best strategy for South East planning was the establishment in 1968 of an entirely new South East Joint Planning Team, specifically to review the alternatives available and to produce its own proposals. This team, the most authoritative body ever to study the planning problems of any British region, and made up of over fifty specialists and planners recruited from government departments, the Planning Council and the Standing Conference, published its *Strategic Plan for the South East* in July 1970.

Rightly arguing that existing local authority plans and government commitments to new and expanded towns will largely determine the regional pattern of population and

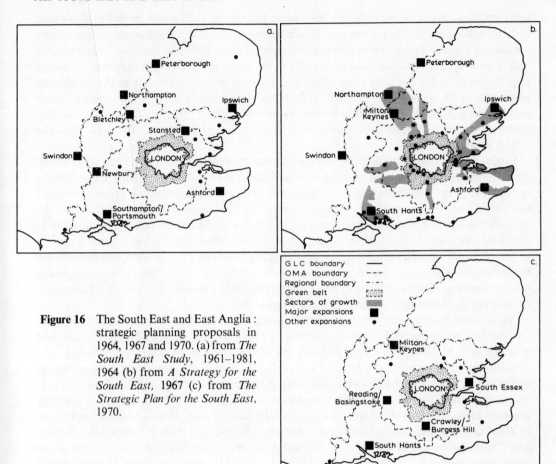

Figure 16 The South East and East Anglia :
strategic planning proposals in
1964, 1967 and 1970. (a) from *The
South East Study*, *1961–1981,
1964* (b) from *A Strategy for the
South East,* 1967 (c) from *The
Strategic Plan for the South East,*
1970.

employment change up to about 1981, the team confined its evaluation of alternative
long term planning strategies mainly to the period 1981 to 2001. By the latter year, the
South East's population may have grown by about 4.5 million from its 1966 level, to a
total of 21.5 millions. The two hypothetical strategies selected for detailed evaluation
by the team deliberately differed in important ways. The first—the 1991A strategy—was
based on the South East Economic Planning Council's sectoral approach, and assumed
the stabilization of London's population at about 7.3 million people, the concentration
of as much regional population and employment growth as possible in new cities and

large counter-magnet developments located in the O.S.E. well away from London (such as Milton Keynes/Northampton and South Hampshire), and the accommodation of any remaining growth in sectors following communications between these counter-magnets and London. The second strategy—1991B—in contrast envisaged a lower eventual population total for London (7 million), and a much greater emphasis in the geography of growth upon areas relatively close to London within the O.M.A. (such as south Essex and Reading/Aldershot). The 1991B strategy thus paid much greater attention to existing, 'natural' trends in population growth, which favour areas closer to London, than the 1991A strategy.

Evaluation of these alternatives was carried out in terms of criteria already determined from detailed study of planning problems and natural trends in the South East. Among the most important of these criteria were the desirability of concentrating growth, whether located in the O.S.E. or O.M.A., into a relatively few large urbanized centres for the sorts of reasons discussed earlier (see pp. 137ff); an emphasis on feasibility, notably in terms of the ease of attracting manufacturing and office employment from London, at the required rate of perhaps 15 to 20 thousand jobs per year in both categories; and the particular need to improve job opportunities, housing and social facilities for lower income families, especially those at present living in inner London. The team's recommended strategy is shown diagrammatically in Figure 16c.

As is immediately clear, this strategy is a blend of the two alternatives considered. Of the five major growth centres proposed, two—Milton Keynes/Northampton and South Hampshire (with eventual populations of 0.8 and 1.4 millions, respectively)—are 'traditional' counter-magnets, located in the O.S.E., while the others—Reading/Basingstoke, South Essex and the Crawley area (with eventual populations of 1.2, 1.0 and 0.5 millions, respectively)—are in the O.M.A. and close to London. Of the less important medium growth areas, three—Ashford, Eastbourne/Hastings and Bournemouth/Poole—are in the O.S.E., while four—Maidstone/Medway, Aylesbury, Bishop's Stortford/Harlow and Chelmsford—are in the O.M.A. Growth centres are thus located in all sectors of the South East, and at a variety of distances from London. However, in terms of their general balance, and compared with those of the *South East Study* and *Strategy,* these proposals do imply a significant shift away from a policy of long-distance transfers of London population and industry to the peripheries of the region, in favour of a more flexible plan catering for considerable but still nucleated growth closer to the metropolis. This shift seems to stem from an awareness of the strength of natural trends, of the limited distances over which many London manufacturing and office firms are prepared to move, and of the social and economic advantages, especially for lower income families, of planned growth close to the capital. The urgent need for redevelopment and rehabilitation in inner London, and recent population trends, also lead the team to anticipate an eventual metropolitan population of only about 7 million inhabitants.

The *Strategic Plan for the South East* thus eschews the drama of counter-magnets or growth sectors in favour of a more varied, pragmatic and perhaps realistic approach than earlier planning studies. Although certain aspects are open to criticism (Keeble 1971), the plan on the whole provides a flexible and appropriate framework within which to shape the future human geography of the region. Not surprisingly, therefore, it was approved by the Government in October 1971 with only minor modifications (such as the abandonment of the Bishop's Stortford/Harlow medium-growth area). Its significance for the South East England of 2000 A.D. may well therefore be as considerable as that of its great predecessor, the Abercrombie Plan, for the South East England of the nineteen seventies.

REFERENCES :

Abercrombie, P. (1945). *Greater London Plan* 1944, H.M.S.O., London.
Brown, A. J. (1968). Regional Problems and Regional Policy. *National Institute Economic Review*, **46**, 42–51.
Brown, C. M. (1966). Living and working in the New Towns. *Town and Country Planning*, **34**, 53–57.
Buchanan, C. (1966). *South Hampshire Study : Report on the Feasibility of Major Urban Growth*, 3 Vols., H.M.S.O., London.
Buswell, R. J. and Lewis, E. W. (1970). The Geographical Distribution of Industrial Research Activity in the United Kingdom. *Regional Studies*, **4**, 297–306.
Cambridgeshire County Planning Department (1965). *First Review of the County Development Plan : Report of Survey*, Cambridgeshire County Council, Cambridge.
Clark, C. (1966). Industrial Location and Economic Potential. *Lloyds Bank Review*, **82**, 1–17.
Daniels, P. W. (1969). Office Decentralization from London—Policy and Practice. *Regional Studies*, **3**, 171–178.
Davies, W. K. D. and Robinson, G. W. S. (1968). The Nodal Structure of the Solent Region. *Journal of the Town Planning Institute*, **54**, 18–22.
Department of Scientific and Industrial Research (1958). *Estimates of Resources Devoted to Scientific and Engineering Research and Development in British Manufacturing Industry*, 1955, H.M.S.O., London. (cited by R. C. Estall and R. O. Buchanan (1966). *Industrial Activity and Economic Geography*, Hutchinson, London. pp. 101–103).
Dunning, J. H. (1969). The City of London : a Case Study in Urban Economics. *Town Planning Review*, **40**, 207–232.
East Anglia Economic Planning Council (1968). *East Anglia : A Study*, H.M.S.O., London.
Evans, A. W. (1967). Myths about Employment in Central London. *Journal of Transport Economics and Policy*, **1**, 214–225.
Greater London Council (1969). *Greater London Development Plan : Report of Studies*, G.L.C., London.
Hagerstrand, T. (1968). Diffusion : The Diffusion of Innovations. In D. L. Sills (Ed.), *International Encyclopedia of the Social Sciences*, *Vol.* 4, Macmillan, London. pp. 174–178.
Hall, P. (1969). *London* 2000, 2nd Edition, Faber and Faber, London.
Hall, P. G. (1962). *The Industries of London since* 1861, Hutchinson, London.
Hammond, E. L. P. (1964). The Main Provincial Towns as Commercial Centres. *Urban Studies*, **1**, 129–137.
Heraud, E. J. (1968). Social Class and the New Towns. *Urban Studies*, **5**, 33–58.
Howard, R. S. (1968). *The Movement of Manufacturing Industry in the United Kingdom* 1945–1965, H.M.S.O., for the Board of Trade, London.
Jones, E. and Sinclair, D. J. (1968). *Atlas of London and the London Region*, Pergamon, Oxford.

Keeble, D. E. (1968). Industrial Decentralization and the Metropolis : the North-West London Case. *Transactions of the Institute of British Geographers*, **44,** 1–54.

Keeble, D. E. (1969). The Proper Place for Industry. *Geographical Magazine*, **41,** 844–855.

Keeble, D. E. (1971). Planning and South East England, *Area*, **3,** 69–74.

Keeble, D. E. and Hauser, D. P. (1971). Spatial analysis of manufacturing growth in Outer South East England 1960–1967. I. Hypotheses and variables. *Regional Studies*, **5,** 229–262.

Martin, J. E. (1964). The Industrial Geography of Greater London. In R. Clayton (Ed.), *The Geography of Greater London*, George Philip, London. pp. 111–142.

Martin, J. E. (1966). *Greater London : an Industrial Geography*, Bell, London.

Ministry of Housing and Local Government (1964). *The South East Study*, 1961–1981, H.M.S.O., London.

Myrdal, F. (1957). *Economic Theory and Under-Developed Regions*, Duckworth, London. (For a discussion of Myrdal's ideas in relation to growth centres such as London, see D. E. Keeble (1967). Models of Economic Development. In R. J. Chorley and P. Haggett (Eds.), *Models in Geography*, Methuen, London, Chap. 8).

South East Economic Planning Council (1967). *A Strategy for the South East*, H.M.S.O., London.

South East Joint Planning Team (1970). *Strategic Plan for the South East*, H.M.S.O., London.

Thomas, D. (1970). *London's Green Belt*, Faber and Faber, London.

Thomas, R. (1969). London's New Towns : a study of self-contained and balanced communities. *Planning*, **35,** 373–473.

CHAPTER 4

The East Midlands

Kenneth Warren

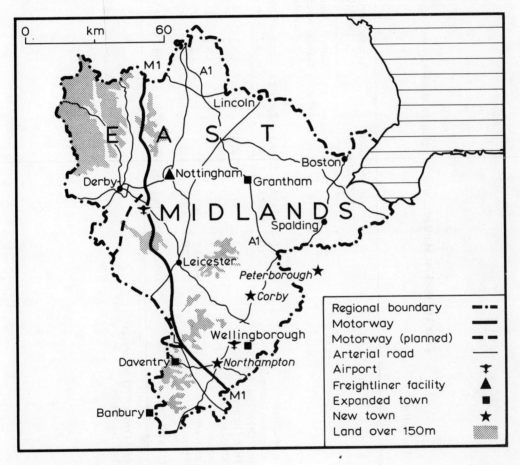

Figure 17 The East Midlands: location map.

Table 11. The East Midlands: selected regional and sub-regional indicators

A. Population

Thousands

	Mid-year estimated home population				Average annual change 1961–1966			Average annual change 1951–1961		
	1971[1]	1966[2]	1961[2]	1951[2]	Natural change	Armed forces change	Net migration	Natural change	Armed forces change	Net migration
East Midlands	3,385.8	3,298.6	3,139.3	2,913.3	+23.7	−0.4	+8.7	+16.0	+1.5	+3.9
Nottingham/Derbyshire	1,773.0	1,782.9	1,704.1	1,587.1	+12.7	—	+3.1	+9.0	+0.6	+0.8
Notts./Derby coal-field and High Derbyshire	754.2	780.2	744.3	689.6	+5.2	—	+2.1	+4.0	+0.3	−0.1
Nottingham-Derby	1,018.9	1,002.7	959.8	897.5	+7.5	—	+1.1	+5.0	+0.3	+0.9
Leicester	740.7	692.0	657.1	610.4	+5.3	−0.1	+1.9	+3.2	+0.4	+1.1
Eastern Lowlands	404.2	393.0	377.6	355.5	+2.6	−0.1	+0.7	+2.0	+0.1	+0.1
Northampton	467.8	430.8	400.4	360.2	+3.1	−0.2	+3.1	+1.8	+0.4	+1.8
BRITAIN	53,821.4	53,176.1	51,380.0	48,917.5	+328.2	−0.5	+22.6	+231.4	+12.9	+1.9

1. 1971 Census; 1971 boundaries.
2. 1966 boundaries.

B. Employment

	Employment		Male employment		Proportion of women at work		Unemployment range		
	1966	Change 1961–1966	1966	Change 1961–1966	1966	Change in % 1961–1966	1968	1967	1961–1966
	'000s	%	'000s	%	%	%	%	%	%
East Midlands	1,440	+6	930	+4	40	+2	1–2	1–2	1–2
Nottingham/Derbyshire	760	+6	500	+4	38	+2	2–3	1–2	1–2
Leicester	340	+5	210	+5	47	+1	1–2	1–2	0–1
Eastern Lowlands	160	+4	100	Nil	36	+2	2–3	2–3	1–2
Northampton	180	+7	110	+5	40	+2	1–2	1–2	0–1
BRITAIN	23,550	+4	14,900	+2	40	+2	2–3	2–3	1–2

C. Industrial Development Certificates

	Estimated additional employment from i.d.c. approvals			
	Total	Annual averages		
	1956–1967 '000s	1964–1967 '000s	1960–1963 '000s	1956–1959 '000s
East Midlands	53.1	4.3	4.6	4.4
Nottingham/Derbyshire	25.2	1.8	1.9	2.6
Leicester	9.7	0.8	0.9	0.7
Eastern Lowlands	4.7	0.6	0.5	0.2
Northampton	13.5	1.1	1.4	0.9
BRITAIN	1,245.2	121.8	108.1	81.2

4.1 Introduction

To the traveller the East Midlands frequently seems to be only an amorphous zone of passage to areas of more definite regional personality. Mining is widespread but until recently has faced no problems as acute as those in the Development Areas; industrial prosperity here is the result of activities whose expression in the landscape is less impressive than that of shipyards, textile mills, oil refineries or steelworks; and the region's affluence has not yet been accompanied by either the congestion or the spectacular public works which this has demanded in the South East or in parts of the West Midlands. Nevertheless, the region has one characteristic which has been recognized by nearly all commentators, namely, that it is an area whose economic potentials are undeniably greater than any past achievement. Twenty years ago, a careful assessment led to the conclusion that here was '. . . a case for planned development under relatively favourable conditions' (Edwards, 1949); the 1966 *East Midlands Study* was prefaced by remarks about prosperity and regional potential; and the Economic Planning Council's second report in 1969 was boldly titled *Opportunity in the East Midlands*. Before the possibilities of realizing these potentials are assessed, however, it is important to consider the nature and the extent of the region.

The East Midlands is not a formal region, but rather an area for descriptive or planning convenience. In the north east, there is a tract of generally low-lying, sparsely populated and rural land. The Lincoln Edge separates this area from the Trent Lowlands which contain (or are fringed by) larger agglomerations of people, and where the existence of major lines of national communication, nearness to coal and to major conurbations have caused the growth of a larger urban and industrial population. The Edge widens south of Grantham into a broad upland covering most of Northamptonshire and Leicestershire, where agriculture still dominates the landscape. However there are also some big towns and in parts—especially in the Northampton, Kettering, Wellingborough area and in west Leicestershire—the spread of the boot and shoe and hosiery industries has built up larger, industrialized villages. Within the broad arc of the Trent is the densely populated zone of the East Midland coal-field, which has a small outlier straddling the Derbyshire-Leicestershire border in two basins east and west of Ashby. The main coal-field has already an associated loose conurbation dominated by the urban growth centred on Nottingham and Derby; it houses just one million people at the southern end, and part of the bigger Chesterfield-Sheffield-Rotherham agglomeration spreads over its northern parts. In the centre of the arc traced by the Trent, the land rises to the high limestone core of the Peak District with its pasture, rough grazing, small population and high recreational importance.

Functionally, these several contrasting components of the East Midlands group into a somewhat tenuous regional entity. There is no outstanding regional focus like Manchester, Newcastle or Norwich. Nottingham approaches nearest to this preeminence, but Leicester provides scarcely inferior service functions—and certainly has ambitions not one whit less. As a result, Lincoln folk travel with a good deal of impartiality for higher quality shopping to both these centres and in some cases to Sheffield (outside the region and part of Yorkshire and Humberside) as well. Similarly, in the south west of the region, Birmingham is tending to exert an ever-stronger pull upon higher order retail activities, and in the south the electrified London-Midland line now affords a remarkably convenient access to London. The characteristics of a region of convenience are more amply demonstrated through a glimpse at the East Midlands' boundaries (see Figure 17).

When the economic planning regions were being delineated it was made clear by the Secretary of State for Economic Affairs that county boundaries would be used in all but exceptional cases, in order to facilitate the provision of statistics. In many instances this has split urban centres from their hinterlands, and divided distinctive economic sub-regions. The East Midlands has a substantial share of such cases. In the southeast, for example, lies the Soke of Peterborough which Edwards in 1949 included within the East Midlands. Thereafter, however, Peterborough and Ely began to cooperate closely with the counties of Huntingdonshire and Cambridgeshire, a development essential for a more efficient administration of their combined population of well under 500,000. Partly for this reason, Peterborough was excluded from the new East Midlands region of the Department of Economic Affairs in 1965, and included in East Anglia; it was a decision which was subsequently confirmed by the Report of the Royal Commission on Local Government in England (1969), under the chairmanship of Lord Redcliffe-Maud, which proposed that Peterborough and a large additional part of the Holland Fens should be included within its proposed East Anglia province. Meanwhile, Peterborough had been designated as an overspill 'city' for the South East region, a development which will undoubtedly have a considerable impact upon the East Midlands, for already there is a substantial journey to work in the borough from as far north as Bourne.

Similarly, although it has traditionally had strong links with major East Midlands' communities, Northamptonshire had begun to benefit from the overspill proposals of the *South East Strategy* (see pp. 148–151), the county town being designated for major expansion during the nineteen seventies. Responding to this new emphasis in its regional affiliations, the Maud Report recommended the transfer of the whole county to the South East province. The East Midlands' southwestern boundary presents similar problems of delimitation. Coventry, understandably, has always been excluded from all definitions of the East Midlands, although there is a marked two-way flow of commuters across the regional boundary between it and Leicester, 40 kilometres (24 miles) away. Already, the East Midlands Economic Planning Council has noted that the relations of Hinckley and its associated communities with Nuneaton, Coventry and the West Midlands are hardly less than with Leicester and the East Midlands, and these will certainly be increased if the proposed motorway link from Tewkesbury via the West Midlands and Hinckley to Enderby (to the southwest of Leicester and on the M1) is ever built.

Burton-on-Trent is excluded from the East Midlands region as a result of the decision to adhere to quirks of ancient county boundaries. In its submission to the Maud Commission, the county borough suggested that a future association with neighbouring areas in Staffordshire and with Swadlincote in south Derbyshire, together with the accep-tance of overspill from the West Midlands, might create a unit of 200,000, '. . . to form a cohesive, sound area of local government standing free from and complementary to the nearest large centres of Derby, Nottingham and Leicester'; Maud chose instead to suggest a link with Derby. As one makes the short journey between Derby and Burton-on-Trent, the artificiality of any boundaries in such a closely knit economic complex as the Midlands is brought home. The traveller notes the relationship between Rolls Royce in Derby and Pirelli tyres in Burton, and remembers the widespread effect on West Midland suppliers of Rolls Royce's financial troubles early in 1971. He might also recall the common owner-ship of—and the considerable linkages between—Raleigh of Nottingham and all the other leading cycle firms in the West Midlands, and then the component and foundry links which also tie the fortunes of firms in Leicester and Northamptonshire with the Birmingham and Coventry motor industry assembly lines. East Midland coal and electricity, generated on Trentside, continue to power much of the industry in the West Midlands conurbation, as well as that of the South East; whilst in the West Midlands there originates a large share of the problem of polluted Trent waters which troubles the planners not only within the East Midlands region, but also in Yorkshire and Humberside. Interregional recrea-tional linkages are no less strong. In the open spaces of the Peak District, weekend motorists and youth hostellers from Birmingham, Manchester and Sheffield, as well as the East Midlands, share the enjoyment of a National Park which falls across two of the country's planning regions.

The northern boundary of the East Midlands region poses problems of no smaller magnitude. In the Chesterfield-Sheffield district, despite the belated designation of an intervening green belt, the selection of a satisfactory line is impossible as a consequence of earlier conurbation sprawl. The 1965 choice of the Department of Economic Affairs, which made use of an old county boundary, however, is possibly one of the least acceptable solutions, since the continuously built up area of Sheffield extends somewhat beyond it. East of the Trent, on the other hand, the Department's boundary between the East Mid-lands and Yorkshire and Humberside signified an important regional planning decision. Until this time, south Humberside had always been part of the East Midlands. The decision that the prospect of estuary-based development justified the inclusion of Lindsey in the Yorkshire and Humberside region was inevitably challenged by many in the East Midlands. Certainly today south Lindsey looks towards Lincoln and the East Midlands, rather than northwards, for many of its middle and higher-order services. Skegness and its seaside neighbours have been largely developed with Nottingham or Leicester capital, and cater primarily for East Midland visitors; and in winter Skegness folk make their more special shopping trips to Boston or Lincoln, not to Grimsby. In this regard, the Maud Commission suggested a reasonable amendment. It proposed the retention of the local authorities immediately adjacent to the estuary within the Yorkshire and Humberside region; but advised the transfer of south Lindsey—which is still overwhelmingly rural—to the East Midlands province in the form of a new Lincoln and Lincolnshire authority.

As a consequence of these and other boundary changes the economically buoyant yet amorphous region of the East Midlands has tended to be defined as a progressively smaller area during the last twenty years (Table 12). Whilst the significance of these changes and the difficulties of regional delimitation must be taken into account, the East Midlands region which is examined below is essentially that defined by the Department of Economic Affairs in 1965.

Table 12. Concepts of the East Midlands

Concepts of the East Midlands	Area		Population (millions) and year
	square kilometres	(square miles)	
K. C. Edwards (1949)	16,835	(6,500)	3.2 (1946)
Department of Economic Affairs (1965)	12,201	(4,711)	3.2 (1965)
Maud Commission (1969)	11,847	(4,574)	3.0 (1968)

Viewed from a national standpoint, the region occupies a middle position—in situation, in wealth and in economic growth. Main railway lines, motorways and trunk roads run through it, or fringe its southwestern edge, as they link London with the West Midlands, the North and the North West. The region is prosperous, but until 1970 it ranked below the West Midlands and still more below the South East in most indicators of prosperity. The proximity of both these regions with their problems, congestion, and rapid development, with tight controls on their industrial building and—between 1966 and 1970—on office development as well, has undoubtedly stimulated economic growth in the East Midlands in recent decades. Overspill manufacturing industry moved into the area on a large scale in the nineteen fifties and sixties. More recently there has been a considerable spurt in office building. Between 1964 and 1969 the increase in office floor space was only 10 per cent less than in the West Midlands, where the existing accommodation was twice as large and the population is almost double.

Over a longer period, 1953 to 1963, employment in manufacturing industry in the East Midlands went up by 45,000—whereas in the four planning regions lying to the north there was a 142,000 decline in the manufacturing work force. Total employment in industries and services increased by only 15,000 less than that in the combined North West, Northern, Scottish and Welsh regions, whose workforce in 1953 was almost six times as big. In new industry as opposed to net growth, the performance has been less impressive, for more of the old industrial structure has been preserved here. The East Midlands had 6.6 per cent of the manufacturing labour force of Britain in 1953, but industrial development certificates granted between 1956 and 1967 were expected to provide additional employment amounting to no more than 4.2 per cent of the national total; it is well to remember that workforce estimates by firms applying for an industrial development certificate are generally pitched low outside the Development Areas. At the same time, it should be noted that the region in the past has been a major generator of what is now, fashionably, called 'mobile' industry, suitable for diversion to the Development Areas (Table 13). In spite of the very large increase in Development Area assistance since 1966, however, there is no evidence to suggest that the East Midlands as a whole is being injured by these policies. Even by the early seventies, the considered opinion of those closely identified with economic planning in the region confirmed this view.

Table 13. Movements of industrial firms and employment from and to the East Midlands and other regions, 1945–1965

	To other regions		From other regions	
	Number of moves, 1945–65	Employment at end of 1966 ('000s)	Number of moves, 1945–65	Employment at end of 1966 ('000s)
East Midlands	128	31.0	106	26.9
West Midlands	215	92.6	58	8.7
South East	732	221.0	104	31.6
Yorkshire and Humberside	138	43.0	112	31.3

Source : Howard (1968).

The latest figures, those of the 10 per cent Sample Census in 1966, show that the East Midlands is in the remarkable position of being an area of net inward migration from every other economic planning region in Britain. Its 1965–1966 net gain by migration was 11.7 thousand. By 1971 its population had reached nearly 3.4 millions, which represented one of the fastest regional rates of growth since 1951 (see Table 1).

4.2 The Eastern Lowlands

While buoyancy and expansion is the keynote of the East Midlands, the region is not without its problem industries and areas. The largest section of slow overall growth is the subdivision described by the Economic Planning Council as the Eastern Lowlands. The area includes much of High Leicestershire lying beyond the labour hinterland of Leicester, Rutland and the Kesteven and Holland divisions of Lincolnshire (see Figure 18). The sub-region has almost one third of the total area of the East Midlands, but in 1951 its share of population was only 12 per cent. Over the next twenty years, population growth was just under 10 per cent of the regional figure. This situation is not the result of economic decline, but of the rationalization of activity in what is generally a highly efficient and prosperous agriculture. In 1963 only 3.1 per cent of the East Midlands labour force was in agriculture, forestry and fishing (overwhelmingly in the first) but in the Eastern Lowlands the proportion was 15.4 per cent. The sub-region includes almost half of the Fenland, the fine corn growing soils derived from limestone on the Lincoln Edge, and the grassland of mixed but generally good quality on the drift soils of High Leicester-shire. There is much evidence of agricultural wealth and in some cases—particularly in the Fens—an impressive business organization. However, between 1959 and 1963 the farm labour force in the Eastern Lowlands fell by 15 per cent and further contraction is inevitable. Other activities are poorly represented in the sub-region as a whole. *The East Midlands Study* (1966) listed 12 categories of industrial employment for the Nottingham-shire/Derbyshire sub-region, but in the Eastern Lowlands only three were big enough to justify examination. Almost one-fifth of industrial employment was in the 'food, drink and tobacco' industries, largely concerned with the processing of agricultural products. Nearly 15 per cent of employment is in distribution, compared with 10.5 per cent in the Nottinghamshire/Derbyshire or Leicester sub-regions—and the Eastern Lowlands' percentage indicates a less economic rather than a fuller provision of services.

On the western edge of the limestone uplands, Lincoln and Grantham are important foci of manufacturing activities; but, to the east, the sub-region is even more heavily dependent on primary activities. The North and West Kesteven rural districts (tributary to Lincoln and Grantham respectively) had 9.0 per cent and 17.0 per cent of their work force in farming in 1966. Although this was high compared with the national figure of 3.2 per cent, in the rural districts of East and South Kesteven the proportion rose to 27 per cent. Economic growth in the recent past was—and in the future is likely to be—closely related to proximity to the larger centres fringing the sub-region. Although the population of Lincoln rose only 7.4 per cent between 1951 and 1966, in North Kesteven rural district (which supplied almost all of the 7,000 who commuted from Kesteven to Lincoln in 1966) there was a 33.2 per cent rise. Even from Boston, which is less than one-third the size of Lincoln, there has been a growth of population outwards from the borough into the Boston rural district. In the south, Bourne and Stamford have both grown as a result of the extension of the Peterborough commuting zone—and in part also because of an overspill of some of its industrial activities. For Stamford, this was a major cause of the 33 per cent increase in the borough's population between 1951 and 1971. Even in rural South Kesteven, the area of depopulation has been shrinking as an increasingly mobile industrial population in the sub-region seeks a rural home. The expected increase in the population of Peterborough from 81,000 in 1966 to 164,000 by 1981 will intensify this effect, for plans exist to create a further 50,000 jobs there between 1971 and 1985. Away from these fringe area growth points, however, the declining agricultural employ-ment has not been fully replaced and population has stagnated or fallen. Sleaford, for example, grew by only 2.6 per cent between 1951 and 1966; the population of the East

Kesteven rural district fell by 4.6 per cent, and that of the East Elloe rural district by 7.2 per cent. The threatened withdrawal of rail passenger services is likely to hinder any adjustment to this decline in the agricultural workforce (East Midlands Economic Planning Council, 1969, para. 107; Kesteven County Planning Dept., 1969).

The deep countryside of the eastern half of the Eastern Lowlands sub-region presents special problems, and ones which regional planning in Britain seems ill-equipped to tackle. The Economic Planning Council and Board in Nottingham are naturally preoccupied with the problems of the industrial and urban communities nearer at hand, with guiding burgeoning new conurbations, and dealing with the problems of mine redundancy. There has as a consequence been something of a failure to appreciate the peculiar difficulties of a rural area. This may be illustrated by a local study which the Nottingham headquarters has now set in hand. In reaction to complaints by the rural areas that they were being neglected, a study of part of the Holland Fens has been commissioned; yet to the consternation of less well-endowed Eastern Lowland communities, this was characterized as an analysis of a 'typical' rural area. As an exasperated local planner concisely put it, 'How can an area, in which farmers drive to their fields in Rolls Royce cars, be fairly labelled typical?' In their turn, of course, the remoter agricultural sections of the Eastern Lowlands seem to wish to preserve as much as possible of their past independence, and to turn their backs on the problems of the bulk of the East Midlands population. This attitude is clearly demonstrated in the evidence submitted by the County of Holland to the Maud Commission. 'In an area of evenly spaced rural population with no big towns and no big industries other than intensive farming and horticulture on the most productive land in the country, and ancillaries such as canning and sugar manufacture, there would appear to be no advantage in altering the present system of local government which, with the aid of grants from central government funds, is able to and does provide all necessary modern services, and with a truly local control which is treasured by the countryman. From afar one hears of a crisis in local government and of the frustrations of the present system, expressions which have no meaning in an area the modernization of which consists only in improvements in scientific farming methods, the redevelopment of parts of the centres of small county towns, the provision of up-to-date public services and the introduction of urban amenities such as sewerage for the larger townships' (Royal Commission on Local Government in England, 1968, p. 187).

The Wash has great potential importance as a source of water for the industry and urban population of both South East England—where water demand is expected to double by the year 2000—and the East Midlands. The East Midlands Planning Council has recognized the possible importance of a Wash barrage and of the need for cooperation with the East Anglia Economic Planning Council which this will involve. In 1968 the Water Resources Board announced a £25,000 study of the feasibility of a Wash reservoir. Given the contemporary vogue for postulating rapid industrial and urban development on estuarine sites, it is understandable that some have thought it desirable to add to this water scheme a vision of a Wash City of ¾ million—built upon reclaimed land, and with a deep water 'British Europoort', a national freight airport, and an extensive industrial area. The architect originator of the scheme, Teggin (1969), has based his proposal on the observation that '. . . the Wash is the (one) area on the east coast which is at present under-developed, underpopulated and unexploited'. But, apart from the suggestion that it has the advantage of being near enough to London to relieve certain development pressures there, the idea seems to be another example of the absence from so many planning proposals of a spatial perspective which would recognize the superior advantages of, and the substantial groundwork already laid on, Humberside or Teesside. The prescription 'if there is an estuary, develop it' is grossly inadequate in a country where the number of estuaries physically suitable for large scale industrial development is considerable, and when the costs involved—an estimated investment of £1,000 million over a thirty year period in the case of the Wash—are so high. In May 1969, the Chairman of the East Midlands Economic Planning Council concluded 'We can see at present no case for a major Wash City, first class port or industrial centre'.

In 1951 the County Borough of Lincoln and North Kesteven rural district, much of which was within the city's commuting hinterland, had 30.4 per cent of the population of the Eastern Lowlands sub-region. Between 1955 and 1968, the sub-division had an estimated population growth of 43.1 thousand, of which 19.5 thousand (or 45.2 per cent) was in the County Borough and the neighbouring rural district. Lincoln has traditionally been dependent on heavy engineering. Its two chief companies, which are closely associated, employ 11,500 workers, a large number for a city of only 76,000. Over the last decade, however, new, lighter electronics manufacture has developed, although the merger between the General Electric Company and Associated Electrical Industries in 1969 is a possible threat to some of this employment. Having a rather poorly developed central shopping area, Lincoln as yet does not perform adequately the service functions for which its location fits it. Although the increase in shopping floor space during the nineteen sixties has been proportionately much greater than in Derby or Leicester, city planning estimates suggest that there is a 'leakage' of the order of £10,000 each week to the shops of Nottingham (*Times Review of Industry and Technology*, 1967).

The long term prospect for economic growth in the Lincoln area is good despite the fact that by 1970/1971 rationalization and recession in heavy engineering were causing higher unemployment. With easy access to the A1 trunk road, it is well placed in relation to national markets. The construction of the Humber bridge by 1976, the development of better approach roads and further economic growth on Humberside (see pp. 351ff). together will widen Lincoln's market area, and there is a fair prospect of the city receiving a growing amount of overspill employment from the more congested parts of the country. The Lincoln 'district', which includes the centre's commuting zone, is already estimated to contain 120,000 people, and local planners have suggested the possibility of an increase of 50,000 before 1981, followed by rather slower growth. The Maud Commission proposed a Lincoln and Lincolnshire authority (which would cover the centre of the present county), and postulated a smaller though still significant increase in population. Their figure was a growth of 51,000 between 1968 and 1981 throughout this larger area—some 18,000 more than that proposed for the neighbouring Nottingham and Nottinghamshire authority, whose 1968 population was half as large again (Royal Commission on Local Government in England, 1969; Grimsby Chamber of Commerce, 1969).

Grantham has grown more rapidly than the city of Lincoln, and in the 1966–1981 period is expected to expand from 25,000 to 36,000. Much of this will result from reception of London overspill, since its position in the rail and road network of England makes it an attractive location for new industry. There are, however, points of weakness in its situation. Overspill has so far proceeded only very slowly; and meanwhile the town is overdependent on two major heavy engineering firms. Already, in December 1968, reorganization within the English Electric Company resulted in the closure of a third major employer, the works of Alfred Wiseman which had employed some 400 people. And for the economic growth prospectively to be captured by the eastern part of the planning region there will be many competitors. Some of them such as Peterborough and Northampton are planning for major population expansion, and have obvious advantages over Grantham in seeking to attract new industry.

4.3 Northamptonshire

In the past, with its pasturelands, boot and shoe factories, ironworks and iron ore quarries, Northamptonshire was a closely identified part of the East Midlands. Now, new means of communication, the arrival of growth industries, and planned large influxes of overspill population—partly from the West Midlands but mainly from the South East—are changing its regional affiliations (see Figure 18). Functionally it is becoming an outlier of the South East. The Maud Report recognized this, and proposed its transfer to a new South East province, a suggestion which was received with dismay in Northamptonshire local government circles. Meanwhile, as the new links become stronger, some of the old staple trades are adjusting or disappearing.

Between 1960 and 1964, the annual output per worker in clothing and footwear nationally increased at a rate almost twice that of production. In footwear alone the difference was less marked. This welcome increase in productivity, however, has adversely affected the economy of some of Northamptonshire's highly specialized but small towns. In the south east, for example, the borough of Higham Ferrers and the urban districts of Rushden and Raunds have long concentrated on medium to low quality men's shoes and military footwear. Between 1951 and 1966 their combined population increased by only 8.4 per cent (2.1 thousand) whereas that of the county went up by 18.0 per cent. Whilst the important A6 trunk road passes through Higham Ferrers, the area is 24 kilometres (15 miles) from the M1 and almost as far from the A1; with possibilities of industrial development much nearer these major national arteries, the replacement of jobs lost in the footwear industry is unlikely to proceed swiftly.

Only ten years ago the night-time traveller by rail would still be surprised by the sight of the white runnels of iron being poured from the blast furnaces alongside the line north of Kettering; coming southwards, the much bigger works at Wellingborough towered away to his right until the mid nineteen sixties. But now they have closed. Other works at Cransley and Islip—and at Holwell near Melton Mowbray in Leicestershire—have also been demolished in the years since 1945. Although large extensions to the associated Northamptonshire iron ore workings took place in the nineteen fifties, there is now a steady contraction in this phase of the industry also. However, these changes have in general affected only small and scattered labour forces. The long term prospects for the integrated iron and steel works at Corby are far more important in a sub-regional economic sense.

The 37 year old plant at Corby is still wholly dependent upon ore worked within a few kilometres of the furnaces. This ore is becoming increasingly less economic to use as more favourably located plants smelt rich foreign ores or concentrates. There seems little likelihood of a precipitate writing down of the Corby plant; but major expansions are also improbable even though in 1970 expenditure of £4 million on new ironmaking plant was announced. Rationalization is likely to reduce still further the work force—by 1971 already reduced by 1,000. The original, single industry, boom town was designated a new town (in 1950) in order to ensure speedy yet planned development. Its 1951 population was only 16.7 thousand; by 1966 it was 43.7 thousand. Stewarts and Lloyds, then still a private steel concern, was at the time planning a substantial increase in capacity, so that the Development Corporation raised the town's target population, and the new Master Plan of 1967 looked to a 1981 population of 65,000. By 1971 the population of Corby was 10,000 below the target planned for that year in 1966. The present economy, and still more the future growth prospects of the town, are threatened by its extraordinarily high level of dependence upon the steelworks.

In 1964, when the population of the town was 43,000, Stewarts and Lloyds employed 12,400 at Corby—although many of them journeyed into it daily from communities some distance away. At this time twenty-one factories on two light industrial estates employed only 2,500 people—and these were mainly women. Since then, other firms have arrived, and in the summer of 1969 a Leicester hosiery concern announced plans for a Corby dye works which will eventually employ over 400 men. Twenty years ago, at a predesignation public meeting, the future Lord Silkin stated that he 'did not anticipate any difficulty in getting the necessary diversification' of employment. The planners, however, then failed to realise that possible newcomers would not like the predominating influence of the steel industry in the local labour market. There has also been a disturbingly rapid turnover in factory occupants on the industrial estates, and only two somewhat larger firms have proved reliable sources of employment. By the late nineteen sixties diversification was being frustrated by the refusal of the Department of Trade and Industry to grant industrial development certificates to firms wishing to move to Corby. The town is rather poorly provided with road transport facilities and it is still surrounded by much land badly scarred from iron ore working, even though active restoration is going on.

If the corporate planning decisions of the British Steel Corporation ultimately allocate to the Corby plant a role which implies a still more rapid contraction of its work force, the town will have some difficulty in attracting alternative employments against the pull of Northampton and Milton Keynes. On the other hand, it does offer some compensating advantages in the form of the vigour associated with an established and still rapidly growing new town, and the magnificent open country beyond the ore workings, particularly in the Welland Valley. And from the viewpoint of the British Steel Corporation, the problems of attracting new employment to Corby are small compared with the enormous difficulties in many other iron and steelmaking centres threatened with rationalization and even closure (Pocock, 1965).

Kettering has grown, and is expected to grow, only slowly. But elsewhere in the county, rapid expansion will in future be the leading theme. In the southwest, Daventry was a small town of only 4 thousand in 1951 and 6.6 thousand in 1966; now, with a town development scheme agreed with Birmingham, plans exist for it to rise to 36.6 thousand by 1981. However, not only does such a rate of growth clearly imply that the existing community will be swamped by an incoming culture group, but there are some doubts as to whether it can in fact be realized. By mid-1969 some hundreds of new homes in the Daventry area were tenantless as a result of the failure of manufacturing industry to disperse from the West Midland conurbation. Without a matching willingness on the part of industry, and perhaps some form of public financial inducement to movement there, the expansion programme is doomed. Overspill agreements between the Greater London Council and Wellingborough are already being put into effect. In this case, however, an even larger total expansion will not so completely overwhelm the indigenous population. In 1968 the Minister of Housing and Local Government accepted the suggestions of the planning consultants Wilson and Womersley for the reception of 70,000 Londoners in Northampton by 1981. By that time the town, which has already grown from its 105,000 of 1961, will be a city of some 220,000. The new city of Milton Keynes will be only 19 kilometres (12 miles) to the south, and the M1 runs through the country which separates them. Obviously, this area is prospectively a major pole of economic growth.

As in the recent past the various component parts of Northamptonshire are expected to grow at widely varying rates, the old boot and shoe centres of the Kettering-Higham Ferrers belt in the east-centre of the county being an area of especially slow growth. Between 1955 and 1965, the annual average increase of population for the county was 5,000; in the next three years it was 7,000. The changes planned for the period between 1968 and 1981 will require a growth of between 15,000 and 19,000 each year. As early as 1966, forecasts of the East Midlands Economic Planning Council suggested a growth rate for population in Northamptonshire about 150 per cent greater than for the planning region as a whole. The Report of the Royal Commission on Local Government in England (1969) provided a useful outside appraisal of growth prospects. For Northamptonshire it anticipated a 47.4 per cent increase in population between 1968 and 1981 (Table 14); for the four other proposed unitary authorities within the East Midlands it expected a

Table 14. Northamptonshire : recent and planned population growth, by districts, 1955, 1968 and 1981 (est.)

(thousands)

	1955	1968	1981 (target)*
Northamptonshire	373	445	697
Rural North East	21	22	34
Higham Ferrers, Raunds, Rushden	25	27	30
Kettering district	62	67	76
Corby	24	48	65
Wellingborough-Irthlingborough	48	55	120
Northampton district	143	162	258
South West	49	63	114

*NOTE : In many cases village figures represent the population which could be accommodated rather than a specific target : this affects the county total by perhaps 50,000.

Source : East Midlands Regional Development Conference, 1968.

combined growth rate as low as 11.7 per cent. This was the rationale for the recommended transfer of Northamptonshire to the outer belt of the more dynamic South East province, and even within that setting Northamptonshire's growth rate was expected to be one of the most rapid.

The Chairman of the Economic Planning Council has suggested that the East Midlands will have two conurbations of national significance by the end of the century, though both will be of a rather looser texture than the existing ones. To the southeast, the Northampton-Milton Keynes-Bedford-Wellingborough conurbation will straddle the existing planning region boundary. The 56 kilometres (35 miles) stretching northwards from Nottingham and Derby to Sheffield will form the second conurbation. The linkages which carry the latter conurbation further northeastwards to Doncaster and northwards to Leeds will clearly pose difficult problems of cooperation and coordination for the relevant planning authorities in both the East Midlands and in Yorkshire and Humberside.

4.4 Nottinghamshire and Derbyshire

In its 1966 regional study, the East Midlands Economic Planning Council expressed the fear that between then and the year 2000 urbanization between Nottingham and Sheffield would accelerate, and that a closely knit conurbation comparable to that of the West Midlands might emerge. The conclusion begged all the questions concerning the costs and benefits of concentrated urban growth. It also overlooked the wide variations in the economic status and the development prospects within the sub-region.

Within this area, Nottingham is the largest city and its capital by almost every criterion

(Figure 18). Old rivalries with Leicester do not seem to have been obtrusive since regional economic planning has been added to its many functions. Nottingham shares with Sheffield service functions required by the densely populated coal-field in between. The traditional trades of the city such as lace and hosiery have been joined by a host of new ones—including some for which the city seems to have no particular locational advantage, such as with those associated with the names of Raleigh, Players and Boots. Growth in these sectors meant that Nottingham was barely touched by the dilemmas and afflictions of the inter-war depression years and, like Leicester (though to a smaller extent) it was able to achieve a certain amount of urban renewal. The impressive Market Square and Council House date from that time. Between 1955 and 1968, the redevelopment of inner residential areas caused a decline of 7,000 (2.3 per cent) in the city's population, but this has been accompanied by impressive growth in the urban and rural districts on its fringes. The increase of population in Arnold, Beeston, Stapleford, Basford and Bingham alone was more than seven times the decline in the city. Although West Bridgford (south of the Trent) in evidence to the Maud Commission argued, by no means convincingly, that its links with Nottingham were growing weaker, a continuing outwards spread of housing and industry can reasonably be expected. Especially is this likely on the west side of Nottingham, which comprises part of a highly urbanized industrial belt stretching almost continuously to Derby—and now traversed by the M1.

Derby is a peculiar anomaly. Although only half the size of Nottingham, it attracted a net in-migration almost half as large again in the 19 years to 1965. It is a major national research and development centre, with key employments in the hands of British Rail and the Rolls Royce organization. The latter has dispersed many of its activities to other parts of Britain, but by the mid nineteen sixties the Derby aero engine division employed 20,000, some 40 per cent of whom were in research and development work. Inexplicably, the potentialilites for city growth, which this science and technology base might have been expected to generate, have demonstrably not been realized; there are extensive tracts of poor housing, and a general drabness within which is located a far from impressive central commercial district (*Times Review of Industry and Technology*, 1964). In 1971 the prolonged uncertainty following the financial collapse of Rolls Royce threatened to undermine the economy of the whole town.

Northwards from Nottingham, and straddling the border with Derbyshire, stretches the East Midlands coal-field. Its population lives in a wide scatter of mining villages or larger urban units linked by a dense network of twisting local roads. There is much low quality housing and the usual dereliction associated with mining is here (as in South Yorkshire) made worse by the large scale of the operations. Although they are set within an attractive natural environment, mining activities have made the landscape depressing over extensive tracts, and the descendants of the scenes which Lawrence pilloried have in some parts become more bizarre than anything he knew as a result of open cast workings. The major sub-divisions of the coal-field recognized by the East Midlands Economic Planning Council—the Erewash valley, Chesterfield, and the Mansfield-Worksop dis-

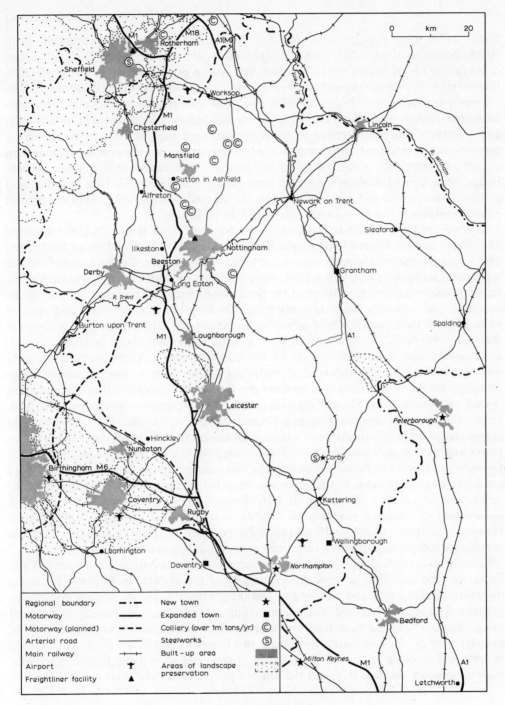

Figure 18 The East Midlands: principal economic and land use features, 1971.

tricts—had a 1965 population of 575,000. The largest centres are Chesterfield (with 70,000 people) and Mansfield (with 55,000); but north of Belper and Hucknall urban districts, there is one other urbanized authority with a population of more than 35,000, four others with over 20,000, and a further six with populations between 10,000 and 20,000.

Twenty-five years ago Fogarty (1945) described this area as a bridge between two economic regions—a southern one with hosiery and lace well represented in its activities, and a northern one characterized by the manufacture of tools and cutlery and marking the approach to Sheffield. These trades are still important, but the previously large iron industry survives only in the big works at Stanton. The furnaces at Clay Cross, Sheepbridge, Staveley and Renishaw have all been abandoned since 1957. Iron founding and pipework also remain and are more widespread. The basis of their past growth and present economic status is the most productive coal-field in Britain.

In 1966 the East Midlands Division of the National Coal Board (N.C.B.) operated 74 collieries and employed 85,000 people. These were mostly to be found in east Derbyshire and Nottinghamshire, although over one-seventh of the divisional output came from the separate Leicestershire and South Derbyshire fields. At a rough estimate, mining directly supports nearly half the population of the three sub-divisions which lie at the heart of the coal-field, and indirectly supports many more. The long-term future of this field appears to be brighter than that of almost any other in the country. Output per man is high—in the year 1966–1967, 562 tons of coal were won for each man above or below ground, as compared with a national average of 390 tons and even a Yorkshire figure of only 400 tons. Such a relatively high level of productivity stems from the development of major new pits—for example at Cotgrave, south of the Trent—and the application of automation —such as is found at the £18 million remote controlled Bevercotes colliery near Tuxford. In addition, as the Economic Planning Council has put it, the East Midlands coal-field has an annual 'in built' advantage of a large local market in the form of the string of major power stations set up along the river Trent during the last 20 years. 43 per cent of the Division's coal went to power stations in the mid nineteen sixties, and the 7,450 MW of capacity being constructed at that time was expected to approximately double the deliveries. One new station alone, that at Ratcliffe-on-Soar, was designed to consume five million tons of coal each year, and so to provide employment for some 10,000 miners. However, the future of the coal-field must also be assessed against a recognition of the new highly competitive situation in which the coal industry is now finding itself.

Existing national fuel policy, which was ushered in with the Minister of Power's White Papers of 1965 and 1967, accepts the sovereignty of the market. Its forecasts recognize the widening role for oil and natural gas, and the continuation of the nuclear power programme. The logic it exposed was a contracting role for the coal industry in national energy markets, and the need for a more open acknowledgement of cost factors in the industry. For the East Midlands this meant two things in particular. First, that changes in costs had to be more speedily reflected in prices—and so in 1969, following a major wage concession, the N.C.B. raised the pithead price of East Midlands coal for the first time since 1960. Second, that in the search for cost reductions the substitution of capital for labour must proceed apace, and the higher cost units would have to be phased out of production. In 1967, it was forecast by the Board that the labour force of the East Midlands division would fall by 40,000 in the eight years to 1975—and that there would be a further, though smaller concentration in the years after that.

This decline falls unevenly on the different parts of the coal-field, for the last decade has seen a general north eastwards drift in the centres of low cost production. In 1959, the 73 collieries at work in the East Derbyshire and Nottinghamshire coal-field produced 37.5 million tons; of this, about 57 per cent (20.6 million tons) came from the 41 collieries of the Alfreton, Ilkeston and Nottingham areas. In 1967, the output from 56 collieries in the whole field was 35.7 million tons; the Alfreton, Ilkeston and Nottingham areas had been reduced to 27 collieries, and they produced only 48 per cent (17.1 million tons) of the total. In the year ending March 1969 (after the boundaries of the East Midlands division of the N.C.B. had been changed to include the Warwickshire field, and the sub-divisions within the field had been changed also) the number of collieries fell from 49 to 42, but the decline was confined to two of the three sub-divisions. In that year, these two, North Derbyshire and South Nottinghamshire, even with five collieries producing over 1 million tons each, made a profit on each ton of saleable coal of only £0.004 and £0.037 respectively *before paying interest*. In North Nottinghamshire, on the other hand, with four units of a million tons/year (Figure 18), the profit was £0.379 per ton. It is clear that, of all the changes in prospect on the coal-field, those facing the communities of the Erewash valley along the Derbyshire-Nottinghamshire border are likely to be the most difficult.

Between 1958 and 1968, 16 out of the 18 pits in the Erewash Valley were closed. From 1951 to 1967, colliery employment there fell from 17,000 to 2,000 (Table 15). By 1969, male unemployment in Alfreton was at times over 9 per cent. The county councils and local authorities alike have long realized the urgent need for more diversification. Alfreton has been striving to widen its economic base with one industrial estate dating from 1949 and another from 1964 (in the latter case on the old Cotes Park Colliery site). As early

Table 15. East Midlands coal-field : population change in principal districts, 1955–1968

(thousands)

District	1955	1968
Erewash Valley	75.9	76.2
Chesterfield*	124.0	130.7
Mansfield-Worksop	236.2	256.3

*Districts are those of the East Midlands Study except Chesterfield where Dronfield U.D. and Chesterfield R.D. (affected by changes involving Sheffield) are excluded.

Source : General Register Office.

as 1963, a study undertaken for Derbyshire County Council recognized the suitability of Alfreton as a location for light manufacturing enterprise; and much progress has been made. The increase in manufacturing employment in the Alfreton-Heanor district between 1959 and 1963 was about 18 per cent (compared with 7.3 per cent for the East Midlands as a whole). However, a large part of this new work was for women—on the older Alfreton estate Aertex employs some 2,500 women—and manufacturing growth was more than matched by the rapid colliery run down. Industrial promotion has unfortunately been penalized initially by the lack of certainty that an industrial development certificate would be granted, and later by the absence of financial inducements comparable to those available in the Development Areas. Public improvements to the urban-industrial environment were also delayed because government grants to local authorities for reclamation stood for many years at only 50 per cent (compared with the Development Area rate of 85 per cent). However, in 1968, in the hope of a higher rate of central government support, Nottinghamshire and Derbyshire County Councils committed themselves to reclamation expenditures of £150,000 and £200,000 respectively over the following three years. That support was forthcoming in 1972 (see front end-paper).

In 1969, in spite of the Hunt Committee's recommendation to the contrary, the government gave Intermediate Area status to four exchange areas in the East Midlands coal-field. Worksop, in the northeast, is administered with the exchanges of the Yorkshire Intermediate Area; the Heanor, Alfreton and Sutton-in-Ashfield exchange areas constitute the Erewash Valley Intermediate Area. This assistance, plus the fact that almost all parts of the valley are within easy commuting distance of the large growth centres to north and south, should help revival. In the mid nineteen sixties, the construction of the M1 through the middle of the coal-field potentially improved its economic prospects; but far better access roads are clearly necessary before the motorway's full effect can be realized. If Intermediate Area status is continued, and the M1 brings its due crop of new jobs and easier journeys to work, there is every reason to expect that by the year 2000 this coal-field zone will have become a diversified and prosperous part of the integrated but rather open-textured conurbation which the East Midlands Economic Planning Council has envisaged. The present haphazard settlement pattern, the crisis in its basic industry, the widespread dereliction, and the low quality of its urban environment together indicate that such an embryo conurbation must be actively and closely planned—the very antithesis of the mischievous non-plan doctrine suggested by Hall and others (1969) as appropriate to this area. Later in 1969 a report commissioned by the area's local authorities proposed detailed physical planning for the development, including a new major city located between Alfreton and Mansfield and astride the M1. By the year 2000 the population of this city would be 350,000.

4.5 Leicestershire

The regional planners' Leicester sub-division had a 1968 population of 518,000. The city itself contains only 280,000 people. In both the city and in much of the Soar valley and the south west of the county the traditional trades of footwear and hosiery-knitwear are still of great importance. Engineering was originally largely related to their needs, but in the twentieth century an autonomous engineering industry has risen to dominate the city's industrial structure. Leicestershire has a much higher proportion of its employment in engineering and electrical goods than have Nottinghamshire and Derbyshire. Its expansion was especially rapid during the consumer durable boom of the nineteen fifties, and before rationalization occurred in its two nuclear engineering groups. Even in the nineteen sixties, however, the Leicester sub-region experienced a faster rate of growth in this category of employment than did the bigger Nottinghamshire-Derbyshire sub-region—in 1966–1967, for instance, the new floor space devoted to engineering and electrical goods employment was almost twice as large. In all categories of new industrial employment, in fact, the Leicester sub-region recorded a more rapid growth during the years 1965, 1966 and 1967 than its neighbour. Since these trends are associated with a much smaller proportion of employment in declining industries—and especially in mine employment—the dynamism of the sub-region, and above all of its core, can be sensed. As *Opportunity in the East Midlands* (1969) put it, '... but for the restraints imposed by government policy in the location of industry, Leicester would grow rapidly in terms of population and industry'. Following the abolition of o.d.p.s at the end of 1970 there was a surge of activity in Leicester. By the spring of 1971 planning permission had been granted for new floorspace equal to almost one third of the office accommodation existing in 1968.

Between 1955 and 1965, the growth of population in the Leicester district was 11.7 per cent, as compared with 8.4 per cent in the Nottingham district. From 1965 to 1968, however, the difference narrowed—the growth rates then being 2.5 per cent and 1.9 per cent respectively. Projections suggest, in fact, that there will be slower rate of growth in future than in the Nottinghamshire-Derbyshire sub-region through to 1981, although those made by the Economic Planning Council in 1969 are rather more favourable to the Leicestershire sub-region than those made three years earlier. The Report of the Royal Commission on Local Government confirmed this slower prospective rate of growth for Leicester, but suggested that it fell between the high rate anticipated for Nottingham and Nottinghamshire and the low rate for Derby and Derbyshire (Table 16).

The physical form of growth in the greater Leicester area is the subject of important new planning proposals. So far much of it has been peripheral to the city. Whereas in the 13 years from 1955 Nottingham's satellites of Arnold, Beeston and Stapleford added 21,000 or 28.9 per cent to their population of 73,000, a similar absolute increase in the urban districts of Oadby and Wigston—5 kilometres (3 miles) to the south of Leicester—represented an 89.8 per cent rate. Responding to the opportunities of the near approach by the M1, Leicester began extensive new housing and industrial developments in the Braunstone section of the city. Later, however, it was realized that continued urban accretion in this fashion was undesirable. The city and county engaged consultants, and

Table 16. East Midlands : population by sub-regions, 1965, 1967 and 1981 (est.)

(thousands)

	1965	1969	1981	
			Estimate of 1966	Estimate of 1969
East Midlands	3,272	3,349	4,002	3,837*
Nottingham Derbyshire	1,769	1,778	2,124	1,982*
Leicester	684	712	799	791
Eastern Lowlands	384	405	444	447
Northamptonshire	422	454	622	640

*To compare with 1966 estimates, add 90,000 for territory transferred to Sheffield.
Source : East Midlands Economic Planning Council, 1966; 1969.

in 1969 published their report as the *Leicester and Leicestershire Sub-Regional Study*. In it, a completely new strategy is proposed. The growth of greater Leicester is expected to continue at a rapid rate, its population rising from 400,000 in 1966 to 538,000 by 1991. It is suggested that part of this should be diverted into two corridors. The first, stretching between the M1 and Coalville, the chief focus in the Leicestershire coal-field, will help to counteract both the problems caused by the National Coal Board's rationalization there, and Coalville's perennial problem of overspecialization. Later, this corridor will be extended further to the neighbourhood of Ashby, where favourable conditions for growth will be created when the proposed Birmingham to Nottingham motorway is built. A second growth corridor will run southwestwards from Leicester.

4.6 Conclusion

The physical planning problems of the East Midlands as a whole are largely concerned, like those of Leicester, with growth. However, as has been noted there is also a substantial problem of dereliction. Although it is concentrated in the coal-field, the problem is also serious in the iron ore districts of south Lincolnshire, Northamptonshire and Rutland, and in the sand and gravel areas, mainly in the Trent Valley. The preservation of amenity is also a universal and major planning problem in such a densely populated area. Mines and their associated settlements were carved out of the fine landscapes of Sherwood Forest in the early twentieth century; the need to prevent any further major incursions of industry into it will be clear to any visitor who motors through on a summer Sunday, when it is thronged with visitors from the nearby conurbations. Perhaps the range of pressures on the environment and the necessity for careful physical planning can best be seen in the wide

Trent lowlands, south of Nottingham and Derby. Giant power stations have proliferated here in the last 20 years. Their marshalling yards, cooling towers and, still more, their mesh of transmission lines add to and spread their impact. Wide tracts are worked for sand and gravel, and these are being extended as construction activity increases. Abandoned gravel pits sometimes become marinas or provide other forms of amenity; at other times they are a convenient dumping ground for power station ash; but often they become wastelands, the old ridge lines which marked the progress of their operations poking through scum covered waters. Sewage works for neighbouring great cities are a further element in the landscape. It is true that there are still fine, wide rural views but as the population expands and as the lowlands become a corridor for more motorway links, the pressures will increase. The area could become a major derelict landscape of the twenty-first century. The economic buoyancy of the East Midlands, and the salvation of its distressed coal-field sections, will have been dearly bought if this is the price.

All authorities agree that the East Midlands will increase its share of national population through into the nineteen eighties. Steady economic growth will be much easier to secure here than in either the 'black' Development Areas or in the 'grey' Intermediate Areas to the north. On the other hand, there is no sign that the region will quite match the traditional dynamism of the West Midlands or the South East. In the future, as in the past, the East Midlands will have an 'off white' ranking in regional economic expansion, and that general hue will continue to be comprised of a variety of sub-regional shades.

REFERENCES :

East Midlands Economic Planning Council (1966). *The East Midlands Study,* H.M.S.O., London.
East Midlands Economic Planning Council (1969). *Opportunity in the East Midlands,* H.M.S.O., London.
East Midlands Regional Development Conference (1969). *Policies of the Local Planning Authorities in the East Midlands Region at Mid-1968,* January 18–20 (unpublished papers).
Edwards, K. C. (1949). The East Midlands. In G. H. J. Daysh, *Studies in Regional Planning,* George Philip, London. pp. 135–168.
Fogarty, M. P. (1945). *Prospects of the Industrial Areas of Great Britain,* Methuen, London.
Grimsby Chamber of Commerce and Shipping (1969). Report on Humber Feasibility Study. *Lincolnshire Echo,* 20 August.
Hall, P. and others (1969). Non-Plan : An Experiment in Freedom. *New Society,* 20 March, pp. 435–445.
Howard, R. S. (1968). *The Movement of Manufacturing Industry in the United Kingdom 1945–1965,* H.M.S.O. for the Board of Trade, London.
Kesteven County Planning Dept. (1969). *A Statistical Study based on the 1966 Sample Census,* K.C.C., Sleaford.
Leicester City and County Councils (1969). *Leicester and Leicestershire Sub-regional Study,* L.C. and C.C., Leicester.
Minister of Power (1965). *Fuel Policy* (Cmnd. 2798), H.M.S.O., London.
Minister of Power (1967). *Fuel Policy* (Cmnd. 3438), H.M.S.O., London.
Pocock, D. C. D. (1965). Town Size and Diversification. *Town and Country Planning,* January, pp. 49–53.

Royal Commission on Local Government in England (1968). *Evidence of the County Councils,* H.M.S.O., London.

Royal Commission on Local Government in England (1969). *Report* (Chairman : Lord Redcliffe-Maud), (Cmnd. 4040), H.M.S.O., London.

Secretary of State for Economic Affairs (1969), *The Intermediate Areas* (Chairman : Sir Joseph Hunt), (Cmnd. 3998), H.M.S.O., London.

Teggin, H. (1969). Quoted in *The Times,* 20 January.

Times Review of Industry and Technology (1967). Survey of Lincoln, October.

Times Review of Industry and Technology (1964). Survey of Derby, October.

CHAPTER 5

The West Midlands and Central Wales

BRIAN RODGERS

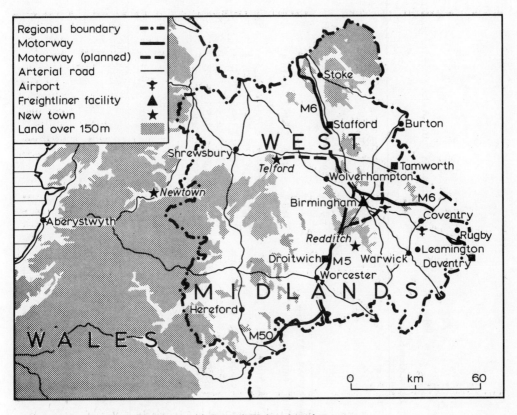

Figure 19 The West Midlands and Central Wales: location map.

Table 17. The West Midlands and Central Wales : selected regional and sub-regional indicators

A. Population :

Thousands

	Mid-year estimates home population				Average annual change 1961–1966			Average annual change 1951–1961		
	1971[1]	1966[1]	1961[2]	1951[2]	Natural change	Armed forces change	Net migration	Natural change	Armed forces change	Net migration
TOTAL West Midlands and Central Wales	**5,188.7**	**5,083.6**	**5,846.1**	**4,516.4**	**+41.3**	**−0.5**	**+6.8**	**+27.8**	**+1.1**	**+4.1**
West Midlands	5,104.7	4,998.9	4,760.6	4,426.1	+41.1	−0.8	+7.1	+27.6	+1.1	+4.7
Central	1,201.8	1,072.3	957.1	847.3	+8.9	−1.0	+15.0	+5.3	−0.7	+6.4
West Midlands conurbation	2,369.2	2,416.8	2,369.8	2,256.9	+21.1	+0.6	−12.3	+14.3	+1.5	−4.5
Coventry	695.2	672.8	623.3	532.9	+6.4	−0.1	+3.5	+4.3	+0.3	+4.4
Western	330.5	330.3	315.3	308.2	+1.9	−0.2	+1.3	+1.4	−0.3	−0.4
North Staffordshire	508.0	506.5	495.1	480.8	+2.8	+0.1	−0.6	+2.4	+0.3	−4.3
Central Wales	84.0	84.7	85.5	90.3	+0.2	—	−0.3	+0.2	—	−0.6
BRITAIN	53,821.4	53,176.1	51,380.0	48,917.5	+328.2	−0.5	+22.6	+231.4	+12.9	+1.9

1. 1971 Census; 1971 boundaries.
2. 1966 boundaries.

B. Employment :

	Employment		Male employment		Proportion of women at work		Unemployment range		
	1966	Change 1961–1966	1966	Change 1961–1966	1966	Change in % 1961–1966	1968	1967	1961–1966
	'000s	%	'000s	%	%	%	%	%	%
TOTAL West Midlands and Central Wales	**2,410**	**+6**	**1,560**	**+5**	**42**	**+1**	**2–3**	**1–2**	**1–2**
West Midlands	2,390	+6	1,540	+5	44	+1	2–3	1–2	1–2
Central	380	+9	240	+6	33	+1	1–2	1–2	0–1
W. Midlands conurbation	1,330	+4	850	+5	50	+1	2–3	1–2	1–2
Coventry	330	+10	220	+7	44	+4	2–3	2–3	1–2
Western	120	+10	70	+9	35	+2	2–3	2–3	1–2
North Staffordshire	240	+4	150	+3	46	+1	1–2	1–2	1–2
Central Wales	20	+5	20	−1	27	−1	3–4	2–3	2–3
BRITAIN	23,550	+4	14,900	+2	40	+2	2–3	2–3	1–2

C. Industrial Development Certificates :

	Estimated additional employment from i.d.c. approvals			
	Total 1956–1967 '000s	Annual averages		
		1964–1967 '000s	1960–1963 '000s	1956–1959 '000s
TOTAL West Midlands and Central Wales	**86.3**	**6.2**	**6.1**	**9.3**
West Midlands	84.3	5.9	6.0	9.2
Central	20.0	2.0	1.4	1.6
Conurbation	37.1	1.6	2.7	5.0
Conventry Belt	7.9	0.4	0.5	1.1
Rural West	7.6	0.5	0.4	0.9
North Staffordshire	11.9	1.3	0.9	0.7
Central Wales	2.0	0.3	0.1	0.1
BRITAIN	1,245.2	121.8	108.1	81.2

5.1 A Profile of the Region

No other major industrial region of Britain has enjoyed such sustained economic progress, over so long a period and with so little interruption, as the West Midlands. It is almost true to say that the last general brake on the region's growth and prosperity was the charcoal famine of the early eighteenth century. This was ended by the coke-iron revolution that led to the massive concentration of iron-smelting and metal-working on the South Staffordshire coal-field, which was producing a quarter of the nation's pig iron by the early decades of the nineteenth century (Johnson, 1951; Johnson and Wise, 1950). Certainly, parts of the region have had their problems, from time to time. Coventry was a troubled city after the French commercial treaty of 1860 removed the protection on which the silk industry relied. Some of the heavy metal-working towns of the central and southeast Black Country were as depressed, briefly but acutely, during the early nineteen thirties, as were many parts of less prosperous Britain. And today Kidderminster depends largely on a carpet industry that has become weak in terms of labour demand. Yet so great has been the versatility and adaptability of West Midland industry that these problems of readjustment have been local and temporary. The occupation of Coventry's empty silk workshops by a bicycle trade, from which the modern vehicle industry is a lineal descendant, is an oft-told tale; but it is typical of the enterprise of the region and the resilience of its economy.

Thus the graphs of population growth, both for the region as a whole and for the Birmingham-Black Country conurbation that is its industrial core, show smoothly rising curves from 1801 to the present day. They are unbroken by decline and, until the First World War, very closely mirror the national trend, but since the nineteen twenties the regional growth-graph has steepened in relation to the national trend. Since 1951 the population of the West Midlands has been growing at an average rate of 0.77 per cent per annum, compared with a value for England and Wales of 0.53 per cent, and the region had steadily increased its share of the national population—from 7.9 per cent in 1921 to 10.5 per cent in 1971. This is the crux of the region's problems: like the North West, the West Riding and the North East, it is an area in which quick nineteenth century growth pre-empted considerable tracts of land in and near to the congested industrial core; unlike them it is an area of unabated—even accelerating—expansion. Indeed, to a greater degree than in any other British industrial region, the conurbation at its centre has continued to grow both in population and employment, and has resisted the dispersal both of people and of work; though the 1971 census reveals that the growth of the conurbation has recently been checked at a population of 2.37 million, a figure similar to that of 1961. In recent years, centralizing forces have remained strong enough to frustrate an admittedly feeble public policy for the dispersal of work and people to distant sites.

In summarizing the general character of the West Midlands in a national context, a profile of one of the country's 'fortunate' regions of rapid urban and economic progress, peopled by a segment of the affluent society, clearly emerges. Yet the region has not shown quite such feverish growth as the greater part of Metropolitan England, nor is there a level of personal prosperity to match southeastern standards quite so widespread, either in social or spatial terms. There are pockets of industrial difficulty associated with environmental decay. The Potteries conurbation in North Staffordshire, for example, with a population of half-a-million, is quite atypical; it is an area still heavily dependent on stagnant or declining industries (ceramics and coal mining), an area with a long history of population loss by migration and a low rate of population growth, an area struggling with the problems of a Victorian urban environment and disfigured by two centuries of vigorous economic growth based on extractive industries (Beaver, 1969). The Cannock Chase and East Warwickshire coal-fields, despite the relatively high productivity of their mining industries, have been caught up in the rationalization of the coal mining industry, and so face problems of redundancy and pit closures; indeed, East Warwickshire (like North Staffordshire) was included in the Hunt Committee's study of the 'grey areas'. The rural western fringes of the West Midlands, in Shropshire and Herefordshire, lie far enough outside the boundaries of the English megalopolis to be suffering from rural depopulation of a classic type, uncorrected by suburban dispersal or the social transformation of the rural community by an 'intrusive' element of urban origin. Even here, however, the larger towns have shown a capacity to grow by attracting mobile industry, and the rather isolated industrial area based on the East Shropshire coal-field has shown a surprising level of industrial vitality and population increase.

Two of these outlying sub-regions (North Staffordshire and East Shropshire) are sufficiently significant and distinctive to merit separate treatment as case studies (pp. 204–212, and 212–217). Even more distinctive, and faced with even graver problems, is the rural area further west in Central Wales (pp. 217–219) where an actual decline in population has for some time been experienced. The 'rural west' and North Staffordshire are areas of relatively slow population growth—6.1 per cent and 2.2 per cent respectively compared with a West Midlands increase of 7.3 per cent between 1961 and 1971. Thus, the industrial heartland of the West Midlands (the three counties of Worcester, Warwick and Stafford, less the north) not only contains the great bulk of the region's population, but it also generates an even higher share of its growth and, so far, has absorbed its population increase without any significant long-range dispersal. In this 'heartland' population grew by almost 18 per cent—an increment of nearly 640,000—during the period 1951–1971.

Given these sub-regional inequalities in growth, it is perhaps surprising that the West Midlands as a whole has proved itself a region of such vitality during the years since 1945. Yet its population increase of 15.3 per cent over the period 1951–1971 is amongst the highest regional rates in the country, even higher than that of the South East (see Table 1). Given the degree of immobility that seems to characterize industry in and near the West Midland conurbation (and which restrains dispersal planning), the regional growth rate is accelerating in a fashion that is positively alarming. From an annual rate of about 0.51 per cent in the early nineteen fifties it had more than doubled to well over 1.00 per cent per annum by the early nineteen sixties. The conurbation itself was not only still growing substantially until very recently (which alone makes it unique among British conurbations as officially defined), but its rate of increase actually quickened, from about 0.26 per cent per annum in the early nineteen fifties, to 0.66 per cent per annum by 1961; there has, however, been a distinct slackening of the growth rate since then, and the present evidence is that it has passed its population peak.

To this rapid increase in population, in-migration has made only a small and varying contribution. This is the chief contrast between the nature of population growth in the West Midlands and the South East. Heavy net out-migration during the nineteen twenties (of almost 70,000) was more than balanced by a net inflow of a little over 100,000 during the nineteen thirties and the subsequent war years. In-migration slackened after 1945 and became a small net outflow during the early nineteen fifties. Since 1956, however, the balance of movement has again been reversed, with a net regional inflow rising from 14,000 per annum in the late nineteen fifties to over 20,000 in the early nineteen sixties. Part of this recent rise is associated with the establishment of non-European communities in the older parts of the conurbation and in Coventry; and it has been reduced by the recent tightening of controls on Commonwealth immigration. In short, there has been a surprisingly small net inflow to the West Midlands from other parts of Britain, though a huge actual movement of people from the northern regions, Wales and Scotland was largely balanced by an outflow of families to the South East; the rest of the in-movement to the region is explained by overseas migration—of the Irish over the whole period, and of Commonwealth migrants since the middle of the nineteen fifties.

Overall, however, less than one-fifth of the region's population increase since 1945 can be explained by net in-migration. The rest arises from a relatively high rate of natural increase; at 9 per cent over the period 1951–1964, this was much higher than either the national rate (6.8 per cent) or the rate in the South East (6.6 per cent). This characteristic reflects, of course, the influence of in-migration during the nineteen thirties, giving the region a favourable age structure and a high level of fertility during the early post-war years. Clearly, the fact that population growth in the West Midlands owes little to migration and much to high fertility means that in comparison with the South East, it is relatively uncontrollable. The national distribution of industry policy has sought to damp-down interregional migration southwards by limiting employment growth in the more prosperous parts of England; and it has had some measure of success in reducing the inflow into the South East during the nineteen sixties. But these policies came at least a decade too late to have any great influence, at any rate in the short term, on the course of population growth in the West Midlands, where the consequences of earlier in-movement must continue for another generation.

The West Midland region has had not the slightest difficulty in generating new employment to absorb both the whole of this great natural increase in its population and the smaller migratory additions. Despite the 'steering' of about 92,000 jobs of West Midlands origin to the Development Areas, the total volume of work available has not only grown (by about 1.2 per cent per annum between 1953 and 1963, compared with a national rate of 0.9 per cent), but it appears to have accelerated to an annual growth rate of 1.5 per cent during the early nineteen sixties. Yet there are weaknesses in the structure of employment in the region. It depends too heavily on the manufacturing sector. This provides 53 per cent of the region's work, but only 38 per cent in the country as a whole; and jobs in manufacturing are growing more slowly nationally than is employment in the service trades. Within the manufacturing sector there is intense specialization on a narrow range of metal working, engineering and vehicle manufacture. Some of these are growing far more slowly in the region than nationally; the vehicle industry increased its employment in the West Midlands by only 1.7 per cent during the decade 1953–1963, while nationally its growth was by over 11 per cent. This was a direct consequence of the Board of Trade's control over the geography of industrial expansion, and the steering of new projects to the Development Areas. Moreover, a number of the region's major industries are sensitive to demand cycles (for example, the manufacturers of power station equipment and heavy electrical machinery), or to the Treasury's use of economic regulators to reduce national consumption (for example, firms making domestic equipment and cars). Thus, short periods of localized unemployment have interrupted the general condition of labour scarcity that has been the norm in the region since the nineteen thirties, at least until 1971.

In fact, a major change is slowly coming to the regional employment structure of the West Midlands, as manufacturing is replaced by service activities. The latter are of somewhat stunted development—in 1963, they provided only 38 per cent of the work available, compared with 56 per cent nationally and almost 60 per cent in the South East—but they are growing more quickly in the West Midlands than in any other region. The industrial vitality and the high level of personal prosperity in the region are the chief driving forces of this growth in service activity. The symptoms are diverse and impressive. The huge investment represented by the almost total remodelling of the Birmingham city-centre; the fact that shop and restaurant floorspace is growing six times as fast in the West Midland conurbation as in the Manchester conurbation, and office floorspace more than twice as quicklv; the very high rates of increase in financial, professional and distributive employment (all expanding at rates much above the national rates of increase); these are all evidence of a major economic—and indeed social—transformation.

Perhaps the best known expression of the economic vitality of the West Midland region is the very high level of income enjoyed by the mass of the population. Although the region is not free from environmental poverty, it is almost without personal poverty. The terraced street along which the cars are packed as tightly as the houses is not an untypical regional image. Indeed, the Coventry car workers have become almost a new social archetype, a community of manual workers with an average income level that permits them to develop their own variant of a middle-class life style. But Midland prosperity is easily exaggerated. Data on taxable incomes, available only on a county basis, suggest that earnings in Staffordshire are scarcely above the national average, though they are undoubtedly pulled down by the low-wage area in the North, and, whilst Worcester and Warwick are certainly more prosperous counties, their average incomes are to some degree inflated by the suburban development of their margins against the conurbation. Male earnings in the region as a whole were the second highest in Britain in 1965 but were only 2.7 per cent above the national average, and are 8 per cent below the level of the South East. Certainly, the West Midlands has a very high activity rate among both men and women of employable age; as a result the number of wage earners per household is above the average for the country, and household income levels are somewhat more above the national average than are personal incomes. The family expenditure survey put the region's household income in 1968/69 at 3.2 per cent above the national average. However, the gap between West Midland and national income levels is probably tending to close. In 1959/1960, employment income was about 4.0 per cent above, and manufacturing earnings about 5.5 per cent above, the national mean. But all these measures are somewhat meaningless in a region that includes both a Stoke on Trent and a Coventry.

There are many reasons, all interacting and complex, for the vigorous economic development of the West Midlands during the present century and particularly since 1945. A relative absence of stagnant or declining industries, and the dominance of what are, in a national context, the growth sectors in the manufacturing economy are the two chief background causes. In short, there is a structural explanation for the prosperity of the regional economy; but such an explanation is not in itself fully adequate. Except for those industries that have been most effectively retarded in their regional development by government intervention (particularly vehicles and electrical goods), the growth industries have expanded even more quickly in the West Midlands than in the country as a whole (especially mechanical engineering and the miscellaneous metal trades); and some of those trades which are declining nationally (such as railway engineering, clothing and textiles) have contracted much more slowly in the region. Clearly, there is evidence of powerful non-structural factors at work.

Some of these geographical factors are discussed at greater length later. They include the extraordinary versatility of so many West Midland metal working firms producing components, semi-products, and the like; such producers are not tied to specific market outlets, but rather adapt their products and processes to take advantage of new market opportunities, and so gear themselves to what are, for the time being, growth sectors. There is little of the monolithic specialization that has been so serious a problem elsewhere. Similarly, the West Midlands has always enjoyed a high birth-rate of new industrial enterprises, a process which is facilitated by the important—indeed, the dominant—role of the small firm in the complex of metal-processing trades. Entrepreneurial vigour and enterprise have never been lacking in the region, which probably gives the 'small man' a better chance of developing a new business than any other part of Britain. This is one of the primary reasons why government action to guide industrial development out of the region has been rather ineffectual in halting the growth of industrial employment, and it is certainly a powerful balance to the dispersal of industry from the conurbation to fringe locations. As fast as employment is decanted, either from the conurbation or the region, new and growing enterprises occupy the vacant floor space in a game of musical chairs. In any case, while industrial development certificate approval was necessary only for projects of over 464 square metres (5,000 square feet), a good deal of new floor space was bound to be created without licensing in a region of relatively small industrial units. Certainly, throughout the nineteen sixties the region's industrial impetus showed no signs of slackening : in the two years 1967 and 1968, almost 1.8 million square metres (19 million square feet) of manufacturing space was approved in the region, a greater two-year total than for any pair of consecutive years in the previous decade.

Almost from the beginnings of significant industrial growth on the South Staffordshire plateau, two spatial factors have been a continuing stimulus to economic advance : the centrality of the region within Britain, and the progressive development of an infrastructure of communications which has quickly responded to each new revolution in transport technology, thereby translating centrality into real nodality. Even before the canal age, the improved Severn-Avon system of navigable rivers brought water transport to the western threshold of the region, and so connected its metal finishing trades with sources of pig-iron supply in east Shropshire and the Forest of Dean. The location of the Birmingham-Black Country metal working complex, straddling the central English watershed, inevitably made it the focus of the evolving canal system. One of the earliest waterways, the Staffordshire-Worcestershire canal of 1772, at once established the region's focal position in the national system of inland navigation by linking the Severn, Trent and Mersey; later the Birmingham and Worcester, the Stourbridge and the Stratford canals all provided alternative links to the Severn and the port of Bristol. The Coventry and Oxford canals gave connection to the Thames and London, via the Grand Junction canal and Thames navigation respectively. As early as 1790, Birmingham lay at the focus of a system of slow but cheap transport for bulk commodities that extended from Bristol to York and from London to Lancashire. No other part of Britain has since rivalled the West Midlands in terms of interregional accessibility.

Railway development quickly confirmed the focal role of Birmingham. By 1850 the London and North Western system had been pieced together to link the capital with Carlisle and the Scottish lines, via the West Midlands. The Midland Railway had not yet emerged as a system but its constituent lines, from Bristol via Birmingham to the east Midland cities and York, were already complete. Timetables for the period provide an interesting commentary on Birmingham's superb advantages of position : Sheffield and the West Riding, the South Lancashire cities, Bristol and London were all within an easy morning's journey. A two-hour service between London and Birmingham was an early achievement of the Victorian railway companies, so that for more than a century a Midland business man has been able to spend a working day in London and return to dine in his Edgbaston villa. Indeed, Birmingham's passenger communications with the rest of the country in the late nineteenth century were so good that they have been capable of only marginal improvement since. Isochrones drawn from Birmingham as centre, for the fastest available means of land transport, would show little radical difference if the 1870 pattern were compared with that for 1970. Intercity air transport has done less for Birmingham than any other major provincial centre, while a century of railway improvement, culminating in electrification, has reduced the Birmingham-London journey time by only twenty minutes.

Modern developments in transport have only marginally improved Birmingham's nodality in terms of interregional personal accessibility, but they have transformed the journey times involved in the movement of commodities. The West Midland conurbation is quickly becoming the node of the national motorway system, and it has become the focus of the only major system of main line electrification in the British railway system. The latter already takes the form of a main trunk route from London to Crewe, and then forks to serve Manchester and Liverpool. In the nineteen seventies it will be extended northwards to Carlisle and to Glasgow. The main line itself is in fact multiple: there are alternative routes northwards from Rugby, via Birmingham or the direct Trent Valley line; a loop to serve Northampton; and a direct link (avoiding Crewe) via Stoke to Manchester. Although railway electrification has transformed intercity accessibility within the English megalopolis, its relative effect has been least within the West Midlands. Certainly, freight movement has accelerated almost to passenger speeds, but the short-range of so much commodity movement within the West Midland region limits the effect of railway improvements. It is significant, for example, that the Midlands' car firms use rail transport much less than their southeastern and south Lancashire rivals.

Motorway development promises a far greater acceleration of commodity flow than of passenger movement, over short ranges as well as long. It therefore has a more vital significance for the region than railway improvements. There will clearly be a period, probably lasting several decades, during which the West Midlands will dominate the developing British motorway system, as it did the early expansion of the canal and railway nets. The M1 London-Yorkshire motorway skirts the region on the east, and the short M45 spur runs from the M1 westwards towards Coventry. From the North the M6, newly extended beyond Lancaster to Carlisle, deeply penetrates not merely the region but also the conurbation; similarly the M5 Birmingham-Bristol-South Wales motorway enters and crosses the conurbation to join the M6 south of Walsall in the very heart of the Black Country. The essence of the motorway plan for the region is to carry an east-west route from this junction across northeast Birmingham, and, skirting Coventry on the north, to link up with the M1 near Rugby; this was completed in 1972.

These Midland link motorways are much the greatest task of urban motorway construction firmly planned and largely completed in Britain. They are not only key links in the national system, joining the M5–M6 and M1–A1 routes running independently north-south through western and eastern England respectively; but they will clearly also become the chief arteries of intraregional traffic flow. Slicing through the densely built-up urban area and some of the most congested industrial zones, they will give this conurbation a distinction, long likely to remain unique, of being intersected by 'main-line' motorways. The effect on the speed and cost of commodity flow is likely to be dramatic. Hitherto, the incomplete system has given local advantages to particular sectors of the conurbation. South Lancashire is within three hours of Wolverhampton for a typical delivery vehicle, while Severnside and South Wales are about as far from the south west of the conurbation; and neither London nor industrial Yorkshire lies much beyond the 3-hour isochrone from Coventry. Much cross-conurbation movement has been slower than ever on a tortured road system. Given the completion of the system, however, these advantages are now generalized. The whole of the industrial heart of the region once again enjoys that immense relative advantage over the rest of the country that it possessed most strongly during the early phases of both canal and railway development. In brief, with the completion of the motorway links, some 68 per cent of the nation's population, almost 75 per cent of its manufacturing employment, and an even higher share of its purchasing power, are within the three-hour isochrone. Can it be hoped that industry will voluntarily leave the conurbation for the fringes of the region—as it is asked to do in order to implement overspill policies—in the face of accessibility advantages of this magnitude?

5.2 The Spatial Framework and Population Growth of the West Midlands

A smooth plateau with a surface ranging between 120 and 240 metres (400 and 800 feet) lies from north to south across central and south Staffordshire. Bounded by sub-parallel fault systems it is, tectonically, a horst that has uplifted Carboniferous materials above the Trias-filled grabens to the west (between Wolverhampton and mid-Worcestershire) and the east (between Lichfield and west Warwickshire). Except in the extreme north and south, coal was available throughout the plateau. In the north the seams are lost under the great thickness of Bunter Pebble Beds in the high plateau of Cannock Chase and in the south they thin and disappear. On the eastern and western margins, coal is workable beyond the boundary faults at some depth under the trias, as narrow concealed extensions. To the east coal has been proved at Lichfield at a depth of more than 3,000 feet (915 metres) so that the seams are probably continuous with the similar succession in the lesser horst of the east Warwickshire coal-field.

In terms of both the succession of seams, and the history of exploitation, the West Midland coal-field is divided into two by the east to west line of the Bentley faults, north of Walsall. To the south of these lines lies the Black Country field, itself divided into a pair of basins by the Dudley ridge of older rocks. This is Britain's most perfect example of an exhausted coal-field. Output peaked as early as 1860, and now lingers only in small coal and fireclay workings in the southern sub-basin, though three pits working the concealed reserves east and west of the boundary faults survived into the post-war period. In the Cannock Chase coal-field to the north of the faults, active mining has retreated to the deeper measures on the northern margins. Thus the setting of the greater part of the conurbation is that of a largely abandoned coal-field, with a surface more tortured than most. The chief seam, the 9 metre (30 foot) Thick Coal, lay at shallow depth and caused devastating subsidence on extraction, while the feverish early growth and prolonged decline of iron smelting added its massive contribution to surface dereliction.

The urban and industrial heart of the West Midlands has formed upon and about this coal-rich plateau, although the coal-field and the industrial region are by no means co-extensive. At the core lies the Birmingham-Black Country conurbation of some 2.4 million people (Figure 20). This itself is divided between what may be described as Greater Birmingham (the city, together with its suburban extensions chiefly into Solihull and Sutton Coldfield) in the east and south east, and the Black Country towns perched on the coal-field plateau to the west. A surprisingly tenuous ribbon of dense urbanization pinched between semi-rural salients joins Birmingham to the Black Country; and the two halves of the conurbation—in fact they have roughly equal shares of the total popu-lation—are complexly contrasted, though less sharply today than a half-century ago (Rosing and Wood, 1971).

Industry in Birmingham is varied. The emphasis lies, of course, on the light metal trades and the assembly industries, but there is diversity outside the metal working group and service employment considerably exceeds manufacturing. The services, in contrast, are only weakly developed in the Black Country; there the bulk of work is provided not only by the manufacturing sector, but dominantly by metal working, and with a strong accent on semifinished materials and components. The urban landscape of the Black Country is that of a confused patchwork. Old housing and industry—clustered about the town and village nuclei, and ribboned along a chaotic road system—alternate irregularly with areas of modern public and private housing that have been forced into the interstices of the Victorian urban framework. Similarly, both large and small modern factories rise everywhere from the obsolescent remains of the old industrial zones, that are aligned along canals and railways or embedded in the urban cores. Birmingham displays a much simpler dichotomy between a collar of nineteenth century development (an amalgam of both industrial and residential slums, now well advanced towards renewal) and the suburban spread to the south and east, with its dispersed and chiefly large-scale industrial development. The problem of substandard housing (a total of about 157,000 houses in urgent need of renewal in 1964) is roughly equally shared between the Black Country and the city; however, the problem is much more localized in the latter. The Black Country has the bulk of the derelict land problem—still about 1,600 hectares (4,000 acres) after twenty years of active reclamation and continuing to spread to new localities. This, then, is a bipartite conurbation, structurally unusual in that the dominant city lies eccentrically placed towards the southeast margin, whilst powerful sub-centres on which the strong sub-regional consciousness of the Black Country is focused play a distinctive role in the west.

Beyond the margin of the conurbation, and separated from it by a planned green belt that is in fact very grey and scarred, lies a ring of free-standing industrial towns. Most of them lie beyond mass-commuting range of Birmingham, but they are bound closely enough by ties of industrial linkage and social affiliation to be, in a real sense, part of the West Midland city region. Kidderminster and Worcester to the southwest, Stratford, Warwick and Leamington to the southeast, the towns of east Warwickshire, namely

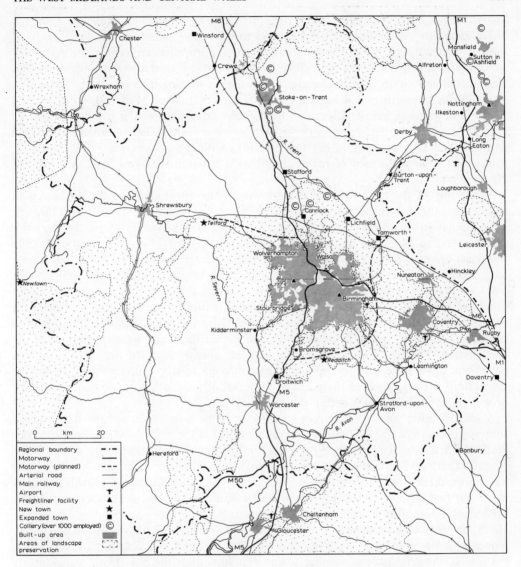

Figure 20 The West Midlands : principal economic and land use features, 1971.

Tamworth, Nuneaton, Rugby and Coventry itself, and Lichfield, Rugeley, Cannock and Stafford to the north are all firmly tied to the conurbation and its dominant city, though in quite diverse ways. The small towns of east Shropshire are as yet more isolated— yet they are quickly becoming more directly bound to the conurbation with their development as the new city of Telford, expanding to receive Birmingham overspill. Burton on Trent in the far north east is anomalously placed in the West Midlands, with which it has little in common industrially; in all roles except administration, it is more commonly associated with the urban complex of the middle Trent Valley. The conurbation of North Staffordshire, too, has only rather tenuous links with the core of the West Midlands; it lies astride the watershed of regional affiliation between the West Midlands and the North West.

The nature of the links between these towns of the outer girdle of the urban region and its core, and their relationships with each other, are most simply demonstrated through an examination of journey to work patterns. There is a hierarchy of journey to work systems, and so of labour market areas, in the urban West Midlands. Clearly the Birmingham-oriented commuter flow dominates the hierarchy. Most of the in-movement to the city is from the adjacent suburban districts of Sutton Coldfield and Solihull, and from those parts of the Black Country that immediately border Birmingham. Feebler flows are generated by areas far beyond the conurbation margin—as far as Tamworth on the east, Stratford on the south, and Worcester on the southwest—but there is little commuting to Birmingham from areas beyond the northern and western margins of the conurbation. The Black Country to the west has always deflected the city's suburban outgrowth towards an arc from the northeast through to the southwest and, except for the Telford project, most of the planned dispersal of population of the conurbation is, or will probably be, to sites within the same arc.

A second, lower 'order' of journey to work systems in part overlaps the Birmingham commuter zone. Each of the major freestanding towns of the city region margin (especially Stafford, Coventry, Rugby and Worcester) and the major employment foci of the Black Country (particularly Wolverhampton) is a major net importer of labour. Most of them have strengthened their role in this regard since 1951. Their industrial growth has been rapid but few have attracted any considerable addition to their dormitory population dependent upon distant employment in Birmingham or the conurbation generally. Much the greatest of these second-order labour market areas is that based on Coventry. Indeed here a semi-independent sub-conurbation is evolving. Not only in Coventry itself, but also in the semicircle of smaller towns that surrounds the city (from Nuneaton to the north, through Hinckley, Rugby and Daventry to the east, and to Warwick-Leamington on the south), the growth of employment, population and the built-up area has been at rates far above the regional average. A complex pattern of daily labour interchanges binds the 'Coventry belt' together into an integrated urban-industrial unit, with a population of over 600,000. Its rate of growth is so rapid that it is the principal pressure point in the region. Worcester, to the southwest, has emerged as a somewhat similar dominant focus of a semi-independent journey to work system. It draws labour from an area that extends to Malvern and Evesham, and that on the north overlaps the conurbation margin at Bromsgrove and Redditch. Another focus within a 'second order' of labour market areas, Stafford, has even more complex spatial relationships in that it is the only point of contact between the labour market of the West Midland conurbation and that of North Staffordshire. A fairly symmetrical area of inflow to Stafford extends from Newport on the west, Rugeley on the east, and bites deeply into the mining communities of the Cannock coal-field. However, a feature of recent development in the Stafford journey to work system has been its strong extension beyond Stone to the Potteries. At the same time, a long-standing out-movement from Stafford to Wolverhampton has continued. In short, Stafford imports labour from the north and exports it to the south; to a degree, therefore, it bridges and links an area of labour scarcity (the conurbation) with an area of incipient labour surplus (North Staffordshire). Wolverhampton has the most distinctive journey to work pattern among the Black Country towns. It imports from a curiously elongated zone, bordering the conurbation from Bridgnorth on the southwest to Cannock and Stafford. There is little movement from the conurbation, but a considerable extension of its commuting hinterland westwards reaches to the towns of East Shropshire, a feature that will certainly strengthen as Telford grows.

Apart from this in-movement of labour to important industrial towns, most of them beyond the conurbation edge, a third 'order' in the hierarchy of journey to work systems may be discerned. This takes the form of a set of complex patterns of interchange between the smaller towns. Many of these third order systems straddle the conurbation boundary and are a factor linking it with the periphery of the city region. For example a Walsall-Cannock-Aldridge-Rugeley sub-system straddles the margins of the Wolverhampton, Stafford and Birmingham journey to work areas; a Leamington-Warwick-Kenilworth-Stratford sub-system exists in an area in which the Coventry and Birmingham commuter zones overlap; while in the southwest, Bromsgrove, Droitwich and Redditch have close commuting links with each other as well as with both Worcester and the conurbation. These third order commuter sub-systems on the conurbation margin have developed strongly since 1951. They represent some degree of both industrial and population dispersal, and they reflect the new mobility associated with very high levels of car ownership in a prosperous region.

Thus, the urban framework of the region may be discerned. At its heart is the compact Birmingham-Black Country conurbation, itself divided into two contrasting halves, of which the western is relatively self-contained in journey to work terms. Beyond the conurbation lies a ring of freestanding cities, each one of which is the focus of lesser sub-system capable of definition in terms of daily labour flows. Between the conurbation and the ring of peripheral towns, increasingly complex affiliations are being shaped in the form of the third order journey to work systems described above. This is, of course, very much the model to which the London city region has developed during the last quarter century, and in many respects the Birmingham city region repeats the trends that have shaped urban growth in Metropolitan England, but on a lesser scale. There are, however, some profound and significant differences. The London conurbation, the continuously urbanized area within the green belt, is no longer growing; indeed its population is in the process of decline (see Figure 10), while that of the West Midland conurbation has continued to grow. This contrast is not the consequence of a mere trick of definition; the Birmingham conurbation was not delimited more generously than others by the inclusion of large semi-rural fringe areas. Indeed, on the north especially, it was rather underdefined. It is, however, a conurbation of relatively open texture, broken by many pockets of open (though often derelict or damaged) land in the Black Country, and penetrated by deep semi-rural salients. Its mean population density is only 33.6 persons per hectare (13.6 per acre) compared with London's 43.7 (17.7). Thus it has been able to absorb much of its own growth both of population and employment and this, together with the immobility of conurbation industry, has worked against any marked decentralization from the conurbation.

Birmingham itself has now reached a point of population stability—even of slight decline—at a size of just over 1 million. In effect this means that a massive slum clearance operation has been almost balanced by new construction, both on 'virgin' land and on redevelopment sites. In the single year 1964/1965, some 3,800 houses were demolished in Birmingham, and 6,000 new units were built. The rest of the older core of the conurbation (in effect the Black Country) has followed a very unusual population trend in the post-1945 years. After heavy, short-range migrational losses during the early nineteen fifties (more than balancing a high rate of natural increase), there was a marked actual growth of population later in the decade, when out-migration fell far below the increment by natural increase. Subsequently, during the early nineteen sixties, dispersal to new areas (on balance) almost ceased, and the population grew by a quantity roughly equivalent to its natural increase in population. In short the tendency to decentralization from the Black Country is weakening, not strengthening. Overall, the Black Country's population grew by 2.3 per cent between 1951 and 1964, but most of this took place late in the period and seems to be continuing. The 'newer' conurbation, the developing dormitory districts on the fringe, accommodated most of the growth and population there increased by 55 per cent during the 1951–1964 period. Meanwhile, piecemeal development in both the urban and rural areas of the green belt produced a further growth of about 130,000, most of which must be seen as conurbation overspill. Against the background of vigorous overall population growth, this is a relatively feeble decentralization process, confined to piecemeal short-range movement.

The impression is left, therefore, that the West Midlands houses a quickly growing urban population that clings tenaciously to the conurbation and its immediate margin— for the primary reasons that manufacturing industry holds on to its conurbation or fringe sites with equal stubbornness, whilst service employments grow briskly at the centre. The very limited population dispersal that has taken place has been balanced by a high rate of natural increase and by in-migration (from other parts of Britain, Ireland and the Commonwealth). But the importance of the migrational factor in population increase, both in the region and the conurbation, is easily overstressed. The 1966 census showed that the ratio of migrants (those who have moved to their present homes during the year prior to the census) to total population was only 83 per thousand for the West Midlands, and 79 per thousand within the conurbation. These values are much the same as those for the North West and the Yorkshire and Humberside regions, and they are far below the 96 per thousand of the South East region. Data for migration over the full five year period to 1966 also confirm this strong suggestion that in-migration is a relatively small element in the population growth of the region and its dominant conurbation.

Despite the uniquely vigorous growth of population within the West Midlands conurbation and on its immediate fringe, the performance of the outlying towns of the city region has been even more impressive. In a general sense the 'central division' of *The West Midlands: a Regional Study* (1965) defines the Birmingham city region. Within the central division excluding the conurbation, population grew from 1.4 millions in 1951 to over 1.7 millions by 1964, an increase of almost 20 per cent. About 60 per cent of this growth was migratory (both short-range from the conurbation and long-range from the rest of Britain and overseas), but rates of natural increase were far above either the regional or the national averages in these outer towns of the city region. Their population growth is both explosive and, in the short term, irreversible, for it derives in part from their 'young' age structures. There are a number of pressure points of exceptional expansion. The 'Coventry Belt' of the *Study* (virtually the Coventry labour market area as defined earlier) increased its population by a quarter between 1951 and 1964 to a total of 612,000. About half of the growth has been by in-migration, but the rate of natural increase is almost twice the national average. Without a significant slum clearance problem, almost all housing development here represents net growth. Yet there are some signs that growth in the Coventry Belt has come up against problems of land availability. House building there during the year 1965–1966 was running at a rate of only 5.9 completions per 1,000 of population; this was lower than the conurbation figure of 7, and far below a value of about 11 per 1,000 for the rest of the city region beyond the conurbation boundary. Between 1961 and 1971, the population increase of Coventry itself was slow by West Midlands' standards—5.6 per cent. This suggests that growth is now being deflected within the labour market area to smaller towns like Kenilworth (with a population increase of 39 per cent between 1961 and 1971) and Rugby (13.9 per cent). There is a clear need for a sub-regional plan (see pp. 219–229) to give a rational framework within which these pressures can best express themselves.

During the inter-war and early post-war periods, Coventry and its neighbours were the region's outstanding growth point. More recently, however, rates of population expansion have been higher in the towns of mid-Staffordshire, within or beyond the conurbation green belt on the north, particularly within the Stafford-based journey to work system. Growth here has been stimulated by a number of small-scale dispersal schemes to which not only Birmingham families but also, to a limited degree, conurbation industries have moved. Stafford itself (with a 1971 population of 55,000) grew by 14 per cent during the nineteen sixties; Cannock (56,000) grew by 18.5 per cent, and Rugeley and Lichfield by 71 per cent and 61 per cent respectively. Served by the M6 motorway and a generally improved trunk road system, with an expanding indigenous industrial base (especially Stafford's electrical engineering complex), and already demonstrated to be an alternative location that some conurbation firms are prepared to accept, mid-Staffordshire has an obvious growth potential. It already contains a population of about 320,000, and it has the incalculable advantage of being (and will largely remain) a single area in terms of planning responsibility, under the Staffordshire County Council. On the other hand, a substantial mining industry still exists there in the Cannock coal-field, and with it a potential problem of labour redundancy. The evolving strategy of West Midland planning is likely to assign a substantial role to mid-Staffordshire in the housing of the region's population growth. The largest project here is a scheme developed on county initiatives to expand Tamworth to a total population of at least 70,000.

The last of the major peripheral areas within the Birmingham city region to merit brief discussion is that based upon Worcester. It falls largely within the journey to work system orientated towards this old county town that has only recently passed through an industrial revolution. Excluding a few small rural districts that as yet have only feeble links with the industrial West Midlands, the Worcestershire sector of the city region has a present population of about 340,000. Close to the conurbation, it is growing fairly quickly—by 21 per cent at Bromsgrove, and by 20 per cent at Redditch, between 1961 and 1971. But Worcester's own growth (10.9 per cent) has been more modest. As the build-up of population at the Redditch new town progresses, and as both 'voluntary' and planned overspill beyond the conurbation fringe continues especially into north Worcestershire, growth will certainly quicken within this sector; however, it will have to accelerate considerably to match the rates of the northern and eastern sectors of the city region. Apart from Redditch, there is an agreed overspill scheme for Droitwich, and a longer-term project for a massive expansion of Worcester's population. Thus, an increase in the area's population to over half a million is envisaged by the nineteen eighties.

5.3 The Economic Base of the West Midlands

As it had developed in its classical form by the middle decades of the nineteenth century, the West Midland industrial region (then still largely confined to the Black Country coal-field and its margin) had developed a complex of metal-working manufactures which were characterised by a high degree of self-sufficiency, almost perfect vertical integration and close linkages between their several branches. The pits working the Thick Coal, the limestone quarries of the Dudley ridge, and the many shallow ironstone workings fed coking coal, flux and ore into a multitude of small blast-furnaces, of which there were 172 in 1865. Much of the pig iron output went to puddling furnaces (there were 2,100 of them in 1865) and so into wrought iron products. As mild steel replaced wrought iron in many markets, the Black Country turned to steel conversion, but relatively late in the century and never on a massive scale. Alongside the iron trades grew a complex of non-ferrous metal industries, refining and alloying lead, zinc, copper, brass, pewter and the precious metals, especially in Birmingham. These primary branches fed an immense variety of metal processing and shaping trades, which cast, rolled, forged, slit, stamped, pierced and machined the metal, to make both finished and intermediate products. At the 'market' end of this linked chain of metal industries were those concerned with finished, and often complex, manufactures: guns and locks, bolts and buttons, chains and anchors, steam machinery (though never locomotives except on a small scale), tools and many engineering products. It is an oversimplification to describe Birmingham as the great focus of the finished-metal trades and the Black Country as its primary supplier, but this was, in a general sense, the relationship of the city with its evolving conurbation (British Association, 1950).

This classical industrial structure reached its zenith in the eighteen sixties, and has now been modified by a century of progressive change. Coal output declined after 1865, through exhaustion and drainage problems, and shifted northwards to Cannock Chase. By 1913 the Black Country coal-field had entered a relic stage in working; output had declined to an annual 3 million tons, and was to shrink to one million tons by 1945. Ironstone production declined even more quickly from levels of about one million tons each year in the late eighteen fifties. Partly because its local resource-base was disappearing, partly because cheap steel (based on imported or Cumberland ores) was rapidly eroding the traditional wrought iron trade, iron smelting passed quickly into decline. Today the primary branch of iron working is represented only by specialized steel production on a relatively small scale, together with scrap remelting and alloying. Thus the primary base of the integrated structure of the Victorian West Midlands has been removed.

The fate of the secondary stages in the working of iron and steel has varied considerably. Some of the trades have prospered; others have declined. During the inter-war depression some of the heavier branches of metal shaping became seriously depressed in the Black Country—for example heavy rolled and forged products and tubes—and these have subsequently tended to disperse from the West Midlands to the major steel producing districts. Other lighter branches—light pressings and sheet-metal work, for example—have grown strongly. The key to this success is versatility in relation to the market. In parts of the Black Country, and especially in the southwest, the metal-shaping industries are highly specialized in equipment and skill and so serve a single market; they have had their difficulties. In the northwest Black Country and Birmingham, on the other hand, these trades are less tied to traditional market outlets in this way. More adaptable, they serve a complex of sub-assembly industries, and so can easily respond to the changing needs of the region's growth industries. Metal presswork firms may serve the car, central heating, and office furniture industries as opportunity offers; a maker of anchors can serve only a single 'assembly' industry. But overlying these structural contrasts is a general tendency towards rationalization and technical innovation in metal processing. The casting trade, for example, is passing through a somewhat belated change in its technology, in which the many small foundries of the past are being replaced by larger automated units.

It is chiefly on the manufacture of 'finished' metal products—and in particular the assembly industries making a wide range of both capital and consumer goods—that the present prosperity of the region depends. Few of these are of long standing in the area. Some have a nineteenth century origin—for example machine tools—and have subsequently developed in a much more sophisticated modern form, but most are products of the present century, like the motor vehicle industry, electrical engineering, the aircraft industry, and the radio-electronic group. Locationally, most of these newer trades are much better developed in Birmingham than the Black Country, but they are even stronger, relatively, in the towns of the outer girdle of the city region than they are in the central city. Nevertheless, they are closely dependent on the secondary metal processing trades of the Black Country, and the sub-assembly industries of the conurbation as a whole. Thus the metalworking-engineering complex is still highly integrated vertically; it has lost its primary branch, but has enormously strengthened its assembly stages. The interlinkages are as close as ever, though differently structured and now much more strongly market orientated. The car assembly plants alone draw body-pressings, forged suspension parts, tubes, zinc fittings, engine castings, machined cylinder blocks, pistons and many hundreds of other components from the metalworking complex. Indeed sub-contracting is a much more important activity in the vehicle industry of this region than elsewhere.

This is one obvious reason for the immobility of so much conurbation industry in the West Midlands. Each part of the complex clings tenaciously to the main mass, and so to the conurbation, for to move would mean some sacrifice of access both to customers and suppliers. More than in any other British industrial region there is here close integration in the locational sense accompanied by disaggregation in the organizational sense. Processes performed by the same firm and in the same factory elsewhere are here performed in separate factories by different firms. The complex as a whole, it may be argued, is indivisible. No longer rooted in local mineral resources, its association with the Black Country coal-field is now incidental and historic. It has been said that the complex could be located anywhere in central England without disadvantage—but only if the system moved as a whole. It cannot be dismantled and dispersed without loss of efficiency. This is the rationale of a continuing concentration of development upon the conurbation, and the counter argument to the attractions of decentralization.

Today, four major 'stages' can be identified in the metal working complex: metal production, refining and alloying (now chiefly confined to the non-ferrous group); secondary metal processing and shaping; components and sub-assembly work; and, lastly, assembly industries marketing a final product. Taking the region as a whole (and so including North Staffordshire and East Shropshire), about 1.2 million people are employed in manufacturing, three-quarters of them in the metalworking-engineering groups. Primary iron and steel production accounts for only 2 per cent of the total, and this lies largely outside the Birmingham city region. Metal fabricating industries producing components and intermediate products employ about 300,000 workers (about 25 per cent of the total in manufacturing), while the assembly and sub-assembly industries employ at least 420,000 workers (35 per cent of the total). Among the last group, the most important individual trades are motor vehicles (164,000), aircraft (34,000), tool making (65,000), mechanical engineering (97,000), and electrical and electronic manufactures (128,000). The strength of what are, nationally, the growth industries in this list is self evident; so is the absence of weak sectors, like railway engineering. Outside the metal working groups are other industries directly related to the assembly stages within them—for example the production of tyres and plastics. Indeed there are few major manufactures in the region that are totally unconnected with the dominant metal fabricating complex, and most of these—such as brewing at Burton, carpets at Kidderminster, shoes at Stafford and Stone, knitwear in east Warwickshire, and the pottery group in North Staffordshire— lie either on or beyond the margins of the Birmingham city region.

Spatial contrasts in industrial structures, reflecting a complex pattern of sub-regional specialization, is an important aspect of West Midland industry. To simplify (and leaving aside North Staffordshire and East Shropshire which are treated separately later) three zones may be recognized: the Black Country towns, Birmingham and its immediate satellites, and the freestanding manufacturing towns beyond the conurbation and its green belt. Among the latter the 'Coventry Belt' is so outstanding that it must be regarded as a distinctive sub-region (see Figure 20). The contrasts between these zones are not limited to the structure of industry inside and outside the dominant metal-using group. They extend also to the place of industrial employment in the overall economy, the size distribution of manufacturing plants, the nature of linkage patterns, and the rates of employment growth.

5.3.1 *The Black Country*

The Birmingham-Black Country contrast is not easy to discuss in the absence of detailed published research of recent date but it is clear that the old relationship between the two has not survived without considerable change. Both by indigenous development and by the receipt of persistent overspill from the city, the Black Country has acquired a considerable range of assembly activities—though it is still more concerned with sub-assembly than with the final stages of production for the market. Two superimposed patterns of contrast can be seen in the Black Country: the traditional local specializations in distinctive branches of metal processing, and a manufacturing geography of more recent origin keyed to the degree to which lighter assembly industries have penetrated the sub-region. Traditional interests have died hard in the Black Country. Cradley Heath is still the centre of anchor and chain making, lock and safe manufacture is tightly focused on Willenhall, West Bromwich and Wednesbury are major centres of tube-making, while Smethwick's specialization is in nuts, bolts and other light machined products. Casting is more widespread, with a strong emphasis on the central Black Country, about Bilston and Tipton, but malleable castings are particularly concentrated upon Walsall. This, in summary, is the traditional pattern of Black Country industry. Perhaps more important is the growth of subsequent activities in the region.

Studies made during the nineteen thirties showed a developing contrast between the northwest of the area (the Wolverhampton district) and the southwest (in Dudley and its surroundings). The former, like Birmingham, had metal fabricating trades that were not strongly specialized as to process, plant and skill. They thereby had a strong versatility of product. Wolverhampton firms were able to serve new component and sub-assembly industries that looked to the major producers in the vehicle and engineering groups for a market. In this situation, the birth and survival rates of new enterprises were high, and there was both a quick growth of employment and strong progress towards industrial diversity. With its important sub-assembly industries, and its interest in the vehicle trade (once cars, now heavy vehicles), Wolverhampton is the closest to Birmingham, among Black Country towns, in its industrial structure. In the southwest of the Black Country, in contrast, the metal fabricating trades were more specialized in their plant, skills, processes and markets. Less flexible, they were not easily able to diversify their products to serve new outlets. Sub-assembly and component enterprises grew less quickly here, the overall birth rate of new firms and units was lower, and employment growth less strong. In the Dudley district, therefore, a more strongly traditional structure of industry survives. These contrasts are to some degree reflected in the distribution of industrial plants of various sizes. Those districts with a strongly traditional industrial structure naturally have a large number of very small units; Wolverhampton and the central Black Country, on the other hand, have a much higher proportion of workers in larger units.

5.3.2 Birmingham

Structural contrasts of industry in Birmingham itself have a strong spatial element also. The inner city is dominated by a very large number of tiny firms largely concerned with rather traditional products and processes. In contrast, the outer, radial industrial zones are dominated by large units of modern assembly activities. The inner city in its old form was (and in part remains) a zone of almost unparalleled industrial concentration and congestion. It contains almost a quarter of the conurbation's factory workers, in an area of 24 square kilometres (9.3 square miles), at an average density of almost 6,000 per square kilometre (15,000 per square mile). Large plants are almost absent, and the typical unit is virtually of workshop size. In part of the old gun and jewellery quarters close to the city centre, there were 923 works in a single kilometre square in 1948. A pattern of industrial quarters with strong specializations had evolved from the middle of the eighteenth century: the gun and jewellery trades were dominant to the north of the city centre, the brass industry to the south west, and mixed metal trades to the south east. An indescribable variety of light metal working industries has been added to these traditional interests.

This inner factory zone is today a formless confusion of obsolescent industrial premises aligned along abandoned lines of communication. It is inextricably alloyed with grossly substandard housing and it closely encloses a city centre in an advanced stage of redevelopment. Already the blade of the bulldozer has sliced away huge areas of the industrial collar. But the tiny firms typical of the zone need—or believe they need—a near-central location and immediate contact with their suppliers, customers and rivals. They are in general reluctant to accept (and possibly cannot afford) a peripheral trading estate type of site. Although the city has built a number of 'flatted factories' to house them close to the centre, many of the small firms compelled to relocate by clearance have seeped away into the surviving factory slums or they have moved a short distance to the very similar urban environment on the nearer fringe of the Black Country. This clustering of so many small firms, providing collectively so large a share of industrial employment in the city and conurbation, is part of the cause of the immobility of employment in the region. It presents also an intractable planning problem.

From the nucleus of the old industrial collar drawn so tightly round the city centre, manufacturing zones radiate outwards along the major lines of communication, becoming fragmentary in the modern suburban fringe. Industry in these radial zones has its own distinctive characteristics. The size of the average unit is much larger; virtually all the city's factories employing over 2,500 workers, and almost all the conurbation's factories employing over 5,000 workers, are to be found in the radial ribbons or their broken suburban extensions. Most of the key assembly industries, especially the car plants, and most of the major units outside the metals group, are sited in these zones. The first of them to form—and one quite untypical in its industrial mix—was the belt of chiefly heavy, metal working industry which follows the Birmingham-Wolverhampton railway and canal across the central Black Country. More modern radial extensions follow the Tame valley northwards to Perry Bar, and eastwards to Castle Bromwich. There, large sites available on low-lying land have attracted a number of very large employers, including the Dunlop Rubber Company. To the southeast from central Birmingham, along the Warwick canal and the former Great Western main railway, a ribbon of factories extends continuously to Tyseley; it is dominated by heavy metal working firms and electrical engineering. Further out, this zone extends brokenly into Solihull, where the Rover car plant is the major unit. South from the city, beyond the break in factory development interposed by the Edgbaston-Moseley areas of high income housing, another radial ribbon extends along the Bristol railway. This has more than its fair share of factories outside the metal group—for example, the Cadbury works at Bournville—but it also has the conurbation's most important single industrial employment complex. This is the British Leyland Motors plant at Longbridge, which is important not only for its sheer size, but also because it is the focus of so many complex chains of sub-contracting and component supply. In their own distinctive way, these large firms of the radial zones and the urban periphery contribute to that spatial inertia of industry that is the chief regional problem. Many are firms of national importance, and they come under Department of Trade and Industry pressure to take their major extensions to Development Areas rather than to West Midlands overspill sites. Others are so closely connected to their pyramids of suppliers in the conurbation that they have little interest in moving from their present sites.

In fact Birmingham itself is passing quickly through a transitional phase in which it is being converted from having a manufacturing to a service base. In the city and its immediate industrial satellite Solihull, 65 per cent of all employment was provided by manufacturing in 1951; but by 1963 the proportion had fallen to 56 per cent. Since 1960 the number of jobs in manufacturing has fallen steeply both for men and women (by 2 per cent per annum), while the volume of work in the services has been rising by 4 per cent per annum. This reduction of manufacturing work is no proof of the movement of industry from the city. In part it reflects productivity increases and labour economies. Yet over the same period, manufacturing jobs in the Black Country have grown substantially—by about 10 per cent and roughly at the same rate as the region as a whole. In short, whilst there has been no industrial dispersal of any consequence (except interregionally, to Development Areas), a redistribution has occurred within the conurbation. This interpretation is borne out by data on factory floorspace construction. Of a total of about 1,200 thousand square metres (13 million square feet) of factory floorspace 'exported' from Birmingham, only about 140 thousand (1½ million) went to the rest of the region outside the conurbation; the remainder was about equally shared between the Development Areas and the Black Country. But apart from this new construction, a huge amount of existing Black Country factory space has been reoccupied by enterprises moving from the city (Eversley, Jackson and Lomas, 1965).

In this natural shift of industry from the city to the Black Country, two forces have been particularly important. These are the reclamation of derelict land for factory development and the rise of the industrial property company. The latter is chiefly responsible for the proliferation of industrial estates, of which there are now over 100 in the conurbation. Many of them are located on derelict land; others on sites abandoned by declining manufactures or on old railway land.

5.3.3 *The Coventry district*

Among the physically separate towns that form an outer girdle to the Birmingham city region, the Coventry cluster is so important as to deserve special treatment. Put into its regional context, the industrial structure of the Coventry district takes the contrasts between Birmingham and the Black Country a stage further in the direction of an increasing emphasis on the assembly stages of the metal-vehicle-engineering complex. In Coventry these stages are completely dominant. In the nineteen fifties, for example, the earlier stages in ferrous and non-ferrous metal working accounted for about 10 per cent of factory employment in the conurbation as a whole, but only about 2 per cent in Coventry; similarly, miscellaneous metal goods, which provided almost a quarter of the conurbation's factory employment, occupied only 5 per cent of Coventry's industrial labour force. On the other hand, motor vehicle manufacture provided jobs for 43 per cent of Coventry's operatives, but only 15 per cent of the conurbation's, while machine tools (9 per cent), radio and electronic engineering (10 per cent), and aircraft manufacture (10 per cent) were the other distinctive manufactures of the Coventry district.

This appears to be an industrial structure ideally geared to derive maximum advantage from the direction of national growth over the last twenty-five years. But, in fact, the growth of factory employment in Coventry itself has been relatively slow, though some of its near neighbours (such as Leamington, Warwick, Daventry and Nuneaton) have added one-third or more to their total volume of manufacturing jobs since 1945. This is in part a natural enough decentralization within the Coventry sub-system but it also reflects more general restraints upon growth. The car industry has not been a growth sector (in employment terms) in the West Midlands since 1950. Part of its growth, both at the assembly and component levels, has been deflected to the Development Areas. Moreover the two assembly firms most closely associated with Coventry (Rootes and Triumph) both fell into financial difficulties early in the nineteen sixties and were absorbed by larger enterprises (Chrysler and Leyland respectively). This underlines a risk inherent in Coventry's economic character, the dominant position of a few very large employers in highly competitive industries. The aircraft industry too has had some grave problems. In general the smaller towns of the Coventry cluster have had fewer of these difficulties to face. Not only their vehicle industries, but also other branches of manufacturing, are concerned more with components than with final assembly—components firms supply 90 per cent of manufacturing employment in Leamington, and 58 per cent in Warwick—and so they are more flexible in relation to the market, and less prone to its vagaries. On the other hand, so close are the journey to work links within the Coventry belt that these town by town contrasts are not very meaningful. Taking the sub-system as a whole, there is considerable diversity outside the dominant industries. Coventry itself manufactures artificial fibres, and the East Midland knitwear zone (see p. 173) overlaps into east Warwickshire generally. Rugby is essentially an electrical engineering town, though the recent merger of the two chief companies here (Associated Electrical Industries and English Electric) with the General Electric Company must cause some anxiety as rationalization proceeds. In brief, the sub-region as a whole continues to grow as strongly in industrial employment as in population, though Coventry's own performance has more recently been much less spectacular than in its inter-war and immediate post-war phases of feverish expansion.

5.3.4 *Other Towns*

The other free-standing communities of the Birmingham city region are mostly county and smaller country towns that remained essentially unindustrialized until the nineteen thirties. Partly for this reason, and also because of their strong recent population growth, the service sector is relatively more important to them than it is in the conurbation as a whole; it provides about 42 per cent of their total jobs, compared with the conurbation's 34 per cent. But two active coal-fields are included within this outer zone of the city region— the Cannock and East Warwickshire fields. Extractive employment, therefore, provides 14 per cent of the total work, and very much higher proportions of male employment in the Cannock-Rugeley-Brownhills and the Nuneaton-Tamworth areas. In the Cannock coal-field the regrouping of the mining industry upon a relatively few units (by 1969 there were only four pits employing 5,050 men) continues, with an inevitable run down in labour demands; mining redundancy here, however, generally seems to have been absorbed by the vigorous general industrial growth of the area. This has not been the recent experience of the Warwickshire coal-field, however. Since 1959, the total of active collieries has declined from 12 to 5, over 10,000 jobs in mining have been lost and by 1969 the field employed scarcely more than 5,000 men. A local pocket of quite serious un-employment has been created as a result in the Nuneaton area, where the rate was as high as 4.8 per cent in June 1968. Indeed North Warwickshire's case for some degree of government assistance was considered (but rejected) by the Hunt Committee.

In the outer zone, manufacturing employment (which provides 44 per cent of all the jobs there) is both distinctly less important than in the conurbation (where it provides 65 per cent) and very much more diverse. Locally, there are important food and drink industries (brewing, milling, baking) that derive ultimately from the rural past of such country towns as Uttoxeter and Evesham. Other manufactures that are anomalous to the region are also traditional. Stone and Stafford in the north and Daventry to the south-east have important footwear manufactures. Kidderminster has its carpet industry. The latter industry is one of the least dynamic aspects of Midland manufacturing, yet about three quarters of all operative employment in the town is within the industry. New processes, and an associated dispersal of carpet making more widely within Britain, have reduced Kidderminster's share of the trade from about one-third to one-quarter and employment has been virtually static at 10,000 in the town and its hinterland during the last decade. In general (but with notable exceptions) there has been a relatively feeble development of conurbation types of industry in these towns of the outer ring. Taking the zone as a whole, iron founding accounts for only 6 per cent of the total job supply, miscellaneous metal goods only 10 per cent and vehicles (chiefly their components) 6 per cent. In contrast electrical engineering (dominant at Stafford and Rugby) is the strongest single manufacture with 17 per cent of total employment, and hosiery, carpets, footwear and mechanical engineering each account for some 5 per cent to 7 per cent of employment. These general figures naturally conceal strong local contrasts. Some of the outer towns, for example, are very strongly specialized, often in vulnerable industries. The situations of Kidderminster and the mining areas have already been noted. Both Stafford and Rugby are uneasily dependent on decisions made in the General Electric Company-English Electric board room. Other towns, in contrast, have great industrial diversity. Worcester, for example, combines employment in machine tools, foundry work, non-ferrous metals, mining machinery, metal cans, and car components with a range of county town trades and a strong service sector. Lichfield and Stratford have almost equal variety on a smaller scale.

There is another approach to the classification of these towns on the fringe, based less on product than on 'stage'. Some towns show a strong emphasis (within their metal working-engineering-vehicle complex of industries) on the 'early' metal processing or shaping trades, or alternatively on the production of capital goods like engineers tools. Others have strong component and sub-assembly industries, and a third group is dominated by final assembly. This last group of assembly towns (chiefly Stafford and Rugby, Rugeley and Uttoxeter) assembles equipment, such as heavy electrical machinery and earth-moving vehicles, not strongly represented in the conurbation. Although some of their components are drawn from the conurbation, they also come from dispersed national suppliers and the firms' markets are national or international. Industrial linkages with the conurbation are therefore weak. Other towns have a far stronger development of 'early' process work of a conurbation type. A zone to the north and northeast of the conurbation, and relatively close to it, produces forgings, castings, bearings, tools, and aluminium shapes. This is essentially industry of the conurbation type. Indeed, much of it has moved out in recent years, to Cannock and Aldridge-Brownhills, and also over the greater distance to Lichfield and Tamworth. Significantly, most of these towns are also receiving population overspill from Birmingham. As a result, genuine dispersal and decentralization of people and work is taking place to areas close enough to the core so that the close links with the total industrial complex that are needed by process firms can be maintained. Similarly, in the southwest, metal shaping and machine tool work has dispersed strongly to the Worcester-Bromsgrove-Redditch area, another district taking overspill. The group of towns in the outer zone which have a strong component specialization include Warwick, Leamington and Nuneaton as the clearest cases—although both Bromsgrove and Redditch have also attracted a components industry on a large scale. Where the component stage is dominant, linkages both with the conurbation and especially with Coventry are likely to be close. Indeed many components firms are of conurbation origin (Wood, 1966).

These contrasts have a clear relevance to the problem of industrial dispersal from the conurbation, the key to a regional planning strategy. Process firms need immediate contact with the industrial complex. They have grown up in, or moved to, areas on the northern and south western fringes, generally within 19 to 32 kilometres (12 to 20 miles) of Birmingham. But they have shown no taste for more distant sites. Component firms, too, have grown far more strongly within 32 kilometres (20 miles) of Birmingham (or 16 kilometres of Coventry) than outside these ranges. Are these the limits to which conurbation industry is prepared to move? If so, from what source would more distant overspill schemes in, say, East Shropshire or North Staffordshire draw their industrial employment? Certainly Telford has had great difficulties in attracting conurbation firms. Outside these distance limits, most industry—as much as 90 per cent of employment in Stafford and Rugby—comprises assembly firms and not closely associated with the Midland complex.

There is some evidence that the ring of towns from Worcester to Droitwich, Leamington, Nuneaton, Lichfield and Cannock, marks a critical distance beyond which industrial decentralization from the conurbation is not likely, in practice, to take place. If this is accepted as a planning constraint, then perhaps short-range overspill and peripheral expansion must be relied upon to meet the main mass of the conurbation's housing demand and population growth, at least in the immediate future.

It is equally noteworthy, nevertheless, that very little of the considerable growth of manufacturing employment in the outer zone of the Birmingham city region between 1951 and 1963 (an increase of over 20 per cent, compared with 5 per cent within the conurbation) has been through the actual transfer of conurbation firms. Moreover, service employment (a 26 per cent increase, with 37 per cent increase among females) has been growing far more strongly than manufacturing employment, so that the ability of these towns to attract mobile conurbation industry is no yardstick of their capacity to absorb overspill. In almost all the larger towns of the outer zone, nine-tenths of the 1963 factory employment was in concerns established before 1947; intraregional mobility of employment, therefore, has been largely irrelevant to their growth. Only in some of the smaller towns has new industry (by no means all from the conurbation) made a real contribution to growth. For example, new enterprises provide almost half of Cannock's factory jobs, and four-fifths of those in Aldridge—although the latter is a special case, almost the only really succeessful example of industrial overspill from the core of the conurbation. However, the total number of jobs created by guided industrial movement from the conurbation to planned trading estates beyond its margins has not been large. Staffordshire has attracted about 12,000 new jobs to planned estates, but almost 8,000 of these have gone to Aldridge-Brownhills on the conurbation's northern margin, and another 3,000 to Cannock, not far beyond. Lichfield, Stafford, Rugeley, Tamworth and a few smaller places have shared less than 2,000 jobs between them, and in these areas most of the new firms are not of conurbation origin.

Two conclusions seem clear. There are sharp and relatively close limits to the distance conurbation firms generally are prepared to move. Nevertheless, beyond these limits, considerable increases in manufacturing employment have occurred since 1951, based on the growth of indigenous industry, new enterprises and moves from areas outside the conurbation. Overspill to relatively long-distance sites needs a completely different strategy, with less insistence upon drawing employment from the conurbation, and more upon the development of an adequate industrial base. In seeking for this, the major problems do not relate to the issues of decentralization, but rather to the competitiveness of these sites—such as Telford—in comparison with the Development Areas and their package of incentives.

5.4 The Potteries Conurbation

North Staffordshire contains a relatively small industrial conurbation, compact to the point of congestion, with a 1971 population of about 450,000. It is centred on Stoke on Trent (population 265,000), which is itself an amalgam of. six formerly separate towns of fierce local loyalty from which a County Borough was formed in 1907. The conurbation also includes the strong and growing borough of Newcastle under Lyme (76,000), plus the smaller urban districts of Kidsgrove, Biddulph and Alsager (see Figure 20). From this compact urban mass, dormitory growth is reaching out strongly into the surrounding rural districts, so that most rural villages—especially the market town of Stone to the south, and the mining district of Cheadle to the east—all show clear signs of suburbanization. This pronounced decentralization reflects not only a growing land shortage in the conurbation—exacerbated by a serious problem of dereliction—but also the unattractiveness of its core as a residential environment.

Thus defined, the conurbation and its suburban outposts constitute a sharply defined labour market area. There is a complex system of labour interchanges between the constituent parts, but only slight movements of workers across its boundaries, the main ones being the journey to work links with Stafford and the towns of south Cheshire. Beyond this well integrated urban complex lies a broader region with a total population of about 750,000. It is linked more tenuously with the Potteries. The local evening paper circulates westwards to Crewe, southwards to Stafford, northwards to Congleton, and eastwards to Leek and Uttoxeter. This is also the service area of Hanley as a high-rank central place, and of Radio Stoke. The existence of a Stoke-oriented city region was accepted in the Maud proposals for the reform of local administration, and the new unitary authority suggested included the whole of north and central Staffordshire together with much of southern Cheshire.

Whether defined in the narrow context of the conurbation, or the wider context of the city region, this is an urban complex that straddles both county and regional boundaries. It lies not only on the divide between the Trent and Mersey drainage systems but also on a watershed in terms of social and industrial affiliations. Both Birmingham and Manchester (neither more than an hour's journey away) attract the occasional shopping of Potteries people. The textile tradition of Pennine England reaches strongly to Leek and Congleton—even Newcastle had a cotton mill until the late nineteen sixties— but the chief growth industries of the conurbation have stronger links with the West Midland vehicle and engineering groups. Newcastle is typical of the Midland industrialized market town in its structure of employment, its vigorous growth, its great prosperity and its urban form. The County Borough of Stoke, on the other hand, shows distinctly 'northern' features. It has to face the problems of its Victorian urban landscape, large areas of sub-standard housing, an overdependence upon a low-wage industry with declining demands for labour, and a failure to attract new sources of employment in the growth sectors of the economy. The boundary between Newcastle and Stoke is a margin of 'grey' Britain.

In its economic fortunes North Staffordshire is anomalous within the West Midlands, the region of which it officially forms a part. Between 1951 and 1964, while the population of the region grew by 12.1 per cent that of the conurbation grew by only 4.7 per cent. While the region attracted a net inward balance of migration of 2.2 per cent, North Staffordshire suffered a net outflow of 2.8 per cent. While the West Midlands as a whole had a high rate of natural increase (9 per cent), the age-selective migration of young adults from North Staffordshire altered the balance of births and deaths sufficiently to bring the sub-regional rate of natural increase down to only 6.6 per cent. The causes of this unfavourable comparison lie in North Staffordshire's poor economic performance since 1945. In the decade from 1953, the sub-region experienced an increase in total employment of only 5.8 per cent, compared with a West Midland rate of 13 per cent. Here then is a distinctive industrial sub-region, burdened by an archaic economy, and failing to secure a fair share in the national growth of population, industry and personal prosperity. Yet it has never suffered industrial distress sharply enough to develop a serious problem of unemployment and so to benefit from Development Area status. In this respect, too, it is typical of Pennine England. Indeed, part of the growth of North Staffordshire's most dynamic industries has been deflected elsewhere by the operation of the government's location of industry policies.

5.4.1 *The Urban Structure*

The urban structure of the conurbation reflects the underlying regional geology and its associated landscape features with remarkable clarity. The Potteries coal-field fills the trough of a south-pitching syncline, one of the several steep folds in the Carboniferous strata of the southwest Pennines. Thus the field is triangular, with an apex to the north and a broad base to the south, the latter defined by a bold scarp in Bunter pebble beds. In the centre of the syncline, the productive measures are concealed beneath marls and sandstones of Upper Coal Measure age. On the east and west, bounding ridges of Millstone Grit enclose the field, and converge northwards to the fine prow of The Cloud. Three inverted 'V's therefore nest within each other : an outermost 'V' of the gritstone ridges, an inner 'V' of exposed Middle Coal Measures, and an innermost 'V' of Upper Coal Measures. Four parallel streams are trenched (from NNW to SSE) across the landscape. The dominant valley is that of the Fowlea Brook. This guided both the Trent and Mersey canal of 1766, and the later North Staffordshire railway (part of an alternative Manchester to London trunk route) to tunnels at Harecastle through the gritstone ridge. The railway in fact abandoned its tunnel on electrification in favour of a new line following a steeply graded glacial spillway. Thus the Fowlea valley was the main axis of communication during the conurbation's formative decades. From its broad floor of Etruria Marls, the valley rises eastwards to the dipslope of a minor scarp, but one that gives a spine to the urban structure—the Blackband outcrop. Along its windswept scarp, there grew the line of the Pottery towns—from Tunstall in the north, through Burslem and Hanley, to Fenton and Longton in the south. They had the canal and railway to their west, as well as a clay supply in the Etruria Marls. Beneath their foundation, and to the east, were rich resources of longflame coals, coarse clays and iron in the Blackband series. On this scarp, the pottery industry rooted itself permanently, showing little inclination to move downhill to the railway and canal—except for minor outliers at, for example, the industrial village of Stoke as it was in the nineteenth century.

Thus there is a marked linearity in the urban framework of the conurbation, and a quite remarkable site-stability on the part of its staple manufacture. The Blackband ridge provided the basic raw materials. The bottle-ovens of the potbanks sprouted along its entire length. Pit-heads in their scores threw their spoil banks across it. Row after row of terraced houses climbed across the ridge, competing for space with the marl holes and the shraff-heaps of pottery waste. The evolving town centres fought for space—and against each other for trade and influence—as each of them developed the simple urban equipment of small Victorian industrial communities. Here was the disorder of laissez-faire industrialism at its very worst; and most of it survived to the mid-twentieth century to present the planner with almost insoluble problems of urban re-design (Moisley, 1951; Beaver, 1964).

Except for scattered iron working and coal mining, there was little spread of industry either east or west from the line of towns smoking furiously on the ridge. Large areas of open land survived close to the old towns; it accommodated their inter-war and post-war expansion into both publicly owned and speculatively built housing estates, under the shadow of the general smoke pall that was dissipated only during the last decade. The most favoured direction of suburban expansion was westwards, both uphill and upwind, to the old market town of Newcastle. Between it and the line of pottery towns the Fowlea valley lies largely open despite the presence of major rail and canal communications. Only small clusters of pottery works sought canalside sites—at Stoke and Longport, for example—for few followed Wedgwood's example in developing the Etruria works and its industrial village beside the waterway. Some ancillary trades processing waterborne raw materials, such as the potters' millers, sought canalside sites. Yet the largest industrial unit in the Fowlea valley is the Shelton steelworks, the last major survivor of the once widespread iron industry. On a 100 hectare (250 acre) site, this plant draws coking coal by conveyor from a nearby colliery and has recently been rebuilt to produce an annual 0.4 million tons of steel by the Kaldo process.

Beyond the Fowlea valley and on the higher ground of the Upper Coal Measures, New-castle stands apart from the pottery towns. Nevertheless, it has not wholly escaped their destiny. There are several working collieries on its outskirts, and a line of brick and tile works follows the Etruria Marl outcrop. Since the nineteen thirties, however, Newcastle has developed its own distinctive manufacturing base, with an accent on industries with some growth potential; car wiring systems, electrical and electronic engineering and bakery products are three examples.

It is a general characteristic of the newer manufactures of North Staffordshire that they have taken up a peripheral location, away from the urban tangle of the six towns. Many are aligned along the much improved north-south trunk road (with motorway access) of the A34. The Michelin factory in Stoke is not far from the southern margin of the urban mass, while the English Electric complex at Kidsgrove is at the northern limit. Two Ordnance factories, at Swynnerton to the south and near Alsager to the north, pioneered this dispersal of employment to the fringes. Thus, industrial employment is declining quickly in the core of the conurbation—it fell by 8 per cent in the County Borough between 1953 and 1963—but it is growing quite strongly on its margins. Population, too, is decentralizing but it is doing so less quickly than employment; Stoke lost only 5.3 per cent of its inhabitants between 1951 and 1971. In this faster dispersal of jobs than people North Staffordshire is unusual among British conurbations.

Until the nineteen sixties, little radical change came to the urban texture of the core of the conurbation, though it was by then enveloped in its suburban spread. However, the changes which are now coming to this well-preserved Victorian townscape, though belated, are sweeping. One of the weaknesses of the County Borough as a regional city has been the rivalry of the five town centres as retail foci, which has long hindered the growth of a totally dominant central business area adequate in stature to perform a major sub-regional role. Hanley has long been the chief retail centre, but as first among near-equals. Happily, policy is triumphing over parochialism, and Hanley is emerging as the dominant focus, with a growing range of department stores and multiple businesses. Commercial expansion is creating strong pressures for physical renewal and the improvement of traffic flows, so that the developer and the bulldozer are at last erasing the confused landscape of tiny houses and workshop industry. Thus this conurbation without a centre is at last acquiring one. A second and even more powerful force in the reshaping of the urban structure is the D-shaped loop motorway from the M6 to the west and through the heart of the conurbation, the first stage of which was begun in 1971. When complete, it will give the Potteries the almost unique distinction of being bisected by a motorway, and its influence will clearly be profound.

5.4.2 *The Industrial Structure*

'Pits and pots' have long been, and remain, the chief supports of the unusually narrow-based economy of North Staffordshire. However, a clear distinction can be drawn between the core (the County Borough) and the rest of the sub-region. In 1952, 41 per cent of the City's (but only 33 per cent of the sub-region's) employment was in the pottery group. Even by 1966, pottery employed a third of the City's and a quarter of the sub-region's workers. Both in the City itself, and the sub-region as a whole, mining provided 16 per cent of male employment in 1952, and this proportion remained as high as 15 per cent even in 1965. Metal manufacture by 1966 employed only 3 per cent of the sub-regional total, and the engineering and electrical group almost 9 per cent—the bulk of it outside the City. In brief, some 35 per cent of male employment, and 37 per cent of female jobs, depend on two old staple industries, both with declining labour demands.

The future of mining in the region clearly depends more on external influences affecting the national energy market than on local factors. This is a relatively rich, productive and profitable field with exemplary man-shift productivity. There are some 43 metres (140 feet) of coal in 30 seams, some of coking quality, worked to a depth approaching 1,220 metres (4,000 feet). Mining has retreated from the shallow margins of the field to the centre and south of the syncline, where 11 large pits are at work. One is a post-1945 sinking, and several others have been extensively reconstructed. Some stow waste underground and are better neighbours within the urban mass than most pits elsewhere. The closure of uneconomic collieries has had little effect on output, which has been stable at about 6 million tons annually since 1945, but rising productivity has progressively reduced labour requirements from a total employment of 24,000 in 1957 to 16,000 in 1965. Whether the field's excellent productivity record can save it from further rationalization is doubtful. The mines have lost their chief local market—for longflame coal was used almost exclusively in the pottery kilns until their recent and almost universal conversion to alternative fuels. If the pits of North Staffordshire employ even 5,000 men in 1980 they will be doing rather better than the probable national trend. Thus one of the region's few relatively high-wage industries seems doomed to be reduced to a remnant during the next decade.

Although it is convenient to refer to the 'pottery' manufacture, in fact this is not one industry but several, with varying records and prospects. Firms in the tableware section tend to specialize either upon earthenware or china, the latter being concentrated in the south, especially at Longton. The electrical ceramics and the sanitary ware industries are separate branches, and there is also a large but declining brick and tile industry. Ancillary trades include the milling of clay, flints and bones, and the preparation of glazing materials, dyes and transfers. The common characteristics of all these branches is their declining demand for labour, though at varying rates; the tile industry, for example, has shrunk quickly following the development of other and cheaper roofing and flooring materials. This is one of the common problems of the ceramics industries, that their products are open to competition from other types of material (especially plastics) that lend themselves better to cheaper mass-production.

Perhaps the most distinctive feature of the pottery industries is their small average unit-size. The typical potbank is small and compact; about one-third employ fewer than 100 operatives, and almost 90 per cent have fewer than 500. On the other hand, there are four large firms employing over 1,000 each. Until recently, most firms were in family management, and both their profits and return on capital employed were low—one reason for their locational immobility. Like the Lancashire cotton firms of a generation ago, the potbanks recruit a highly skilled work force from their immediate locality, and there is often a strong family connexion with a particular firm. Labour supply, too, is a constraint on movement. The few firms that have moved away from the line of towns along the Blackband ridge are mostly large units in the tile and sanitary ware sections. Wedgwoods are the exception among the producers of fine pottery, having moved to a rural site; its Barlaston factory to the south of the conurbation is, however, linked to the core by rail and has its own station.

Two great changes, neither locational, have come to the industry in recent years. It has almost entirely abandoned both coal firing, and the bottle kiln, for continuous firing using gas, oil or electricity. As part of this change many potbanks have been rebuilt but almost always on their old sites. If the industry were ever going to shift from its traditional pattern of sites, it would have done so during the last fifteen years. Yet its general location in 1971 is much the same as it was in 1871, or even, indeed, in 1771. Secondly, the old family pattern of ownership has begun to break down as a number of large firms and holding companies have gradually secured control of a large part of the industry. Twenty such groups account for 80 per cent of tableware production and only three firms now dominate wall-tile output. Yet the works themselves remain small. In a trade still so dependent on craft-skill and creativity, there is no necessary virtue in great unit size.

Rationalization has come slowly to the pottery industries. It expresses itself in a gradual reduction in the labour force, without a loss either in the value or in the volume of output. In the decade to 1965, employment in the ceramic group fell from 58,000 to 45,500. Most of the loss has been in female employment. Although this is socially less serious in affecting only the supplementary incomes of most families, it presents a problem in the sense that there is little alternative industrial work for women. The service industries are too stunted in the region to act as an effective replacement, and in a low wage sub-regional economy the income of wives is important not only to the family, but also in terms of its influence upon the sub-region's purchasing power.

There is nothing very surprising in the slow decline of the labour force in a technically conservative craft industry of Victorian growth. A more serious cause for concern is the inadequate development of replacement employment, which has expanded far more slowly in the City than the region as a whole. The growth industries in the national context are also the growth sector of North Staffordshire's economy but their progress in the region has been uneven and uncertain. The electrical and engineering group grew faster in the sub-region between 1953 and 1963 (by 35 per cent) than in the West Midlands (20 per cent) or the nation (23 per cent)—but from a trivial size. Paper and printing and miscellaneous manufacturing also have a good employment growth record but the vehicle industry actually declined in the sub-region. Perhaps the weakest aspect of the economic performance of the Potteries over this decade was the feeble growth of its service industries. The distributive group grew by 23 per cent nationally, but only by 16 per cent in the region and a derisory 1 per cent in the central city. Here is the clearest possible demonstration of the lack of a truly dominant focus, able to attract massive retail investment and capable of challenging the distant influence of Manchester and Birmingham. In sum, the growth of 'replacement' employment has scarcely balanced the decline in the older staples, so that the total volume of work available in the sub-region has become stagnant; indeed between 1962 and 1966 it declined by about 1,200 jobs. This is an east Lancashire type situation in which slow structural change, associated with the replacement of old industries by new, takes place in the context of an overall loss in the total of work available, but it occurs without serious unemployment and is corrected by out-migration and falling activity rates.

The influence of the distribution of industry legislation upon North Staffordshire has been entirely negative. World War II brought the first major progress towards a more diversified economy in the region. Potteries were closed to free labour and new factories were built, later to be converted to more peaceful purposes. Established industries outside the traditional groups—for example tyre manufacture, which dates from 1926—grew strongly during the war and immediate post-war periods. Some of these growth units are very large, and in trades with a great potential: Michelin employs 5,000, and the Rist car-wiring plant in Newcastle some 4,000. But the impetus towards diversification seems to have been lost. Within the area this is blamed on the effect of regional policies and especially the Board of Trade's reluctance to approve industrial development certificate applications by mobile industry for sites in North Staffordshire. There is some evidence that the vehicle industry has been actively discouraged from considering expansion in the area, and certainly the great bulk of certificates actually approved have been from firms in the traditional pottery and metal trades. On the other hand, the real effect of Board of Trade policies has undoubtedly been indirect rather than overt. Whilst few mobile firms have actually been prevented from entering the region by a direct refusal of an i.d.c., many have been deflected elsewhere by the Development Area 'package' of incentives and the known reluctance of the Board to grant certificates in the sub-region.

Certainly North Staffordshire has lost part of the growth of its established 'alternative' manufactures to sites elsewhere. Michelin's recent growth has been largely in Lancashire and Ulster. The making of an advanced range of computers was transferred from Kidsgrove to a new factory at Winsford, the nearest point to the parent plant at which Development Area incentives were available. On the other hand, the closure of the aluminium rolling mills at Milton in 1964—with the loss of 1,000 jobs in a high wage industry—seems not to have been directly influenced by regional policies. For all these reasons, Stoke made a powerfully argued plea to the Hunt Committee to be considered one of the Intermediate Areas, entitled to some Treasury support in modernising both its economic structure and its urban environment. Except for greater financial help in treating its derelict land, the plea went unheard, even with the extension of Intermediate Areas in 1972 (see p. 65).

What then are the prospects of the sub-region? In one sense they are superb. There is no locality in Britain of greater centrality or developing accessibility. London is two hours from Stoke by electric train, Manchester and Birmingham one. The M6 now joins the M1 via the Midland link and will join the M62 via the North Cheshire motorway; this will bring the whole of England from London to Carlisle and from Bristol to Leeds and Tyneside within an easy day's return journey by delivery truck from Stoke. Why then does mobile industry show so little interest in the sub-region? There are, of course, enormous local problems of environmental rehabilitation. Stoke has a greater area of derelict land than any other county borough in the country—almost 700 hectares (1,700 acres) or 8 per cent of the city's area. There is as a result a shortage of industrial sites, at least for large units and in the core of the conurbation. There are the accompanying problems of sub-standard housing and the total 'environmental image' of a Victorian industrial city in which so much of the social capital is decayed and depreciated. About 40 per cent of all the houses in the city date from before 1914. The greater part of the conurbation is liable to mining subsidence—although this is limited by underground waste-stowage and is no serious problem to low structures. But perhaps the greatest obstacle to progress is the absence of any major development proposals in the sub-region.

On many occasions since 1945 a site at Swynnerton, south of the conurbation, has been proposed for new town growth. This is an area of wooded Bunter scarps of high amenity value surrounded by good farmland. There was also a wartime ordnance factory close by, and an M6 interchange is only two miles away. The site has been rejected— doubtless correctly—but the sub-region needs some such project to spearhead its economic growth. Stone has been proposed as a new town site. Stoke itself has offered to absorb an overspill population of 50,000; it is not clear, however, where the land could be found. Yet there remain no firm plans for any major development in or near the conurbation. In the regional planning context, the Potteries conurbation occupies a vacuum, too far from both Manchester or Birmingham to attract growth from either. There are few areas in Britain where such a great development potential is so completely neglected.

5.5 Industrial East Shropshire and the Telford Growth Point

Set within one of the last of the predominantly rural English counties, 48 kilometres (30 miles) north west of Birmingham, lies the tiny Coalbrookdale coal-field, the focus of a compact industrial region that has many of the characteristics of a Black Country in miniature. It suffers all the latter's environmental problems of surface devastation, but it also shares its industrial vitality and adaptability. In little more than a decade, between 1953 and 1964, the total of work available in the area grew by 24 per cent, more than twice the national rate of increase. This outlier of industrial development has often had, in the past, a significance far beyond its modest size. Here, in 1709, the first coke-iron was successfully smelted and by 1780 the area was producing no less than 40 per cent of the entire national output of pig iron. Like east Lancashire it was a district of remarkable fertility in technical innovation in the eighteenth century: the first cast-iron bridge spanned the Severn by 1779, and what was probably the first successful locomotive came from the Darby works in 1802. The region paid the inevitable price for such vigorous industrial development in the palaeotechnic phase. Coal, clay, gannister, ironstone and road metal were won from it by shallow shaft and open pit workings. Spoil and slag heaps were littered over its surface, and abandoned mines and ironworks were scattered along the ruins of a complex canal system. It was, in part, the extent of this industrial devastation that led to the suggestion that East Shropshire might absorb some of Birmingham's overspill.

Here was a district beyond the West Midlands green belt in which a new town could be built with the minimum loss of farmland of any quality, and with the added advantage that its development would restore a tortured landscape. Thus Dawley new town was designated in 1963. Forty-one per cent of its area of 3,700 hectares (9,168 acres) was affected by past or present mineral working. In its first conception Dawley was to be a middle-sized new town, initially to absorb some 55,000 newcomers, and so reach a population of 90,000 by the mid-nineteen eighties, but in 1968 this development programme was augmented to one of new city scale. The designated area was more than doubled to include the towns of Wellington and Oakengates. Dawley as a result became Telford; its present population is 78,000 and to this about 145,000 overspill migrants will be added to produce a total community, with natural increase, of the order of 250,000. Telford is thus the first of the new city projects to make physical progress. It also represents the first time that an entire industrial region has been scheduled for comprehensive redevelopment under a single authority.

The physical setting of this very large project is attractive and impressive. To the west of the coal-field, along the line of a fractured uplift, the Wrekin rises in wooded slopes to 400 metres (1,300 feet). From the upthrust Pre-Cambrian outcrop, the Palaeozoic strata dip away gently southeast and are down-thrown by faulting into the Wolverhampton graben with Trias at the surface. A narrow NE-SW trending outcrop of Middle Coal Measures, rarely more than two miles wide, flanks the Wrekin uplift on the east, and is lost under an overlay of Upper Coal Measures and Trias in a considerable concealed extension to the south and east. Across this low coal-field plateau the Severn is trenched in a post-glacial gorge, which has provided a locally lower base level to which the coal-field tributaries work. Much of the earliest industrial development in the area was located in the lower courses of these deep and incised valleys, especially in Coalbrookdale, where the coal and iron outcropped, the 'hanging' profiles afforded abundant water power, and the navigable Severn was nearby. There are proposals to create, along the wooded slopes of the gorge, an amenity area of a distinctive type in which some of the most interesting legacies of the industrial past will be preserved and restored; it will provide a remarkable outdoor museum of industrial archaeology and a permanent record of the distinctive importance of East Shropshire in British industrial history.

The industrial structure of East Shropshire has always been—and still in part remains—directly based on the local mineral resources. The coal-field itself is at the end-stage of exploitation. The shallower seams of the dissected west and south have long been abandoned for large-scale working, as have the bedded ironstones that once supplied the local blast furnaces. But a considerable volume of open-cast working, for both coal and the associated fireclays, survives in the shallow part of the field towards the slopes of the Wrekin. Since clay production (for bricks, pipes and sanitary ware) is running at some 230,000 tons a year, and open-cast coal output at between 100,000 and 150,000 tons, these surface mineral workings are a very considerable problem in the development of the new city, within the area of which they lie. Underground mining sets fewer constraints on development. The location of collieries is at the last stage in a 'down-the-dip' eastward progression, and large modern pits have penetrated the Upper Coal Measures to reach undisturbed seams below. There were two such pits at work until 1967; the single survivor,

Granville colliery, is thought to have an assured future and a development potential of 1 million tons per year at competitive costs. Thus, there remain possible problems of conflict between active (and especially surface) mineral working and the progress of the new city, quite apart from the costs and technical difficulties of handling urban and industrial development in an abandoned mining landscape.

Metal working in East Shropshire has gone through much the same process of evolution as in the Black Country. Smelting has been dead here since the nineteen thirties, and some of the heavier traditional branches, such as constructional steelwork and heavy castings, have tended to decline. The main growth sector within the metal working group is the production of light, specialized forge and foundry components for the vehicle industry and the domestic equipment market. The influence of the West Midland car assembly industry is seen most clearly in a large plant near Wellington—the sub-region's biggest unit, employing over 6,000 workers—which produces car wheels and other steel pressings. The largest of the ironfounding firms in the area now slants its production towards domestic heating and plumbing equipment, and so is geared to the demands of a buoyant national housebuilding industry. Through these changes in product-emphasis the metal working trades of East Shropshire are quickly increasing their labour demands, and their growth since 1952 has been at much above the West Midland regional rate. The other major growth industry in the sub-regional economy is the engineering and electrical group. This was feebly developed until 1939, but has subsequently made rapid progress. Indeed, one of the strengths of the area's economy since 1945 has been the high birth-rate of young engineering firms, supplemented by some movement from the West Midland conurbation; most of these firms have prospered. There is a great variety of product in this sector, but the strongest single element is clearly the production of both mechanical and electrical components for the West Midland assembly industries, and especially for vehicle manufacture.

Structurally, therefore, the East Shropshire economy has a strength that belies the drab, sub-derelict appearance of so much of the coal-field. Excluding the service sector (the region's chief weakness), employment has grown much faster than in the West Midlands as a whole, by no less than 36 per cent between 1952 and 1966 compared with a regional increase of only 8.5 per cent. All three major manufacturing growth sectors have increased their employment at far above regional rates; metal manufacture by 46 per cent, the vehicle group by 75 per cent and engineering by 68 per cent. These three groups now provide, respectively, 16, 23 and 30 per cent of the total of mining and manufacturing employment in industrial Shropshire. In brief, East Shropshire's manufacturing falls chiefly in the components and sub-assembly groups, and it has demonstrated a marked adaptability and a flexibility in relation to its markets.

There are, however, weaknesses that may perhaps pose serious problems as the new city grows. The service sector is very feebly developed as one would expect in a coal-field without a high ranking town but under the commercial shadow of both a strong county town, Shrewsbury, and the more distant cities of the conurbation. Scarcely 30 per cent of total employment is provided by service activities and their growth since 1945 has been slow compared with the vigorous expansion of the key manufactures. An associated weakness is the lack of adequate employment opportunities for women. The female activity rate has always been far below the national and regional averages, not only because of the limited number of service jobs but also because there was little use of female labour in the traditional metal working and metal-using industries. The presence of this pool of unused female labour, only 32 kilometres (20 miles) from a labour-short conurbation, is a major reason for the vigorous growth of industry in the sub-region from 1950 to 1965. Not only did clothing factories come into the area, but some of the new units in the electrical and engineering trades made far greater use of women workers than most of the established firms. Thus female employment in manufacturing rose by over 50 per cent between 1952 and 1966, a social as much as an economic transformation. A degree of female under-employment nevertheless remains, and may increase with the build up of the incoming population. A last problem facing the East Shropshire economy is continuing exceptional dependence on a very few large employers. The largest single factory employs 6,000, about a third of the industrial labour force in the sub-region. A large defence establishment, which provides chiefly civilian employment of quasi-industrial type, is almost as large. Several units in the metal working group employ over a thousand workers each. Thus, in an age of industrial rationalization, there are clear risks inherent in an economy dominated by a few such giants.

Despite these problems, there would seem to be ample evidence that there exists a sound and successful industrial base from which the growth of the new city can commence. Such a rapidly expanding economy—it might be assumed—would have little difficulty in attracting mobile industry to provide the work necessary for the incoming population. Although indigenous employment is growing fast enough to absorb a higher proportion of the population intake than in most new town projects, it has been estimated that some 15,000 new factory jobs must be brought into the area by the early nineteen eighties to balance planned population growth. So far they have been very slow to appear, despite the area's earlier success in securing mobile enterprises from outside. A small industrial estate has been developed in the south of the designated area, but most of the firms on it are small. A second much larger industrial zone is now growing, with a greater average size of factory unit, but compared with the runaway industrial success of new towns elsewhere, and in competition with Telford for mobile industry, progress has been faltering. There have been complaints of unemployment among the overspill families and there is some degree of commuting to Wolverhampton, the nearest major employment focus, some 27 kilometres (17 miles) away—a huge distance by West Midland commuting standards. There is a real danger, therefore, that the rate of population intake may have to be reduced if a faster flow of new employment into the area can not be achieved.

The reasons for Telford's sluggish industrial growth despite the strength of the sub-regional economy are not particularly obscure. Both in the regional and the national perspective, it is engaged in unequal and perhaps unfair rivalry with alternative growth points for the limited quantity of mobile employment available during a period of slow national economic growth. On the national scale, Telford is almost uniquely disadvantaged as a major development project in that it enjoys neither the attractions of a location firmly within the English megalopolis, nor the powerful counterbalance of development area status. On the former count, it is at a great disadvantage compared with the London new towns or the new cities in the South East. On the second count, Telford is in competition both with growth points in the North West close to the M6—places such as Winsford, Skelmersdale and Runcorn which enjoy various development area allowances through their association with Merseyside—and with more distant alternative sites in Wales, Scotland and Northern England, all with the full development area package of incentives. Skelmersdale's industrial experience contrasts sharply with that of Telford. The two were scheduled at about the same time. By 1969, the former had attracted some 4,700 new jobs in 40 factories, compared with 477 jobs in 28 factories at Telford. Fortunately there were some signs of a quickening movement of new industry into the latter in 1970, a change clearly associated with the Department of Trade and Industry's shift in policy, which began to look more favourably upon the transfer of firms from the West Midlands conurbation. Nevertheless, it is an unhappy coincidence that Telford's early years of growth (in any case confused and impeded by the change in scale of the project) should have been at a time when development area policy was being strengthened by a considerable improvement in the inducements it offered to incoming firms.

Since the area is not likely to be outstandingly successful in the national competition for mobile industry, it must look rather to a regional source for the new employment it needs. Unfortunately West Midlands industry seems to have become less mobile (or less expansionist) in the late nineteen sixties, and enterprises made mobile by growth or the need to relocate must now come under even greater pressure (partly from the Department of Trade and Industry, partly from their own accountants) to consider development area sites. In any case the West Midland economy has long been a milch cow in the implementation of location of industry policy. Up to 1963, the region exported some 200 enterprises, representing about 100,000 jobs, to other parts of Britain, but over the same period only about 115 (on average much smaller firms) moved from the conurbation to other parts of the region; they represented a mere 20,000 jobs. If these quantities are any guide to the future, Telford's prospects are bleak. It has already been noted that Telford alone needs almost 15,000 new jobs over the next decade to sustain its planned growth; but there are other, perhaps more attractive, rivals for any firms which become mobile within the region. Redditch New Town has the great advantage that it lies at the conurbation margin, within the range of movement that conurbation industry seems willing to accept. The towns of mid-Staffordshire lie between the M6 and M1. The proposed Worcester-Droitwich growth point lies astride the M5. Telford, in contrast, is 24 kilometres (15 miles) away from the M6, a journey at present made over a poor road, the A5, still much as it was when the engineer after whom the new city is named built it. A replacement for the A5 is now being planned; but during the next and crucial stage of Telford's growth it must contend with a problem of poor communications, in addition to its other serious disadvantages.

Thus Telford's future is one of the enigmas in West Midland regional planning strategy. Some of the problems that the town faces are institutional in that they derive from public policies which may not prove permanent, or even long-lived, in their present form. Any lowering in the present level of development area incentives, or a relaxation of the controls over the location of industry might transform Telford's competitiveness. Some other contemporary weaknesses of the city may respond to investment, particularly its road connections to the conurbation and the M6. But the site must long remain remote from the main centres of West Midland population and economic activity. The developing regional strategy is based on the concept of growth corridors. Corridors lead somewhere but Telford-Shrewsbury lies rather at the end of a cul-de-sac, against the rural valleys of eastern Wales.

5.6 Central Wales

Central Wales has strengthening associations with the West Midlands, partly as a supplier of water (from the Elan Valley reservoirs to Birmingham) but also, increasingly, as the nearest and most accessible upland recreational region to a city-dwelling population of over four millions. But in moving from a study of the West Midlands to a brief and selective appraisal of some of the problems of mid-Wales we are turning to an area virtually unique in Britain, in that the shaping of regional policy must be related to a distinctive cultural and even political background. The cultural heartland of Wales extends from Snowdonia to the Brecon Beacons and from the upper Severn to the sea. Within these limits a Welsh speaking society—still sustained chiefly by a simple pastoral agriculture—struggles for survival not only against the slow erosion of its linguistic identity, but also against the handicap of an insecure economic base. In general the proportion of the population that can (and habitually does) speak Welsh rises from east to west, from about 10 per cent in eastern Montgomeryshire and Radnorshire to over 90 per cent in a considerable area of southern Cardiganshire. The coastal slope, west of the unsettled summit plateaux of the Cambrian mountains, has become the chief redoubt of a living Welsh culture. Unhappily there is a fairly strong correlation between the proportion of Welsh speakers and the rate of rural population decline by migration. The two areas that are linguistically the most Welsh (the valleys of western Montgomery and the hinterland of southern Cardigan) are also among the districts of steepest rural population decrease; but these are merely the most critical local examples of a more general problem. For generations population has streamed from central Wales and the social consequences of migration—the loss of the young, the able and the best qualified—are sharpened by the emotional issues involved (Jones, 1968). Since 1901 the three counties of Cardigan, Radnor and Montgomery have been losing population at a rate of roughly 4,000 per decade (about 0.5 per cent yearly); but there is some evidence that the rate of loss is slowing for the three counties together recorded a 1.7 per cent increase from 1961 to 1971. Cardiganshire, indeed, has recorded consistent growth since the middle nineteen fifties, although this is largely confined to the resort and University town of Aberystwyth and its locality. In Radnor population decline has slowed but Montgomery continues to lose by migration at undiminished speed. In these latter two counties population growth is largely confined to small towns in the east, that is in the least Welsh parts.

Few regional economies in Britain still depend so largely upon farming as this one. In both Radnor and Montgomery about a third of the working population gets a living directly from agriculture, and chiefly from farms that combine small average size with unintensive types of enterprises, such as extensive sheep and cattle rearing on land of low carrying capacity. Average farm incomes are very low : many farmers take less than a rural labourer's wage from their holdings. Underemployment is common, for over large parts of the area 60 per cent of farms require fewer than 275 man-days of labour annually. Amalgamation of these small holdings continues rapidly : about 20 per cent of Radnorshire farms of less than 40 hectares (100 acres) disappeared between 1957 and 1967. On the coastal slope south of Aberystwyth, and in the Severn valley of eastern Montgomeryshire more intensive dairying has provided a greater security to farmers, but has not arrested population decline. On the higher ground encircling the upland core of the Cambrian mountains—especially above 260 metres (800 feet)—forestry has partly replaced farming. About 46,000 hectares (114,000 acres) of forest land now exist, not only under Forestry Commission control but also in the hands of private groups who have shown a growing interest in commercial forestry here. However, about 24,000 hectares (60,000 acres) of bleak moorland are too high (over 500 metres) ever to be planted successfully.

In essence, policies to arrest the flow of Welsh speakers from the region take three forms : the attraction of industry to the small towns, the development of recreation and tourism, and planned urban growth on a small scale. A Mid-Wales Industrial Development Association was formed in 1957. Though it has had modest success in attracting 23 new enterprises to the three-county area, the most industrialized of the three (Montgomery) has only 10 per cent of its total employment in manufacturing. The Welsh Tourist Board (1969) has analysed the character of tourism in the area with results that are not altogether encouraging. The Cardiganshire coast dominates the holiday industry of the region and here (despite the presence of the 'classical' resort of Aberystwyth) half the accommodation is in the form of holiday caravans. This is the type of tourism that generates the lowest cash input into the local economy, while causing serious planning and amenity problems along a fine stretch of coast. Radnor and Montgomery have tourist industries of trivial size, and indeed are seriously underdeveloped in relation to their considerable recreational resources, especially for open-country pursuits. It is perhaps the inevitable destiny of the greater part of mid-Wales to attract relatively low-spending types of visitor (the day-tripper, the camper, the climber, the caravaner,) rather than the high-spending long-staying residential visitor who generates much greater levels of service employment and injects a far greater cash flow into the economy. The proposal to create a national park in the Cambrian mountains (if the experience of other National Parks is a guide) will do little to generate a greater inflow of tourists of the latter type. The most imaginative and radical proposal to arrest population decline in Central Wales is that for the creation of a new town in the upper Severn valley. This is best seen in the context of regional planning strategies, and is discussed briefly at page 228.

5.7 The West Midlands: A Strategy for Regional Development

The nub of regional planning problems in the West Midlands is relatively simple. How far can, or should, the Birmingham-Black Country conurbation contain its own growth of population by supplying sites to meet its own future housing demand? Ought it to be permitted to enlarge itself peripherally into its own green belt (see Figure 20), and if so where and to what extent? Is it good planning policy to scrape together scattered sites for housing and industrial growth, in a piecemeal fashion, within this rather open-textured conurbation, thus reducing the overspill need at the cost of accepting a denser, more compact urban structure? Only after these questions have been answered, and resolved into a set of policy objectives, can decisions be made about the most rational directions and locations for major dispersal of people and work from the central urban mass. This is an old controversy, in which the problems and the costs of congestion must be balanced against the benefits and economies of concentration, and the environmental attractions of decentralization set against the industrial, infrastructural and social costs involved in massive dispersal. These issues raise the fundamental but unanswerable question: is this conurbation of about two and a half million people already too large for its own efficiency and for the quality of life of its inhabitants? There is perhaps a stronger case to be made than in most other instances for accepting some further areal extension, coupled with interior infilling, of the Birmingham conurbation and so a substantial increase in its population. Certainly the case for dispersal cannot rest on the assertion that the need to contain the conurbation within its present physical limits is a self-evident truth.

The case for permitting some further growth of the conurbation, in terms of population and physical extent, can be briefly stated. Through an accident of its nineteenth century industrial history, much of the conurbation is a mosaic of dense urban development encircling the town and the village centres of the Black Country, interrupted by considerable areas of open but industrially damaged land. The urban fringe is jagged, an alternation of urban and rural salients. The strong suburban development of Birmingham in the two great extensions towards Sutton Coldfield and Solihull has left semirural wedges to either side, which bring a quasi-countryside, pock-marked by suburban development, to within 11 kilometres (7 miles) of central Birmingham. The eccentric location of the central city also means that large areas of open land lie within 16 kilometres (10 miles) of the commercial core. Within this indistinctly defined urban mass, there still remains a huge area of derelict land awaiting treatment and some form of use. In 1945 there were 3,660 hectares (9,044 acres) within the conurbation and other large areas on its margin; over half has been reclaimed, but over 1,660 hectares (4,100 acres) survive. Here is a land-bank, still with a substantial balance, which in the last twenty years has materially improved the site supply both for housing and industry in the Black Country. In sum, the conurbation is not yet at the end of its land supply, and there seems no over-riding reason to fossilize its present somewhat chaotic urban structure by imposing rigorous constraints on some further physical growth. To these factors must be added the reluctance of industry to decentralize—the risk that firms may be steered into a Development Area if they become mobile by expansion or a change in site—and the quick build up of service employment dominantly in central Birmingham. Employment, therefore, is immobile in location, but not, in the manufacturing sector, strongly centralized. The fragmented pattern of Black Country industrial location and the growth of the radial ribbons in Birmingham bring homes and work places close together, so that journey to work distances are low, at least by the standards of Greater London and the South East.

5.7.1 *Housing Needs*

Although the need to impose strong and close restraints on the further spatial growth of the Birmingham-Black Country urban mass is, to say the least, much less obvious than it is in the London case, there can be no doubt that this conurbation is generating far too vigorous a growth of population to absorb it all. Some element of dispersal is inevitable. The alternatives open are, therefore, questions of emphasis. Should infilling and marginal expansion be given a major or a minor role in accommodating population growth? Should the surpluses that arise be dispersed over long or short ranges? These questions must be seen against the background of future housing need. If there were to be no net migration into or from the West Midlands, its population would grow (at present rates of natural increase) by about 778,000 over the period 1964 to 1981. It has been suggested that in-migration may add about another 100,000 to this total, giving a growth of about 880,000 by 1981. And very tentative estimates suggest a further increment of 1.5 millions by the year 2000. Virtually 90 per cent of this enormous growth will be generated by the 'Central Division' of the *West Midland Study* (essentially the Birmingham city region), and about half the total growth (at least in the early stages) will emanate from the conurbation. The quantification of housing need and site-supply is confused by a number of statistical uncertainties, and by contested assumptions as to the quantity of land available in and near the conurbation.

In the region as a whole, there was, in 1963, an immediate shortage of 75,000 houses; new family formation through natural increase will create a need for an additional 275,000 houses by 1981, and if in-movement persists at present rates another 30,000 houses will be needed to accommodate migrant families. The level of need for replacement housing as slum-clearance continues is debatable. A requirement for 250,000 units is probably a realistic maximum by 1981 but this would still leave 120,000 houses standing that, by 1981, will be a century old, and a total of over half a million houses more than 65 years old. The official estimate (in the *West Midland Study*) is a total need for 630,000 houses by 1981 (of which 355,000 is the demand generated by the conurbation). An independent estimate (in which most assumptions are placed nearer to maxima) suggests that the total regional demand could amount to almost 910,000 dwellings by 1986, of which the conurbation and its margins would need almost 580,000 (Eversley, Jackson and Lomas, 1965).

There is also much dispute as to the available site-supply. The official view is that redevelopment sites will accommodate 75,000 new dwellings within the conurbation (chiefly in the high-rise units now becoming the dominant feature of the inner Birmingham townscape), and that the use of 'virgin' sites involving an infilling of the interstices in the urban framework might yield between 65,000 and 95,000 sites. In total about 150,000 to 170,000 sites can be found within the conurbation or at its margin. This would scarcely meet even the existing shortage and the renewal need, and would make no contribution to the demands arising from population growth or in-migration. At least 185,000 houses must be built outside the existing limit of the conurbation during the period 1964 to 1981. Three possibilities exist for finding sites to accommodate this growth : substantial peripheral expansion, short-range movement to satellites within commuter range, or long-range dispersal to sites beyond commuting distance involving a major redistribution of employment. These alternatives are bedevilled by the paradox that marginal expansion and short-range dispersal are likely to carry industry with them (as they have in the last decade), while long range dispersal meets the problem of industrial immobility. In the empirical development of overspill over the last decade there has been a little of all three solutions.

During the decades since 1945 the Birmingham conurbation has been conspicuously successful in accommodating its own population growth. From 1951 to 1963 its population grew by 154,000, so that it retained much the greater part of its natural increase of 178,000. Over broadly the same period, only 25,000 people moved from the conurbation to planned overspill schemes. However, the latter figure is no guide to population dispersal. The ratio of local authority buildings to private development is relatively low, and falling, in and near the West Midland conurbation. Even in the central city, with its huge low-income housing demand, municipal building fell from 81 per cent to 63 per cent of completions between the early nineteen fifties and the early nineteen sixties and, in the districts that form the newer suburban fringe, only a quarter of completions has been in the public sector over the last decade. This is a measure of West Midland prosperity. It means that a progressive, half-controlled seepage of population has taken place from the conurbation, to be accommodated in piecemeal development attached to the villages and small towns of the green belt. These areas have provided sites for about 40,000 houses in the private sector since 1951. This shift of more than 100,000 people is enormously greater than the planned dispersal to overspill sites. There is every sign that owner-occupiers will continue to dominate the outward movement from the conurbation. Yet most of the planning for dispersal is at present found in the public sector. The intense pressures for speculative building development are seen in the many small, and a few large, planning applications for sites within the green belt and on both its margins. This outflow in the private sector is chiefly of white-collar workers whose employment is in central Birmingham. It has therefore a very strong preference for sites tied to the skirts of the conurbation—another powerful constraint on long-range dispersal.

The first of the alternative strategies listed above, further infilling and peripheral expansion, would merely legitimize present trends. Some of the major contemporary housing projects are in fact a peripheral enlargement of the conurbation, and can be described as overspill only in the technical sense that they involve the accommodation of Birmingham population in new homes beyond the city boundary. For example, the movement of Birmingham families to Aldridge, on the northeastern edge of the Black Country, over the last decade has been associated with the development of about 70 hectares (170 acres) of new industrial sites, partly on derelict land; yet 80 per cent of the overspill men work outside the district, and about 50 per cent of them in the city of Birmingham. In a mobile society even vigorous local industrial development is no guarantee against commuting. The new factories of Aldridge merely become part of the general pool of employment available within the labour market of the north of the conurbation.

Having come within sight of the exhaustion of its own land supply, Birmingham has looked for sites for out-of-town estates. One such project has been agreed and is under construction at Chelmsley Wood (in Meriden urban district) just to the east of the city boundary; it is well within 16 kilometres (10 miles) of the central area, and scarcely 8 kilometres (5 miles) from the Tame valley industrial zone. Although there was opposition to this piece of marginal expansion, in fact the site is encircled by patchy suburban growth, and its development is merely a consolidation of the conurbation margin. Houses for 16,000 families (and a population likely to be about 60,000) are being built, and this is likely to make a larger immediate contribution to the solution of Birmingham's public housing problem than any other single project in the near future. Even more controversial is a proposal for a scheme of similar size (about 15,000 houses) to be built close to the southwestern margin of the conurbation in north Worcestershire. Like Chelmsley Wood, this is seen as a 'crash' programme to relieve the city's housing emergency, to commence early in the nineteen seventies and to be completed within five years. Here too, the development is seen in commuter terms, with little if any movement of industry. This must tie it closely to the conurbation, spatially, and a large part of the development is likely to be on the northern margin of Bromsgrove, 19 kilometres (12 miles) from Birmingham but scarcely 8 kilometres (5 miles) from the British Leyland Motors Longbridge plant. Thus, an existing but skeletal salient of suburban development southwestwards from Birmingham to Bromsgrove will be strengthened. These two large public schemes together will quickly accommodate perhaps 120,000 people in conurbation fringe sites, a far greater total than that likely to be removed in the near future to more distant schemes by true dispersal, and the tremendous pressures on rural areas within 24 kilometres

(15 miles) of Birmingham for private house building are not likely to be wholly frustrated. Thus the next stage in the development of the West Midland conurbation will almost certainly be dominated by its peripheral expansion rather than decentralization from it (West Midland Economic Planning Council, 1967).

5.7.2 *Planning for Dispersal*

Planning for dispersal has been at two scales, a middle distance movement to sites within possible commuter range, and a longer range outflow to projects far beyond daily travelling radius from Birmingham (though not necessarily from the conurbation margins). In both cases three alternative development procedures have been used: new town designation, town development schemes, and ad hoc overspill agreements. Middle distance dispersal has been to a substantial new town at Redditch to the south, and to a group of considerable industrial towns in mid-Staffordshire, chiefly Tamworth, Lichfield, Stafford, Cannock and Rugeley. The decision to develop Redditch has been criticized as a misuse of the new town concept, to create an essentially dormitory community in a suburban setting close to the margin of the existing urban mass. This is an old metal working town, almost a Black Country outlier, once dominated by needle manufacture, but now it has a varied industrial base, in which spring making is an important specialism. It is proposed to increase its population from 29,000 to 90,000 within a designated area of nearly 3,000 hectares (7,200 acres) by absorbing an intake population of about 35,000 from Birmingham. Only 23 kilometres (14 miles) from the city, and 8 kilometres (5 miles) from the conurbation margin—from which it is separated by a mere token of a green ribbon—there is an obvious danger that the town will become a dormitory community. Indeed, it was once estimated that 40 per cent of the overspill wage earners would have to commute out daily. In fact it has demonstrated its ability to attract industry from the conurbation and elsewhere. Although new industrial employment totalled only 500 by the end of 1968, a number of significant enterprises have come to the town from Birmingham more recently. The industrial and mining towns of mid-Staffordshire have also attracted a small overspill flow from Birmingham; but dispersal northwards exists chiefly on paper. No fewer than 11 overspill agreements have been concluded between Birmingham or Wolverhampton and various Staffordshire County districts, but most have proved almost abortive. It is still hoped, however, that Stafford, Lichfield and Tamworth will together absorb a population of 50,000 from the conurbation. The most ambitious project is that for Tamworth, a town of 34,000 that is prepared at least to double its present population, and for which there is a firm development plan. Only 21 kilometres (13 miles) from central Birmingham, Tamworth has grown vigorously during the last decade in terms of industrial employment, and it has attracted mobile industry not only from the conurbation but also from elsewhere. In fact, overspill to Tamworth would build on proved industrial success.

Dispersal to ranges beyond easy commuter travel from the conurbation has so far been very limited, despite the fact that this category includes what is by far the largest of the West Midland development projects, the Telford new city. The problems of Telford are reviewed above (pp. 212–217). It is necessary here only to recall that its growth has been slow; by 1969 only about 2,000 new town houses had been built, and until the rate of job formation accelerates dramatically (and there are signs of improvement) a brake upon growth is bound to persist. Two other, much smaller, long-distance dispersal schemes are also in operation, to Daventry and Droitwich, the former almost 48 kilometres (30 miles) southeast of Birmingham and the latter about 32 kilometres (20 miles) to the southwest. Daventry was, in 1965, a small country town of 5,800, with a traditional boot and shoe manufacture and a new bearings industry. Closely linked to Rugby by journey to work ties, Daventry is thus the extreme southeastern outlier of the Coventry-based urban system. Near to the M1, it has obvious attractions as a site for industrial growth, yet very little industrial overspill has taken place from the conurbation to the town.

New firms have come in, but chiefly from elsewhere. Nor have Birmingham families flocked to Daventry in great numbers. Almost three-quarters of the 1,000 new houses built in the late nineteen sixties were taken by city families, but by 1970 the link with Birmingham had been weakened to permit Daventry to allocate houses intended for overspill migrants to workers coming with firms from elsewhere. Thus Daventry's planned growth to about 40,000 may depend little upon its links with Birmingham. Here is yet another proof of the great difficulty found in attempting to decentralize both people and work to the margins of the city region. Droitwich is a small and somewhat faded spa, only 10 kilometres (6 miles) north east of Worcester, and partly suburban to it. A rather limited town expansion scheme was agreed in 1963, to take about 13,000 overspill migrants in the course of a planned growth from 8,000 to about 30,000. By 1968, both an industrial estate and two overspill housing areas were growing. Although the scheme is a small one, it has a certain spatial significance in that it strengthens the southwest salient of development from the conurbation; it may become in time part of a much larger expansion, and a major regional growth point.

Excluding Telford and Redditch, this catalogue of small dispersal schemes, some of them indifferently successful, clearly does not amount to a regional strategy. They embody the results of Birmingham's tactical opportunism in securing overspill agreements wherever there seemed some possibility of success. The city is said to have had talks with over 100 other authorities and has entered into more than 30 agreements, some as far away as Central and southwest Wales; but only about a dozen of these have produced significant transfers of population. Now, however, the responsibility for framing an overspill policy that will become the chief instrument in developing a regional strategy has passed to the Economic Planning Council and the Regional Planning Board. Nevertheless, a local authority consortium has taken the initiative and put forward a set of strategic planning proposals (*West Midland Regional Study*. 1971).

5.7.3 *Corridors of Growth*

Although a regional strategy is still in the melting pot of debate, a few general principles have emerged. The Council is adamant that in principle the growth of the conurbation must be contained (though it is still expanding in fact), and that a true dispersal of people and work must be achieved. To secure this, a strategy of 'corridors of growth' has been proposed. These would permit some short-range dispersal, while encouraging movement to greater distances far outside commuting radii. Such axes of development need not be radial to the conurbation. Indeed the corridor of improved communication from Daventry-Rugby to Stafford, along the electrified Trent Valley railway, and within the V formed by the M1 and Midland link motorways, is an attractive tangential corridor already defined by a number of active or potential growth points. It probably has a much greater capacity for development than so far has been assigned to it. The chief corridors of expansion, however, are likely to be defined in radial terms, extending outwards as a number of sectors from the conurbation. Thus, the future development of the region would be to a stellar model, in which broad but broken urban salients would extend starwise from the outer margin of the green belt; and these would be separated by rural wedges in which growth would be limited to scattered housing development in the private sector. The rural salients would have almost as great a significance in the total design as the urban corridors, for they would contain the short-range outdoor recreational resources for the urban society.

The axes of growth are becoming clear, at least in general terms. Broadly, they follow the major corridors of communications out from the conurbation. Thus, a southwestern salient is already evolving along the approach of the M5/M50 motorway to the threshold of the conurbation. The north Worcestershire overspill proposal and Redditch new town will form the base of this development against the green belt; the growth of Droitwich, and a proposed expansion of Worcester by 50,000 overspill migrants (this is likely to be deferred until the nineteen eighties, however) will extend it. If all the projects under discussion within this southwestern sector were to fructify, a new population of about 150,000 would be added to the M5 axis by the nineteen eighties, when the total population within the corridor would exceed 400,000. This zone has an obvious potential for industrial growth. When completed, motorways will link Birmingham with its nearest port at Bristol and with the growing industrial region of Severnside and coastal South Wales. The West Midlands and South Wales are already closely linked industrially, partly through their complementary roles in the metal industries, and partly through the large number of transfers (often of branch plants) from the former to the latter under Board of Trade direction. Thus the M5 is already a real corridor of commodity flow. Sites close to it are likely to be attractive to conurbation industry, and there is as a result a better hope for a massive dispersal of employment in this direction than in some others. In addition, Worcester provides not only the retail, commercial and social facilities of a high-ranking county town, but also a large and growing pool of service employment.

The northwestern growth corridor consists of the single, massive but rather slowly developing Telford project, although it has also been suggested that Shrewsbury might be considered for planned expansion later in the century. The objections to the latter are the same as those levelled at the Worcester proposal—namely that a county town and historic city of attractive character might be ravaged by the traffic flows and land-use pressures that any substantial growth would generate. But the danger to Shrewsbury is remote, for the contrast between the northwestern and southwestern axes in the matter of development potential is plain. The former lacks direct motorway access and its railway provision has deteriorated quickly—and would be dramatically impoverished if the suggestion to re-route the Crewe-Severnside services via Wolverhampton were pursued. Most seriously, there is beyond Shrewsbury no major industrial complex in a relationship of inter-dependence with the West Midlands. Thus the M5 zone is truly a corridor; urban Shropshire more strictly a salient.

In contrast with East Shropshire, there is a northern axis of possible development that offers a very great potential, but so far it has not attracted any major dispersal project, either active or firmly planned. No part of Britain has seen so radical an improvement in communications as the Birmingham–Stoke on Trent axis. Along the corridor are aligned not only the M6 with its spurs to Stafford and the Potteries, but also the much improved A34 trunk road, together with the duplicate main lines of the London-Midland electrification. These routes, moreover, link the two largest of the English provincial manufacturing regions, the West Midlands and South Lancashire. This is one of the main streets of industrial Britain. Yet only piecemeal development is proposed, in the regional strategy as presently revealed, for this area. There may perhaps be a limited expansion of Stafford; certainly growth is likely to continue at the northern margin of the conurbation. But the key to a policy for this northern sector lies in the future of North Staffordshire. The problems of this region have already been reviewed (pp. 204–212): in essence, any major development is frustrated by the area's gross environmental problems, its massive renewal needs, and the weakness of its economic base. Possible new town sites at Swynnerton, just south of the Potteries, and more recently at Stone, have been canvassed fruitlessly. In fact, the City of Stoke on Trent is both willing and anxious to accept overspill to balance its own population decline—but it has turned away from a possible link with Birmingham in an attempt to recruit migrant families from Manchester.

Without doubt, however, an even greater potential for growth lies not within the Potteries conurbation, but to its west, in the Crewe area of South Cheshire. This is too remote within North West England to be regarded as a candidate for growth in the near future, and since it lies beyond the boundaries of their region, it has not been seriously considered by the West Midland planners. In the long term this area can hardly be ignored as a possible growth location. The whole northern axis of possible development from the West Midland conurbation is, therefore, one of great potential, but of wasted opportunities.

These principal growth corridors to the southwest, the northwest and the north have the greatest capacity for absorbing conurbation overspill. Development in other directions offers slighter prospects. A possible northeastern corridor has been identified, extending beyond Lichfield and Tamworth to Burton. Certainly Tamworth is committed to substantial growth by overspill, but an enlargement of Lichfield would conflict with farmland of high quality and the character of a small and well preserved cathedral city. Burton is seen as a possible reception site for an overspill population of 50,000; in real terms this would be a transfer from the West Midlands to the margins of the Derby-Nottingham urban complex and its virtues must be considered in the context of an East Midland strategy. Population dispersal to the southeast from the conurbation is seriously limited by the indigenous pressures of population growth and land supply within the Coventry belt. In fact, a growth corridor has long been developing here, through the Coventry complex to Rugby and Daventry. Its present population of about 695,000 is bound to rise to over 720,000 by the early nineteen eighties through natural growth alone and there is almost bound to be some in-migration, both intraregional and interregional. The problem here is to develop a sub-regional plan that will accommodate these increases without a total elimination of the diminishing green ribbons that divide Coventry both from its smaller neighbours and from the conurbation. Except for Birmingham's declining interest in Daventry, the southeastern sector cannot absorb significant overspill transfers from the conurbation.

Between these corridors of urban growth, however they may develop in fact and in detail, lie broad rural wedges within which a triangular conflict of interest is already evolving. This is between the need to protect good farm land, the pressures for high-income dormitory development, and the role of the countryside as a recreational resource. The rural area south of the conurbation, straddling the Warwickshire and Worcestershire boundary, illustrates this problem. One of the most concentrated districts of intensive fruit and vegetable cultivation in Britain occupies the Avon terrace lands, centred on Evesham but extending more patchily to Warwick and across south Worcestershire. To the north are areas of intensive livestock rearing, with a varying local emphasis on milk or beef. These are not types of farming that coexist easily with mass penetration by the urban visitor, but the Avon valley and the river itself are recreational amenities of great value, invaded from the conurbations each weekend, even though there is little open-access land. The southern sector is also one of the most favoured by the Birmingham long-range commuter, so that many of the villages and small towns, for example Henley in Arden and Alcester, are pressure points for dispersed suburban growth. The planning problems of the rural wedges, therefore, are no less complex than those of the proposed growth corridors. Rather different conflicts and opportunities are evident in the rural areas immediately to the north of the conurbation. Here the forested Bunter plateau of Cannock Chase is largely open to the visitor and has been carefully developed by the County and the Forestry Commission as a recreation area; but the active Cannock coalfield reaches the borders of the Chase—and indeed penetrates the south—so that commanding prospects of spoil banks and pit villages alternate with views of the fine Bunter scarps. Beyond Cannock lies the Trent, a river punctuated by power stations of great size, for it offers cooling water in a relatively cheap coal area. But it also has great recreational potential. The terraces contain huge gravel resources of great commercial value. As these are worked, the pits flood, and offer opportunities for the development of water-recreation areas in the wake of gravel working. Clearly the most careful local planning is required to reconcile the conflicting interests of electricity generation, gravel working and recreational uses.

Beyond the Severn on the west—another river coming under increasing recreational pressures—lies a more distant hinterland of the West Midlands. This includes the border counties and the upland mass of east and central Wales, an area of immense but under-developed recreational and tourist potential (see pp. 217–219). The central Welsh upland offers not only general resources for mountain and moorland recreation, but also developed facilities for the visitor by car, for example at the Vyrnwy and Elan valley reservoirs of Liverpool and Birmingham respectively. Outliers of the Welsh uplands thrust eastwards almost to the Severn, in Wenlock edge, the Clee hills and the Longmynd. A single main axis of communication crosses this thinly settled region from north to south, the parallel Shrewsbury-Hereford trunk road and railway, the latter with a somewhat suspect future. Spaced along this are small market towns of historic character and tourist potential like Leominster and Ludlow. Apart from small scale overspill to Hereford, and the problematical future growth of Shrewsbury, only a trivial growth of population (and substantial rural decline) is to be expected in this remote region of pastoral farming. Oddly, the only substantial proposal for urban-industrial development lies yet further west, and even more remotely located, in the upper Severn valley at and above Newtown. Proposals were made in 1966 to arrest population decline in mid-Wales by the development of a linear new town, centred on Caersws and extending down-valley to Newtown and up to Llanidloes. The idea was to attract both population and industrial overspill from the West Midlands, and also to make a determined effort to exploit the recreational potential of the area. An ultimate population of 70,000 was envisaged. This was a controversial proposal of doubtful viability, though the relative remoteness of the site would have been balanced by Development Area status. In fact, following a certain amount of local opposition, it was replaced by a very much more limited scheme which would expand Newtown from its existing 5,500 to 11,000 but even this very modest growth has the benefit of new town status.

The regional strategy being shaped to guide the future growth of the West Midlands must be seen in broader than regional terms. It is also a plan for the development of the core of the English megalopolis. There is clearly in process of formation, on the axis joining metropolitan England to South Lancashire and West Yorkshire, a system of city regions that is already coherent and as firmly integrated as its counterpart on the eastern seaboard of the United States of America—both in the complex linkage system between the constituent units, and in their progressive penetration of the remaining rural interstices. The elongated motorway triangle of the M1, M6 and M62 defines the axes about which this megalopolis is developing. It already contains an urban population of about 32 millions; and four zones within it—the London city region, the urban West Midlands, the East Midland city complex and southern Lancastria—will between them generate and absorb the great bulk of the nation's growth of population over the next few decades. The West Midland city region is clearly the hinge of this urban complex. Planning for decentralization from the West Midlands is, in effect therefore, planning for a consolidation of England's megalopolis. Most of the growth corridors of greatest potential in the West Midlands are aligned along the interior communications of this system of city regions. The continuing growth of the Coventry complex, the potential for expansion across Staffordshire to the Potteries, and the development of the towns of the Trent Valley all represent an infilling within the existing urban mass. Only the Telford project can be seen to represent an advance of the urban frontier away from the core of the megalopolis. Thus the development of a regional plan involves the taking of decisions that have as great a national importance as they have a regional significance. The most southerly of the Midland dispersal locations, Daventry, is less than 15 minutes away from one of the more northerly of the major South East projects at Northampton. Any major growth in the Stoke city region straddles a provincial boundary and must be reconciled with two regional strategies. So must any significant development of Burton. This, of course, is simply a restatement of the centrality and nodality of the West Midlands within urban-industrial Britain. If an inadequate regional strategy for the West Midlands were adopted as a blueprint for growth, it would confuse and frustrate national planning for the most efficient distribution of population and economic activity. In this sense, the key to national planning lies in the future shaping of the West Midland region.

REFERENCES :

Beaver, S. H. (1964). *The Potteries, a study in the Evolution of a Cultural Landscape,* Institute of British Geographers, London.
British Association (1950). *Birmingham and its Regional Setting,* B.A., London.
Department of Economic Affairs (1965). *The West Midlands; a Regional Study,* H.M.S.O., London.
Eversley, D. E. C., Jackson, V. J. and Lomas, G. M. (1965). *Population Growth and Planning Policy,* University of Birmingham.
Johnson, B. L. C. (1951). The charcoal iron industry in the early eighteenth century. *Geographical Journal,* **117,** 167–177.
Johnson, B. L. C. (1958). The distribution of the factory population in the West Midland conurbation. *Transactions and Papers, Institute of British Geographers,* **25,** 209–223.
Jones, H. R. (1965). A study of rural migration in Central Wales. *Transactions and Papers, Institute of British Geographers,* **37,** 31–45.
Ministry of Housing and Local Government (1966). *Dawley, Wellington and Oakengates* (Study of John Madin and Partners), H.M.S.O., London.
Moisley, H. A. (1951). The industrial and urban development of the North Staffordshire conurbation. *Transactions and Papers, Institute of British Geographers,* **17,** 151–165.

Rosing, K. E. and Wood, P. A. (1971). *Character of a Conurbation*, University of London Press, London.

Smith, B. D. M. (1970). Industrial overspill; theory and practice. *Urban Studies*, **7**, 189–204.

Stedman, M. B. (1958). The townscape of Birmingham in 1956. *Transactions and Papers, Institute of British Geographers*, **25**, 225–238.

Welsh Council (1970). *Land Use Strategy: a Pilot Report for Cardiganshire, Montgomeryshire and Radnorshire*, H.M.S.O., Cardiff.

Welsh Office (1964). *Depopulation in Mid-Wales* (The Beacham Report), H.M.S.O., London.

Welsh Office (1966). *A New Town in Mid-Wales* (Economic Associates), H.M.S.O., London.

West Midland Economic Planning Council (1967). *The West Midlands: Patterns of Growth*, H.M.S.O., London.

West Midland Group (1948). *Conurbation: a Planning Survey of Birmingham and the Black Country*, W.M.G., Birmingham.

West Midland Regional Study (1971). *A Development Strategy for the West Midlands*, W.M.R.S., Birmingham.

West Midlands Shopping Study (1966). *Journal of the Town Planning Institute*, **52**, 146–149.

Wood, P. A. (1966). *Industry in the Towns of the West Midlands*, unpublished Ph.D. thesis, University of Birmingham.

CHAPTER 6

The South West and South Wales

GERALD MANNERS

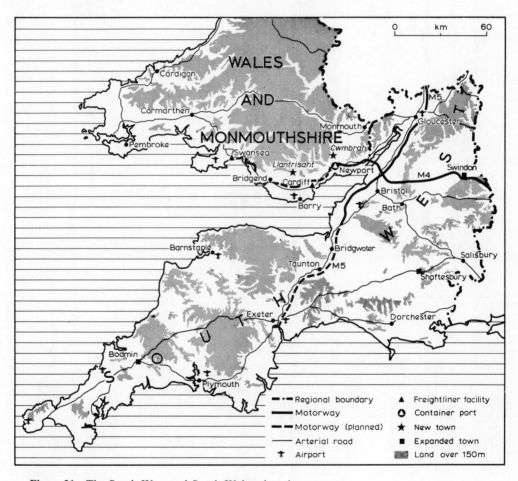

Figure 21 The South West and South Wales: location map.

Table 18. The South West and South Wales : selected regional and sub-regional indicators

A. Population :

Thousands

	Mid-year estimated home population				Average annual change 1961–1966			Average annual change 1951–1961		
	1971	1966	1961	1951	Natural change	Armed forces change	Net migration	Natural change	Armed forces change	Net migration
TOTAL South West and South Wales	**5,829.7**	**5,697.9**	**5,452.0**	**5,215.0**	**+26.8**	**−1.6**	**+23.9**	**+18.1**	**−0.5**	**+7.1**
South West	3,768.1	3,634.8	3,436.0	3,247.4	+16.9	−2.0	+24.8	+10.5	−1.6	+9.9
Central	729.2	694.4	656.9	618.2	+3.3	−1.0	+5.2	+2.4	−0.8	+2.3
Southern	820.8	796.4	758.7	735.3	+1.6	—	+6.0	+0.7	−0.3	+2.0
Western	485.1	453.0	438.6	436.3	+0.4	−0.1	+2.6	+0.3	+0.1	−0.2
Northern	1,733.0	1,690.9	1,581.8	1,457.6	+11.7	−0.9	+11.0	+7.1	−0.6	+5.9
North Gloucestershire	456.5	456.4	424.0	388.2	+3.2	−0.2	+3.4	+2.2	−0.2	+1.5
Bristol/Severnside	926.2	893.7	848.8	792.9	+5.3	—	+3.7	+3.0	+0.7	+1.9
North Wiltshire	350.4	341.0	309.0	276.4	+3.3	−0.8	+3.9	+1.9	−1.1	+2.5
South Wales	2,061.6	2,063.1	2,016.0	1,967.6	+9.9	+0.4	−0.9	+7.6	+1.1	−3.8
Industrial South Wales	1,833.7	1,834.0	1,790.9	1,742.4	+9.5	+0.2	−1.1	+7.2	+1.0	−3.3
Central and Eastern Valleys	632.6	648.9	652.7	679.5	+2.7	+0.1	−3.6	+2.2	+0.5	−5.4
West South Wales	461.7	464.4	457.3	449.4	+1.3	+0.1	—	+1.2	+0.3	−0.7
Coastal Belt	739.4	720.7	680.9	613.5	+5.5	—	+2.5	+3.8	+0.2	+2.8
South West	227.9	229.1	225.1	225.2	+0.4	+0.2	+0.2	+0.4	+0.1	−0.5
BRITAIN	53,821.4	53,176.1	51,380.0	48,917.5	+328.2	−0.5	+22.6	+231.4	+12.9	+1.9

1. 1971 Census; 1971 boundaries.
2. 1966 boundaries.

B. Employment :

	Employment		Male employment		Proportion of women at work		Unemployment range		
		Change		Change		Change in %			
	1966	1961–1966	1966	1961–1966	1966	1961–1966	1968	1967	1961–1966
	'000s	%	'000s	%	%	%	%	%	%
TOTAL South West and South Wales	**2,770**	**+5**	**1,410**	**+2**	**33**	**+3**	**2–3**	**2–3**	**1–2**
South West	1,360	+6	870	+4	33	+2	2–3	2–3	1–2
Central	240	+3	160	+1	32	+1	2–3	2–3	1–2
Southern	270	+6	170	+3	30	+2	3–4	3–4	2–3
Western	150	+10	100	+7	27	+3	4–5	4–5	3–4
Northern	690	+7	450	+4	37	+2	2–3	1–2	1–2
South Wales	810	+3	540	−1	32	+3	3–4	3–4	2–3
Industrial South Wales	750	+3	510	−2	34	+3	3–5	3–5	2–3
Central and Eastern Valleys	240	Nil	170	−5	29	+4	5–10	5–10	3–4
West South Wales	200	Nil	140	−4	31	+3	3–4	3–4	2–3
Coastal Belt	310	+6	200	+3	38	+2	3–4	3–4	1–2
South West	60	+5	40	+2	22	+2	3–4	3–4	3–4
BRITAIN	23,550	+4	14,900	+2	40	+2	2–3	2–3	1–2

C. Industrial Development Certificates :

	Estimated additional employment from i.d.c. approvals			
	Total 1956–1967 '000s	Annual averages		
		1964–1967 '000s	1960–1963 '000s	1956–1959 '000s
TOTAL South West and South Wales	**159.5**	**17.0**	**12.7**	**10.4**
South West	76.0	7.2	6.8	5.0
Central	11.1	1.3	0.7	0.8
Southern	17.7	1.2	2.2	0.9
Western	12.1	2.1	0.7	0.3
Northern	35.1	2.6	3.2	3.0
South Wales	83.5	9.8	5.9	5.4
Industrial South Wales	77.4	9.3	5.6	4.6
Central and Eastern Valleys	26.0	4.3	1.3	1.0
West South Wales	29.5	3.6	2.1	1.7
Coastal Belt	21.9	1.4	2.2	1.9
South West	6.1	0.5	0.3	0.8
BRITAIN	1,245.2	121.8	108.1	81.2

6.1 Introduction

The heightening public interest in Severnside in recent years stems essentially from two parallel developments. In the first place, a national need for more urban space, which caused the Department of Economic Affairs to investigate alternative long-term strategies for the distribution of population (pp. 65–66), has generated the suggestion that the area bordering upon the Severn estuary could house a substantial increase of both industry and people. The reasons for this choice of Severnside stem from the other development which has encouraged a growing interest in the area in recent years, namely, its changed and changing special relationships. Most obviously from the bridging of the Severn and from the construction of the associated M4 and M5 motorways, but also as a consequence of the much improved intercity rail services for both passengers and freight, the relative position of the communities on both sides of the estuary is being radically transformed. Both between each other, and between Severnside and the rest of Britain, a reinterpretation of distance, a new ease of movement, and a reassessment of economic and social opportunity is taking place.

With the opening of the new Severn road bridge in 1966, the road distance between Bristol and Cardiff came to be a mere 50 kilometres (32 miles) instead of the former 130 kilometres (81 miles). This much improved accessibility between the two major cities in the South West and South Wales respectively began immediately to influence a wide range of business decisions from Bridgend to Bridgwater, and more especially between Barry and Bath. The economic interdependence of the two sides of the Bristol Channel began to be progressively strengthened and Bristol was the first community to experience demonstrable gains. For example, many people in South Wales, and more especially in its eastern half, began to take increasing advantage of the wider range of retail and service facilities that were available in Bristol by comparison with Cardiff. The former, with a population of half a million, had an immediate advantage over the latter with its 275,000; and Bristol retailers capitalized upon the situation by advertising extensively in South Wales. Some consumer durable manufacturers, such as the General Electric Company with accounting and servicing facilities in both the South West and South Wales, elected to centralize them in Bristol. A number of wholesaling activities followed suite, with the Cooperative Wholesale Society transferring some 200 jobs from Cardiff to an enlarged depot at Bristol. The Central Electricity Generating Board similarly moved 800 jobs 'across the bridge' into England, where governmental restraints upon the construction of offices in London were simultaneously giving Bristol—with its relatively attractive location and wide range of amenities—a further burst of new central business district activities. Some of the latter were in a very strong position to offer services to people living in South Wales.

Thus, with the opening of the bridge, the economic role, the regional functions and the hinterland of Bristol began substantially to be increased. It is highly unlikely, of course, that Bristol will once again become 'The Welsh Metropolis', a role which it played so effectively in the eighteenth century when water communications exerted the strongest influence upon the spatial patterns of trade and economic life. At that time, Welsh agricultural produce and cattle on the hoof were ferried across the Severn to be marketed in Bristol. However, the industrial revolution and the railways put an end to that relationship over one hundred years ago and focused the economic life of South Wales upon its own ports and London. Although the development of the new motorway and trunk road system will certainly not create a replica of eighteenth century geographical relationships, it has undoubtedly thrown them into the melting pot once again; and it is clear that the economic dependence of South Wales upon Bristol cannot but increase.

Nevertheless, the increasing complexity of the economic linkages between the major urban centres on the two sides of the lower Severn is not working solely in favour of Bristol. Already some manufacturers in South Wales are competing successfully in their new 'local' West Country market. Cardiff has the only British Rail freightliner terminal on Severnside (see Figure 21); indeed, despite earlier plans to the contrary, the whole of the South West remains without such a transport facility. In the short run at least this can not be without some influence upon manufacturing location decisions. Moreover, many distributors are viewing sites in Monmouthshire and East Glamorgan with considerable interest—since the more central locations to serve the population of Greater Cardiff and Greater Bristol together are to be found on the Welsh side of the estuary. Also, the more ready availability of labour in South Wales, to say nothing of the Development and Intermediate Area incentives available there, is a further inducement to both distributors and industrialists serving the whole of the Severnside market to locate in the Principality.

Of equal importance in influencing the pattern of future growth on Severnside is the louder political voice which has been given to Wales in recent years. The creation of the Welsh Office, the devolution to Cardiff of much Welsh administration and the associated growth of a Civil Service, together with those activities which find it advantageous to be located close to the centres of political power, has begun to widen the quality as well as increase the size of the market in the Cardiff sub-region. Moreover, in the performance of administrative and cultural services for the wider Severnside complex, South Wales in the medium run need not necessarily take second place to Bristol. It is not unrealistic to assume, for example, that an attractive redevelopment of the central area of Cardiff to high environmental standards will powerfully assist the city in its attempts to espouse a wider range of higher order activities than have located there in the past. Backed by a strong political will—already 1500 Army Department posts have been designated for dispersal to a new government office building at Maindy, Cardiff—it is highly likely that the redevelopment programme now under way and modified from the earlier and more ambitious proposals of Colin Buchanan and Partners (1966a) will allow Cardiff to counterbalance some of the present advantages of Bristol. As a result, not only will its role and influence continue to extend throughout South (and the rest of) Wales, but it could reach out strongly to areas east and southeast of the Severn bridge as well.

At the same time as this new set of relationships between, and the accelerating inter-dependence of, the cities and towns on both sides of the Upper Bristol Channel are being forged, the new spatial relationships of Severnside in a national context are also generating new economic opportunities. Modern manufacturing and service industries rely heavily upon scale economies. Ease of accessibility to large and growing markets is, therefore, of paramount importance to the successful conduct of their enterprise. The South Wales and the Greater Bristol regions individually, however, are not only relatively small in terms of their population—South Wales houses less than 4 per cent of Britain's people—but traditionally they have been comparatively inaccessible to and from the main centres of British urban development and hence the country's principal markets. Both of these constraints upon their economic development have been significantly reduced by the Severn bridge and the enlarged regional market which it has helped to create, and by the improved interurban road and rail communications which have radically increased the national accessibility of Severnside. The fact that most Severnside communities either are, or shortly will be, little more than two hours road or rail travel time from both London and Birmingham is certainly a most powerful asset for economic develop-ment in Britain today. It is interesting to reflect that London Airport (Heathrow) via the completed M4 is only about one and a half hours from Chepstow and Bristol by road; as a consequence it is now more accessible in terms of time from these locations than it is from many parts of the congested Greater London area. Such an attribute is not unimportant in regional development when an increasing number of export-oriented manufacturers, and many firms in the tertiary and quaternary sectors of the economy, place such a high premium upon easy access to a major international airport.

It is already clear that the newly enlarged market and the transformed accessibility of Severnside is encouraging the development of many manufacturing and service activities which, in response to their scale economies and the small size of the South Wales and Greater Bristol markets individually, were previously performed in larger urban centres. At the same time the possibility of serving the national market, and especially the Greater London and West Midlands regional markets, with a wide range of goods and services from Severnside locations has begun to look extremely attractive. The Portbury dock proposals were a typical response to this situation (pp. 260–261); designed to capture a significant share of the growing national deep–sea container trade, the scheme would have been completely unrealistic without the prospect of the M4 and the M5 motorways.

From a regional and sub-regional planning viewpoint, Severnside is given additional interest by virtue of the contrasting reactions to these new economic and development opportunities on the two sides of the estuary. The South West Economic Planning Council in their *A Region with a Future* (1967), for example, took the view that :

'Having established an up-to-date motorway system ... The national economy cannot afford to waste the opportunities which have been created. The Council regard the Severnside study as a preliminary to deciding *where* development should take place,

238REGIONAL DEVELOPMENT

not *whether* it should take place: they take the latter to be self evident ...' (p. 107). 'The Council foresees natural growth resulting in an increase of nearly one million in the population in the Northern sub-region by the end of the century, but this figure could prove an underestimate if the Government's study of the feasibility of large scale population growth on Severnside leads to planned expansion on the eastern side of the Bristol channel ...' (p. 97). 'We doubt whether the present development policies of the local authorities concerned will be adequate for expansion of the order we foresee without risk to the amenities of the area. Accordingly, we suggest that the Government and local authorities should explore ... alternative methods of development encompassing the area of Bristol, Bath, South Gloucestershire, North Somerset and West Wiltshire, designed to profit from the new motorway system and to build up, by the end of the century, a new complex of settlements of major importance' (p. 120).

The exciting prospect of rapid and major industrial and urban developments on Severnside was thus embraced almost without qualification by the representatives of the South West. In the same year, the Secretary of State for Wales presented to Parliament a long-awaited White Paper in which the prospects for the future economic development of the Principality were discussed. In vivid contrast to the draft strategy for the South West, *Wales and the Way Ahead* (1967) barely glimpsed at the enormous development prospects of Severnside. Under the sub-heading 'Newport' it was noted that :

'(The estuarine zone) is the subject of a feasibility study by the Government, in the light of the expected population increase of Great Britain, to examine its potential as an area for accommodating a large addition of population: the future of much of Monmouthshire may be deeply affected by its results' (p. 106).

But throughout the White Paper, the attention of the reader and the development proposals were focused upon other parts of the Principality on the grounds that :

'It has been argued that the industrial development of Wales could be encouraged most economically and effectively in the districts where natural growth is easiest, and that the secondary effects of such development would gradually extend to neighbouring parts of Wales ... When the Wales Development Area was created in 1966, it was decided to exclude South-East and North-East Wales; because it was judged that, even without special financial inducements for new industrial enterprises, they both possess good prospects of continuing economic development. It was also considered that, if the inducements available in the parts of Wales included in the Development Area were equally available in adjacent districts already more diversified economically, the latter would attract enterprises which might otherwise go to places in Wales where their presence is more immediately required ... The primary object of fostering industrial development where it is most needed could thus be frustrated' (pp. 50–51).

Such contrasting attitudes towards the future of Severnside have been reflected both by local politicians and in the regional press on both sides of the Bristol Channel. The explanation for them can be found in the recent economic history and the changing economic geography of the South West of England and South Wales respectively. It is for this reason that the two regions in the first place are examined separately.

6.2 South West England

The South West region includes the whole of the long peninsula south and west of the Bristol Channel (see Figure 22). Compared with the national pattern of employment, the service sector is especially important in the regional economy. There are more than 100,000 workers in each of the distribution, professional and scientific services, and miscellaneous services (including hotels and catering) orders of the standard industrial classification. A large share of this employment is generated by the needs of the local people, including the considerable number who have retired to the South West from other parts of the country. The sheer physical size of the region and the proliferation of small towns accounts for much of this relative importance of services, since the many small shopping centres and the extended lines of communication place heavy demands upon manpower. In addition, however, services offered to a larger national market provide considerable employment in educational, medical and dental, and national government establishments, as well as in the various activities of the tourist trade. The latter caters for well over half a million visitors each year and represents about one-fifth of the British holiday market.

Despite the fact that manufacturing in the South West accounts for a smaller share of employment than it does in all other regions, there can nevertheless be little doubt about its local and national importance. Its main features stem from the fact that the industrial revolution of the eighteenth and nineteenth centuries largely by-passed the region. Apart from the development of Bristol, which already boasted quite a wide range of manufacturing activities based mainly upon imported raw materials, only the naval dockyard at Plymouth, the ship repairing activities of Falmouth, Brunel's railway engineering centre at Swindon and various engineering developments at Cambourne (related to the non-ferrous mining industry) stem from the era of Victorian economic expansion. Nevertheless, by the beginning of the present century, a sufficiently diverse range of manufacturing activities and skills in the South West—plus other factor endowments—permitted the appearance of a number of important growth industries in the region. During the inter-war years, aircraft assembly and component manufacture were outstandingly successful; in the years since 1945, the development of the engineering and chemical industries has been particularly rapid.

As a result, the contemporary structure of manufacturing industry in the South West is characterized by its diversity, by a relatively fast rate of expansion, and by its ability to attract new manufacturing units from outside the region. Manufacturing is also notable

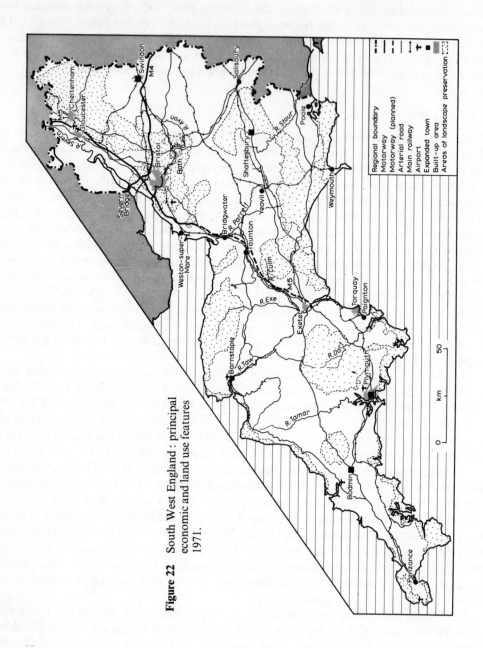

Figure 22 South West England : principal economic and land use features 1971.

for the number of comparatively large units which are located in relatively small towns, and—as with the service trades—its marked concentration in the northern part of the region. The main employers in the manufacturing sector of the regional economy of the South West in 1965 (with a labour force of 402,000) were the engineering and electrical goods industries (104,000 employees), vehicles (especially the aircraft and aerospace industries—63,000) and the food, drink and tobacco industries (62,000). Together these activities accounted for more than half of the region's manufacturing jobs, whilst paper, printing and publishing, the clothing and footwear industries and the shipbuilding, ship repairing and marine engineering group accounted for a substantial part of the rest. Between 1953 and 1963, employment in engineering and electrical goods increased by 40 per cent, a rate well above the national average, and accounted for half of the total growth of manufacturing jobs during the decade. All the other major employers in the region also increased their demands for labour with the exception of the shipbuilding/ship repairing group in which a considerable decline was recorded; nationally, however, employment in this industry contracted even faster.

Part of the growth of manufacturing industry in the South West derived from the growth of the industries already there. But a further component resulted from the arrival of new firms into the region. Between 1945 and 1965, some 189 moves by manufacturing industry into the region have been identified—and of these 56 were in the period to 1951, 52 were between 1952 and 1959, and 81 were in the last five years to 1965 (Howard, 1968). The substantial increase in numbers during this last phase can in part be related to the growing attractions of the region for manufacturing enterprise. In addition, however, it has to be remembered that Development District status was confered upon part of the region in 1960, and, of the 81 moves between 1960 and 1965, 28 were to the Development Districts. The importance of these new industries far outweighs the mere 36,000 jobs they provided in 1965 (about 9 per cent of the regional manufacturing employment in that year), for they were largely in the newer and rapidly expanding science-based areas of manufacturing activity. They are likely therefore to generate both more employment and more firms in the future.

With its large number of small towns, one of the characteristics of the industrial geography of the South West is the degree to which particular localities depend upon a single large firm. Quite apart from the heavy dependence of Plymouth upon its naval dockyard, four small towns—Keynsham, Melksham, Dursley and Chippenham—in 1965 had over 30 per cent of their employment in their largest manufacturing unit, and a further 12 towns had between 10 and 30 per cent of their jobs in their single largest plant. To the extent that some employees journeyed into these centres from their rural hinterlands, the dependence of the town's residents upon these plants was even greater. Geographical specialization of this nature clearly offers the possibility of certain external economies in the local labour market; but at the same time it implies a risk for the dependent communities since the commercial failure of a single firm can generate enormous local distress. This is a problem which the widening of labour market areas through improved employee mobility can in part ameliorate. It is a problem which is least acute in the Northern sub-region.

6.2.1 *The Northern Sub-region*

By far the most important spatial component in the economic geography of the South West is the *Bristol city region*. Whilst for certain administrative and service purposes it extends throughout the whole of the South West peninsula, the city's commuting sphere is more confined. It stretches over South Gloucestershire, West Wiltshire and North Somerset, embracing a population of about one million people. During the present century it has been a remarkably prosperous area, experiencing steady economic growth and low levels of unemployment. To its natural increase in population, therefore, has been added a persistent in-migration of people from other parts of the country. Since 1951, for example, the rather more narrowly defined Bristol/Severnside sub-region has increased its population by 133,000 to reach a total of 926,000 (in 1971), most of it by net in-migration.

The oldest industries of Bristol are related to its long-standing role as a port. Tobacco processing, wine importing, flour milling and food processing have long been a source of the city's considerable wealth—and in the form of such companies as Wills (Imperial Tobacco), Harveys and Frys they continue so today. Port facilities, but this time at Avonmouth, have also encouraged the development of an additional range of raw material processing industries of a primarily chemical and metallurgical nature. One of the largest of these, owned by Imperial Chemical Industries, in fact receives its principal feedstock— ethylene—by pipeline from Fawley, but the manufacture of fertilizers, phosphorus, carbon black, general chemicals and non-ferrous metals, all of which are to be found on the flat alluvial land to the north of the River Avon, rely upon such water-borne raw material imports as petroleum products, rock phosphate, sulphur, potash and lead and zinc ores. It is a good example of a Maritime Industrial Development Area (M.I.D.A.), but, unlike Teeside, one without adequate deep-water facilities for modern bulk carriers (see pp. 380–383). Elsewhere in Bristol and its immediate environs are located other industrial giants such as the British Aircraft Corporation and the Bristol engine division of Rolls Royce. Given the fluctuating fortunes of aircraft manufacturers in Britain, plus the fact that about half the Filton workforce of 24,000 is committed to the highly speculative Concorde project, this particular component of Bristol's economy has been interpreted by some as a potential problem. Certainly the real strength of the city and its region's manufacturing economy lies in the heterogeneity of the many smaller yet nevertheless highly successful firms, especially in the engineering sector. Sometimes in the smaller towns on individual sites, elsewhere on large industrial estates such as tne Chittening and Avonmouth Dock Estates, these industries have grown as fast as post-war Board of Trade, and Department of Trade and Industry policies have allowed.

In the service sector of the economy equally dynamic growth forces are at work. The city region contains a number of smaller centres that depend heavily upon service, and especially white collar, jobs. Bath, with a large Ministry of Defence establishment and a new technological university in addition to its long standing tourist and recreational roles, is a good example. But it is Bristol itself which once again can claim the lion's share of such growth. Port and public utility employments have increased, the university has been considerably expanded, and since 1945 a series of major redevelopment schemes in the central area has provided new shopping and entertainment facilities and the construction of many new office blocks. The floor space of the latter has been increased by more than 60 per cent, so that the City can now claim to be the fourth largest office centre in England outside London. With the old Bristol docks in the centre of the city approaching the end of their useful life, as much as 28 hectares of land and water could in the near future be transferred from transport (both port and associated railway) uses to additional office and amenity purposes in the heart of the central business district.

Most winds blow fair for Bristol. It has a newly acquired accessibility to and from the rest of the country. It boasts a well-balanced and growth oriented manufacturing structure, with a tertiary employment boom simultaneously under way. It has a range of urban amenities that are attractive to the immigrant employer and his employees alike, and it has ample recreational opportunities close to hand (the Cotswolds, the Mendips and the Somerset coast, as well as the urban delights of Bath). Only public policies can deny the city region a continuing industrial and commercial success. The city's economic growth and population expansion have naturally expressed themselves geographically in the spread of urban development on the periphery of the built-up area. Constraining it now, however, is a green belt of considerable extent that encircles both Bristol and Bath (see Figure 22), and that is designed to prevent an indiscriminate and sporadic urban sprawl into the countryside in the case of the former and to preserve a city of exceptional historical and architectural interest in the case of the latter. There will be some further residential development near to the centre of Bristol on its eastern side, but the principal result of this strategy of physical planning has been to encourage the growth of the surrounding villages and towns, both within and beyond the green belt. 'In-filling' and minor expansions are proceeding at such nearby places as Almondsbury, the Patchway area, Alveston and Pucklechurch (all within the green belt); but the major reception areas for Bristol overspill are further away at Yate (where land uses have been designated for a population of 35,000), Thornbury (14,000) and Nailsea (20,000).

Two other prosperous and expanding city regions, at a lower order of the urban hierarchy, are also to be found in the Northern sub-region of the South West. These are the *Gloucester/Cheltenham area* and the district focused upon Swindon. The population of the former has expanded steadily in recent years, from 388,000 in 1951 to 456,000 twenty years later. Spawning and attracting new manufacturing industry, especially in the engineering and transport component fields, North Gloucestershire has been able to take advantage of its location between Bristol and the West Midlands, at the same time as having a good access to the Greater London market. Dowty Rotol at Gloucester and Smith Industries at Cheltenham are but two examples. Since industrial development certificates have only being given to firms in the sub-region with considerable reluctance since 1945 (except in the case of the relatively isolated communities in the Forest of Dean, where the run-down of a small coal mining workforce has not been offset immediately by new incoming industry), the area has grown in spite of government policies. A measure of its inherent strength was provided by the closure of the Gloster Aircraft factory in the early nineteen sixties for, despite the loss of 5,000 jobs, the area avoided any significant short term unemployment. Alternative work was very quickly provided both by the expansion of local firms and the arrival of new companies, including I.C.I. Fibres Ltd. (formerly British Nylon Spinners), to take advantage of an attractive industrial site which did not require an industrial development certificate. A further asset of the economic development of the Gloucester/Cheltenham area, and especially in the growth of service employments, is its amenity attractions. Cheltenham especially—set at the foot of the Cotswolds, within easy reach of the Forest of Dean and able to boast some of the finest Regency architecture in the country—has been successful in attracting from London one of the few longer distance moves of a major (private) office employer, the Eagle Star Insurance Group, as well as several smaller decentralizing offices. In an area such as this, one of the primary tasks of the local planning authorities must inevitably be to ensure that development does not take place in ways that might detract significantly from the present attractiveness of both the older urban centres and the surrounding tracts of rural and natural beauty.

To the east lies *Swindon* set in a prosperous agricultural region and blessed with an advantageous centrality in Southern England. The decline in employment opportunities at the workshops of British Rail since the early nineteen fifties would have been catastrophic for a town in a less advantageous situation, and its recovery would have been slower but for the early advantage which was taken of the Town Development Act. Accepting overspill from London, attracting a diverse range of new employments both from the metropolis and from the West Midlands, and building upon its existing engineering tradition, the Borough of Swindon has increased its population from 69,000 in 1951 to 91,000 in 1971. Its new economic base includes several major establishments in the vehicle trades (Pressed Steel-Fisher Ltd. being the largest) and in electrical and electronic engineering; and the town's employment opportunities have been both widened and stabilized with the arrival of the wholesale organization of W. H. Smith & Son and decentralized office activities. The latter will be substantially increased further with the arrival of Burmah Oil in the early nineteen seventies. The continuing expansion of Swindon, therefore, is without doubt. In 1966, a report by Llewelyn-Davies, Weeks and Partners demonstrated the feasibility of a planned expansion of the Swindon-Newbury area to absorb an additional population of 125,000 by 1981 and a total population of 400,000 by the end of the century. Even with the recent completion of the M4 to the south of the town, however, current ambitions are rather more modest, and an increase of a further 85,000 people by 1981 is now the goal.

Nesting within the Bristol, Gloucester/Cheltenham and Swindon city regions is a geography of settlement which is characterized by a variety of small towns and villages with a diverse range of industry. The employment and population growth there, however, has been impressively steady. The principal foci are the Stroud-Dursley area, with an emphasis upon engineering, and the towns of West Wiltshire (such as Chippenham and Calne) where food processing and rubber manufacture are important.

The Northern sub-region, then, from Weston-Super-Mare in the west to Marlborough in the east, and reaching as far north as Tewkesbury, includes not only nearly half of the population of the South West, but also its most dynamic industrial and urban centres. South of the Mendips and Salisbury Plain, in contrast, the pace of life and the character of economic development changes, and a transitional zone can be delineated.

6.2.2 *The Central, Southern and Western Sub-regions*

The *Central sub-region* is predominantly rural. As in the rest of the South West, dairying is the predominant type of farming, although cereal production is favoured on the well-drained soils of the chalk and the Cotswolds, and there are localities in which horticulture can take advantage of either nearby urban markets or good interregional communications. Prosperous market towns, such as Salisbury and Taunton, serve this rural economy. There are in addition, however, a number of important medium and small towns which play an industrial as well as a service role in the region's economic life. Outstanding amongst these are Bridgwater, which can boast a fairly diverse industrial structure (Britton, 1967, pp. 72ff.), and Yeovil which is nationally famous as a centre of helicopter manufacture. In addition, there are a number of individual towns in the Wellington-Westbury district that are heavily dependent upon a single enterprise for their employment and income: C. & J. Clark at Street (footwear) and John Heathcote & Co. at Tiverton (textiles) are but two examples. The largest town in the sub-region, however, is Poole. There, besides a diverse range of manufacturing activities, the important resort and recreational role of the South West begins in a geographical sense. Poole is nevertheless a community that in many respects 'looks out' of the region, principally in response to its close and growing connections with the Bournemouth area and (to a lesser extent) Southampton. It is noteworthy in this context that the 1966 South Hampshire Study for the former Ministry of Housing and Local Government not only confirmed the feasibility of a major planned overspill of London's population and employment into the Southampton-Portsmouth corridor, but also underlined the likelihood of considerable unplanned migration into the central sub-region of the South West. It is highly unlikely that Bournemouth-Poole will be unaffected by such a nearby growth. Indeed, Poole has benefited considerably since 1966 from its location just outside the zone of office controls and has become a notable centre for decentralized office activities. The Ministry in fact has asked the local authorities to examine the possibility of a town development scheme at Poole that would accommodate at least a further 30,000 Londoners.

With a population of a quarter of a million, the second largest urban centre in the whole of the South West and the focal point for many activities in both Devon and Cornwall is Plymouth. At one time the economy of the city was completely dominated by the Admirality Dockyard at Devonport—and indeed as recently as 1966 the 18,500 employed there represented one-fifth of the city's jobs, and nearly one-third of all male employment— but in recent years continuing attempts have been made to attract new industries in an effort to offset its declining employment opportunities. These have met with some success, more especially in the period 1960–1961 when the city was part of a development district. Nevertheless, unemployment rates have been consistently above the regional and national average—in November 1958, for example, the rate in the Plymouth area was 3.4 per cent, compared with a regional average of 2.7 per cent and the national figure of 2.3 per cent. Despite the counterbalancing effects of a lively tourist industry in the locality and widening employment opportunities in the service sector, since World War II female activity rates have remained relatively low, a net outward migration from the city (particularly of young people of working age) has persisted and the population of the area has barely increased.

The main area of population growth in Devon, in fact, lies to the northeast in the Exeter-Torbay area. The considerable migration into this locality of retired people, who in turn have thrown a considerable strain upon local social services and in particular upon the hospital and geriatric services, in part explains this trend. In addition, however, a range of new employment opportunities have grown in Exeter—which serves as an administrative and distributive centre for much of Devon, as well as performing a distinguished educational role through its university and training colleges—whilst Torbay has emerged as the largest and most successful holiday district in the South West. Out of some 530,000 holidaymakers in the region at the peak of the 1964 season, 125,000 were in the area between the Rivers Exe and Dart (South West Economic Planning Council, 1967, p. 53).

The remaining major elements in the settlement pattern of the South West—in the *Southern and Western sub-regions*—reflect an economy dominated by the service trades and agriculture. Along much of the coast in many small towns and villages, there exists a considerable and expanding tourist industry, which also extends inland to service visitors to the moors of Devon and Cornwall. Whilst it undoubtedly makes a considerable contribution to the wealth of the region, tourism also places fluctuating seasonal demands upon the labour force; with it is associated, therefore, relatively high rates of unemployment in the winter months, particularly in the more remote parts of the sub-region. Agriculture poses even more difficult employment problems. West of the Exe valley, although horti-culturalists can benefit from a favourably mild climate, many farmers engaged in dairying and mixed farming have to contend with poor and infertile soils. All suffer from a remoteness from their main markets. The farms are usually small family businesses. Cornwall has more than twice the national share of land in holdings of less than 20 hectares (50 acres). The result has been a steady rural depopulation, the economic effects of which have been multiplied into the related service activities of the sub-region's towns.

Opportunities for employment in the two other major categories of primary activity in the South West are also declining. The fishing industry has contracted and is now mainly based on Brixham and Newlyn. In contrast, the mining of china clay in the St. Austell district, which has the only workable deposits in the country, is both prosperous and expanding; the United Kingdom remains in fact the largest china clay exporter in the world. The mining of granite and tin is also still of considerable local importance. But the much more famous extraction of tin and copper in the Camborne-Redruth area— an activity which reached its peak about a century ago—had dwindled to minute proportions. Offsetting these declines, there has been some scattered growth of manufacturing employment, in such centres as Newton Abbott and Paignton, Penzance and Redruth. A few old-established industries, such as ship repairing at Falmouth, have been modernized and grown. New ones have been attracted or steered into the region. But this increase in manufacturing employments has not offset the decline in agriculture. However, the new jobs in manufacturing and the service sector, together with the increasing retired population, have meant that the overall population decline, which characterized large parts of the southern and western sub-regions in the nineteen fifties, has at last been checked; the period 1961–1968, for example, saw an estimated net in-migration of 67,000 people. In this reversal of fortune, the central government has played an important role.

The government first responded to the weaknesses of the more remote parts of the South West through the Local Employment Acts of 1960 and 1963. Under their provisions, it was able to assist the City of Plymouth during the period 1960–1961, and parts of West Cornwall (the Camborne-Redruth-Falmouth areas) and North Devon (the Bideford area) over the longer period 1960–1965. The effects of these measures can be seen in the figures for the estimated additional employment generated following the approval of industrial development certificates. Between 1956 and 1959, the annual average gain in employment from i.d.c. approvals in the Southern and Western sub-regions was 1,200, whereas between 1964 and 1967 the figure was 3,300. Since mid-1966 the greater part of the county of Cornwall and North Devon have together formed part of the South Western Development Area, delineated to assist those localities suffering from the worst effects of unemployment and depopulation. Plymouth was excluded from the Development Area by the Board of Trade on the grounds that the remoter parts of Cornwall and North Devon faced even graver economic dilemmas, and that the availability of development incentives in the city would in all probability deny to those areas an opportunity to attract mobile industry. It was a decision which met considerable criticism. Apart from the predictable pleas of local interest groups, the South West Economic Planning Council argued against it on the grounds that the long term economic growth of the remoter parts of the region required a buoyant sub-regional pole of economic growth, and that Plymouth was the only town large enough to perform this role and stand comparison with other urban centres elsewhere in Britain. It was further argued that, rather than denying economic opportunities to more remote communities in the existing development area, such a policy would stimulate complementary developments in the wider Plymouth city region through (for example) sub-contracting. A recent survey revealed that ten of the engineering firms established in Plymouth since 1945 were spending £270,000 each year in 38 towns and villages in the city region, and that two further post-war Plymouth factories have set up branch plants in Cornwall and have spent £400,000 annually in that County.

The Hunt Committee joined in the debate. In their 1969 Report, it was argued that the city had an inherent potential for growth; that it was an attractive area in which to live and work; that it possesses a labour supply with a wide range of skills and backed by appropriate educational facilities; and that its only problem was remoteness. Once its communications with the rest of Britain had been improved, Hunt concluded, the considerable potentials of the area could and would be exploited. Accordingly, the Committee's report advocated the speedy construction of the 'spine' motorway from the M5 in Somerset south to Plymouth (a road which in time, it is planned, will be extended to Penzance), but not any additional development assistance (Secretary of State for Economic Affairs, 1969, pp. 147). The government, on the other hand, possibly making a more realistic assessment of the rate at which the interregional road communications of Plymouth would in fact be improved, decided in 1969 to give the city and its immediate environs Intermediate Area status.

The dichotomy of economic structure, performance and growth prospects within the South West, then, is clear. In the north, history and geography have combined to produce a prosperous industrial and spatial structure with a considerable potential for further expansion; it would be very difficult—certainly it would be unwise—for any government to dampen down too severely the dynamic forces which are to be found there. In the south, in contrast, the opportunities for outstandingly rapid development are very much more limited, both in terms of their magnitude and their location; locally—principally in the more remote parts of the region—serious problems of economic stagnation, above average levels of unemployment and out-migration are to be found. Most people in the South West live in communities with either a considerable or alternatively a modest potential for further economic development. Only a very small minority are faced with the problems and distress of local stagnation and decline. In this respect—as well as in many others— the South West contrasts vividly with South Wales.

6.3 South Wales

The size, the structure and the location of employment, and the broad pattern of urban development, in South Wales still bears the heavy impress of the nineteenth century. It has to be recognized, of course, that since 1945 (and unlike the years before and after the depression) the region has enjoyed a remarkable prosperity. Unemployment stood at between 2 and 3 per cent until the late nineteen sixties when it moved up one per cent. Annual net out-migration was contained to 3,800 between 1951 and 1961, and a mere 900 during the subsequent five years. Employment opportunities in the region have

been significantly diversified through the introduction of new and expanding industries. Huge improvements have been made to the communications both within South
Wales and with other parts of Britain. The services and amenities available within the region
have been substantially improved. In many places the urban fabric has been completely
renewed. All these facts are widely appreciated and as a consequence the image of South
Wales, both nationally and internationally (and such matters are not unimportant in
regional economic performance), has been radically improved. The contrast with 1931,
when one in three of the region's workforce was a miner, and one in five was unemployed,
is all too clear (Minchinton, 1964).

Nevertheless, the structural problems of the economy, which have posed recurring
dilemmas for private and public interests alike since the end of World War I, remain.
The net loss of population has continued. Unemployment rates have persisted above
the national average. Between 1961 and 1966 male jobs in the region—and in the long
run it is male jobs that are most decisive in regional economic development—actually
declined. The gains in female employment still left the regional activity rate substantially
below the national average. The importance of industries which, in terms of employment,
are either contracting or growing slowly persists—coal mining and steelmaking together
directly employed 113,000 in 1966, and through their multiplier effects were probably
responsible for about one-third of the region's jobs in that year. There is, in fact, a good
deal of evidence to suggest that South Wales still lacks within its own economic base a
potential for rapid growth, and certainly not enough to meet the considerable loss of jobs
that can reasonably be expected in the near future. To many a contemporary entrepreneur,
the region remains *relatively* less attractive than many other parts of the country. It
continues to offer him less than other locations in such matters as established labour
skills, external economies, access to markets and the range of social and urban amenities.
In other words, in spite of 35 years of government 'protection', it would appear that for
some time to come various forms of public assistance will be required to maintain the
momentum of structural change.

6.3.1 *The Central and Eastern Valleys*

There are, of course, considerable differences in the economic performance and the
growth prospects of the different parts of South Wales. To speak of the region as a whole
hides certain important geographical truths. The Central and Eastern Valleys stand unique
as a sub-region of relative stagnation and prospective economic decline. Between 1951
and 1971, their population fell from 680,000 to 633,000. The *raison d'etre* of settlement
in this area is essentially the coal mining industry, which dramatically increased its production from 10 million tons in 1860 to 57 million tons in 1913 in response to both domestic
and overseas demands. In the process were created the famous South Wales mining communities, with their rows of terraced housing straggling up the narrow valleys of the Taff,
the Rhondda, the Rhymney and the Sirhowy (amongst others), and competing with the

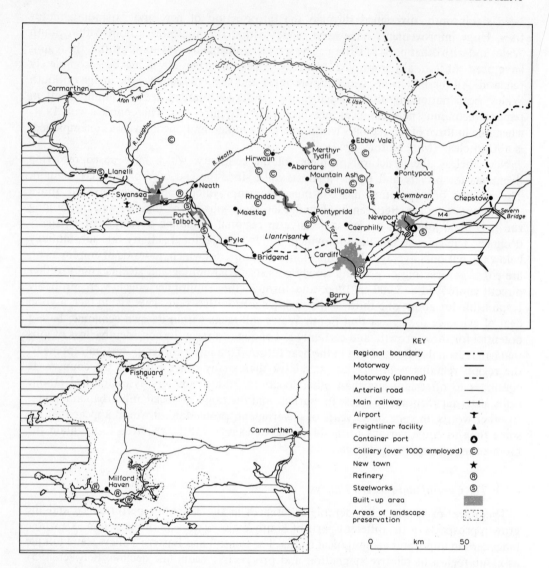

Figure 23 South Wales: principal economic and land use features, 1971.

pithead gear, the railways, the schools and the chapels for the limited amount of reasonably flat land which was available. Since World War I, however, the output of the coal-field has steadily declined. With the initial loss of its foreign markets, and the subsequent inability of the industry to compete profitably with alternative sources of energy at home, sales fell to 20 million tons in 1945 and 12.6 million tons in 1969. The manpower used by the industry contracted even more sharply. From 270,000 in 1913, it fell to rather less than 100,000 in 1945 and 43,000 in early 1970. Paralleling this run-down there has also been a shift in the geography of mining.

Although there has been a revival of interest in open-cast and drift mining in recent years—two new drifts have been opened in the Dulais Valley and a third near Blaenavon—the overall effect of concentration and rationalization has been for the industry to shrink away from the edges of the coal-field and to leave many of the communities in the north and the southwest devoid of deep-mining activities. More than two-thirds of the 300 collieries taken over by the National Coal Board (N.C.B.) in 1948 have been closed down, and those remaining are today concentrated in the heart of the coal-field basin where deep valleys cut into the Pennant Sandstone plateau. Three clusters of collieries stand out. The first is in the east and centred on the deepest part of the syncline to the south of the exhausted north crop area. Here, at Abertillary and in the Ebbw valley, for example, the depth of the seams has meant that the exploitation of coal had to await the arrival of twentieth century technology and economics; the result has been that the collieries tend to be bigger and newer than elsewhere, and the seams have been relatively little worked. The second group lies along the northern edge of the Pontypridd-Maesteg anticline, where mining yields a relatively high quality steam coal and the seams dip more gently northwards. A third group of collieries is located to the west of the Vale of Neath (in the West South Wales sub-region, see p. 252); this is the expensive remnants of the once famous anthracite mining industry—the N.C.B. has spent over £23 million on the new collieries of Abernant and Cynheidre—working the deepest seams beneath the Pennant Sandstone cover, and wresling with a disturbed and unstable geology (Humphrys, 1964).

The prospects for the coal industry in South Wales are distinctly bleak. Within the national energy market, the role of coal is likely to diminish both relatively and absolutely (Ministry of Power, 1967; Manners, 1971; see also pp. 170ff). Compared with the British coal industry as a whole, the productivity of the mines of South Wales is distinctly poor. Output per manshift in the N.C.B.'s East Wales and West Wales areas in 1969 was 1.39 tons and 1.47 tons respectively; this can be compared with a national average of 2.12 tons and the South Midland figure of 3.05 tons. In part the low productivity is a reflection of the underground geology; more especially it stems from the high absenteeism of the workforce, and the relatively small size of the mines—in 1970 the largest produced less than ½ million tons of saleable coal, and most were in the 200,000 to 300,000 ton range. In November 1965, when the N.C.B. announced the introduction of a phased, national programme of pit closures, only 47 of the 91 pits in South Wales were categorized in Group A and expected to have a long life. Two years later, when the employment implications of an even more rapid contraction of production were made public, it was forecast that the 57,000 jobs in the South Wales industry would contract to 39,000 in 1971, 24,000 in 1975 and perhaps only 9,000 in 1980. The exact timing of this forecast might have been in error. But the magnitude very probably was not.

The Central and Eastern Valleys of course offer some employment opportunities outside of the coal industry. A large integrated steelworks was located in Ebbw Vale in the late nineteen thirties with the help of government persuasion; its employment prospects today, however, are not especially bright (see pp. 254–255). In contrast, the variety of lighter manufacturing enterprises which have been steered into the sub-region as a result of the government's wartime and distribution of industry policies—firms such as the Hoover Company at Merthyr Tydfil, E.M.I. Electronics at Treorchy in the Rhondda, and South Wales Switchgear at Blackwood—are likely to increase their labour demands; and other firms might occasionally follow them onto the coal-field when their locational requirements can be matched to the limited number of sites available in the valleys or on the trading estate at Hirwaun. Moreover, the continuing residential and growing dormitary function of the valleys (Humphrys, 1962; 1965) in an increasingly affluent society has implications for the employment opportunities in the service sector there. The employment prospects mean that the sub-region will undoubtedly require over the next fifteen years or so a considerable investment, both private and public, in new homes, for the renewal of old urban centres and in better transport facilities. It will be in the larger centres such as Aberdare, Merthyr Tydfil and the Rhondda that the need will be the greatest. Nevertheless, the prospective decline of the sub-region's basic industry without question implies that the Central and Eastern Valleys as a whole will continue to be the most depressed part of South Wales. It is here that unemployment rates will continue to be the highest. It is here too that emigration will be fastest, that activity rates will be the lowest and that the prospects (and the advantages) of economic development will be the smallest.

6.3.2 *West South Wales*

West South Wales, on the other hand, an area which embraces much of the Swansea city region, enjoys at least a slow rate of growth. Between 1951 and 1966 its population increased from 449,000 to 464,000. In the subsequent five years, however, the population of the sub-region actually fell by 2,700. This decline was clearly a function of employment opportunities. During the period 1961 to 1966 there was no significant change in the total level of employment in the sub-region but the number of male jobs declined by 4 per cent. Clearly the declining employment opportunities on the anthracite coal-field especially, near such communities as Ammanford and Pontardawe, were being only partly offset by the creation of new jobs for men elsewhere in the sub-region and overall employment stability was secured only through the attraction of more women into the work force. The new jobs in the nineteen sixties were partly provided by the expansion of existing manufacturing concerns. These included various non-ferrous metal industries, such as nickel smelting at Clydach, aluminium and titanium rolling at Waunarlwydd, zinc smelting at Morriston and aluminium rolling at Resolven. The B.P. refinery at Llandarcy was expanded to have an annual throughput of 9 million tons in 1970 and spawned an expanding petrochemical complex at Baglan Bay, as well as a nearby gas manufacturing facility. The diverse range of large and small manufacturing concerns that had been steered into the sub-region after World War II—firms such as Cam Gears producing motor components in the Vale of Neath, the Minnesota Mining and Manufacturing Company making business machines at Gorseinon and the Mettoy Company, maker of Corgi toys, at Swansea—also expanded their output and job opportunities. By the middle of the nineteen-sixties a number of new industries that had been steered into the sub-region under the Local Employment Acts also began to make a significant contribution to employment opportunities there. Extensively publicized were the new motor component plants of British Leyland and the Ford Motor Company at Llanelli and Swansea respectively; but equally important were the smaller firms that arrived to adapt old tinplate mills, rented the Board of Trade's advanced factories or located on one of the sub-region's several industrial estates. Further major manufacturing developments were planned by Borg-Warner at Kenfig and Morgan Crucible at Landore. An important geographical characteristic of this employment growth in the manufacturing sector of the economy of West South Wales was its scatter throughout the coastal zone from Pyle to Burryport, with only the occasional industrialist being enticed any distance inland to such places as Ammanford and Ystradgynlais. The widening opportunities for employment in the service sector however—a third important source of 'replacement' jobs—have been concentrated especially in the city of Swansea. In the past this growth was primarily a function of the growing centralization in Swansea of many services both for the West South Wales sub-region and for West Wales generally (especially Carmarthenshire and Pembrokeshire); it was also a reflection of the widening educational role of Swansea through the development of its University College. Prospectively, however, the service sector will receive yet a further boost from the arrival of new government office employments, and in particular from the national Vehicle Taxation, Registration and Licence Issuing Centre and the Land Registry, which together will provide about 4,500 new jobs in the city.

There can be little doubt, however, that the recent employment record and economic performance of the West South Wales sub-region would have been considerably poorer but for the steady expansion of the erstwhile Steel Company of Wales at Port Talbot. During the post-1945 years, the steel industry throughout South Wales has been dramatically transformed. As late as 1953, for example, there were as many as 13 cold metal steelworks in the region. Fifteen years later, all but three of these open hearth plants, unintegrated with pig iron production, had been closed down to leave virtually the whole of the industry at four integrated sites—Port Talbot, Llanwern, Ebbw Vale and Cardiff. Tinplate manufacture, one of the traditional specializations of the region, had similarly been modernized and concentrated upon fewer and fewer sites. In 1950, the South Wales tinplate industry consisted of 36 hand mills, one cold reduction mill and an electrolytic tinning line. By 1961, the last handmill was closed, to leave only three modern plants at Trostre, Velindre and Ebbw Vale producing the whole of the British output. Some of the tinplate was consumed locally—by the Metal Box Company at Neath for example— but most was shipped out of the region to markets elsewhere in the country and overseas. By the time of the 1967 nationalization of steel, two further (prospective) developments were clear. The first was the urgent need to reduce the labour inputs of an industry that was grossly overmanned by international standards; figures of 10,000 to 17,000 redundant jobs in South Wales alone were regularly quoted in the press, and were possibly an under-estimate of the radical changes needed to meet foreign competition. The second prospective development was a further rationalization of at least pig iron and steel production upon yet fewer sites (Manners, 1968; 1971).

In the corporate planning of the British Steel Corporation (B.S.C.), the claims of South Wales for a significant share of future investment are rooted in its specialization in one of the fastest growing sectors of the market—steel strip and its products—and in the size and nature of the capital investment already sunk there. The locational economics of the industry further suggest that the B.S.C. would gain most by concentrating any new iron and steelmaking investments at Port Talbot and Llanwern. Both are large, integrated and coastal plants (although only the former, with its modern, £20 million import terminal capable of handling bulk carriers of 100,000 dwt and over, is in an economic sense coastal), both have ample room for expansion, and both enjoy reasonably good access by rail and road to their markets in the Midlands and the south of England. In 1967 the steel-making capacity of the whole of South Wales was about 7 million tons per year; by the mid nineteen seventies, it is likely to be somewhere between 10 and 12 million tons and largely concentrated in these two plants—as first Ebbw Vale and then possibly East Moors in Cardiff shut down their small blast furnaces and at a later stage end their roles as producers of tonnage carbon steel. Already by 1971 the conversion of Port Talbot to basic oxygen steelmaking had been completed and plans had been announced for a second blast furnace at Llanwern. In addition, of course, rather more specialized and smaller scale steel production is likely to continue for some time at the East Moors plant in Cardiff which has the advantage of being sited next to its chief customer, Guest, Keen and Nettlefolds (G.K.N.). Stainless production, at Panteg, is also likely to remain viable, being more dependent upon skills than scale. The small remaining cold metal works in the private sector—at Llanelli—could also survive for some time through its intimate links with the West Midlands engineering industry, its written-down capital equipment and the low price of British scrap.

The finishing plants of the industry, however, will be more widespread. Apart from the mills at, or near, the two huge integrated works on the coast—the range and the size of which will undoubtedly be expanded—the nineteen seventies will see major invest-ments at Ebbw Vale as it is transformed into the country's largest tinplate and galvanising facility. Partly justified by the B.S.C.'s social responsibility towards its employees there, it is an investment which will protect some 8,000 of the (1969) 9,300 steel jobs in this Monmouthshire valley. Tinplate production will also be expanded at Velindre and Trostre (near Swansea and Llanelli, respectively), as will the capacity of the paint-coated strip plant at Gorseinon. In the private sector, the G.K.N. mill in Cardiff has the greatest potential for expansion. Greater output, however, does not necessarily mean extra jobs. The 58,000 South Wales' steel workers of 1968 could well be reduced to less than 45,000 by 1975. If they are not, then the industry's costs are likely to be too high and its further expansion prejudiced.

Whilst it is clear that the steel industry will for many years be a major component in the economy of West South Wales, therefore, along with coal it is likely to be a diminishing source of employment. Judging from past trends and without a major upsurge in the rate of national economic growth and investment, it is improbable that any new manufacturing industries and decentralized offices steered into the sub-region—together with the continuing centralization of service activities for the whole of West Wales upon the city of Swansea—will be able to do more than simply maintain jobs and population at the present level throughout the nineteen seventies. As a result much of the natural increase of the population will continue to be lost through net out-migration. Geographical adjustments will naturally continue within the sub-region and in this regard the Llanelli-Swansea-Port Talbot coastal zone stands most to gain; this shift will continue to generate both a commuting and a permanent movement of population away from the coal-field communities further inland. It also seems likely that the activity rate of West South Wales will continue to rise. Taking the sub-region as a whole, however, the evidence suggests few grounds for anticipating exceptionally vigorous growth in the near future.

6.3.3 *South West Wales*

West of Llanelli lies the South West Wales sub-region (Figure 23). More extensive than the other parts of South Wales geographically, it is much smaller in terms of its population and employment. The greater part of the area is rural, heavily dependent upon a dairying and mixed farming economy with steadily contracting labour requirements. Its relatively small farm holdings, and the distance of large urban markets, are very reminiscent of the conditions and problems of farming in the southern and western sub-regions of South West England. The tourist industry—albeit less well developed in West South Wales— is a further common denominator. However, the economic development of Pembrokeshire has been distinctively moulded by a major and unique natural resource in the sub-region, and one which has helped to offset the run-down of its military employment. This is the natural deep water at Milford Haven. Here is one of the very few places in Britain where a decade ago it was possible to bring vessels of 100,000 dwt close to the shore without expensive dredging, and where (following the deepening of the channel) tankers of 250,000 dwt could be berthed by 1970. Of the four oil terminals already built, one serves the

Llandarcy refinery at Swansea via a 112 kilometre (70 miles) crude oil pipeline; the others serve the three refineries of Esso (6.35 million tons), Texaco (6.0 million tons) and Gulf (3.9 million tons), which are likely to be joined by a fourth (Amoco) in the near future.

Whilst the scale of the refinery operations is impressive, the employment opportunities created in Pembrokeshire after the initial construction phase are quite limited. A modern 6 million ton refinery might only provide about 300 jobs when fully operational, and even in the construction phase it is not at all certain how much local manpower is employed, since itinerant construction labour tends to be readily available and more adaptable to the work required. Moreover, there is no sign as yet that any associated petrochemical complex will develop in such a remote corner of the Principality and Kingdom. The projected product pipeline to the West Midlands and South Lancashire, when completed, will presumably set back even further any chance of secondary developments other than the large 2000 MW power station of the C.E.G.B. Despite the considerable cost of the refinery complex in terms of lost natural amenity—for the Haven is fringed by an extensive stretch of the Pembrokeshire Coast National Park, and this section of South Wales has an important recreational value for visitors and second homes—the general level of unemployment in West South Wales has persisted above the national average, and the need for further industries remains as urgent as ever. Net out-migration, temporarily checked in the early nineteen sixties, appears to have returned by the end of the decade (see Table 18).

6.3.4 South East South Wales—the Coastal Belt

The final geographical component of South Wales is the so-called Coastal Belt in the southeast. Compared with the other sub-regions it has both a larger population and in recent years a very much better record of economic growth. It is without doubt, the most attractive part of the region both for manufacturing industry and for commercial and office development. During the last 35 years, its economic base has been completely transformed, and the former heavy dependence upon the coal and ferrous industries has been replaced by an increasingly complex manufacturing structure that includes aluminium rolling, electrical engineering, the motor component and assembly industries, plastics and chemical firms and a host of light manufacturing concerns. Many of the new industries have located in and around the coastal towns such as Newport, Cardiff and Barry. Alcan at Rogerston, Monsanto at Newport, British Leyland (Rover division), the British Aircraft Corporation and Powell Duffryn Engineering at Cardiff, and British Geon at Barry are just some of the larger corporate enterprises manufacturing in this zone. However, most of the new industries, either through their own choice or through public policy, are to be found some distance inland at the mouths of the South Wales' valleys. There, they are still near to the services and amenities of the City of Cardiff, but they are also within easy commuting distance of the valley communities which (through them) no longer rely almost exclusively upon coal mining for their livelihood. The new decimal branch of the Royal Mint at Llantrisant, the many industries in the Cwmbran-Pontypool area such as Girlings and I.C.I. Fibres, and the variety of industrial enterprises to be found on the large industrial estates at Bridgend and Treforest are typical of this locational characteristic.

The economic base of the coastal belt, which embraces the core but by no means all of the Cardiff city region, has been further diversified by the growth of service and office employments there; indeed, the post-1945 growth of jobs in the distributive trades, in insurance, banking and finance, in professional and scientific services, and in public administration has been as notable as the changes that have occurred in the manufacturing sector. Some of these jobs have been created in the ports, especially Newport and Barry, which have lost their coal export trade but to which a variety of new traffics have now been attracted. The export of vehicles from Newport and the import of bananas through Barry are but two examples of this trend which has ameliorated but by no means solved the financial problems of the region's ports. Some central government departments have been transferred to Newport. The new town of Cwmbran has emerged in recent years as an important sub-regional shopping centre, as well as providing a new home for the Monmouthshire County Council. However, the greater number of the sub-region's new service jobs are to be found in Cardiff itself, which only in 1948 was recognized officially as the capital of Wales. Since then its economic and geographical influence, and its importance as a business, financial, cultural and educational centre—it has both a College of the University of Wales and the new technological Institute of the University—have greatly increased. With the appointment of a Secretary of State for Wales for the first time in 1964, plus the parallel creation of the Welsh Office in Cardiff, the city has also come to play a much larger administrative role in the life of Wales than it did in the past.

The coastal belt, therefore, offers the contemporary entrepreneur a labour force with increasingly diverse skills. It is the part of South Wales which is best served by the existing communication facilities, and which stands to gain most by the new ones. It also offers the widest range of industrial, commercial and amenity services. This, then, is a zone of quickening immigration, of increasing male as well as total employment, and (by the standards of South Wales) of relatively low unemployment and high activity rates. Nevertheless, in assessing the economic prospects of the sub-region, it must not be overlooked that a significant share of its recent employment growth has been related directly or indirectly to public policies and initiatives. But for the distribution of industry policies in general, and the expanding labour force at the Llanwern steelworks in particular, male employment could well have fallen during the nineteen sixties. It would be unwise therefore to assume that the sub-region will experience net employment growth in the near future without the continuation of some form of governmental assistance. Even with the changing spatial relationships of the area which will undoubtedly work to its considerable advantage, the relative weaknesses of its economy remain. Within the sub-region and throughout the nineteen seventies, the steel industry, the coal industry and the railway and dock industries will all continue to reduce their labour requirements, most of which are of course for men.

In 1971 government development assistance was available to almost the whole of

South Wales. Most of the region was within the Welsh Development Area, and certain localities on the coal-field were eligible for the higher subventions of the Special Development Areas. However, the southeast estuarine and coastal strip (extending from Barry to Chepstow, and reaching inland to Cwmbran and Abergavenney) was only given an Intermediate Area status—and that after being without any assistance at all for about a decade. It was the city of Cardiff that had to offer inducements in the form of relatively cheap land and new service roads in order to attract the then Rover Motor Company into the sub-region. Interpreted in retrospect, the vacillating and at times obscure emphasis of public policies in South Wales since 1945 has been aimed primarily at steering mobile employments as close as possible to the main concentrations of unemployment in the coal-field valleys and in West South Wales. At first determined efforts were made 'to attract industry to restricted valley sites amidst outworn housing in areas relatively isolated from main traffic channels' (Glamorgan County Council, 1964, para, 123). However, with physical space for industry at a premium in the valleys themselves, and with firms reluctant to move to such relatively isolated and environmentally unattractive locations in any case, the policy had to be modified. Firms were found to be more willing to accept sites near the mouths of the valleys, and the Board of Trade thus refocused its strategy to encourage industrial development on the northern edge of the estuarine and coastal plain. The trading estates at Treforest, Bridgend, Pyle and Swansea symbolize this policy, as do the new towns at Cwmbran and Llantrisant.

The Monmouthshire Council in particular has in recent years strongly opposed industrial development in the Coastal Belt. It believes in trying to attract new employments to the existing valley communities where the unemployment rates are the highest, and in reserving the less urbanized parts of the centre and east of the county for tourism, week-end cottages and the like. The development of the coastal strip, it has been argued, would undermine this tourist potential. As Hallett and Randall have recently observed: 'In view of the nature and location of the Llanwern Flats ... this seems an unnecessarily pessimistic view.' (1970, p. 14). Nevertheless, without defining whether the 'need' was short or medium term, the Welsh Office in 1967 argued that :

'If the inducements included in the parts of Wales included in the Development Area were equally available in adjacent districts already more diversified economically, the latter would attract enterprises which might otherwise go to places in Wales where their presence is more immediately required to give employment to men released from declining industries or to help check rural depopulation. The primary objective of fostering industrial development where it is most needed could thus be frustrated.' (Secretary of State for Wales, 1967, p. 51).

The corollary of this policy, of course, has been for industry to be offered no assistance— or since Hunt only limited assistance, albeit contrary to the advice of that distinguished committee—in those localities where the locational advantages are the greatest and where it would be very much easier and cheaper to generate new employments.

Three principal explanations underlie this policy. One is the fear that expansion in the estuarine/coastal zone would be entirely at the expense of the communities further west. There is no clear evidence that developments in the former would necessarily or quickly generate secondary developments in the latter, although many believe that this would in fact happen. The employments created in Cornwall as a result of new Plymouth industry (see p. 248) are suggestive of this possibility, but they are by no means conclusive. The second is the sheer political strength of the valley communities in South Wales—a strength which is of course declining as their population falls. The third is the lack of a widely accepted preference for (or a political commitment to) any particular future of urban form in southeast South Wales. In the past too much energy has been spent arguing about the boundaries of local authorities within the sub-region—between Glamorgan County Council and Cardiff City Council in particular—and too little on a consideration of priorities in the emerging urban complex, the environment of which is their joint responsibility. Even the designation of the two new towns was a response to limited planning problems and goals, and not to the urbanization problems of the Coastal Belt viewed as a whole. In the absence of a vision of the sub-region's future urban geography, it was inevitable that the emphasis of planning policy should have been primarily to preserve, and only marginally to amend, the existing urban geography. The weakness of such an approach to sub-regional urban development is highlighted by the selection of Llantrisant as the site of a new town. Within easy reach of many east Glamorgan valley communities, it also happens to lie within the 130 millimetre (50 inch) rainfall isohyet. Whilst the late nineteenth century coal industry and its associated settlement pattern could not, for obvious geological reasons, avoid such a damp and basically uninviting environment, it is debatable whether 60,000 or so souls working in light manufacturing industry, in the decimal branch of the Royal Mint and in associated service employments in the late twentieth century, should be encouraged to live in such conditions—particularly when environmentally pleasanter and certainly much drier localities exist only a few kilometres away nearer the coast.

Consequent upon this planning strategy to deflect potential growth away from Severnside, industry has tended to select development area sites which are as near as possible to the major urban centres, and/or which will have good access to the M4 once it is extended westwards from Newport to Bridgend. The strategy has even encouraged some firms and employments to move from the estuarine urban complex onto nearby inland sites where development area subventions are available. The shift of Dialoy Ltd., employing 360, from Cardiff to Caerphilly is a case in point. There is also some evidence that a number of firms which were denied the opportunity of locating in the Chepstow to Barry zone have not located in South Wales at all. However, it remains impossible to measure the amount of economic development and the number of jobs that have been foregone by the Principality through the decision not to take full advantage of its locational and other assets on Severnside. One somewhat illogical aspect of the strategy is the continuing exclusion of the still expanding new town of Cwmbran from the Development Area— a decision which has prompted more than one of the town's industries to expand its production facilities a short distance away in Pontypool—whilst the more recently designated new town at Llantrisant is afforded every development area assistance. However, the most important result of this planning policy has been for the emerging pattern of land uses, commuting and urban development to be influenced as much by a Development Area boundary (the arbitrary qualities of which are widely recognized) as by the more legitimate considerations of sub-regional, urban and local physical planning.

In sum, then, the role of the planning authorities in South Wales has been and remains to strike a balance between four fundamental yet contrasting objectives. The first is to ensure a steady and balanced movement of population away from those communities whose existence makes relatively little sense in the late twentieth century. To date, the exodus has largely comprised the young, the healthy, the educated and the ambitious, and has left behind older generations who have neither the will nor the economic resources to move. The second is to promote the economic and environmental redevelopment of those older mining and industrial communities where the chances of adaptation are the greatest. The third is to ensure the continuing general prosperity of communities west of Barry, Cardiff and the coastal zone; these include not only the settlements at the mouths of the valleys and in the Swansea Bay area, but also the rural areas further west in Carmarthen and Pembrokeshire. The fourth objective must be to take advantage of the economic opportunities of Severnside. There can be little doubt that, in the present state of the regional planning art, the most appropriate balance between these four goals is difficult both to formulate and to achieve. However, not a few observers consider that in recent years the second and third have been given an unjustifiable preference over the other two.

6.5 Severnside prospects

Whilst the contrasting political reactions to the opportunities for vigorous economic development on the north and south banks of the Severn estuary can be better understood in the light of their more recent economic history and contemporary economic geography, a partial reconciliation of the two cannot be indefinitely avoided. Central government, as well as common sense, requires a coherent and consistent framework for public investment and physical planning throughout the whole area. Now that the flow of people and goods between the homes, towns, factories and shops on both sides of the estuary has been made considerably easier by the region's new and improved transport facilities (and especially by both the physical and psychological effects of the Severn Bridge), it has become increasingly evident that some of the problems of the Bristol and Cardiff city regions are in part complementary. Their possible solutions are to some degree complementary also.

In the matter of port investment, for example, it is clear that the technological revolution overtaking all aspects of the ocean transport industry demands a coordination of major developments—and particularly new container handling facilities—on both sides of the

Upper Bristol Channel. Moreover, investments need to be made in the context of prospective Severnside and national requirements, rather than in response to the inevitable
local desire to perpetuate an historical port pattern. Events over the last decade, however,
do not give rise to excessive confidence in the wisdom of public policies in this field. The
proposal of the Port of Bristol Authority in 1964 for the construction of a large new
(national) deep-sea container and bulk raw materials importing facility at Portbury was
intially received in South Wales with parochial envy. It quickly generated a number
of alternative proposals for investment in a comparable range of facilities on the north
side of the Channel. When the scheme for a new deep-water berth and entrance channel
for the Llanwern steelworks was being given serious consideration *circa* 1965/1966—
indeed, it was blessed with broad government approval (Minister of Transport, 1965)—
the possibility of multiple use of that channel plus the land available in estuarine Monmouthshire adjacent to the steelworks suggested to Welsh interests in particular that there
were greater advantages in making any substantial container port investments there
rather than at Portbury. In the subsequent study of the maritime industry and port development in South Wales by Hallett and Randall (1970), it was this same Uskmouth site
which was favoured for serious consideration as a Maritime Industrial Development
Area (M.I.D.A.). Meanwhile, the Ministry of Transport had examined and reported
on the original Portbury scheme (Ministry of Transport, 1966); although their analysis
is open to criticism (Tanner and Willams, 1967), the Ministry cannot be faulted for
examining the proposal in the light of national port requirements before they advised
against it. However, four years later, with the proposals for a new entrance channel for
the Llanwern steelworks shelved, the government decided to approve a modified and
less ambitious dock scheme for Bristol. Although its construction is not yet under way,
the government's decision appears to represent a return to a more piecemeal approach
towards port development on Severnside. By September 1972, it is interesting to reflect, a
decade had elapsed since the Rochdale Report on the ports of the whole of Britain (Ministry
of Transport, 1962); that committee had strongly recommended that the ports of Bristol
and Newport should be transferred to the control of 'a new Upper Bristol Channel port
trust which would be responsible for conservancy and pilotage, and which would be
in a better position to judge the merits of alternative port development proposals' (p. 188).
Such a body has still to be created, yet the arguments in favour of it are no less pressing
in the nineteen seventies than they were in the nineteen sixties.

Turning to the matter of employment growth, the complementary nature of the two
sides of Severnside is once again all too apparent. Greater Bristol is a sub-region of labour
shortage. Greater Cardiff has persistently been faced with a labour surplus. Market
forces will ensure that in the future, as in the past, some Welsh people will be attracted
to work in the factories, shops and offices in the Bristol area. Contrarywise, some Bristol
firms might seek a solution to their labour difficulties by establishing branch plants for
manufacture in South Wales. Some people will travel to man these industries on a daily
basis and so intensify commuter flows in both directions across the Severn. Others will

resolve to change their homes and find accommodation nearer to their work. The major uncertainty, of course, is the degree to which each of these alternative solutions will be adopted. To a very large extent, this will depend upon public policy, and in particular upon the attitude of the Department of Trade and Industry towards the administration of industrial development certificates, plus thinking in the Ministry of Local Government and Development and the Welsh Office concerning some of the broader issues of land use and strategic planning. Certainly, there is a *prima facie* case for the future industrial roles of these two areas to be examined and to some extent shaped together.

Turning to urban growth, it is reasonable to expect that the population of South Wales and the Greater Bristol regions will expand by 300,000 to 350,000 people between 1970 and 1981. Most of these people will want to live in towns and the greater number will be located in the Severnside zone. The question naturally arises therefore as to what is likely to be the best form of urban development to house these extra people. Should the bulk of the development be encouraged in and around the two largest centres of population, that is the cities of Cardiff and Bristol? Should several large centres be developed? Or should the population expansion be spread between all the existing communities both large and small? Again, should we continue to expand existing towns, or should new towns be designated and built? And how many? Whilst these are highly complex questions to answer in summary fashion, it is noteworthy that the several local authorities which are responsible for the physical plans of Severnside are in some agreement as to the general form which urban development there should take. Their decisions, many of which were taken from essentially parochial viewpoints, in fact make very good regional sense for a variety of economic, traffic planning, and amenity reasons. Their plans are in fact encouraging a polynuclear form of urban development throughout the area.

The Buchanan *Probe Study Report* (1966) on Cardiff, for example, sought to demonstrate the advantages of restraining the growth of that city to perhaps 350,000 in 1970 and 500,000 in the year 2000, and suggested that provision be made for the population which might otherwise have moved into or grown up in the city in a new town built to the north west of Cardiff. Llantrisant was designated in fact in 1967. The Glamorgan County Council, which had advocated a new town in the same locality for some time, are also planning for the growth of such communities as Bridgend, Barry and Caerphilly. In Monmouthshire, some further expansion of Newport, and the growth of the new town at Cwmbran to its planned size of 55,000, are naturally to be expected; and a second new town in the county in the Caerwent-Caldicot area has been seriously mooted on a number of occasions. In Gloucestershire and Somerset, the expansion of Bristol and Bath are being, and will continue to be, physically restrained by their encircling green belt (see Figure 22); and provisions are being made for the anticipated increase in population in the area by the expansion of a number of smaller centres, with Yate/Chipping Sodbury singled out as a major focus of growth and having a future population of perhaps some 55,000. The Central Unit for Environmental Planning in their 1971 Severnside Study considered three basic options for the expected growth in the area's population. One was a continuation of policies which seek to restrain the spread of the largest towns on Severnside. A second was the development of large new towns in rural areas well away from the existing large communities. The third, and the one ultimately preferred by the Central Unit, was the major expansion of Bristol/Bath, Gloucester/Cheltenham and Newport/Pontypool. Under this third strategy, the expansion of the Bristol area would be made possible by a revision of the green belt policies to the north east of the city and the M4 in the locality of Frampton Cotterell, where urban development could accommodate an additional 300,000 people and thus contribute substantially to a Bristol/Bath sub-regional expansion of between 300,000 and 450,000 by the year 2001. The growth of the Gloucester/Cheltenham area would involve substantial developments on the west bank of the Severn; however, after making a large initial investment in a basic infrastructure there, it was judged possible to increase the population of North Gloucestershire by between 200,000 and 400,000 people. The only clear-cut immediate option for the expansion of population in the Newport area was seen to be northwards in the localities of Cwmbran and Pontypool, where an additional 150,000 inhabitants could be accommodated by the year 2001. By that time, under the accelerated growth estimates of the Central Unit, the Severnside Study Area would have an extra million people and a total population of 2.65 million; of these, 1.35 would be living in the Bristol/Bath sub-region and a further 0.85 million in the Gloucester/Cheltenham area.

Whether or not the proposals contained in the Severnside Study are ultimately accepted by the government, looking ten or fifteen years ahead there is emerging on both sides of the lower Severn a closely related series of towns and cities varying in size from 10,000 to perhaps 500,000. (The population of Bristol proper, of course, is not expected to increase; in fact, through redevelopment and overspill its population would appear likely to fall slightly.) All these communities will be linked together by the new M4/M5 motorway system and by further road investments (including a second crossing of the lower Severn), as well as by the existing trunk roads and railways. They will be functionally interrelated by means of industrial, commercial and service industry linkages, by an increasing amount of intercity commuting and by their common dependence upon the two largest centres of population and services, Bristol and Cardiff. Thus, within this discontinuous urban area, Barry, Llantrisant, Cardiff, Newport, Cwmbran, Chepstow, Gloucester, Cheltenham, Yate, Bath, Bristol and Western-Super-Mare (amongst others) will be separate but closely related nodes of development. They can be interpreted as integral parts of a greater urban whole straddling the lower Severn, as an emerging conurbation, as a new provincial metropolis (Manners, 1966a).

This semi-circular urban zone could prospectively assume characteristics not dissimilar with those to be found in western Netherlands. There, in 'Randstad Holland', Amsterdam serves as the capital city, The Hague as the seat of government, and Ijmuiden the centre for steel production, Rotterdam is the major port, Leiden is a university city and Utrecht is the centre of railway administration. There is, in other words, a diffusion of metropolitan functions between the several separate but closely related towns. In 'Randstad

Severn', similarly, there are several urban nodes, each of which is assuming a distinctive range of economic functions; yet at the same time they all rely in varying degrees upon each other. Newport has an emphasis on heavy industry, Cardiff on an administrative and political role; Gloucester has lighter engineering industries, Bristol manufacturing and commerce; and Bath a new educational role. But together, it is possible to envisage all these (and other) towns growing to provide all the services, amenities and activities of a second order centre, a provincial metropolis. Separated by carefully preserved country parks, as mooted in the Minister of Housing and Local Government's White Paper in 1968 on *Leisure in the Countryside,* and bound together by modern systems of transport and communication, the several towns and cities in this new urban complex could together constitute one of the fastest growing urban regions, or at least one of the most rapidly changing regions, in Britain in the next 20 years. For certain aspects of urban planning, therefore, it is clearly imperative to look at this region as a whole. In particular, Severnside needs some coordination of its land use and traffic plans. The failure of the Department of the Environment and the Welsh Office to insist upon some measure of joint planning by the authorities responsible for the component parts of Severnside could well lead to serious miscalculations of land allocations for housing, industry, open space and the like, as well as wasteful investment in utilities. Even more disastrous would be for these land use allocations to be made without an over-all traffic plan.

In the sphere of recreational planning also, it is abundantly clear that the local and regional planning authorities in the South West must increasingly take cognizance of the new proximity of the Brecon Beacons, the Gower, and other recreational amenities in Central and West Wales, just as their counterparts in South Wales can not ignore the ease with which the Cotswold Hills, Somerset and Devon can now be reached from places north of the Bristol Channel. Rising levels of personal income and greater population mobility together mean that day visits, weekend trips, seasonal holidays and second home purchases across the Severn are likely to increase particularly rapidly and to place severe pressures upon some outstanding recreational resources. The transport and land use planning implications of at least some of these trends can most usefully be examined, and the appropriate policy responses conceived, at the interregional rather than the regional or local level on Severnside. The same will increasingly apply to matters of water resource allocation and to estuarine pollution control.

These and other relationships between the South West and South Wales were given full and balanced consideration in the government's study of Severnside (Central Unit for Environmental Planning, 1971). Initiated in the hey-day of the Department of Economic Affairs in 1966, the study unfortunately suffered from a number of interregional disagreements and a lack of political leadership. The Study Area, for example, whilst embracing all that might reasonably be called Severnside on the English bank, was defined to end at the western Monmouthshire boundary and so to exclude the city of Cardiff and east Glamorgan. Only subsequently was it redefined, for the purposes of the economic analysis only, to include certain critical so-called 'fringe areas' in South Wales and the

South West. The clear reluctance of certain Welsh interests to get closely involved with, or to accept any commitment to, Severnside development inevitably reduced the value of the Study, and in their conclusions the Central Unit state that 'There are almost certainly better sites to the west of the Study Area for the location of the growing population of South Wales' (p. 10). On the other hand, the Study was able cogently to set out the main practical options which appear to lie open for urban development in the next few decades within a narrowly defined Severnside and to indicate something of the benefits and the costs of alternative strategies. The downward revision of the national population forecasts by the Registrar General in the late nineteen sixties naturally reduced the urgency of finding localities capable of housing the prospective increase in the country's population, and hence the Study itself. Nevertheless, the population of even the narrowly defined Severnside Study Area is still expected to grow (from 1.65 million in 1968) through natural increase and intraregional migration to 2.30 million in 2001, and it would be surprising if central government planners did not in addition steer some of the national expansion of population in the direction of Severnside. From this estuarine focus of growth, development opportunities would undoubtedly spread out south and west into the more remote parts of the two economic planning regions.

In accommodating this growth, Severnside presents a microcosm of so many of the nation's planning dilemmas. It poses the problem of how best to balance the advantages of new urban development with the need to renew (where practicable) the old. It raises questions concerning the most appropriate balance between the benefits and costs to both the private and public purse of alternative courses of action. It underscores the difficulties faced in seeking to adjudicate between the conflicting human desires for economic gain and social stability. In the Severnside case, however, these dilemmas are further compounded by political divergences in which the interests of the component parts of Severnside are not always seen to be identical. It would be one of the tragedies of the nineteen seventies if the inadequacies of the planning art, and the indecisions of the political process, combined to frustrate on Severnside what *The Economist* (1968) has described as 'the most brilliant of opportunities, both for economic success and for a pleasant life for its inhabitants'.

REFERENCES :

Bowen, E. G. (1957). *Wales, A Physical, Historical and Regional Geography*, Methuen, London.
Britton, J. N. H. (1967). *Regional Analysis and Economic Geography, A Case Study of Manufacturing in the Bristol Region*, Bell, London.
Buchanan, C. and Partners (1965). *Bath : A Planning and Transport Study*, C.B.&P., London.
Buchanan, C. and Partners (1966a). *Cardiff: Development and Transportation Study. Report of the Probe Study*, C.B.&P., London.
Buchanan, C. and Partners (1966b). *South Hampshire Study : Report on the Feasibility of Major Urban Growth*, 3 Vols., H.M.S.O., London.

Caesar, A. A. L. (1949). Gloucestershire, Wiltshire and Somerset. In G. H. J. Daysh (Ed.), *Studies in Regional Planning*. George Philip, London. pp. 171–195.

Carter, H. (1965). *The Towns of Wales*, University of Wales Press, Cardiff.

Central Unit for Environmental Planning (1971). *Severnside: A Feasibility Study*, H.M.S.O., London.

Economist, The (1968). South Wales and Severnside, Two Sides of the Water, 14 December.

Hallett, G. and Randall, P. (1970). *Maritime Industry and Port Development in South Wales*, University College, Cardiff.

Howard, R. S. (1968). *The Movement of Manufacturing Industry in the United Kingdom* 1945–1965, H.M.S.O. for the Board of Trade, London.

Humphrys, G. (1962). The dormitory function of the South Wales coal-field, *Journal of the Town Planning Institute*, **48**, 73–76.

Humphrys, G. (1964). The coal industry. In G. Manners (Ed.) *South Wales in the Sixties*, Pergamon, Oxford, pp. 75–101.

Humphrys, G. (1965). The journey to work in industrial South Wales. *Transactions and Papers of the Institute of British Geographers*, **36**, 85–96.

Llewelyn-Davies, Weeks and Partners (1966). *A New City, A Study of Urban Development in an Area including Newbury, Swindon and Didcot*, H.M.S.O., London.

Manners, G. (Ed.) (1964). *South Wales in the Sixties*, Pergamon, Oxford.

Manners, G. (1966a). *The Severn Bridge and the Future*, T.W.W., Cardiff.

Manners, G. (1966b). Bristol, South Wales and the bridge, *New Society*, 10 February, 7–10.

Manners, G. (1968). Reshaping steel, *New Society*, 19 December, 907–908.

Manners, G. (1971). *The Changing World Market for Iron Ore, 1950–1980*, Johns Hopkins, Baltimore.

Manners, G. (1971). Some economic and spatial characteristics of the British energy market. In M. Chisholm and G. Manners (Eds.) *Spatial Policy Problems of the British Economy*, Cambridge University Press, Cambridge, pp. 146–179.

Minister of Housing and Local Government (1968). *Leisure in the Countryside* (Cmnd.2928), H.M.S.O., London.

Minister of Transport (1962). *Report of the Committee of Inquiry into the Major Ports of Great Britain* (Chairman: Lord Rochdale), (Cmnd.1824), H.M.S.O., London.

Minister of Transport (1965). *Iron Ore Imports into South Wales* (Cmnd.2706), H.M.S.O., London.

Minister of Transport (1966). *Portbury. Reasons for the Minister's Decision not to Authorise the Construction of a New Dock at Portbury, Bristol*, H.M.S.O., London.

Minchinton, W. E. (1964). The evolution of the regional economy. In G. Manners (Ed.) *South Wales in the Sixties*. Pergamon, Oxford. pp. 1–29.

Port of Bristol Authority (1964). *Portbury. Report on Proposed New Dock Development*, P.B.A., Bristol.

Powell, E. J. (1965). *Glamorgan, A Planning Study*, Glamorgan County Council, Cardiff.

Secretary of State for Economic Affairs (1969). *The Intermediate Areas* (Chairman: Sir Joseph Hunt), (Cmnd.3998), H.M.S.O., London.

Secretary of State for Wales, (1967). *Wales: The Way Ahead* (Cmnd.3334), H.M.S.O., Cardiff.

Shorter, A. H., Ravenhill, W. L. D. and Gregory, K. J. (1969). *Southwest England*, Nelson, London.

Smith, R. D. P. (1970). The changing urban hierarchy in Wales, *Regional Studies*, **4**, 85–96.

South West Economic Planning Council (1967). *A Region with a Future, A Draft Strategy for the South West*, H.M.S.O., London.

Tanner, M. F. and Williams, A. F. (1967). Port development and national planning strategy: the implications of the Portbury decision. *Journal of Transport Economics and Policy*, **1**, 315–324.

Walker, F. (1965). Economic growth on Severnside, *Transactions and Papers of the Institute of British Geographers*, **37**, 1–13.

CHAPTER 7

The North West and North Wales

BRIAN RODGERS

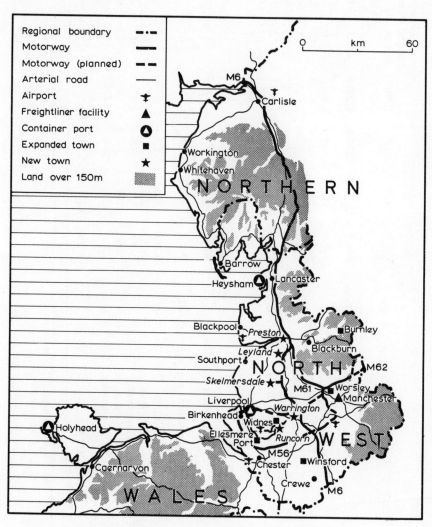

Figure 24 The North West and North Wales: location map.

A. **Population**

Thousands

Table 19. The North West and North Wales : selected regional and sub-regional indicators

	Mid-year estimated home population				Average annual change 1961–1966			Average annual change 1951–1961		
	1971[1]	1966[2]	1961[2]	1951[2]	Natural change	Armed forces change	Net migration	Natural change	Armed forces change	Net migration
TOTAL North West and North Wales	**7,669.0**	**7,635.3**	**7,437.7**	**7,298.6**	**+41.1**	**+1.2**	**−0.1**	**+24.8**	**+1.6**	**−13.4**
North West region	6,726.3	6,712.8	6,545.3	6,416.8	+38.0	+1.2	−5.7	+23.5	+1.7	−12.4
S. Cheshire (High Peak)	541.4	502.2	464.4	443.1	+2.4	+0.2	+5.0	+1.4	−0.1	+0.8
South Lancashire	651.0	624.0	596.4	605.8	+3.8	+0.1	+1.3	+2.6	−0.5	−3.1
Manchester	2,459.0	2,511.9	2,474.7	2,454.7	+14.5	+0.5	−7.5	+7.5	+1.3	−6.8
Merseyside	1,750.3	1,785.8	1,744.1	1,666.9	+15.2	+0.4	−6.9	+12.5	+0.6	−5.2
Furness	107.6	104.6	104.4	106.1	+0.2	+0.1	−0.2	+0.1	+0.1	−0.4
Fylde	294.0	280.4	272.7	252.9	−0.6	−0.2	+2.4	−0.8	−0.3	+3.1
Lancaster	123.5	119.7	114.1	110.3	—		+1.0	—	+0.1	+0.3
Mid Lancashire	325.3	310.5	296.8	283.3	+1.9	+0.1	+0.8	+0.9	+0.2	+0.3
North East Lancashire	474.3	473.5	477.8	493.7	+0.5	+0.1	−1.4	−0.7	+0.4	−1.3
Cumberland and Westmorland	364.7	366.2	358.7	350.9	+1.7		−0.2	+1.5	−0.1	−0.7
North Wales	578.0	556.3	533.7	530.9	+1.4		+5.8	−0.2		−0.3
North East	230.2	215.3	205.6	201.2	+1.3		+0.6	+1.0		−0.5
North West	347.8	341.0	328.1	329.7	+0.1		+2.6	−0.3		+0.1
North coast	116.3	108.4	100.2	94.2	−0.3	+0.1	+1.9	−0.3	−0.1	+1.0
Remainder	231.6	232.7	227.9	235.5	+0.4	−0.1	+0.7	+0.1	+0.1	−0.9
BRITAIN	53,821.4	53,176.1	51,380.0	48,917.5	+328.5	−0.5	+22.6	+231.4	+12.9	+1.9

1. 1971 Census; 1971 boundaries.
2. 1966 boundaries.

B. Employment

	Employment		Male employment		Proportion of women at work		Unemployment range		
	1966	Change 1961–1966	1966	Change 1961–1966	1966	Change in % 1961–1966	1968	1967	1961–1966
	'000s	%	'000s	%	%	%	%	%	%
TOTAL North West and North Wales	**4,560**	**+1**	**2,870**	**−3**	**40**	**+1**	**3–4**	**3–4**	**2–3**
North West region	3,030	+1	1,870	Nil	43	Nil	2–3	2–3	1–2
S. Cheshire (High Peak)	190	+1	120	−3	36	Nil	1–2	1–2	1–2
South Lancashire	270	+1	170	Nil	39	Nil	2–3	1–2	1–2
Manchester	1,220	−1	740	−2	46	−1	2–3	1–2	1–2
Merseyside	810	+4	500	+4	43	+1	3–4	3–4	3–4
Furness	40	Nil	30	−1	33	+1	2–3	2–3	2–3
Fylde	100	+5	60	+4	33	+1	4–5	4–5	3–4
Lancaster	50	−2	30	−3	34	−1	2–3	2–3	1–2
Mid Lancashire	140	−5	90	−4	40	−4	1–2	1–2	1–2
North East Lancashire	230	Nil	130	+1	47	Nil	2–3	1–2	1–2
Cumberland and Westmorland	1,340	+2	880	−8	35	+2	4–5	3–4	3–4
North Wales	190	+6	120	+2	45	+2	3–6	4–6	3–4
North East	80	Nil	60	−2	26	+1	2–3	2–3	2–3
North West	110	+10	60	+6	59	+3	4–8	5–8	3–4
North coast	40	+13	20	+12	33	+2	3–4	4–5	2–3
Remainder	70	+9	40	+3	26	+4	5–10	5–10	4–5
BRITAIN	23,550	+4	14,900	+2	40	+2	2–3	2–3	1–2

C. Industrial Development Certificates :

	Estimated additional employment from i.d.c. approvals			
	Total 1956–1967 '000s	Annual averages		
		1964–1967 '000s	1960–1963 '000s	1956–1959 '000s
TOTAL North West and North Wales	**235.0**	**24.0**	**23.0**	**11.7**
North West region	204.6	20.0	20.5	10.6
South Cheshire (High Peak)	13.2	2.2	0.7	0.5
South Lancashire	17.3	2.4	1.2	0.7
Manchester	32.6	2.2	2.5	3.4
Merseyside	109.5	10.1	13.4	3.9
Furness	6.2	0.9	0.6	0.1
Fylde	5.4	0.6	0.5	0.3
Lancaster	1.4	0.2	0.1	0.1
Mid Lancashire	5.1	0.7	0.3	0.3
North East Lancashire	14.0	0.8	1.3	1.5
Cumberland and Westmorland	11.0	1.8	0.7	0.3
North Wales	19.4	2.2	1.8	0.8
North East	9.3	1.3	0.7	0.3
North West	10.1	0.9	1.1	0.5
North Coast	4.5	0.3	0.5	0.3
Remainder	5.6	0.6	0.6	0.2
BRITAIN	1,245.2	121.8	108.1	81.2

7.1 Regional Contrast in North West England

Taken as a whole and placed in a national perspective, the North West must be recognized as one of those less prosperous regions that have failed to secure their fair share of the national growth in population, employment and personal prosperity. Indicators of its general economic debility are so easy to assemble that there is risk of tedious repetition. Its population growth rate was only 0.19 per cent per annum between 1951 and 1961 and 0.15 per cent from 1961 to 1966, compared with national values of 0.53 per cent and 0.40 per cent respectively. However there has been a recent recovery in the region's population growth, shown in an increase of 0.24 per cent per annum for the entire decade 1961–1971. Losses by out-migration each year were removing 0.19 per cent of the region's population during the nineteen fifties and, although the rate fell to about 0.05 per cent during the period 1961–1966, it may now be rising again. The selective migration of young adults has changed the age-structure and depressed fertility so that the rate of natural increase has fallen to 0.55 per cent per annum, distinctly below the national rate of almost 0.7 per cent. Between 1961 and 1966 the North West experienced only a 1 per cent growth in the total volume of work available (one-quarter of the national rate) whilst employment in manufacturing actually declined. Regional unemployment rates have ranged between 2 per cent and 3 per cent in the years since 1945, and have consistently exceeded the national mean. Average male earnings have been running at about 3 per cent below the national mean, and some 13 per cent below the level of the South East. And so one could go on.

All these values have one characteristic in common. They are meaningless if they are thought to apply to any specific part of the region. They are merely averages for an area whose dominant feature is its dualism, a sharp intraregional distinction between zones of exceptionally rapid growth in industry and population, and others of equally dramatic decline. In the North West, areas that belong to 'fortunate' and 'unfortunate' Britain are brought into close juxtaposition; indeed the prosperity watershed between the 'two nations' crosses the region, dividing it with remarkable clarity (see Figure 25). A line drawn on the map southwards from Lancaster via Preston to Wigan and St. Helens, looping eastwards to bisect the Manchester city region from northwest to southeast, and finally running southwards along the Pennine flanks, broadly defines these contrasts and divides the region. This is a familiar enough line. Much of its course lies along the western and southern borders of the coal-field, so that all areas to the east and north of it have a textile and mining tradition and a history of precocious nineteenth century economic growth. In contrast, the areas to the south and west attracted little industrial and urban development in Victorian times, except locally on Merseyside and on the Cheshire salt-field; they have as a result largely escaped the complex of economic and environmental problems that the older towns of eastern Lancastria face.

Almost every economic and demographic indicator adds strength to this intraregional contrast. Population trends since 1951 show consistent and heavy losses over the whole of eastern Lancastria, reaching maxima of 5.3 per cent (for the period up to 1964) in North

East Lancashire and Rossendale. Although the Manchester city region grew over the period by 2.2 per cent (only half the regional rate), virtually all its constituent parts lost population except the southern suburban fringe. The 1971 census shows a sharp actual loss of population overall in the late nineteen sixties. In contrast, every sub-region of west and south Lancashire, and all Cheshire except the northeast, grew from 1951–1964 at rates that not only exceeded the regional, but, in many cases, the national average. The Merseyside city region grew by 7.1 per cent; the Chester and Macclesfield sub-regions increased by about 14 per cent, and the Fylde by 13 per cent. The first results of the 1971 census suggest that these contrasts persist, but much less sharply: 'textile' east Lancashire suffered a population loss, but only of about 1 per cent, over the decade 1961–1971; while the Fylde and Macclesfield sub-regions increased by 6.9 per cent and 16.4 per cent respectively over the decade. The chief immediate cause of this contrast is differences in migration, both from the northwest and within it, balanced against a sharply varied pattern of natural increase. On a sub-regional basis (and so discounting local population shifts to suburban areas or overspill sites) migrational losses in the textile areas were as high as 6.2 per cent in Rossendale; they were between 3 per cent and 5 per cent in most of the spinning towns of southeast Lancashire, while the Manchester city region lost over 3 per cent. Though the contrast is blunted by the high rate of migration from Merseyside (a consequence of its very high rate of natural increase) the whole of south Cheshire and west Lancashire gained substantially by a net inward flow of migrants; in the Fylde, however, this is largely a movement of the retired and so of limited economic significance.

The influence of prolonged migratory movement on population structure and fertility is as clear as it is difficult to correct. Many of the textile towns of the east are now experiencing a natural decrease of their elderly populations, and they are among the very few towns in Britain (outside the retirement resorts) to do so. The Blackburn, Burnley and Rossendale districts, a contiguous area with a total population of over half a million, have all suffered an overall natural decrease since 1951. In almost all the spinning towns that form the northern and eastern border of the Manchester conurbation natural increase was scarcely over one per cent for the period, compared with a national value of almost 7 per cent. Merseyside in contrast recorded an increment to population by natural increase of 10 per cent, and in south and central Cheshire the rate varied from 5 per cent to 7 per cent. Here is one of the keys to the industrial future of the North West.

In every textile town the labour force has been not only reduced but seriously aged by the migration of its younger members. A high proportion of the workers left are approaching retirement age, and recruitment into the labour force is reduced both by low birth rates and by continuing migration. Thus projections of the total size of the labour force, in the short term at least, suggest a sharp contraction over much of eastern Lancastria, but a very quick increase in the west and south, especially on Merseyside. Indeed the latter region will generate about half the total regional increase in employable population to 1981. This is the chief reason for the condition of labour shortage that already, paradoxically, troubles the textile towns. It is not only a factor in the decline of their traditional industries, but it also prejudices their chance of attracting alternative employment. As a consequence the incidence of unemployment reverses the patterns of sub-regional contrast reviewed so far. During the nineteen sixties, rates have varied between 1 per cent and 2 per cent of the insured population in the textile areas (and have rarely exceeded the national mean), while on Merseyside the range has been between 3 per cent and 4 per cent, with occasionally higher peaks. In the Fylde the rate has been as high as 5 per cent, though here unemployment is largely seasonal. Unemployment rates have traditionally dictated the delimitation of Development and Intermediate Areas, and eligibility for Distribution of Industry funds; yet in the North West they are weakly or inversely correlated with most other measures of economic debility. Development Area policy, therefore, has added its very powerful influence to strengthening the contrast in economic trends between the two broad divisions of the region. Thus government intervention has reinforced a 'natural' trend in the North West, the converse of its general influence (and its intent) on the national scale.

Indexes of employment growth sharpen this broad pattern of intraregional contrast (see Table 20). Total employment, in all sectors, fell in northeast Lancashire by 10 per cent over the decade 1953 to 1963, and by slightly lower rates over most of the rest of eastern Lancastria. In the Manchester conurbation it grew by 3 per cent (scarcely half the Merseyside rate of 6.4 per cent) but this increase was wholly confined to the city and its southern industrial outliers. Elsewhere growth ranged from 5 per cent in South Cheshire

Table 20. The North West : employment change, by sub-regions, 1953–1967

	Annual percentage change in total employment in selected manufacturing industries			
	The North West		The Textile areas	Manchester
	1953–1959	1959–1966	1958–1967	1958–1967
Food, drink, tobacco	+2.1	+0.1	−1.4	−3.8
Chemicals	+1.7	−1.2	+0.1	−1.3
Engineering and electrical	+1.1	+2.7	+0.6	+0.1
Vehicles	+0.7	+2.1	−3.5	−9.5
Textiles	−3.6	−3.7	−4.5	−5.4
Clothing and footwear	−2.0	−0.7	−2.7	−4.5
Paper and printing	+2.1	+1.8	+0.9	−0.4
All industries and services	+0.1	+0.3	−0.3	−0.8

Source : Department of Employment and Lancashire and Merseyside Industrial Development Association.

to 13 per cent in the Fylde. This was the decade of the cotton industry's quickest contraction, and so perhaps atypical. But data for the period 1961–1966 are even more disturbing. Virtually the whole of the textile zone (including the Manchester sub-region) suffered losses of from 1 per cent to 5 per cent in total employment, compared with growth rates of 4 per cent for Merseyside and 5 per cent for the Fylde. Trends in manufacturing employment repeat these contrasts but with even greater emphasis. The rate of net job losses in the Manchester sub-region was 4.4 per cent for the period 1959–1966, in North East Lancashire it was 3.4 per cent, and in mid-Lancashire it was almost 7 per cent. On the other hand growth reached almost 8 per cent on Merseyside, and over 13 per cent in the Fylde. Throughout the textile areas male employment decreased (by as much as 3 per cent) over this period, but it grew by over 4 per cent on Merseyside and 5 per cent in the Fylde, both much above the national mean. The volume of female work and the proportion of employed women declined sharply over much of the east—a feature completely at variance with the national trend—while female jobs increased, though rather slowly, in the south and west of the region. The decline of the cotton industry was bound to lead to a very heavy loss of work for women in the mill towns, but the total rate of loss is far higher than can be explained in terms of the former structure of female employment and its degree of dependence on the textile mills. Paradoxically, the female activity rate has not fallen seriously in some textile districts; many former mill workers were of retirement age when their mill closed (Smith, 1969).

The textile region of eastern Lancastria, therefore, has an economy of extraordinary weakness. Almost every indicator (except unemployment) picks out this area as consistantly the weakest in the whole of Britain, inside or outside the Development Areas. The most obvious cause—too great a dependence on two sharply contracting industries, mining and textiles—is not, by itself, a sufficient explanation. It is possible to assess the influence of an unfavourable structure of industry on the overall trend of employment in an area by applying national rates of growth (or decline) to each of its industries for some period of time. This, in effect, gives a prediction of the change in total employment that the area ought to have experienced, had each industry (or service activity) within it grown or declined strictly in conformity with national trends. It therefore measures a structural component in total employment change, isolating a residual component that reflects the operation of factors peculiar to the areas concerned. Such an exercise, applied to the sub-regions of eastern Lancastria for the period 1961–1966 produces alarming results: both in male and female employment, the total decline was greater than the structural factor would suggest it should have been. A technical comment of caution must be attached to this finding.

The two chief studies (Smith, 1969; Secretary of State for Economic Affairs, 1969) so far made of the influence of economic structure on employment trends in the North West have reached partially contradictory conclusions. This is because they treat data for different periods in dissimilar ways. They agree, however, on one fundamental point. Merseyside and much of nearby South Lancashire have experienced a far quicker rate of economic growth than can be explained by their industrial 'mix', while the Manchester city region has lost employment far more seriously than its relatively favourable industrial structure would have led one to expect. There are many reasons for the unhappy experience of so much of east and southeast Lancashire as judged by this yardstick. They are examined in detail later (pp. 296–314): they include the rapid conversion of mining and textiles to capital intensive industries using less labour more productively, the existence of weak sectors like textile and railway engineering in what are, nationally, dynamic growth industries, the slow development of service employment, the effects of physical remoteness, poor communication, and land shortage, and, most powerfully of all, the influence of industrial guidance policies in retarding new growth over almost the whole of the east of the region. This last factor is so crucial that a separate section is devoted to it (pp. 276–287). In fact the total area of new industrial floor-space approved by the Board of Trade in the textile districts after 1947 was derisory (except in the short lived North East Lancashire Development Area), while the south and west, and especially those areas grouped about the Mersey estuary, have benefitted significantly. Thus over the twenty years to 1965, coastal Lancashire and south and west Cheshire secured new factories employing a total of about 63,000 workers while the figure for the textile province was 9,000.

Not only in economic vitality but also in the quality of environment are there to be found profound contrasts within the North West. Textile Lancastria contains the great bulk of the region's sub-standard housing. Official returns of slum housing are notoriously variable and unreliable, but more objective measures suggest that, of rather more than 500,000 sub-standard houses in the region, about 250,000 are in southeast Lancashire; one house in every four there (and in some of the spinning towns one house in every two) is of unacceptable standard. Housing conditions in Rossendale and North East Lancashire are at least as bad as this, though the dimensions of the problem are smaller here, but there is very marked improvement westwards and southwards. Non-industrial Cheshire has virtually no slum problem, while in coastal Lancashire it is virtually confined to north Merseyside; but even here the total number of houses involved is considerably less than 100,000. There are no figures to quantify the extent of the industrial slums—the old valley-bottom and canal-side factory zones, rotting, obsolete and half abandoned—but this, too, is a problem largely confined to the east, where about 68 per cent of the cotton mills operating in 1947 were built before 1900. These environmental contrasts have a social dimension. Several east Lancashire towns habitually compete for the unhappy distinction of the highest national death-rate by bronchitis. Except for the coastal retirement colonies, they are also among the areas returning the highest gross death-rates. That this is not merely a function of their distorted age-structures is shown by their high infant mortality experience. On all these counts, except for inner Merseyside, the coastlands and Cheshire have much happier and healthier records.

Although it may seem to be almost an exercise in neodeterminism, these economic and social contrasts within the North West can be put into a physical context. Almost the whole of the area below the 75 metre (250 foot) contour has recorded quick increases in population and employment during the period since 1945, while the areas enclosed within the 120 metre (400 foot) contour are those of steepest economic and demographic decline. The generalized course of the 875 millimetre (35 inch) isohyet, similarly divides the region between its zones of growth and of decline perhaps more neatly than any single economic or social indicator. The major geological boundary separates a triassic Lancastria of sustained economic progress from a carboniferous Lancastria of decay, decline and painful industrial readjustment. This is not a search for determinist explanations, but a distinction between two sorts of environment.

The dissected uplands of east Lancastria and the low plateau of the coal-field offered every possible attraction to those Victorian industries that were tied, locationally, to specific physical resources : the abundant energy source of the upland streams, the superb water supply of deep valleys bathed by the weeping Pennine climate, the cheap coal so readily available from shallow resources. Inevitably, eastern Lancastria dominated the growth of industry and of towns, and largely shaped the evolving pattern of communications, prior to 1914. It clearly has much less to offer to modern industry, little influenced by immediate access to physical resources. In contrast the low, drift-smeared, plains of the west Lancashire and Cheshire Trias are crossed by improved communications and especially by the rail and motorway arteries leading into the West Midlands; they are served not only by the Mersey but also by other specialist ports. They have only a small share of the region's burden of almost 450 hectares (10,000 acres) of derelict land. The lowlands of the west and south are now the region of greatest industrial vitality and quickest urban growth. They also remain the areas of highest agricultural productivity from intensive arable and dairy farming, so that a heightening conflict between town and farm must continue to be one of the chief regional policy issues.

Whether the rather neat and simple dualism of the contemporary North West will persist, is open to some doubt. The M6 motorway follows, across Lancashire, almost the line of contact between sub-regions of growth and of decline. It must clearly dominate the evolution of a regional planning strategy, and is already seen as the major axis of economic growth. Much of central Lancashire must respond to its influence. Over a longer period the M62 (Lancashire-Yorkshire) and M61 (Manchester-Preston) motorways, both open by 1971, must broaden this impact of improved communication on the sub-regional economies. The heart of the textile province, in Rossendale and North East Lancashire, has no place yet on the motorway map—except for a new spur road along the Irwell valley from the south. If a nucleus of contraction and decline persists here, it will be thrown into ever sharper contrast with the areas of continuing growth, or of progressive recovery, further west and south.

7.2 Development Area Policy and Industrial Mobility

Through all the many changes in government policies affecting the location of industry during the post-war decades (pp. 47ff) high and persistent unemployment has been the chief qualification for Development Area status. The great paradox of the economic history of the North West since 1945 is that, despite the catastrophic decline of its two staple industries and the marked contraction of several other sectors (for example, engineering and vehicles), serious unemployment has been ephemeral and has occurred chiefly outside the textile zone. Only one part of the region, Merseyside, has had the advantage of Development Area status throughout the greater part of the period; elsewhere only the fine-weaving towns of North East Lancashire, a part of the South Lancashire Coalfield and the Furness district have been scheduled long enough for the status to show any effect on the local structure of industry. During the policy vacillations of the early nineteen sixties a number of resorts and textile towns were scheduled, briefly, nominally and fruitlessly, as Development Districts. Thus the positive impact of government policy towards the location of industry is confined to a few compact regions; the negative influence of the policy, the restraining of economic growth in areas that failed to qualify for assistance, is much more widely evident through the region. The North West is almost unique among the regions of Britain in that the two aspects of the policy can be studied in closely juxtaposed districts.

7.2.1 *Development Areas*

Immediately after the Second World War, in 1946, a section of the *South Lancashire* coal-field, centred on Wigan and St. Helens, was created a Development Area. Here all the classic causes of distress were clearly evident. There was high and prolonged unemployment caused by the contraction of coal mining in a difficult and part-exhausted section of the field; and this was coupled with the long-term decline of a weak manufacturing industry, cotton, plus a lack of replacement employment in adequate volume. Here, too, were towns with perhaps the gravest problems of environmental decay and surface devastation in the entire region. Hindsight leads to the conclusion that the scheduling of South Lancashire was neither necessary nor successful. Mining has survived quite strongly near St. Helens (though it is extinct in Wigan) and the textile industry has suffered a slower contraction here than almost anywhere else in the region. Moreover the continued growth and technological vitality of the St. Helens glass industry has helped to balance the loss of male employment following pit closures. This Development Area attracted little interest by mobile industry before it was descheduled in 1960—though two small industrial estates were developed, and other large new enterprises making, for example, canned foods and asbestos products came to sites near Wigan. Although incoming firms have made a substantial contribution to the area's modest growth of employment between 1945 and 1965, of a total 14,000 jobs brought in by them, only 4,000 were in firms that had built new factories. The remainder were new enterprises in existing buildings, most of them converted mills. Since moves of this kind at the time derived little or no benefit from Development Area status they would presumably have occurred in any case. In brief, the scheduling of South Lancashire had only a marginal effect on employment growth; the construction across it of the M6 motorway early in the nineteen sixties almost certainly had a more powerful impact. Indeed the inflow of new employment accelerated strongly immediately after the descheduling of the area and on the eve of motorway construction. Thus the present relative prosperity of South Lancashire (the area grew by 5.4 per cent in population between 1951 and 1964, and by 4.2 per cent in manufacturing employment from 1959 to 1966) can scarcely be counted as one of the great triumphs of Development Area policy (Board of Trade, Manchester, 1969).

Chronologically, the next part of the North West considered to merit Development Area status was *Merseyside,* where a considerable area, on both sides of the estuary and reaching eastwards to Widnes, was scheduled in 1949. This region has a long history of male unemployment, rooted historically in the feeble development of manufacturing coupled with the port's declining share in the nation's trade, and nourished since 1945 not only by a relatively high birth-rate but also by continuing Irish and—more recently—Commonwealth immigration. In 1932 some 28 per cent of the Merseyside labour force was out of work; after 1945 serious male unemployment returned again and reached 7 per cent within a year. Since then the Merseyside unemployment rate has been persistently between two and three times the national average and reached 5 per cent in 1963. This region is the subject of a separate study (pp. 287–296) so that there need be only a very summary treatment here of its fortunes during its period of government assistance. In fact Merseyside has been perhaps the most successful of all Development Areas in the country in attracting mobile industry, particularly those with a dominantly male labourforce. Between 1952 and 1966 new industrial enterprises employing 81,000 workers entered Merseyside; this was 70 per cent of all the mobile employment entering the North West during the period, which itself represented one-sixth of the national total of interregional movement. Without this transfusion of new industrial activities, Merseyside would have suffered an 8 per cent decrease in its volume of manufacturing employment. Unhappily Merseyside is attracting new work not only from the rest of Britain (and especially from the South East), but also from the rest of the North West region. Partly for this reason the Hunt Committee on the Intermediate Areas unsuccessfully recommended that Merseyside's assisted status be withdrawn. With or without any special status, Merseyside would probably remain the region's dominant growth point. Apart from the new and modernized facilities of the port, there are motorway spurs in preparation on both sides of the estuary as links to the M6, and Liverpool is now scarcely more than 2½ hours from central London by rail. The multiplier effect of Merseyside's new motor vehicle industry in bringing component firms to the region has almost certainly not yet exhausted itself, while the parent industry, too, has plans for expansion. In fact the graph of employment growth is steepening sharply. Perhaps Merseyside illustrates the truism that the ultimate measure of the success of Development Area policy in any locality lies in the descheduling of that area.

Although the creation of a Development Area on Merseyside was intended to correct the chronic ailments of an economy that had never developed a satisfactory manufacturing base, the institution in 1953 of the North West's third area with assisted status—in *North East Lancashire*—was a response to a crisis of more immediate origins. The fine-weaving towns aligned along the Burnley-Nelson-Colne axis had been protected by their specialization in high qualities of work from the worst of the decline of the cotton industry in the years before and after the Depression; and the trade was quickly rebuilt after 1945 in an area of little industrial diversity and slight labour competition. In 1952, about 45 per cent of total employment was in the mills, and an economy of Victorian simplicity survived. However, it was brought close to collapse by the first of the post-war textile recessions, in 1952. Unemployment quickly rose to levels reminiscent of the nineteen thirties, and the district was briskly scheduled as a Development Area. In competition with Merseyside and South Lancashire, it had little to offer to mobile industry except an abundant labour supply of high quality, but even this became less certain as the textile trade-cycle moved towards its next crest and unemployment disappeared. Remote in its hill-girt valley, separated from the main mass of industrial Lancashire by the Rossendale upland and an execrable road system, and as far from London as is Carlisle in terms of journey times, this was one of the least promising Development Areas in the country. Yet it did surprisingly well—for a time. Having already acquired a foothold in some branches of industry new to it by wartime dispersal, a variety of diverse enterprises moved into the area and by 1969 were providing 11,000 jobs. Thus kitchen equipment, vehicle electrical components, electric heaters and tyres are all now produced by flourishing industries in the locality, which today depends for less than a third of its work on the textile trades.

This better economic balance has been brought about, however, more through the rapid decline both of textiles and the overall size of the labour force, than it has by the growth of new employment. The area lost 19,000 jobs in the mills in the decade 1953 to 1963. The number of women in employment dropped by 13 per cent, and of men by 7 per cent; total population fell by 5.3 per cent between 1951 and 1964 but has become more stable since, as is shown by the loss of only 1 per cent between 1961 and 1971. Thus, the traditional processes of migration and a reduction in the proportion of women at work have been more significant than new employment in correcting both existing and potential unemployment. Moreover, of the total of new jobs brought to the area since 1952, about a half (5,000) are provided by firms that have arrived since 1960 (when the area was descheduled) and have occupied existing factories, mostly old mills. Thus the net employment gain directly attributable to the area's status as a Development Area represents scarcely more than 4 per cent of its present reduced total in manufacturing. All that can be claimed for government intervention here is that it provided the first impetus towards the evolution of a more diverse economy, but the processes of migration, retirement and mill conversion—east Lancashire's universal response to its economic problems—have carried industrial readjustment much farther.

For a brief period late in the nineteen fifties, when for a time government industrial guidance policies became more flexible, a number of other parts of the North West were scheduled as assisted areas. *Blackpool,* for example, was accorded Development District status partly because of the inevitable problem of seasonal unemployment in a resort town, and partly following the local collapse of aircraft manufacture—an activity which survived the war but disappeared at an early stage in the rationalization of the industry, leaving the huge Squire's Gate factory, one of the largest in the region, empty for many years. Another crisis in the cotton industry between 1958 and 1960 also produced enough unemployment to warrant the scheduling of a number of *textile towns* (for example, Blackburn, Accrington and a few small spinning communities), but these quickly lost their status after the passing of the 1960 Local Employment Act. Only one other part of the region has had—and still retains—assisted status, the *Furness* peninsula.

This is a remote area detached from the rest of Lancashire by the sands of Morecambe Bay. Barrow is as far from Manchester, in terms of journey time, as is London. It remains a remarkably well-preserved example not merely of a one-industry town, but of a one-company town, for its fortunes depend utterly on the Vickers shipyards and their associated marine engineering works. A new town of the Industrial Revolution, Barrow grew quickly from being a mere ore dock, especially after the beginning of iron smelting in 1859 and of shipbuilding in 1869. Local hematites were smelted in the locality, and the shipyards were established along the sheltered inlet between the town and Walney Island. Far from the main centres of shipbuilding, the Barrow industry became a remarkably self-contained and vertically integrated system. It survived with a little radical change until quite recently, sustained partly by its specialization in naval construction. The yards are still independent, having escaped the consequences of the post-Geddes rationalization of the shipbuilding industry (see pp. 379ff; 394ff). But this perfect survival of a Victorian economy is beginning to crumble.

The chief local iron works closed early in the nineteen sixties, leaving only a single small steel works as a relic of the area's long metal working tradition. Employment in the shipyard complex has fallen progressively, though the engineering plant has diversified away from marine work. There was a 4 per cent fall in total male employment during the decade 1953–1963, accompanied by a persistent rise in unemployment. As a result, in 1963 the area was designated a Development District. Despite its poor landward communications (even Lancaster is two hours away by heavy truck via the poor road eastwards around the heads of the Furness estuaries), Barrow and its sub-region managed to attract a number of new firms making, for example, footwear and pharmaceuticals. Most of this movement predated scheduling, however, and was almost certainly a response to the large reserves of non-employed female labour which characterize a metal working and shipbuilding economy. Almost half of the total of 5,000 jobs in 'immigrant' firms were for women and the total of female employment rose by 17 per cent in the decade 1953–1963, as much a social as an economic transformation.

Furness is another district in which the Distribution of Industry policy seems almost impotent. The movement of new employment into the area has slowed markedly during the nineteen sixties. Despite their contraction, shipbuilding and engineering still provide a quarter of total employment; this is dependent not only on a single firm, but largely on a single defence programme, for the construction of nuclear submarines is presently the corner-stone of Barrow's prosperity. The brightest hope for the town is that a More-cambe Bay barrage, topped by a motorway, would transform its position. The possibility of such a scheme coming to fruition in the next decade or so seems slight, yet without a radical improvement in road communications Barrow can scarcely compete on equal terms with Merseyside for mobile firms.

Furness has only a tenuous attachment, not only in terms of physical connection but also in the sense of economic and industrial linkages, with the remainder of the North West Economic Planning region, of which it forms a part largely because it is in the county of Lancaster. In all other senses its associations are with the discontinuous ribbon of urban and industrial development which follows the coastal coal-field of *West Cumberland*. For regional planning purposes, this area is part of the Northern region, and has enjoyed Development Area status since 1945. Few industrial areas grew with such pace or on so narrow an economic base as this during the second half of the nineteenth century. Both coal and ore mining had developed chiefly for coastwise shipment prior to the eighteen forties, but two almost simultaneous events led to the dramatic growth of steel making after 1860. These were the introduction of the Bessemer converter (to which the local high grade hematite was especially adapted) and the opening of the South Durham to Furness railway in 1861, which cheapened the import of Durham coke. Between 1851 and 1901 the population doubled to 100,000.

West Cumberland emerged from the war of 1939–1945 with its traditional economic base fundamentally unmodified, although each of the three chief sectors within it had contracted to almost token proportions. Ore mining contracted sharply during the nineteen thirties through a combination of dwindling resources and rising costs. By 1956 output had dropped to 400,000 tons and in 1968 the last of the major deposits, at Hodbarrow, was abandoned leaving an estimated 16 million tons of uneconomic ore unworked; only a little activity now persists near Egremont. Fortunately the contribution of ore mining to male employment had been relatively small since the nineteen thirties but the parallel contraction of the coal mining industry has had far more serious social conse-quences. This is geologically an unusually complex field. A narrow, fault-broken strip of coal measures encircles the western and northwestern flank of the Lake District dome, off which the Carboniferous strata dip steeply. In the south the field is coastal, with a concealed component under the Trias and an extension off-shore which is as large as the landward field. Today the main mass of the reserves is off-shore. All the collieries that survived into the nineteen sixties perch on the low cliffs, and the working faces are as much as four miles out to sea. Long underground hauls together with complex faulting make the field a high cost producer and it has suffered the inevitable consequences. Fourteen pits were at work in 1947; by 1966 there were three and the future of at least one of these is uncertain. Employment dropped from 6,000 in 1954 to 2,500 in 1967, and there is at present speculation whether even a single pit will survive for long. Thus coal mining too has reached the relic stage, and has made its cont ibution to the persistently high male unemployment. In 1959 the unemployment rate of the area was 5 per cent, when the Northern region's rate was 3 per cent and the national rate 1.9 per cent.

The last of the trio of basic industries, metal manufacture, has had a more secure recent history, but it faces equally bleak prospects. Rationalization came early to the Cumberland steel industry; the many small works of the nineteenth century were replaced, in the nineteen thirties, by a single integrated plant of the United Steel Companies at Workington. This has employed about 4,600 men in recent years. The plant continues to produce West Cumberland's traditional specialization, railway track, although it also rolls special sections. Despite a £12 million investment programme since 1945, West Cumberland's share of national steel output has steadily fallen from 3 per cent to less than 1 per cent. In any major reshaping of the British Steel Corporation this isolated plant, operating in one of the least buoyant sectors of the market, must be at some risk. Its only companion, the Millom ironworks, closed in 1968, leaving a local male unemployment rate of 25 per cent. Millom has been declared a Special Development Area, and it is hoped that a crash programme of 'advance' factory construction will give this town that has lost its *raison d'etre* a new economic base. There are, however, those who have pleaded for an act of mercy-killing under the slogan 'Let Millom die'.

Despite the prolonged agony of the traditional industries of west Cumberland, the region has grown more quickly in population during the post-1945 years than for several decades previously. The population in the coastal strip rose from 133,000 in 1951 to 144,000 in 1964 and about 150,000 in 1971. Whitehaven increased by almost 11 per cent, much above the national rate. Migration dwindled to a net loss of only 1,400 over the 1951–1964 period, and the economy has shown itself able to absorb the greater part of a higher than average rate of natural increase—though with some degree of unemployment. Since 1953 almost 90 new industrial projects have been granted industrial development certificates, and these have created about 6,000 new jobs, a little over half of them for men. This new employment is very diverse; it includes the manufacture of food products (Quaker Oats and Rowntrees), paper (Thames Board), carpets, clothing and pharmaceuticals. But two of the new employers have had a dominant influence on the region's prosperity. Marchon Chemicals (at Whitehaven) employs 2,000 chiefly in the manufacture of detergent materials; it is alone among the new industries in depending in part on local physical resources, for it exploits anhydrite in the Trias as a source of sulphur. The other major newcomer is the Atomic Energy Authority which produces plutonium at its Windscale plant; alongside is the first of Britain's atomic power stations, Calder Hall. A third major development is pending: British Leyland is to have built an automated bus plant (to employ 500) at Workington, in a project in which the State will have a 49 per cent interest. The reasons officially given for the choice of location—that the area might expect serious redundancies in the steel industry—have an ominous ring. But, as part of the agreement, the trunk road to Penrith and the M6 extension will be improved, so that the isolation of the sub-region, its most persistent problem, will be partly corrected. Thus

West Cumberland's relative prosperity, after its disastrous experience in the nineteen thirties (when unemployment in Maryport peaked at almost 70 per cent), may be counted a solid achievement of distribution of industry policies: the structure of employment has been transformed. However, whether the whole of the projected population increase of 25,000 by 1981 can be absorbed into local work is clearly doubtful. There are massive physical as well as economic problems to be faced. Much sub-standard housing survives as part of a Victorian urban environment. And there are over 1,200 hectares (3,000 acres) of derelict land in the areas of once-vigorous coal, iron and metal working. Yet beyond the scarred surface of the mineral fields, not 16 kilometres (10 miles) away, is the magnificent back-drop to the sub-region, the western slopes of the Lake District. They offer a reminder that the fastest developing sector in the national economy is the recreation-based group of manufacturing and service industries.

North East Wales has long had close association with North West England, and especially with Merseyside. Chester served, traditionally, as a *de facto* regional capital for much of the north of the Principality, though it was partly supplanted in this role by Liverpool, with the development of modern communications. Certainly the future of both the coal-field of North East Wales and the coastal ribbon of industrial, residential and resort development from Deeside to the Conway estuary must be seen in the context of the future growth of the Merseyside complex (see pp. 319–320). In this section we are concerned with the influence of regional policies on North Wales, for the greater part (excluding Deeside and the resort coast) is within the Welsh Development Area. The coal-field of North East Wales is divided into two parts, not only geologically but also in terms of industrial structure and economic potential. Dipping eastwards off the uplift that brings Silurian rocks to the surface to form the Clwydian range, the Coal Measures form a threshold to the Welsh upland in an outcrop broadened by minor flexuring and disturbed by complex faulting. A major east-west fracture divides the field into the Flintshire and Denbighshire sections. The former extends to and continues beneath the Dee estuary; it was much the more accessible of the two parts and was worked early in association with local metal industries (lead, copper and brass) and for an Irish export trade. Without a concealed extension eastwards, the field reached its peak output early and mining had become residual by 1939. A single small pit stubbornly survives, at Point of Ayr, where it works the sub-estuarine seams. But this northern portion of the field has no significant problems of reemploying a redundant mining labour force. Not only a new structure, but also a new alignment of industry has developed along the shore of the estuary, in three major concentrations. At Hawarden a war-time aircraft factory has survived the rationalization of the industry, though with a reduced labour force. At Shotton a large integrated strip-steel plant occupies reclaimed land, while at Flint and *see p 289* Holywell a man-made fibre industry has been developing since 1917. If present proposals mature this estuarine zone has great potential for further urban-industrial development in the future.

In contrast the Denbighshire section of the coal-field shows all the classical problems of a declining mining area. Later to develop through its relative inaccessibility, this area had a greater long-term potential since there is a concealed eastward extension of the field, where the Coal Measures dip beneath the Trias, and towards which the mining industry had largely migrated by 1939. As late as 1959 five substantial pits were at work here, with a total employment of 15,000. Three survive, with a labour force reduced, by 1969, to only 2,600. Alternative employment, traditionally, has been available chiefly in an iron industry of vigorous early development, but today represented only by a plant at Brymbo producing electrical steels. But there has been a strong and quickening growth of new employment in firms attracted by Development Area status. Much the largest is the Monsanto chemical plant at Ruabon; at Wrexham an old Ordnance factory has become the nucleus of a trading estate with a diversity of light industry on it. It is illustrative of the short-range locational shifts that regional policies sometimes cause that Wrexham has attracted investment by Courtaulds (whose chief local interests are at Flint) and by a Crewe clothing firm. In 1970 the Pilkington group announced plans to invest £8 millions in a glass-fibre plant at Wrexham, a development thought likely to be sited in the Merseyside area. On the coal-field as a whole population has grown strongly during the post-war period, by 7 per cent since 1951 to a 1966 total of 215,000, but with far greater pace on Deeside than elsewhere. Out-migration has been halted, and even in the Wrexham area the population has reached stability at a total of just under 100,000 for the town and rural district combined.

The same distinction between quick coastal population growth and a progressive decline in the hinterland is repeated in *North West Wales :* here the coastal belt grew by 15 per cent between 1951 and 1966, while the population of the interior declined by 2 per cent over the same period. Population increase in the coastlands is related at least as much to the development of the residential-retirement function of the resorts as to the further development of their holiday industries; indeed the latter have attracted little major recent investment except in the proliferation of caravan camps, the form of tourist development that has the slightest impact on the local economy. The North Wales resorts have a serious problem of seasonal unemployment. Population decline in the interior of the sub-region reflects the contraction both of agriculture and primary industry. Slate quarrying at Blaenau-Ffestiniog and in north Caernarvonshire has shrunk almost to extinction; 1966 employment was only about one tenth of that of 1900 and the primary sector in the economy of North West Wales as a whole lost 30 per cent of its employment between 1959 and 1966, largely a reflection of the closure of the last survivors among the major slate producers. Attempts to revitalize the economy of North West Wales have taken two forms. A number of very large capital investments have been located here, for example the Trawsfynyth and the more recent Wylfa Head nuclear power stations, the Tanygrisiau pumped storage scheme and the aluminium smelter under construction on Anglesey. These have created—or will create—large volumes of localized male employment, but chiefly during construction. Secondly a rather slow flow of manufacturing enterprises, offering more permanent employment, has been attracted through the Development Area status of the sub-region; for example Pilkington's have an optical glass plant at St. Asaph and Ferodo a friction-materials plant at Caernarvon. Even limited and localized growth of factory employment has a considerable impact in an area in which (in 1966) only 15 per cent of employment was in the manufacturing sector and 78 per cent in the services.

7.2.2 *Industrial Mobility*

The whole purpose of the policies of government intervention in the location of industry which have evolved from the Distribution of Industry Act of 1945 is to persuade or coerce mobile enterprises to move to areas of greatest need for new employment, and from areas in which the further growth of industry would only serve to overheat economic systems growing too quickly for their own good. The acid test of the success of these policies therefore lies in an evaluation of the patterns of industrial movement that they have helped to generate and guide, both interregionally and intraregionally. Neglecting for the moment West Cumberland and North Wales, three sorts of movement need to be considered : the entry of new enterprises (whether by total transfer or branch development) into the North West from other regions of Britain; the intraregional movement of mobile industry from sub-region to sub-region within the North West; and lastly the movement of enterprises from the North West to other parts of Britain. The salient facts are quickly stated. Of intra-regional movement into the North West since 1945, Merseyside secured much the greatest share, some 70 per cent of the total. In intraregional shifts within the North West, the Manchester sub-region was by far the greatest 'exporter' of employment, and Merseyside the leading beneficiary; the former provided 15,000 of the 21,000 jobs involved in intraregional movement, while the latter secured 40 per cent of this total. In the movement of employment out of the North West entirely, Manchester was again the chief sub-region of origin, providing 17,000 of a total of 28,000 jobs lost by the region to locations elsewhere. This pattern of industrial movement, at its simplest, is a pronounced westwards shift of employment, both in relative and actual terms, from southeast to southwest Lancashire.

In the movement of mobile industry between regions the North West has been a very substantial net beneficiary : 108,000 jobs were created by incoming industry between 1945 and 1967, compared with a loss to other regions of only 28,000. Moreover the attractiveness of the North West is progressively increasing; it secured only 13 per cent of the interregional movement of manufacturing between 1952 and 1959, but 25 per cent during the period 1960 to 1965. This is clearly the direct result of Merseyside's success in attracting mobile firms; but other parts of the region shared more modestly in this inflow. South Lancashire and North East Lancashire attracted 14,000 and 11,000 jobs respectively, while the inflow into Furness of 5,000 jobs is the highest share relative to total sub-regional employment (to which it represents a 12 per cent addition). The Manchester area secured a substantial share of employment inflow (9,000), but the outflow was almost four times this size (Board of Trade, 1969).

Apart from Development Areas policy, a second major influence at work in shaping this pattern is the availability of cheap mill premises for conversion. This not only makes possible the growth of a new enterprise at minimum capital cost, but it also evades the industrial development certificate controls. In all parts of the North West except Merseyside and Furness, a majority of new jobs is attributable to the conversion of existing premises; and in the region as a whole just over half the total of new employment is in converted rather than newly-built accommodation. Even this does not give a full measure of the importance of mill conversion to the changing regional economy, for neither very small firms nor young firms newly born within the region and which have taken up space in old mills are reflected in these figures.

The structure of employment in 'immigrant' industry is significant, for the great bulk is in those growth sectors of which the North West has had an inadequate share. Taking the period 1953 to 1966, some 83 per cent of all new employment entering the region was in the growth sectors, defining these in terms of national trends. The vehicle industry was much the most important, providing 23,000 new jobs within the region, largely concentrated on Merseyside. Electrical products and instruments (7,000), mechanical engineering (7,600) and the food and drink industries were the next most important. All of these, but especially vehicle manufacture, made very great contributions to the overall change in the structure of North Western industry. Over one-fifth of regional employment in the vehicle industry in 1966 was the result of in-movement; in food and drink and engineering the proportion was about one-tenth. But the pattern of industrial in-movement has changed with time. In the chemical industry, 90 per cent of the new jobs are in firms that entered the region between 1945 and 1951, and half the new employment created in engineering dates from the same period. The North West seems to have become distinctly less attractive to these two industries, despite their traditional importance here, during recent decades. Without the huge inward movement of the vehicle industry between 1960 and 1965, the North West would have attracted little employment in the major growth sectors over this period, and this is not a move likely ever to be repeated on so great a scale.

Not surprisingly, the greater part (77 per cent) of the mobile employment that has left the North West since 1945 is also in the growth sectors; by their nature these are inevitably the most mobile sections of the economy. But the loss of industry from the region contains a larger proportion from what are, both nationally and regionally, declining trades—especially textiles and clothing. Over recent years the outflow of employment has tended both to decline overall and to become increasingly dominated by the declining sectors : textile and clothing employment accounted for over half of the outflow between 1960 and 1965. The nature of spatial industrial exchanges between the North West and other regions therefore has been increasingly to the advantage of the former, in terms of their structure. Almost exactly the same pattern is true of intraregional movement. It has shrunk in overall volume in the recent past, and has become more strongly dominated by declining industries, especially textiles and clothing. This might be seen to be no bad thing for those areas of southeast Lancashire and northeast Cheshire that are the chief areas of 'export' for intraregional shifts of employment; but in textiles at least the migrating firms are among the more enterprising, for migration is almost inevitably associated with re-equipment and the construction of more modern plants.

Only the more salient features of a most complex pattern of industrial movement have been presented here, but a number of conclusions as to the operation of industrial guidance policies in the North West are clear. Only Merseyside has derived major and lasting benefits directly from the 'steering' element in Development Area policies. Of the other assisted areas, both Furness and South Lancashire made their fastest acquisition of new employment either before scheduling (the former) or after descheduling (the latter); while in North East Lancashire, despite the 'spearhead' role of guided enterprises, the uncontrolled process of mill conversion has provided the bulk of incoming employment. Mill conversion is in a sense the antithesis of Development Area policy. The extraordinarily low cost of space in old mills balances the incentives that Development Areas offer, and the reuse of industrial premises avoids the operation of industrial development certificate procedures. The process appears to have brought a greater volume of new employment to the region than the steering powers of government intervention. Without it, the whole of the textile zone, except perhaps North East Lancashire, would have a miserable record of industrial attraction. But even the availability of such cheap premises was unable to prevent southeast Lancashire and parts of Cheshire and Derbyshire—in short, the Manchester city region—from suffering a far greater outflow than inflow of new enterprises. This was the principal source of both intraregional shifts and extraregional losses of mobile employment, which cost the area a total of 26,000 jobs. These are the circumstances that led regional interests in southeast Lancashire to make such a powerful case in 1968/69 to the Hunt Committee for 'Intermediate' status in the operation of industrial guidance policies.

It is not possible to analyse the movement of employment to and from North East Wales or West Cumberland in the fineness of detail available for the North West proper; but the overall effect of regional policy on both can be stated very simply, for it is remarkably similar in the two cases. Neither has attracted much mobile employment while regional policies were being weakly implemented, but both have done much better as the development area 'incentives package' has been strengthened. Thus North East Wales was securing only about 300 jobs a year through industrial development certificate approvals during the late nineteen fifties, but about 1,300 a year between 1964 and 1967; the figures for West Cumberland follow the same trend at about the same values. Both had something to fear from the Hunt proposals, but neither area recorded any significant increase in total employment from 1961 to 1966; in both cases the effect of regional policy has been to speed structural change in archaic economies rather than to increase overall employment.

7.3 The Economic Miracle of Merseyside

On any map to show the location of industrial expansion in Britain since 1945, Merseyside is an outstanding node of growth. By any measure—the volume of new employment created, the total of industrial floor-space built, or size of capital investment—Merseyside ranks with Teesside, Severnside and the lower Thames as one of those estuarine growth-points that have attracted so large a share of the nation's recent heavy industrial development. Yet the Merseyside of 1945 had an economic structure with little capacity for expansion, and much potential for further decline. Indeed there seemed every prospect in the immediate post-war years that the area would repeat its lamentable inter-war experience. The scheduling of a large part of Merseyside as a Development Area in 1949 saved the region. Without the influx of new work that this has brought, it has been estimated that factory employment on Merseyside would have fallen by 7 per cent over the decade 1953–1963, and total employment would have been barely stable. The economic miracle of Merseyside is therefore one of the undoubted achievements of the Development Area concept. It can be argued that the price of success on Merseyside has been too high, for it has meant not only that most mobile industry entering the North West has been steered into Merseyside, but also that there has been a substantial intraregional transfer of employment to it from the textile towns. In answer to this view, it is plain that with or without the incentives and constraints of industrial guidance policies this great estuary and its port-complex must inevitably be, in the long term, the North West's most attractive growth point.

The first half of the twentieth century was an unhappy one for the port of Liverpool. As the century dawned, a newly created port at the end of the 60 kilometres (37 miles) long Manchester Ship Canal, was gradually eroding the trade of Liverpool's traditional hinterland. There followed the developing catastrophe of the Lancashire cotton industry, which for so long had been a vital source of Merseyside's commerce. During the nineteen thirties no major British port had so depressed a hinterland; by 1935 the value of exports passing Liverpool fell to less than half the average of the early nineteen twenties. In contrast, industry and population grew without interruption in London's hinterland, and Liverpool was quickly overtaken as the country's leading port. There had been only a feeble development of manufacturing on Merseyside, and most industry was import-based, so that the bulk of all employment depended directly or indirectly upon the docks and their trade. Thus unemployment rose to a sub-regional rate of 28 per cent in 1932, remained as high as 20 per cent even at the trade-cycle crest in 1938, and rose again to a post-war peak of 7 per cent in 1946.

So much attention has centred on Merseyside's industrial progress as a Development Area that it is easy to overlook the revolution that has come, slowly and painfully, to the port itself. There is not one port on the Mersey estuary but several. The Mersey Docks and Harbour Board controls not only the 10 kilometre (6 mile) long line of docks that forms Liverpool's water front, but also the dock complex based on Wallasey Pool on the Cheshire shore. Down-river are the private Unilever port at Bromborough on the Cheshire side and the former railway port at Garston on the Lancashire shore, while the terminal facilities at the entrance to the Manchester Ship Canal are, geographically though not technically, part of the Merseyside port system. Of the main mass of the

Liverpool-Birkenhead docks it may be said that it entered the second half of the twentieth century admirably equipped to handle the trade of the late nineteenth. Almost 263 hectares (650 acres) of docks provided 60 kilometres (38 miles) of quays—although many of the entrances set serious restrictions of draught and beam—while the great landing stages at the Pierhead provided mass facilities for an overseas passenger trade that has now dwindled almost to extinction. In short, this was a general cargo and passenger port ill-equipped to handle shipping of increasing size and specialization, and served by an immense, casually employed dock labour force for whose manual skills there was a diminishing demand. The size of the port sets its own obvious problems of adaptation, but progress has been made. There has been general improvement to handling facilities and to dock access, especially at the Canada group, and part of the Gladstone dock has been converted into a container terminal. Huskisson dock has been adapted for semi-automatic bulk-sugar handling, some of the southern and Birkenhead docks have been further developed for bulk-grain discharge, while Birkenhead also has an ore terminal handling over 1.5 million tons annually for the Shotton integrated steel strip mill on Deeside. A new drive-on ferry service will strengthen Liverpool's position in competition with specialist ferry-ports for the Irish trade, now largely dominated by the container and road-trailer. But much the most ambitious scheme in Liverpool's dockland is the Seaforth extension, at the seaward end of the system: a £33 million investment here will create ten new deep water berths (three of them for container handling) which will be able to accommodate shipping with a 48 foot draught; the first berths opened in 1972.

Up river from the main mass of the port, the outlying dock facilities have always been more specialized in function. Bromborough dock handles bulk cargoes of vegetable oils by a pipeline system, and uses conveyor belts for dry cargo to serve the Unilever food, fat and soap plants. Garston has always specialized in timber, and for both this and chemical raw materials it has advanced equipment. Quick ship-to-rail transfer brought the banana trade to Garston; it also has coal-handling facilities that dealt with exports of a million tons annually even into the nineteen sixties. Along its first 8 kilometres (5 miles) from Eastham locks, the Manchester Ship Canal is virtually a linear port; and woodpulp and petroleum are discharged for the Ellesmere Port-Stanlow industrial complex. The development of the oil trade illustrates more clearly than any other the problems that the Mersey ports face. Oil docks to accommodate 16,000 dwt tankers were built at Stanlow in 1922, close to which the Shell refinery was later sited. A realization that tanker sizes would rise led to the development of a new oil dock at the Canal entrance to handle 30,000 dwt vessels, during the middle nineteen fifties. Initiative then inevitably passed out of the hands of the Manchester Ship Canal company to the Mersey Dock Board which, in association with Shell, built the Tranmere oil terminal with its twin jetties to take tankers initially in the 60,000 to 100,000 dwt range, but now able to accept 200,000 dwt vessels. There is a probability that two new tanker terminals will be constructed nearby. Yet there seems little hope that any estuarine site within the shallow off-shore bar, constantly and expensively dredged at the entrance to the estuary, can be developed for tankers of the larger sizes now coming from the yards. A project has been mooted for an artificial island, beyond the bar and joined by pipe to the mainland, to take vessels of 1,000,000 dwt, but this is much less likely than a new import facility at (and pipeline from) Amlwych on Anglesey, a development for which the Shell company has sought planning and other permissions. There remain therefore certain doubts as to the future of the Mersey as a major oil port; one company is known to have considered a Merseyside site for a new refinery, but has withdrawn. On the other hand, if in the future tankers of immense size serve Bantry Bay type terminals and smaller vessels distribute from them, or if short-haul North Sea oil becomes a major source of Stanlow crude, Merseyside is at no serious disadvantage.

In the growth of manufacturing on Merseyside two themes can be seen : both the development and the decline in the range of traditional industries based directly on the trade of the port itself, and the much more recent growth of manufactures entirely new to the region but only tenuously linked with the port. Some of the traditional trades have grown vigorously since 1945, partly in response to the stimulus of Development Area status, but others have declined (Table 21). The worst hit has been shipbuilding and repairing. After weathering the immediate post-war stresses surprisingly well, employment in the industry shrank by 32 per cent (compared with a national decline of 20 per cent) between 1959 and 1963. The major yard, Cammell Laird at Birkenhead, has remained independent during the reconstruction of the industry (see pp. 379ff; 394ff), though it has technical links with the Barrow yards with which it shared the nuclear programme. In 1970, partly as a consequence of the transfer of nuclear submarine work to Barrow, Cammell Laird were plunged into a financial crisis that threatened the yards with closure. Like other major shipbuilders in Britain they were saved only by a massive injection of Treasury finance : loans to a total of £6 millions were made available and the Government acquired a 50 per cent equity holding in what is now partly a nationally-owned company.

Whatever the future prospects for shipbuilding on Merseyside, ship repairing appears unlikely to make any recovery. Its size is inevitably a function of the number and complexity of ships using the port, and the loss of so much of the passenger liner traffic was a serious blow to it. For major overhauls and refits, lower cost foreign yards have presented ever-growing competition. Jobs in another of the port-based industries, the food, drink and tobacco group, grew quickly to the late nineteen fifties (by 24 per cent, four times the national rate between 1953 and 1959), but since then employment in them has been relatively stable. This is a diverse group; it includes sugar refining, flour milling, and especially the production of soaps, lard, margarine and cattle food. Much the biggest unit is the Unilever complex at Bebbington with 11,000 workers, although Tate and Lyle employ 5,000 at a plant in Liverpool. Since new firms have been attracted to the area (for example Birds Eye, Cadbury, Kraft), the tailing off in the growth of employment suggests some decrease of labour demand by the older branches. Much the same pattern of employment growth—brisk expansion in the nineteen fifties followed by slower progress —is true of the engineering and electrical group; an overall growth rate of 27 per cent

Table 21. Merseyside : trends in employment, 1951–1967

	1951	1962	1967	Change 1951–1967	
TOTAL	**701,000**	**761,100**	**779,200**	**+78,200**	**(+11.2%)**
Primary sector	14,900	12,000	8,400	−6,600	(−44.0%)
Manufacturing sector	300,000	304,700	323,500	+23,500	(+7.8%)
Food and drink	50,700	53,100	51,100	+300	(+0.6%)
Chemicals	47,800	47,800	45,200	−2,600	(−5.4%)
Engineering and electrical	73,100	58,600	70,200	+11,600	(+19.7%)*
Ships and repairing		15,200	17,300	+2,000	(+13.3%)*
Vehicles	12,500	9,600	29,500	+17,000	(+136.0%)
Other metal goods	13,100	14,300	16,100	+2,900	(+22.0%)
Clothing	13,000	12,700	10,500	−2,500	(−19.4%)
Bricks, glass	26,300	27,300	26,800	+500	(+2.0%)
Paper and printing	14,000	18,700	18,000	+4,000	(+29.0%)
Service Sector	318,400	394,300	385,600	+67,200	(+21.0%)
Transport	105,700	95,900	82,300	−23,400	(−22.0%)
Distribution	79,000	101,200	93,700	+14,700	(+19.0%)
Finance	14,300	17,700	18,200	+3,900	(+27.0%)
Professions	48,100	69,600	83,600	+35,000	(+73.0%)
Public administration	25,700	29,000	28,600	+2,900	(+11.6%)

*Since 1962.
Source : Department of Employment.

over the decade 1953 to 1963 is nevertheless impressive. In more recent years, some branches of engineering were depressed through their links with local shipbuilding and with the textile industry. Other branches have been affected by entirely external factors: for example, English Electric is well represented on Merseyside, and serious rationalization involving factory closures has followed from the merger with the General Electric Company.

Over the last twenty-five years, both on Merseyside and nationally, the chemical industry has made enormous investments, which have both improved its productivity as well as increased its output; its labour inputs as a consequence have tended to decline. Thus, between 1953 and 1959 employment in the industry remained stable on Merseyside (while it grew by 11 per cent nationally); since then Merseyside employment has fallen slightly while the national trend has been stable. In fact this net trend conceals a marked reduction in the labour force used by some of the traditional branches of the industry in the area, and a general change in its character. Petrochemical plants have grown in association with the Shell refinery at Ellesmere Port, and products are exchanged with the Carrington plant, 37 kilometres (23 miles) further up the Ship Canal, through a multiple pipeline. Work has recently begun upon a major £225 million expansion of the whole complex which will more than double Shell's chemical production and raise the capacity of the refinery from 10.75 million tons to 18.25 million tons by 1975. Organic chemicals based on oil undoubtedly have been the industry's chief growth point. The 'indigenous' branches, especially at the twin towns of Widnes and Runcorn at the head of the estuary, have had difficult problems of readjustment to face. Widnes was traditionally an alkali producer, using Lancashire coal and Cheshire salt in the long-obsolete Leblanc process. The industry here was overtaken by technological progress almost a century ago, when the Solvay process for alkali production was first applied on the Northwich salt field, at what has now become the Winnington-Wallerscotes complex of plants. However, the Leblanc process died hard at Widnes; and since it involves the production of acids and chlorine-based by-products it has left the town a legacy of miscellaneous chemical manufacture. Appropriately, the town is the headquarters of the General Chemical Division of Imperial Chemical Industries. Other firms also produce fertilizers, phosphorus compounds, ammonia and potassium products. Runcorn, in contrast, has had a simpler and more stable involvement in the chemical industries. Brine piped from Cheshire is used by a large vacuum-evaporator saltworks, and is also converted into industrial alkali at an electrolytic soda plant. The one theme common to these diverse industries— and to soap and detergent manufacture both at Warrington and Bebbington—is that technical advances have reduced the specific labour demand in almost every branch.

A broad conclusion stems from this selective review of some of the traditional manufacturing industries of Merseyside. None has generated a vigorous growth in labour demand over the post-1945 period; all have weak sectors or their problems of adjustment and adaptation. Almost all suffered a marked reduction in employment (or a sharp fall in the rate of growth) during the nineteen sixties after a stronger performance during the nineteen fifties. In short, the port-based industries alone were proving themselves entirely incapable of absorbing the very rapid growth in employable population that the region was generating by its high birth-rate—this despite their reinforcement by 'mobile' enterprises guided to Merseyside by the distribution of industry legislation, which provided some 12,000 new jobs in the 'old' trades. It was a happy accident (rather than carefully planned timing) that the growth of Merseyside's car industry came as the older industrial base was passing into a period of weak labour demand. Moreover, recent work has shown that by 1959 the initial impetus of Development Area policy had spent itself, since by then the opening of new factories was roughly balanced by the closure of others (Lawton and Cunningham, 1970).

The origins of car assembly in the sub-region lie in the series of bargains struck between the government of the day and the major assembly firms early in the nineteen sixties by which, in effect, their expansion was divided between their traditional locations and the Development Areas. Three of the companies affected chose to expand on Merseyside :

Ford, Vauxhall and Standard-Triumph. They doubtless saw good reason, apart from government pressures and the incentive provisions of the 1960 Local Employment Act, to prefer sites here rather than other possible locations. There was the obvious advantage of a major port to an export-orientated industry. There was the further attraction of surplus labour resources (which were continually being replenished by a high birth rate), an existing components industry in industrial Lancashire, and a major steel strip producer at Shotton. Moreover, at the time, progress was advanced both on the building of the M6 motorway and on the electrification of the London-Midland main line, so that communications with the parent plants were in process of radical improvement.

This was industrial growth on a grand scale, and a remarkable act of faith on the part of the firms concerned. Their total investment by 1969 was of the order of £160 million; their direct employment was over 30,000 workers. Yet all three have brought quite different approaches to their development on Merseyside. The Ford site at Halewood (closer to Widnes than Liverpool) lies alongside the electrified railway line which provides a high speed daily shuttle service linking the Halewood and Dagenham production lines. Thus, all engines are made by the latter, whilst all transmissions are made by the former. Assembly is divided between the two: Halewood builds the company's small-car range, at the same time as it shares in medium-car production. Vauxhall's original intention was to develop its Ellesmere Port facilities only for components. These were to be transported to Luton for assembly, despite the new factory's poor rail access and indifferent links with the motorway system. In fact, this policy has been reversed. The Ellesmere Port plant has been developed as an almost self-contained unit for small-car production, which it monopolises, and it also supplies components to the parent plant. Bodies, engines, and transmissions are all produced at Ellesmere Port, which is thus a highly integrated and automated, low-cost, single-model unit, allegedly the most efficient producer of its kind in Europe. The Triumph factory at Speke (the only one of the three actually in Liverpool) was initially a body and trim plant, sending complete car bodies to Coventry for assembly. Its role within the British Leyland Motors' complex has, however, changed; Pressed Steel are now part of the group and supply most of its bodies, and the Speke plant has now been developed for assembly of the complete car as well as bodies.

The impact of the creation, so quickly, of so much new work in a high-wage industry has been enormous. It has far more than balanced the downward drift of employment in the older industries, so that total factory employment on Merseyside grew by 8 per cent between 1953 and 1966. On the other hand, it has not removed (or even much reduced) unemployment, which is still running at over 3 per cent; and because of their peripheral sites the benefits of the new firms are by no means confined to central Merseyside. Halewood is easily accessible from the mill and pit towns of central Lancashire, while Ellesmere Port is much closer to Chester (facing problems of rationalization in the aircraft industry) than to any part of north Merseyside. But the motor vehicle industry cannot, itself, guarantee the region's future. Nationally, it no longer has a quickly growing demand for labour, and Merseyside's share of future investments will doubtless depend on factors as diverse and unpredictable as the future of Development Area policy and local experience in labour relations. The strength of the 'multiplier-effect', too, is problematical. It was expected that component firms would flood into both Merseyside and the North West generally following the growth of the assembly factories. Certainly, some firms have come into the area—to make, for example, spark plugs and brake assemblies. Others were already established in the region; for example, Dunlop were at Liverpool, and both Lucas and Michelin had plants in North East Lancashire. Others are known to have considered Merseyside sites, and rejected them. In fact, the patterns of sub-contracting in vehicle manufacture are so complex, the ease of movement between Lancashire and the West Midlands now so great, and the scale economies and externalities of production in the latter so formidable (pp. 196ff; 398), that it would be naive to see the components manufacturers as tied, locationally, to the shirt-tails of the assemblers.

Despite these radical changes in the manufacturing sector, Merseyside's economy is still based upon service activities, as it must be in a sub-region dominated by a great port, and performing the role of a provincial metropolis. Service employment still represents 61 per cent of the total, and in the pattern of changes since 1945 the dominant trend has been a replacement of the port-based activities by a more general structure of service employment typical of the great city rather than the great port. An accelerating decline (much stronger in the nineteen sixties than the nineteen fifties) in transport and communication jobs reflects the reduction of the dock labour force and associated employment in rail and road transport. This sector of service employment had shed 8 per cent of its 1953 labour force of over 90,000 men by 1963; and the fall continues. Miscellaneous service employment, too—although it is growing nationally—is declining steeply on Merseyside, especially among women; this trend reflects the rise and decline of the football pool industry, once a most important employer of Liverpool women. The other service sectors have been characterized by relatively slow rates of growth on Merseyside, in most cases distinctly below the national figure. For example, distributive work grew, between 1953 and 1963, by 18 per cent in the sub-region but by 23 per cent nationally, the finance group by 22 per cent compared with 36 per cent in the country as a whole, and professional and scientific employment by 28 per cent compared with 38 per cent. That these sectors should be growing here less quickly than nationally is perhaps not surprising, but most are also growing more slowly than in the rest of the North West region.

There is some evidence that, as a centre of office employment in the most general sense, Liverpool is not growing as quickly as other cities in the same size-range. Between 1958 and 1961, the gross rateable value of commercial offices increased in Liverpool by only 7 per cent, compared with rises of almost 17 per cent in both Manchester and Birmingham. Part of the reason for this is to be sought in the fact that the existing level of office development in Liverpool was far greater, whether measured in value or area, than in other cities with a comparable (conurbation or city region) population. For example, until recently it was twice that in Leeds, and almost the equal of Manchester or Birmingham. This relatively high level of office development reflects the diverse commercial interests of a great port, and it has clearly been affected by the decline of the port's trade and its changing role. Moreover, Liverpool falls in the shadow of Manchester in seeking to attract those types of offices that normally seek a location in the regional capital—and there is little evidence that the relative industrial weakness of southeast Lancashire has led to a weakening in Manchester's regional role as the chief focus of tertiary employment.

Economic progress on Merseyside since 1945 has been driven along by an exceptionally rapid growth of population. This is an area that must run hard, in terms of the creation of new jobs, merely to stand still in terms of activity rates. The rapid population increase of the nineteenth century eased during the nineteen twenties and fell to a minimum of 0.29 per cent per annum in the nineteen thirties. Since then, the rate has more than doubled, to about 0.65 per cent per annum during the early nineteen sixties. Although this is below the national average, it is low because the area's annual migrational loss remains at about 0.35 per cent. Without migration, the population of Merseyside would be rising at about 1 per cent each year, considerably above the national trend. In fact, migration has consistently removed about one-third of the natural increase since 1951. With a birth rate that has varied between about 19 and 21 per thousand, rising gradually through the nineteen fifties, and always several points above the national average, but with a death rate close to the national value, Merseyside has an exceptionally high (and slowly rising) rate of natural increase. The primary reasons lie in the high proportion of Roman Catholic families in total population (at least one-quarter), and the even greater proportion in the lower income groups. The preliminary report of the 1971 census suggests, however, that Merseyside's quick population increase may have halted : there was virtual stability between 1961 and 1971.

There is an obvious dilemma confronting any attempt to formulate a rational subregional plan for Merseyside. If out-migration is seen as an evil that ought to be corrected, and if projections are made on this basis, then the total population would rise from 1,664,000 in 1963 to 2,026,000 in 1981. The volume of additional employment required would be over 120,000. The net rate of new job creation would have to rise from 5,000 to 7,000 per annum over the period. Whether the region's economic base can stand such an increase is debatable. That its land resources can not is already clear. There has already been a very marked decentralization of population from core to periphery that has matched the dispersal of employment caused by the decline of old, centrally situated, port-based activities and the growth of new enterprises at fringe locations. The four county boroughs of the conurbation core (Liverpool, Bootle, Birkenhead and Wallasey) housed 82 per cent of the region's population in 1921, but only 63 per cent by 1964; the share of the suburbs beyond their limits grew from 10 per cent to 20 per cent; meanwhile, the more distant suburban fringes beyond the conurbation limits increased their share from a mere 8 per cent to 17 per cent.

Most of this outward shift of population so far has taken the form of short-range peripheral expansion, closely associated with the growth of industry in outlying locations. The advance of the great seas of municipal housing from southeast Liverpool beyond the Speke industrial estates towards the Ford plant at Halewood, the growth of a Liverpool overspill population of about 50,000 at Kirkby close to the very large industrial estate that is separated from Liverpool by the mere formality of a green ribbon, and the movement of some thousands of Liverpool families to new estates at Ellesmere Port near the Vauxhall works and the canal-side industrial zone are all typical of the outward spread of the conurbation to its industrial outposts since 1945. This piecemeal expansion at the margins cannot go much further, especially on the Lancashire side, without very seriously eroding the belt of superbly fertile arable land that lies in the conurbation's immediate hinterland. Thus there has been a search for new town sites.

The new towns growing at Skelmersdale and Runcorn, and the large town expansion projects at Widnes and Winsford, are discussed in the section on the strategy of population dispersal in the North West as a whole (pp. 314–325). Only a measure of the scale of the problem need be given here. Taking the period 1964–1981, and assuming that Merseyside continues to lose about one-third of its natural increase by migration, the housing demand generated in the sub-region by all causes (population growth, new family formation, and slum clearance) will be about 220,000 units. The conurbation itself and land available on its margins can probably offer sites for about 160,000. This leaves 58,000 families needing to be accommodated in dispersal schemes at some distance. If, on the other hand, migration from the region was to cease, this overspill to distant sites would rise to 95,000 families. In short, if Development Area policy achieves its ultimate objective, which is to eliminate net migration, then huge problems of dispersal planning will ensue. Merseyside itself simply cannot contain its population growth physically, and must lose part of it either by extra-regional movement or by planned dispersals to new communities within the North West. Thus, the future economic performance of Merseyside, and its capacity to generate jobs to absorb its natural increase of population, are the biggest imponderables in attempting to shape a regional planning strategy. But there are uncertainties also about the future rate of population increase on Merseyside : lower projections of population growth coupled with a shift of housing demand from the public to the private sector have led Liverpool to revise its estimate of overspill needs sharply downwards.

7.4 The Textile Zone : An Industrial Portrait in Shades of Grey

Location of industry policy in Britain has always been geographically naive and therefore regionally insensitive. It has contained an implicit assumption that Britain could be neatly and simply divided between regions of growth and of decline, and that high and persistent levels of unemployment are an infallible indicator of economic ill-health and social distress. There is growing realization, given its most articulate expression in the Report of the Hunt Committee, that there are large areas of Britain that have quite failed to share in the vigorous economic expansion of midland and southern England yet, despite the contraction of their traditional industries, they have never suffered serious unemployment and so have never enjoyed the artificial stimuli of Development Area status. The 'Intermediate Areas' are regions of economic stagnation rather than dramatic decline, of persistent outmigration that has balanced falling labour demands within their archaic economic structures, of environmental deterioration and industrial dereliction, and of inadequate levels of investment in the replacement and improvement of their wasting capital assets, in housing, industry and communications. In all these respects the textile zone of eastern Lancastria is archetypal (Smith, 1968).

A general profile of the nature and symptoms of the wasting illness that has reduced the textile areas to so debilitated a condition has been sketched already (pp. 271ff). This section is concerned chiefly with their causes and with the possible cures. In varying degrees (for there are considerable sub-regional contrasts) the textile towns are the victims of population loss by age-selective migration so persistent that most are no longer generating any significant natural increase in population. Local economic structures of Victorian simplicity, based on textiles, mining and their ancillaries, survived late into the twentieth century. Yet the contraction of employment in the cotton industry to scarcely more than one-sixth of its peak of over 600,000 workers has left no residual unemployment. The decline was gradual and spread over forty years; out-migration, natural 'wastage' in an elderly working population, and the retirement of women from the labour force as the mills closed down have all contributed to this remarkable situation. Indeed there has been over-correction, for the mill towns are now short of labour; for this reason alone, and there are many others, they are unattractive to mobile industry. Development Area policy has steered employment away from, rather than into, the greater part of the textile zone, which since 1945 has suffered a net loss of 'mobile' industry (pp. 285–287). In the absence of new factory building—except locally and on a limited scale—mill conversion has been the spearhead of economic progress but this is industrial diversification 'on the cheap' and it is no long term solution.

These, then, are the economic measures of 'greyness', but there are the social and physical dimensions to the dilemma too. In an area that roughly corresponds with the textile zone, Burnett and Scott, using the data of the 1951 census, found that 14 per cent of all dwellings had three rooms or less, and 42 per cent lacked a bath. In 1958, some 32 per cent of all houses were rated at £10 or less, and almost two-thirds below £18. In one of the worst districts (which it is kindest not to name) 36 per cent of the housing was officially unfit, about 60 per cent lacked baths, over 30 per cent had no exclusive use of a water closet (indoor or out), over a quarter were back-to-back, and some hundreds were basement or 'back to earth' dwellings. Agreed, there has been considerable clearance since but this is the housing environment from which the migrants have moved. Added to the physical obsolescence of much social capital (for example schools and hospitals), the limited service provision of all but the largest towns, and also the out-moded life-style associated with a Victorian urban fabric and community structure, these factors of environment are at least as important as questions of job security in helping to explain the heavy out-migration from within the 15–44 age-band. Nor is this a complete stocktaking of the problems of the area. Its road communications system is largely unimproved

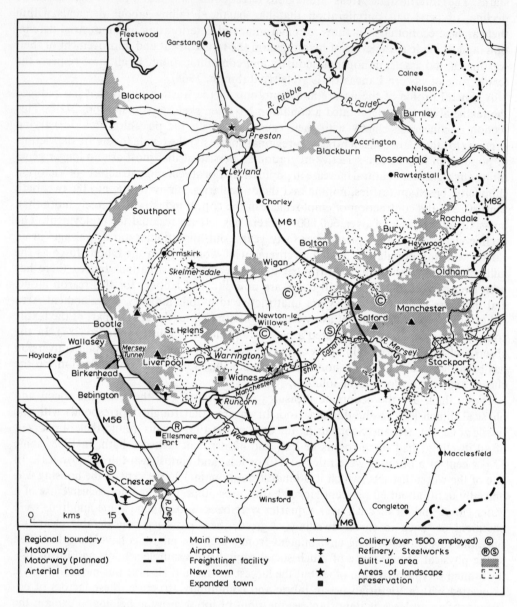

Figure 25   The North West: principal economic and land use features, 1971.

(apart from the M62 and Irwell valley spur road), and its railway net is half abandoned. In the textile areas with the strongest mining interests, chiefly in central Lancashire, land dereliction is a problem of appalling size. Ince-in-Makerfield has almost 40 per cent of its entire area standing derelict. Wigan is encircled by a devastated collar. Leigh stands on the shores of a subsidence lake over a kilometre long. There are areas in south Lancashire incapable of finding sites for the new industry they so desperately need, because of these problems of surface devastation.

To analyse the industrial problems of eastern Lancastria and to make any appraisal of the region's future involves studies of the fate of the old staple industries, the rise of alternative manufactures, the changing structure of employment, and the factors that are likely both to promote and to restrain its progress towards a new economic stability on a broader base.

7.4.1 *Cotton and Coal : the Geography of Rationalization*

One of the greatest changes in the British economy during the last quarter-century has been the collapse and disintegration of the Lancashire cotton manufacture, which at the peak of its fortunes in the early nineteen twenties provided not only almost 40 per cent of all employment in the textile region, but also over a quarter of the total value of the country's exports. This once-great manufacture may now be pronounced extinct. From its wreckage there has risen a new industry, a general textiles manufacture, very different both in its materials and products, and increasingly also in its technology and structure, from the old cotton trade. Both in labour force and the volume of output, the new textile industry is much smaller than the old. It is no longer the base of the regional economy but rather an important (but not the largest) element in a much better diversified structure. It now dep s almost as much upon the chemical industry as upon raw cotton imports for its raw materials and traditional types of fabric are a diminishing proportion of its output. No longer is it divided between a multitude of small firms, many of the 'family' type, but it has now come to be concentrated in the hands of a few large and very powerful companies. By 1966, four combines controlled 45 per cent of the spinning, 25 per cent of the weaving and 30 per cent of the finishing capacity. These changes have gone hand in hand with a belated technical modernization. New machinery has been installed, and is worked harder—and over longer periods—than was the old. As a consequence, what was a labour-intensive industry has become much more capital intensive, with a far lower specific labour demand. Lastly, the old cotton industry was very much Lancashire's monopoly. The new textile manufacture, in contrast, has already shown itself to be locationally much less tied to the mill towns of North West England.

The decline and fall of the cotton industry may be summarized briefly. It employed almost 600,000 before the beginning of contraction in the early nineteen twenties, about 330,000 at the peak of its post-war recovery in the early nineteen fifties, but only 190,000 on the eve of its crisis and reshaping in 1959–1960. Now (1969) the mills and finishing works employ only 127,000. The causes of its early contraction are now matters of economic history. Especially important initially was the rise of local cotton industries in countries like India and Brazil, which had once been major customers of the Lancashire mills. Later, Japan appeared as a powerful low-cost competitor for the declining volume of world trade in cotton products. During the post-1945 period, however, other factors have been paramount, especially the increasing technical obsolescence of the industry. This was the radical cause of its inability not only to maintain its share of world export markets but also even to prevent imports capturing an increasing share of the British market for cotton textiles. Imports exceeded exports for the first time in 1958. Today they are five times greater in volume, although the balance is better in terms of value (imports were valued at £56 million in 1965, exports at £41 million). Lancashire's output of cloth is currently about 1,400 million metres (1,500 million yards) annually; imports of cloth are some 730 million metres (800 million yards) and of 'made up' goods the equivalent of 180 million metres (200 million yards). Exports, which include a substantial re-export element of imported grey cloth that is 'finished' in the region, are a mere 180 million metres (200 million yards). Thus imports are now responsible for roughly 40 per cent of the domestic consumption.

For over a decade, spokesmen for the industry have held that this is an intolerable level which, by threatening its future, has deprived it both of labour and investment resources, and they have sought either tariff protection or some physical restraint on the inflow. From 1960, bilateral agreements putting limits on the volume of cotton imports into Britain were made with the chief suppliers—the low-cost Asian producers who enjoyed a commercial advantage through their membership of the Commonwealth—but imports from other more 'advanced' countries, for example Portugal, continued to rise. In 1966, therefore, a quota system was adopted, which for the first time included made-up clothing, a quickly growing aspect of the import trade. In 1969 it was announced that, after 1972, a 15 per cent tariff would apply to all cloth imports, thus giving that direct measure of protection that the industry has sought for so long. The commercial environment of the trade changed radically during the nineteen sixties, therefore, from an open-market policy to one of direct protection.

There have also been immense changes in the structure of the textile industry. By 1959 much of it had reached an enfeebled and moribund condition. Mills had closed in their hundreds, about 550 during the period between 1951 and 1960; over half of the surviving equipment lay idle, much of it almost unbelievably aged and obsolete, and over one-third of the mill labour force had been lost in less than a decade to other more secure employment. The industry was clearly powerless to save itself by its own initiative. A government-sponsored rationalization scheme, therefore, was proposed within the Cotton Industry Act of 1960—the first direct intervention by government to secure the reshaping of a major private industry. The Act was limited in its objectives. It sought, first, to reduce the size of the industry to a level more appropriate to its prospects, by offering compensation for the scrapping of machinery. This, it was hoped, would eliminate both the weak firms and the weaker units of stronger firms. In a simple sense, this part of the Act worked. Half the spindles, and 40 per cent of the looms, were offered for scrapping. Much of this machinery, however, had been idle for years, and there was only a slight drop in employment as the direct consequence of the Act. Its other main provision, the offer to subsidize the re-equipment of those firms who remained in the industry, was less immediately successful. Uncertainties not only concerning the state of future markets, but also about the future of the labour force, were powerful restraints on expensive schemes to re-equip mills, which would then have to recruit labour for two or three shifts to show an acceptable level of return on the capital (Rodgers, 1962).

Paradoxically, the cotton industry has been seriously short of labour during its period of reorganization. Workers have left it faster than the industry has abandoned them. Migration, longer-distance commuting, retirement and the attractions of alternative employment have all contributed to the labour scarcity, while the unpopularity of shift work in a trade which had never known it was also a problem. Shift working has now become more widespread, although full three–shift operation is still uncommon: on average spindles are worked for about 3,800 hours annually and looms 3,300 hours. These are much higher rates than previously but internationally they remain almost the lowest values amongst the major textile producing industries; American spindles, for example, are worked for over 6,000 hours each year. Since machine-utilization is the key to investment and re-equipment, these are discouraging figures. However, progress has been made, for the proportion of automatic looms has risen from 14 per cent in 1955 to about 50 per cent in 1969.

Unhappily the 1960 Act also had some less praiseworthy results. In particular, it reduced the size of the industry without radically changing its structure. This has been left to the forces of industrial politics restrained by the oversight of the Monopolies Commission. The changing raw material supply is the key to the process of restructuring. Even between 1962 and 1969 the proportion of cloth made wholly or partly of man-made fibres rose from about 37 per cent to 43 per cent of the total produced in northwestern mills, while man-made filaments and mixtures now account for more than half the yarn-supply. In short, the fate of the industry has increasingly become a matter of crucial concern to those companies with chemical interests who produce the bulk of the man-made fibres. Of this output about two-thirds consists of cellulosic rayons (of which 80 per cent is viscose and 20 per cent acetate), while the truly synthetic fibres account for one-third (of which half is nylon and the rest shared between terylene and the acrylic group). The production of each of the major man-made fibres is dominated by a single company. Courtaulds supply the great bulk of rayon output (and have smaller nylon and acrylic interests), while Imperial Chemical Industries are the major producers of both nylon and terylene. Almost all the other producers of synthetic fibres (Du Pont, Monsanto, British Enkalon, Beyer) are British branches of overseas companies, and so have a more marginal interest in the Lancashire market. Clearly therefore it fell to Courtaulds and

I.C.I. to initiate the restructuring of the Lancashire textile trade in order to save it as a major market for their products. These two giants have developed contrasting philosophies in their approaches to the problem.

Courtaulds sought to save the Lancashire textile industry by absorbing large parts of it. I.C.I. have tried to stimulate a restructuring within the industry itself, especially by means of large capital injections designed to make amalgamation and merger possible; their hope was that two or three big groups would emerge. Both policies have had substantial success. Courtaulds absorbed the Lancashire Cotton Corporation, and Fine Spinners and Doublers; these became the basis of the group's Northern Textile Spinning Division, in which 15 of the 52 mills originally acquired have since been closed. Courtaulds now possess about one-third of Lancashire's spinning capacity, and about 20 per cent of the filament weaving. Meanwhile amalgamation has proceeded within the Lancashire industry in a 'fish-eat-fish' fashion. To illustrate the process, Tootals merged with English Sewing Cotton, which later amalgamated with Calico Printers Association to form English Calico, which then attracted a bid from Courtaulds on which the Monopolies Commission reported adversely. Viyella International and Carrington and Dewhurst, the two remaining giants, both grew with the help of large I.C.I. capital holdings. By 1970 these two companies had merged under the control of I.C.I.

These changes amount to a financial and managerial revolution, the necessary pre-condition for further technical progress. The giants have together absorbed about 100 other companies since 1960. Not all branches of the trade have been equally affected, however. In 1964, there were 350 weaving firms and 180 finishers, but only 75 spinning firms. Each of the remaining great combines has an identifiable 'personality', and a distinctive range of activities. Carrington and Dewhurst, for example, are Europe's biggest filament-weavers; they are highly specialized in this branch and so represent the traditional Lancashire pattern of 'horizontal' specialization carried to its logical extreme by progressive amalgamation. Viyella, on the other hand, is distinctive in having grown 'backwards' from the merchanting branch, and has a balanced vertical structure with about 10 per cent of the industry's total spinning, weaving and warp-knitting capacities. English Calico has its dominant stake in the finishing industry, of which it owns about 40 per cent. Beyond these three (and the Courtauld empire) are many smaller amalgamations and specialist independent firms, particularly in the weaving section.

Any major industrial reconstruction has its locational consequences. Lancashire cotton is no exception. For over forty years the spatial pattern of decline in the industry has exhibited strong areal contrasts. Before and after the Depression the coarse cloth producers of the Blackburn area suffered almost twice as sharp a contraction as the fine-cloth weavers of the Burnley district. The Bolton-based fine-spinning industry was long relatively stable, but when its decline ultimately came, in the nineteen fifties, it was catastrophic. In the valley towns of the Rossendale upland, with a strong specialization in heavy industrial textiles and access to a labour supply less eroded by industrial diversification, mill employment has declined more slowly than in almost any other area. But the post-1960 reconstruction of the industry has produced complex and indecisive, though nevertheless important, locational changes. Along the western border of the textile region, in central Lancashire, the industry has shown great stability; this is associated with the local importance of fabrics made from man-made fibres and the success of Carrington and Dewhurst, a firm historically based in the locality. In southeast Lancashire, after the immense number of mill closures during the nineteen fifties, there has been much greater stability; one of the most significant results of the 1959–1960 contraction was to leave a high proportion of the industry's looms in this traditional spinning area. As a result, there is now a better balance of spinning and weaving in the textile towns of the Manchester conurbation, for them a distinct advantage given the trend for the two main branches of the industry—after a century of regional segregation—to become re-integrated geographically, operationally and commercially. Moreover, two of the industry's major combines, and many smaller ones, are Manchester-based. In contrast the old 'weaving area' of the north, from Blackburn to Colne, has suffered a quick decline in its share of both the industry's equipment and employment during the period of reorganization; also the dominant companies are less strongly represented here.

It is too early to deduce firm patterns from these trends. The evidence is mounting, however, that the industry's capacity for survival is greater in west-central and southeast Lancashire than elsewhere. Paradoxically, these are areas in which there exists the broadest general diversity of employment, and the greatest apparent potential for economic growth; the weaving towns further north, in contrast, depend more heavily on their shrinking share of textile employment, and have a far slighter potential for attracting replacement industry. But perhaps the most significant locational trend in recent developments is for new textile investments to be made entirely outside the traditional area of concentration in eastern Lancastria. Courtaulds has recently announced major plans to increase its share of weaving capacity by building four new factories: a site at Carlisle was chosen for the first of these, another is at Skelmersdale, and almost certainly the other two will be in Development Areas. Indeed it is generally agreed in the industry that no group building a new plant *ab initio* can afford to ignore the Development Area investment assistance. The 1969 refusal of the government to categorize the whole of east Lancashire as an "Intermediate Area", and so to provide greater investment allowances, was a serious blow for the greater part of the region; fortunately the decision was reversed in 1972 when the government included the whole of the North West region (outside the Merseyside Development Area) in an enlarged Intermediate Area. If there is a dominant growth region for the British textile industry, it is Ulster. It has attracted huge investments by both British and overseas man-made fibre producers, and since it can offer the full range of locally produced raw materials, plus a surplus labour supply and an enticing package of incentives to migrant firms, it has also attracted investment by a wide variety of fibre-using firms.

The rationalization process in northwestern coal mining has been governed by very different circumstances from those that have prevailed in the reconstruction of the textile industry. Government intervention in the latter was for long timid and limited, and it was left to the chemical industry to supply the final initiatives. In the case of coal mining, however, rationalization reflects the decisions taken by a single national agency, working within the framework of a changing national energy market and policy. But there are themes common to the two cases. Both have come to have the reputation of industries in which employment prospects are uncertain; neither therefore has been able to retain a labour force adequate in size and quality against competition from other employers. In both, the process of rationalization has taken the form of an increasing concentration of production into a smaller number of large units, and has transformed their geographical expression.

In the Lancashire coal-field the greater part of the workable resource is 'exposed' in the sense that it occurs in areas in which the productive coal measures form the sub-drift surface. Only in a narrow and fault-interrupted strip along the southern border of the field are there coal resources concealed under a Triassic overlay. Partly because of its almost total 'exposure', but also because of the huge regional demand generated by early and vigorous industrial growth, almost all parts of the field were being worked to their full capacity by the end of the nineteenth century, when this relatively small field was producing as much as 25 million tons each year. By the nineteen thirties, the consequences were becoming clear. Much of the best, shallowest and most profitable coal had gone. Costs were rising to the point at which Yorkshire coal could enter the north-western market in increasing quantities, so that scores of marginal producers west of the Pennines were forced to close—and thereby initiated a first stage not only in the contraction of the industry but also in its rationalization by amalgamation. By 1930 output had dropped to scarcely 16 million tons, and sub-regional amalgamation of pits, for example Manchester Collieries, were being formed to defend their share of a shrinking market. Further closures reduced the number of pits rather than output. About 130 pits, many very small, produced some 14 million tons annually in the mid nineteen thirties, while twenty-five years later about 50 pits were responsible for an annual tonnage of about 12 millions. The National Coal Board, in sum, acquired an industry which had already made some progress towards concentration.

Certainly by the nineteen fiftees the spatial changes associated with rationalization were well developed. The heart of the triangular Lancashire field consists of sterile Millstone Grit, so that mining has always been unequally divided between a number of distinct districts. At the northern apex is the almost detached Burnley basin, a shallow syncline of limited resources and exceptionally thin seams. Obituaries were being written for the mining industry here as early as the nineteen thirties; it struggles on, though now only five pits survive, largely because part of the coal is of coking quality, and part is mined in association with valuable fireclays. Reaching along the Pennine flank east of Manchester lies a section of the field almost detached from the main mass by complex faulting along the line of the Irwell valley. This 'Manchester coal-field', enormously productive in its day, was physically exhausted by 1960. Then mining was extinct, except for a single very large and modernized pit, at Bradford, working rich and deep seams profitably under the Trias of east-central Manchester. The Bradford pit was the perfect example of the incompatibility of mining with intensive urban land use. At the same time as its output was used to generate much of the city's electricity—it being efficiently linked to an adjacent generating station by means of a conveyor belt—the mine caused subsidence damage on a grand scale. To the unconcealed joy of its neighbours, it closed in 1968, having made a loss of £800,000 in a single year, after a period of great profitability. The cause of death was a common one in the fault-shattered Lancashire field, the occurrence of unexpected minor fracturing which abruptly cut off the best seams.

Since nationalization, the great bulk of active mining has been confined to the southern border of the field. This comprises the deeper 'exposed' Coal Measures to the north, and the narrow, fault-broken extension concealed under Trias to the south. Along the boundary a long line of some 25 pits stretched from Salford in the east almost to the suburbs of Liverpool in the west. Ten of these were reconstructed giants, each employing an average of 2,000 men. Together with two new sinkings at Agecroft and Parkside, they employed almost two-thirds of the entire labour force of the field in 1960, and were seen as the collieries of the future. Nowhere was this narrow zone of vigorous mining and massive investment in modernization more than eight kilometres (five miles) wide, except where it intersected the Wigan-Chorley fault trough, which carried a line of working pits northwards through these two towns. This extension to Chorley has now been abandoned and in Wigan, for so long the mining capital of South Lancashire, the only evidence of what was so long its dominant industry is the broad belt of derelict and subsidence-damaged land which virtually surrounds the town.

Thus, the spatial pattern of mining in Lancashire has been much simplified. Except for the relict survival about Burnley, the logical conclusion of a gradual 'down the dip' progression has been reached in the long corridor of active working, clinging tightly to the southern, deeper border of the field. Mining is prevented from reaching further southwards, in search of untouched and concealed reserves, by the steepening of the dip in the seams under the Trias, which quickly carries them to uneconomic and unworkable depths. It was known that many of the older pits here had short lives because of their limited reserves, but it was believed until very recently that perhaps a dozen pits in this zone would survive for a prolonged period. This appraisal has been brought seriously into question by recent developments in the national energy market and the associated response of fuel and power policy.

In 1965, within the National Coal Board's Northwestern Division (which by then had been broadened to include West Cumberland and had long included North Wales) fourteen pits, employing a total of 19,000 men, were categorized as Class A 'long-life' collieries. Another six pits (employing 6,000) were put in Class B with a less certain future. Fifteen were placed in Class C1 (likely to last no longer than five years), and three in Class C2 (likely to disappear very quickly). The Class C pits together employed 9,000 men.

For obvious reasons the allocation of pits to classes was not made public. Nevertheless it was clear that at least ten of the Class A collieries were spread across South Lancashire—for there were probably only three pits in North Wales, and scarcely even one in West Cumberland, with any potential for long survival. It seemed reasonable to deduce, therefore, that of the thirteen collieries in the southern zone in 1967 the great majority were safe for some years and that the 18,000 jobs they provided were relatively secure. In fact, three of the largest and most extensively modernized of these have already closed. These three pits alone involved a total of 5,300 jobs. In addition, it is known that the future of a number of other pits in this zone is now being questioned.

There is no good reason to assume that, even by existing yardsticks of profitability, the field has any long-term potential. Its recent performance has not been entirely unfavourable, alternating between modest operating profits and minor losses; in 1967–1968, despite the burden of loss-making collieries chiefly outside Lancashire, the Northwestern Division made a very small loss of £0.058 per ton. This loss could well have been converted to a profit by the closure of Bradford and Mosley Common pits, for the latter alone lost £750,000 during its last six months of 'probation' working. Both in terms of its profit and loss account, and in terms of output per man shift (at 5.28 tons, about 0.76 tons below the national average), the Lancashire field falls between the low-cost East Midland and Yorkshire fields and the high-cost Northern, Welsh and Scottish mines. It seems much more likely to share the fate of the latter than that of the former.

Two great problems trouble the uncertain future of the Lancashire coal-field, one technical, the other essentially social. As a field much disturbed by faulting, the life of many of its pits can be brought to a premature and sudden end by relatively minor fractures interrupting profitable seams. It is clear that development work to restore faces to operation is likely to demand too long a period of unprofitability to be tolerated under present circumstances. This was the fate of the Bradford pit and of many others in the past, but the problems at Mosley Common—for so long the show pit of the field, and one that had absorbed £6 million of N.C.B. investment—were human rather than technical. On the western fringe of the diverse labour market of the Manchester conurbation, this colliery has always faced severe competition for labour; latterly it recruited much of its workforce from the abandoned field in the Wigan district. It had a disastrous record of absenteeism and labour turnover, and consequently of low productivity, and this seems to have been partly associated with the lengthy journey to work of most of its miners. In short, mining labour in Lancashire is not readily mobile. The redundant miner, used to a workplace near his own home, is not readily transferable to a pit many kilometres away, and the increasing diversity of employment in the old mining districts reduces his mobility. This problem has its parallel in the textile industry, in which it was naively assumed that labour made redundant by mill closures would be available for multi-shift working in the re-equipped mills. There is a complex social dimension in industrial planning which is by no means easily understood; both the mining and textile industries of the region have been victims to it.

7.4.2 *The Growth of Alternative Employment*

The progressive decay of an archaic economy based on two staple activities—one a low-wage industry and the other a dirty and dangerous occupation—need occasion no regret. Indeed, the ultimate decline of both coal and cotton was always inevitable. What is much more serious and alarming is that replacement jobs have grown at so inadequate a rate over all but a few parts of the textile zone. Table 20 summarizes employment trends in the area since the crises of the textile industries in the late nineteen fifties. Since then, about 140,000 jobs in the mills and pits have disappeared; but the rest of the manufacturing base has been quite unable to generate new employment—either by indigenous growth or by attracting mobile enterprises—to replace this loss. Indeed, several of these alternative industries are themselves declining as quickly as the traditional staples, and what (nationally) are the 'growth industries' have had a lamentable record of expansion in the textile North West. The service trades have experienced modest growth, especially in the larger mill towns, where between 40 per cent and 50 per cent of all work is now provided by service activities, but the record of the service sector in the sub-region is by no means good. Employment in transport has declined at about five times the national rate. Employment in the distributive trades has grown only half as quickly as in the country as a whole. Indeed, the increased relative importance of service jobs in the mill towns is the product of the decline of their manufacturing base, rather than any real expansion in the service sector. The massive withdrawal of women from the labour force, reducing the number of families with multiple incomes, has seriously reduced purchasing power in the textile zone, and in turn depressed the demand for many services.

There is no great mystery involved in the slow growth (or occasionally the serious decline) in the textile area of industries that are making rapid progress both nationally, and elsewhere in the North West. In eastern Lancastria, many of these broad industrial groups are burdened by weak sectors, declining rapidly both in the region and the country. Within the engineering industry of the mill towns, for instance, there has always been a strong emphasis on textile machinery. This has passed through its own process of contraction, rationalization and modernization in parallel with that in the textile industry itself. A small number of dominant companies has emerged. Stone-Platt Industries unites several of the largest of the formerly independent concerns. Other textile engineers have sought salvation through diversification, and have turned to more general engineering. Today the chief growth point in textile engineering is the production of equipment for the man-made fibre section of the industry—but this is by no means confined to the North West. In short the rationalization of textile machine-making has not only led to concentration and the closure of many factories, but also some degree of spatial redistribution. It nevertheless remains an important branch of engineering in many mill towns, for example Blackburn, Bolton and Macclesfield.

Some contraction of textile engineering was to be expected, but the uncertain recent trend of employment in electrical engineering in the textile zone is more alarming. This

seemed, until the nineteen sixties, perhaps the most successful of the 'replacement' manufactures. It is an industry of great diversity, ranging from the making of heavy electrical
equipment to intricate electronic assemblies. The 'heavy' end of the east Lancashire
industry, especially, has been seriously affected by its recent national reorganization,
and the Metropolitan-Vickers plants on the Trafford Park estate at Manchester exemplify
the regional impact of this process. These once employed well over 20,000 workers and
were the largest single industrial unit in the textile zone. Merged initially into Associated
Electrical Industries and subsequently absorbed by the General Electric Company, these
plants are now a relatively minor part of the General Electric Company-English Electric
empire. Clearly, some of the enterprises conducted in them are thought to be uncompetitive
and are to close—just as English Electric is closing some of its factories and reducing
the labour needs of others in the Merseyside region. In general, the North West has come
rather poorly out of the British electrical industry's reorganization by merger in recent
years. This is chiefly the result of the region's concern with the heavier, capital-equip-
ment side of the trade, and its rather feeble development of consumer goods production.
Thus what was, in the nineteen fifties and nineteen sixties, one of the vital growth industries
of the textile towns now faces grave problems of its own.

Of all the alternative industries, the vehicle group has the worst record. Indeed, in
Manchester it has declined at a rate far exceeding that of even the textile industry. Again
the reasons lie in the detailed composition of the trade. In and near the textile zone, the
manufacture of railway locomotives and rolling stock once dominated the vehicle industry.
Until a decade ago, there were six large railway engineering plants in the North West,
and all but one (the Crewe works) were within the textile sub-region. Four of these plants
have closed entirely and the two survivors both have a much reduced labour force. Given
the trend of both national and international demand, this represented the inevitable
contraction of an old industry but a decade ago it seemed possible that a much newer
sector of the vehicle group, aircraft manufacture, might grow to balance this decline.
In northeast Manchester, at Bolton and at Preston this had grown to a considerable size,
Unhappily, not only were the firms concerned caught up in the general rationalization
of the British aircraft industry, but they were also victims of changes in national defence
strategy. Thus yet another potential replacement industry of the mill towns has itself
gone into decline. As Table 20 shows so clearly, the vehicle industry is growing strongly
in the North West as a whole, but declining even more quickly in the textile zone. These
figures reflect the location of car assembly plants on Merseyside and (on a much smaller
scale) at Crewe, and of the heavy vehicle branch of the industry at Leyland and Sandbach.
The only growth sector in eastern Lancastria is the construction of car and truck components, but even this is increasingly being attracted to Merseyside.

During the inter-war and early post-war years, the growth of the clothing industry
seemed to offer the prospect of some replacement jobs for those female employments
being lost through mill closures. Long established in the Manchester area, this industry
was tending to disperse more broadly to the textile towns, where it often took over the

premises as well as the labour of the cotton industry; but after reaching its employment peak in the early nineteen fifties, the industry has declined at an accelerating pace. Its contraction has been quicker in the North West than in the nation and far faster in the textile towns than elsewhere in the region. The causes are complex and obscure. They include changes in fashion, in production techniques and the progressive improvements of productivity in what was a labour-intensive trade not outstanding in its efficiency. The effects are simple; the decline of labour demand in the clothing factories now almost rivals mill closures as a cause of the reduction in female employment opportunities in the mill towns. Yet, surprisingly, in the North West outside the textile zone, it is an industry of quite marked growth in recent years.

Very little evidence of industrial growth in the textile zone is presented in Table 20. The brightest feature is the modest expansion of engineering, despite the effect of the weak sectors; even so, employment has grown at only about a quarter of the regional and national rates Chemicals are at least a stable employer, and have escaped the effect of those technological changes that have reduced labour demand in the mid-Cheshire and mid-Mersey regions. Papermaking is still fortunately a growing industry in parts of the textile zone (for example at Bury and Darwen), and there has been some change from older activities to new, for example to wallpaper manufacture. But the food and drink group, a growth industry outside the textile area, is an industry of decline within it. One fact stands out with great clarity from the table. The working populations of textile towns within daily travelling range of Manchester cannot now rely on the more diverse economy of the city for employment as their local economic base contracts.

The figures for the Manchester group of exchange areas (both central and suburban) show that the city has an economy of quite extraordinary weakness, certainly the weakest of all the major British cities. Virtually the entire manufacturing base is contracting, and (in all the industries listed) more sharply than in the textile region as a whole. Service employment, too, is declining overall in the city, chiefly because sharp falls in transport and distribution more than balance a very substantial growth (at rates of about 1½ per cent and 4½ per cent per annum respectively) of the financial and professional groups. Clearly this is not a city that can spare any industrial employment to implement either Development Area or overspill policies—although in effect it is being obliged to do so. Appropriately, as the regional capital of a grey area, Manchester's economy is slowly drifting downhill. It is experiencing an annual loss of not far short of 1 per cent in its total employment, and yet it has no significant unemployment problem. All the indicators give clear expression to the multiplier effect of economic decline. The contraction of the old staple industries has caused other related manufactures and services to shrink also; activity rates have fallen, the growth of family income has been arrested, and the development of the service sector stunted. Economic failure, like economic success, is cumulative, with an unhappy tendency to be self-perpetuating.

During all the changes of fortune that have affected the non-textile manufactures of the North West since the late nineteen forties there has been one major factor only making for growth and diversity in employment, the conversion of textile mills for other types of industrial use. This is no new trend. Some of the largest firms in the region's most important growth industries grew from infancy in this way—for example the Avro Aircraft Company and Ferranti, the electrical engineers. But the massive contraction of the textile industry during the last twenty years has freed cheap space for new enterprises on a very great scale indeed. Of the thousand or more mills and finishing factories that have closed their gates since 1945 many are so old and ruinous, or so poorly sited in deep valleys or beside silting canals, that they can interest no one save the demolition contractor or the industrial archaeologist. Others, in the congested factory zones that enveloped the centres of Victorian cotton towns, have been demolished as part of clearance schemes to improve central areas and their traffic flows. Yet at least four hundred old mills have been reoccupied, wholly or partly, by new enterprises which now provide a total of rather more than 120,000 jobs. Indeed, at least two-thirds of the jobs lost in cotton since 1953 have been replaced by the reoccupation of textile factories. In general, single-storey weaving sheds have proved more adaptable than multi-storey spinning mills. Many of the latter in fact offer such large areas of floor space, but with restricted clearances, that there are few potential tenants who can use a whole mill; some, therefore, have been turned into flatted factories to accommodate many small firms. In this they play a most important role as industrial nurseries, sheltering the immature firm with a low rent until it can look for better premises elsewhere.

It is impossible to generalize about the types of industry that have come into old mills. Almost every order in the standard industrial classification is represented, although engineering in a wide variety of forms, clothing, plastics and plastic foam, surgical dressings, food and tobacco products and paper manufacture are among the most important. Many of the new firms are not manufacturers at all, but rather wholesalers or distributors; mail-order houses, for example, are common users of converted mills. In general, this type of accommodation has proved most adaptable to labour-intensive enterprises without the need for complex and heavy plant. This is fortunate in that the ratio of operatives to site area almost rivals that in many textile mills, and is indeed often higher than in a modern mill with automated machinery. The advantages of a converted mill are two-fold. First, space in them can be bought or rented at an exceedingly low cost, so that they probably represent the cheapest industrial floor space in the country. Second, they avoid the need to secure an industrial development certificate and so they provide a considerable loophole in industrial guidance policies. For both these reasons, the converted mill has permitted the textile region to compete on more equal terms with the development areas and the attractive package of financial incentives that is available there, and it has been quite vital to the economic progress of many mill towns. This is, however, industrial diversification on the cheap. It may bring a sort of first-aid relief to alleviate the sufferings of the stagnant textile economy, but it is clearly no long term solution. Even the vital nursery role of the converted mill is to some degree frustrated by the application of the location of industry legislation. Cases have occurred in which a small firm has successfully come to be established in an old cotton mill, and subsequently expanded until the mill could no longer contain it; but, when its management has applied to rebuild their premises in or near to the town in which they mean so much, thus committing themselves more firmly to their present location, the necessary industrial development certificate has been refused. Instead they have been invited to move to a Development Area. It was to encourage both new firms in converted mills (and indeed all industrial enterprises in physically obsolescent accommodation) to modernize their factories, and so to commit themselves more firmly to the region by greater capital investment, that the Hunt Committee recommended that a system of rebuilding allowances should be introduced throughout the textile zone. In 1969 only a limited part of North East Lancashire was scheduled as an Intermediate Area. However, the 1972 decision to accept the advice of the Hunt Committee and to include all of the North West region (outside the Merseyside) in an enlarged Intermediate Area does at last afford the textile area some small measure of hope that twenty-five years of unhampered downhill drift night now be arrested.

7.4.3 *A Typology of Local Economies in the Textile Zone*

The recent industrial history of the textile zone has been nothing if not eventful. The dramatic decline of cotton manufacture, clothing and coalmining, the emergence of the general textiles industry, the progressive reconstruction of the engineering trades, the near-extinction of railway engineering, the quick rise and fall of the aircraft industry, and the medley of new trades in old mills, have all contributed to a set of revolutionary changes varying in pace and nature from town to town in a way that almost defies summary. The Industrial Revolution of the nineteenth century produced almost a 'standard' economy in eastern Lancastria, but the economic transformation of the middle twentieth century has converted this to a patchwork of local contrasts. Figure 26 attempts to resolve this patchwork into a system by suggesting a typology of local economies in the textile zone. At its simplest, this shows a series of stages in a progression from almost total specialization in textiles (in some areas supported in varying degrees by mining or other old established 'alternative' industries) to diverse economies, without undue specialization in any single manufacture or related group. This goes hand in hand with an alteration in the balance of the service and manufacturing sectors, although this is also clearly a function of settlement size. Thus, the cases at the top of the table are survivals of 'classical' economies of Victorian type, the cases at the botton are their diversified derivatives, and in-between are examples of intermediate stages in the process. The time-scale involved is relatively short. Only twenty years ago, even Preston and Stockport had employment profiles close to the present condition of Rochdale.

Across the top of the table are a number of variants of the classical economy of eastern Lancastria. Rochdale still has almost 40 per cent of its employment in the mills, engineering is a quite minor employer and the service sector is one of stunted development (despite the town's relatively high rank) even by eastern Lancashire standards. Nelson and Colne,

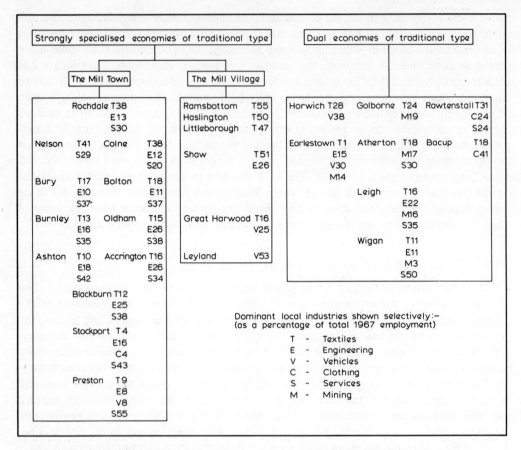

Figure 26 North West England: a typology of local economies in the textile sub-region.

neighbours and twins, are very close to Rochdale in their structure of employment. In the mill villages or small towns (such as Haslingden, Littleborough and Ramsbottom) half of all the work available is still in the mills; even this, however, shows a reduction from proportions as high as 70 per cent in the late nineteen forties. Traditional 'dual economies' existed widely, and still survive in little modified form. The most common was the mill-and-pit type, so widespread in the worked coal-field, and represented by Golborne. But even here, textiles and mining now supply less than half the jobs, while as recently as the nineteen fifties they jointly provided two-thirds of employment in some of the smaller towns and pit-villages of central Lancashire. Horwich is almost unique in its class as a railway town with a cotton industry; Earlestown is a less specialized parallel, with only a relic textile industry. Rawtenstall typifies the distinctive economy of Rossendale, in which textile mills and footwear factories (the latter an outgrowth of an early felt slipper trade) are codominant. Bacup shows a condition of change-by-decline from this, since both its textile and footwear industries have contracted, the former more sharply. Whether Bacup's greater specialization in a more slowly declining industry confers an advantage over Rawtenstall's more balanced dependence on two contracting manufactures is a moot point.

These, then, are the surviving variants of the Victorian economy. Most of them cluster spatially into the Rossendale upland and its flanks, the remote inner core of the North West region. From these as archetypes, a number of stages in the process of industrial reconstruction can be identified. Among the mill towns, Bolton and Bury exhibit a distinct change from the 'Rochdale' type of employment structure. Textiles remain the chief single source of work but their share of the total is only half what it is in Rochdale. Both have rather stunted engineering industries, but other trades (for example paper making) provide some breadth. Neither has the northwestern average proportion (52 per cent) of total employment in the service sector, though both are high-rank towns. With Burnley a critical break-point is reached in the succession of types, for here engineering employment exceeds textiles (and partly reflects its former Development Area status). Indeed the category in which Burnley is placed—with Oldham, Ashton and Accrington—is the norm for the mill town of the present time. Textile firms provide only between 10 per cent and 16 per cent of total employment, chiefly for women, while engineering absorbs about one-fifth to one-quarter of the labour force and almost half the men. There is some slight development of metal-working, chemicals and vehicle components but the share of service employment is regionally below average. Stockport and Preston represent the extreme of industrial diversity, at least as found in the textile zone, excluding Manchester. In both, textiles are something of a relic industry and neither depends on a single dominant replacement but rather on a broad spread of opportunity. In Preston, the county town, the service group employs over half the working population, a proportion only just below the national average. That diversity is a guarantee of growth is questionable in the light of Manchester's experience. There, the service sector provides 58 per cent of work, and five manufacturing industries employ between 3 per cent and 11 per cent each; yet, as has been noted, decline continues.

In the mill villages and smaller towns the process of industrial change takes a different form. These are too small, and of too low a rank as service centres, for this sector to make much contribution to replacement employment. There is as a result a distinct tendency for a single industry (sometimes even a single firm) to replace the once-dominant role of cotton manufacture. Shaw illustrates a common case—the strong growth of engineering in a small mill town. In Great Harwood, vehicle manufacture has replaced textiles as the chief employer. In Leyland, although the cotton industry was always rather feebly developed there, the vehicle group is entirely dominant.

None of these settlements has had, in the recent past, a mining industry of significant size. The chief variants in the economic profiles of the mill and pit communities are illustrated on the right-hand side of Figure 26. Atherton is a large enough settlement to have a significant development of the service trades, though it has attracted only a limited amount of replacement employment in the manufacturing sector. Leigh has left only remnants of its mining and cotton industries but a considerable range of new engineering and electrical employment, mostly in converted premises. Wigan represents perfect diversification, at least in so far as it is found in the coal-field. Mining is dead, textiles a minor (and largely female) employer, but food, paper, engineering and a service group of employments sustain a broad-based economy.

There is only an indistinct relationship between these contrasts in economic structure and either total employment or population trends. For example, Preston's total employment has fallen sharply, despite its diversity, while Wigan's has grown. However, where textiles still provide the bulk of work, the total number of jobs has declined consistently— by 16 per cent in Rossendale between 1951 and 1965, and by 12 per cent in Rochdale. Yet not all of such localities have suffered rapid population decline. Certainly Rossendale lost 7 per cent of its population between 1951 and 1966 (and, more seriously, about 14 per cent of its population of working age), but Rochdale's population was more stable; indeed it grew by 6 per cent from 1961 to 1971. Rather oddly, a group of towns in the middle of the order of diversity (Ashton, Bolton, Bury, Blackburn) suffered only slight losses in total employment, or even recorded modest gains, and they exhibited parallel population trends. There is at least a strong suspicion that they have achieved a degree of economic stability. Perhaps their present employment structures are a pointer to the future of what, until recently, could be called the textile town.

7.5 Dispersal Planning and Regional Strategy

Regional planning is a many-sided problem. In its simplest definition, it is the rational location of investment, in housing, industry and commerce, and in the infrastructure of communications and social equipment. Seen in these terms, the dispersal of 'surplus' population from the great cities and conurbations is the point of departure for the shaping of regional policies, for this is much the largest consumer of investment funds. At the prices of the last twenty years, it has cost a little below £4,000 to house each new town family, and a total investment in the range of £50 to £80 millions has 'bought' only a middle-sized new town. Since industrial investment largely follows the pattern of social investment, the strategy of regional development is, in practice, governed by the tactics of dispersal planning. Certainly, in the North West this contention is easily demonstrated. There is, as yet, no overriding strategy for future development. However, many tactical decisions concerning the dispersal of population have been made, and these collectively— in the absence of a broad policy—are in practice the most powerful factors in shaping the region's growth.

The regional total of house sites needed for new town and major town development schemes (and so the total of investment funds in practice available to implement a regional planning strategy) largely depends upon calculations of housing demand likely to be generated by the two major conurbations set against the shortfall of sites within them. Liverpool and Manchester are bound to generate substantial overspill movements, but elsewhere in the region local land resources seem to be adequate to meet housing demand. No precise estimate of the total quantities of population overspill from the two conurbations are possible. Both entered the nineteen sixties with huge areas of congested slum housing. As late as 1961, gross population densities were still over 40 persons per hectare (100 persons per acre) in part of inner Liverpool; but both cities have made accelerating progress in clearing their worst slums, and little of the pre-bye-law housing now survives. The size of the population surplus each city is likely to generate during the next quarter of a century now depends partly on their rate of household formation. It also will rest upon the policies towards the massive districts of post-bye-law housing that still encircle the high density renewal areas now rising close to their central business districts. There are other imponderables, too. Will migration away from the Manchester and Liverpool city regions persist at the general levels of the last twenty-five years? In an increasingly affluent society, will 'voluntary migration' to suburban housing in the private sector reduce the relative importance of municipal housing in total housing activity? What proportion of the populations of the slum clearance areas can be rehoused in situ? (Salford, in particular, has much reduced its earliest estimates of overspill by building high density, high rise, schemes on the sites of former slums).

The now somewhat dated official estimates of housing need and population surplus in the two conurbations suggest that their total housing demand to 1981 cannot be less than 470,000 (all assumptions at minima) or more than 520,000 (all assumptions at maxima). By redevelopment, infilling and minor peripheral expansion, they may be able to accommodate a little over 420,000 new houses. The surplus of families who will be obliged to leave the conurbations or their near vicinity for homes elsewhere (including movement to dispersal schemes on which progress is already being made) is most likely to be between 106,000 and 190,000—but this will meet housing demand only to 1981. All of these values depend upon predictions concerning future rates of natural increase, geared to the vital statistics of the mid-nineteen sixties. A slight but persistent fall in the national birth-rate has already led to substantial downward revision in the Registrar General's estimates of future population growth. This, combined with other factors, has led authorities on Merseyside to question their previous assumptions about overspill needs and there has even been doubt expressed as to the necessity for a major central Lancashire new town project.

7.5.1 *Anti-planning and Overspill*, 1945–1961

In a timorous fashion, planning for some degree of dispersal began early in the nineteen fifties. It was entirely in the form of short range movements, chiefly of small bodies of population, and arranged by *ad hoc* agreements between the cities and some of their smaller neighbours. Perhaps a typical, but also the largest, scheme of the period was the 'export' of Liverpool families literally only two or three kilometres beyond the city boundary to Kirkby. Then a mere rural parish, Kirby has become an urban district of almost 50,000 people, a close-packed 'one class' community with a flourishing industrial estate developed from the nucleus of a war-time factory. It scarcely represents the planner's art in its highest form. Other pieces of peripheral enlargement to the conurbations were simultaneously in progress. Salford had begun the export of about 16,000 people to overspill estates clustered around the mining town of Walkden to the west; this was a scheme which, whatever its lack of visual amenity, at least took no good farmland and reclaimed a semiderelict landscape.

Manchester had by now exhausted the potential of its huge Wythenshawe complex of estates in the far south—a salient thrust deep into the countryside of north Cheshire, which quickly consumed a district of intensive market gardening—and was looking for alternative sites. Manchester's experience is typical of the frustration of the early post-war period. As early as 1946 the city attempted to secure a site for new town development. Mobberley, some 24 kilometres (15 miles) south of the city centre, and with a rail link to it, was its first choice. The quality of the first-class grassland that formed the site, and its supposed potential liability to brine-pumping subsidence, led to the abandonment of the project. The small town of Lymm, 27 kilometres (17 miles) to the southwest, was the subject of the next proposal. At a Ministry enquiry in 1958 the project failed, again largely because of the weight of agricultural opposition. In the interim, there had been desultory discussions concerning the possibility of overspill on a new town scale at Congleton, more than 32 kilometres (20 miles) to the south.

Sensing that expansion into Cheshire, its traditional direction of suburban growth, would continue to be checked by a combination of agricultural and political opposition, the city turned to Lancashire. In the early nineteen sixties it wooed the little mining town of Westhoughton. This had already been abandoned by the mining industry and little was left of its textile manufacture; indeed no weaker existing economic base for a large planned growth of population could have been found anywhere in Britain. But at least the site was of almost no agricultural value, and much was semi-derelict. Although at one time it seemed probable that a development project on a new town scale would begin here, the proposals failed largely through local political opposition. Meanwhile a site at Risley, a little east of Warrington, had been examined; part consisted of derelict war-time installations and part of reclaimed peat under intensive arable farming. The first proposals here, like all the others, proved abortive but from the Risley scheme grew the concept of developing Warrington itself under new town precedures to take Manchester overspill. It may seem odd that proposals to create new towns deep in pastoral Cheshire should ultimately fructify with the designation of Warrington—a very old town indeed, and a large one of over 75,000 inhabitants—as a new town. But such has been the achievement of regional planning in the north west.

During its twenty-year-long search for a major reception site capable of development on new town principles, Manchester was forced to the expedient of short-range piece-meal population dispersal. It is almost literally true to say that it 'got rid of' surplus popu-lation, in consignments of a few hundred or a few thousand families, to any local authority in or near the conurbation that would take them. Some nine agreements were made with Cheshire suburban authorities (all on the southern fringe of the conurbation), five with Lancashire authorities (all of them small textile towns within the northern zone of the conurbation), and one with a Derbyshire authority, Glossop. In short, this was a process of infilling, and minor peripheral expansion of the conurbation. By 1959, some 37,000 people had been moved from the city to overspill estates; yet, of the 9,700 houses built for them, all but 400 were within the conurbation as officially defined. The major new project of the nineteen sixties—the Hattersley scheme to the east of Hyde—is another peripheral addition. It can, of course, be argued that the very fact that the rest of the conurbation could house the Manchester population surplus is the best demonstration possible that no long-range movement to a new town was necessary. Certainly the absorption of (mostly young) Manchester families into the ageing communities of a number of textile towns has helped to repair the demographic damage of out-migration to their population structures. However, this can also be interpreted as the pouring of water into leaking vessels.

Dispersal planning for Merseyside has pursued a far more orderly course, after the emergency rehousing operation of the mushroom growth of Kirkby. While Manchester's overspill has gone either to suburbs without industry or textile towns with declining economies. Liverpool's overspill has gone to major industrial growth points, though chiefly at the edge of the conurbation rather than beyond. For example, overspill develop-ment at Halewood accompanied the growth of the Ford enterprise there; the transfer of several thousands of Liverpool families to Ellesmere Port helped to provide a local labour force for the Vauxhall factories. Such a planned transfer of population to conurbation-margin sites was inevitable given the strong tendency for the dispersal of employment on Merseyside—though any expansion of industry or population at the margins of the urban mass almost inevitably meant the loss of farmland of high quality. It was on Mersey-side that the first stage of population dispersal in the North West—piecemeal, short-range overspill—came to an end; this was with the designation of Skelmersdale and Runcorn, in 1961 and 1964 respectively, as new towns.

7.5.2 *Towards a Regional Strategy*

In the shaping of a regional strategy to guide growth into the twenty-first century, three alternative principles at once suggest themselves, and all have received serious consideration in the current debate about the region's future. In brief, the main mass of population growth might be accommodated by the further expansion of the two major conurbations, by development athwart the east-west axis between the two conurbations (along the line of the Ship Canal and the planned Manchester-Merseyside motorways), or by the selection of growth-nodes along the north-south axis of the M6 between Lancaster and Crewe. These alternatives are clearly not mutually exclusive. The present pattern of change contains a little of all three, and the debate about their relative merits is essentially a discussion of emphasis.

For twenty years after 1945 it was accepted almost as dogma that the major conurbations were already too large and that their outward growth must be restrained. This view was held to be as self-evidently true of the conurbations of feeble growth, for example Manchester, as it was of London itself. This gigantic assumption, and the green belt policy that gives it physical form and legal force, has since been challenged. Certainly a *prima facie* case exists—on the physical grounds of land use and land availability—for the Manchester conurbation to contain much more of its projected population increase than is at present envisaged. It is, especially in the north and east, an open-textured conurbation of cellular structure. At its margin, 13 to 16 kilometres (8 to 10 miles) from the city, is the outer girdle of the cotton-spinning towns, cities in their own right by size and urban rank, and joined to each other and to the core by long-established ribbons of development along the main roads. Between these ribbons are large semirural interstices of low farming value. Already these open enclaves have absorbed some tens of thousands of families both by planned intraconurbation rehousing (especially at Middleton, Heywood, Worsley and Hyde), and by the usual processes of speculative housing development. Their capacity is by no means exhausted. There are other cogent arguments for encouraging the conurbation to 'solidify' and expand peripherally in this way. All the major towns of the outer girdle have attracted considerable investment in central area redevelopment, and they are much better equipped than a decade ago to meet the service needs of new populations brought into their hinterlands. The M62 motorway, presently under construction, traverses these half-developed areas, and ought to stimulate the quicker reconstruction of the declining economic base of the spinning towns.

There are, of course, counter-arguments to the thesis that a combination of infilling are limited peripheral growth could largely solve the problem of population surplus in the Manchester region. Expansion to the north and east would quickly meet the physical barrier (expressed in slope rather than altitude) of the Pennine flanks. Advance to the south would meet the equally difficult problem of high-grade farmland in the north Cheshire arable-dairy zone. There is little open land left here that is not earmarked for green belt. On the other hand the conurbation has an open flank, to the west and northwest, against the abandoned coal-field. There, the major physical problem limiting expansion is the extent of derelict land and it is clearly capable of solution (at a cost). The most powerful argument against the proposal that the conurbation should retain all or most of its population growth is the economic one—the area's general industrial weakness, and the overall decline in employment. Even if population growth were to be contained physically, it might not be capable of being supported in the economic sense. Even with southeast Lancashire now scheduled as an Intermediate Area, hope of quick industrial progress through the offer of direct incentives must be tempered with the knowledge that employment in manufacturing industry is growing slowly throughout the whole country, and that the Development Areas still can offer more substantial inducements to footloose enterprises. The report of another government committee has an obvious relevance for the future of overspill policy in southeast Lancashire. If a metropolitan administration takes control of the city region (as both the Maud Committee and the 1971 White Paper proposed, in different forms), replacing the present fragmented structure in which 52 authorities govern the conurbation alone, it would be surprising if the need for population transfer to sites outside the new boundaries were not re-examined and possibly modified. The reconstruction of local government is now in progress.

The Merseyside conurbation, far more strongly mono-focal than Manchester, has a different framework of urban growth. On the Lancashire shore, development around the core is compact and continuous, without any open enclaves which could be used for expansion. Beyond, however, well-developed salients reach out some distance, their tips defining the urban region. Suburban settlement follows the electric railways discontinuously to Southport along the coast, and to Ormskirk inland and to the north. A continuous ribbon of urban uses joins Liverpool to St. Helens, while to the southeast the Speke-Halewood expansion with its massive industrial development now virtually joins Liverpool to Widnes. On the Cheshire shore, a similar ribbon of estuarine settlement extends continuously to Ellesmere Port. Why not allow these salients to solidify, to grow, to thicken and perhaps even in part to coalesce, and so to contain the bulk of Merseyside's population increase? Green wedges—in fact mostly deep brown wedges of mossland agriculture—could remain between them, so preserving the richest farmland. Indeed, Merseyside lends itself well to such a 'stellar' model of urban development. It can be argued that such a form of urban growth would maximize the advantages of its estuarine location and port facilities. There is still some open land on both sides of the Mersey estuary with a potential for industrial development, notably the Frodsham marshes with a frontage along the Manchester Ship Canal.

The crucial policy decisions for the Mersey estuary have in fact already been taken piecemeal. Runcorn has been scheduled as a new town, to grow from its present population of 31,000 to 90,000 by migration from Merseyside. With limited dock facilities along the Ship Canal, and with hope of an early connection to the M6 via the north Cheshire motorway, it ought to be able to secure the new industry it needs to reduce its almost total dependence on the salt and chemical group. Its first major industrial acquisition, however, is likely to be a new Imperial Chemical Industries plant on marshland beside the Ship Canal. Across the narrows of the estuary, joined by a new high-level bridge, Widnes is also planning to grow quickly under the Town Development Act. It, too, desperately needs non-chemical employment to diversify its economic base and provide female work. In effect these decisions mean that the estuary will be almost continuously enveloped in urban-industrial development, virtually to Warrington. But estuarine development from a Liverpool core can be seen in a much broader context. The recently completed second Mersey tunnel, an improvement to trans-Wirral road links, and a

Dee Barrage across sand-spreads that are rapidly reclaiming themselves by salt-marsh colonization, would bring the whole of the Welsh shore of the Dee estuary, and the resorts beyond, much more firmly into contact with Merseyside.

Despite its lack of port facilities the Dee has attracted considerable industrial growth. A discontinuous 13 kilometres (8 miles) ribbon of industry extends along reclaimed land from Chester to Shotton and more brokenly to Flint. Aircraft, steel, man-made fibres and engineering are among its chief activities (see p. 283). In short, a Dee barrage would open up the North Wales coast as far west as Rhyl to Merseyside suburban expansion. It might also promote industrial growth on reclaimed land to match the estuarine developments along the Mersey, and the environs of Flint have in fact been suggested as a potential new town site. The potential of coastal North East Wales for substantial urban-industrial development in the long term has been investigated in two consultancy studies (Ministry of Housing and Local Government, 1967 and 1970). The first of these identified no serious technical problems in the engineering aspects of a new Dee crossing to the neighbourhood of Flint, associated with a considerable acreage of land reclamation. The second study proposed a population build-up to about 280,000 by the year 2000 in the triangle between Holywell, Mold and Queensferry. But this is yet another project that would look to Merseyside for its population intake, and the recent scaling down of Liverpool's overspill needs (and Merseyside's likely rate of population growth) already imperils other schemes elsewhere to which investment has already been committed. Moreover the possible siting of a nuclear power station at Connah's Quay raises further problems. Certainly, there is at present no firm policy for the future of the Deeside area, although in 1972 (along with other parts of North Wales excluded from the Wales Development Area) it was offered Intermediate Area status.

The planning philosophy expressed in the view 'let the conurbations grow' has its attractions. It recognizes present 'natural' trends, though it would shape them more rationally. It perhaps makes sounder economic sense on Merseyside than Manchester. However, in effect, the guided peripheral expansion of the conurbations would quickly lead to the second general principle for which a planning strategy could be developed. This is the deliberate merging of the Manchester and Liverpool city regions into a single continuous city system, of at least five millions in its developed form, reaching from the Pennines to the Wirral coast. This model of regional development has an almost mystical appeal to some of its proponents. Here, it has been argued, is the only prospect for the creation of an urban unit large enough almost to rival London. Here is that northern equipoise to the overweening growth of the metropolis that, alone, can restore some balance of urban and economic power in Britain. This is plainly a false prophesy. The two dominant cities would clearly continue their independent existence, and their regional rivalry. No new central and dominant focus within the entire urban mass could replace them, and so develop service and social facilities appropriate to the total population of the entire city system, except in the distant future. Thus no real challenge to London's hegemony could develop. Yet it is significant that already a project has been mooted, and reported on at some length, for a new 'out-of-town' regional shopping centre at the junction of the M6 and the East Lancashire road (Kantorowich, 1964). Had this Haydock Park scheme succeeded as a planning application, this could have created a retail complex of departmental and specialist shops able to rival and compete against both the established central business districts in Liverpool and Manchester; in addition, it would have been far more accessible than either to the car-owning families in an ultimate hinterland of almost seven million people extending from Lancaster to Stoke.

The basis of any 'east-west' development strategy in the region lies in the excellence of communications between Manchester and Liverpool. The Ship Canal, an ocean waterway, and potentially a linear port, the improved east Lancashire road, a direct trunk route of the nineteen thirties, the proposed South Lancashire and North Cheshire motorways, and three main railway lines with high-density services, all provide for an enormous mass movement of people and commodities along this axis. Two airports, Speke and Ringway, in addition afford the zone easy European and inter-continental contact; the latter is the leading international airport outside the London region. Moreover, the Manchester-Merseyside axis is already largely committed to an urban future. Discontinuous urban growth, accompanied by considerable industrial development, now links southwest Manchester with Warrington. The latter is already a town of almost 130,000 population, including its suburban extensions both in Lancashire and Cheshire; designated a new town, it will take at least 13,000 families from southeast Lancashire, chiefly on open areas to the east and bordering the peatland of Risley moss. Warrington's growth towards the 200,000 mark is thus already accepted. In every sense—in terms of physical urbanization, social affiliation and industrial linkages—Warrington is the bond between southeast and southwest Lancashire. In terms of journey time, it is much closer to Liverpool, but in social linkages it will become more closely bound to Manchester as overspill develops. Its soap-detergent-chemical group of industries are part of the chemical complex of the mid-Mersey region, and so look westwards; metal working and engineering have closer links eastwards, at one time particularly with the small (formerly integrated) Irlam Steel plant on the Ship Canal 11 kilometres (seven miles) away.

Warrington stands close to the place at which the M6 crosses the Ship Canal, one of the few points of contact between the national motorway system and salt water. One suspects that the former is likely to be much the greater industrial stimulus. The Ship Canal has had a diminishing impact on industrial location, after its early success. The growth of the great Trafford Park industrial estate (at its peak employing over 50,000 workers but now scarcely 30,000) near the terminal docks began at the turn of the century, and was virtually complete by 1950. The 0.6 million ton Irlam steel works, using the canal for ore transport, was a development of the early nineteen thirties; though subsequently modernized, a decision has been taken by the British Steel Corporation within the context of their corporate plan to close the plant except for a small finishing facility. The growth of oil refining and petrochemicals at Stanlow and Carrington reflected the increasing importance of the canal as an oil port in the nineteen fifties; in this case, however, continuing expansion is assured. But in the last decade, it is clear that the impetus of canal-side industrial growth has slackened. New enterprises have grown alongside it, to be sure, but many (like the Vauxhall factory at Ellesmere Port) are neighbours for reasons other than any direct transport relationship. Moreover, though there is apparently a lot of space still undeveloped beside the waterway, not all of it is likely to be available for urban and industrial use. There is a dredging problem that makes necessary the retention of land for spoil discharge. And much canal-side land (Chat and Carrington mosses, and the flood plain alluvium at Lymm, for example) is first-class quality farmland. The east-west motorways, too, will cross dairy and arable areas of high productivity. In short there are powerful constraints upon the implementation of an east-west strategy pinned to the Ship Canal and adjacent motorways and, unless present green belt policy is much modified, Manchester and Warrington will remain separated by a broad gap in urban development (see Figure 25).

The third possible alternative in shaping the region's future—the alignment of growth-nodes along the north-south corridor of movement traversed by the M6—is currently the most fashionable, and part of the declared policy of the Regional Economic Planning Council. The latter's endorsement does not necessarily follow entirely from the strategy's technical merits; it is also politically highly acceptable in so far as it pleases the maximum number of the local interests. The line followed by the M6, fixed by the uplands on the east and the heads of the estuaries on the west, is an old corridor of movement; indeed the parallel trunk road is in part of Roman origin. Across Lancashire, the M6 and the railway to Glasgow (shortly to be electrified) are rarely more than two or three kilometres apart. Long before any attempt at coherent regional planning began, this zone had attracted interest as a location for urban investment. About ten new town and major town expansion projects (active, proposed or abortive) are threaded along it like beads on a string. Two major developments within about 8 kilometres (5 miles) of the motorway have actually been started (at Skelmersdale and Winsford), two others (at Warrington and in the Preston-Leyland-Chorley area) have been agreed in principle, while another two (in the Crewe and Lancaster areas) have been proposed as long-term possibilities by the regional council.

The new town under construction near the old mining village of Skelmersdale, 24 kilometres (15 miles) northeast of Liverpool is to absorb at least 14,000 Merseyside families, chiefly on land of low fertility left half derelict by a long-dead mining industry, and has a population target of 80,000, Winsford, 45 kilometres (almost 30 miles) southeast of Liverpool, is planned to grow under the procedures of the Town Development Act, but virtually on a new town scale, from 12,000 to at least 60,000—though its future is threatened by Liverpool's reappraisal of overspill needs. This was, in the early nineteen sixties, a salt town with an almost moribund economy, largely dependent on the employment offered by the Northwich chemical complex. Almost every possible factor favours the industrial expansion of both towns. They can offer an ample and quickly-growing labour supply, excellent communications southwards and (since they are linked by overspill agreements with a Development Area) major investment incentives too. Both have already attracted a broad range of firms, some from Manchester and Merseyside, but most from outside the region and so a net gain to the North West. Skelmersdale, especially, has been outstandingly attractive to industry. By mid-1968, it had 240 thousand square metres (2½ million square feet) of factory space built or under construction, and almost 4,000 jobs in an indescribably diverse range of manufactures; but some of the industrial acquisitions of both towns underline the artificialities inherent in Development Area policy. Skelmersdale is the site of one of Courtaulds' new and technically advanced weaving factories, to employ 900 operatives; it is thus located at the nearest point to the textile zone (and to experienced labour) at which Development Area incentives are available. Winsford was chosen for the location of a large new factory (since affected by merger and rationalization) of the English Electric Computer Division; once again, this was at the nearest point to the parent plant at Kidsgrove, North Staffordshire, at which the Development Area incentives 'package' was available. Even a cursory examination of the origins of firms that have come, or are likely to come, to the three major Liverpool dispersal sites at Runcorn, Skelmersdale and Winsford suggests that there has been a distinct movement to them of firms, attracted by the offer of incentives, from areas further east. In short, these projects are attracting mobile industry on terms that dispersal sites in the Manchester city region cannot match.

There are two further growth points on the M6 that are to take overspill population chiefly from southeast Lancashire, though both are still at the preparatory stage. One of these, the expansion of Warrington, has been discussed above; the other is the proposed central Lancashire new town. In fact, the latter is a project of new city scale, designed to receive a population of about 150,000, and so to create an urban unit, based on Preston, with a total population of about half a million. This is a development that has been debated for almost 20 years. The immense commercial success of Leyland motors created a complex of factories in the Leyland-Chorley area with a labour demand that far outstrips local resources. As early as 1951, it was suggested that this area could absorb a substantial overspill from southeast Lancashire. With the completion of the M6 and the belief (since questioned) that inadequate provision had been made to accommodate the regional growth of population, what had been seen as a modest overspill scheme became a new city project. No longer was it confined to Leyland-Chorley; instead it was recentred upon Preston, with a possible spur reaching up the Ribble valley. This is, however, an area of quite serious economic weakness. Apart from the troubles of its textile industry, it has seen the contraction of what was once its chief growth sector, the aircraft industry, through the cancellation of military contracts upon which it largely depended. Certainly the Leyland Company has had continued success. Perhaps it has had too much success, from the area's point of view. By absorbing the greater part of the British heavy vehicle industry, and then assuming the leadership of that conglomerate of firms that incorporates what remains of the British-owned car industry, 'Leylands' have become a national and international rather than a regional enterprise and there is no longer any guarantee that its expansion will be chiefly within Lancashire. Indeed for its most recent project, the firm has turned to the Development Areas, and specifically to West Cumberland.

In brief, the central Lancashire new town cannot look to any certain expansion of its own economic base to provide for its growth of employment. Moreover, even with its recently acquired (1972) Intermediate Area status, the town may find itself in unequal competition with Liverpool-linked rivals for mobile industry. Despite having its own limited but specialist harbour facilities at Preston, the new city is farther than its potential rivals from a major port. On the other hand, there is the long-term possibility of estuarine reclamation on the Ribble, which might create attractive new areas both for industry and for coastal residential growth and recreational development. Indeed one of the strengths of the Preston site, in an age of increasing leisure, is its access to superb recreational resources. The fine moorland mass of the Bowland Fells rises as a magnificent backcloth to the northeast, the site of one of the first of the country parks to be established under the 1968 Countryside Act. The southern border of the Lake District is scarcely 30 minutes drive along the M6, and access into the heart of this tourist region will be much improved by the new road proposed to link the M6 with Grange via a crossing of the Kent estuary.

The two potential growth nodes on the M6, suggested by the regional council as worth detailed consideration for expansion later in the century, are in the Lancaster-Garstang and Crewe areas. On the grounds of access and centrality—for it occupies the centre of the Liverpool-Manchester-Birmingham triangle, and is only an hour away from all three—the latter has clear advantages. On the other hand, there are constraints on growth. The farmlands to the southwest and west are dairying areas of high productivity, while the lower-quality land to the north and northeast has a salt-subsidence risk that will remain as long as uncontrolled brine-pumping is tolerated. Two tentative design studies have suggested ways to avoid these problems. Cheshire County has proposed a linear city on the Crewe-Winsford axis. And from the Potteries has come a suggestion for the development of a 'molecular' city to extend from Stoke to Nantwich; this would join North Staffordshire with the south Cheshire towns through a series of intervening developments, loosely integrated into what is essentially a dispersed city framework.

Has a regional strategy yet emerged? Clearly not. The population growth of the next decade will be shared between all three possible alternatives, although most of it will be contained within the conurbations or in extensions to their margins. Infilling between the two conurbations, through the growth of Warrington and the dispersal schemes at the head of the Mersey estuary, is also an obvious short-term trend. How quickly dispersal to the new town schemes strung along the M6 will progress (and how soon the growth sites in the far north and south will be required) depends on a number of imponderables. Will extraregional migration from the North West diminish or accelerate? What will be the effect of the development of major growth nodes elsewhere in the country, or of possible future changes in location of industry policy? Will the slight but persistent fall (nationally and regionally) in the birth-rate continue? How will the North West—England's remotest province from continental Europe—react to a British entry into the Common Market? These become the major uncertainties in the region's future, rather than the possible fate of its older industries. In 1971, the Secretary of State for the Environment set up a North West planning strategy study group to examine these factors and to produce an outline plan to guide the region's future growth.

References :

Board of Trade (1969). *The Movement of Manufacturing Industry in the United Kingdom : Study of Movement Affecting the North West Region,* B.O.T. Regional Office, Manchester.
Carter, C. F. (Ed.) (1962). *Manchester and its Region,* British Association and Manchester University Press, Manchester.
Department of Economic Affairs (1965). *The North West : a Regional Study,* H.M.S.O., London.
Department of Economic Affairs (1965). *Problems of Merseyside,* H.M.S.O., London.
Freeman, T. W., Rodgers, H. B. and Kinvig, R. H. (1966). *Lancashire, Cheshire and the Isle of Man,* Nelson, Edinburgh.
Kantorowich, R. H. and others (1964). *Regional Shopping Centres in North West England,* University of Manchester Department of Town and Country Planning, Manchester.
Lancashire and Merseyside Industrial Development Association (1950a). *The Spinning Area,* L.A.M.I.D.A., Manchester.
Lancashire and Merseyside Industrial Development Association (1950b). *The Coal-Chemical Area,* L.A.M.I.D.A., Manchester.
Lancashire and Merseyside Industrial Development Association (1967a). *Decline of Cotton and Coal Mining Industries of Lancashire,* L.A.M.I.D.A., Manchester.
Lancashire and Merseyside Industrial Development Association (1967b). *Closure and Reoccupation of Cotton Mills,* L.A.M.I.D.A., Manchester.
Law, C. M. (1970). Employment Growth and Regional Policy in North West England, *Regional Studies,* **4,** 359–366.
Lawton, R. and Cunningham, C. M. (Eds.) (1970). *Merseyside : Social and Economic Studies,* Longman, London.
Lloyd, P. E. (1964). Industrial Changes in the Merseyside Development Area, 1949–1959. *Town Planning Review,* **35,** 285–299.
Miles, C. (1968). *Lancashire Textiles; A Case Study of Industrial Change,* Cambridge University Press, Cambridge.
Ministry of Housing and Local Government (1966). *Expansion of Warrington,* H.M.S.O., London.
Ministry of Housing and Local Government (1967a). *Central Lancashire—Study for a City,* H.M.S.O., London.
Ministry of Housing and Local Government (1967b). *Expansion of Winsford,* H.M.S.O., London.
Ministry of Housing and Local Government (1967c). *Dee Crossing Study, Part* 1, H.M.S.O., London.
Ministry of Housing and Local Government (1968). *Central Lancashire New Town Proposal : Impact on North East Lancashire,* H.M.S.O., London.
Ministry of Housing and Local Government (1970). *Dee Crossing Study, Part* 2, H.M.S.O., London.
Robson, R. (1957). *The Cotton Industry in Britain,* Macmillan, London.
Rodgers, H. B. (1962). The Changing Geography of the Lancashire Cotton Industry, *Economic Geography,* **38,** 299–314.
Rodgers, H. B. (1964a). Recent Industrial Changes in North West England and their Social Consequences. *Problems in Applied Geography II,* Polish Scientific Publishers, 211–228.
Rodgers, H. B. (1964b). *Overspill in Winsford,* Winsford U.D.C.

Salt, J. (1967). The Impact of the Ford and Vauxhall Plants on the Employment Situation of Merseyside, 1962–1965. *Tijdschrift voor Economische en Sociale Geografie*, **58,** 255–264.

Secretary of State for Economic Affairs (1969). *The Intermediate Areas* (Chairman : Sir Joseph Hunt), (Cmnd.3998), H.M.S.O., London.

Smith, D. M. (1968). Identifying the "Grey" Areas : A Multivariate Approach, *Regional Studies,* **2,** 183–193.

Smith, D. M. (1969). *Industrial Britain : The North West,* David and Charles, Newton Abbot.

Smith, W. (Ed.) (1953). *A Scientific Survey of Merseyside,* British Association and University of Liverpool Press, Liverpool.

Wallwork, K. L. (1956). Subsidence in the mid-Cheshire industrial area. *Geographical Journal,* **122,** 40–53.

Wallwork, K. L. (1962). The cotton industry of North West England, 1941–1961, *Geography,* **48,** 241–255.

CHAPTER 8

Yorkshire and Humberside

KENNETH WARREN

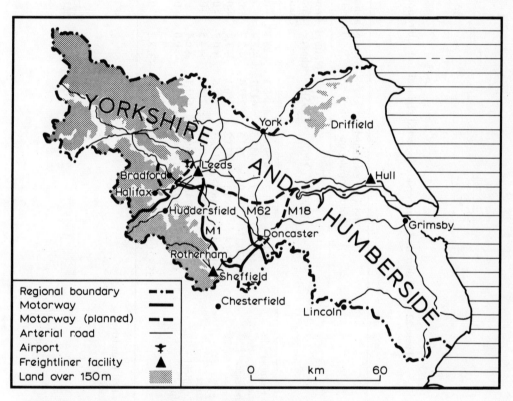

Figure 27 Yorkshire and Humberside: location map.

Table 22. Yorkshire and Humberside : selected regional and sub-regional indicators

	Mid-year estimated home population				Average annual change 1961–1966			Average annual change 1951–1961		
	1971[1]	1966[2]	1961[2]	1951[2]	Natural change	Armed forces change	Net migration	Natural change	Armed forces change	Net migration
Yorkshire and Humberside	4,793.6	4,731.2	4,595.9	4,488.3	+28.1	+0.1	−1.0	+19.5	+2.3	−9.6
North Humberside	466.9	471.7	457.5	442.7	+3.4	+0.1	−0.7	+2.9	+0.2	−1.6
South Humberside	320.1	305.0	287.5	262.4	+2.7	+0.1	+0.7	+1.9	+0.1	+0.5
Mid Yorkshire	409.4	396.1	373.2	366.1	+1.4	−0.3	+3.4	+0.9	−0.3	+0.1
South Lindsey	150.4	146.4	142.3	141.6	+0.7	−0.4	+0.4	+0.6	−0.1	−0.5
South Yorkshire	746.4	720.9	714.9	713.7	+4.5	−0.2	−3.3	+3.0	+0.5	−2.0
Yorkshire Coalfield	778.7	774.0	736.0	693.1	+6.4	—	+1.2	+5.6	+0.6	−1.8
West Yorkshire	1,921.7	1,917.2	1,884.5	1,868.8	+9.0	+0.4	−2.8	+4.6	+1.3	−4.3
BRITAIN	53,821.4	53,176.1	51,380.0	48,917.5	+328.2	−0.5	+22.6	+231.4	−12.9	+1.9

1. 1971 Census; 1971 boundaries.
2. 1966 boundaries.

B. Employment :

	Employment		Male Employment		Proportion of women at work		Unemployment range		
	1966	Change 1961–1966	1966	Change 1961–1966	1966	Change in % 1961–1966	1968	1967	1961–
	'000s	%	'000s	%	%	%	%	%	%
Yorkshire and Humberside	2,110	+3	1,360	+2	40	+1	2–3	1–2	1–2
North Humberside	200	+9	130	+5	39	+4	3–4	2–3	1–2
South Humberside	130	+6	90	+4	34	+2	2–3	2–3	1–2
Mid Yorkshire	150	+7	90	+5	37	+2	2–3	1–2	1–2
South Lindsey	40	+2	20	−3	25	+2	3–4	3–4	2–3
South Yorkshire	370	+3	240	NIL	44	+4	2–3	1–2	1–2
Yorkshire Coalfield	310	+4	220	NIL	31	+3	3–4	2–3	1–2
West Yorkshire	910	NIL	560	+1	44	−1	1–2	1–2	0–1
BRITAIN	23,550	+4	14,900	+2	40	+2	2–3	2–3	1–2

C. Industrial Development Certificates :

	Estimated additional employment from i.d.c. approvals			
	Total 1956–1967 '00s	Annual averages		
		1964–1967 '000s	1960–1963 '000s	1956–1959 '000s
Yorkshire and Humberside	82.6	8.4	6.3	5.8
North Humberside	7.9	0.8	0.6	0.6
South Humberside	11.3	1.2	1.1	0.5
Mid Yorkshire	4.6	0.5	0.4	0.2
South Lindsey	3.0	0.2	0.4	0.1
South Yorkshire	11.9	0.8	0.8	1.3
Yorkshire Coalfield	18.9	2.4	1.3	1.0
West Yorkshire	25.1	2.6	1.5	2.1
BRITAIN	1245.2	121.8	108.1	81.2

8.1 Introduction

. A product of forward-looking regional planning, the composite Yorkshire and Humberside region has gained recognition only within recent years. Forty years ago, the essays in regional geography edited by A.G. Ogilvie (1928) dealt separately with the Don Valley, the South Yorkshire coal-field, Holderness and the Humber, and the large and varied, so-called Yorkshire region which surrounded them to northeast and northwest. In 1962 a new collection of essays edited by J.B. Mitchell divided the area between four authors and chapters. The emphasis was on formal regions in both these cases. Yet even when a focus was placed on problems and planning, the connections between Humberside and the rest of Yorkshire have long been ignored. The West Riding and Humber ports were considered separately by M.P. Fogarty in 1945, and four years later K.C. Edwards included the Humber south bank within the East Midlands in *Studies in Regional Planning* (1949). Whilst the two-part regional title is to some extent merely a convenient grouping to prevent too great a national proliferation of regions, there is more substance in it than there could ever have been previously, for the traditional links between the West Riding and the Humber are being matched increasingly by newer ones.

Hull has long handled much of the import traffic for West Riding textile mills; Immingham and Goole are the traditional ports for the foreign coal sales of Yorkshire pits; and Scunthorpe from its beginnings as a metal centre 100 years ago has had close links with the Yorkshire coal-field and with Sheffield, both in its raw material and finished product flows, and in the steel industry's organizational structure. This is not to deny, of course, that historically Hull has also served the East and West Midlands, or that the steelworks of Scunthorpe throughout most of the twentieth century have been closely linked with South Wales firms as well.

In recent years, the eastwards shift of coal mining and the construction of big new coal-field generating complexes at Drax (4,000 MW) and Eggborough (2,000 MW) has begun to close the gap of rural land between West Yorkshire industry and the industrial/port complex on the Humber. The most decisive factors forging a new regional unity however are the post-1945 industrialization of South Humberside, the prospects of major new economic and population growth in the areas fringing the estuary, and the planned links between west and east Yorkshire with roads of motorway standard. In the pattern of economic growth within Yorkshire during the last quarter of the present century, the Humber estuary will undoubtedly be more important than in the past. In planning there will inevitably be tensions between those interests which desire to speed up the process of adaptation and those which, for a variety of reasons, seek to slow it down. While each of the major regional sub-divisions have their own pressing and peculiar problems, this is a basic theme of long term significance for the region. Essentially, as in many other areas of Britain, the dilemmas concern how much of the nineteenth century pattern of economic activity and population can or should be refurbished, and so preserved well into the middle half of the twenty-first century, and how much expertise and investment should, conversely, be given to new foci of economic growth.

The boundaries of the Yorkshire and Humberside Economic Planning Region are inevitably unsatisfactory in detail (see Figure 27). Too close an adherence to county boundaries is (here, as elsewhere) a common source of difficulty. To the west, the boundaries are generally unexceptional. It is no indictment to point to the interdigitation of the wool and cotton industries along the Yorkshire-Lancashire border, for no workable boundary could have disentangled them. The emphasis on cotton and the problems of Todmorden, its closer proximity to both Burnley and Rochdale than to Halifax and its likely future as a commuter town for the southeast Lancashire conurbation, is just one example. Saddleworth Urban District is growing more rapidly than its Yorkshire neighbours because it already is a residential growth point for Lancashire, with Oldham its nearest service centre (Y and H Economic Planning Council and Board, 1969, p. 4). The converse of this situation is found on the edge of South Yorkshire, where Sheffield overspill is flowing across into Derbyshire; indeed, in April 1967, parts of Derbyshire were transferred to the County Borough. Further east, no wholly satisfactory line can be drawn through the coal-field which is shared with the East Midlands region; this situation was recognized in the spring of 1969 when the Worksop Employment Exchange Area in the East Midlands was grouped with several Yorkshire exchanges and given Intermediate Area status. Further east again, the city of Lincoln, whose influence dominates much of South Lindsey, lies outside the Yorkshire and Humberside region; to the north, in contrast, the city of York with a population of 104,000 has a substantial urban field which extends well beyond the boundaries of the region. The Maud Commission on Local Government in England in 1969, giving primacy to administrative requirements rather than regional economic planning, suggested a reshaping at these points : South Lindsey, it argued, should be transferred to a Lincoln and Lincolnshire unitary area which for regional economic planning purposes should be part of the East Midlands; York, on the other hand, should be made the administrative centre for a wide rural hinterland which would include the southern part of the North Riding. In neither of these solutions, however, do prospective administrative changes appear to threaten the economic linkages within the Yorkshire and Humberside region, either those which already exist, or those which seem likely to develop. Since statistical sources deal with the sub-divisions of the established planning region, these are used in the discussion which follows.

Yorkshire and Humberside shares several general economic characteristics with the planning regions both to north and south but in its economic structure, its general level of prosperity, and its medium term prospects considerable contrasts are to be found with both. Like the East Midlands to the south it contains a relatively low-cost coal-field— although it has a larger labour force, 93,000 as compared with 72,000 in 1967. Its steel industry, centred on Scunthorpe and Sheffield, is half as big again as that of the North East even in tonnage terms, but the emphasis on quality steels in the Sheffield area renders the value of output in the Yorkshire and Humberside region several times greater. As in the East Midlands, textiles are a major economic interest but the emphasis is upon spinning, weaving, finishing and clothing manufacture as opposed to the hosiery and knitwear industries. The growth prospects of the East Midlands are clearly centred in the west near existing foci of population, or along the new highways; in the North East the favoured development zone is unquestionably coastal. Like the East Midlands, the existing concentrations of population in Yorkshire and Humberside and the new motor-ways are in the west, but, as in the Northern region, a considerable potential for future industrial and urban growth exists in the estuarine east. Although the Eastern Lowlands and West Durham political interests may protest, power both to the north and the south lies in the favoured area: in Yorkshire and Humberside there is an uneasy balance bet-ween the region's two principal component parts.

Overall, the Yorkshire and Humberside economic planning region shows all the signs of an Intermediate Area, as spelled out in detail in the Hunt Report (Secretary of State for Economic Affairs, 1969, pp. 55–66). The downward drift in the region's share of national population is long established, and the absolute decline has in fact been more than that of the Northern region (Table 23). Although there have been relatively low

Table 23. Yorkshire and Humberside, East Midlands and Northern Regions : percentage of national population, 1921–1981 (est.)

	Economic Planning Region		
	East Midlands	Yorkshire and Humberside	Northern
1921	5.7	9.5	7.1
1931	5.8	9.6	6.8
1951	5.7	9.2	6.4
1961	6.0	9.0	6.3
1965	6.2	8.9	6.2
1981*	6.5	8.7	6.1

*as estimated 1966.
Source : Economic Planning Councils.

levels of unemployment, out-migration from Yorkshire and Humberside has been con-siderable. The rates of economic growth and of increase in per capita income have been intermediate between those of the boom and the Development Areas of Britain, and there are severe environmental problems, notably a very large area of derelict land and much poor housing. Generalizations about such a large region are however dangerous. For economic planning purposes it has been divided into seven sub-divisions. Three of these—west of a line running north from Thorne, along the eastern limit of coal mining, skirting Leeds and reaching the high (and almost empty) northwest corner of Yorkshire—have 72 per cent of the region's population yet less than 39 per cent of its area. North and South Humberside, more than half as big in area, in 1965 had only 16.4 per cent of the region's population; and in agricultural Mid Yorkshire and South Lindsey the population densities are one eleventh and one twenty-seventh respectively of those in urbanized South Yorkshire. At one end of the urban-rural spectrum is the new urban highway system of Leeds and the glass and concrete melange of the reconstructed central area of Bradford; at the other end are the amazingly antiquated villages to be found in the northern Wolds of Lindsey.

8.2 The West Riding of Yorkshire

The West Riding dominates the whole planning region with 79 per cent of its population in 1965. Part of the east of the county is occupied by the good land and the mainly rural pursuits of the Vale of York; it is included in the Planning Council's Mid Yorkshire division, which includes the very different Wold country and the coast from Filey almost down to Hornsea. The most extensive division of the West Riding, anomalously included by the Planning Council with the West Yorkshire conurbation, is the high grit country to the north of Ilkley and Otley in mid-Wharfdale. This area is very sparsely populated with pastoral farming confined to the narrow valley bottoms. Yet the proximity of the conurbation is important in two ways: commuting by the more affluent presses into its southern margin, and the recreational needs of an increasingly mobile population in part are satisfied there at weekends. Some of its roads, for instance that across Blubberhouses Moor, in addition have important functions within the total pattern of east-west communications in northern England, although they are not adequate for the purpose.

Southwards is the west Yorkshire conurbation—now designated West Yorkshire—whose urban core lies within the irregular line joining Leeds, Keighley, Halifax, Huddersfield and Wakefield. Textiles and engineering are the principal supports for its 1.9 million people. Eastwards and southwards is the Yorkshire Coalfield sub-division; its chief urban foci are Barnsley and the newer growth point of Doncaster, and coal mining remains the dominant economic activity. South and west of a line from Penistone to Conisborough and Maltby is a third sub-division of the West Riding. It is much smaller in area than the coal-field and it has a smaller population; it nevertheless has a larger workforce. South Yorkshire is preoccupied with steel making and engineering, and one large centre—Sheffield—dominates the area, in contrast to the multiple foci of the other two densely populated regions. Leeds and Sheffield are only 45 kilometres (28 miles) apart, and Barnsley lies between, but each of these neighbouring though distinctive economic areas has its own (and serious) planning problems.

In *West Yorkshire* there is still an extraordinarily high dependence on textiles. Nationally, by 1965, only 3.3 per cent of workers were employed in textiles, but in the 'textile zone' of West Yorkshire this proportion was 20.4 per cent and in some parts the share was a good deal higher—as at Morley, Shipley and Keighley, where the proportion was between 31 and 35 per cent, and at Elland, where the figure was an unusual 54.1 per cent of the workforce. The woollens and worsteds industry made up over 80 per cent of the textile employment throughout most of the industrial region, but on the fringes (notably at Todmorden, Barnoldswick and Skipton) cotton was more important. Since 1953 some 200,000 jobs have been lost in Lancashire textile employment (see pp. 299ff); the decline in Yorkshire has been smaller yet it has still been substantial. In December 1960 there were almost 153,000 production workers in wool textiles; by the end of August 1968 the figure was just over 112,000 and by the end of 1970 only 94,000. This steady decline appears likely to continue. In a study of the national industry—some 73 per cent of whose workforce is in the West Riding—W.S. Atkins suggested to the Economic Development Committee (E.D.C.) for the Wool Textile Industry (1969) that employment ought to drop from 144,000 (in early 1969) to 121,000 by the mid nineteen seventies. However, no large displacement of workers will be necessary since natural wastage will account for most of the reduction. With female activity rates in the woollen textile zone relatively high, unemployment rates very low and unfilled vacancies usually at a high level, these traditional sub-regional economic indicators might be interpreted as signifying reasonably healthy conditions. However, by 1970/1971 unemployment rates were creeping up and the situation in the textile communities remains far from satisfactory.

Wage levels are relatively low, so that skilled workers have drifted away from the textile industry and frequently left the region. This is a feature related to the economic structure of a trade in which the firms are still small and mainly privately owned. By the mid nineteen sixties, the 20 largest public companies still operated only about one fifth of the 750 to 800 mills in Yorkshire. The average number of production workers employed per mill was well under 200. In addition the industry appears unable to make a return on its capital sufficient to finance desirable reorganization and reequipment. Modernization costs have been put at over £4,000 per worker in a new mill. With such a level of investment beyond the resources of most firms, operations have remained labour intensive, and with a relatively low value of output per worker. This low productivity naturally makes it difficult for the industry to pay wages competitive enough to retain many, especially the more skilled, in its labour force; in turn this makes the increased mechanization (which cannot be afforded) still more desirable. One development has been to employ increasing numbers of Commonwealth immigrant workers, who are prepared to work under relatively difficult conditions, and for low wages. In 1964 about 10 per cent of the workers in Bradford mills were Pakistani.

Although it is clearly not going ahead rapidly enough, the desired change from '... a craft-based, labour intensive industry to a scientific, technological, capital-based industry' (*Voice of Yorkshire and Humberside Industry*, January, 1969, p. 10), is underway. Between 1963 and 1968, several of the larger firms alone made an average annual expenditure on capital development of £15 million. Shift working, which is a necessary accompaniment to mechanization, increased by 50 per cent between 1954 and 1964, and there have been some outstanding cases of productivity increases following a switch from a 5½ to a 7 day working week and the installation of new high speed equipment and quality control.

The E.D.C. study of 1969 suggested the national need for a continuation of this policy, with the number of worsted spinning establishments being reduced from 140 to 90, and in weaving from 120 to 60, by the mid nineteen seventies. Indeed, already the number of mills is falling. In the primary sector, three topmakers and seven spinning firms went out of business in the first eight months of 1967, partly through the effects of rationalization but also as a result of the loss of export markets and the shortage of labour.

Labour shortages have been singularly important in the changing economic geography of the industry. They have restrained the growth of the clothing trade in its major centre, Leeds (where it employed 13.4 per cent of all workers in 1964). They have caused the textile industry to look beyond West Yorkshire to tap the underutilised female workforce on the coal-field. In the mid nineteen sixties, up to 6,000 women each day travelled from the mining communities to the mills of West Yorkshire, and busloads of workers were commuting as far west as the upper Calder. However, this movement appears to have reached its peak in 1961, and to have declined by about 200 persons each year since then. Branch factories have meanwhile been built on the coal-field in order to tap the available supplies of labour on the spot. Between 1959 and 1965, employment in textiles in general and clothing in particular on the coal-field rose by 50 per cent and 26 per cent respectively—although compared with West Yorkshire the industries remained quite small there. Meanwhile, a number of other textile and clothing firms have elected to move further afield and especially into the Development Areas, where labour supplies are easier and where government financial assistance has for some time been available to ease the costs of the transfer. Paton and Baldwin's early post-war movement to Darlington was an unusually important example, but there are many others: in clothing, for example, Hepworth's of Leeds employ almost 2,000 workers in Sunderland and Ashington. In times of difficulty the outlying factories have sometimes been victims, but in exceptional cases it has been the parent West Yorkshire plant which has been closed.

Engineering in West Yorkshire was originally closely linked with the textile trades. Later it became concerned additionally with railway equipment. In the twentieth century, it has widened greatly. The emphasis of activities within the sub-region, however, is on heavier lines for which demand has generally grown more slowly than for lighter products. As a result the post-1945 growth in engineering employment has been at only a little more than half the national rate. Within the sub-region there have been widely varying experiences in this and related trades. Since the mid nineteen fifties, for example, Bradford has lost its role as a car manufacturing centre as Jowetts felt the effects of remoteness from Midland components and from assured supplies of car bodies. In Leeds some of the industry on the south side is physically so crowded that it has been described as operating in an engineering ghetto sn higgledy-piggledy that it looks llke a parody on modern industry (Hodson, 1968). And in Huddersfield, textile engineering has declined, but there has been a counterbalancing growth in both electrical engineering and in the tractor production of the David Brown organisation.

Other new industries have also come into the West Yorkshire sub-region—but not on a scale to match the area's past industrial importance, or to compensate fully for the decline in the old staple trades, especially textiles. In certain respects it has fared much worse than other parts of the Yorkshire and Humberside region. In 1965, for example, the South Yorkshire and Coalfield sub-regions together had a workforce only 73.6 per cent that of West Yorkshire. However, the estimated additional employment from industrial development certificate permissions over the period 1956 to 1967 was 22.7 per cent greater (Secretary of State for Economic Affairs, 1969, p. 228)—much of this increase of course was merely keeping pace with the loss of job opportunities there, overwhelmingly in coal. So far, the West Yorkshire industrial area has offered few attractions for new industry with markets wider than the conurbation. The labour supply situation is tight, the internal transport facilities are overburdened and, until the mid nineteen sixties, motorway access to national markets was poor. Relatively cheap premises were available in the form of old textile mills, but such multi-storey buildings are not well suited to modern, flowline, production processes. Heavy floor supports break up their floor space and they have low ceilings and problems of lighting, ventilation and noise. Many on riverside or canal sites lack room for expansion. In addition the whole conurbation presents the would-be entrepreneur with a host of environmental deficiencies. As these are shared with the two other economic sub-regions in the West Riding, an examination of them is deferred until later.

Developing several decades after the West Yorkshire conurbation, the economy of the *Yorkshire Coalfield* has remained much more dependent upon primary industry. There was no preexisting textile industry to provide a market for engineering goods and there were no major iron ore resources in the coal measures to stimulate a metallurgical industry (and there was an increasing dependence by this time in all coal-field metallurgical centres on Jurassic or foreign ores). In any case, the large mines required by the deeper coal measures in the east around Pontefract—or, still more, in the concealed coal-field developed around and to the east of Doncaster in the twentieth century—provided ample employment for all the available male labour and excellent railway communications enabled their output to be delivered to distant markets. In 1959, the primary industries employed the extraordinarily high proportion of 40.5 per cent of the labour force in the sub-region. Mining, almost all of it for coal, had 117 thousand out of a total insured workforce of 301 thousand. However, between 1959 and 1965 this staple activity began to shrink and to displace labour even quicker, so that the number of men engaged in mining fell dramatically to 97,000. There was some compensating growth of female employment in the service and manufacturing sectors but, overall, there was only a 1.3 per cent increase in insured employees on the Coalfield, compared with 2.6 per cent in the West Riding, 4.3 per cent in Yorkshire and Humberside and 7.0 per cent nationally.

The South Yorkshire coal industry has a considerable output, relatively high productivity, and a largely local market in electricity generation (44 per cent) and in the coke ovens at Scunthorpe, in the Sheffield district and at Corby (21 per cent). In 1967–1968, some 28.4 million tons of an output of 40.5 million was delivered to consumers within Yorkshire. The pattern of profitability within the coal-field, however, varies widely. The so-called South Yorkshire area of the National Coal Board (N.C.B.) made the largest profit of any area within Britain in the year 1967–1968; the Doncaster area, in contrast, recorded a substantial loss. Some of the industry's old outlets now seem much less assured. By 1969, the Central Electricity Generating Board was moving strongly in favour of alternative primary fuels for firing its conventional stations, and of nuclear power. Desk studies have demonstrated, under certain assumptions, the lower cost of modern reactors for generating power on the coal-field itself. Even the Ministry of Power was initially hesitant to commit itself on whether a second installation at Drax (on the Ouse only 15 kilometres north of Thorne, the most easterly pit in the field) would be coal-fired. In the event a decision was made in favour of the coal industry, but only because existing investments could be shared with the new plant. Whether coal would have been preferred on a greenfield power station site is a very open question. Another eighth of the output of the Yorkshire field at present finds an outlet in the domestic and smokeless fuel markets; however, the present drive towards central heating, the competitive stance of oil, and the new supplies of natural gas all appear likely to erode its position there. In the year to March 1970 Yorkshire coal output fell to 36 million tons. Rationalization in order to lower costs is clearly essential but in the process more men are displaced. Concentration in bigger pits is going on— seven were closed in 1968–1969—and other mines are being reconstructed with impressive productivity increases. At Bentley colliery, northwest of Doncaster, the labourforce was cut from 2,300 to 1,300 between 1965 and early 1969, but weekly coal output went up from under 10,000 tons to 16,000 tons. Output per man-shift thus rose from 1.4 tons to nearly 2.8 tons and by spending as little as £0.2 million more the N.C.B. was expecting to raise it to 3.5 tons. Late in 1967, the Board employed 88,500 workers in Yorkshire. all but a small proportion of them in the Coalfield sub-region. Its own estimates, regarded by many as optimistic in the light of an increasingly competitive energy market in Britain, suggest that this work force will decline to 78,000 by 1971, to 42,000 by 1975 and to 18,500 by 1980.

In some communities as much as three-quarters of male jobs are in coalmining and, after low unemployment levels into the late nineteen fifties, rates are now high. In November, 1967, for instance, when the rate for Britain was 2.5 per cent, it was 3.4 per cent in the Coalfield sub-division. In its thirteen employment exchange areas, the rate varied from as little as 0.9 per cent (in Knottingley where a favourable combination of factors such as the opening of the new Kellingley colliery in 1965, the construction work on the Ferrybridge power station, and a new bypass and bridge on the A1 together boosted local employment opportunities) to 9.5 per cent in Thorne (the furthest community from alternative employment in the textile zone of West Yorkshire). Between 1971 and 1975, it has been estimated, up to 7,000 new jobs will be required each year to compensate for the inevitable decline in the mining industry's workforce; this compares with the need for only 1,500 jobs in the year 1968–1969. Commuting to the bigger neighbouring urban centres will obviously help but for the rest, the rationalization of the coal industry will mean either out-migration, intolerable levels of unemployment, or steering new jobs onto the coal-field. To ease the last solution, the West Riding County Council, in its submission to the Hunt Committee, suggested that the coal-field should be given full Development Area status, while the rest of the county should be granted Intermediate Area status. The Hunt Committee (p. 57) admitted that, outside of the Development Areas, they 'found no other problem which was comparable in scale, given the size and the speed of the rundown and the key position of the (coal) industry in the area'. They did not, however, recommend special action other than the Intermediate Area status suggested for the whole of the economic planning region. The government initially (in 1969) designated the coal-field as the only Intermediate Area in the West Riding, and offered it the benefits of building grants (as in the Development Areas), the construction of advance factories at public expense, and additional spending on roads and housing. With the new programme for industrial and regional development in 1972, however, the whole of Yorkshire and Humberside was given Intermediate Area status.

The most obvious attraction for new industry here is the large male workforce likely to become available as pits close, plus a good deal of so-far untapped female labour. Activity rates for women have traditionally been extremely low, 27.8 per cent in 1965, as compared with 39.7 per cent for the West Riding as a whole. The major disincentives are the drabness of the settlements and the unsightliness of a landscape dominated by huge pits and waste heaps; large areas have also been made unattractive by the steam and gases from coke ovens, and by extensive subsidence. Considerable net additions to the area of wasteland accrue each year as a result of mine closures, which leave pithead gear, railway sidings and general waste littering large areas of the sub-region. *The Review of Yorkshire and Humberside* (1966) suggested that there were about 2,5000 hectares (6½ thousand acres) of derelict land in the whole of the West Riding but the County's own planning department has suggested a figure over four times this level, most of it in the coal-field. Success in the levelling and developing the old pitheaps, and research's progress in the seeding of others to improve their amenity value, have been restrained in particular by the fact that, whereas in Development Area reclamation grants of 85 per cent have been available for some years, in the Yorkshire coal-field the assistance was only 50 per cent of project costs until 1969. Meanwhile, a very promising and well-advanced West Riding project to landscape the M62 corridor to improve the attractiveness of the county had to be cancelled when the Ministry of Housing and Local Government insisted that narrow economic criteria had to be applied to such a project, and that a relationship had to shown between the landscaping and reclamation on the one hand and jobs created on the other—in the narrow sense of so many jobs in a new factory on the site.

Yet the importance of central government assistance in these matters is clear. It can be illustrated by the problems associated with the proposed development of a 312 hectare (770 acres) site for industry at Whitwood, in an area of the Aire valley terribly afflicted by dereliction, as the traveller on the A1 may see as he looks down from the Magnesian Limestone escarpment just north of Ferrybridge. The purchase and reclamation costs were estimated to be £1 million. Assuming that half of this represented the cost of re-claiming the 180 hectares (450 acres) of land covered with colliery waste, then the lack of Development Area status would have cost the West Riding an extra £175,000. Fortu-nately the government has moved some way towards the Hunt Committee suggestion that equality with the Development Areas should be accorded the Yorkshire coal-field in matters of land reclamation by offering 75 per cent grants for land to be used for indus-try—in this case throughout all Yorkshire and Humberside.

In the southeast of the coal-field lies Doncaster, the largest urban centre in the sub-region. It exemplifies the considerable possibilities and problems of the zone as it tries to diversefy away from coal. It became an important railway engineering town after 1853 when the Great Northern Railway moved its workshops from Boston; nevertheless in 1901 (with a population of 36,000) it was still much smaller than Barnsley. In 1907, the exploitation of the deep coal around the town began, and Doncaster's population surged upwards. In the nineteen thirties new industry came in; there was further industrial expansion in the late nineteen forties and early nineteen fifties, and even predictions at that time that the town would have 100,000 by the mid nineteen sixties. In fact, growth was less rapid, and the 1965 population was 87,000. The town and its hinterland have long had a low ratio of female to male jobs, and the main industries of the town's post-1945 expansion have been male employing. British Ropes, Imperial Chemical Industries (Fibres Division) and International Harvester employed some 9,000 men between them by 1968. The Department of Trade and Industry (D.T.I.) deny that they have refused any applications for i.d.c.s in the West Riding for many years but it is widely believed in the county that the Department's obligation to draw the attention of industrialists to the attractions of the Development Areas, plus the fear of an adverse decision following an application, have persuaded many firms either not to apply or to go elsewhere. In 1962 the Ford Motor Company closed down its Doncaster assembly plant and the town lost 2,000 jobs. The company argued with justice that the Doncaster operation was too small for cost-reducing mass production. but in Doncaster it is still widely believed that the D.T.I.'s refusal to grant an industrial development certificate for a major expansion was the fundamental cause of the move, and it is pointed out that Halewood, a part bene-ficiary of the closure, now employs over 14,000.

The town is clearly a major regional focus. Only 40 per cent of its retail income is esti-mated to come from the borough's own population. Within the Doncaster city region, with a population of 250,000, some 22,000 travel each day to work in the borough. A substantial redevelopment of the centre, and a new industrial estate on 100 hectares (250 acres) of Doncaster Carr by the main railway, have been proposed. However, these and other developments are at hazard. Early proposals from the West Riding County Council that Doncaster should be made into a major industrial growth focus were coldly received by the central government. Nevertheless, there was subsequently conducted (apparently with the fullest cooperation with the regional representatives of the central ministries) a joint study of the Doncaster area (JODAS), which resulted in the publication in August 1969 of *Doncaster—an Area Study*. This showed clearly enough the long term growth prospects of Doncaster and its area. Simultaneously it demonstrated that a short term hurdle must be overcome before these can be realized. A manpower budget analysis has shown that in this area with a workforce of approximately 100,000 there will be, largely because of colliery closures, a shortfall of 7,000 to 10,000 jobs by 1975. To overcome this difficulty, sites for new employment must be provided which must be serviced, dereliction must be reduced, new housing must be made available and the town centre must be improved. Although Doncaster is now in a designated Intermediate Area, its share of the £20 million allocated annually for all such areas—and for certain wider functions also in both Yorkshire and Humberside and the North West—can only be small. Here is but one example—often repeated throughout the country—of the apparent inadequacy of the means to tackle a necessary and fundamental economic transformation.

To the southwest of the Coalfield is the *South Yorkshire* sub-region. Here, in mid-1965, there were some 350,000 insured employees—compared with 305,000 in the Coalfield and 833,000 in the West Yorkshire sub-regions. Less than 3 per cent of its workers are engaged in coal mining and only a small proportion in textiles. In 1965, three orders of the Standard Industrial Classification (S.I.C.) had 42.7 per cent of the total insured employees in the sub-region (a much higher proportion than textile and clothing employment in West Yorkshire), and since the late nineteen fifties employment in them has been steady. There are, however, substantial differences between the four employment exchange areas within the sub-region (Table 24).

In South Yorkshire it is impossible to generalize reasonably about either the steel or the engineering industries. The former produces not only common carbon steels, but also a whole range of more specialized products through to the finest alloy steels. Engineering output runs all the way from large chemical plant and oil refinery pressure vessels and from marine engineering through to the fine and delicate products of the cutlery trade. The two activities are frequently closely interwoven, as they are within such renowned firms as Firth-Brown, the English Steel Corporation and United Steel Companies, but within Sheffield and Rotherham there is still a clear division of activities between the areas which almost 70 years ago (the future) Lord Aberconway described as 'Sheffield on the Sheaf' and 'Sheffield on the Don'. One is concerned with light products, the other with heavy lines, and both localities face serious planning problems.

The former division covers much of the west and centre of Sheffield. Industry there is conducted in what are frequently highly congested premises, operating on slopes of inconvenient steepness and with difficulties of access. The second division reaches eastwards from near the centre of Sheffield to Rotherham and beyond. It focuses on the valley of the Don, which is almost filled to capacity with heavy industry. It is a splendidly impressive sight from the train or from the Tinsley viaduct of the M1 but on closer examination it can be recognized as a haphazard growth, with a lack of room for well laid out expansion and with the various units of one company's works frequently separated by sub-divisions of its rivals. The road access is inadequate, the housing stock is of low

Table 24. Britain and South Yorkshire : employment structure, by districts, 1965 (percentages)

	Britain	South Yorkshire				
		Total sub-region	Employment Exchanges			
			Sheffield	Rotherham	Stocksbridge	Chapeltown
Primary industry	4.8	2.9	1.8	7.9	1.3	12.2
Service employment	57.0	43.7	46.5	40.5	13.5	19.7
Manufacturing employment	38.1	53.2	51.7	51.6	85.2	68.1
Iron and Steel	1.3	20.0	15.9	33.5	67.0	6.0
Metal Goods	2.5	11.2	13.6	0.6	8.8	8.8
Engineering and electrical	19.7	10.3	11.0	5.1	—	32.5
All others	24.6	11.7	11.2	12.4	9.4	20.8
Proportion of sub-regional workforce	—	100.0	77.8	16.2	3.0	3.0
Female/male employment ratio	58.0*	51.0	55.7	40.4	18.2	38.3

*1966.

Source : Minutes of Evidence of the West Riding County Council to Hunt Committee on Intermediate Areas, 1968 (unpublished).

quality and is intermixed with manufacturing, and the environmental problems are intensified by industrial and power station effluent—steam, smoke, gases, heavily polluted water and piles of scrap. Through it all winds the river which gave its name to this famous industrial belt—a small, dirty, tired and neglected stream.

From the most congested parts of the valley, and from the centre of Sheffield, a certain amount of out-movement is taking place. Since the early nineteen sixties, the English Steel Corporation has built a major new works at Tinsley, and Osborn Steel, which for ten years has been planning to move out of its congested central area premises, is now (as part of a wider steel group) about to concentrate the activities of its several Sheffield plants—plus those of the Low Moor works at Bradford—on a 12 hectare (29 acres) site just north of the city boundary at Ecclesfield. Since 1945, house construction has pushed the built-up city to the edge of Ecclesfield, and the new move will transfer 1,000 jobs across the city boundary. An unexpected additional bonus was the plant's qualification for Intermediate Area assistance. Further out, Chapeltown-Thorncliffe has lost its old iron trade, but retains important engineering and chemicals activities, while Stocksbridge, in a narrow tributary valley of the upper Don, remains heavily dependent upon an important, but anomalously located, steel plant.

As in West Yorkshire, employment in engineering has shown much less favourable trends than in Britain as a whole. There has been decrease in the machine tools industry, and indeed overall, in the Sheffield area, the S.I.C. order VI—engineering and electrical goods—showed a decline of 4.8 per cent between 1959 and 1965, as compared with a national growth of 17.9 per cent and a smaller increase in West Yorkshire. Moreover, between 1952 and 1968, the Sheffield district's share of national crude steel production fell from 13.9 to 12.4 per cent, and employment declined more rapidly than nationally. The area remains dominant in quality steels—although even its share of alloy grades fell from 65.6 to 62.7 per cent British output in the twelve years from 1952. Between 1956 and 1960, expenditure on development schemes (costing over £100,000) was only 7.2 per cent the national total. However, the proportion rose to 16.9 per cent in the next six years, with the construction of the new Tinsley Park works of the English Steel Corporation, the reconstruction of the Parkgate works, and the conversion of the big Rotherham cold metal works of the Steel Peech and Tozer subdivision of United Steels to electric furnace practice.

Examined from the viewpoint of national, rather than company, strategy the last two of these important projects are of questionable wisdom. The result, nevertheless, has been to assure for some time to come the industrial future for the Don valley—and from this stem a host of geographical consequences, in particular the prospective general environmental conditions there, the inevitable demands for new housing, and the journey to work pattern. The peculiar process by which old industrial locations and economic and social distributions are perpetuated may be seen very well in the case of these works. Lacking a blast furnace, a decision was taken within United Steel Companies to build what, on its completion in 1965, was the world's largest electrical steelmaking facility. The plant is now being modified to raise its capacity from 1·4 to 1·8 million tons. But the new steel furnaces supply an extremely elderly primary mill complex and clearly the most desirable next step would be to replace this—and then, soon afterwards perhaps, the ancillary plant there or the finishing mills at the associated works of the British Steel Corporation (B.S.C.). At the Parkgate works, now equipped with new Kaldo and electric furnaces with a capacity of over 0.5 million tons, plus two small blast furnaces, yet another old rolling mill will soon have to be replaced. In this fashion, the investment decisions at any one time are compromised by the need to maximize the advantages gained from previously installed plant. Yet at no time is it at all easy to draw back and ask whether the long term development of steelmaking might be more profitably effected in an entirely different location. The recent investments undoubtedly mean that steelmaking will remain a major component of the Sheffield district for many years to come—although rationalization amongst the formerly independent units is already underway, both within the B.S.C. and, with the assistance of the (former) Industrial Reorganization Corporation, amongst the still private concerns now making new affiliations. In 1971 plans for the reorganization of the B.S.C. Special Steels Division seemed likely to cause the loss of up to 4,500 jobs at the River Don works over a two year period; although this particular development was strongly resisted by the unions and deferred, further rationalization and consequent redundancy in the Sheffield/Rotherham steel trades must be expected.

So far, therefore, there has been no change in the economic structure of the steel area of South Yorkshire as disturbing as those in the other two industrial sub-regions of the West Riding. The Sheffield employment exchange in August 1969 had only a 2.1 per cent rate of unemployment. Rotherham, with heavy industry more prominent in its overall employment structure, had a 4.1 per cent rate—hence its early inclusion in the Intermediate Area.

In all directions except the northeast, the built-up area of Sheffield has been extended considerably in the years since 1945. With rebuilding taking place at lower densities than are found in the small houses at the centre of the urban area, or the dreary Victorian industrial rows of Attercliffe and Brightside, the city population fell from a peak of 512,000 to some 489,000 in 1965. However, on 1st April 1967, the Sheffield boundary was extended to take in parts of the West Riding, and certain (larger) areas of Derbyshire centered on Mosbrough 9 kilometres (6 miles) south east of the centre of Sheffield. As a result, the 'official' population has 'increased' by over 47,000, and Sheffield once again has become the largest city in Yorkshire. In this Mosbrough area, Sheffield has planned a new type of development, designed to house 85,000 people; many of them will be employed locally, and the whole scheme has an estimated cost of £70 million. Progress towards its realization, however, was briefly threatened by the 1969 designation of the Yorkshire Intermediate Area, for it was feared that industry would be attracted a few kilometres to the east, or into the Rotherham exchange area, in order to benefit from this assistance. In 1970 Sheffield was assured that the Mosbrough scheme would not be penalized, and in 1972 Intermediate Area benefits were extended to the whole planning region. Nevertheless, this was one example of an increasing problem within the West Riding—the need to coordinate sub-regional and area policies at a time when the spatial relationships conditioning the problems and the possible solutions are rapidly changing.

Thus, the *West Riding* has in full measure the problems of an old industrial district—dereliction, urban decay, transport congestion and, central to the whole difficulty of tackling these, a fragmentation of planning control. The Local Government Commission in its 1964 Report on the urban core of the West Yorkshire subdivision of the county noted that the proportion of unfit housing was 1 in 8, or twice the national average. Leeds has 90,000 houses built before 1900, and its target by the end of the century is to replace all poor quality housing of pre-1914 age. In the Halifax and Calder Valley study of 1968 it was shown that the proportion of dwellings in the area with a rateable value of not more than £30 was 56.6 per cent, as compared with 15.4 per cent in England and Wales; only 17.4 per cent of the 1966 housing stock had been built since 1945, compared with 30.8 per cent nationally. Transport conditions are also bad. Traffic congestion is at present severe in much of the conurbation and prospectively is unlikely to improve; the number of cars in the 2,590 square kilometres (1,000 sq. miles) of the West Yorkshire Transportation Study area is likely to treble and the proportion of the journeys to work across local authority boundaries which are made by car is likely to go up from 50 per cent at present to about 70 per cent by the end of the century. Urban renewal too requires both drastic action and coordination. Can a major new shopping centre, at present proposed for Morley midway between the bigger foci of Leeds and Batley/Dewsbury, be a success without prejudicing the role and future of those older centres? What is likely to happen to the service functions of Bradford's reconstructed centre if the county planning authorities permit large, new, out of town shopping centres some distance beyond the city's outskirts?

In reaction to these and similar puzzles, the vision of the several local authorities in the area has sometimes seemed extraordinarily narrow. Joint sewage schemes, common in other parts of Britain, have often been rejected in the West Riding by local authorities jealous of every inch of independence. Their reactions may be seen in a more extreme form in the written evidence submitted to the Maud Commission by Garforth Urban District in October 1966. In 1964 the Local Government Commission had suggested that the district (with a population of 18,000) should be merged with the slightly larger Rothwell and Stanley urban districts, plus two parishes from the Tadcaster Rural District, to form a new unit of 60,000 people. Garforth U.D. now wrote : 'The Commission will also be aware of the objections forcefully put forward against this unwanted marriage. Garforth's attitude to this merger remains the same and is unlikely ever to alter'. At a higher level of administration, that of the local authorities with planning powers, the same absence of cooperation is only too clear. There are twelve local planning authorities in the West Riding—the County Council and eleven County Boroughs including York. The average population of the ten in the industrial part of the county was 189,000 in 1965; excluding Leeds and Sheffield, it was only 111,000. It is doubtful whether this is a viable size in terms of being able to recruit all the necessary planning skills. Equally critical is the fact that the spheres of influence of the several authorities so overlap that the fragmentation is an undoubted impediment to efficient administration and planning. The arrangement poses even more difficult problems when set within a time framework. Under the 1947 Town and Country Planning Act, twelve development plans had to be prepared, but they have been submitted to the Ministry of Housing and Local Government at quite different times, so that any coordination of their proposals (especially those affecting the boundary zones between the various authorities) has been extremely difficult. The obligation to review the development plans every five years has compounded the problem until (in the words of the County Council's written evidence to the Royal Commission on Local Government in England) '... the position has now been reached where coordination between the respective development plans is almost impossible'. Such are the difficulties in physical planning. They are matched by those in the broader field of regional economic planning for the industrial area. The case of Sheffield is particularly instructive in this regard.

Its distinctive pattern of industrial development has made the Sheffield area very different from the West Riding conurbation, or the more diffuse coal-field zone, and for long the city has nourished ambitions to make a reality of the South Riding of literature. This separatism comes out in the comments made by the Sheffield and Rotherham Chambers of Commerce on the 1966 *Review of Yorkshire and Humberside*. Neither the M62 nor a possible Humber Bridge is seen as of much significance for this area; and they proposed another motorway standard road over to Manchester. Cooperation with neighbouring parts of the East Midlands region was also suggested. Indeed, early in 1968, the so called '44 Committee'—comprising representatives of 44 local authorities from South Yorkshire, North Nottinghamshire and North Derbyshire—met in Sheffield to formulate plans to attract new industry, and to urge more assistance for grey areas. This was interpreted by some as a move by Sheffield to carve out a new economic region, of which it would be the leader. If such intentions existed they were frustrated by the designation of an Intermediate Area which excluded Sheffield, but which included Rotherham and employment exchanges to the east, in 1969. Later that year, however, Sheffield relaxed its opposition to cooperation with the West Riding and other planning authorities, and withdrew its objections to the designation of a major economic growth point at Dinnington-Maltby about 17 kilometres (11 miles) to the east.

In 1964, the Local Government Commission tried a halfway solution to the problem of multiple local authority units in West Yorkshire. It proposed a sharp reduction in the number of authorities, through the retention of the five county boroughs and the division of the rest of the area between municipal boroughs and the West Riding County Council. The Maud Commission report five years later suggested a much more radical change. Its proposals divided the industrial West Riding between seven unitary authorities, which were to be associated with the North Riding of Yorkshire (except Cleveland) and a smaller portion than at present of Lindsey in a new Yorkshire Province for regional economic planning purposes. Within the suggested new groupings Sheffield and Leeds would have retained their preeminence (Table 25). The provincial rate of population growth was estimated, before the Registrar General's downward revision in 1969, at 8.6 per cent between 1968 and 1981. The major areas of growth, however, were expected to be in the east—in the short and middle term in the eastern part of the West Riding, and in the longer term in Humberside—whilst in the western industrial area the Maud prospect was for population decline, stagnation or at best only a slow rate of growth. Even the regional commercial and service capitals such as Leeds and Sheffield would barely hold their position within the wider economic region. Their futures would have been even bleaker but for the coming of the motorways.

The changing pattern of transport facilities, and above all the emerging motorway network, is a major new element in the economic geography of the West Riding. Yorkshire and Humberside as a whole contains about 240 kilometres (150 miles) or almost 11 per cent of the British motorway programme as outlined at the end of 1968. It is widely believed that this will improve the region's economic status within Britain. Equally certain it will alter the economic prospects of the component parts of the economic region. The Doncaster by-pass (of motorway standard) has been open since the early nineteen sixties. In 1968, the M1 was completed to Leeds, and the M18 was opened from the M1 east of Sheffield to the A1(M) west of Doncaster. By 1972, the M62 will run from Stretford and

Table 25. The Yorkshire Province : suggested units and their population, 1968 and 1981 (est.)

	1968 '000s	1981* '000s	Increase %
Yorkshire Province	4,849	5,271	8.6
York	432	477	10.4
Bradford	500	518	3.6
Leeds	840	912	8.5
Halifax	195	185	−5.2
Huddersfield	207	218	5.3
Sheffield and South Yorkshire	1,081	1,161	7.4
Doncaster	284	325	14.4
Mid Yorkshire	469	543	15.8
North Humberside	536	577	7.6
South Humberside	305	355	16.3

*1968 forecast.

Source : Report of the Royal Commission on Local Government in England, 1968.

Worsley (west of Greater Manchester) to Lofthouse on the M1 south of Leeds. It was suggested in the study on *Huddersfield and Colne Valley* (Y and H Economic Planning Council, 1969, pp. 13–14) that by the mid nineteen seventies the number of people within four hours travelling time of Huddersfield will have increased from the present 22 millions to probably 37.5 millions. The impression is given that this is Huddersfield's market area, and that the latter compares very favourably in size with an estimated 36.2 million for Doncaster, 28.2 million for Hull and only 20.3 million for Middlesbrough. Meanwhile, the Ministry of Transport had commissioned an economic impact study of the M62. This is the first to be undertaken in connection with a motorway development in Britain, and it seeks to analyse the situation before the road is opened, soon after, and three years later. Its leader, the Professor of Transport Economics at Leeds, has already stressed the permissive rather than the automatic economic effect of motorway construction. He has pointed out, for example, that the M1 might allow into Yorkshire for the first time goods which have more efficiently produced in the Midlands and South East. Stressing that the effect of the M1 on the aggregate level of activity in the West Riding is indeterminate, he has observed that the new motorway might be more seriously viewed as challenge requiring positive response from local industry, rather than a magnet which will automatically ensure its growth.

Within the West Riding, motorway access has nevertheless been regarded as a prize worth fighting for. Local agitation has secured more access points than were originally planned on those parts of the M62 which form the common boundary between the Halifax and Upper Calder Valley and the Huddersfield and Colne Valley study areas. In the east, it was originally believed by central government planners that it was impracticable to route the M1 through the old mining and industrial areas between Sheffield, Barnsley and Leeds and an alternative alignment was planned curving eastwards towards the A1 and then back to Leeds. Together the local authorities pressed the Ministry of Transport to think again and at a considerable cost (the most spectacular of which is the £4 million viaduct across the Don Valley at Tinsley) the present route was chosen, running to the west of Barnsley and snaking northwards to the outskirts of Leeds. An academic member of the Economic Planning Council, speaking of the cost of the Tinsley viaduct, has argued that '... to have the West Riding on the motorway system is worth £4 million' (Page, 1969).

Any gain to the county, however, will clearly not accrue to all points within it. Foci of growth at the motorway interchanges are widely expected. The Halifax and Upper Calder Valley study identified Brighouse and Elland as most likely to benefit from the M62 because of this. The response of private enterprise was revealing. Slough Estates Limited, almost 50 years ago pioneers in industrial estate development in Britain and noted for the perception of their location policy, have opened a new factory and warehouse estate on the edge of Wakefield, almost at the M1/M62 interchange. West Riding planners have also responded to the opportunities of good motorway access in their proposed pattern of new population foci which is designed mainly to relieve the problems of the coal-field. One of the three 'primary' growth points which they have listed lies between Dinnington and Maltby, within 5 kilometres (3 miles) of the M1/M18 junction and well placed for the interchanges both to north and south. A second is at Adwick/Bentley, between Doncaster and the A1(M) and south of the proposed 'South Yorkshire Highway' from Hoyland to the M18 when it is extended eastwards. The third growth point is the so-called Five Towns development, centred on Castleford, Pontefract, Featherstone, Knottingley and Normanton which together already have a population of 115,000. In each of these centres it is proposed that by the year 2000 there will be an increase in population of over 50,000. In the Five Towns, which is to be given some priority, the increase will bring the population to 200,000 by the end of the century. Three other 'major' growth points have also been proposed; these are smaller and are strung out along the South Yorkshire Highway at Penistone, Hoyland and South Elmsall. Associated with these proposals are three 'strategic' and five 'major' industrial sites located in the area between Doncaster, Leeds and Hoyland.

The plans for developing this area—which are a response to the problems of the coal-field and the patterns of labour availability, as well as the improved road transport facilities—received a further boost when fifteen of the Coalfield exchange areas (all, in fact, except Rothwell in the Leeds commuting zone), the Rotherham exchange area in the steel district, and the Wakefield area in the textile district were made into the Yorkshire Intermediate Area in 1969. This briefly reinforced the natural (relative) attractiveness of the area as a growth zone. Sheffield, although troubled with doubts about its Mosbrough

project, had to withdraw its opposition to Dinnington/Malty as a growth point. Fears
were also expressed in the Calder and Colne Valleys that one effect of the M62 link to
the Intermediate Area would be to tempt industry to relocate or expand in the east, in
order to qualify for the 25 per cent building grants. However, the 1972 extension of the
Intermediate Area to the whole planning region reduced these fears. Nevertheless,
new and equally disturbing factors have begun to complicate the planning situation
further.

In 1966 the Yorkshire and Humberside Economic Planning Council, working on
Register General regional estimates made in 1964, estimated a natural increase to 1981
of 650,000; a prospective net out-movement of 135,000 gave a 1981 population of 5.2
million, and an annual increase of 30,000. In 1966, these figures were revised. Both natural
increase and net out-movement were forecast at lower levels but the overall figure was
still 5.2 millions. In the light of these estimates the growth points on the coal-field were
chosen. In the three 'primary' and three 'major' growth points, the increase would be at
least 275,000 by the end of the century, assuming minimum levels of expansion for the
primary points (except the Five Towns for which full growth has been assumed) and middle
range levels for the three major points. New estimates made by the Registrar General in
1969, however, suggest a slower rate of growth in the national population, and for Yorkshire and Humberside both a smaller natural increase and a bigger net out-movement
are now expected. The figure for 1981 as a result is more than 150,000 less than that forecast
in 1964 and 1966. This may not in the long run prevent the growth of the Five Towns
or the other growth points, but the Registrar General's new forecasts are said to have
evoked a regrettable reaction at the Regional Planning level. The view has been expressed
there that the growth points should feel the full impact of this reduction, and that growth
and reconstruction in the conurbation should be little affected. The wider issues of the
patterns of growth in the whole economic region seem in danger of being affected by
the same philosophy. Humberside appears likely to be the main area to suffer.

8.3 The Rural Middle

Between the industrial West Riding and Humberside the rural districts mainly comprising the East Riding and Lindsey extend in a great arc. The country and its agricultural
economy is highly diverse. The drained glacial drift and improved outwash gravels of
the Vale of York support a varied and generally prosperous farm economy. To the south
and southeast it is replaced by the fens and warplands of Thorne, Axholme and Ancholme.
The Jurassic escarpment of the Lincoln Edge has great grain fields but at its northern end
are the sandy heaths and coniferous plantations around Scunthorpe. The rolling landscapes of the Lincolnshire Wolds support a grain (largely barley) and sheep economy.
Accessibility varies greatly from the proximity to main routeways in the Vale of York
to the remoteness of many Wold villages. Apart from agricultural processing and the
servicing of agricultural machinery the towns have little industry. Towards the fringes

of the belt many are mushrooming as commuters to the bigger industrial centres choose rural homes.

The city of York dominates the northern part of this agricultural zone. As a route focus and industrial centre, as well as a fine historic city with major tourist and cultural activities, it is plagued with traffic and physical planning problems. History and location at first sight make it an extremely attractive location for a regional capital standing above the partisanship of either the West Riding or Humberside. In his minority report to the Maud Commission, Senior even suggested it might become capital of a province extending from the Humber to the Tweed. The power of the great conurbations and the very different character of the North East region and of Yorkshire and Humberside alone suggest that York is unlikely to be capital of either the smaller or the larger province. This rural middle is also increasingly related to the urban-industrial economy of Yorkshire and Humberside as well.

In the northwest of the *Mid Yorkshire* planning sub-division—a very different area from the similarly named unit in the Maud Report, it should be stressed—there is already a good deal of commuting into the industrial area to the south. Harrogate, Ripon and Northallerton indeed straddle the bridge between the industrial West Riding and Tees-side, and in Harrogate especially brisk residential growth has already been accompanied by a growth of science-based industry and research establishments. There is every indica-tion that these communities will continue to grow, and the West Yorkshire Transportation Study in 1969 urged an improved rail service over the 30 kilometres (18 miles) of the Harrogate-Leeds track. By 1971 Harrogate was resisting inclusion in a West Yorkshire metropolitan county which had been proposed in the White Paper on local government reorganization.

On the southern border of the Mid Yorkshire sub-region there is substantial develop-ment along the Humber bank, which is influencing the rural hinterland to its north. Industry is centred on Hull, and also near the major railway junction point on the Ouse between Selby and Barlby. Much of the southern part of the East Riding is already within the industrial and commuter zone of Hull, and future economic growth (plus the impact of the Humber Bridge) will tend to push development still further out. Haltemprice, with a population of over 49,000, is essentially part of greater Hull—inspite of its own industrial estate, and its evidence to the Maud Commission that councils under 60,000 are viable and can support a full range of local authority staff. Beverley, only 13 kilometres (8 miles) from central Hull, is also within the commuter zone, and between 1956 and 1968 the population of both the Borough and rural district went up by approximately 29 per cent. Beyond Beverley, however, is an overwhelmingly rural area, where popula-tion trends are very different. In the same twelve years, the Driffield urban and rural districts experienced a 2.8 per cent population decline. Bridlington on the coast has grown and has its own industrial estate, but it is faced annually with the seasonal economic problems of small seaside resorts.

In *Lindsey* much larger areas are remote from main centres of industry or lines of com-

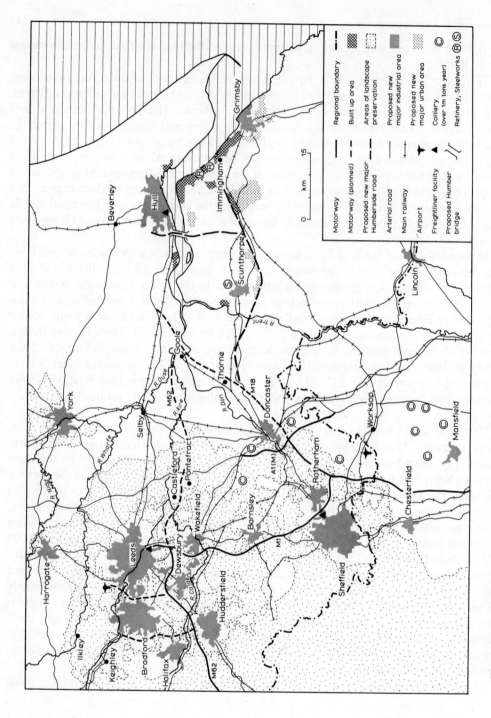

Figure 28 Yorkshire and Humberside : principal economic and land use features, 1971.

Legend:

Motorway
Motorway (planned)
Proposed new major Humberside road
Arterial road
Main railway
Airport
Freightliner facility
Proposed Humber bridge
Regional boundary
Built up area
Areas of landscape preservation
Proposed new major industrial area
Proposed new major urban area
Colliery
Refinery, Steelworks (R,S) (over 1m tons year)

Map labels:

Grimsby
Immingham
Beverley
Hull
Scunthorpe
Lincoln
R. Trent
Goole
Thorne
Doncaster
Worksop
Mansfield
York
Selby
R. Ouse
R. Aire
R. Don
M62
M18
A1(M)
Rotherham
Chesterfield
Castleford
Pontefract
Wakefield
Barnsley
R. Wharfe
R. Nidd
Harrogate
Ilkley
Keighley
Bradford
Halifax
M62
Huddersfield
Dewsbury
R. Calder
Leeds
M1
Sheffield

15
0   km

munication. Rural society and village structure have possibly changed less than in almost any other part of lowland Britain. In most of the rural districts, there has been slight population growth; in one or two a small decline since the mid nineteen fifties. The market towns also show no marked tendency to grow. The combined population of the five urban districts of Alford, Gainsborough, Market Rasen, Woodhall Spa and the municipal borough of Louth, for example, increased only from 39.2 thousand in 1956 to 39.9 thousand twelve years later. Skegness, Mablethorpe and Sutton have a vigorous holiday traffic, but they offer little alternative work; their population increased by only 1.6 per cent over the same period. However, the situation is changing.

In both the southwest and the northeast of Lindsey more vigorous population growth is being experienced near to important centres of industrial development. In the south, the population overflow from Lincoln (in the East Midlands region) accounts for the increase of 6.5 thousand (40.8 per cent) in the population of Welton rural district between 1956 and 1968. In 1966, Gainsborough agreed with the Greater London Council to take 1,000 overspill families over a number of years—an agreement welcomed in the area and across the Trent as a means of stimulating both the town and the surrounding countryside. And in the northeast, Louth and Grimsby rural districts experienced a population growth of over 24 per cent (compared with the regional figure of 4 per cent) between 1955 and 1964. The prospect of further economic growth in Scunthorpe and along the Humber bank—especially with the building of the Humber Bridge and new motorways in the middle and late nineteen seventies—will undoubtedly transform development opportunities in south Lindsey. A Hull-Humber Bridge-Lincoln-Nottingham motorway, for instance, could greatly alter the economic growth pattern in interior Lindsey. Southeast Lindsey, on the other hand, already an area of slow economic growth, may be expected to become still more a relative backwater (or haven of peace, depending on the point of view).

Between Gainsborough in the south and Goole in the north, the industrial West Riding is separated from Humberside by a belt of low-lying, mainly rural and sparsely populated land. This is an area of enormous growth propsects. Proposed motorways could associate it closely with both the banks of the Humber, with West and South Yorkshire, and so with the M1 and Lancashire. The same area is also an important rail focus. Taking into account the facts of existing and prospective accessibility to considerable concentrations of population, consultants have even advised the development of an international airport in the area by 1980 (Stratford and Associates, 1967). Thorne Waste, the suggested airport site, may paradoxically be the centre of a major new urban and industrial complex by the end of the century.

8.4 Humberside

Humberside, with a population equal to that of the Yorkshire Coalfield sub-region, but covering a much larger area, is almost universally acknowledged to have great development prospects. The sobriquet 'Britain's Europoort' is commonly used. Both regionally and nationally there has been a failure to recognise how very different is the planning context from that of Europoort. And so far there has been a distinct lack of resolution concerning how best to handle the development of the area's full potentialities. The broad Humber estuary divides the region into two sub-divisions (Table 26). South Humberside. comprising the northern half of Lindsey, has a number of economic foci. Major

Table 26. North and South Humberside : population change, 1956–1968

	1956 '000s	1968 '000s	Change %
Humberside	720.0	784.0	+8.8
North	448.9	472.4	+5.2
South	271.1	311.6	+14.9
Britain	49,234.3	53,780.5	+9.2

Source : Registrar General.

activity in the *North Humberside* sub-region, on the other hand, is concentrated at one—Kingston upon Hull, which with the neighbouring urban district of Haltemprice has a conurbation population of over 350,000 (approaching half that of Humberside as a whole).

Hull is served by docks stretching more than 11 kilometres (7 miles) along the estuary. The approach channel so far has been deep enough for vessels carrying its main primary imports of timber, grain, wool and oil. The early docks along the river Hull are now redundant. The city, and more recently the British Transport Docks Board, has spent liberally on new facilities, with the King George dock, to the east, as the centre of modernization work. Recently, new container berth facilities have been developed both there and at Alexandra dock. Looking ahead, there is a scheme for new deep water facilities yet further down the estuary between Spurn Head and Hawkins Points. Modern dock development always involves new patterns of urban expansion and demands improvements in land transport. The physical setting of Hull has meant that these changes have created serious planning problems.

There were no major variations in rock type or topography on the lowlands of the river Hull and there were no important agricultural villages to provide nuclei for suburban development as very rapid economic growth occurred in Hull towards the end of the nineteenth century. The urban area seems to have spilled out across the lowlands with, as

Hull planners have put it, 'little to control the flow except sheer distance from the centre'. Within this expanding conurbation, only a little above sea level, railway construction involved the proliferation of level crossings which, with the subsequent growth of road transport, have become a serious cause of traffic congestion. Essential urban renewal and a reconstruction of the circulation system, however, have been made easier by the extensive bomb damage to the central district during the second world war.

Hull has failed to become a major industrial centre. Of the five county boroughs in the country nearest in population, it has the lowest proportion of its rate income provided by industry, or even by commerce and industry together. It has of course a complement of port industries but the shipbuilding and ship repairing activities have been adversely affected by the lack of Development Area status, which is reckoned generally to reduce labour costs in shipbuilding by about 12 per cent. There is some metallurgical activity, as for instance at the Rio Tinto tin refinery at North Ferriby (west of the conurbation). In 1925, in a development stemming from a traditional port activity, the Distillers Company acquired a plant at Salt End (to the east) to make industrial alcohol from molasses; this has now become an important and diverse chemical operation, with an improved tanker terminal. Engineering is a prominent activity also, and at Brough an aircraft industry employing some 4,000 has been built up since 1945 as an overspill from Leeds enterprise. There are large tracts of land suitable for further industrial development, for example, some 267 hectares (660 acres) near Salt End and the former pit wood storage land on the dock estates. To make further progress it seems essential that the relative remoteness, and still more the perceived remoteness, of Hull should be broken down.

The existing main road to the West Riding has been described as an 'archaic disgrace', and the tortuousness of rail links with the Midlands has long been a joke. A Hull planning report at the end of the nineteen fifties unconsciously betrayed the psychological remoteness which these conditions engendered. There were, it mentioned, commercial connections with the North Midlands and the West Riding '. . . but these links with distant centres of population are commercial only. There are no large towns near enough for Hull to have close social contact, and much of the day-to-day life of the city is bound up with the predominantly rural East Riding' (Kingston upon Hull, c. 1959). After the Department of Economic Affairs linked Hull with the West Riding for regional planning purposes, the city seems to have been careful from the start to guard its interests; and the Council set up a Regional Development (Special) Committee in October 1965 to give '. . . continuous consideration to the problems associated with the encouragement of regional development, and the safeguarding of the interests of the city . . .' (Kingston upon Hull, 1965/1966) There can be little doubt however that in future these must be seen in a wider context than hitherto. The proposed motorway links with Doncaster and West Yorkshire, and the suggested improvements of the road to York, will bring Hull into easier contact with a wider hinterland and the decision to build the Humber bridge by 1976 opens wider (if hazier) horizons. This investment will bind the future of Hull much more closely than ever before to the people and places south of the Humber estuary.

During the last 20 years, population and employment have grown much more rapidly on *South Humberside* and there seems every sign that this difference will continue. In 1951, the population on South Humberside was 59.3 per cent of that on the north; (1966) projections, on the other hand, suggested a figure of 72.4 per cent by 1981 (see Table 25). There has been substantial industrial growth on both sides of the estuary in the nineteen sixties but although half of the industrial development certificates approved for the whole of Humberside between 1956 and 1967 were for projects in the Hull and Hessle areas, their yield in additional employment has been considerably less than half. One estimate is that only 7.9 thousand new jobs were created on the north bank, compared with 11.3 thousand on the south. Such figures reflect the way in which South Humberside increasingly has come to be preoccupied with larger schemes and heavy industry, in contrast to the increasing prominence of service employment in Hull. Whilst the late nineteen sixties saw a net out-movement of 800 to 900 persons annually from the north bank of Humberside, the south experienced a net immigration of some 200 each year. This pattern may be changed following the opening of the Humber Bridge, and with the 1969 designation of a North Humberside Intermediate Area it appeared that public policy would endorse such a change. However, with the extension of the Intermediate Area in 1972 it seems more likely that South Humberside will maintain the forward thrust which it has acquired over the last 20 years, even though there remain some weaknesses in its industrial structure.

One hundred years ago Hull already had a population of 120,000. Grimsby was then only one sixth as large and there was no other important centre in the whole of Humberside. Fogarty's 1945 analysis of Humberside was by no means optimistic, and suggested only limited possibilities for the south bank. During the late nineteen thirties, even Goole had done better than Immingham as a port. Grimsby had, of course, its fishing trade, its port activities, a small amount of ship construction and repairing (mainly of fishing craft) and for the rest its manufacturing was largely confined to biscuit and jam making. Since then, however, this part of Humberside has become an outstanding boom area. Between 1956 and 1968, the growth of population in Cleethorpes, Grimsby and Grimsby rural district was 13 per cent (over 18,000). Housing expansion and town centre development, which have accompanied this economic growth, have begun to transform the once isolated Immingham into an attractive town.

The prosperity has been founded on the close proximity of a deep water channel, suitable for further dredging, and an abundance of low-lying, flat land available for bulk reducing industries—plus the perceptiveness of the local authorities which realized the existence of this potential over thirty years ago. Immediately before World War II, Grimsby rural district began to acquire land specifically for industrial development, and the Borough of Grimsby soon followed suite. By 1967, Imperial Chemical Industries and Fisons had invested £16 million in ammonia and nitrogen plants respectively in the Immingham Dock Estate, and Laporte and other chemical firms also erected big plants in the 10 kilometres (6 miles) between Grimsby and Immingham. Beyond the latter (in Glanford Brigg rural district) is the area best favoured with future growth prospects for space extensive industry, and near Killingholme there are already large electricity generating and petrochemical developments—partly associated with the fact that this is a landfall for natural gas (Leafe, 1967). Two oil refineries have been built in this locality since 1966. They are served by a new terminal at Immingham capable of handling 200,000 dwt tankers. In addition to its suitable sites, Humberside offers locational attractions to the oil companies. It is close to the Yorkshire and Midland markets, and provides interesting possibilities of linked development with European operations. These are clearly being exploited both by Petrofina/Total (with a 6.5 million tons per year facility) and by the Continental Oil Company (4.0 million tons); the continental refinery interests of this latter group are in Karlsruhe at the other end of the important markets which it has cultivated in Britain, Benelux and West Germany.

The small upswing in coal exports by the National Coal Board, especially following devaluation and the accumulation of surface stocks, is largely through the Humber ports. The traffic has been concentrated at Immingham, to which all former shipments through Hull have been diverted. At the end of 1970 a new deepwater terminal at South Killingholme came into operation, designed initially to handle coastal and foreign coal shipments up to 6 million tons each year. The National Coal Board at an early stage expressed the hope that the British Steel Corporation might make joint use of this facility for its iron ore imports, taking advantage also of empty wagons returning through Scunthorpe to South Yorkshire pits. By 1969, the Steel Corporation had decided not to locate any steelmaking capacity on a greenfield site at Immingham—for reasons which, though logical and economic in the short term, appear highly questionable as part of a long term development strategy (Warren, 1969a; 1969b)—but rather to concentrate its investments on an existing site inland at Scunthorpe. A year later they had agreed to join with the N.C.B. and the British Transport Docks Board to extend the existing terminal to make it capable of handling 70,000 dwt bulk carriers and 9 million tons of import and export traffic each year. The additional £6 million investment for the extension has to be seen against the £250 million already invested in the industries of the Immingham area since 1945, and the £110 million which was being spent on schemes underway there in the spring of 1969.

There are other, though smaller, foci of heavy industry along the south bank of the Humber. Barton-upon-Humber, for example, was already important before Albright and Wilson opened a new fertiliser plant there in 1969 to supply the considerable markets of Yorkshire and Lincolnshire. In the Flixborough-Keadby area, where the Trent is still navigable for vessels of some 2,000 dwt, the ammonia plant of Nitrogen Fertilisers is now linked through raw material and product flows with the joint Fisons/Dutch/National Coal Board caprolactin plant nearby. Eastwards is the very different but equally dynamic economy of Scunthorpe, land based and until recent years dependent in the main on local resources.

Scunthorpe, Brigg and parts of the rural districts nearest to them—the area which in 1966 the Leeds School of Planning defined as the Scunthorpe study area—doubled in population between 1900 and 1961 to 112,000. Growth at the heart of the area has been very much more impressive. Scunthorpe itself seems to have increased by just short of 15,000 between 1951 and 1966, a 28.2 per cent increase. This growth has been overwhemingly dependent upon three steelworks. The degree of specialization in metal manufacture in Scunthorpe, as indicated by a 'coefficient of town specialization', is greater than in any of the 70 British towns outside the conurbations with a population of over 50,000. The industry in the town is now at a major new stage of development.

Scunthorpe's share of national steel output went up only from 10.0 to 11.8 per cent between 1952 and 1968. By the mid nineteen sixties, it had been decided by the private companies then controlling the industry and notably by United Steel Companies that major capacity extensions should be made in North Lincolnshire; after some hesitation it was decided that they should be at the existing works in Scunthorpe. The subsequent common ownership of the three plants under nationalization gave the B.S.C. the opportunity of considerable cost reductions through rationalization. For instance, the present nine blast furnaces produce only about 3.3 million tons of pig iron each year, a tonnage which could be produced by three large furnaces and high quality feed. A decision was in fact taken to switch to a much higher proportion of foreign ore in the blast furnaces of the district in order to reduce the use of Frodingham stone which is so lean that it has even been called ferruginous limestone! The Corporation also elected in 1969 to make Scunthorpe one of its major sites under its corporate planning proposals for the early nineteen seventies. Its investment programme will not only replace the old open hearth and rotary furnaces by three basic oxygen convertors, but will also provide a new continuous casting plant and rolling mills. Steelmaking capacity will be raised from 3.4 million tons to 5.2 million tons by 1973. As output expands, however, so will the steel industry's workforce be reduced. The Corporation have announced that up to 3,500 will be affected initially and it is in this context that Scunthorpe's lack of industrial diversification is a glaring problem. The 1966 planning study of the area failed to identify any industries which appeared likely to generate new job opportunities in the next few years. However, it argued that a Humber Bridge and improved road communications would sweep Scunthorpe into a new growth spiral. This prospect for the whole of Humberside has been widely anticipated but rarely closely analysed. There are a number of weaknesses in the area's economy which should not be ignored.

In the mid nineteen sixties, the sharp increase in the rate of assistance given to industry in Development Areas showed no sign of checking growth in Humberside. The advantage of greater proximity to national markets was a substantial countervailing asset for the heavy trades—for instance for the costs of operating the estimated 1,800 or so road tankers which will serve the Humber refineries in the early nineteen seventies. Even more than on Teesside there remains an abundance of land to accommodate development on almost any conceivable future scale and there are equally good conditions for the disposal of effluent or the dispersal of atmospheric pollution. The provision of deep water is not likely to present insuperable difficulties and now, for the first time, a detailed study of the whole Humber estuary is under way. However, water supplies are potentially perhaps a very serious problem and one which in the past has served to frustrate major metallurgical plans for Immingham. A remedy may be found in the use of Trent river water, which estimates suggest would be capable of supplying another 500 million gallons of water each day, but this would involve a huge investment and a comprehensive basin-wide water improvement programme (which would involve pollution control as far away as the Black Country and even the Potteries). Another difficulty may be a shortage of labour, although most of the new activities have relatively small work forces—one report on the Continental Oil refinery noted that, while it was costing £15 to £20 million, its employment would barely be over 100. Finally improvements in land transport in the sub-region are clearly long overdue.

The Humber estuary has undoubtedly been a major barrier to movement in the past. By 1961, when there were 13,000 daily journeys to work between Hull and Haltemprice, the movement to work across the estuary was only about 500. Believing that better access to the south will improve its economic prospects, Hull has actively promoted the idea of a bridge across the Humber for over 40 years. South bank communities have been much less enthusiastic. Grimsby for instance promised its support in 1964, but did not back it with any financial commitments; many argued that better road links to the national motorway network should be given priority. In 1966, the Central Unit for Environmental Planning began work on the feasibility of major urban and industrial development on Humberside. Earlier, the Minister of Housing and Local Government proposed a new city of 750,000 on the south bank, though with a timetable which would postpone construction until the nineteen eighties. The Leeds School of Town Planning had also produced a scheme for a new town of 130,000 in the vicinity of Killingholme and Barton on Humber. A little later, there were suggestions of a 'million city', probably in the lowlands between Selby and Goole, and thus north of the new Thorne motorway (Lane, 1966). These schemes give the impression of ever-escalating dreams.

The Humberside feasibility study (Central Unit for Environmental Planning, 1968) considered the area's future under two different assumptions, and suggested a population increase over present levels of either 550,000 or 1 million by the end of the century. A variety of forms for expansion were considered, with an emphasis on sites some distance away from tidewater; a conclusion was reached that a very promising development would be a new city at Limber some 16 kilometres (10 miles) north west of Grimsby, together with a new town in the North Cave area on what by then will be a motorway link from Hull to West Yorkshire. The cost of the larger development scheme would be £1,800 to £2,000 million over a 25 year period. However, there have been subsequent suggestions that no major Humberside industrial developments should begin before 1980—even though the Humber bridge will be completed by 1976 at an overall cost (including the approach roads) of some £23 million. These recommendations point up a number of serious weaknesses in the planning strategy of the Yorkshire and Humberside region as a whole.

8.5 Continuing dilemmas

There is first, and most important, the unresolved dichotomy of interest between the industrial west and Humberside. Alone among the country's great conurbations, that of the West Riding has never shown any desire for planned overspill or for new town construction. Partly no doubt this reflects both the dispersed pattern and distinctive physical framework of the conurbation, but it is also a response to its economic status intermediate between the dynamism of the London, West Midlands and even South East Lancashire conurbations on the one hand, and the more depressed but overcrowded ones in the Development Areas on the other. The Humberside City of the Leeds School of Town Planning was designed largely for West Riding overspill. When the representatives of the Central Unit for Environmental Planning first discussed their study with the Economic Planning Council in 1966, they also envisaged that some population should be transferred from the West Riding. Yet, as was shown in the Halifax and Calder Valley study, the Council itself preferred to give redevelopment in West Yorkshire precedence over new developments on Humberside. Their attitude was to provoke a mild rebuke from the Hunt Committee: '... we think that any deliberate designation of regional growth points ought preferably to be made in a wider context' (Secretary of States for Economic Affairs, 1969, p. 61). By this time, of course, forecasts of national population growth were being revised downwards, and the prospects for major new developments in the region had worsened. For some time, therefore, it was clear that opportunities were going to be foregone in a locality where—as the Humberside feasibility study had shown, even on the least favourable assumptions—development costs would only be 5 per cent or so higher than in the lowest cost area of Britain, and where (it might have been added, though it would have been difficult to quantify) the benefits were likely to be exceptionally high.

From the postponement of major Humberside plans for population growth and economic development stems the second weakness of the strategy. The Humber Bridge, its associated roads and other related motorway developments in the sub-region will cost relatively little in comparison with the estimated expense of a major population expansion there. The bridge and its approach roads would require an investment equivalent to less than 2 per cent of the total urban development costs under the Central Unit's assumptions for a population growth of ¾ million by 2000 A.D. Nevertheless, the two projects should be examined together. Instead they are being considered, judged and programmed separately, with the result that the full economic benefit which might have been derived from the bridge and the road investments will not (at least for some time) be secured, and what undoubtedly could be a major national growth zone will be handicapped. Yorkshire and Humberside are indeed an object lesson in the dilemmas of a mature industrial economy unwilling to go fully for long term economic gain, for fear of short term economic loss. Old areas can be made viable, but in a case such as this the price may be a high one.

REFERENCES :

British Iron and Steel Federation (1966). *The Steel Industry. The Stage* 1 *Report of the Development Coordinating Committee,* B.I.S.F., London.

Central Unit for Environmental Planning (1969). *Humberside : A Feasibility Study,* H.M.S.O., London.

Economic Development Committee for the Wool Textile Industry (1969). *The Strategic Future of the Wool Textile Industry,* H.M.S.O., London.

Edwards, K. C. (1949). The East Midlands. In G. H. J. Daysh (Ed.), *Studies in Regional Planning,* George Philip, London. pp. 138–168.

Forgarty, M. P. (1945). *Prospects of the Industrial Areas of Great Britain,* Methuen, London.

Hodson, R. (1968). Survey of Yorkshire and Humberside, *Financial Times,* 30 October.

Kingston-upon-Hull (c. 1959). *Planning in Action,* City Council, Kingston-upon-Hull.

Kingston-upon-Hull (1965/66). *Town Planning Officer's Annual Report,* City Council, Kingston-upon-Hull.

Lane, L. (1966). *The Guardian,* 18 January.

Leafe, R. Y. (1967). The Port of Immingham. *The East Midland Geographer,* **4,** June, 127–142.

Local Government Commission (1964). *Report on the West Yorkshire Special Review Area,* H.M.S.O., London.

Mitchell, J. B. (Ed.) (1962). *Great Britain : Geographical Essays,* Cambridge University Press, Cambridge.

Ogilvie, A. G. (Ed.) (1928). *Great Britain. Essays in Regional Geography,* Cambridge University Press, Cambridge.

Page, J. K. (1969). In H. R. Wilkinson (Ed.), *Regional Planning in Britain.* University of Hull, Kingston-upon-Hull. Miscellaneous series in Geography, p. 28.

Royal Commission on Local Government in England (1969). *Written Evidence,* H.M.S.O., London.

Secretary of State for Economic Affairs (1969). *The Intermediate Areas,* (Chairman : Sir Joseph Hunt), (Cmnd.3998), H.M.S.O., London.

Stratford, A. and Associates (1967). *An Airport Programme for Yorkshire and Humberside,* A.S.&A., Maidenhead.

Voice of Yorkshire and Humberside Industry (Monthly).

Warren, K. (1969a). Coastal Steelworks—A Case for Argument. *Three Banks Review,* **81,** June, 25–38.

Warren, K. (1969b). Recent Changes in the Geographical Location of the British Steel Industry, *Geographical Journal,* **135,** 343–364.

West Riding County Council (1968). *Evidence to the Hunt Committee,* W.R.C.C., Wakefield.

West Riding County Council (1968). *County Development Plan—Second Review,* W.R.C.C., Wakefield.

Yorkshire and Humberside Economic Planning Council (1966). *A Review of Yorkshire and Humberside,* H.M.S.O., London.

Yorkshire and Humberside Economic Planning Council (1968). *Halifax and Calder Valley. An Area Study,* H.M.S.O., London.

Yorkshire and Humberside Economic Planning Council (1969). *Huddersfield and Colne Valley,* H.M.S.O., London.

Yorkshire and Humberside Economic Planning Council (1970). *Doncaster : an Area Study,* H.M.S.O., London.

CHAPTER 9

The North East

KENNETH WARREN

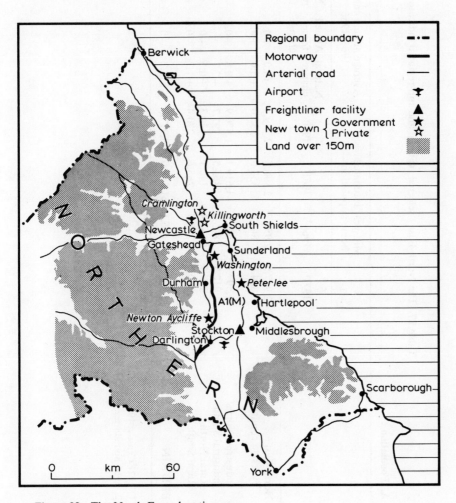

Figure 29 The North East: location map.

Table 27. The North East : selected regional and sub-regional indicators

A. Population :

Thousands

	Mid-year estimated home population				Average annual change 1961–1966			Average annual change 1951–1961		
	1971[1]	1966[2]	1961[2]	1950[2]	Natural change	Armed forces change	Net migration	Natural change	Armed forces change	Net migration
North East	2,927.5	2,950.7	2,890.3	2,779.4	+19.0	+0.1	−6.9	+17.9	+0.4	−7.9
Tyneside conurbation	804.4	844.0	853.0	835.0	+5.0	+0.2	−6.6	+5.1	+0.5	−3.8
Industrial North	1,597.1	1,634.6	1,619.1	1,570.9	+9.6	+0.3	−6.8	+9.9	+1.1	−6.1
Industrial South	912.3	895.0	865.5	797.7	+7.7	—	−1.9	+6.7	+0.5	−0.4
Rural North	137.7	142.4	140.1	140.3	+0.5	+0.1	−0.1	+0.5	+0.1	−0.6
Rural South	280.4	278.7	265.6	270.4	+1.2	−0.4	+1.8	+0.8	−1.1	−0.1
BRITAIN	53,821.4	53,176.1	51,380.0	48,917.5	+328.2	−0.5	+22.6	+231.4	−12.9	+1.9

1. 1971 Census; 1971 boundaries.
2. 1966 boundaries.

B. Employment :

	Employment		Male employment		Proportion of women at work		Unemployment range		
	1966	Change 1961– 1966	1966	Change 1961– 1966	1966	Change in % 1961– 1966	1968	1967	1961– 1966
	'000s	%	'000s	%	%	%	%	%	%
North East	1,200	+2	790	+2	35	+3	4–5	3–4	3–4
Industrial North	700	+2	460	−2	37	+3	4–5	3–4	3–4
Industrial South	380	+3	260	Nil	35	+3	4–5	3–4	3–4
Rural North	50	+2	30	−4	29	+3	3–4	3–4	2–3
Rural South	70	+6	40	+3	25	+2	3–4	2–3	2–3
BRITAIN	23,550	+4	14,900	+2	40	+2	2–3	2–3	1–2

C. Industrial Development Certificates :

	Estimated additional employment from i.d.c. approvals			
	Total 1956–1967 '000s	Annual averages		
		1964–1967 '000s	1960–1963 '000s	1956–1959 '000s
North East	136.5	20.2	9.8	4.1
Industrial North	72.7	9.8	6.2	2.2
Industrial South	57.2	9.4	3.0	1.9
Rural North	3.3	0.4	0.4	—
Rural South	3.3	0.6	0.2	—
BRITAIN	1,245.2	121.8	108.1	81.2

9.1 Introduction

The outsider commonly has a stereotyped mental image of North East England. In it a poor, slow-growth economy, a heavily unbalanced social structure and a cultural desert is given form in pit heaps, derelict factories, belching chimneys and drab urban landscapes of terraced housing, the whole within a harsh physical setting. Each of these elements may indeed be found in various parts of the region but, as a general evocation of regional personality, the image is of the same order of accuracy as a view of the 'congested South East' which portrays an absence of uninterrupted rural landscapes and an environment dominated by the rush of cars and the stench of their petrol fumes. The North East is much richer in its variation than the outsider believes (Cherry, 1967).

Although Durham and Northumberland are obviously its core it is a difficult region to delineate in any realistic sense. The functional economic heart until the nineteenth century was in the tidewater zone from which small coal pits could be tapped, especially along Tyneside and Wearside. Beyond were county and market towns and rural villages. Rail transport, a growing demand for coal and industrialization subsequently spread economic growth throughout most of the coal-field—a roughly triangular area from Amble, 40 kilometres (25 miles) north of the Tyne, to a point west of Bishop Auckland, and from there east to Hartlepool. South of this line Darlington and Teesside also became major industrial centres. Further out still, industrial development made new calls on the rural fringe, partly for food but also for minerals; lead, iron ore, barytes, fluorspar, limestone and even coal were mined in the Pennines or their fringes, and ironstone was quarried in the Cleveland Hills. In the twentieth century, there has been something of a reversion to older patterns. The last Cleveland ore mines closed in 1964; Pennine lead, iron ore and coal working died out long ago. The other minerals are still worked, and potash has recently become a Cleveland product. The fall in coal output in the main field implies a focusing of economic prospects within the core area, and in the absence of an active planning policy there can be little doubt that these would crystallize around the bigger regional focuses of Darlington, Teesside and Tyneside and to a lesser extent in the so-called 'growth' zone which links the last two.

In many ways the North East is similar to two other British Development Areas—South Wales and Scotland. Problems of coal and steel are shared with both, and in engineering and shipbuilding there are close parallels with the Scottish scene. However there are significant differences too. In part these stem from important historical contrasts in the industrial structure of the three regions. The greater buoyancy of the contemporary Welsh steel industry, and the more rapid diversification of Scottish engineering are rooted in past patterns of growth. They also reflect different space relations with the core area of the British economy centred in the West Midlands and the South East. South Wales increasingly has opportunities to serve as a heavy industrial outlier of this area. Mid-Scotland is sufficiently far away, and within a big enough regional economy, to justify a highly complex industrial structure. The North East in some ways falls sadly in between. Another factor of some importance in these Development Area contrasts is political. Wales and Scotland have a power to influence the central government's decision-taking processes which the North East has so far struggled hard but unsuccessfully to match. One of the more recent examples was the decision to site the British Steel Corporation's general products division headquarters in Glasgow, even though Teesside will have a far larger share of its capacity. Moreover northeastern influence is still unfortunately lessened by local authority internecine wrangling.

In 1971 the North East, defined for convenience as Northumberland, Durham and the whole North Riding of Yorkshire, contained nearly 3 million people or 6.0 per cent the total for England and Wales on 9.1 per cent of its area. Although they hide some widely varying sub-regional trends, generalizations about the northeastern economy as a whole provide a valuable standard of reference for comparisons between the region and other parts of Britain. Unemployment rates, for example, are generally twice the national average and now, as in the nineteen thirties, variations in national prosperity affect the region to a magnified degree. The deflationary measures of July 1966 had severe repercussions in the North East : even 18 months later seven of the government's advance factories in the region were still tenantless, and the continuation of the squeeze into 1969 killed some big capital development schemes from outside firms. Activity rates and income levels continue to be low by national standards; a family expenditure survey in the mid nineteen sixties revealed a regional gross household income before tax averaging only 88.6 per cent of the national figure, and the lowest in Britain. Net out-migration continues; consequently, the population growth in the region is slow, and in some sections there has been decline. The region's share of the national population continues to drift downwards; in a rough and ready way the various aspects of its changing fortunes are summed in the fact that 6.7 per cent of the 1931 population of England and Wales lived in the North East, whereas this proportion had fallen to 6.3 per cent in 1951, 6.0 per cent in 1971 and (prospectively) 5.9 per cent by 1981 (Northern Economic Planning Council 1969a, pp. 20–21).

There is a common cause for all these signs of distress. The staple trades on which past economic expansion was built have declined, and new growth industries have not arrived sufficiently quickly to offset the effects. The new employers have different requirements from the old in the number and skills of their workers, in their raw material needs and outlets, and so in their location. Change in the economic geography of the North East is thus inevitable. The coal-field, as the fountainhead of the former industrial growth, has become the chief problem in a new age. Accordingly, its economic and social dilemmas are examined before consideration is given to the contemporary growth areas of the North East which mark the coal-field's coastal and southern edge.

9.2 The Coal-field

Until recently coalmining was the largest single source of employment in the region, and the one whose influence was most widespread. The coal seams dip generally seawards, and beyond a line from South Shields to a point east of Bishop Auckland are concealed beneath a thick cover of Magnesian Limestone. The grade of the coal generally decreases outwards from a node around Consett in northwest Durham. Both west Durham and southeast Durham have coking coal, but gas and steam coals become more common away from the northwest. Just before World War I, the so-called Great Northern coalfield was second only to the combined Yorkshire and East Midlands fields in output with an annual average of over 54 million tons. Pre-1914 peaks were almost reached again in the early nineteen twenties, and the Tyne's record coal shipments of over 20 million tons were made in 1923. The mid and late twenties were years of creeping depression, and were followed by the apocalyptic experience of the Great Depression. By 1937 employment in coal mines had fallen to 162,000—64,000 less than in 1913. Post-1945, reconstruction and rationalization following the nationalization of the mines was accompanied by an increasing output until the late nineteen fifties. After that, in response to increasing competition from alternative fuels and steadily contracting markets, the decline began again. In the year ending 31 March, 1969, the northeastern field produced 23.2 million tons of deep mined coal.

The concentration of operations and an accelerating shift eastwards are leading characteristics of the process of adjustment. As late as 1947 there were 225 working pits; by March 1969 there were only 56. An even more rapid shrinkage is now anticipated (Table 28). In 1966, only 37 of the 105 existing pits were described by the National Coal Board

Table 28. The North East : number of coal-mines and output, 1959, 1967, 1969 and 1975 (est.)

	Number of pits at work (and date)	Output (million tons)
1959	174 (end June)	35.1
1967	84 (end March)	27.2
1969	56 (end March)	23.2
1975 (est.)	12–14	?

Source : National Coal Board.

(N.C.B.) as 'long life' units; 20 were said to have a doubtful future and the other 48 were scheduled for closure within the subsequent few years. The 1967 White Paper on *Fuel Policy* (Cmnd. 3438) forecast—and implicitly gave government approval for—an even more rapid movement from coal. Northeastern productivity is low—in 1968/1969 when national output per man-shift was 2.13 tons, the figure for the Northumberland area was 2.00 tons, for South Durham 1.79 tons and for North Durham 1.69 tons—and of the three subdivisions only the Northumberland area made a profit before interest payments in 1968/69. The operations in both North and South Durham were both conducted at a working loss of £0.133 per ton. In addition the North East lacks a major local market for coal comparable to that of the Yorkshire and East Midland pits which for many years will serve the power stations along the Aire, the Calder and the Trent. There are, to be sure, some large existing agglomerations of generating capacity along the Tyne, and the two units at Blyth alone consume over 3½ million tons coal a year (over 40 per cent of the output of Northumberland pits), but the new 1,250 MW power station for Seaton Carew, which might have provided assured employment for up to 9,000 Durham miners, is to be nuclear. By the mid nineteen seventies, the prospect is for a continuing important output from a handful of pits in the Blyth-Ashington area, with Ellington-Lynemouth alone producing 2½ million tons; but in the whole of County Durham there will probably be no more than seven pits, all of them coastal. These will include Westoe pit in South Shields, Wearmouth Colliery (Sunderland) and five in the Seaham-Horden area, and will represent the final stage in the long established eastward trend in the centres of mining.

As late as 1958 some 140,000 men worked in the coal mines of the North East. In 1965 there were 94,000; in January 1969 only 63,000 remained. By 1975 the figure is expected to have shrunk to a mere 25,000. Lord Robens has even spoken of as few as 6,500 miners in the region by 1980. In the past, the N.C.B. has had considerable success in finding jobs for displaced miners in the region's remaining pits. Some 79 per cent of those displaced between 1958 and 1966 were found new work in this way; and in addition, from 1960 to 1968, a further 5,000 men were transferred to Midland pits—a policy which was stopped in the latter year when the displacement of men in the reception areas became rapid also. In the future—quite apart from the fact that local transfers and a longer journey to work will become increasingly impracticable for many miners as the pits become more highly concentrated—it is clear that new industries will have to replace the job opportunities lost in coal mining. The prospective contraction of N.C.B. employments will represent far and away the largest component in the forecast loss of perhaps 150,000 jobs in the old basic trades of the Northern Region; and most of these will disappear from the North East (Northern Economic Planning Council 1969 a, pp. 6–8). It has been estimated that merely to replace coal mine labour which is likely to be lost between 1969 and 1980 will require an annual provision of over 5,000 new jobs; and up to 1975 the rate will be over 6,000. Both east and west Durham face immense problems of adjustment. The substantial problems of the Northumberland section of the field will be examined later.

East of the Great North Road (A1), many communities have already lost their pit. The loss of what is generally their only source of employment has not only disturbed their patterns of work but also threatened their standards of living. Older men find it difficult to find a new job, and for all ages most alternative employment pays less well than mining (House & Knight, 1967). In the early nineteen seventies whole districts, rather than localities, will lose their mine employment. However, *east Durham* has more favourable topographical and climatic conditions than the county to the west. Its mining settlements, although still unattractive, were built later; as a result they have better housing, and are rather larger. This eastern section of the coal-field—lying between Tyneside and Teesside, and between British Rail's main London-Edinburgh main line and its coastal line—was in fact recognized by the government in its White Paper on the *North East* (Secretary of State for Industry, 1963) as a 'growth zone'. Its northern and southern parts are within easy commuting distance of either Tyneside and Wearside or the nascent Teesside conurbation; indeed there is already a daily flow of labour throughout the whole zone.

Within the coal mining belt itself, there are important new foci of employment at Peterlee and Washington (see Figure 30). The former, although established as a new town as early as 1948, developed only slowly and with difficulty until the early nineteen sixties. In recent years, however, it has become a much more significant growth point. In the 2½ years to mid-1968, Board of Trade approval was given for projects which are estimated to provide 1,027 male jobs and 1,912 jobs for women. Since the autumn of 1967, when the government introduced Special Development Area (S.D.A.) status for localities affected by coal mine closure, a 100 hectare (240 acre) area west of the A19 and beyond the previously planned limits of the new town has been scheduled for industrial development. There are ambitious plans for a science-based industrial park in the town, but these may yet fall foul of intraregional rivalries in the form of developments connected with the proposed Teesside Technological University. Some years ago a new linear city along the Durham motorway was proposed and more recently the need for a new city of some 500,000 population—along the lines of the Central Lancashire new city (see p. 323)—has been suggested to serve as a much needed focus for new developments (Northern Architect, 1969, pp. 28,29). Neither scheme appears to be more than a physical planner's dream, but already impressive growth is occurring at long established centres along or near the motorways such as Team Valley, Birtley, Spennymoor and (another new town, designated in 1947) Newton Aycliffe.

There will nevertheless be problems enough in the east as rationalization in coalmining continues. Journeys to work will lengthen, there will be much individual hardship, family income will fall in many cases and some communities will shrink. In *west Durham*, on the other hand, the problems are even starker and much more intractable. The major redeeming factor is that in some parts the process of contraction is already far advanced. In 1831 the population of County Durham to the west of the Great North Road was some 50,000. By the early nineteen fifties some 300,000 lived there. Pits which turned out about 13 million tons of coal a year then employed 40,000 workers (Daysh and Symmonds, 1953, pp. 3–4). As late as 1957, at the end of the period of post-1945 expansion, there were still 81 pits in this section although they were generally much smaller than those in the east, and very few employed over 1,500 men. Yet by 1965 only 29 remained in production, and all but ten were scheduled for imminent closure. Already the industry had almost disappeared in some localities. Within little more than 5 kilometres (3 miles) from Consett, there were nine pits in 1957; there were 11 in a similar area around Bishop Auckland. In each case only three pits, all threatened with imminent closure, survived eight years later. Between 1947 and 1968, the mine labour force in west Durham fell from 42,000 to 7,000. By mid-1970, 11 pits employing 4,800 men were still at work west of the A1. Only three of these with 1,390 were in southwest Durham. However, in the 14 years to December 1969, other employers granted industrial development certificates were expected to provide employment for 23,700 persons in west Durham. Much of this new employment is in the bigger centres of population such as Bishop Auckland, Spennymoor and Stanley. In addition, of course, new jobs have been found beyond the boundaries of the zone on Tyneside, at Team Valley or in Darlington, for example. But the more remote parts of the coal-field, having lost their traditional source of employment, are unable to attract a new one.

West Durham is served by one important trunk route, the A68 from Darlington to Edinburgh. Elsewhere, roads of only fair quality link the communities along the western edge of the coal-field with the main axis of movement in central Durham. In the nineteen thirties one of these was improved from Durham to Lanchester in order to help to open up the northwest, but it still does not penetrate into the sub-region's heart. Whilst, in hauls to midland or southeast markets, the extra time and length of the journey from such west Durham communities as Crook or Tow Law is insignificant, prospective manufacturing industries are deterred by a number of adverse factors.

One, difficult to quantify, but important partly for that reason, is the psychological view of distance. It is common to regard anywhere more than about 8 kilometres (5 miles) away from the Great North Road or Durham motorway as a remote location. Second, although there is grand, open country in west Durham, the physical environment is harsh even when compared with the bracing conditions of the northeastern lowlands. Third, in an area of such scattered population, the assembly of a labour force is far from easy. Fourth, man-made amenities in west Durham are relatively few, and depressingly narrow in range. New foci of employment may be provided by the larger centres of the zone, but it is futile to expect that the pattern of new work can be matched to the scatter of population which mining supported in the past. The North East Development Council— a body representing local authorities, industry and commerce and with access to Department of Trade and Industry grants in aid—has made a compromise proposal that industrial estates, each with six or seven firms on them, should be developed within reasonable travelling distance of every mining village.

In the past, ever-lengthening journeys to work in the remaining mines of the zone and to alternative sources of employment in east Durham, plus the creation of new jobs in the west, have checked an overall population decline to a remarkable extent. In the coal-field district of northwest Durham, which gained only 6,000 new jobs between 1956 and 1968, the population of the three local authority areas (Consett and Stanley urban districts, and the more extensive rural district of Lanchester) has declined steadily but slowly. Their peak population was 111,000 in 1921. By 1951 the total was 103,000; by 1961 it was 100,000; and it had fallen to 91,500 by 1971. In view of the change in the employment structure of County Durham, however, and the accelerating concentration of coal production, it is doubtful whether the population decline can be held at a comparably low rate in the future. Combined with the new projections of national population growth, this has caused the Northern Economic Planning Council to write down its earlier forecasts for West Durham population (Table 29). This step has given added point to the controversy over the Durham County Council plan to concentrate new housing and services in only a limited number of the existing communities—essentially a programme for organized sub-regional contraction, but aimed to minimize the discomforture of the population living in that area.

Table 29. County Durham : population of the east, northwest and
southwest sub-regions, 1964–1981 (est.)

(thousands)

	1964 (actual)	1981 (1966 estimates)	1981 (1969 estimates)
North East	2,937	3,316	3,188
of which :			
East Durham	190	204	193
Southwest Durham	166	166	152
Northwest Durham	98	98	83

Source : Northern Economic Planning Council, 1966, 1969a.

The County Development Plan of 1951 classified towns and villages of Durham into four categories, A to D. Of the villages, 70 were grouped in category A; these were reckoned suitable for substantial growth and therefore for further investment. The 143 category B villages were to be allotted sufficient funds to meet the changing needs of a static population, and 30 category C villages, likely to have a slowly declining population, were scheduled for minimum investment. The rest, 114 villages or almost one third, were expected to lose a substantial part of their population, and were therefore reckoned unsuitable for further development. When existing houses in these category D villages were abandoned, they were not to be replaced in the same village. This scheme was approved by the Minister of Housing and Local Government in 1954, and again in 1968 in the amended Development Plan. By this time one or two of the very small D villages had been completely demolished, but numbers in the group had increased slightly as a result of reclassification. A very high percentage of these villages lie to the west of the Great North Road (Table 30). The changes in mining, and the prospective population trends, make the policy even more rational than when it was first announced.

On the other hand it has been argued by the supporters of preservation, now institu-

Table 30. County Durham : distribution of villages as classified in 1951, east or west of the A1 road

Category of village	Location in relation to the A1 road (Gateshead-Durham-Darlington)	
	West	East
A	30	24
B	72	63
C	7	21
D	87	26

Source : Durham County Council, 1951.

tionalized as the County Redevelopment of Villages Action Committee (C.R.O.V.A.C.), that with improved transport the remote villages could readily become dormitory communities. The point of increased personal mobility must be taken, and the dormitory function of west Durham is in fact already growing. However, there can be little doubt that investment per capita would be increased by scattering it. It is also clear that not all modern amenities can be widely distributed and, if places of work and residence are not reasonably matched, there can be no long-term assurance of the viability of the villages, however vigorous their present community life—something which is in any case more commonly claimed than proved. New, evolving patterns of settlement in west Durham are obviously desirable, and attention must be switched from narrow, preservationist views to these new horizons. Individual hurt is unfortunately inevitable in this process. Superficially Durham County Council appears to have compromised its policy by a recent decision to invite district councils to prepare a case for the removal of any village from the D category, but in fact few believe that in the long run the County will be willing to recant. Larger villages and towns are looked on as 'anchor' or major 'regrouping' points for the population displaced from the non-viable village communities, and the centre of many of these towns is being or is to be redeveloped.

9.3 The Iron and Steel Industry

Whilst the prospective evolution of the coal industry and the settlement pattern of west Durham appears reasonably clear, one major doubt concerning the economic future of the zone remains. This centres on the town of Consett, a community of 40,000 which is very largely dependent upon the local steelworks, and which may be looked upon as an outlier of the coastal metallurgical complexes. The problem lies in the fact that within the framework of a new, nationalized steel industry, Consett may be transformed from an outlier to a troublesome appendage inviting surgery.

Ironmaking was once widely spread throughout County Durham and even Northumberland. Steelmaking was much more concentrated, and the removal of the Tudhoe works from Spennymoor to Middlesbrough in the first years of the twentieth century marked the penultimate stage of concentration on the coast. The industry disappeared from Tyneside with the closure of the Newburn works and the much bigger plant at Jarrow between the years 1925 and 1932. Thereafter, only three large centres of steelmaking remained—on the south bank of the Tees estuary (from Middlesbrough to Redcar), at West Hartlepool and at Consett (Warren, 1969). Skinningrove on the Cleveland coast survived as a very small but integrated works. The decline and eventual abandonment of the Cleveland ore supplies made the whole of the northeastern industry completely dependent upon foreign iron ore. This has been imported through the Tyne for Consett, at West Hartlepool for the nearby furnaces, and through two points on the south bank of the Tees estuary. The industry's coking coal comes from Durham pits and (as working has moved down dip) increasingly from the rather poorer coking seams of the east. Skinningrove, exceptional in its lack of coke ovens, obtains its supplies from N.C.B. ovens in southeast Durham.

Since the early nineteen fifties, the growth of iron and steel making capacity and output has been almost inversely related to the intrinsic suitability of the several locations for low cost production. Annual capacity at Consett has expanded fivefold since 1946 and is now approaching 2 million ingot tons. At West Hartlepool, with its wholly inadequate ore port, expansion went on against the intentions of the British Iron and Steel Federation, and in 1958 work was begun on a wholly new plant at Greatham, 3 kilometres (2 miles) to the west. The Dorman Long complex on Teesside has grown less, and in the nineteen sixties performed very badly as a result of its emphasis on heavy steels, notably structurals and plate. Yet there is no doubt that the Dorman Long plants are in the ideal situation for any expansion of steel production in the North East. For this reason, the British Steel Corporation, as part of its corporate planning, is to build up capacity there adjacent to a new £15 million ore terminal at Redcar, which will be able to handle 100,000 dwt ore carriers initially—and eventually vessels of perhaps 200,000 dwt (Warren, 1969). The planned expansion of the new, high capacity, Lackenby oxygen steel plant initially to 2 million ingot tons, and eventually to 5 million tons or more, will be followed by the closure of steel making plant (though not necessarily the rolling mills) at Cargo Fleet, Redcar and Skinningrove. Although the older Hartlepool works will be abandoned, some additional expansion at Greatham will still leave a major production facility awkwardly located on the north bank. All of the ore for this complex will be imported through Redcar, possibly by means of a long rail haul via Stockton, although foreign operations have shown that there are alternatives such as a shuttle service of barges or even a high-level conveyor belt across the estuary. By the nineteen eighties all steelmaking will probably be concentrated on the south side of the Tees estuary with new developments towards Redcar. Consett's relative importance will be reduced, although for some time its furnaces will be supplied by rail from the Tees. Already the blast furnaces at the Cargo Fleet works are making good the Consett deficiency in iron capacity; a daily shuttle service of hot metal has been arranged on a circuitous rail route which brings the trains up the east side of the county through Pelaw and Gateshead, followed by the long climb up to the plateau. The social factor is brought into the forefront of locational discussions when Consett's longer-term prospects are assessed.

The modern plant at Consett is a direct descendent of an ironworks built in 1840 and based on local coal and coal measure ore. As such it is analagous to the works of mid-Lanarkshire and, even more closely, to the plant at Ebbw Vale. Like them, it is now wholly dependent on imported ore. As local coking coal collieries have closed, so has the length of haul on its fuel also increased; within a few years the prospective concentration of mining near the coast means that the nearest pit will be over 32 kilometres (20 miles) away by rail. To these relatively high raw material assembly costs (and the fact that the North East is a scrap–deficient region) has been added a progressively less advantageous market situation. In particular, changes in the amount and the type of steel used in the shipyards, plus keen competition from Teesside and Lincolnshire plants, have made its former Tyneside and Wearside markets relatively less important than in the past. Yet, as locational conditions have moved against it, Consett has been modernized and extended. As nearby mining employment dwindled, the Consett Iron Company adopted a policy of laying off more distant rather than local workers at time of hardship, so that the works has become increasingly important in sub-regional employment. By 1968 the steel works was said to spend in the order of £25 million a year on salaries and services in the area. From this it is easy to make a superficially plausible case that the closure of Consett is unthinkable to any humane man. 'Every business in northwest Durham would face bankruptcy. The waste of social capital, in towns, schools and other facilities would be incalculable. The human suffering could not be measured' (Watkins, 1968).

Like many other towns or villages in west Durham, Consett presents a bleak prospect to the outsider. The marked atmospheric pollution, the universal dustiness as a result of a steelworks only a few hundred metres west of the town centre, and the poverty of the town's housing stock, all suggest that there is little social capital worth preserving in terms of physical structure. The question of the values of its social life, of the future for its society rather than its material possessions, is a much more serious issue. It has been suggested that the social cohesion, and the identification of this with a particular (albeit ill-favoured) place, is characteristic of the older age groups. It is also noted that the young are moving away quickly, and that any reconstruction will be too slow to retain the potential community leaders of the next generation. In the narrow terms of steel making economics, the perpetuation of what will undoubtedly prove to be a steadily worsening location is indefensible. The gradual closure of the works, combined with the most assiduous care to assist the attraction of new footloose trades, to facilitate the outmovement of people and to minimise hardship, can be argued as the best policy.

At the same time, it is also clear that the prospects for Consett have been delineated by many in colours of too dark a hue, for several reasons. First, even if the ironworks and steel plant do close within 5 years or so, the Consett rolling mills will be kept at work for a number of years working up semi-finished steel from Teesside. Second, as a fairly large community, Consett is proving able to attract new sources of employment. In 1968, for example, an American firm began to produce a carpet backing which, it is claimed, is greatly superior to the more traditional jute. Showing great vigour, it antici-pates an employment of over 1,000—more than one-sixth of the steelwork's labour force. Whilst this development will help to reduce the unemployment problem of Con-sett, it will incidentally shift some of the burden to other afflicted areas of Britain (and curbs on national consumer spending have already led to a sharp decline in demand for carpets and for Dundee's common jute backing). Third, in other ways too the possibility of new industrial growth is being repeatedly demonstrated in several parts of northwest Durham. Ball bearing manufacture, for example, is already important at Annfield Plain. Ever Ready Batteries are made—largely for export markets--at Stanley. In 1969, new Board of Trade advance factories were announced for Team Valley, Consett and Stanley, and Durham County Council is planning a new industrial estate at Tanfield Lea.

9.4 The Expanding Conurbations

Already the changing status of the Consett steelworks has affected the larger, river-based, industrial complexes to the east. For some years, at least, hot metal for Consett (later iron ore, and eventually slabs for finishing) will come from Teeside, thereby boosting investment and employment there. The process of run down at Consett could also affect *Tyneside*—in general by removing an important outside source of purchasing power for its services, and more specifically through its effects upon particular localities within the conurbation. The closure of the Consett billet mill, for example, might put at hazard the Consett Iron Company's rerolling mills at Jarrow. More certain are the effects upon the port of Tyne.

For some years, the Tyne dock at South Shields which is able to handle vessles of 35,000 dwt has been the deepest draught iron ore terminal in Britain and iron ore is currently the largest single import of the river. Indeed, thanks to the past buoyancy of the Consett works, that trade has varied much less since the mid nineteen sixties than has ore traffic on the river Tees. However, when the new £15 million Redcar terminal is completed in 1972, the Tyne Dock will close, and the port of Tyne will lose a most valuable revenue. Its grain and timber trades will remain important, but the traffic in refined oils to nearby tank farms on both sides of the river—an import which has grown rapidly in recent years—is also imperilled by new developments in transport. Now that the new Shell refinery is in production at Teesport, Shell Mex and British Petroleum are handling their product distribution for the Tyneside conurbation in 70 ton capacity rail tank cars over the 64 kilometre (40 mile) route, rather than in small tankers loaded at Grangemouth or on Thamesside. Taken with the rapidly dwindling coastwise shipments of coal, as other fuels and rail shipments of coal together cut into its old outlets, the decline of the port seems inevitable. New east coast container facilities, first at Hull and then on the Tees and at Grangemouth—facilities which are scarcely matched by the Port of Tyne's new (1969) North Shields terminal for Esbjerg—have been another adverse development and, except on a few routes such as those to Scandinavia or to the southern shores of the North Sea, it is clear that ports elsewhere offer better services by cargo liner than does the Tyne. These conditions account for the considerable use which the conurbation's industries make of other ports for their overseas shipments. Tyneside fears when the National Ports Council failed to include the port in its list of the 14 to share in a £150 million improvement programme have been amply justified by subsequent events. Yet, in spite of this, the conurbation has economic prospects as bright as those of any part of the North East.

Tyneside has an official population of 0.8 million but when the conservative nature of conurbation definitions and lengthening journeys to work are taken into account, 1 million is a more realistic figure. Its economy is far bigger and more diverse than that of any other area within the region and although the magnificence of its riverside industrial landscape seems to indicate a nineteenth rather than a twentieth century greatness, it has the formidable momentum of a large going-concern. Shipbuilding and heavy electrical engineering are distinctive trades but the rest of its manufacturing employment is spread through a wide range of activities. To these are added the tertiary employments appropriate to a second order commercial, shopping and cultural capital, plus a range of regional offices of central government. Both industry and office employment now show strong centrifugal tendencies.

A large acreage of derelict land on both banks of the river, but predominantly on the south side, is a legacy of the once considerable alkali industry whose last representatives were eliminated about 45 years ago. Some of this land has been used for other industrial premises, including the shipyards, and since 1968 a large area at Felling has been landscaped to form the first stage of a riverside park which will help to remedy the marked deficiency of recreational land in the centre of Tyneside. This dereliction, together with the difficult topography throughout the whole length of the river in the conurbation where it trenches through the Coal Measures, forced early twentieth century factories onto the plateau top if they had extensive space requirements. (Only recently has the ending of coal shipments from Tyne dock, and proposals to fill in the nearby Jarrow Slake, offered the prospect of another 70 hectares, approximately 170 acres, of riverside lowland available for industry). Post–1920 housing has taken up many of the remaining sites on the plateau, and incidentally filled in the open spaces between formerly distinct urban nuclei to create today's continuously built-up conurbation.

The subsequent need for good road access, and the trend to single storey buildings, provided further inducements to build new factories on the edge of the conurbation or, more recently still, beyond it. In exceptional cases firms have moved away from the area altogether, as with the closure of the Heaton Junction works of Metal Box in 1968 which cost the conurbation 700 jobs, but usually, even when displaced from congested areas, industrial firms and warehousing operations have found new peripheral sites. By 1968, for example, the Team Valley industrial estate, which was begun 22 years earlier in a newly drained valley bottom to the southwest of Gateshead and a kilometre from the A1, housed some 100 firms and employed 18,000 workers. Work was then begun to extend its area by one-fifth, although Team Valley already suffers from substantial peak hour traffic jams and is running out of room for further expansion. Smaller estates at North Shields, and between Jarrow and South Shields, were based on the Team Valley experience. Since 1945 there has also been impressive industrial development on the Newcastle to Tynemouth coast road, which has now been greatly improved; further industrial growth points can be recognized on the edge of the built up area at Ryton, Throckley and Westerhope.

This movement of manufacturing activities has been paralleled by shifts in service employment. Central Newcastle remains the focus both of existing office accommodation and of its growth; however, the centrifugal forces are strong (Ely, 1969). Government office accommodation provides a good example. The main regional offices of the several national ministries are grouped in an office block on the edge of the central business district. On the northern fringe of the conurbation, in contrast, are the head offices of the present Ministry of Social Security which were transferred from London to Long Benton in the years immediately after 1945. The Land Commission occupied a similar peripheral position at Kenton Bar. Somewhat nearer the heart of the conurbation, the extensive redevelopment of the centre of Gateshead, which is now under way, will include a new government office complex.

Both industrial and office employments are being dispersed still more widely to the planned new communities at Killingworth, Cramlington and Washington, which will in large part house overspill population from the Tyneside conurbation (Figure 30). In 1962, Northumberland County Council began work on its own new town for overspill population, industry and office employment on a 300 hectare (760 acre) site of marshy, derelict colliery land at Killingworth. Only 1.6 kilometres (1 mile) north of the conurbation's edge, the town is planned to house 20,000 people and its factories, warehouses and offices will eventually employ 7,000 of them. Additionally, it is intended that Killingworth will serve as a focus for another 30,000 people living in the drab, ill-serviced mining villages around it. A year after work was begun there, Ministry approval was given for a bigger, joint County Council and private enterprise, new town five kilometres (3 miles) further north at Cramlington. By the summer of 1968, some 11,000 lived in this area, and the initial target population for the early nineteen eighties (50,000) had been increased to 62,000. Its communications are good. Having the A1 only 1.6 kilometres (1 mile) to the west, a new spine road will link it to Long Benton and to Ashington, to the recently completed Tyne tunnel and to the North Eastern Regional Airport only 6 kilometres (4 miles) away to the southwest. Cramlington thus provides ideal locational conditions for industrial growth. Three industrial estates with an area totalling 280 hectares (700 acres)—equal to the whole site, still not fully developed, at Team Valley—

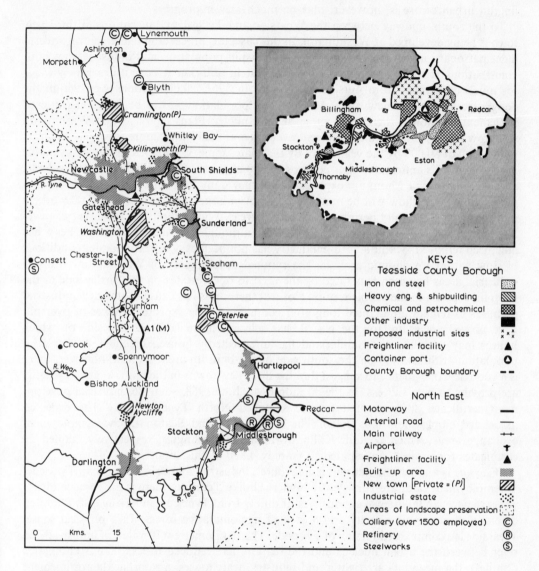

Figure 30 North East England: principal economic and land use features, 1971.

have been laid out and occupation is proceeding well. The development of the Cramlington urban centre is, however, making much slower progress.

To the south, midway between the Wearside and Tyneside conurbations, a third new town is being developed at Washington. In this case, it is proceeding under central government patronage and the New Towns Act. Overspill population and industry from both conurbations is to be accommodated there but in addition it constitutes a new focus for much investment from outside the region. In 1961, 20,000 people lived within the designated area of the new town. Much of this population was to be found in scattered settlements, although there were three distinct nuclei. Plans envisage that Washington will grow rapidly into the mid nineteen seventies and then rather more slowly to its target population of 80,000 by the year 2000. By that date, some 38,000 jobs should be available in the town. It is anticipated that perhaps 17,000 of these will be filled by local residents, an equal number of whom are expected to journey daily to neighbouring centres of employment. This outflow will be matched by an even larger daily influx of 21,000 workers into the town's generally peripheral industrial areas. Washington has a number of development problems. There are site difficulties—although the great central pit heap has now been removed. Manufacturing industry has not been easy to secure under conditions of slow national economic growth. The rational development of Washington's various industrial areas has been frustrated by the need to open estates on the Birtley side of the town in response to the problem of pit closures there; this has caused some new industrial premises to remain untenanted long after completion. The expected sources of overspill have proved uncertain, for the N.C.B. has released more land on Tyneside on which houses may be built, and Sunderland has unexpectedly housed much of its displaced population at Silksworth on the south side of the built up area. Overall, however, there is a good deal of evidence to suggest that the three new towns in the hinterland of Tyneside are proving to be a success. In the 30 months to June 1968, some 86 industrial development certificates were granted for the so-called North Tyneside area. The expected associated employment was 7,460. The West Moor and Seaton Delaval employment exchange areas, which contain Killingworth and Cramlington respectively, gained 23 certificates for projects anticipated to employ 4,890 of this total.

Wearside is a much smaller and less favoured industrial and urban area than Tyneside. Unemployment rates are persistently higher. Unlike Teesside, there is an absence of impressive new capital intensive industries. It differs from Tyneside, in having only a limited diversity of economic activity and a lack of agglomerative forces. In a physical sense, Wearside is a compressed version of Tyneside. The 16 kilometres (10 miles) of industrialized river between the urban nucleus and the sea are here reduced to less than 3 kilometres (2 miles), the meanders are tighter and industry, warehouses, a ramshackle arrangement of houses and the principal lines of communication all crowd in more closely upon a gorge which is much narrower, in this case cut through the Magnesian Limestone. Coal exports are still significant, but they have declined more rapidly even than those through the Tyne. Wearmouth colliery, however, sited within the conurbation, is one of the few

Durham pits whose long-life status survived the rescheduling of 1967. On the west side of the urban area, the Pallion industrial estate has the usual assembly of light industries and marks a valuable diversification of the area's economic base: but there is little room for further expansion and the recent history of some of its firms, notably in electronics, has not been at all stable. Although the heart of Wearside is less than 19 kilometres (12 miles) by road from central Newcastle, it seems strangely remote. The new Tyne Tunnel approach roads and the upgrading of the A19 to Teesside may help to improve this situation, and so assist in the attraction of new diversifying employments. On the other hand, the adjacent new town of Washington provides an economic growth point with many superior attractions to firms coming to the North East. Much more than with either Teesside or Tyneside, the economic prosperity and prospects of Wearside are associated with shipbuilding. Even in that activity, however, it lacks their advantages. The status of this northeastern staple can best be examined as a whole.

Into the early nineteen sixties over a dozen firms built ships on the North East coast. As foreign competition stiffened a number failed and their yards were closed. William Gray, the last Hartlepool firm, and (in 1966) the Blyth yard which had employed 1,000, are two examples. The 1966 Geddes Report on British shipbuilding stressed the necessity for a wholesale reorganization which would concentrate the industry into some five regional groups, and would bring economies from centralized design, purchasing, production control and the rationalization of separate workshops. The typical new unit was to employ 8,000 to 10,000 men, and to turn out up to 500,000 gross tons a year. In 1967 the Shipbuilding Industry Board was set up to make government loans and grants to help along this rationalization process. From the start it was realised that the obstacles were substantial. As an industrial correspondent put it 'It means uprooting physical and human barriers that have stood as long as the shipyard communities can remember; new places of work, new loyalties, promotion and disappointment, a lot of argument' (*The Guardian,* 25 March, 1966). The northeastern yards differed in their ability to respond to this challenge.

The large Wallsend firm of Swan Hunter predictably became the main coordinating force. It linked up with yards in North Shields and at South Bank (on Teesside) in 1966 and early in 1968 merged with all the other Tyne yards to form a new group known as Swan Hunter and Tyne Shipbuilders, which now employs 10,000 on that river. Since 1966, the size of tankers launched at its Wallsend yard has been stepped up from 65,000 dwt to 253,000 dwt and the firm speaks confidently of the prospects for building vessels twice or even four times as large through the construction of sections which would be joined together after launching. However, even if launch problems can be solved in this way, Tyneside provides by no means ideal conditions for modern ship construction. The little room left between the river cliff and the river is already highly congested with houses, other industries, railways and roads; as a result the layout of the shipyards is often poor, and modern assembly line construction techniques cannot be fully adopted.

Wearside's five important firms have now been merged into two, both of which have been very successful with dry cargo vessels. Neither has the capacity or sites to match the potentialities of the Swan Hunter group, however, and in spite of their high reputation and valuable contacts with foreign lines it is doubtful how long they can survive separately in an increasingly competitive business. The Shipbuilding Industry Board has recommended that Austin and Pickersgill and the Doxford group should merge, but so far long negotiations have not produced a link. It is pointed out on Wearside that, although past mergers made it possible to build bigger ships through the elimination of old yards and the construction of new ones across old boundaries, the five surviving yards are separate; as a result, further amalgamation will not permit larger berths. Organizational economies might still, of course, be substantial (*Financial Times,* 1968).

Shipbuilding problems on Teesside are of a completely different nature. There are ideal site conditions, but the river at present lacks the construction capacity to secure the necessary scale and overhead economies. The one major unit, the Furness Yard at Haverton Hill, had its lay-out improved and was splendidly reequipped at a cost of over £5 million after 1964. It was able to fabricate 1,000 tons of steel each week, a national record. In spite of this it lost over £8 million before the decision to close down was announced early in 1968. Some 3,000 men were directly affected, although Trades Union estimates suggested that, through the multiplier effect, 8,000 would be a more realistic figure. In spite of the disadvantage of its remoteness, which had seemed likely to rule out a link, Swan Hunter took over the Furness yard in the autumn of 1968. Only £2.5 million was paid for it, and £1 million of this was a government grant. Soon afterwards Haverton Hill was allocated orders for three 166,000 dwt vessels by its new masters, a size of ship twice as large as anything previously built there. The prospects for concentrating a considerable share of the group's larger tonnage work on the Tees would seem therefore to be favourable.

Teesside has long been the main industrial growth zone in the North East (Warren, 1968). The estuary, from above Middlesbrough to the sea, contains the most impressive agglomeration of modern bulk processing industries in Britain, and the rate of growth of this sub-regional economy has been rapid. Its chief contemporary asset is an estuarine river capable of improvement to take very large vessels, plus ample fringing areas of flat land suitable for space-extensive industrial operations. At its heart lies the new Teesside County Borough (created in 1968) which has a population of 400,000. A more realistic figure for the whole of the economic area, an emerging conurbation, is nearly 500,000.

The Northern Economic Planning Council's *Regional Ports Survey* (1969b, p. 22) recognized the Tees as the only port in the region for which big developments should be recommended. It approved planning for vessels of 200,000 dwt or more and it indicated that at the seaward end of the north bank alone there were over 700 hectares (1,750 acres) of land fit for reclamation, together with another 2,800 hectares (7,000 acres) suitable for industry needing good access to deepwater. On the south side, Bran Sands plus the land between Redcar and Lackenby provide similar major sites for future developments. Already a new port complex has been developed at Teesport between Grangetown and Lackenby, and there are new special-purpose jetties on the north bank. Between 1965

and 1967, some 13 million tons of material were dredged from the estuary at a cost of
£5.25 million to make it navigable for vessels up to approximately 250 metres (800 feet)
long, and of 65,000 dwt, to points as much as 6 kilometres (4 miles) above the entrance.
In 1969 the British Steel Corporation announced plans for the £15 million deep-water
ore terminal at Redcar which was noted earlier. The dredged material has already been
used to reclaim shallows and to provide ideal sites for processing the raw materials, which
will be brought in the huge vessels using the improved waterway. These bulk-reducing,
space-extensive and often pollution-creating activities are best sited in such relatively
isolated locations within the industrial conurbation.

Traditionally, Teesside has had a rather narrow range of staple trades : steel, a comparatively small amount of heavy engineering and shipbuilding, and (mainly since the
nineteen twenties) a heavy chemical trade. Since 1945 a new oil-based chemical complex
has been built up at Wilton and more recently Billingham too has shifted from coal to
oil as its main raw material. By the end of 1969, Imperial Chemical Industries (I.C.I.)
was estimated to have spent in the order of £500 million on Teesside, some of the products
of which are transferred by feedstock pipeline to Runcorn over 200 kilometres (136
miles) away. There was no oil refining industry until the mid nineteen sixties when, first
a cooperative I.C.I. and Phillips refinery (5.5 million tons) was built on the north bank,
and then a Shell plant at Teesport came into production. By 1969, with 11 million tons
refining capacity, Teesside already had an estimated 13 per cent of the United Kingdom
total and two further oil companies are said to be interested in possible developments
there. In addition, by 1972 it had become increasingly apparent that North Sea oil from
the (Norwegian) Ekofisk and related deposits, initially moved to various refineries by
tanker, would eventually be piped ashore to Teesside and be in part refined there. Already Phillips Imperial naptha becomes an I.C.I. feedstock. Although it has been suggested
that Shell might develop a petrochemical and particularly a fertilizer base at Teesport,
this further development has not yet occurred, Shell deciding instead on very big developments in the North West region. But other chemical companies are moving into Teesside.
Monsanto is building a plant to produce raw material for its acrilon fibres on Seal Sands
and Lennig Chemicals from Jarrow is investing in the same area. The evidence of a developing chemical complex is impressive.

In steel the situation is less favourable. As was noted earlier, there is to be considerable
expansion of production, above all at Lackenby and later between there and the new
Redcar terminal. This will involve the partial closure of works elsewhere on Teesside.
More important, however, is the continuing absence of any real progress in local fabrica-
tion. This is one sign of a basic weakness in the Teesside economic structure. Although
its industrial landscape is impressive, and although its installations are vast, its economy
remains immature. To a dangerous extent, Teesside has a bulk reducing economy; it is
concerned with the production of semi-manufactured goods which are finished elsewhere.
The very antithesis of the West Midland industrial complex, this situation is not entirely
satisfactory from a development planning point of view.

In recent years, Teesside has been more successful than the Tyne or the Wear industrial areas in obtaining industrial development certificates. But the Tees remains dependent upon its traditional trades. Whereas I.C.I. employed 30,000 on Teesside, and the British Steel Corporation's Northern and Tubes Group 27,000 in 1969, the Swan Hunter and Tyne Shipbuilders employment of 10,000 was Tyneside's largest single commitment to the old basic trades. In these, increasingly, a high level of investment is required for each job produced and they are commonly activities in which, as rationalization proceeds, old output levels can be exceeded with a shrinking labour force. Even if Teesside steel production is increased from its present 3 to 3.5 million tons to 5 million tons by 1975, it is quite likely that its labour requirements will fall, though probably by less than really efficient management would permit. The Teesside industrial structure has meant, therefore, that industrial development certificates approved there have on average created a smaller additional employment than they have in the industrial centres further north, and much more of it has been for male workers (Table 31). It was in fact the capital intensive characteristics of many of the industries granted industrial development certificates on Teesside, plus the high level of public assistance provided for each additional worker employed in them (at times rising to over £20,000), which prompted Bray (1970) to question the investment incentive premium in development area assistance, and to call for policies better designed to make use of the sub-region's labour reserves.

Table 31. Teesside and Tyneside-Wearside : population and industrial development, *circa* 1967

	Population mid-1967 (thousands)	Industrial development certificates granted 1966, 1967, and the first half of 1968				
		Number	Hectares (acres) involved	Expected additional employment	% male	Additional employment per i.d.c.
Teesside	571	110	1,110 (2,742)	6,440	79.5	58.5
North Tyneside	583	86	1,197 (2,957)	7,460	66.4	86.7
South Tyneside (incl. Wearside)	753	94	1,049 (2,593)	6,650	68.4	70.7

Source : Board of Trade Statistics.

In 1969 the so-called *Teesplan* was produced by consultants after three years of analysis. Looking to 1991 it anticipates a population increase of 220,000 over the 1966 level. Some 120,000 new jobs will be needed, of which 53,000 will be in manufacturing. To accomplish this it will be essential to create a more diverse industrial structure with, amongst other newcomers, firms finishing the products of the large bulk-reducing units. Some progress has been made in this direction. For example, British Enkalon are in the process of investing about £2 million at Thornaby in a plant which will texturise polyester fibre (brought from its Antrim works), and provide employment for 300. This investment/employment ratio contrasts starkly with Monsanto's investment of £10 million to make acrilon fibre on a 40 hectare (99 acre) site on Seal Sand which will offer only 100 jobs. *Teesplan* suggests that new light industries should be steered into the sub-region to employ some 50,000 people in expanding communities beyond the present built up area at Wolviston, Hemlington, Crathorne, Nunthorpe, Marske and further away on the Cleveland coast at Loftus. To this end in April 1969 the Teesside County Borough, together with eight other local authorities, formed the Teesside Regional Organization for Industrial Development in order to sponsor industrial development and diversification.

Service employment is poorly developed on Teesside as compared with Tyneside. This frequently means that people in the former conurbation go without higher services, rather than journey 64 kilometres (40 miles) north to secure them. The contrast between the central commercial districts of the two is acute, even accepting that Teesside suffers in part from the wide geographical spread of its previously autonomous units (and above all from the division of the higher functions between Middlesbrough and Stockton). Big new shopping centres have been built in Thornaby and Billingham, and are now to be provided in both Stockton and Middlesbrough also. The latter, however, will be developed as the heart of the sub-region, and present plans envisage that its inadequate central district will be reconstructed and doubled in area by 1991. In the process the remarkably diverse, if individually undistinguished, architectural styles of its characteristically Victorian Town Hall square will unfortunately disappear. Immediately behind this square, the dreary rows of working class housing show clearly enough that, despite the huge recent investments on the estuary, all on Teesside is far from golden.

It has been suggested by some in the North East that, whilst Teesside's growth will be automatic, that of Tyneside is less assured and as a consequence the latter must secure as much government help as possible in order to escape the beginnings of a downward spiral (House, 1969, p. 234). In practice, however, as the activities of certain construction firms show, Tyneside is near enough to share in buoyancy of Teesside's capital investment; whilst at the same time its own concentrated purchasing power, plus its more complex economy, is able to attract new and especially labour intensive firms. It may well be Teesside which will require special assistance to aid its diversification, and to ensure a rising level of sub-regional income. There are, however, doubts as to whether growth on the dimensions of the Teesside Survey and Plan is practicable or regionally desirable. There are other localities in south Durham which are competing for development.

In particular Darlington (with a present population of 86,000) offers very substantial advantages for new industries. In the past it grew as a manufacturing point because of its railway nodality. Now, with the Durham motorway nearby, it is even more attractive. It has an excellent position, both to serve the biggest regional markets of Tyneside and Teesside, and as a 'gateway' from the North East to the main centres of national demand.

At the same time new industrial growth there benefits from all the special provisions made for the Development Areas. Newton Aycliffe nearby, with a major industrial estate, has the additional advantages of new town status. Economic growth in this locality has been rapid, and unemployment rates are low. Some of the light industries which could help to diversify Teesside, therefore, may well be attracted to the Darlington area, where they will also help to provide new employment for workers displaced from the pit villages of southwest Durham.

9.5 Northumberland

Beyond the Durham coal-field and the conurbations the only considerable urbanized tract in the North East is in the heart of the Northumberland coal-field, and is centred on Blyth, Ashington and Newbiggin. A number of pits have closed in recent years, but important long-life ones survive. There is an assured local market for large tonnages in the two units of Blyth's 1,350 MW power station. Coal shipments from the port of Blyth have fallen away sharply, from 5.5 million tons as recently as 1963, to 2.8 million by 1968. The liquidation of the Blyth Dry Docks and Shipbuilding Company in 1966 was a severe blow to the community, for the town and its neighbours afford few attractions to the outside industrialist. They lie on the wrong side of the Tyneside conurbation for easy access to the national market, though the 'spine' road and the Tyne Tunnel will improve this. Their colliery waste heaps, subsidence and general drabness give them an unattractiveness which has undoubtedly repelled many firms from developing there. Yet in spite of all this, they have had noteworthy successes in attracting new employments too. Hepworths, the tailors, have a major plant at Ashington. Glaxo are to build a big, new pharmaceutical plant at Cambois, Blyth. Between 1956 and 1968 the estimated additional employment from industrial development certificates granted for this locality has been estimated at 5,060, a higher proportion in relation to population than for the North East as a whole; 2,800 of this total provided jobs for men.

So far, therefore, although there has been some out-migration, the area has managed to hold onto its people surprisingly well. Between 1957 (a halycon time for coal) and the middle of 1968, the population of the municipal borough of Blyth and of the adjacent urban districts of Newbiggin, Ashington and Bedlingtonshire fell by less than 400 to 101,700. In 1966, in line with its generally optimistic population forecasts, the Economic Planning Council suggested a small but sustained rise for the Northumberland coal-field. By the time of its 1969 strategy document, however, the Blyth sub-region was one for which a larger than average decline was anticipated by 1981. For the 1967–1981 period, it suggested a growth of 57,000 (4.3 per cent) for the North and South Tyneside areas, but a decline of over 7 thousand (more than 7 per cent) was forecast for the Northumberland coal-field subdivision, an area almost identical with the four local authorities considered above.

The 1968 decision on build an Alcan smelter at Lynemouth may be criticized as a national strategy (see pp. 419–421; also Manners, 1968), but it will certainly make an important contribution to the maintenance of population in the area, even at the lower forecast level. Costing £50 million, it is expected to employ 900. It will also ensure continuing work for perhaps 1,000 miners in the local coal industry whose output will supply its power plant. With others working in the improved docks which will handle alumina, and additional local railway jobs, an overall direct employment boost of 2,000 seems likely, giving an investment/employment ratio which compares favourably with that in many new Teesside industrial developments. Teesside certainly resented the 'political' decision which rejected the offer of an ideal, deep-water site at Seal Sands in favour of Lynemouth.

9.6 In conclusion

The intraregional controversy over the siting of the new aluminium smelter is but a variation upon the wider national issues already raised in Chapter 1. Does an old industrial area like the North East deserve preferential treatment in national economic development? Can its economy eventually be made viable and self-renewing? Will there ever be a time when special assistance from Whitehall will no longer be required to bolster the region within an ever-changing national economic structure?

Most of the growth industries which the North East is attracting manufacture either components for the consumer goods trades, or those consumer goods themselves. The latter have a mass market, and location near to the centre of gravity of demand is theoretically highly desirable. However, since the product is easily transported, transfer costs are of small significance as compared with those carried by the region's traditional heavy products; they are more than offset by the provisions of government assistance to Development Areas. Yet problems of the distance from southern England remain, in particular the lack of speedy access to and direct contact with suppliers, the absence of a local ancillary trade complex and the psychology of distance. The way in which the entrepreneur thinks about these matters is as important as the way in which in fact it touches his pocket. For instance, the management of a Hartlepool works making metal stampings in weights from 0.68 to 68 kilograms (1.5 to 150 lbs) reckons that it must do so about 3 per cent cheaper than its Midlands competitors in order to cover transport costs. Perdio Ltd., making transistors, radios and record players, closed its Sunderland factory in 1965 after only three years in the north; the plant was only 480 kilometres (300 miles) from its main component suppliers, but it was found that delivery frequently took up to 10 days. A few months later Volkswagen decided to locate a new distribution centre at Doncaster rather than on Teesside allegedly because of the bad communications from the latter. The Confederation of British Industry's regional evidence to the Hunt Committee referred to the 'remoteness' of the North East, to the 'consequent communications difficulties', and to the likelihood that these would be increased by the provisions of the 1969 Transport Act. As it was put, 'Though the differentials may not be high, *the thought of them* and the possible delays will divert orders from customers in other parts of the country'. In fact, the North East is now well provided with trunk roads, especially following the completion of the Durham motorway to the edge of Gateshead, but even if remoteness is partly the product of a mistaken value judgements, it clearly impedes northern progress. And within the region it helps to focus development in the areas near to the main lines of movement such as Darlington-Aycliffe, Spennymoor or Cramlington.

The economic argument against considerable national subventions for the North East is unsound : the regional economy must be put right. Socially the case for such a policy is stronger still. The chief indication of its necessity may be derived from a simple question which should follow a study of the regional economy : what would have happened without Development Area assistance? Individual mistakes and political blunders apart, reassurance concerning the general wisdom with which that policy has been applied may be gained as the signs of a new and more vigorous economy are traced amongst the ruins of the old.

References :

Bray, J. M. P. (1970). *Decision in Government*, Gollancz, London.
Cherry, G. (1967). The ambiance of the North : the image of an unfavoured region. *Northern Architect*, July, pp. 834–835.
Daysh, G. H. J., and Symmonds, J. S. (1953). *West Durham*, Blackwell, Oxford.
Durham County Council (1951): *Development Plan*, D.C.C., Durham.
Ely, G. (1969). Newcastle builds for the future. *The Times*, 2 June.
Financial Times (1968). Shipbuilding survey, 1 April.
Fullerton, B. (1960). *The pattern of service industries in North-east England*, University of Durham King's College, Newcastle.
House, J. W. (1969). *The Industrial North East*, David and Charles, Newton Abbott.
House, J. W. and Knight, M. (1967). *Pit Closures and the Community*, Papers on Migration and Mobility in Northern England, University of Newcastle upon Tyne, Newcastle.
Manners, G. (1968). Misplacing the smelters. *New Society*, 16 May, 712–713.
Minister of Power (1967). *Fuel Policy* (Cmnd.3438), H.M.S.O., London.
Northern Architect (1969). March, 28–29.
North East Development Council (quarterly). *North East News*.
Northern Economic Planning Council (1966). *Challenge of the Changing North*, H.M.S.O., London.
Northern Economic Planning Council (1969a). *Outline Strategy for the North*, H.M.S.O., London.
Northern Economic Planning Council (1969b). *Regional Ports Survey*, H.M.S.O., London.
Secretary of State for Industry, Trade and Regional Development (1963). *The North East* (Cmnd.2206), H.M.S.O., London.
Teesside Survey and Plan (1969). *Teesplan*, H.M.S.O., London.
Watkins, D. M. P. (1968). Pros and cons at Consett Iron. *Voice of North East Industry*, September, 27–29.
Warren, K. (1968). Teesside—the shaping of an industrial region. *Advancement of Science*, **25**, 185–199.
Warren, K. (1969). Iron and steel in North East England. The regional implications of development in a basic industry. *Regional Studies*, **3**, 49–60.
Warren, K. (1970). *The British Iron and Steel Sheet Industry since* 1840, Bell, London.

CHAPTER 10

Scotland

KENNETH WARREN

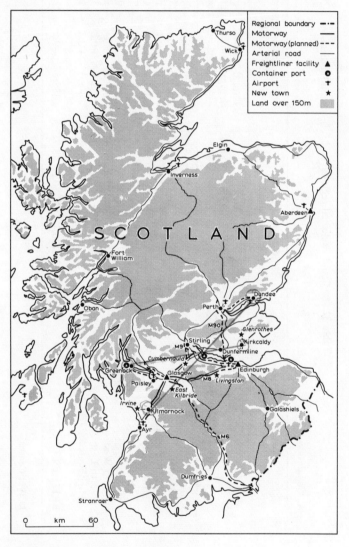

Figure 31 Scotland : location map.

A. Population :

Thousands

Table 32. Scotland : selected regional and sub-regional indicators

	Mid-year estimated home population				Average annual change 1961–1966			Average annual change 1951–1961		
	1971[1]	1966	1961	1951	Natural change	Armed forces change	Net migration	Natural change	Armed forces change	Net migration
Scotland	5,227.7	5,190.8	5,183.8	5,102.5	+38.7	+1.6	−38.8	+33.9	+2.4	−28.2
Glasgow	2,508.8	2,476.6	2,495.5	2,434.1	+22.5	+0.4	−26.7	+19.5	+1.1	−14.5
Falkirk/Stirling	251.3	272.4	253.2	240.4	+2.1	+0.1	+1.7	+1.8	+0.1	−0.6
Edinburgh	1,030.1	1,011.9	996.2	966.5	+7.1	+0.5	−4.5	+6.1	+0.3	−3.4
Tayside	451.1	449.8	452.6	450.5	+2.2	—	−2.8	+2.0	+0.4	−2.1
Borders	102.0	102.6	105.1	111.2	+0.1	—	−0.6	+0.1	+0.1	−0.8
South West	150.4	151.6	152.3	153.6	+0.9	—	−1.0	+0.9	—	−1.0
North East	450.6	448.5	453.1	462.8	+2.8	+0.2	−3.9	+2.8	+0.3	−4.1
Highlands	283.4	277.3	275.9	283.9	+1.0	+0.3	−1.0	+0.7	+0.1	−1.6
BRITAIN	53,821.4	53,176.1	51,380.0	48,917.5	+328.2	−0.5	+22.6	+231.4	−12.9	+1.9

1. 1971 Census

B. Employment :

	Employment		Male employment		Proportion of women at work		Unemployment range		
	1966	Change 1961–1966	1966	Change 1961–1966	1966	Change in % 1961–1966	1968	1967	1961–1966
	'000s	%	'000s	%	%	%	%	%	%
SCOTLAND	2,190	+1	1,370	−2	40	+2	3–4	3–4	3–4
Glasgow and West Central	1,110	+1	690	−2	44	+3	4–5	4–5	3–4
Falkirk/Stirling	110	+2	70	−2	38	+1	3–4	2–3	2–3
Edinburgh and East Central	430	+2	270	Nil	40	+2	2–3	2–3	2–3
Tayside	190	Nil	110	−2	42	+2	2–3	2–3	2–3
Borders	40	−2	30	−3	40	+1	1–2	1–2	1–2
South West	50	−5	30	−7	31	Nil	5–10	5–10	4–5
North East	170	+1	110	Nil	34	+1	3–4	3–4	3–4
Highlands and Islands	90	+2	60	−1	28	+2	5–10	5–10	5–10
BRITAIN	23,550	+4	14,900	+2	40	+2	2–3	2–3	1–2

C. Industrial Development Certificates :

	Estimated additional employment from i.d.c. approvals			
	Total 1956–1967 '000s	Annual averages		
		1964–1967 '000s	1960–1963 '000s	1956–1959 '000s
Scotland	166.0	20.0	14.8	6.7
Glasgow	84.1	8.6	9.0	3.4
Falkirk/Stirling	11.7	1.5	0.6	0.8
Edinburgh	49.5	7.5	3.9	1.0
Tayside	9.7	1.0	0.5	0.9
Borders	1.1	0.2	—	0.1
South West	3.1	0.5	0.3	—
North East	4.6	0.5	0.3	0.3
Highlands	2.2	0.2	0.2	0.2
BRITAIN	1,245.2	121.8	108.1	81.2

10.1 Introduction

The student of the Scottish economy is immediately presented with inconsistencies. Spectacular success has been achieved in the attraction of new employments, and to a much greater extent than elsewhere in Britain this has involved foreign firms. Whilst Scotland had 8.4 per cent of Britain's manufacturing workforce in 1967, its share of the national jobs gained from incoming foreign firms since 1945 was 46.4 per cent. With firms from both foreign and home sources, Scotland has in the process gained a large share of the rapidly growing electronics trades, which now employ more Scottish workers than does coal mining. Under the Local Employment Acts, between 1960 and 1968 Scotland received 43 per cent of all the financial assistance given in the United Kingdom and in the latter year received approximately 40 per cent of the Regional Employment Premium. If road development plans for the nineteen seventies were worked out on a population basis, Scotland would get £270 million of the allocation for Britain; instead it will have £480 million.

In spite of all this, the signs that Scotland remains a problem region are numerous. Between 1964 and 1967, there was an average annual net loss of population by migration of 42,000, mainly to England, and in 1970 the rate was still 20,000. Employment rose by only 1 per cent between 1961 and 1964, and for males fell by 2 per cent; these figures compare unfavourably with the plus 3 and minus 1 per cent for Wales and the plus 2 and minus 1 per cent for the Northern Region over the same period. In Great Britain as a whole there was a 5 per cent increase for all employment, and a rise of 4 per cent in the male labour force. Between 1956 and 1967 the Scottish share of national employment has fallen from 10.0 to 9.3 per cent and in the Development Area—the whole of Scotland except a very small area around Edinburgh—only in three of the last 13 years has the unemployment rate been less than twice the national average. Merseyside alone amongst British Development Areas has had an unemployment history since the mid-fifties as bad as this, and since *circa* 1964 even there it has been noticeably better. In October 1968 the Scottish rate was 3.6 per cent, half as much again as the national figure, and by April 1971 unemployment in Scotland had climbed to 123,000 or 5.7 per cent.

As in other Development Areas the explanation for such continuing economic distress, in spite of very substantial government assistance, is to be found in a past dependence upon a few basic trades which have either shrunk or been rationalized, and which have consequently shed labour. Between 1959 and 1969 almost 100,000 jobs were lost as a result of changes in the coal mining industry and in the Scottish railways alone. And the decline goes on. In the two years to June 1967, employment in mines and quarries, transport and communications, metalworking, shipbuilding and marine engineering fell by 21.8 thousand, or 5 thousand more than the gains in the main growth categories of industrial employment.

Scotland's population of 5.2 million is bigger than that of any economic planning region except the North West and South East. Areally, Scotland is more than one third of Britain. Naturally within a kingdom of this size the problems and prospects vary considerably. There is, first, a highly concentrated industrial belt some 145 kilometres (90 miles) long at its most extreme from Kilmarnock to Dundee, and less than 100 kilometres (60 miles) in extent at its mid-Clyde to Musselburgh-Kirkcaldy core. Its width is nowhere more than 50 kilometres (30 miles). 75 per cent of Scotland's population and 80 per cent of manufacturing employment is included in this central industrial belt— sometimes defined as the Glasgow, Edinburgh and Falkirk/Stirling sub-regions—and if Tayside is included the share of population rises to 82 per cent. To the south is a predominantly rural area, and northwards in the Highlands is a region which by virtue of its size, remoteness, and its physical and economic character poses development problems which are unique in Britain. The solution of the lowland's difficulties is, however, the key to the future of Scotland.

10.2 The Lowlands

Coal, iron and steel and heavy engineering, especially shipbuilding and railway work (and their associated trades) were the traditional staples of the Scottish industrial economy. As in all other nineteenth century coal-based industrial areas, they were adversely affected by the economic events of the period from 1920 to 1940, but in spite of their substantial decline, Scotland remained heavily dependent on them. The West Central District (see Table 33), the key economic area of Scotland, typifies this.

Table 33. Britain and West Central Scotland : number employed in major industry groups as a percentage of all employed, 1935

	Britain	West Central Scotland
Mechanical Engineering	6.0	14.6
Shipbuilding	1.1	5.2
Iron and Steel	7.5	10.6
Coal Mines	10.6	10.2
Electrical Engineering	3.4	0.5
Motors and Cycles	3.9	0.8

Source : Fogarty (1945), p. 152.

Since 1945 *coal* production, historically the fount of growth for all the other basic trades, has shrunk and still more noticeably changed in its location pattern. Compared with its peak output of 42.5 million tons (or 14.7 per cent of the British total) in 1913 when 139,000 were employed, output in 1945 was down to 21.7 million (11.7 per cent) and the labour force stood at 84,000. By 1967, ten years after the end of a period of post-1945 expansion, Scotland produced only 15.7 million tons (including its open cast operations) and two years later annual output of deep mined coal had contracted further to no more than 12.5 million tons. Labour productivity remained well below the national level, and in 1966–1967 was under 60 per cent of that in the East Midlands. The labour force and the number of pits have declined in parallel with production. In 1960, 133 pits still employed 72,000 workers, but by 1969 there were only 37 units and a workforce of 31,500. The effects of the decline have been increased by geographical shifts in production, above all the decline in the central field of Lanarkshire where many small pits had exploited the valuable upper seams of the productive coal measures—as late as 1947 Lanarkshire's output of 9 million tons came from 179 pits (compared with an output of 6.5 million tons from the 47 mines in Fife and Clackmannan). In 1910, 58.5 per cent of Scotland's coal came from Lanark, in 1950 34.7 per cent and in 1967 the central field produced only 18.0 per cent of the Scottish total. Some new development has occurred around the fringes of this coal-field but most investment in recent years has been elsewhere, and some sub-sections of the field have lost all their old employment. For instance in Shotts, on the Slammanan plateau at the eastern edge of the Lanarkshire field, the last colliery closed in 1961; eight others had been abandoned in the previous twelve years.

In Ayrshire, mining has been moving southwards and the main longlife pits of Killoch and Barony are located west of Cumnock. Two of Scotland's four 1 million ton pits are in the Midlothian field within 6 miles of Edinburgh. In Fife the shift has been east and west from a declining central district centred on Cowdenbeath, a boom town of the second half of the last century. To the east, near Kirkcaldy, is the big new Seafield mine; westward is the Logannet complex, which combines a number of units. Marketing conditions are relatively favourable for the east of Scotland fields, the Kincardine (760 MW) and Cockenzie (1,200 MW) power stations being within a few miles of the Logannet and Midlothian pits respectively. The completion in 1971 by the South of Scotland Electricity Board of the Logannet (2,400 MW) power station almost doubled deliveries to the Board from Scottish pits. By the early nineteen seventies electricity generation is expected to take about 65 per cent of Scotland's 12.5 million tons output. Another 2.5 million tons (20 per cent) will go to the steel industry's coke ovens, but whereas the biggest new power stations are near to the lowest cost coal-field, the second largest market for Scottish pits is in the declining Lanarkshire field.

In 1965, after Scottish self-sufficiency in coking coal had at long last been secured, local ovens carbonized 1.8 million tons of coal, but it is now feared that N.C.B. closures and higher prices together may jeopardize supply once again. The ovens which use the coal are at Ravenscraig (near Mothwell) and at the Clyde Ironworks in Rutherglen (on the southeastern fringe of Glasgow). The Scottish *steel* industry in its traditional, scattered and unintegrated form made 23 per cent of Britain's steel in 1920. By 1951, with integration and rationalization already going ahead, its share had fallen to 13.5 per cent. Its 1968 output at 3.07 million tons was 45 per cent greater, but the share of the national total had fallen yet further to only 11.8 per cent. Scottish steelmaking is much more localized than that of either the North East Coast or South Wales, Motherwell and Glengarnock

(handwritten margin notes:)
Decline of Lanark's. c/F

F'n c/F's fav⁴ ×

Main Mkts Elec. (65%) Steel Ind (coke) (20%)

STEEL etc

decline in Steel (rel)

(handwritten at bottom:)
Sc Steel output. (% of Br Tot).

1920	1951	1968
23	13.5	18.8
	(integ⁴cte)	

being only 45 kilometres (28 miles) apart. More also than in any other major British district except the East Midlands, the industry has been controlled by one concern—Colvilles—which in 1965, the year of British record output, made over 77 per cent the Scottish total. Once noted for its cold metal practice, Scotland still has a low hot metal rate for a heavy steel district and only two integrated works. The mineral supply situation is unfavourable. Coking coal comes from the fringes of the central field or from Stirlingshire; all the ore is imported. It is anomalous that among 'coastal' steel districts Scotland is unique in that for many years it has been both wholly dependent on imported ores and yet all its ironmaking plant is inland. Yet, when reconstruction began in the nineteen thirties, locational choices were probably freer of material hindrances to a new coastal development than anywhere else in Britain. A study of this development reveals starkly the complicated processes of locational decision taking (Warren, 1965). The result was to preserve the old metallurgical communities, but to burden the plants—which have grown substantially since they were built—with costly land hauls on their ore. The General Terminus Quay in Glasgow is unable to handle ore carriers bigger than 21,000 tons. In 1965 and 1966 plans were outlined for a new terminal at Clydebank to handle 45,000 ton vessels and later 65,000 tonners but it soon became clear that this was inadequate as a long term project, and by 1968 the Clyde Port Authority and the Scottish Office's Clyde Estuary Development Group were suggesting major schemes either between Dumbarton and Greenock or, more commonly, on the Firth of Clyde.

Here, at Hunterston, a major new terminal to handle 250,000 dwt vessels, and later possibly vessels up towards 500,000 dwt, will eventually be built. Whether the British Steel Corporation's tentative proposal for a £300 million, 5 to 6 million tons steelworks on an adjacent green field site will be adopted is much more doubtful. Colvilles lost the ideal opportunity for such a desirable development when in 1954 they decided to build at Ravenscraig. Within the British context a Clyde estuary plant is not a priority project, and there has been no indication that the British Steel Corporation has shifted from the views of the British Iron and Steel Federation (1966) that no major further expansion in Scottish steel is justified. Estimates made by the latter suggest that steel demand in Scotland will be equal to about 2.8 million tons of crude steel in 1975—some 0.2 million tons below the Scottish 1968 record. For Britain as a whole production was expected to go up by 31 per cent. Steelmaking has, in the past, been closely identified with Scottish and Ulster shipbuilding. Although still important, this market is now less critical, and by 1967 the production of plate was only 30.2 per cent finished steel output and was far exceeded by sheet products destined mainly for the new industries attracted to Scotland since 1945.

In 1947, 23 yards capable of constructing 600,000 tons of shipping were still in business on the Clyde. There were difficulties, notably in steel supply, but markets seemed insatiable, yards were reshaped and output remained at a high level until 1958. After that, as competition in world markets became keener, output shrank. Between 1960 and 1969 the labour force in Scottish *shipbuilding and marine engineering* went down by well over one-quarter—19,000 men. Famous yards closed, such as Denny's of Dumbarton, the Govan yard of Harland and Wolff, and Swan Hunter's Clydeholm yard. At the end of the nineteen fifties there were still 20 companies, but by 1967 only seven important yards remained. They were already clearly divided into two groups. Scott's of Greenock and Lithgow's of Port Glasgow, well down the estuary, were able to build vessels of 100,000 dwt and more; they had, moreover, shown vigour in coping with the technical and other changes in shipbuilding. The Upper Clyde yards, on the other hand, are all about 20 kilometres (more than 12 miles) up river from Lithgows, three of them being well into the heart of the conurbation at Partick and Scotstoun. Yarrow, the naval builder of Scotstoun, seems to have been the only one in this group to make profits in recent years. All the upper Clyde yards are limited to building vessels of under 100,000 dwt and, although in the middle nineteen sixties John Brown of Clydebank outlined a scheme for altering the course of the river so as to permit 250,000 ton vessels to be built there, the limitation remains.

Early in 1966, the Geddes Committee on British Shipbuilding recommended the grouping of firms to create new units of 8,000 to 10,000 men each, and capable of building ½ million tons yearly. On the labour and capacity side the Clyde could not be neatly divided according to this scheme. Location, type of work and profitability however, as has been seen, clearly separated the firms into an upper and lower group. In 1967 the Shipbuilding Industry Board was established and provided with a fund of well over £200 million to use as a revolving credit to speed up the modernization of British yards, and it was understood that the qualification for loan assistance would be appropriate mergers, the precondition of rationalization. Lithgows and Scotts, whose connections were already close, merged almost immediately, and a year later Stephens, Connell, Yarrow, Fairfields and John Brown joined together as Upper Clyde Shipbuilders (U.C.S.). Losses within this group soon mounted, partly due to an inadequate assessment of the situation before the merger (there were no common accounting systems) and partly due to high levels of absenteeism and an extremely low steel throughput. The performance of U.C.S. was even worse than the national level of 80 man-hours per equivalent ton, a figure which should be compared with German and Swedish labour inputs as low as 40 man-hours. However, in the Fairfields' (Govan) division, recently reconstituted, productivity was higher. By the spring of 1969 the group was on the verge of failure and facing the inevitable closure of some of its yards. Emergency government support amounting to as much as £12 million was requested, and eventually U.C.S. was granted loans of £9.3 million by the Shipbuilding Industry Board on condition of changes expected to cut the labour force by 2,600 within twelve months; this figure was raised to 3,500 early in 1970, although natural wastage seemed likely to reduce the need for dismissals to something below this figure. In many quarters, a merger of the upper and lower Clyde shipbuilding groups was regarded as desirable. Before that happened, however, the profitable Scott-Lithgow group were believed to favour the elimination of the Clydebank yard, said to need expenditure of £3 million on improved steel handling to make it economic. Early in 1971 Yarrow, largely preoccupied with naval work, left U.C.S. In June the group's working capital ran out and the jobs of 7,500 shipyard workers and possibly 25,000 others in supplying industries were threatened. After some months of protracted uncertainly, early in 1972 three of the yards were revived as Govan Shipbuilders Ltd. and with the promise of £36 million in government aid; the fourth yard—Clydebank—was shed to American interests for oil rig construction.

Govan Shipbuilders

In *mechanical engineering* too there has been contraction. The Glasgow area was once of great importance for the production of railway equipment, and as late as 1953 the North British Locomotive works in the heavy industrial area on the east side of the city employed 5,000 men. In 1962 it was closed. Employment changes in the old staple industries of Scotland, then, have been widespread. However, because of the localization of steelmaking, shipbuilding and mechanical engineering, and the centrifugal tendency in coal mining, their impact has fallen especially severely on the Clydeside conurbation. New industry has come into Scotland but it is concentrated in this area to a smaller extent.

Mech Eng

Locos

* concl

Industrial diversification began in Scotland as in other Special Areas in the late nineteen thirties, and already by 1950 about 100,000 persons were at work in projects which had started since 1937. 42,000 of these worked for 'immigrant' firms. These were mainly from other parts of Britain although 36 out of 298 concerns new to Scotland had come from North America (Survey of Industry and Employment in Scotland 1950–1951). A number of these industries were concerned with the production of consumption goods; others with rapidly growing new lines in capital equipment—Hoover at Cambuslang, Pressed Steel in Linwood, Rolls Royce at Hillington, National Cash Register on the fringes of Dundee. After 1950, the flow of firms from the United States quickened, and *electronics and telecommunications* emerged as major new Scottish specializations, with British as well as American firms prominent in it. Indeed, by 1966, instruments, electronic equipment and business machines represented an investment of £65 million, or 22.5 per cent of all the capital in new Scottish industry. More impressive still, outlay in this sector almost doubled between 1964 and 1966. The implications for employment were naturally considerable. By 1959, there were some 7,500 jobs in electronics in Scotland; ten years later, 80 firms employed about 30,000. As a result of these developments, major new centres of employment growth are appearing in such otherwise unlikely areas as Cowdenbeath in the declining centre of the Fife coal-field.

The manufacture of electronics equipment, business machines and electrical domestic appliances is—to varying degrees—'footloose'; their components can be transported considerable distances at relatively small costs and provided that deliveries are reliable they are locationally highly flexible. As skills are developed, however, so any area which has a number of factories affords external economies to other firms in the industry, becomes a centre of agglomerative forces and is able to attract more. As a result of its early success, Scotland has become a much more important centre in these growing lines than, for instance, the North of England; the latter has the advantages of a closer proximity to the centres of national demand, but significantly less in the way of world-wide contact or reputation, a matter of some importance with trades which have a large export sector.

Unfortunately electronics is not by any means a full answer to the contraction of the heavy trades. Its employment is growing less rapidly than job losses in the older industries, it is mostly for women, it will grow less than output in the next few years and it is located mainly in the East away from the centres of high unemployment. Foreign firms, though providing a major contribution, have in general failed to locate research and development work in Scotland along with their manufacturing activities. By 1971 some were already cutting back their work forces. Burroughs Machines for instance announced plans to reduce the number of its employees by 1000 within a year.

The *motor industry* has become another important new Scottish trade. As Lord Polworth, Chairman of the Scottish Council (Development and Industry) put it in 1963, the opening of the Rootes factory at Linwood symbolized the 'revolutionary changes which are taking place and mark the beginning of a new era to which Scots look forward eagerly'. The new motor activities there, and at the British Motor Corporation (B.M.C.) commercial vehicles and tractor plant at Bathgate, were looked upon as a major step towards the provision of a Scottish market for the new strip mill at Ravenscraig, and at the same time as a leader trade for the growth of a host of new component suppliers—the creation of a South Wales-West Midlands type relationship in the Central Lowlands (see p. 225). There were early successes. But soon a number of difficulties which revealed grave weaknesses in the Scottish industrial structure and in national planning came to light. They are worth fuller examination.

Until 1960 the heavy commercial vehicle manufacturing firm of Albion in Scotstoun was the only survivor of a once flourishing Scottish motor industry killed thirty years earlier by mass production in other areas and remoteness from component suppliers. At the end of 1958 the government announced the plan to build a wide strip mill at Ravenscraig and—as it was clear that much of its product would have to be sold in England— agitation for new sheet using trades in Scotland grew. Early in 1960 there were rumours of negotiations with a number of English firms and these eventually crystallized into schemes for a new light car factory for Rootes at Linwood (Renfrew) and a new B.M.C. tractor and commercial vehicle plant at Bathgate (West Lothian). The Bathgate factory, opened in 1961, had a capacity of some 50,000 commercial vehicles and 35,000 tractors, and Linwood production began in May 1963 with a capacity of 150,000 cars. To meet their needs the Pressed Steel Company Ltd. made extensions to its Linwood pressings plant, Colvilles extended its hot and cold strip mills at Ravenscraig and Gartcosh, and component making firms began to set up Scottish branch factories. By the autumn of 1964 about 20 had been said to have taken this decision. All seemed set fair for a classic multiplier growth of metal and metal fabricating activities in central Scotland.

Unfortunately, a number of factors—partly Scottish, partly British—dimmed these bright hopes. By the late nineteen sixties only Albion was paying its way. The other two units (employing together almost 13,000) were not covering their costs in spite of all the apparatus of government assistance to plants under the Development Areas legislation. As a *Times* correspondent put it, many felt that results so far '... point to the conclusion that the experiment ought never to be repeated'. By mid-1968, B.M.C. was operating at only 55 per cent of its capacity, and its labour force had shrunk from 5,000 to 4,100 (though by the early summer of 1969 it was back to 4,600). In Spring 1971 the Bathgate plant was operating at only 45 per cent of its capacity. Built to make 3,000 cars a week, six years later Linwood was still making only 300 medium range and 1,200 small units weekly. National curbs upon consumer spending, especially in the crisis measures of 1966 which also checked the buoyancy of the English Midlands, severely affected the new Scottish hopes. In particular, the mass market for the small 'Imp' car of Rootes contracted severely. As with previous growth, there was an inevitable regional snowball effect so that by the autumn of 1966 the new Colville strip mill was operating at only half capacity. Beyond these immediate problems of the Scottish motor industry, however, there were emerging other and more fundamental difficulties that are related directly to its location and to the supply of workers and components.

Scotland is deficient in an intermediate range of industries. It has more than its share of old, heavy trades; it also has spectacular new ones, turning out products with a very high value-to-weight ratio. The former demand specialized skills, and a good deal of unskilled labour. The latter need highly skilled workers. The motor industry lies somewhere between the two. Albion motors—long-established, renowned for the quality of its products, and benefiting from a wise (Leyland) policy which devolved extensive responsibilities to plant management—has a relatively satisfactory labour situation. It has built up over the years a reliable and skilled group of workers who are well used to the rhythm of work in the motor trade. In contrast, the other plants have had to train workers in new skills, to introduce them for the first time to the psychology of the mass production line, and to make them accept companies far bigger and more impersonal than the firms in which they worked before. Initially they had to bear the cost of unacceptable rates of material wastage. Although wage rates were set at lower levels than in the Midlands, and although there were only three unions at Linwood (compared with the 20 or so in Midland car works), it was some time before a smoothly running organization for consultation with management was established. As a result there have been tense labour relations and frequent walkouts at both Linwood and Bathgate.

In the summer of 1963 only 20 per cent of the components used in the 'Imp' were Scottish. The rest came from established suppliers mostly 480 to 640 kilometres (300 to 400 miles) away. In the case of Albion, there was even a steady decline in the share of parts derived from Scotland—from 22 per cent in 1958 to 10 per cent a decade later. After their arrival, Rootes and B.M.C. both examined the structure of Scottish industry in an effort to increase the proportion of local supplies, the former even organizing a 'component exhibition' to encourage a greater Scottish participation. The number of items available locally to B.M.C. was in fact increased from 15 to 32 in a little over 18 months to the summer of 1963. However, such an achievement must be measured against the fact that as many as 4,000 components were said to be required for the trucks made at Bathgate.

One explanation of the slow growth of component manufacture lies in the traditional structure of Scottish industry. By 1968, for example, over one-quarter of the material brought from England to Bathgate was in the form of iron castings worth £5 million. Although Scotland has an iron castings industry (in the Falkirk area), it has traditionally been concerned with large and heavy products and it is deficient in the precision, light castings needed for the motor trade. Another explanation is the relatively low level of transport costs on components brought in from the Midlands. In real terms these are getting lower as the efficiency of transport operations and the size of road and rail loads increase. It is sometimes even possible to carry components back to Scotland exceptionally cheaply as a return freight from England, especially now that half the output of body shells from Linwood goes to the Rootes works in Coventry. Meanwhile, evidence increasingly suggests that the actual cost of component transport is of decreasing importance to the overall performance and economics of the industry. In the middle nineteen sixties the cost of rail transport from the B.M.C. Wellingborough foundry in Northamptonshire to Bathgate was some £2.50 per ton but the firm saw an advantage in using lorries at a cost of approximately £3.50 per ton in order to avoid damage and ensure regular delivery. For many components even apparently high carrying charges are not especially significant, whereas breakdowns in production flows caused interruptions in activity, the need to layoff labour and consequent labour troubles at Bathgate.

More crucial even than the costs of transport are the economies of large scale component manufacture in the Midlands. These, a central location, a fuller market knowledge, and the external economies which can be derived from the possibility of using 'off-cut' material (metal discarded by others), give Midland firms a decisive advantage in serving the national market, and in so far as vehicle makers sometimes share the tooling costs of their component suppliers, they are naturally reluctant to duplicate this investment in Scotland. As a result the new entrant into a small regional market is at a considerable disadvantage, the magnitude of which may be judged by a recent Scottish example. A Scottish sub-contractor offered a part to a motor firm for £0.246 of which approximately £0.096 was reckoned for material and the rest was made up of process costs and profit. A Midland competitor, using off-cut material, and with numerous other advantages of scale and location near the centre of demand, offered the same part delivered to Scotland for £0.096.

By early 1967 new component firms in Scotland, or transfers from England, had produced some 1,800 new jobs in the Kingdom but most British firms were deterred from doing more than open or extend their existing depots in Scotland because of the small size of the regional market. The latter was estimated by five of the largest component manufacturers to be no more than 5 per cent of their total sales. Under such circumstances, it is not surprising that Scotland is still seen by many to be a marginal proposition for such a mass production, mass market, durable goods trade as components manufacture. However, it is also noteworthy that B.M.C.—since the 1968 merger reorganized as Leyland (Scotland) within the new British Leyland Group and with more control over its own operations—have recently sought to eliminate some of the uncertainties in their production schedule by beginning themselves to make some of their own components. Between early 1967 and the middle of 1968, Bathgate began to manufacture 400 components which had previously come from the Midlands. Whether such further integration is desirable remains doubtful, but the peculiar circumstances of the Scottish motor industry have clearly forced it upon the company.

From the viewpoint of Scottish employment needs, this development—plus the acquisition of Rootes by Chrysler, the purchase of the (former Pressed Steel) Linwood body shops, and their decision to concentrate any major new investments in Scotland—suggests that prospectively job opportunities in the motor industry will grow rather than diminish. Ten years after the decision to inject a new motor industry into the Scottish economy, however, it is clear that whatever the economic and social gains to the region, the British economy as a whole has paid dearly for the establishment of a trade described in 1968 by the late Professor Donald Robertson as 'an important symbol of industrial regeneration'.

10.2.1 *The Glasgow and West Central Sub-region*

Within the industrial belt, therefore, and indeed in Scotland as a whole, there is impressive evidence of the changing economic status of various sub-regions. Simultaneously, glaring conflicts in the aims for development planning have begun to emerge, and not all the regional schemes which have been proposed are compatible with each other. Within the Lowlands, the Glasgow and West Central sub-region remains economically the most important area, one which is much more dominant in Scotland than is the South East region within the English economy. It houses 48 per cent of Scotland's population, and in 1966 it offered employment to 50.6 per cent of total workers and 50.3 per cent of male workers in the Kingdom. In many respects, however, the sub-region has been losing ground. Employment for men, for example, grew rather quicker in the nineteen sixties in the Edinburgh and Falkirk/Stirling sub-regions; the rateable value of industry went up 2 per cent between 1961 and 1965 in the Glasgow region, but 12 per cent and 16 per cent respectively in the other two; and between 1956 and 1967 the share of new employments from industrial development certificates in the Glasgow and West Central sub-region was smaller than its share of population. Much of West Central Scotland was made into a special Development Area in February 1971. This is an area, however, which is big enough to include several distinctive sub-divisions.

Mid-Lanarkshire, with a declining coal industry and with the changing steel and heavy engineering trades, is an area of industrial dereliction, acute problems of urban renewal and a slow growing population. Industrial diversification has sometimes taken the form of the conversion of old factories for new trades—as with some old engineering works in Airdrie. The most spectacular new industries, such as motor manufacture and electronics, have passed the area by, and only on the fringe of this industrial belt—at Newhouse, Hamilton, Blantyre and Larkhall, for example—have important new activities been established.

Glasgow has long been recognized as a grossly congested city with an average population density in 1945 of two-and-one-half times that of Birmingham. Much more recently, and probably conservatively, the Glasgow Corporation has estimated that 41 per cent of the city's housing stock is sub-standard. At the end of the nineteen fifties, a long term urban renewal programme and attempts to speed up the city's painfully slow traffic were begun. Simultaneously, a decision was taken to try to rehouse between one-quarter and one-fifth of the population, some 200,000 to 250,000 people, beyond the city boundaries. Overspill agreements have been negotiated with a large number of local authorities throughout Scotland, although mainly in the central belt and, whilst outmovement has proceeded relatively slowly, in 1966 the city population fell below 1 million for the first time since 1911. By the early nineteen sixties, four new towns, largely intended for Glasgow overspill, had been designated. Three—Glenrothes, Cumbernauld and Livingston—are beyond the sub-region. East Kilbride, the most successful of all, lies only a little way beyond the built-up zone. In 1966 a further new town project was begun at Irvine on the Ayrshire coast and designed to take a population increase of 55,000. More recently still, the Scotish Development Department decided on the desirability of a new town type of development at Erskine (near the new Clyde bridge) and at Lennoxtown (northeast of Glasgow and just over the border into Stirlingshire). Early in 1969 the government rejected the idea of a new town at Stonehouse, six miles south of Motherwell, but in principle it accepted the idea of a major expansion of the burghs of industrial Lanarkshire, especially Hamilton and Motherwell-Wishaw. The complex renewal of these old centres would proceed alongside the rehousing of Glasgow overspill. However, the attractive idea of combining renewal and overspill hides innumberable difficulties of execution. One problem for Glasgow itself is to prevent too much dispersal of light industry, needed to diversify its own industrial structure, along with the overspill population.

Within Glasgow the difficulties and dilemmas remain acute. The sheer shortage of room has led to incredibly costly—and far from satisfactory—high density redevelopment. Some blocks of flats have been built as high as 30 stories, and sites which in other circumstances would be regarded as unsatisfactory (such as the old St. Rollox chemical works) have been used for rehousing. There remains still an enormous problem of old and congested properties, and the situation has not been helped by the shifting foci of economic activities within the area. Whilst the heavy east-end industries have suffered severely from the changes of the last 15 years, much of Glasgow's new manufacturing growth has been on the south side. Here, 15 kilometres (9 miles) from the centre, is the booming industrial centre of East Kilbride, already housing 58,000 of its planned 100,000 inhabitants. Here also is the pioneer Hillington industrial estate, and the motor industry at Renfrew-Paisley. Each represents a key element in the emerging pattern of urban growth. Another is the congestion and high rates of central Glasgow, which seem likely to boost such outlying shop and office centres as Paisley. Less certain in its medium-run impact upon the form of the city region is the existence of the great labour resources of some of the old industrial districts like Springburn, which it has been suggested make Glasgow itself the most suitable manufacturing growth point in the Kingdom.

Much of the *upper Clyde estuary* to the west is cluttered with docks, shipyards, engineering works and their attendant services. Greenock and Port Glasgow have the two most successful yards on the Clyde, important dock facilities and a new container terminal. On the north bank of the river, these activities extend as far as Duntocher but on the south bank large open tracts of flat land stretch down river beyond Renfrew and Paisley. Once considered as a possible relocation point for Scottish steelmaking—a function for which the increased size of ore carrier would now render it unsuitable, though still better than the existing Lanarkshire centres—and also for oil refinery construction, it clearly now has a quite different economic potential. By reason of its improved road links to Greenock, the new Erskine bridge and the proposed major housing developments at Erskine, the range of development opportunities has widened immeasurably. Areas further down the estuary and out along the Firth of Clyde have now become the favourites for the industrialists and engineers contemplating new locations for large-scale bulk importing and processing industries.

The Finnart terminal of British Petroleum and its pipeline link to Grangemouth were the first intimations of an emerging re-evaluation of the deep waters off the west coast of Scotland. Opened in 1951, Finnart can now handle vessels of over 200,000 dwt and a second pipeline is being laid across to the refinery. By 1968, however, public attention was being focused increasingly upon the Wemyss Bay-Hunterston-Ardrossan section of the Firth. Already this area has an industrial importance. Ardrossan is a considerable port. Irvine has a Monsanto chemical plant, a silicon works of Imperial Chemical Industries and a new nylon plant belonging to that same firm. At Hunterston, adjoining the existing 300 MW (magnox) nuclear power reactor, is being constructed a new 1,200 MW (a.g.r.) plant to be opened in 1973, and at Inverkip the South of Scotland Electricity Board (S.S.E.B.) is proposing to build its next (oil fired) conventional power station.

By mid-1968, the (former) Scottish and Northwestern Group of the British Steel Corporation had shifted its preferred location for a new ore terminal from Ardmore Point on the north bank of the Clyde opposite Greenock to Hunterston; and early in 1969 the Clyde Port Authority proposed to build there a major terminal capable of handling up to 8 million tons of ore each year from vessels of 250,000 dwt initially and possibly 500,000 dwt later. Included in the proposal was the idea that 40 per cent of the ore imports would be sent in smaller vessels or in part-loaded carriers to other, shallower iron ore ports elsewhere in Britain. The B.S.C. has now approved the plan for a Hunterston ore terminal, but has otherwise not completed its review of Scottish development prospects. Two big oil refineries have also been proposed. The site of the smaller, Murco, refinery was at Longhaugh Point near Bishopton on the Clyde estuary; well up-river on the previously undeveloped southern shore, it was to be linked by a 24 kilometres (15 miles) pipeline with a deepwater terminal on Wemyss Bay. Although approved by the consultants of the Clyde Estuary Development Group, it failed to obtain the approval of the Secretary of State for Scotland on grounds of pollution hazards, and the company was asked to look for an alternative site further down the estuary or on the Firth. By 1971 Murco was involved instead in plans for new refinery capacity on Canvey Island. The other and larger scheme was for a 5 million ton Chevron plant 19 kilometres (12 miles) to the south and on the Firth at Portencross; the proposals envisaged that 320,000 dwt tankers could be docked initially, and even bigger ones later. In May 1971 the Secretary of State for Scotland rejected the Chevron scheme on environmental grounds. Soon after the firm announced a major expansion of its Pernis (Rotterdam) refinery.

Certain aspects of these proposals deserve fuller attention. Initially their contribution to economic growth as measured by employment would be quite small. Chevron, investing £35 million would have employed perhaps 200. The iron ore terminal will naturally have a much smaller workforce. However, in terms of their prospective growth, the developments could be more significant. It is possible, for example, that any oil refinery or refineries would produce petrochemical feedstocks; there is a possibility, therefore, that in time a petrochemical producing and processing industry could develop in the locality in much the same way as has occurred at Grangemouth. Although it was noted earlier that the British Steel Corporation remain uncommitted on their Scottish plans, and a green field site development there is unlikely, it is not impossible to envisage at some future date a 5 to 6 million ton steel plant at Hunterston, such as was once proposed by Colvilles. Were it to be developed, perhaps 8,000 people would be employed. However, the results of such developments would not be unqualified gains, for three reasons in particular.

First, to support a Clyde Estuary steel plant it would be necessary to run down the existing works in Lanarkshire, and to close some of them altogether, unless the new coastal works had such low costs that it would concentrate on foreign outlets; past experience and consideration of the world steel situation (Manners, 1969; 1971) suggests that such a role is unlikely. On the other hand it was being suggested by mid-1971 that, without a new deep-water works, perhaps 10,000 out of the 25,000 jobs in Scottish steelmaking might be lost within five years as a result of the plant closures under consideration by the B.S.C. Second, the iron ore, steel, oil, chemical, and power station developments all threaten amenities. The Murco refinery was denied an estuary site on the grounds that the emission of sulphur fumes would cause discomfort and a possible health hazard to the nearby population of 1.25 million. The waters and adjacent land of the Firth of Clyde is an area of growing recreational importance to the Clydeside conurbation and one in which an increasing number of the more wealthy, mobile workers make their home. The North Ayrshire Coast Development Committee has suggested an attractive development strategy based upon recreation, and is at odds with the Ayr County Council with their plan to rezone the Hunterston peninsula for industrial use. Third, it is not entirely clear how the developments and their associated urbanization would relate to the proposed population growth zone to the south, centred upon Kilmarnock and the new town of Irvine.

Central Ayrshire now has a population of only 87,000, but in 1968 a Joint Land Use Working Party suggested a target population of 200,000. The need to integrate physical with economic planning, and to see individual projects within an overall plan for both the sub-region and indeed the whole of the central valley, does not appear to have been met. The same can be said of the developments on and near the Firth of Forth.

10.2.2 *The Edinburgh, Falkirk/Stirling and Tayside Sub-regions*

The economic standing of the zone about the Firth of Forth is becoming rather more comparable with that of the Clyde as it has increasingly become industrialized. Along the Firth itself are major foci of electricity generation and oil refining. The Cockenzie (1,200 MW), Kincardine Bridge (760 MW) and Logannet (2,400 MW) power stations have their main source of coal nearby in the Lothians and Fife. The refinery at Grangemouth was established in 1924 when oil tankers were only 10,000 to 12,000 tons; since then it has become the focus of a vigorous and continuously ramifying petrochemical complex which has brought in such major concerns as the Distillers Company, Monsanto and Union Carbide to supplement and cooperate with the refinery owner, British Petroleum. (B.P. has recently taken over most of the chemical interests of the Distillers Company). With the decision of B.P. to pipe the oil from its North Sea Forties field ashore at Peterhead and then southwards to Grangemouth for refining and for export, there is every likelihood that these developments will continue apace. Already there are firm plans for a refinery throughput of some 20 million tons per year by the middle nineteen seventies. Away from the Firth, the common denominator is economic and geographical change dominated especially by the designation and growth of three new towns—Livingston. Glenrothes and Cumbernauld, the first two in the Edinburgh sub-region, the third in the Falkirk/Stirling sub-region (Figure 32). The present small population living in their designated areas, 76,400, will be increased eventually to 275,000 and will comprise a large element of Glasgow overspill. In turn this immigration will provide the manpower and the justification for more industrial growth.

Edinburgh dominates the very small enclave which, alone in Scotland, lacks the benefits of Development Area status. This district is made up of the employment exchanges of Edinburgh, Leith and Portobello and contains 0.24 million employees or 11 per cent the Scottish total. The unemployment rate is usually less than half the national average. The reason for this is to be found in the diverse employment structure which in turn reflects Edinburgh's national role in culture and government and its regional-national service function. Whereas one third of the employment in Scotland is in manufacturing, in the three exchanges of this district the proportion is only one quarter.

However the situation has proved unstable. In the first place, parts of the district and notably the port of Leith are heavily dependent on manufacturing. Secondly congestion has increased as population, traffic and the capital's service functions have all grown. Whereas between 1951 and 1961 the population of Glasgow fell by 39,000 or 3.5 per cent that of Edinburgh went up by 7,000 or 1.5 per cent—although in the case of the latter a small increase in area was also involved. In addition to those 'push' factors, a strong 'pull' was exerted by the adjacent the Scottish Development Area. This outward movement has accelerated, 2,300 manufacturing jobs or 4 per cent of the district total

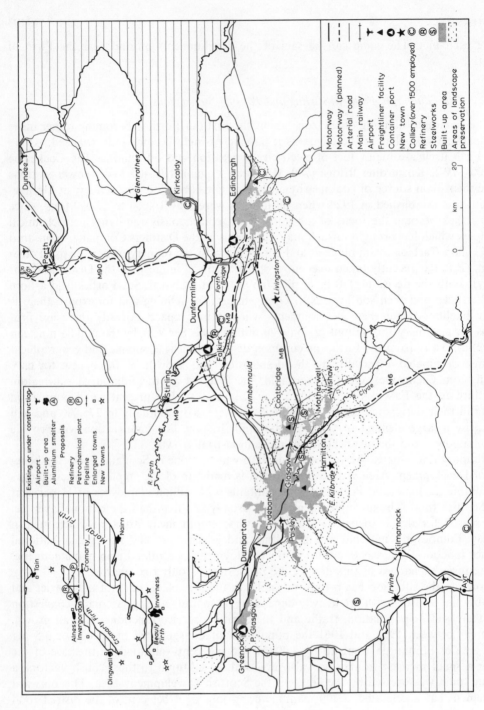

Figure 32 Central Scotland and the Moray Firth : principal economic and land use features, 1971.

being involved in the moves undertaken to September 1968. However in many cases the moves were short enough for workers from Edinburgh to retain their jobs at the cost of a longer journey to work. A notable example was the relocation of Uniroyal (North British Rubber) at Newbridge, Midlothian, less than eight kilometres west of the Development Area boundary. The Hunt Committee concluded that, although there was a need for periodic review of the situation, the district did not qualify for preferential treatment. Later in 1969 the government designated the Leith exchange as an Intermediate Area.

The 1963 White Paper on *Central Scotland* (Cmnd. 2188) recognised Livingston as the major potential growth centre for the *Lothians*. These counties have already benefited from the movement of industry out from Edinburgh-Leith, and West Lothian additionally has received new employment to make good the collapse of its oil shale industry. The workforce in this traditional industry steadily declined from 10,000 in 1913 to 1,800 in 1960, and—apart from that at the small Pumpherston refinery, now working on East Midland crude—was eliminated two years later. It was in this area that the development of the new town of Livingston was begun in 1965. Then its population was 2,000. By the year 2000 it is planned to have a population of 100,000, and a major service and cultural centre for a sub-regional population of one-quarter of a million. The viability of such a centre only 24 kilometres (15 miles) from Edinburgh, with its population of 0.5 million and many higher-order activities, is an open question; at the least it will involve some changes in the present economic and social role of the Scottish capital, changes which as yet remain unspecified.

In the *central Fife* section of the Edinburgh sub-region the new town of Glenrothes has come to serve as a focus for new developments, whilst coal mining has gradually been displaced as the major source of employment. The attraction of new industries has undoubtedly been made easier following the opening in September 1964 of the Forth road bridge, which reduced the distance between Edinburgh and central Fife by about one-quarter from 80 to 19 kilometres (50 to 12 miles). It cost about £20 million, but annual savings from reduced distances, lower vehicle operating costs, the reduction of accidents, the ending of ferry charges and other benefits were estimated by Stewart (1964) to be £2.4 million; with maintenance costs £175 thousand per year, this gives a direct annual return on the capital cost of the bridge of some 9.7 per cent. An even higher return might be shown from a fuller cost-benefit study of the bridge, which would take account not only of the costs of the associated motorways (such as that, still to be completed, into central Fife), but would also seek to measure the benefits of Fifeshire's new accessibility. The bridge has made central Fife not only more attractive to light industry but almost as near as the West Lothian growth area for commuting to Edinburgh or for the receipt of Edinburgh overspill industry. A toll of £0.13 for all vehicles was levied at the beginning, but in 1969 new and varying tariffs were introduced—£0.15 for cars, and £0.50 for commercial vehicles, with a reduction to £0.30 for regular crossings. These charges could be a deterrent to those projects in Central Fife which demand easy and inexpensive access to the south bank of the Firth, and a consequent spur to developments in the Lothians or in the Falkirk-Grangemouth area.

Two growth points were designated in 1963 in the *Falkirk/Stirling* sub-region. The more westerly was the new town of Cumbernauld, which has attracted international attention through its uncompromising treatment of pedestrian and vehicle segregation, and which has the advantage of being the nearest new town—East Kilbride apart—to the Glasgow source of overspill. The more easterly was the Grangemouth-Falkirk urban and industrial area with its dispersed and long-established pattern of heavy industries. It has a good location within the rail and (still more important) the new motorway and trunk road system of central Scotland and it has in Grangemouth one of the three container terminals in the whole central belt. However, it lacks the vital image of a new town centre of growth, and undoubtedly it has felt the strong pull of the surrounding ones at Cumbernauld and Livingston. As a consequence, economic expansion been disappointing, and a Joint Planning Advisory Committee of local authorities has criticized the (former) Board of Trade for failing to steer an adequate volume of new employment into the area. Present plans envisage an increase of 50,000 upon the present population of 128,000, an increase which will require 20,000 to 25,000 extra jobs, of which about half should be in manufacturing. There are some doubts whether this target will be achieved.

The remaining industrial area of the central belt has not performed at all well in recent years but has most ambitious growth plans. The extensive *Tayside* economic sub-region (whose boundary runs from north of Montrose to Rannoch, irregularly through south central Perth, and then east to include the northern and eastern parts of the Fife peninsula lying beyond the coal-field) has a population of 448,000. One third live in Dundee. The recent economic history of the sub-region is a distinctive amalgam of bright and dark. The rateable value of industry in the sub-region went up by 15 per cent between 1961 and 1966 (compared with 2 per cent for the Glasgow and West Central sub-region, 12 per cent for Edinburgh, 16 per cent for Falkirk/Stirling, and 7 per cent for Scotland as a whole), and the unemployment rate has remained low. Yet the sub-region has received relatively few i.d.c. permissions in the last decade or so, and its overall level of employment has not increased; between 1961 and 1966, in fact, male jobs contracted by 2 per cent. The diversity of these indicators stems essentially from the economic past of Tayside.

Following the decline of its old coarse linen industry 100 years ago, a long tradition of fibre production plus the absence of alternative opportunities eased the shift of Dundee (and to some extent of its neighbouring towns) into jute production. A boom in this trade was the chief factor pushing its population from 61,000 in 1851 to 175,000 in 1931. As late as 1937, some 38 per cent of the insured population worked in jute; there were also textile and engineering industries related to it. In the subsequent thirty years production has declined by about 30 per cent; productivity has increased as much as 50 per cent since 1949 as a result of an investment of £12.5 million; and in the process the labourforce has shrunk from 38,000 to 16,000. Almost all of this decline occurred before 1960. Any compensating growth has depended upon the arrival of new light trades, a development which began with the location of National Cash Register in the town in 1946, and was followed by the location of a range of new employers especially in the town's two peripheral industrial estates. There have been some disappointments, notably the closure of the 20-year-old refrigerator plant of Morphy Richards in 1967, and the decision in the same year by both Plessey and Associated Electrical Industries not to go ahead with big electronics and telecommunications developments which had reached the advanced planning stage. Nevertheless, overall the economy of this focus of the Tayside region has been transformed. The opening of the £6.5 million Tay road bridge has been followed by ambitious sub-regional growth plans. In 1966 it was said that Tayside might eventually have an urban centre of 1 million. Even when this extraordinary figure was scaled down, Scottish planners in 1969 still spoke of a rise of between 175,000 and 300,000 for the sub-region by the year 2000—although the detailed study of the area's development potential by the Scottish Office in the light of national population growth (see p.65) had not then been published.

The incompatability of the various schemes for Central Scotland is obvious. The population of Glasgow will fall by perhaps as much as 250,000 as urban renewal proceeds; there will also be some dispersal from Edinburgh. Elsewhere, however, as in the old industrial area of central Lanarkshire, the rehousing of population will take place in existing urban areas. The five new towns already under construction—East Kilbride, Cumbernauld, Glenrothes, Livingston and Irvine—are expected to grow by various terminal dates by some 237,000. To this may be added 50,000 for the Falkirk-Grangemouth growth area, and an additional 45,000 to 50,000 for Central Ayrshire, the population of the other proposed new towns of Lochwinnoch in southwest Renfrewshire, Lennoxtown and Larkhall, and the proposed 175,000 to 300,000 for Tayside. Even making conservative assumptions—that only two of the three proposed new towns will be built and that each will grow to only 40,000, and that the lower figures for Central Ayrshire and Tayside are realistic—and ignoring the fact that a substantial part of conurbation overspill will go to a variety of small towns in central Scotland, existing schemes appear to involve 290,000 people in excess of a total overspill need of perhaps 300,000. Since 1951, the total population increase of Scotland has been 85,000. The unrealism of the proposals in population terms—and neglecting the equally important financial considerations—is made even more remarkable when it is noted that in addition to the schemes for Central Scotland, there are plans for the expansion of population in the Borders and the Moray Firth area which involve further increases of over 200,000. The case for a more objective scrutiny of the population, migration and economic base assumptions of the various sub-regional plans of Scotland is difficult to resist.

10.2.3 *The South West and Borders Sub-regions*

The large area of the *South West of Scotland*—the counties of Dumfries, Kirkcudbright,

Wigtown and southern Ayrshire—has a population of only 153,000. There are no major centres of population. Dumfries (28,000) and Stranraer (9,000) at opposite ends of the region are far and away the biggest towns. Road communications are circuitous and of only moderate quality away from the excellent Glasgow-M6 link through Annandale. The railway through the peninsula from Dumfries to Stranraer has now been closed, so that the only routes surviving are the two between Glasgow and Carlisle (through Annandale and Nithsdale) and the Glasgow, Ayr, Stranraer line for Ulster traffic. There are no major mineral resources, and the main activities are sheep rearing, dairying—in which improved transport has spread liquid milk and creamery activities at the expense of cheesemaking—and tourism. The days when Dumfries was a name to be reckoned with in motor manufacture are almost forgotten, though near the town is an important plant of Imperial Chemical Industries.

South West Scotland has high unemployment rates comparable to those of the Highlands. The 5 per cent decline in employment there between 1961 and 1966, although it involved only some 3,000 jobs, was proportionally bigger than in any of the other seven sub-regions in the Kingdom. The fall of 7 per cent in male employment contrasts with a 2 per cent decline for Scotland as a whole. Between 1956 and 1967 i.d.c. permissions were expected to produce only 3.1 thousand new jobs, a 1.9 per cent share for a sub-region with 2.9 per cent of the Scottish total population.

The economic prospects of the area are naturally the concern of the Scottish Office, but there seems little hope of any major economic developments. Two areas present possibilities, but in each case they stand up badly when examined in a national context. In the mid nineteen fifties Luce Bay was suggested by the Board of Trade as a possible site for a new steelworks. Even at this time it was a rather wild suggestion; the subsequent growth in size of ore carriers makes it even less credible today. Nonetheless the extensive flat area at the northern end of the bay, at the moment used only for pasture, forestry and military purposes could ultimately have an important development potential. The second area is the Solway Lowland in southern Scotland and Cumberland. In 1964, R.L. Drew of the Atomic Energy Authority produced a scheme for the wholesale development of the Solway. Central to the project was a causeway from Bowness to Annan carrying greatly improved communications into the south of Scotland and creating an enormous freshwater reservoir. Associated developments were to include a deepwater port, an international airport, and nuclear power development whose energy would be used in the production of such products as aluminium, soda and magnesium. Later the scheme was elaborated into a Solway plain development embracing considerable population and urban growth. Even in its early form the call on the national Exchequer was put at almost £3,000 million. This, the fashionability of other estuarine schemes such as the Dee (p. 00) and the Humber (p. 00), and national indigence, as well as its own inherent weaknesses, have caused the scheme to fade into the background. But in any case there is nationally little appetite for developing a wholly new area almost from scratch when, with the groundwork already laid by past development, expansion can be integrated with the revival of less favoured communities as on the Clyde, the Forth or the Tees.

To the east, the *Borders* have no such mesmerising growth possibilities, but they do have serious problems and contrast with the southwest in the importance of their industry. The four Border counties of southeast Scotland have a population of just over 100,000. It is heavily concentrated in the mill towns of the Middle Tweed (from Galashiels, through Melrose to St. Boswells) and at Selkirk and Hawick. For their high quality woollens and tweeds there is expanding demand, but, as in the very different environment of the West Yorkshire textile industry (pp. 333–335), a dwindling labour force, and frequently labour shortages. Organized in small units, the textile industry in the Borders has proved even less able than elsewhere to attract skilled and better educated workers and, as there are few other job opportunities, the young and ambitious have drifted away. Mechanization in farming has caused men also to move from the area and with them went their women folk who provided the main labour force of the mills. Between 1951 and 1961 population in the Border counties fell by 7,000 and at one time in the late summer of 1963, when there were only 430 people unemployed (a 1 per cent rate) there were over 1,150 unfilled vacancies. In these circumstances, as in West Yorkshire, firms have built factories elsewhere; one, Lyle and Scott of Hawick, which opened its first factory in the Team Valley estate near Newcastle in 1958, within nine years had a second factory there and an employment of 250 (*Industrial Tyneside,* 1966; *Voice of North East Industry,* 1967).

The spiral has been downward. The increase in industrial rateable value between 1961 and 1965 was only 1 per cent (compared with 7 per cent for Scotland as a whole). Overall employment fell by 2 per cent. There was a net outward migration and an ageing of the population. Environmental circumstances have not helped. Flat land suitable for building is in short supply, the roads are tortuous and the 'Waverley Line' of British Rail which linked Edinburgh and Carlisle through Hawick and Melrose has now been closed after losing as much as £250,000 a year. Services generally are costly to provide for a small and rather scattered population for which the biggest centres are Hawick and Galashields with populations of only 16,000 and 12,000 respectively. The report, *The Scottish Economy* 1965 *to* 1970 (Cmnd. 2864), published early in 1966 recognized the need to reverse these trends. It saw an increase in population and industrial employment as the only means of saving the Border counties from a 'distortion of the age and community structure and a draining away of youth, vigour and the capacity for innovation' which Peter Self (1966) has seen as a danger for the whole of Scotland.

An Edinburgh University study was begun as a joint physical planning and economic exercise but, even before it was published in 1968 as *The Central Borders,* an emergency scheme for settling 4,500 people and matching industry on a site at Darnick (between Melrose and Galashiels) had been set in motion. The scheme faced strong opposition from those whose first priority was the preservation of the natural beauty and historical traditions of the area, and from a predictable rural lobby. The Central Borders plan involves a further increase of 20,000 inhabitants through industrial development. For a time there was controversy as to the best form such a population infusion could take—whether it was to be mainly near Galashields, in a new centre, or divided between the existing small towns. In the summer of 1968 Roxburgh County Council rejected the

Borders plan, taking issue with the proposal that 10,000 should be grafted onto the very small communities of St. Boswells and Newtown St. Boswells. Late in 1968 a compromise agreement was reached in which growth there was reduced to 5,000, whilst both Hawick and Galashields will be expanded by over 6,000 and Jedburgh by over 2,000. The problem could well be to find matching sources of employment. One early and promising suggestion was that 'research and development' types of employment, for which small sites and even remoteness are no particular hazard, may be suitable (Johnston and Hood, 1968). The means whereby this type of enterprise can be induced to locate in the area have yet to be explained.

10.3 The Highlands

North of the central lowlands, there are two very different areas. The coastlands, plateau and foothills northeast of a line from Montrose through Ballater to Nairn have a population of 450,000. Employment is almost equal to that of Tayside, but the area has a consistently higher rate of unemployment and a much slower rate of industrial growth; estimated employment from i.d.c. permissions between 1956 and 1967 was well under half that on Tayside. There are excellent farmlands, and in some areas—for example, along the coastal plain of Moray—every sign of rural prosperity. Recent studies of parts of this area conducted by Aberdeen University (Gaskin 1969) suggest the need for efforts to stabilize population by the mid-nineteen seventies—and, in order to achieve this, the creation of some 8,000 new jobs. Growth, it is suggested, should be focused upon Aberdeen and on Elgin. The population of the Aberdeen city region should be increased by one-twelfth from its present level of 240,000, a goal which will not be difficult to achieve now that the city is becoming the principal land base for much North Sea oil exploration and development. The proposed 10 per cent increase in the population of 66,000 currently living in the area between Buckie and Forres, and extending half way up the Spey valley towards Grantown, is likely to be more difficult to generate.

The Highlands and Islands include the crofting counties of Caithness, Sutherland, Ross and Cromarty, Inverness and Argyll, and all the islands in the wide sector from the peninsula of Kintyre to the Isles of Shetland. This huge area has a population of only 280,000. Even general economic and social indicators show their plight—very low activity rates, a small female labour force, consistently high unemployment levels and very much less new industrial employment than in any other sub-region in Scotland. Here, as opposed to most other parts of the Kingdom, the problems have roots penetrating deeply into a period even before the industrial revolution.

Defined roughly by the seven counties—a definition which excludes such eminently highland areas as much of the Cairngorms and Rannoch—the Highlands occupy 47 per cent the area of Scotland and over one-fifth that of Britain. Yet they contained in 1965 only 0.5 per cent of the British population. In no part of Europe west of a line joining west central Anatolia to Stavanger are population densities so low over such a large area.

It is indeed another world from the crowded, bustling central valley with all its problems of an old industrial economy, though improved roads and weekend ski trips render its differences rather less romantic than when Samuel Johnson reckoned Lowlanders were still as ignorant of the Highlands as they were of Borneo or Sumatra (Thomson and Grimble, 1968, p. 17).

The existence of a Highland problem is indisputable. Only since about 1920 has there been a population decrease in Scotland as a whole, but in the seven crofting counties population decline has been going on for a century. Between 1871 and 1965, whereas the Kingdom's population increased by 1.82 millions (or 54.1 per cent), there was a decline of 96,000 (25.8 per cent) in that of the Highlands. Rates of natural increase have been high but they have been more than cancelled out by net outward movement so that, in the 1871 to 1949 period in which natural increase was 103,000, the Highland population fell by 75,000. The younger age groups, the more vigorous and often the more enterprising or intelligent have left. As a result, 14.4 per cent of the population in 1961 was over 65, compared with 10.6 per cent for Scotland as a whole. In more remote parts decline has proceeded even further, so that Lochcarron District in southwestern Ross and Cromarty had 22.8 per cent of its population over 65 and only 17.7 per cent under 15 (less than three-quarters the Scottish average). In one Assynt township, no child has been born for over 35 years (Mitchell, 1962). In spite of the loss of population by emigration, unemployment rates are high—usually twice the Scottish average—and standards of living are low. In their degree, in their origins, and in the great size of the area involved, the development problems of the Scottish Highlands are unique in Britain (Thomson and Grimble, 1968, pp. 17–24).

The traditional activities of the Highlands were grazing and fishing, with cultivation confined only to the coast or valleys. These were activities which supported a dispersed population. The system changed after the Jacobite rebellions, as landlords replaced communal run-rig farming with independent peasant holdings and moved families out of the glens. Simultaneously, sheep rearing gradually ousted the traditional cattle economy. Displaced Highlanders swelled the shift to the Lowlands, to England, to America or to the crofts of the western coastal belt which became steadily more overpopulated. Late in the nineteenth century, clearances for deer forests at a time when hunting was in vogue for the wealthy speeded the process of decline. When large concentrations of population, mineral wealth or rich land were the basic prerequisites of success in urban and industrial, or agricultural, activity respectively, the Highlands had neither. Highland society disintegrated.

For almost seventy years after the Highlands were first recognized as a national problem, action on their behalf was based upon primarily social rather than economic criteria. Although the Napier Committee of 1884 seems to have been quite clear about the economic and social arguments, the Crofters Acts of 1886 and 1892 which gave the peasant security of tenure ossified the system by sheltering it from economic forces, which would have secured the amalgamation of units and might have given a more reasonable income to the crofter. Originally writing in the nineteen twenties Demangeon (1939, p. 160) still described the authentic, traditional Highlands—its cultivation, pasture, fish and the shoots of the rich. 'In their desolate moors and among the cottages, with their smoke-grimed dry walls and their roofs of turf or reed-thatch, it is still possible to breathe a calm and healthy old-world atmosphere'. Behind this colourful facade the Highlands continued to decay. Twenty years later planning still contained the same bias. Geddes and Spaven in Daysh (1949) described the region's prime asset as the Highlander's way of life; they criticized any trend to ranching, which would only 'lead to further breakup of communities and emigration', and they looked forward to a time when (perhaps by 1960) the Highlands and Isles might become 'an example to Western Europe and the Dominions in rural rehabilitation'. As late as 1954 members of the Taylor Committee on crofting recorded their unanimous conviction '... that in the national interest the maintenance of these communities is desirable because they embody a free and independent way of life which in a civilisation predominatly urban and industrial in character is worth preserving for its own intrinsic quality'.

By the nineteen sixties, however, there was a strong reaction in favour of applying economic criteria to any assistance. In the *Scottish Economy* 1965 *to* 1970, it was stressed in relation to the Highlands that the Scottish Office were concerned with applying '... the same criteria as were employed in other study areas, to limit examination rigorously to those elements which offered some possibility of being integrated with the economy of the United Kingdom as a whole and to determine which economic and social objectives were worth spending resources on' (p. 52). By this time the focus of development planning was shifting too. Although still concerned with improved crofting and farming, with fishing, forestry and tourism, the Highlands and Islands Development Board (formed in 1965) saw as its most urgent task the need to foster industrial employment. With only 10 per cent of employment in the Crofter Counties in manufacturing, more than one-quarter of the loans and grants of the Board were made to manufacturing industries in 1967.

The uniqueness of the Highland problem, however, can not be overstressed. This is not meant to suggest that the Highland planner cannot learn much from the way development problems are tackled in other areas of the world, but that analogies are sometimes too lightly suggested. Quite irrationally, Geddes and Spaven proposed the relevance of the Tennessee Valley Authority's experience as if it had some substantial lessons for the Highlands. More commonly and more recently, frequent references have been made to the vigour with which the Scandinavian countries have tackled the problem of their northern regions, and to the success of Norwegian policy in encouraging the growth of major manufacturing activities using hydro-electricity. In fact, of course, in Scandinavia generally (and especially in Norway) the north is a much bigger part of the whole than are the Highlands in the British economy. Britain, and indeed Scotland itself, both have tremendous problems in their old industrial areas, where the great bulk of population lives and which are without their parallel in Scandinavia. Moreover, whereas in

Norway—as in the Tennessee valley—physical conditions do permit the production of low cost hydro-electricity; in Scotland the cheapness of hydro-power is a chimera. Similarly, it is unreasonable to attempt comparisons between Danish farming and that of the remote northwest of Scotland (Daysh, 1949, p. 45; Thomson and Grimble, p. 291; Martech Consultants, 1964, p. 15). The various strands of the Highland economy must be understood in the context of their distinctive problems and opportunities.

In 1966 *agriculture* was estimated to provide the equivalent of 17,000 full time jobs, work for 16 per cent of the employees in the Highlands. In economic terms, three-quarters of the industry comprised full-time, mainly pastoral, farming operations concentrated on the better land. The other quarter of farm income was derived from crofting. Located in the poorer areas of the western and northern seaboard, the 20,000 crofts are four times as numerous as the farms, but offer only part time employment to some 16,000 workers. As in the rest of Britain, the rationalization of farming is proceeding steadily in the north of Scotland, but the crofts present innumerable special problems. They are grouped into some 700 small communities or 'townships'. Rainfall is heavy, sunshine totals are low, winds are strong, the land is poor and the croft units are small and dispersed. Crofting is often an ancillary to a range of other part-time occupations, and unemployment and underemployment levels are high. Some 80 per cent of the crofts are said to provide less than two days work a week. Per capita income is low and, although it is common to argue that poor economic returns are matched by a satisfying life, it is a case which the decay of crofting does little to support. An awareness of high standards elsewhere, the frustrated desire of young people to have a home of their own outside the communal croft house, and the (relatively) high prices offered by urban dwellers for holiday homes are new disintegrating factors. But many obstacles bar the way to a more economic organization.

The crofts are far from main lines of communication to markets. Their remoteness is both general and particular, for the individual crofting townships are also cut off by sea lochs and bogs from one another. The progress of the crofter counties road construction programme introduced by the Ministry of Transport in 1935, when 100 per cent grants were promised for the upgrading of nearly 2,000 kilometres (1,200 miles) of classified roads, has been slow. Thirty years later 568 kilometres (354 miles) of this total still awaited authorization. The last few years, however, have seen the programme speeded up (Report of the Highland Transport Board, 1967, pp. 14–15). A second obstacle is the rigidity of the crofting organization, in spite of the obvious need to merge the minute and un-economic units. In 1955 a new Crofters Commission was established but it quickly passed from enthusiasm to dismay at the intractability of the problem. An attempt was made to ease its tasks by the Crofting (Scotland) Bill 1961, but ideas of preservation rather than proposals on the reshaping and reinvigoration of crofting prevailed in the new Crofters Act. The old crofter prefers to hold onto his land, even if he does not work it, and even though the returns are notably smaller than those from the exceptional localities where crofts have been reorganized, such as Westray in northwest Orkney. But without extensive reorganization, bountiful assistance in the improvement of land, in the fostering of tourism and in the attraction of industry will not go the whole way to solving the crofting problem (Mackie, 1969).

In the past, the typical Orcadian has been characterized as 'a farmer with a boat' and *fishing* has been one of the staple activities of the crofters. The loss of overseas sales, and competition from bigger trawler fleets with bases nearer large urban markets, caused the industry to shrink. In 1937 there were 5,800 fishermen in the crofter counties, of whom over 4,000 were part-time crofters. By 1964 the part-time fishermen were 900 but 2,200 full-time workers were still employed. Although canning and freezing have improved the livelihood of landing points remote from the market, the scattered nature of the activity and the uncertainty of supply make it difficult to secure an economic loading for some of the processing plants. It is nevertheless widely agreed that, although fishing cannot be a growth sector of the Highland economy, it has a role in any general population holding operation there and locally is crucial in improving standards of living. The Highlands and Islands Development Board is financing research, training, the further development of processing and the purchase of second hand boats. Most important of all, it has a Fisheries Development Scheme for the provision of new boats, which were financed by grants from various fishing authorities, loans from the Board and contributions from the applicant. In 1966 a scheme was introduced for the construction of 25 fishing boats by 1971 at a cost of £750,000; the scheme went so well that in 1967 approval was obtained for the financing of an additional ten new boats (Highlands and Islands Development Board, 1967, Appendix V). It has been estimated that one fisherman provides work ashore for two men in processing and ancillary trades.

Forestry development in the Highlands is under both private owners (43 per cent) and the Forestry Commission. Whilst earlier Commission policy was severely criticized on grounds both of economy and amenity—for breaking up estates only part of which were used for planting, for taking sheep lands or for planting whole areas in a dull uniformity of species—these faults have in general been corrected. By the summer of 1965, the Commission had planted 128,000 hectares (316,000 acres), almost 37 per cent of its landownings in the Highlands. This was divided into 95 separate forest areas with an average size of 1,346 hectares (3,325 acres). Although this scattered pattern of operations raised costs, it spread geographically the stabilizing effect of forest work. Whereas sheep rearing, deer or grouse lands provide work for no more than one man per 405 hectares (1,000 acres), forestry operations directly employ more than six. There are wider implications too. Yields from the maturing forests are now increasing rapidly, and at the same time the rate of new planting is going up—from about 4,000 hectares (10,000 acres) per year at the end of the nineteen fifties to 5,500 hectares (14,000 acres) by 1967, and prospectively as much as 20,000 hectares (50,000 acres) a year by 1976. As yields increase more opportunities develop for sawmill operations and the woodworking trades. At still higher levels of yield, new and bigger industries can be considered; the Fort William pulp and paper mills, although perhaps a premature investment, are a good example. Their prospects can be considered along with other industrial projects associated with two further Highland resources, waterpower and natural deep harbours.

The significant development of Highland *waterpower* dates from the years 1896 to 1906 when the Foyers and Kinlochleven plants of British Aluminium were built in or near the Great Glen. From then on, however, there were no further developments until the Lochaber and Rannoch and Loch Tummel schemes in the late nineteen twenties and nineteen thirties. Then, in 1943 the North of Scotland Hydro-electric Board was established and given a mandate which was social as well as commercial; it was charged to produce electricity, to attract industry, to improve the standard of living and to check the outward drift of people. It was instructed also to export power to the Lowlands as a means of subsidizing the provision of power in the scattered Highland communities. Hopes in the Board were at times unreasonably high; Geddes and Spaven (p. 52) considered in 1949 that 'whereas for 150 years power (in the exclusive form of coal) drew Highland hands to Lowland factories, hydro-electricity from Highland streams may henceforth employ them at home'. The Board was bedevilled both by its difficult physical environment—variable rainfall, small catchment areas and the consequent need for many small dams or expensive linking tunnels—and by the social commission.

Nevertheless, substantial progress was made. The projects of the Hydro Board can be divided into three groups : the bigger power stations such as Errochty and Loch Sloy, the (less profitable) projects designed to produce and sell power to the South of Scotland Electricity Board at times of peak demand there and the provision of small units, often diesel-fired, for the islands. By the late nineteen sixties, some £50 million had been paid by the Board to workers in the Highlands. There were new roads, the availability of electricity had improved social conditions and signs of modernization in the form of power stations, dams and powerlines had given the region a moral boost. However, although some employment had been created, the more extravagant hopes—for instance, for a Corpach (Fort William) calcium carbide works, or for magnesium production on Cromarty Firth using Hydro Board power and Eriboll-Durness limestone—have not materialized. The transformation of the Highlands by the Hydro Board in other words has been less than revolutionary and as an economic operation it has simply not been a success.

Moreover, the economies of hydro-electricity generation are not improving in the Scottish context. The most favourable sites have already been developed, and the cost of new ones mount steeply. In addition, the Board has increasingly to face amenity objections and the steadily falling costs of conventional (and nuclear) power generation. The situation may be illustrated by the ill-fated Glen Nevis scheme, which raised major amenity issues in the early nineteen sixties. The project would have employed some 400 men during its construction but when completed it would have provided permanent jobs for only ten. Generating costs were estimated at 0.31 pence (or possibly a little less) per unit but the Kincardine Bridge coal-fired station, burning Fife coal and opened in 1960, had production costs of only 0.24 pence a unit. Since then, in a new generation of Firth of Forth stations, costs have been cut even further. By 1965 only about half of the estimated potential Highland power resources had been developed but it looked increasingly uncertain whether the case was strong enough for their further exploitation.

The elusiveness of *industrial development* in the Highlands has tempted the unwary to throw caution to the wind and to propose schemes there which take little note of the needs of other parts of Britain, or even of their likely effects upon the character of the Highlands themselves. For instance, through the Scottish Trades Union Congress, one of the members of the Highland and Islands Development Board (H.I.D.B.) has demanded a 30-year tree planting programme to cover 1.2 million hectares (3 million acres), ten times the present Forestry Commission lands. This would involve a rate of sustained annual planting double the apparently very hopeful forecast once made by Harold Wilson for 1976. The cost was estimated at £750 million, in return for which it was optimistically suggested that 130,000 new jobs would be created. The Scottish Nationalist Party has also advocated a big planting programme without observing that in the process the Highlands would be transformed, farming interests would suffer and (with the trend to specialized contract work) the effect on local employment could well be small. Above all, the commercial viability of such a programme is highly suspect—as indeed are the economics of not a few related industries.

There are many small sawmills in the Highlands, a response to the scattered nature of the forests. Their smallness makes it impossible to secure many of the economies open to larger concerns, especially in the use of waste. In the late nineteen sixties, the earlier Forestry Commission planting began to mature, and there was a prospect of a rapid growth in output—possibly a fourfold increase in timber yield in the subsequent twenty years. At the same time there was talk of reducing the existing sawmilling industry to four or five large units which would be able to compensate for their longer hauls on timber through the economies of their bigger throughput, which in turn would justify the installation of plant to use what now is merely waste. The same conditions were also judged to favour a pulp and paper mill for the Highlands.

A decade earlier, the Forestry Commission had explored the feasibility of small British pulp, chipboard, fibre and building board factories. However, Canadian consultants showed that a successful plant in those trades would have to be large, and would consequently need to be located near to very large forests. Water and rail access would be essential and, if there were doubts about the adequacy of home timber supplies, a coastal location would be required to handle supplementary foreign imports. Only two areas in the Highlands fit these locational requirements—the Moray Firth, and the area at the opposite end of the Great Glen around Fort William.

Although the major British paper firms—Bowater, Reed, Thames Board Mills—were all involved in investigations, it was Wiggins Teape which in 1962 decided to build a mill at Corpach, Fort William. Costing £20 million (of which £10 million was a government loan) the plant was at work by 1965 and had a capacity to handle 260,000 tons of Scottish softwoods plus 110,000 tons of imported hardwoods each year. Construction brought the usual multiplier effects—1,500 employed in construction, the purchase of 40 per cent of the plant from the Scottish economy, an expenditure of over £1 million on roads, new piers to handle the imported timber and the continued operation of the West

Highland railway line which had been threatened with closure. Initially, 700 were employed at the mill, rising to 1,300 by 1970; 2,000 more will work in the forests, on the railway or at the piers in order to service the operations. In the process the population of Fort William will double to 7,000 by the early nineteen seventies. This employment growth has offset the dwindling job opportunities at the nearby British aluminium plant. It has also created a new if unquantifiable mood of expansion in Highland thinking, especially in regard to the possible stimulation of a host of small industrial projects. However, there are shadows behind this story of apparent initial success. The early operations of the mill have not been commercially very successful. The plant has proved to be too small to secure economies available to its overseas rivals and although the rise in Scandinavian pulp prices—said by some to be aimed at squeezing unintegrated British paper firms—seemed to justify the integrated Fort William concern, there is no doubt that its operating costs are extremely high.

Some of the basic issues facing the development of Highland manufacturing have come into still greater prominence since the Highlands and Islands Development Board (H.I.D.B.) was appointed in 1965. In line with its broad development strategy, the Board has spoken of a three-level approach to industrial growth in the Highlands : the encouragement of any industry wherever a developer wishes to locate, the establishment of major growth points for large-scale industrial development and a methodical programme of facilitating manufacturing in small industrial centres '... in scale with the possibilities of the West and Islands'. The last is easily overlooked but is of vital importance, for as Gillanders (Thomson and Grimble, 1968, pp. 138, 149) remarked of his native Applecross '... a small industry, like boat building, for example, employing only ten to twelve men would make the difference between a decadent community, without hope, and a human growth point'. In pursuit of this aim, in 1967 the Board made 51 grants to manufacturing or processing concerns expected to produce an average additional employment of less than 6 per grant. Between 1965 and autumn 1968, 28 new small factories providing 460 jobs had been approved or set up between Shetland and Kintyre (H.I.D.B., 1967, Appendix V).

In its new growth point policy the Board has run into greater difficulties. Apart from its general programme for further development at Fort William (and the removal of impediments there such as the housing shortage) its so-called area development planning or growth point strategy is focused upon two areas in the northeast Highlands : Wick-Thurso and the Moray Firth. In the first, it aims to build upon the notable achievements of the last 15 years; the second is a clearer case of development planning.

Between 1931 and 1951 the population of Caithness fell by 3,000. In the next decade, it went up by 4,700. The key to this change of fortune is found in the decision of the Atomic Energy Authority (A.E.A.) to build an experimental reactor at Dounreay seven miles west of Thurso. Some 2,000 new houses were built in the area to serve the workforce; and the younger age range of the A.E.A. employees, their high levels of education and their keenly active social life, were basic to the revival of the area. In 1966 it was decided to build a prototype fast breeder reactor at Dounreay to incorporate the results of the successful experimental work carried out there. There remained nevertheless the prospect of a gradual decline of the workforce after the mid nineteen seventies when, if its operations proved successful, the reactor would become merely another power producing unit with a small labour force. By the late nineteen sixties local agitation, backed by the Highlands and Islands Development Board, was urging the need for new research activities and facilities. It was argued that such a 'mini-Harwell' could serve Scottish industry in a host of ways—and might be accompanied by new energy intensive industries employing local (nuclear) power and (possible) deep water facilities at Scrabster just along the shore of Thurso Bay. In 1969 consultants made a market survey of a project which had been anticipated in slightly different form at least 20 years earlier—a magnesia plant using dolomite from Sutherland, hot sea water and energy from Dounreay. No firm plans have yet been announced, however. Locally it is believed that the government is obliged to keep up the momentum that has transformed the area. How it can do so, particularly in the light of the bigger developments on and proposed for the Moray Firth, remains an open question.

No focus of population comparable to the Moray Firth lowlands exists anywhere else in the Highlands. In the seven crofting counties there are only 10 communities of over 3,000. Of these, two—Inverness and Dingwall—are in the zone between Dornoch Firth and the southern shore of the inner Moray Firth. Moreover, the crofting counties have 53 communities in the 400 to 3,000 population range of which 14 are in the same belt. Of all employees in the six northern crofting counties (that is excluding Argyll), 40 per cent are in the Inverness-Dingwall-Invergordon area. In 1963, two-thirds of the freight received on the 264 kilometres (165 miles) of railway between Inverness, Wick and Thurso was handled in the 55 kilometres (33 miles) between Inverness and Invergordon. Like Fort William this has been recognized as a suitable growth area for some time. Early in 1949 it was designated as a Highland Development Area not merely because of the need to tackle local unemployment problems but '. . . because of its suitability as a focal centre of industrial development for the Highlands as a whole' (Scottish Home Department, 1950, p. 20). In the summer of 1964 Martech consultants submitted their report *Highland Opportunity* to the 'extra political' Scottish Vigilantes Association. In it the need for high volume production, as opposed to the existing scattered and small industrial output was stressed. Cheap power was recognized as an asset but a change in the Hydro Board's pricing policies was strongly urged in order to benefit major consumers very near to the power source. Among other tentative power intensive projects, a mineral-petrochemicals complex at Loch Eriboll was mentioned.

At about the same time, Frank Thomson was the moving force in the idea for a £30 million petrochemical complex at Invergordon: a 2 million ton refinery, a 330,000 ton ammonia plant, a 75,000 ton fertilizer unit and a 80,000 ton plastics factory (Martech, 1964, pp. 28–29). Thomson, who had been associated with the major new grain distillery at Invergordon, was the chairman of the Scottish Vigilantes Association. When he joined the Highlands and Islands Development Board as a part-time member, he seems to have transferred to their councils the idea of big new mineral processing complexes.

In January 1966 the White Paper *The Scottish Economy* 1965–1970 (pp. 59 and 151) spoke of the increasing attractiveness of the Beauly and Cromarty Firths for industry and as a new foci for population growth. It suggested an urban population increase in the Nairn-Tain belt from the present 75,000 to some 165,000 by an unspecified date. Between March and August 1966 Product Planning Limited studied and confirmed the feasibility of a major Moray Firth development (see Figure 32) and by the year end they had submitted a plan for a substantial urban-industrial development there with a population rising to 300,000. The area was recognized as having an unusually favourable range of assets for large scale industry, such as '. . . a sheltered deep-water harbour capable of taking very large tankers up to 200,000 tons and all the biggest bulk cargo carriers likely to be built; ample supplies of fresh water, and the very unusual situation where suitable areas of flat land lie adjacent to the deep-water . . .' (H.I.D.B., 1966). The locality's disadvantages, in particular the relatively high costs of bulk product distribution to the national market, were not explored. In their Second Report the Highlands and Islands Development Board summarized (p. 14) what it was hoped would be gained from such a development by the Highlands; these included the creation of a major centre of 'modern job opportunity', able to offer the region a full range of modern commercial, social, cultural and other activities, a 'home market' of reasonable size for regional products such as food, a related justification for the improvement of transport and social provision and a more balanced economic structure as a result of an increase in manufacturing industry. In 1967–1968, several specific studies and a more general one were carried out.

In 1967 Occidental Petroleum of California seems to have seriously examined in a £120,000 feasibility study a £50 million petrochemical project for Invergordon. It failed to obtain governmental approval, however. Whereas the profit would have been Occidental's, the associated suggestions of the H.I.D.B. would have involved the national Exchequer in almost 80 per cent of the overall costs, either in loans or grants for buildings and machinery, or in the estimated £20 million of infrastructure spending on docks, roads, housing and the like (Thomson and Grimble, 1968, pp. 126–147). In response, one full-time member of the H.I.D.B. resigned, observing that the Scottish Office seemed to believe that 'the Highlands was a place for little things, not a place for big things'. Within two months another big project, this time an aluminium smelter was under consideration.

In 1967 Britain used approximately 400,000 tons aluminium but produced only about 35,000 tons from the British Aluminium plants in the Highlands, the first of which was built over 70 years before. The national import bill for aluminium by 1969 was about £85 million. Forecasts suggested that by 1974 consumption would be equal to some 500,000 tons. The lack of a home industry is at first sight incomprehensible. At one time in 1968, when metallic aluminium was £196 a ton, alumina (aluminium oxide) the chief raw material was £27.5 a ton; with two tons needed for every ton of metal, an apparent foreign exchange saving of £140 a ton could be obtained by manufacture at home. The historical impediment has always been the high cost of electricity, the chief element in the industry's cost structure. Prices paid by the smelters in Canada are as low as 0.12 pence per unit, whereas the cheapest power in prospect in Britain—that from the nuclear a.g.r., apart from the politically untenable conventional oil fired generation—in 1967 looked likely to be 0.29 pence. Nevertheless, faced with acute balance of payments difficulties, and with the prospect of a large expansion in aluminium imports, even before devaluation the British government was willing to consider smelter proposals from aluminium companies which were already major fabricators in Britain. By late summer 1967 the Scottish Office had ensured that Scotland should be seriously considered and three sites were soon proposed; one was in Fife, one on the Firth of Clyde, and a third was undecided. Eventually, Invergordon was chosen as the most suitable. Six companies were interested, but all asked for power at prices some 30 per cent or so below the minimum levels envisaged by the Hydro Board. The dilemmas and the debate reached Cabinet level. However, an arrangement was concluded whereby the companies were permitted to purchase electricity at a rate which allegedly reflected the very low running costs which power production for their regular bulk demand implied, plus a contribution to the generating authorities' capital costs; by implication they were freed from the normal obligation to contribute a proportionate share of the capital costs of the whole industrial supply system.

Originally, all the smelter proposals envisaged the purchase of electric power. Subsequently however Alcan decided to generate its own power and to negotiate for supplies of coal at special pithead rates. It was able to purchase from the N.C.B. coal at a prospective f.o.t. price of 1 penny per therm, compared with the average price of 2.1 pence per therm for coal sold to the C.E.G.B. Although for a time Alcan continued to compete for the Invergordon site with British Aluminium, and had plans for piers to handle 40,000 dwt colliers running from Northumberland, in the course of 1968 it responded to the logic and lower transport costs of a location near the pit. It withdrew from Invergordon in order to build both a power plant and a smelter almost at colliery mouth near Blyth. Rio Tinto Zinc opted for a site at Holyhead near to the Wylfa Head nuclear station, and British Aluminium was left to develop the Invergordon site, which could be integrated with its existing Scottish fabricating, smelting and alumina operations. All three plants, therefore, neglected the possibility of a gradual fall in the beach-head price of natural gas. All three took advantage of considerable public assistance to firms locating in the development areas (Manners, 1968).

After complaints from Norway that investment grants to private companies contravened E.F.T.A. agreements, the government scaled down the projects initially to 60,000 annual tons at Blyth, and 100,000 tons at Holyhead and Invergordon. By 1971 the Invergordon smelter was at work employing some 600 persons. At the public enquiry at Dingwall which led to rezoning of over 280 hectares of good farmland for the smelter, the spokesman of the H.I.D.B.—their chief planning and research officer F. D. N. Spaven, who with A. Geddes had endorsed the development of the Moray Firth 20 years earlier—summarized

Table 34. Invergordon : financial aspects of farming and aluminium
smelting on a 280 hectare (700 acre) site

	Farming	Aluminium Smelting
Capital investment	£70,000	£40,000,000
Wages annually	£ 5,000	£ 1,000,000
Rateable value	£ 200	£ 200,000
Annual output	£20,000	£27,000,000
Import saving	£20,000	£20,000,000
Direct employment (persons)	6	700 to 1,200

Source : *The Guardian* 6 March, 1968.

the impact of big industry in the area (Table 34). Later development may involve an alumina plant nearby at Ord. This would process some 230,000 tons of bauxite a year, and increase the British Aluminium Company's overall investment by 50 per cent to about £52 million. This development is said to be in part conditional upon governmental permission to increase the aluminium refining capacity from 100,000 to 120,000 tons.

Very soon after the Invergordon smelter issue was resolved, the oil refinery and petrochemicals scheme was revived, this time under the name Grampian Chemicals which was controlled by American interests. And in July 1969 the Secretary of State gave approval for its construction in spite of opposition from farmers who likened the decision to the infamous Critchel Down case. The site was approved against the advice of the chairman of the public enquiry who had recommended the reclamation of land in Nigg Bay to the east—a site already rejected by the aluminium interests as unsuitable for heavy plant—and 545 hectares (1,100 acres) of farmland have been rezoned for industry, more than two thirds of this to be occupied by the proposed £100 million complex. A workforce of 500 to 600 would be engaged in the processing of 7 million tons of crude oil each year and the production of chemical feedstocks. Two companies were reported to be considering plant nearby in order to further process the Grampian Chemical products but, with the domestic petrochemical market firmly in the grip of the existing large producers such as Imperial Chemical Industries and British Petroleum, it was not surprising that the stated aim of the project was to export the greater part of its output. Such an achievement could make the eccentric location of the complex within the national market less important. Early in 1970, however, an announcement was made that the project had been indefinitely postponed, the reason being a shortage of capital in the European market. It could also be that marketing problems began to loom large, for it is not at all certain what would be the attitude of other E.E.C. countries to a flood of imports from a plant receiving heavy government Development Area assistance.

However, on the assumption that both the aluminium smelter and the oil and chemicals complex had been constructed by 1973–1974, it is worthwhile examining the benefit-cost situation in broad terms. By that date about £140 million would have been spent at Invergordon to produce perhaps 1,200–1,400 jobs directly. Plant, machinery and investment grants from the government would mean that public funds would have provided between 33 and 40 per cent of the investment and there would be a continuing public commitment to maintain low labour costs through the R.E.P., although the latter will be phased out from 1974. The investment to employment ratio would have been extremely high and the possible results by no means ideal. Clearly this is no adequate foundation for the population increase in the Moray Firth lowlands from its present 70,000 to the 250,000 or 300,000 which the Jack Holmes Planning Group scheme outlined to the H.I.D.B. in 1968. Even with high multiplier effects of say 3 to 1, the total employment generated by these two developments would still be no more than 4,500, sufficient to support a population increase of some 20,000 for the Moray Firth growth area. Recognizing this, the H.I.D.B. is actively fostering the growth of lighter industry particularly at the southern edge of the region in Inverness and to the east at Dalcross. Its plans propose that between Evanston and Tain the urbanized population will grow to 64,000, with employment for 19,500 concentrated on two major industrial sites at Invergordon and Evanston. For the other 191,000 urban dwellers between Dingwall and Dalcross industrial estate employment will provide jobs for only 13,500; this will remain the administrative and service hub of what will be a substantial albeit dispersed conurbation. Inverness, its undoubted centre, will have increased from 30,000 at present to 65,000.

There remain a number of doubts. Is expansion on this scale necessary for the health of the Highlands? Eric Linklater (1969) has suggested that plans for development on this scale suggest that Highland planning has now become a pastime rather than a necessity. There will be a loss both of some of the best agricultural land in the sub-region and of amenity—although it has been made clear from the start that the highest standards of effluent and of atmospheric pollution control will be maintained. Bearing in mind the H.I.D.B. arguments concerning the economic and social advantages of a thriving new Highland nucleus, two questions remain. Does it have to be on this scale? More to the point, where is the increase of over 220,000 people to come from? This is 20,000 more than the total population at present living in the whole of the Highlands outside the Moray Firth lowlands. As noted earlier, overspill from Glasgow and Edinburgh is already more than provided for in the new growth centres of the central Lowlands, the Borders and Tayside. There seems a danger that growth in the newly affluent, well-serviced zones either around Inverness-Invergordon or along the Thurso-Wick axis will denude the rest of the Highlands of still more population. Many of the services there, which are already heavily subsidized, would then reach the point at which maintenance would be quite impracticable and the outmovement would become uncontrollable. Consequently the improved roads, the modernized fishing fleets in which the H.I.D.B. is investing and the west coast crofts which the Crofters Commission are still trying to reshape, all will be rendered insupportable. If this should happen, the clearances which began 200 years ago for self interest will have been all but consumated by the well-intentioned schemes of the planner. It appears after all that the Highland way of life and the popular image of the region are incompatible with modern social and economic conditions. In this sense at least the Highlands problem is insoluble.

REFERENCES :

British Iron and Steel Federation (1966). *The Steel Industry. The Stage* 1 *Report of the Development Coordinating Committee*, B.I.S.F., London.

Clydesdale and North Scotland Bank (annually). *Survey of Economic Conditions in Scotland*, C.N.S.B., Glasgow.

Daysh, G. H. J. (Ed.) (1949). *Studies in Regional Planning*, George Philip, London.

Demangeon, A. (1939). *The British Isles* (English translation by E. D. Laborde), Heinemann, London, p. 160.

Department of Agriculture and Fisheries for Scotland (1967). *Highland Transport Board Report*, H.M.S.O., Edinburgh. pp. 14–15.

Fogarty, M. P. (1945). *Prospects of the Industrial Areas of Great Britain*, Methuen, London.

Gaskin, M. and others (1969). *North East Scotland : A Survey of its Development Potential*, H.M.S.O. for Scottish Office, Edinburgh.

Geddes, A. and Spaven, F. D. N. (1949). The Highlands and Islands. In G. H. J. Daysh (Ed.), *Studies in Regional Planning*, George Phillip, London. pp. 1–54.

Glasgow Herald Trade Review (annually). January.

Highlands and Islands Development Board (annually). *Annual Report*, H.I.D.B., Inverness.

Industrial Tyneside (1966). August.

Johnston, M. and Hood, N. (1968). On the Border. *Scotland*, January, 30–34.

Linklater, E. (1968). Highland planning : pastime or necessity. *Scotland*, September, 20–21.

Mackie, R. (1969). Three articles on crofting problems. *The Scotsman* 23, 24, 25 July.

Manners, G. (1968). Misplacing the smelters. *New Society*, 16 May, pp. 712–713.

Manners, G. (1969). Steel surpluses : fact or fiction? *Area*, **4,** 42–45.

Manners, G. (1971). *The Changing World Market for Iron Ore* 1950–1980, Johns Hopkins, Baltimore.

Martech Consultants (1964). *Highland opportunity* Scottish Vigilantes Association, Invergordon. p. 15.

Mitchell, J. B. (Ed.) (1962). *Great Britain : Geographical Essays*, Cambridge University Press, Cambridge. p. 556.

Secretary of State for Economic Affairs (1969). *The Intermediate Areas* (Chairman : Sir Joseph Hunt) (Cmnd.3998), H.M.S.O., London.

Secretary of State for Scotland (1946–1954). *Industry and Employment in Scotland*, H.M.S.O., Edinburgh.

Secretary of State for Scotland (1950). *A Programme of Highland Development*, H.M.S.O., Edinburgh. pp. 20–21.

Secretary of State for Scotland (1963). *Central Scotland* (Cmnd.2188), H.M.S.O., Edinburgh.

Secretary of State for Scotland (1966). *The Scottish Economy* 1965 *to* 1970 (Cmnd.2864), H.M.S.O., Edinburgh.

Self, P. (1966). Scotland's opportunity. *Town and Country Planning*, April, 195–196.

Stewart, M. (1964). Quoted in *The Guardian*, 4 September.

Thomson, D. C. and Grimble, I. (Eds.) (1968). *The Future of the Highlands*, Routledge and Kegan Paul, London.

Voice of North East Industry (1967). July.

Warren, K. (1965). Locational problems of the scottish iron and steel industry since 1760. *Scottish Geographical Magazine*, **81,** April and September, 18–37 and 87–103.

CHAPTER 11

Regional Development : The Continuing Policy Dilemmas

GERALD MANNERS

Over the last forty or so years regional and sub-regional planning in Britain has passed through a number of clearly recognizable phases. Throughout the nineteen thirties the limited political response to the problems posed by differential regional development was rooted in an essentially emotional base. The latter was fed by the widespread poverty and distress caused by the long-term unemployment localized in the industrial economies of the north and the west. The achievements of the policies were small. Throughout the next twenty years, but with fluctuating degrees of political commitment, regional planning objectives were much more vigorously pursued. Formulated against the background of the Barlow *Report* (Royal Commission, 1940), which reflected thinking in and the experience derived from the inter-war and war years, they were pursued within the framework of a substantial body of new legislation passed in the years immediately following 1945. Its many successes are undeniable. However, this legislation was more a response to the geographical consequences of the country's industrial and urban history than it was to farsighted regional, land use and environmental priorities and goals. In consequence, by the nineteen sixties the rationale and precepts of this post-war phase of regional planning had become increasingly inappropriate to the problems of the day. Policies were accordingly amended and, as was seen in Chapter 1 (pp. 7ff), their objectives were endorsed and widened by a new economic rationale. Nevertheless, doubts persist in regard to both the interpretation of the dilemmas which are posed by the spatial characteristics of economic development in Britain and the adequacy of the policies that have been embraced for the amelioration and solution of these problems.

An examination of the Hunt Committee's report on *The Intermediate Areas* (Secretary of State for Economic Affairs, 1969) strongly underlines this point. Although it was somewhat cavalierly treated by the government of the day and was primarily concerned with questions pertaining to interregional resource allocation and development, the report stands as a crucial benchmark in the history of British regional planning. It was, after all, the outcome of the first major governmental enquiry into the location of economic

425

activity and employment since Barlow. The report mirrors many of the advances that have been made in the understanding of both the symptoms and the causes of spatial variations in the pattern of socio-economic change. It naturally reflects something of the considerable experience gained by the British government in regard to public intervention in the processes of regional development. In addition, the Committee both clarified and reformulated a number of important issues in the field of spatial policy-making and thereby advanced our understanding of them. Nevertheless, it is clear that on a number of crucial issues the Hunt Committee had to reach its judgements against a background of both factual and conceptual uncertainty, and these same doubts continue to qualify the confidence with which any government can address itself to regional and sub-regional problems. More specifically, public policy in the nineteen seventies still has to operate within three key areas of uncertainty. These concern the nature of employment mobility, the establishment of policy goals, and the effectiveness of alternative measures and controls. Each deserves a brief comment.

The procedures used to influence the location of firms and the mobility of employment continue to leave a considerable amount of discretion to the Department of Trade and Industry for industrial development certificates and to the Department of the Environment for office development permits. There are, of course, substantial differences in the history and in the policy context of these floorspace controls (see Chapter 1). Yet there undoubtedly remains in both cases widespread doubt concerning the precise yardsticks that are used by civil servants in the two departments when they are considering development applications. Statements by government spokesmen stressing the need to maintain a 'flexible approach' in their administration of the legislation reflect the executive's highly empirical approach towards the problem; they also mirror the infinite diversity of industries and firms, and the undoubted administrative advantage of being able to consider each case 'on its own merits'. However, the absence of clear criteria not only frequently causes frustration and irritation to industrialists and office developers who might be denied the opportunity of investing in the place of their first choice; it also leaves justice, if done, to some extent unseen. Especially is this the case when changes occur in the emphasis of public policies, and when developments denied in one year are subsequently allowed in another. To a large extent, of course, this absence of declared and clear criteria is a reflection of the uncertainties that still surround our understanding of employment mobility, and there is an urgent need for a conclusive body of research findings that will demonstrate for the widest possible range of firms, industries and groups of economic activities their sensitivity to locational costs, to movement inducements and to distance.

Notwithstanding the very important work associated with such names as Toothill (Report of a Committee, 1961), Luttrell (1962), Cameron (1966) and Keeble (1971), there has still yet to be prepared a full categorization of industries on the basis of their sensitivity to locational costs. It can be argued, for example, that industries which are highly sensitive to such costs—the steel, oil refining, and aluminium smelting industries come readily to mind—should be excluded from i.d.c. procedures and that the full effort of the distribution of employment policies should be focused upon these activities whose costs are insensitive, or alternatively only slightly sensitive, to differences in location. These industries would naturally include many of those basic service employments whose reluctance to move from the London city region has remained one of the more disturbing challenges to interregional employment policies in recent years. Certainly there remains a real question—and it was not squarely faced by the Hunt Committee—as to whether the country can afford to support indefinitely in the less prosperous parts of Britain those industries whose locational costs make them a continuing economic liability there. Chapter 10 exposes the particularly acute problems of the Scottish case.

Related, but by no means identical to this characteristic, is the sensitivity of firms to movement incentives. A firm's or an industry's response to such inducements as free depreciation, relatively high investment incentives, the regional employment premium, advance factories and the like is not only a function of its locational costs. It is also related to the firm's investment decision-making procedures, and to its management's perception of the map of spatial opportunities. The structure of a firm, its size, its accounting procedures and the 'traditions' of its industry are all important in this matter. It is probable that a number of firms and industries which are insensitive to locational costs are also insensitive to the various inducements to movement, but it remains unclear what or how many they are, and whether they are becoming more or less important in the total spectrum of employment. Movement, of course, is a relative matter. Because of their linkages, their reliance upon external economies and the like, some firms can only be induced to transfer relatively short distances from their initial location; others, without impairing their efficiency, can be persuaded to move further. Once again, however, the proportion of firms, industries or economic groups which fall into each of these categories remains unknown.

A reduction in these uncertainties would obviously be invaluable in the search for a clearer formulation of those criteria that can most appropriately be used in the consideration of i.d.c. and o.d.p. applications, and it would permit a more transparent administration of government employment location policies. In addition, evidence of this sort would for the first time begin to indicate just how much employment is capable of being steered into the less prosperous parts of the country, and/or into the new towns and cities of southern England, at different stages of the investment cycle and at different rates of national economic growth. Such evidence would also begin to demonstrate whether, over time, a greater or smaller share of total national employment is likely to be available for use in regional development and redevelopment programmes. Enquiry along these lines, therefore, is imperative if any attempt is to be made to answer, even in general terms, the question of whether or not it is reasonable to assume that large metropolitan counter-magnets planned in the South East and the Midlands can be provided with a satisfactory economic base within a period of twenty or twenty-five years. It is also fundamental to the debate concerning the feasibility of steering enough alternative employments into the development and intermediate areas, during periods of rapid structural change and slow economic growth, in order to reduce unemployment and check out-migration there. The question undoubtedly remains open as to whether it is technically feasible to redevelop the economies of all the coal-field industrial areas simultaneously, and the argument that some interregional spatial priorities must be formulated can not be completely discounted. Naturally the Hunt Committee recognized the limited availability of footloose industry at any one time for regional planning purposes, including the development of overspill communities, but they were unable to approximate how much it exceeded or fell short of these areas 'needs'—however the latter might be defined—even within a British context, let alone the prospectively wider setting of Britain within an enlarged European Community.

A second area of uncertainty that continues to affect the confidence with which spatial planning decisions are taken follows from the difficulties encountered in trying to formulate and to justify objectives or goals, especially those that are primarily of a positive nature. 'It is a telling comment . . . on state intervention in the location of industry, and planning generally', wrote Lomas (1969) with allowable exaggeration, 'that Hunt was scarcely better placed than Barlow for getting to grips with the costs and benefits of different courses of action and hence with the geographical options available to us.' At the most generalized level of spatial resource allocation, adequate guidelines to indicate the most desirable interregional and intraregional distribution of population and employment in the future remain highly elusive. Should planning decisions be taken, and investment resources in the public sector allocated, on the basis of the 1971 patterns of population and economic activity, and on the assumption that they should and will persist until the end of the present century, or is some alternative economic geography likely to prove more desirable? Should the share of the national population living in Yorkshire and Humberside or in the South West region be encouraged to increase or to remain stable in the forseeable future? What is the most desirable size of the West Midlands' or Scotland's population and economy? The Central Unit for Environmental Planning was established in the middle nineteen sixties in part to consider such questions; whilst there has been much governmental committee work as a result (Inter-departmental Study Group, 1971), there is little evidence that much real progress has been made. The basic problem stems essentially from the very nature of the interregional economic and social system, the complexity of which eludes accurate description. Yet without such a description, any attempt to optimise the system through planning policies and public decisions inevitably can have only a limited logic. Observers and planners as a consequence have come out of necessity to concentrate increasingly upon marginal analyses of spatial changes within particular sectors, or sub-systems, of the economy. Chisholm (1971), for example, has made one such attempt in the transport sector, and his findings suggest that the national freight transport bill is insensitive to major variations in the interregional distribution of population. Many more studies along these lines are required to throw further light upon variations in the costs of other factor inputs in the space-economy, plus of course some counterpart studies of the corresponding range of alternative benefits.

At the intraregional scale, the formulation of planning goals may be concerned with smaller populations and economies, but the intellectual dilemmas are compounded by even greater problems of data, by a more articulate set of political interests and by the recent emergence of a cluster of environmental issues the main elements of which pose huge difficulties of quantification. Earlier chapters of this book have pointed to the conflicting interests between, say, the Greater London Council and the local authorities in the Outer Metropolitan Area, between Merseyside and East Lancastria, between Humberside and the West Riding of Yorkshire. At what point should dispersal planning for the conurbations be phased out? At what stage should new urban developments be given priority over the rehabilitation of older towns and cities? Have the compromises of regional development and planning in the past stood the test of time? In what ways, and with what emphases, could the planning of South Wales or the London city region have been significantly improved? What lessons are afforded there for the future? A few of the possible answers to these questions have been suggested in earlier chapters of the book. Within every region, some localities will tend through time to increase their employment opportunities, their population, the range of their amenities and the like, whilst others will tend to decline in either relative or absolute importance. Some areas present natural opportunities for further development; others exhibit the need for public assistance if they are to avoid unemployment and stagnation. Such contrasts in spatial economic prospects have long been widely recognised, but a particular difficulty facing the planner in the first instance is the need to define them with confidence upon the map. Of the two, it is the second type of area—the 'problem area' or 'area of need'—that presents the lesser challenge of delimitation.

Until the early nineteen sixties, the designation of Development Areas and Development Districts in Britain was based upon a single criterion—the level of unemployment. Under the 1966 Industrial Development Act, however, the new Development Areas were defined as 'Those parts of Great Britain where... special measures are necessary to encourage the growth and proper distribution of industry; and... regard (shall be had) to all the circumstances actual and expected, including the state of employment and unemployment, population changes, migration and the objectives of regional policies'. The width of this definition allowed virtually the whole of Wales and Scotland, and extensive tracts of northern and southwest England. to be offered assistance, as was noted in Chapter 1 (p. 57). A considerably more selective, and certainly more scientific, approach towards the definition of areas of need, however, could be based upon the ten causes for (local or regional) 'concern' that were listed in the Hunt Report. These were sluggish or falling employment, a slow growth in personal incomes, a slow rate of addition to industrial and commercial premises, significant unemployment, low or declining proportions of women at work, low earnings, a heavy reliance on industries whose demand for labour is growing slowly or falling, poor communications, a decayed or inadequate environment and serious net outward migration. On the basis of these criteria, the techniques of factor analysis and related grouping procedures can be usefully employed for region-building purposes (Smith, 1968). However, further work is certainly required in this context on the quantification of such factors as regional transport and communication facilities (and costs), and on the measurements of environmental characteristics and quality, other than simply an estimation of the area of derelict land such as was noted in the Hunt Report. Moreover, if this method of delimitation is to be improved, in the matter of amenity evaluation especially a number of non-quantifiable values need also to be embraced in any final assessment. Even then, of course, such an approach lacks normative guidelines, and any governmental response to areas of need must of necessity stem from quite different economic, social and political considerations which can assist in determining whether anything *can* be done, whether anything *should be* done and over what time period any reaction should be phased.

The delimitation of the counterpart 'areas of opportunity' presents much greater problems for the planner. For example, the contrast between the locations for new towns that were recommended by Abercrombie in 1945 and those that were subsequently designated by the government in the post-war years was noted in Chapter 1 (p. 27). It represents in large measure the uncertainties which at that time surrounded the growth prospects of the Outer Metropolitan Area and especially its less accessible parts. Similarly, the designation of the growth districts within the less prosperous regions in the 1963 White Papers—the 'areas' of Central Scotland and the 'zone' in North East England—was rooted essentially in intuitive formulae which allowed the selection of specific areas offering what were termed 'especially favourable growth prospects' within those broader regions. After 1964 the growth centre concept as applied to the redevelopment of the less prosperous regions lost favour in government circles, at least in public. Nevertheless, what were in effect three extensive areas of opportunity—Humberside, Severnside and Tayside—were placed under close scrutiny by the Central Unit for Environmental Planning in order to understand more clearly their development potential. Officials within the county planning machine also continued to examine smaller localities, such as south Gloucestershire (for Bristol overspill) and central Lancashire, with a view to their accelerated development. In southeast England the designation of further new and expanded towns and cities was also an important feature of the late nineteen sixties (see Chapter 3), and it is especially noteworthy that the overspill proposals in the 1964 *Study*, the 1967 *Strategy* and the 1970 *Strategic Plan* (see pp. 145–151), whilst not without certain common denominators, stand in some contrast to each other. The criteria used to delimit these and other growth areas in different parts of the country have tended to be unique to each case, and in its report the Hunt Committee deliberately avoided identifying with precision the Intermediate Area 'growth zones' for which it argued. There are many economic, sociological and political uncertainties beneath and hence reasons for this failure to discover explicit criteria for delimiting areas of opportunity. In particular, however, the failure stems from the absence of a conclusive body of evidence that spells out with some clarity the magnitude of external economies, and the benefits and costs, of different scales of local economic concentration. As a consequence, it remains impossible to identify what might be termed 'opportunity thresholds' which would indicate at what levels of sub-regional income and purchasing power, with what size of labour pool, at what index of market accessibility—and the like—regional economic growth would be more advantageous and hence would be better assured.

Progress in understanding these matters would without doubt permit a more meaningful exploration of alternative planning goals at the sub-regional scale, and in particular it would clarify those of a primarily economic nature. Even this, of course, would still leave unresolved many of the problems facing society in connection with the growing desire to preserve and enhance the quality of the environment, and it would in no way assist in the evaluation of alternative urban life-styles. Both of these matters are powerfully influenced by sub-regional and regional planning decisions, are becoming increasingly important features of public debate, need to be considered in the formulation of planning goals and yet are areas upon which our intellectual grasp remains unsure (Chisholm and Manners, 1971).

The third area of uncertainty concerns the effectiveness of alternative public measures and controls. Throughout the Hunt Report there is an awareness of the high and increasing cost of regional policies and the need radically to improve the cost-effectiveness of the measures used. Despite nearly forty years of deliberate governmental intervention in the location of economic activities, however, the relative merits of alternative measures still remains unclear. In seeking to steer manufacturing industry into the Development Areas, is it more effective and economical for the Department of Trade and Industry to offer free depreciation or substantial investment grants? Are grants and subsidies direct to firms more or less effective than improvements in the regional infrastructure? Having dramatically improved the intraregional road systems of North East England and Central Scotland, would it be reasonable for the government to expect a significant upturn in their economic fortunes? Is one set of measures more effective than others over different time-scales? In assisting the Development and Intermediate Areas, should there be more emphasis upon offering public funds to reduce the costs of buildings and plant, or should priority be given to subsidies of the costs of labour? Will the prospective withdrawal of the Regional Employment Premium in 1974 substantially reduce the attractiveness of the Development Areas for private investment, or not? Would a 'congestion tax' in the conurbations of southern England be more or less effective than alternative inducements to development in the less prosperous parts of the country? Will the new Industrial Development Executive, created in 1972 under a Minister for Industrial Development (Secretary of State for Trade and Industry, 1972) provide a new dynamic and a long-awaited flexibility for regional industrial policies? Should interregional office policy have been brought under the same directorate, or is it better to leave it in an entirely separate government Department? And so on. These are all questions on which both theoretical and empirical—and to some degree interdisciplinary—evidence remains singularly elusive. They raise, of course, a host of long-standing issues concerning the measurement of real and opportunity costs, the quantification of direct and multiplied achievements and the calculations of private and social gains. Inevitably, therefore, regional planning decisions have to be taken, and policies must be initiated, in the knowledge that it is possible to specify only in broad terms what their benefits are likely to be.

The persistence of these and other uncertainties must not detract from the considerable progress made in the description, modelling and the understanding of the regional development process in Britain of late (Brown, 1969; Manners, 1972), nor in the achievements of British regional planning in recent decades. Testament enough to the latter is to be found in the earlier chapters of this book—although the impossibility of knowing exactly what would have happened without public intervention in the process of regional development makes it impossible to measure the magnitude of these achievements. Above all, however, the continuing problems besetting the management of regional and sub-regional change pose an intellectual and practical challenge to the government, the planning profession and to the social sciences. The challenge is to improve yet further our understanding of the processes and policy options of regional change. For one thing is clear : the problems posed by shifts in the economic and social geography of the country will persist for many years to come.

REFERENCES

Brown, A. J. (1969). Surveys in applied economics : regional economics, *The Economic Journal*, **79,** 759–796.
Cameron, G. and Clark, D. B. (1966). *Industrial Movement and the Regional Problem*, Oliver and Boyd, Glasgow.
Chisholm, M. (1971). Freight transport costs, industrial location and regional development. In M. Chisholm and G. Manners (Eds.). *Spatial Policy Problems of the British Economy*, Cambridge University Press, Cambridge. pp. 213–244.
Chisholm, M. and Manners, G. (Eds.) (1971). *Spatial Policy Problems of the British Economy*, Cambridge University Press, Cambridge.
Inter-departmental Study Group (1971). *Long Term Population Distribution in Great Britain—A Study*, H.M.S.O., London.
Keeble, D. (1971). Employment mobility in Britain. In M. Chisholm and G. Manners (Eds.), *Spatial Policy Problems of the British Economy*, Cambridge University Press, Cambridge. pp. 24–68.
Lomas, G. M. (1969). The Hunt Report : a geographer-planner's view. *Area*, **3,** 13–15.
Luttrell, W. F. (1962). *Factory location and industrial movement*, N.I.E.S.R., London.
Manners, G. (1972). Regional development. In M. Chisholm and B. Rodgers (Eds.), *Studies in Human Geography*, Heinemann, London.
Ministry of Housing and Local Government (1964). *The South East Study*, 1961–1981, H.M.S.O., London.
Report of a Committee (1961). *Inquiry into the Scottish Economy*, 1960–1961 (Chairman : J. N. Toothill), Scottish Council, Edinburgh.
Royal Commission on the Distribution of Industrial Population (1940). *Report* (Chairman : Sir M. Barlow), (Cmnd.6153), H.M.S.O., London.
Secretary of State for Economic Affairs (1969). *The Intermediate Areas* (Chairman : Sir Joseph Hunt), (Cmnd.3998), H.M.S.O., London.
Secretary of State for Trade and Industry (1972). *Industrial and Regional Development*, (Cmnd.4942), H.M.S.O., London.
Smith, D. M. (1968). Identifying the "grey" areas—a multivariate approach. *Regional Studies*, **2,** 183–193.
South East Economic Planning Council (1967). *A Strategy for the South East*, H.M.S.O., London.
South East Joint Planning Team (1970). *Strategic Plan for the South East*, H.M.S.O., London.

Index